WORLD ATLAS OF GOLF

The Publisher would like to thank Mark Rowlinson
for his hard work and enthusiasm in producing
this updated edition

Additional text contributions by Peter Doereiner,
Michael Gedye, Peter Hildyard, Derek Lawrenson,
Keith Mackie, Marven Moss, Arvid Olsen, Mark
Rowlinson, Donald Steel, Larry Wood, Alfred Wright

Illustrations: Harry Clow, Allard, Chris Forsey, Brian
Delf, Charles Pickard, Peter Morter, Tony Garrett,
Arka, Shaun Deal and Line and Line

This revised edition first published in Great Britain
in 2002 by Hamlyn, a division of Octopus Publishing
Group Ltd, 2–4 Heron Quays, London E14 4JP

Copyright © Octopus Publishing Group Ltd 2002
First edition published 1976, Reprinted 1979, 1981,
1983, 1984, 1986 twice, 1987
Second edition 1988
Third edition 1991
Fourth edition 1998
Fifth edition 2000

10 9 8 7 6 5 4 3 2 1

ISBN 0 600 60720 8

A CIP catalogue record for this book is available
from the British Library

Printed and bound in China

Every effort has been made to ensure that the
course cards and text in this book are as accurate as
possible. However, golf courses are frequently being
adjusted and redesigned. Some of the artworks in this
book represent courses at a certain time and may not
include particular changes to the course layout. The
Publishers will be grateful for any information which
will assist them in updating future editions.

Throughout *The World Atlas of Golf* distances are
quoted in yards, still in use throughout most of the UK,
the USA and Japan. In many other countries metres are
standard. The difference (less than one percent) may
not seem great, but it is enough to make a difference of
one club at 100 yards. To convert to metres multiply the
yardage by 0.9144.

WORLD

ATLAS OF GOLF

PAT WARD-THOMAS, HERBERT WARREN WIND,
CHARLES PRICE, PETER THOMSON

hamlyn

Contents

Introduction

By Mark Rowlinson

More than a quarter of a century has passed since The World Atlas of Golf first appeared in print, immediately opening the eyes of a vast readership worldwide to the intricacies and subtleties of the greatest courses on earth through ground-breaking illustrations and the incomparable wisdom and glorious prose of four of the finest commentators the game has known. It was part of a series of books building on the immense success of Hugh Johnson's World Atlas of Wine, in which the precise differences of flavour distinguishing one Grand Cru Burgundy from another were revealed to those of us who could never afford to drink the stuff through the interpretation of vineyard geology, grape varieties, vinification techniques, and all the rest of it. So vivid were the descriptions that we could almost taste the wine as we read.

To most of us a round of golf at Augusta National or Cypress Point is no more likely to come our way than a case or two of Romanée-Conti or La Tâche, but through the word painting of Pat Ward-Thomas, Herbert Warren Wind, Charles Price, and Peter Thomson we are still able to get a very real feel for these courses. We can almost sense the overwhelming pressure of standing on the 18th tee at Augusta holding a one-stroke lead on Sunday or savour the Pacific breezes wafting over us at Cypress Point.

In 1976, when the Atlas was first published, the United States celebrated its bicentennial, Jimmy Carter was elected President, Concorde completed its first commercial supersonic transatlantic flight, Abba had massive hits with Fernando and Dancing Queen and the last Cadillac Eldorado Convertible rolled off the production line. In golfing terms it was hardly a vintage year, although Raymond Floyd equalled Jack Nicklaus's record low score of 271 in winning that year's Masters. For the sake of completeness, Jerry Pate won the US Open at Atlanta, Johnny Miller took the Open Championship at Royal Birkdale and Dave Stockton triumphed in the US PGA at Congressional. Woods were still made of wood, and a drive of 220 yards was about as much as most amateurs could hope for.

Since then there has been a technological revolution in golf equipment, with quantum leaps made in the performance of clubs and balls. Professional golfers (just as other athletes) have become even fitter and stronger. So the leading tour stars are now averaging over 300 yards with their drives. Holes that were a drive and 3-iron to the professional of 1976 are no more than a 3-wood and sand wedge to Tiger Woods. Many classic courses (Augusta National and the Old Course, St Andrews come to mind) have had to be lengthened considerably in an attempt to keep pace with contemporary professional play. This new edition of the World Atlas of Golf reflects the latest revisions to over one hundred great courses throughout the world. An opportunity has also been taken to expand the entries for Oak Hill, the Inverness Club and Muirfield Village, which are now included in the main section of the book, rather than the gazetteer. Two courses which had not even been built when the first edition appeared, the Stadium Course at the Tournament Players Club and Valhalla, are also added to the main section, while two distinguished old courses, Ganton and The National Golf

The state of the art at the close of the 20th Century: the 1999 Wentwood Hills Course at Celtic Manor designed jointly by Robert Trent Jones Snr. and Jnr. It encapsulates a lifetime's work in its brilliant combination of lakeland, highland and forest holes: Florida, California and The Alps transported to South Wales. The award of the 2010 Ryder Cup matches to Celtic Manor is an early acknowledgement of the quality of the design – although as many as six new holes will be incorporated in the final layout.

Links, have been restored to their rightful place. In the gazetteer there are new entries for the Bay Hill Club, TPC of Scottsdale and Sahalee in the United States, Slaley Hall and the Marquess Course at Woburn in England, Waterville and Tralee in Ireland, and Emirates in the United Arab Emirates, a current European Tour venue and one of a number of exciting recent developments in a region where water to irrigate the course is dearer than petrol!

Almost all the courses selected for inclusion in the first edition as being the best the world then had to offer are still to be found high up in the league tables so fashionable in today's golfing press. Indeed, in a recent survey of the world's top 100 courses by Golf Magazine, 78 courses are at least 50 years old. Yet the compilers of that first edition were doing much more than simply provide a league table. Somehow they contrived to put together an astonishingly varied collection of courses: ancient, modern, linksland, parkland, mountain, swamp, Major championship venues, even courses which have never been subjected to the hullabaloo of the professional circuit. The original text was incomparable and it has been left intact except where recent developments have rendered it obsolete.

Where possible, the course details quoted are those as they stood in the early months of 2002. Sincere thanks are due to the officials of the many clubs who took immense trouble to bring the details fully up to date. But it is inescapable, when writing about golf, that no sooner has it been stated in print, "This is the longest hole on the course", than a course rebuild is undertaken and the facts are immediately out of date. The Publishers will be grateful for any information that will assist them in updating future editions.

Links courses

Nature's gift to golf

Golf architecture is now recognized as a distinct art, the creation of a great golf course being achieved with a subtle alchemy of skill, imagination and technology upon which another dimension of greatness can be conferred by the staging of a championship. But not every championship setting owes its quality to the hand of man. St Andrews, Prestwick and Carnoustie are relics of the old, natural links on which the game first became popular. To this day nobody knows who laid them out, but even they are refinements of the earliest golfing arenas used when the game was played across country. There were no fairways, no tees and no greens, simply agreed starting and finishing points. The game had reached St Andrews, Carnoustie, Leith, Dornoch, Montrose, North Berwick and Musselburgh by the beginning of the sixteenth century. Golf thus became established on linksland. These strips of coastal land, left when the seas receded after the last ice age, were once a wilderness of sand. Slowly, sparse vegetation grew up and something akin to a fairway with fine-bladed grass threaded its way amongst the gorse. St Andrews became – and still is – one long fairway, with nine holes out to a distant point and nine holes back. Those unfamiliar with links courses expect it to have more definition and more colour. Yet the Old Course's influence on generations of golf architects has been immense – so pervasive that every golf course is essentially built in imitation. The Old Course served as a model for the early architects, Old Tom Morris, Willie Park Jr and the Dunns, who in their early days did little more than site 18 teeing grounds and greens on the splendid golfing ground that was put at their disposal. Unfortunately, for a period the blessings of nature were often overlooked and some courses took on a stiff and unnatural appearance. Designs incorporated stone walls, blind shots, hedges, regularly shaped mounds and greens in geometric shapes.

Left and below: The par-four 17th (Alps) at Prestwick is typical of the many blind holes that once existed on the old links course. It used to be considered a sporting hole, but its emphasis on the vagaries of fortune – their cruellest twist epitomised by the deep bunker, below – to the almost total exclusion of skill, makes the Alps an anachronism. A number of large bunkers on courses around the world have been named Sahara on account of the vast expanse of sand. The first to be so named was the bunker that protects the 17th green at Prestwick, left.

Right: The hidden bunkers that riddle the Old Course's 12th fairway started out as natural sandy depressions and were probably enlarged by sheep sheltering from the wind. These are common on links courses where the first bunkers were not designed but evolved through use.

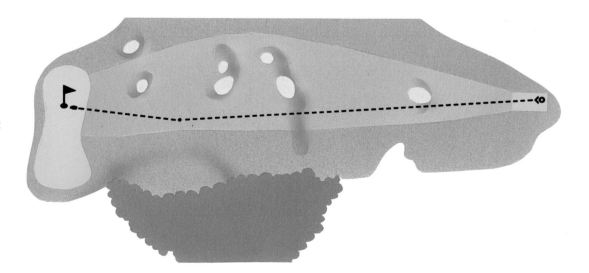

The birth of golf architecture

Towards the end of the 19th century came a welcome return to simplicity and naturalness. Great courses continued to be built on traditional linksland (Muirfield and Portmarnock, built in the 1890s, were routed in refreshingly new ways), but due to a radical decision to build on the sandy heathland west of London, they were for the first time created inland. Courses had previously been built away from the sea – but on non-porous soil, soggy in winter and rock hard in summer; this new land was superbly drained and easy to contour, and on it the genius of Willie Park Jr, Herbert Fowler, Tom Simpson, H.S. Colt and Charles Alison flourished. In America, Charles

Above and right: The 2nd at Pine Valley is one of the most dramatic and fearsome holes on a course which, apart from being considered the most difficult in the world introduced the concept of island fairways. These fairways dictate not only line but also length and are isolated amongst vast areas of sandy scrubland which, along with the more formal bunkers set around the greens, are never raked.

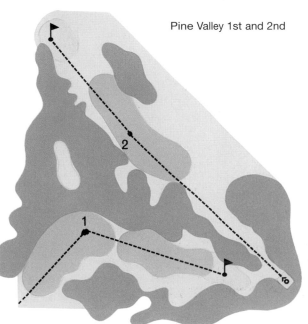

Pine Valley 1st and 2nd

Blair Macdonald created the National Golf Links, the first course of real quality built beyond the shores of Britain and Ireland, and in the years until the end of World War I some exceptional courses were carefully nursed into existence by truly gifted men – George Crump (Pine Valley), the Fownes family (Oakmont), A.W. Tillinghast (San Francisco GC) and Hugh Wilson (Merion).

All of these men, British and American, made careful studies of the fine old linksland courses and incorporated the best features into their designs, but they also introduced new ideas of their own and formulated two divergent schools of thought on golf architecture – the strategic and the penal. A penal hole dictates the line of play and punishes a player who strays from it out of all proportion to the degree of his error. The strategic hole offers a number of routes of varying difficulty and, while hampering the poor shot in subsequent play, rewards the good one. These men also understood the value of good drainage, the virtues of suitable grasses, the subtleties of green size in relation to the approach shot, and they did away with the lottery of blind holes, building instead holes that made no secret of their hazards. In their knowledge and its application golf architecture, part intuition, part science, was born.

Left: A feature of the daunting Oakmont layout is the bunkers that protect virtually every hole, not least the par four 14th.

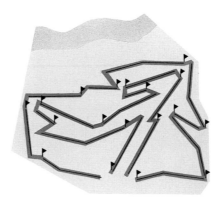

Muirfield 8th   Hagen 1929

Muirfield 8th
Although Oakmont was the first penal course earlier individual holes were decidedly penal, including Muirfield's 8th, an example of insurance bunkering. In the 1929 Open, before trees made the shot too difficult, Walter Hagen used an ingenious route to a birdie-three.

Muirfield   Portmarnock

Muirfield, left, and Portmarnock, right, were among the earliest courses to depart from the then accepted principle of nine holes out to a distant point and nine holes back. On both courses only once do three successive holes pursue the same direction, forcing the golfer to play the wind from all quarters.

The golden age

A universal quest for perfection

Golf's popularity soared in the period between the wars, particularly in the United States, where the feats of Bobby Jones caught the public imagination. Thus, when he retired and built his ideal course, it was bound to be influential. Fortunately, Augusta National, which Jones designed with Alister Mackenzie, proved to be a worthy model. Its wide fairways, sparing but telling use of bunkers, subtle mounding, huge greens and its capacity to test golfers of all abilities, demonstrated irrefutably that strategic design was superior to penal design, which had enjoyed an inexplicable vogue in the 1920s.

Other design features emerged as, with a sounder knowledge of the technical problems of building and maintenance and with increasing subtlety, architects pitted their wits against players whose consistency was considerably enhanced by the switch from hickory to steel-shafted clubs. They patiently sculpted their greens, angled them and tilted them; they held out baits, forced decisions, encouraged boldness, indulged the growing taste for spectacular drop-shots and popularised the heroic, all-or-nothing type of hole. Their growing preoccupation with

Left: Between the wars came the transition from hickory (left) to steel shafts. The change was dramatic because steel eliminated the torsion present in hickory, which had made the shaft twist as well as bend when swung. The changeover took time, the first perforated steel shaft (right), devised by Allan Lard of Massachusetts in 1903, proving inadequate. The breakthrough came with the development of the seamless steel shaft, legalized in Britain in 1929, which led to matched sets of clubs with consistent feel and characteristics.

Left: Pebble Beach. The 8th: 431 yards par 4.
The 8th at Pebble Beach is a magnificent example of the heroic hole which came into its own in the years between the wars. Unlike so many other death-or-glory holes the 8th does offer a less adventurous alternative to the player who has hit a bad drive: he can play to the left and get home in three. However, for those who dare to go for it, the second shot, seen from the small, heavily bunkered green, far left, is a thrilling experience, requiring a carry of some 150 yards to clear the sea and the cliff-edge bunker short of the green. Pebble Beach, on which work was begun in 1918, has eight holes set along the rock-bound coast of Carmel Bay and it was the forerunner of a host of imitative, and usually inferior, spectacular seaside courses.

balance was best summed up by Donald Ross, creator of Seminole and Pinehurst No. 2: "The championship course … should call for long and accurate tee shots, accurate iron play, precise handling of the short game and, finally, consistent putting. These abilities should be called for in a proportion that will not permit excellence in any one department of the game to too largely offset deficiencies in another."

In those years many other architects were given marvellous land on which to build, and on it they created some unforgettable courses: Jack Neville at Pebble Beach, A. W. Tillinghast at Baltusrol, Stanley Thompson at Banff, Charles Alison at Hirono, Mackenzie at Royal Melbourne. They made the period between the wars into golf architecture's Golden Age.

Right: When restoring Turnberry's Ailsa Course after the Second World War Philip Mackenzie Ross reinstated the traditional defences of the golden age: deep bunkers, unpredictable rough, and lightning fast greens.

The modern era

The land yields to the machine

Few courses were built in the years immediately following World War II, the prime concern being the reinstatement of courses that had been neglected or partially destroyed. Then in the late 1950s more money, more leisure time and the magnetism of Arnold Palmer again made golf into a boom sport.

Increased mobility led to a demand for courses in exotic vacation areas where golf had barely been heard of, and a championship golf course became an essential for every chic resort, just as it did for the proliferation of expensive real estate developments. Elaborate water systems, new construction techniques and better machinery made them possible, just as these were instrumental in the transformation of desert, mountain and marsh into land that was fit for golf. Some of the results have been predictably disastrous, but one welcome by-product has been the creation of a plethora of heroic holes in glorious settings around the world.

Water has become a dominant feature of design, particularly around the green. Fairway bunkers are now commonly staggered, though all too often flat and far too easy to escape from. Small greens are again finding favour, ensuring the survival of the art of chipping. Golfers of all abilities are catered for by long tees or, more imaginatively, by numerous smaller tees scattered to provide variations not only in length but also in the line of attack.

The technological revolution in club and ball performance during the 1990s has suddenly thrown an undue emphasis back on length. The magic figure of 7,000 yards is no longer magic and par-4s approaching 500 yards are commonplace on championship courses. Even so, a 300-yard drive (average length for today's top golfers) still only leaves a mid-iron approach to the longest two-shot holes. The challenge for the contemporary architect is to restore the long-iron approach shot, the hardest shot of all under pressure, immortalised by Ben Hogan at Merion in 1950.

Far left and left: The modern practice of staggering flanking fairway bunkers is perfectly illustrated by Pete Dye's 1969 design for the 13th at Harbour Town. The ideal tee shot must be threaded between the left-hand bunker and a lone oak tree but kept out of the right-hand bunker. Dye also made interesting use of trees, a device which became increasingly popular, by using two oaks to guard the entrance to the green.

The Dunes Golf
and Beach Club
The 13th: 590 yards par 5

Far left and left: Robert Trent Jones has always championed strategic design, the 13th hole at Dunes being an excellent example of his approach. From every tee the golfer can decide on the extent of the challenge he wishes to take on.

Like all the early courses actually built to a design, Muirfield was constructed by hand with the help of horses pulling shallow scoops, or drag-pans. The architecture benefited from the limitations of this slow but controlled method because it was easier to give earthworks constructed in this way a pleasing natural contour.

The science that transforms
design into reality

Since World War II it has been possible to build a golf course almost anywhere – given the two major requirements, money and the technical knowledge. Swamps can be reclaimed, jungles cleared, deserts irrigated and mountains moved. However, only in the last 50 years or so has it been necessary to even contemplate such radical action to bring a golf course into being. It was finally forced by soaring demand, combined with the rapid escalation in the cost of land and the scarcity of suitable sites. Previously, architects had, with comparative ease, found land that without too much effort could be made fit for golf. With the limited means at their disposal, usually hand labour and horses hauling drag pans, they were able to create courses with the naturalness they so coveted. Occasionally the very earliest designers were unable to route their courses around unwanted sandhills and blind holes resulted, but they were almost the only insurmountable problem.

Today the challenge is altogether different. While it is physically possible to undertake the most ambitious land transformations in order to construct a superb course in the unlikeliest of situations, the biggest obstacle to completing the project may well be consideration for the environment. When Robert Trent Jones was building a course at Kiahuna in Hawaii construction was delayed for a whole year by the blind spider, the world's smallest daddy long-legs. His son Bobby had a project at Edgwood Park in California held up for ten years by conservationists seeking to protect the bay checkerspot butterfly – 7,000 yards of golf course held in check by a one-and-a-half-inch butterfly. Wetlands and woodlands, archaeological finds and sites of special scientific interest are fiercely protected, and the best designers utilise them to advantage. "In most cases," says Tom Fazio, "the natural environment is better than a man-made one, so the more of it we have, the better golf courses will look."

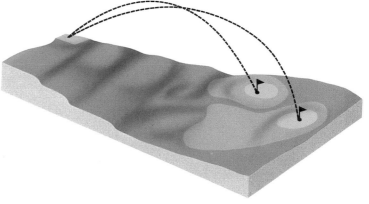

Above: The old 3rd hole at Royal St George's offered "sporting alternatives", a euphemistic way of describing a capricious blind hole. A new green –wholly visible – was later built on a rise.

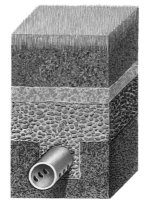

Left: The consistency and distribution of materials in a modern green are tailored to climatic conditions, but the aim is to ensure controlled growth through use of a balanced seedbed mixture – so important that it is often imported – and good drainage. The sand absorbs excess water, which filters through gravel to be drained off through perforated piping.

Right: The 1st hole at Muirfield Village, with its numerous bunkers, rolling fairways, thoughtfully contoured green and carefully shaped multiple tees, is typical of the course – and of what $2 million could buy back in the 1970s. Today the maintenance bill for a state-of-the-art course is likely to be around $2 million per year.

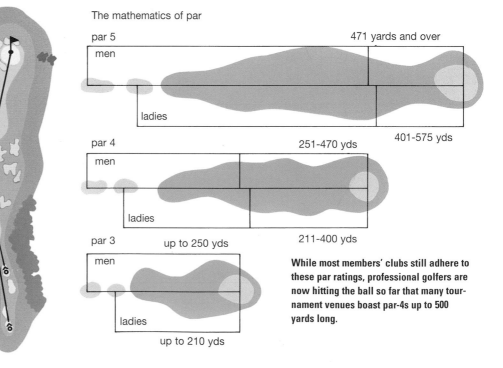

The mathematics of par

par 5 — 471 yards and over
men
ladies
401-575 yds

par 4 — 251-470 yds
men
ladies
211-400 yds

par 3 — up to 250 yds
men
ladies
up to 210 yds

While most members' clubs still adhere to these par ratings, professional golfers are now hitting the ball so far that many tournament venues boast par-4s up to 500 yards long.

Left and below: On the 386-yard 11th at Winged Foot the green is tilted to present a good target and its contours, shown in detail below, are formed in such a way that balls hit to the pin positions on either side may roll off into flanking bunkers. The position at the back is easier, but any overhit would leave a chip or pitch to a downhill green. The front position allows the greatest room for error.

green:
3 inch contours

0   10ft

Greens
the ultimate target

No part of the golf course can have as much influence on a golfer's score as the greens – the ultimate target. They form the most important part of the construction work and often are the most costly item. No two are alike, but their nature has had an obvious bearing on the difficulty of a course ever since the principles of golf architecture became accepted.

Greens influence scoring in two ways: in the target they present for shots hit into them, and in the effect which they have on putting – that controversial game within a game. At first greens were little more than cut extensions of the fairway, though sometimes they were sited in hollows or on plateaus; some were flat, others eccentrically undulating, but all were natural. It was unreasonable to expect a golfer to flight a mashie shot with a feathery or gutty over greenside bunkers and stop his ball on a rough, unprepared surface. Thus in the early days greens were relatively unguarded, but later were given protection, as a

means of calling for more control and as a counter to the ever improving clubs and balls. First sand and later water, sometimes both, were used, often completely encircling the putting surface, their severity depending on the type and length of approach to be played. Greens were angled, raised or lowered to favour those who had hit their previous shot to the ideal place.

With the advent of watering and improved strains of grass, it was not so much a question of hitting the green as one of hitting it in the right place. Pin placement became an art in itself, practised, with weather conditions in mind, to vary the severity of the test. It came to be universally accepted that if a player aimed for the fat of the green he might face difficulty in getting down in two putts, whereas should he be bold enough to play for the pin the margin for error was slight but the potential rewards great. The putting surface itself should be receptive to the well-struck shot and, ideally, be firm, fast and true.

Above: The fast, undulating 18th green is typical of those at Oakmont, which are generally acknowledged to be the most terrifying in America, not simply because of the premium they place on putting but because they call for such perfect placement of approach shots. In spite of their fearsome contours, Oakmont's greens are fair because they contain no grain, which affects not only the distances putt will roll but also in which direction it will bend.

Above: The short 7th hole at Pebble Beach is famous for its beauty. Despite its length of only 107 yards, it is a great golf hole, its challenge lying in the size of the green – 8 yards wide and 24 yards long – its siting along the line of approach and the tight ring of bunkers which enclose it.

Right: These three very short holes, Pebble Beach 7th (left), Augusta 12th (centre) and Country Club of North Carolina 3rd (right), show how the size and angling of the green can affect the difficulty of a par-three hole.

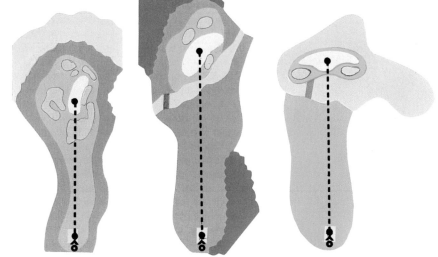

As the 21st Century opens golf has reached another turning point – some might call it a breaking point. It has been said that, if club and ball technology continues to advance at the same extraordinary rate it does at present and the physical fitness and technique of the finest players also develop equally rapidly, every championship course as we know them will be obsolete inside ten years. There have been mutterings about using only one type of ball with a limited performance and about putting a stop to any further innovations in club design, especially with regard to new manufacturing processes and materials. But the golf equipment business is enormous, its wealth and power colossal, and it would be a very thick-skinned golfing bureaucrat who tried to halt this progress through legislation alone. It is not the first time golf has had to come to terms with major upheaval caused by the latest technology, nor will it be the last, but, as always, it falls to the golf course architect to try to stem the tide. It is under such circumstances that the imperishable genius of the master architects is never more apparent.

There is probably no greater challenge to the modern architect than to have to make alterations to a course so famous that it could be described as a national monument. Tom Fazio was given a budget of millions of dollars to equip Augusta National to withstand the onslaughts of today's big hitters such as Woods, Daly, Love, Duval, Mickelson and Cabrera. He did a brilliant job, contriving to provide a leader board with six of the world's top seven golfers in contention entering the last round. Visually there was not a scar on the beautiful face of Augusta. This was not painting a moustache on the Mona Lisa. Inevitably, it

The imperishable genius of
the master architects

cost a fortune. Moving in dozens of 50-foot trees just to cut out a safe drive on the 18th brings with it an enormous price tag. $500,000 alone is reputed to have been spent purchasing a plot of land enabling the 13th tee to be moved back a mere 25 yards. It is a far cry from the fee of £4 paid to Tom Morris for laying out the Royal County Down links towards the end of the 19th Century or the £2,000 that was all it cost for Mackenzie Ross to build Southerness, a fine and challenging championship course in southern Scotland, just after the Second World War, at much the same time that he was restoring Turnberry to its full glory.

Although the best players of their day have always been involved in the laying out of courses, golf design as an art or science is really a creation of the 20th Century. Harry Colt, in the early 1900s, is credited with being the first designer who regularly used a drawing board, and at least ten of his courses still figure in most credible lists of the top 100 courses in the British Isles. However, such lists, so popular with the golfing press and eagerly scoured by an informed readership ready to argue the case for their own particular favourites, frequently throw up unfamiliar names. Who, for instance, was Arthur Croome, credited with the design of Liphook, currently ranked 100th in Golf World's British Isles league table? For the record, Croome was a talented amateur sportsman who

went on to be a business manager and publicist for a golf design company involving Herbert Fowler, J.F. Abercromby and Tom Simpson. Why he should have ventured into golf design himself is not recorded, but Liphook is the only course known to have been designed by him, a little gem of a Surrey heath-and-heather course giving the visitor all the fun of Sunningdale at a third of the cost. Who, for that matter, was Tom Bendelow, whose name lives on through the illustrious No.3 course at the Medinah Country Club in Illinois, which has hosted three US Opens and the 1999 US PGA, albeit after many a rebuild? Nothing, it seems, will change the reputation of poor Tom, described as an "eighteen stakes on a Sunday afternoon" phenomenon, referring to his capacity for marking out a course in a few hours for no more than $25. He was hardly unique. Even Donald Ross descended to this mediocrity more than once.

In the introduction to this edition it is noted that 78 of the world's top 100 courses are at least fifty years old. It would be easy to assume that they must all be old-fashioned links on the coasts of the British Isles. Not so. A great many of these venerable courses are in the United States, a fact recognised by the USGA in its choice of venues for its Open Championship. How many present day courses have been considered good enough to host the US Open since the first edition of the Atlas in 1976?

The answer is only one, the Atlanta Athletic Club, which was allocated the 1976 event almost as a tribute to the memory of Bobby Jones who had written the club's letter of request but had died before the decision had been notified. We have seen, at last, the recognition of Pinehurst No.2, a Donald Ross creation of 1907, with its staging of the 1999 US Open, and there is much rejoicing in the decision to hold the 2002 tournament over the Black Course at Bethpage State Park, A.W. Tillinghast's last design (1936), a public course thankfully restored to robust health after it had fallen into serious disrepair during the 1970s.

Like so many of the golf designers of the early years of the 20th Century Tillinghast was quite a character. Sadly, it seems that he lost interest in golf course architecture as his personal fortune ebbed away during the Depression, ending his days running an antiques shop in Beverly Hills, but he left an impressive roster of inspired designs which continue to challenge to this day. He was born in 1874 and it was fitting that during his centenary year no fewer than four USGA championships were played on courses of his design, Winged Foot (hosting the US Open), San Francisco G.C., Brooklawn, and Ridgewood. As a colourful figure, Tillinghast is rivalled by the wealthy Englishman, Tom Simpson, who habitually appeared to view the site of a potential new golf course wearing an elaborate cloak, sporting a beret, and driving a Rolls-Royce. While his submitted design was being considered it was not unknown for him to drive his Rolls-Royce round and round outside the meeting room, not allowing anyone out until he had been given the contract. That his designs at Chantilly, Morfontaine and Fontainebleau are still ranked amongst the top twenty in continental Europe shows that his self-belief was hardly unfounded. His work in Belgium is no less distinguished, with Royal Belgique at Tervuren and RGC des Fagnes in the hills above Spa as the pick of a delightful bunch.

Slightly senior to both men was Alister Mackenzie, whose golfing reputation is summed up for most of us by his masterpiece at Cypress Point and his collaboration with Bobby Jones at Augusta National. But a glance at the spread of his outstanding designs from the Jockey Club in Argentina to New South Wales in Australia shows the extent and lasting effects of his enormous influence. His very earliest course, Alwoodley in Leeds, has recently been restored as closely as possible to his original plans, and it provides an object lesson to all contemporary architects in the art of understatement. This should come as no surprise when it is realised that this former army surgeon studied the art of camouflage during the Boer War and he was credited, by Marshall Foch no less, with saving thousands of lives during the First World War, cutting casualties on the western front by a third! Mackenzie's genius was in using the natural contours of the land, or imitating them, to deceive the golfer's eye. The great and prolific architect Robert Trent Jones credited Mackenzie with having more influence on modern course design than any other architect, so it is perhaps at this point worth quoting Mackenzie's "essential features of an ideal golf course", for they are as relevant today as they were in Mackenzie's own time, over seventy years ago:

- The course, where possible, should be arranged in two loops of nine holes.
- There should be a large proportion of good two-shot holes, two or three drive-and-pitch holes, and at least four one-shot holes.
- There should be little walking between greens and tees, and the course should be arranged so that in the first instance there is always a slight walk forwards from the green to the next tee; then the holes are sufficiently elastic to be lengthened in the future if necessary.
- The greens and fairways should be sufficiently undulat-

The 11th hole at Augusta is a completely different challenge now than that presented to players in the 1950s. The advances made in golf club and ball technology, plus fitter and stronger golfers, often means a wedge approach to the green rather than a three or four iron. Ben Hogan used to play away from the water that protects the green's left hand side. In 1998 the green was raised to present a less receptive target. The pond was also raised and widened, making it once again a significant threat. For 2002 the downhill fairway was levelled to lengthen the approach shot.

ing, but there should be no hill climbing.

- Every hole should have a different character.
- There should be a minimum of blindness for the approach shots.
- The course should have beautiful surroundings, and all the artificial features should have so natural an appearance that a stranger is unable to distinguish them from nature itself.
- There should be a sufficient number of heroic carries from the tee, but the course should be arranged so that the weaker player with the loss of a stroke or a portion of a stroke shall always have an alternative route open to him.
- There should be infinite variety in the strokes required to play the various holes – viz., interesting brassy shots, iron shots, pitch and run-up shots.
- There should be a complete absence of the annoyance and irritation caused by the necessity of searching for lost balls.
- The course should be so interesting that even the plus man is constantly stimulated to improve his game in attempting shots he has hitherto been unable to play.
- The course should be so arranged that the long handicap player, or even the absolute beginner, should be able to enjoy his round in spite of the fact that he is piling up a big score.
- The course should be equally good during winter and summer, the texture of the greens and fairways should be perfect, and the approaches should have the same consistency as the greens.

It is remarkable how many of the world's greatest courses embrace most, if not all, of these "essential features".

Slightly older than Mackenzie was John Frederick Abercromby. Only now is it being recognised more widely just what a genius he was, too. "Aber" was a fine player, but had no experience of golf course design when he undertook in 1908 to locate a site and build a course for his wealthy employer. He found a spot at Worplesdon in Surrey and laid out a course entirely by instinct. It is said he measured nothing, nor made sketches, yet Worplesdon remains largely unaltered and it is a course greatly respected to this day for its challenging design.

The following year "Aber" went up in a balloon to ascertain the best routing through the woods at Coombe Hill in Kingston, which later became one of Bing Crosby's favourite British courses. He then went on to design The Addington, a course full of unique character (including a couple of world-class short holes) only a few miles from the centre of London, where he lived for the rest of his life as its "beneficent despot".

But it is not only old British or American architects who have been re-evaluated as the 20th century has been reviewed. The reputation of Canadian Stanley Thompson's courses at Banff, Capilano and Cape Breton is as high as ever. Perhaps his greatest legacy, though, is his influence on Robert Trent Jones, the most prolific of the many fine architects whom he trained.

The German, Bernhard von Limburger, did much to re-establish golf in Germany after the Second World War, and each German Open for thirty years from the end of that war was played on one of his designs. More recently, Bernhard Langer, who has been the most successful German golfer of the modern era, has now also made a successful entry into golf design with fine layouts at Bad Griesbach and Schloss Nippenburg in Germany and also in Ireland, Spain and Italy.

In fact just about every significant player of the post-war era has got in on the golf architecture business. But do not be fooled by names! Who has heard of Eddie Hackett? Try one of his many Irish courses and you will want to search out others by him. Hackett's a fine and prolific designer, if shy, who very often had to work within a minimal budget. Until the last quarter of the century few knew much of the work of the Spanish architect, Javier Arana. Now, however, he is recognised as a master craftsman, his layouts amongst the best in Spain, a country to which all the best contemporary designers have been drawn, occasionally equalling his work, but never really outshining it.

Neither should one be fooled by the fact that a particular course regularly hosts a tour event. The plain fact is that the sponsor who enables the tournament to take place is in a very strong position to select the course on which it is played. Money and politics determine far more than the examination set by the host course, and, the majors apart, only a few tour venues qualify for the adjective, great.

But the best golfers of recent years *are* designing many good and some great courses: Arnold Palmer, Gary Player, Tom Watson, Severiano Ballesteros, Nick Faldo, Ben Crenshaw, John Jacobs, Johnny Miller, Dave Thomas, Peter Alliss, Peter Thomson, Des Smyth and Christie O'Connor Junior, to name but a few, have put their names to an impressive portfolio of fine courses.

There is an equally strong list of late 20th Century architects who were not quite so famous as players but have proved to be no less accomplished as architects: Robert von Hagge, Pepe Gancedo, Robert Muir Graves, Joe Lee, Rocky Roquemore, Pat Ruddy, Tom Craddock, Arthur Hills, Geoffrey Cornish, Dan Maples, Martin Hawtree, Donald Steel, Hamilton Stutt, Frank Pennink and C.K. Cotton have all delivered exceptional goods when given a reasonable site and an appropriate budget, and many continue to do so. A number of them have also been capable of producing a rabbit out of a hat, a decent course on a restricted site with a very limited budget. In fact, for many of them, the bulk of their work is making revisions to existing courses – to bring them into line with current technological advances, to enable courses to withstand the wear and tear of play at saturation level, and (in an era of trigger-happy litigation) to remove potentially dangerous holes. It is a great skill.

In the past, fine courses tended to proliferate wherever the wealthy enjoyed their leisure. Golf followed money. Nowadays almost the opposite is happening, with golf courses being constructed specifically to attract visitors – and money – to holiday destinations. Golf is a compulsory part of tourism in South-East Asia, the Iberian Peninsula, the more liberal of the Gulf oil states, the Caribbean Islands, Turkey and Cyprus, South Africa, Egypt, and even the former Iron Curtain countries (with the world class Moscow Country Club leading the way), as well as the traditional leisure resorts of the United States, Canada and the British Isles.

To be able to cope with the enormously different demands of golf design in such dissimilar climates the contemporary architect has to be a polymath combining the skills of a civil engineer, environmentalist, economist, marketing manager and salesman, surveyor, psychologist, philosopher, artist and conjuror. It is simply not enough to be able to distinguish bentgrass from fescue, bluegrass from zoysia, or to differentiate between a collection bunker and a carry bunker.

Huge sums of money are now involved in the construction of a top class golf course, and it is a major exercise in estimating and subsequent project management. Tom Fazio's sample construction figures are along these lines:

General earthwork
(moving up to 1 million cubic yards of soil)
$1.5 million
Hole shaping
$180,000 – $360,000
Grassing
$12,500 per acre
(with between 20 and 100 acres to be turfed)
Greens construction
(including blower/vacuum/heating systems)
$500,000
Landscaping
(for instant maturity)
$500,000 – $2 million
Irrigation
(computer controlled sprinklers etc)
$1.2 million
Erosion control
$100,000 – $500,000
Maintenance complex
$350,000 – $800,000

Already we are talking of between $4 million and $8 million and there is no clubhouse, no fees have yet been paid to consultants and legal advisors to obtain all the necessary planning permission and environmental approvals, the architect has not yet claimed his fee (which may be $1 million or more in the case of a "big name"), and a staff of between 15 and 40 will need to be recruited to maintain the course at a cost in excess of $1 million per year. The figures get even more horrific when the terrain is extreme. No wonder there have been a number of highly publicised bankruptcies amongst the "instant" golf courses when income and expenditure have not quite kept pace with each other. In many ways the most successful new ventures have been those which were begun at the bottom by getting a few simple holes in play and adding facilities and extra holes only when the cash flow permitted. It may take 30 years or more to produce a half-decent course in this way, but their proprietors are still in business when those whose ambition could not be matched by income long ago returned to selling used cars.

The introductory chapters have told the story of the development of the golf course, pointing to the achievements of the great architects of the 20th Century. The dawn of the new Millennium sees Jack Nicklaus, Pete Dye, Tom Fazio, Robert Trent Jones II and Rees Jones at the pinnacle of world golf design. It is no coincidence that they are all Americans because, ever since Donald Ross and Charles Blair Macdonald took the principles of the best Scottish architecture across the Atlantic Ocean to the United States, the Americans have produced the greatest players and their architects have been required to be more resilient and more innovative in order to keep their brilliant players in check. The year 2000 also saw the passing of the most renowned architect of them all, Robert Trent Jones Snr. His career lasted 70 years, he built or remodelled over 500 courses in 30 countries, and no fewer than 20 US Opens, 12 PGA championships and 47 other national championships were played on his courses. He devised his own study programme at Cornell University, including agronomy, horticulture, landscape architecture and hydraulics. Hardly surprisingly his courses were always at the cutting edge of strategic design and technical invention. Many of the courses in this book are testament to his particular imperishable genius.

At the 7th at Muirfield, a par-three played to an exposed green, a golfer is completely at the mercy of the elements and club selection is dictated accordingly.

Europe

Born, cradled and nurtured on the wild coasts of Scotland, golf is native to the British Isles and an exotic plant everywhere else – although, like many exotics, it has often found conditions as much to its liking where it has been imported. Scotland's pride are the natural links where time and the seasons were the principal architects of courses like Royal Dornoch, that noble links of the north, and the austere, patriarchal St Andrews, the shrine to which the greatest still return to pay homage. Golf began its travels when it was taken south to England by the Stuarts and then to the four corners of the earth by the men of both nations in the Empire-building days of the nineteenth century. Progress remained tardy on the European mainland until as late as the mid-1980s when the emergence of players like Bernhard Langer from Germany and Spain's Severiano Ballesteros, allied to victories for Europe in the Ryder Cup, had a dramatic effect.

Among the earliest of courses on the Continent of Europe were those built during Queen Victoria's reign at watering places to which the wealthy British migrated annually to take the cure: spas like Baden-Baden in Germany, Karlovy Vary and Marienbad in Czechoslovakia (then a realm of the Hapsburgs), and Pau in the foothills of the Pyrenees, the earliest of them all (1856). At first most progress, outside Britain, was made in northern Europe – the Low Countries (where there are echoes of Scottish linksland), Sweden and Germany.

But changing patterns of wealth and tourism have seen the emergence in more recent times of a plethora of courses at Europe's other extreme, the Mediterranean and Atlantic coastlines of the Iberian Peninsula. In 1997 the importance of Spain in particular to European golf was recognised when Valderrama, in the province of Andalusia, was chosen as the first continental venue for the Ryder Cup.

Similar in appearance and atmosphere to the resort courses of North America, these new venues have largely been built as commercial developments by entrepreneurs and have had the benefit of some of the best architects that money can buy. Their sunlit, Sybaritic ambience seems a world away from the windswept linksland of the Scottish coast where the game took root, almost organically, as part of the life of small, tightly-knit communities.

1. St Andrews 2. Royal Troon 3. Carnoustie 4. Royal Dornoch 5. Muirfield 6. Turnberry
7. Loch Lomond 8. Royal Liverpool 9. Royal Lytham St Annes 10. Sunningdale 11. Royal Birkdale
12. The Belfry 13. Royal St George's 14. Ganton 15. Royal Porthcawl 16. Royal County Down
17. Royal Portrush 18. Portmarnock 19. K-Club 20. Ballybunion 21. Kennemer 22. Royal Antwerp
23. Falsterbo 24. Halmstad 25. Club Zur Vahr 26. Le Golf National 27. Chantilly
28. El Saler 29. Las Brisas 30. Valderrama 31. Sotogrande 32. San Lorenzo 33. Vilamoura

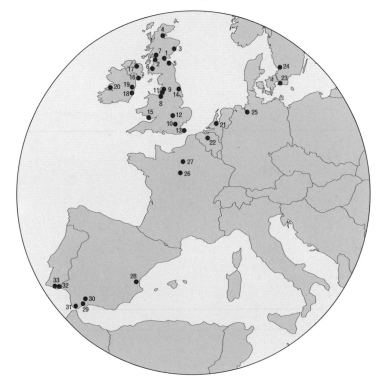

Nature fashions an
ageless masterpiece

With the patronage of King William IV in 1834 the Society of St Andrew's Golfers became known as the Royal and Ancient Golf Club.

For centuries, the eyes and thoughts of golfers everywhere have turned towards St Andrews: in all their world there is nothing to compare with the ancient university city and the Old Course spreading away from its doors. Here is the very heart of golf, the very breath of its history on links that, for countless ages, have known so little change. Every golfer there ever was has wanted to play at St Andrews, and down the years it has attracted more pilgrims than any other course in the world.

At first sight, the Old Course may not seem remarkable. One will have been charmed by the intimacy of its approaches from within the city and the beauty of the spacious rectangle of green, sweeping down from the Royal and Ancient clubhouse, grey, four-square and slightly forbidding. On one side are the smaller clubs, Old Tom Morris's shop, hotels and houses; on the other a rolling sward of putting green and beyond, the superb bay, leagues and leagues of golden sand curving away towards the distant estuary of the Tay.

The old links has been condemned as an anachronism and cursed as being unfair, but no course has commanded greater affection and respect from those who have learned to appreciate its subtleties and charms. It can be as tantalising as a beautiful woman, whose smile at once is a temptation and a snare, concealing heartbreak and frustration for some, joy and fulfilment for others, but possession only for the very fortunate few. It does not yield its ancient secrets lightly or take kindly to contempt and impatience, but it does reward those who give their best in thought, temper and technique. Furthermore, St Andrews is the setting for the Royal and Ancient Club. It was founded on May 14, 1754, when 22 "Noblemen and Gentlemen, being admirers of the ancient and healthful exercise of the Golf", met to

subscribe for a silver club, to be the trophy of an annual competition. Since then its sphere of influence has become almost universal, except in America, which has its own governing body in the United States Golf Association.

There is no telling when golf began at St Andrews, but the earliest written evidence was a licence, issued in 1552, which permitted the community to rear rabbits on the links, and "play at golf, futball, schuteing ... with all other manner of pastimes". The proprietor was bound "not to plough up any part of said golf links in all time coming" but to reserve them for the comfort and amusement of the inhabitants. So, for more than 400 years, every golfer has enjoyed a right to play over the course, and only within the present century has a green fee been imposed. In recent times, this has grown to the point where the cost is outside the means of many golfers, a sad development since the last thing the Old Course was meant to be was a testament to wealth.

It remains, nonetheless, a monument to the origins of golf as a game played on links by the sea. In the beginning it knew no architect but nature; it came into being by evolution rather than design; and on no other course is the hand of man less evident.

In all the years since the Royal and Ancient Club was formed, the outline of the course has never changed. It was then no more than 40 yards wide, a rolling strip of linksland between the gorse bushes in the shape of a huge billhook. There was not room for separate holes going out and home, so the golfers played eleven (later nine) out to a distant turn by the shining waters of the Eden estuary, and returned using the same fairways and greens.

St Andrews must have had its perilous moments in those days – and it still can, for seven of the double greens remain – but nowadays there is more delay than danger on a crowded day. The double greens are so huge that only an extremely wayward shot will find its way on to another man's province. If so, the player can face a length of putt undreamed of on any other course in the world. Nowhere does the old excuse for an indifferent score of taking three putts hold more water.

The greens are further evidence of nature's bounty; most of them are on plateaus, sometimes only slightly raised above the level of their surrounds but plateaus nonetheless. When the wind stands firm and the turf is hard and swift, the man who pitches to the hole can be lost; the pitch and run or the plain running approach must be used, though such conditions nowadays are the exception rather than the rule at St Andrews. In common with many other links it has lost something of its seaside character; the grass on the fairways is richer, the greens more holding than of old. Often enough, it is possible to pitch to them and good scoring is easier in consequence. This is most readily seen at the Alfred Dunhill Cup, which is played at St Andrews every October, when the turf is invariably lush and the greens soft. Add a windless day and anything becomes possible: in 1987 Curtis Strange went round in just 62 strokes to set a new course record. Ten years later, a Swede called Joakim Haeggman played the front nine in level threes, a wonderful effort given the formal regulation mark of 36.

Another remarkable feature of the course is the mul-titude of bunkers, most of which are named, ranging from vast sandy caverns to little holes of varying depth, often allowing room only for an "angry man and his niblick". All are natural, many are relics of the days when people dug for shells deposited by the sea before the links were formed, while others were made by sheep sheltering from the wind. Over the years great numbers were filled, but enough remain to test and infuriate the mightiest, because they are not always visible and seem to lurk in the most unexpected places.

Lying within the curve of a bay on the north eastern shores of Fife, the course is vulnerable to every caprice of the wind. Many are those who have played to the turn against it and then, hoping for assistance on the home-ward journey, had to face it all the way back. The strate-gy of play can change within the hour. Such are the

The first and 18th holes at St Andrews, flanked by some of Scotland's finest architecture. On the left is the magnificent club house of the Royal and Ancient G. C. the governing body (with the USGA) of golf.

The Course Card

The Old Course, St. Andrews, Fife

Record: 62, Curtis Strange, Dunhill Cup, 1987

Hole	Name	Yards	Par
1	Burn	376	4
2	Dyke	413	4
3	Cartgate (out)	397	4
4	Ginger Beer	464	4
5	Hole o' Cross (out)	568	5
6	Heathery (out)	412	4
7	High (out)	388	4
8	Short	175	3
9	End	352	4
10	Bobby Jones	379	4
11	High (in)	174	3
12	Heathery (in)	314	4
13	Hole o' Cross (in)	430	4
14	Long	581	5
15	Cartgate (in)	456	4
16	Corner of the Dyke	424	4
17	Road	455	4
18	Tom Morris	357	4
Out		3,545	36
In		3,570	36
Total		7,115	72

whereabouts of the hazards that the slightest variations in the wind can mean the difference between being trapped in an infuriating little bunker and having a straightforward shot to the green. There is no standard way of playing the holes, except for the first and the last. Everything depends on the wind; an approach may be a metal wood one day, a short pitch the next.

The Old Course makes a wonderful play on courage and fear but, above all, it is an examination of a golfer's thinking: he can never relax. In view of this, it is not surprising that nearly all the great golfers throughout the ages have grown to respect the place, and some, like Bobby Jones, to love it. With Jones it was not love at first sight. In the third round of the 1921 Open he was a dozen or more strokes over par and, after taking six on the short 11th, tore up his card. The world knows how he redeemed

that failure with a famous victory six years later, and another in the Amateur championship, the first stage of the "Grand Slam" in his imperishable summer of 1930. When, almost thirty years later, Jones was given the freedom of St Andrews and made an Honorary Burgess of the city – a distinction not conferred upon an American since Benjamin Franklin – he said: "The more I studied the Old Course, the more I loved it and the more I loved it, the more I studied it, so that I came to feel that it was for me the most favourable meeting ground possible for an important contest. I felt that my knowledge of the course enabled me to play it with patience and restraint until she might exact her toll from my adversary, who might treat her with less respect and understanding."

The beginning of the course seems innocence itself. The widest fairway in existence – shared by the first and last holes – looks inviting, but at its limit winds the Swilcan Burn, an immediate menace to peace of mind for it must be carried by the first shot to the 1st green, and this invariably is longer than it looks. From the second tee the long trail outwards begins down the narrow ribbon, perhaps a 100 yards across, of crumpled, saffron links, broken only by the emerald pools of the double greens and the countless folds, falls and hummocks of the ageless land. This second hole is a perfect example of the course at its best, especially when the flag is towards the left of the green. The only reasonable approach is from the right, so either the drive risks bunkers and gorse or the second shot must be played to the right-hand part of the green, leaving a long and formidable putt.

The problem at the 3rd is the same – a measure of risk must be taken from the tee for a clear pitch to the pin; likewise at the 4th, with its drive along a valley between a plateau and the inevitable gorse and bunkers on the right. A host of bunkers awaits the drive to the 5th which is aimed too straight at the distant pin; this is the Hole o' Cross, the longest of all, which forces a decision whether to attempt to carry a hill with two large bunkers in its face or play short, leaving a longish third to the green. In the

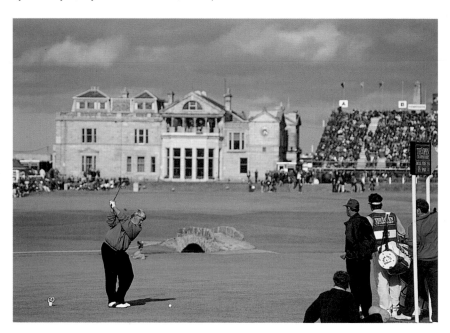

John Daly drives off from the 18th hole on his way to an emotional victory in the 1995 Open Championship.

The 17th

Hardest Par Four in Golf

When Tom Watson stood on the 17th tee during the final round of the 1984 Open he was, unquestionably, the finest golfer in the world. In an astonishing eight-year period of supremacy he had won eight majors and he was on the point of equalling Harry Vardon's record of six Opens.

When Watson stood on the 18th tee he was a different golfer entirely. He had misjudged his second shot and with it went his dream of winning the Open at the Home of Golf. He had also lost that feeling of imperiousness, that self-belief that gave him his edge. Watson never did

win another major. Vardon continues to stand alone.

If a single hole can do that to a player of Watson's stature, what hope the rest of us? Not much, for only the best of the pros expect to walk off with a par. This is one hole that has withstood the demands of technology, offering advantage to the long hitter only if he shows the utmost courage from the tee. For John Daly to find the 17th fairway with his driver in the 1995 Open play-off, he had to practically aim at his suite balcony in the adjoining Old Course hotel. Daly plotted the route perfectly, drawing the ball back from the building and into the

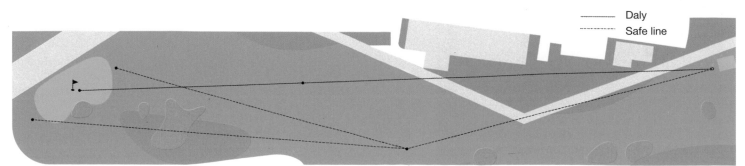

———— Daly
- - - - - Safe line

1933 Open, with the ground bone-hard and a gale behind him, Craig Wood drove into one of these bunkers, almost a quarter of a mile from the tee. A slight ridge protects the 6th green and makes the approach seem shorter than it is, a common feature of the Old Course. The stranger is forever under-clubbing.

·The next six holes form what is commonly known as the Loop, where the foundation of low scores invariably is made; on occasion they have been played in 18 strokes or fewer. The drive to the 7th is one of the most testing, practically blind, with a sea of gorse to punish the slice – but the 8th is not a severe short hole. Good drives make threes readily possible at the next two holes, but the little approach to the 9th is dead flat. It has caught many a player in two minds as to whether to pitch or run it, and has often resulted in a scuffle.

Of all the great short holes, the 11th stands high. The green is on a considerable slope, with the waters of Eden beyond; to the left is the deep Hill bunker. The essence of the shot is to avoid these and yet not to have a fiendishly difficult putt. To finish above the hole with the wind off the estuary is to invite three putts; men have been known to putt off the green. Gene Sarazen once took six there, with three shots in the Hill bunker, and eventually lost the championship by one stroke.

There never was a hole more obviously the work of the Devil than the 12th, where seeming innocence conceals all manner of evil. However well one knows the hole, it is hard to realize that so much danger exists between tee and green, only some 300 yards away. None of it is visible, but the fairway, a gentle green slope, is infested with bunkers.

After the 13th, the task is stern indeed. No single hole in golf has brought more championship competitors to grief than the 14th; the number of great golfers who have taken sevens and worse there is legion. In any kind of wind, save a helping one, the prospect from the back tee is fearsome indeed, with the five Beardies bunkers clustered together to trap the slightest pull and a low grey stone wall jutting into the line from the right. Only the bold or the very strong attempt to carry the great Hell bunker and its attendants, and then remains the problem of judging the third shot over a sleek, steep bank. The 15th presented no great difficulty for years, because the professionals could easily carry its main hazard, the wretched little Sutherland bunker, which stands precisely on the cautious line from the tee. But now the hole has been lengthened by 46 yards and many a pro will now find himself echoing the thoughts of one Greens Committee long ago, who ordered its removal. On that occasion the rebels went in the night, opened it again and there it remains.

Similarly the 16th has been lengthened by 44 yards ·to bring the Principal's Nose bunker back into play. The confident or the unthinking will continue to drive between the railway and the hazard, a threateningly narrow approach. The railway, whose fences remain, is nowadays out-of-bounds. But in olden days, when it was a cart track, golfers carried a track iron, one of which can be seen in the Royal and Ancient Museum. The prudent line from the tee is to the left, but the Wig bunker by the green must be avoided. Then at last the golfer stands on the tee of the most famous hole in the world.

The drive over the corner of the hotel grounds, where black railway sheds once stood, is not as alarming as it looks, but the green on a little plateau is an awesome sight. On the left, "eating its way into its very vitals" as Bernard Darwin once wrote, is the Road bunker, while beyond the narrow green is the road itself, at the foot of a sharp little shelf with nothing to prevent the ball rolling down. The second may be anything from wood to short iron, but only the brave go for the top level of the green. The majority play short, but even the little approach is fraught with danger. The ground draws into the bunker, from where there is no more terrifying recovery, with the road awaiting any overhit.

Whatever may have befallen the golfer on the 17th the broad, guileless swoop of the last fairway is infinitely appealing. The drive can be aimed anywhere to the left;

---

middle of the fairway. From there he had just a seven iron to the flag.

Besides the bold second shot, where a player tries to hold the sliver of green, there are several approaches possible. A golfer can aim to take the bunker out of play, and aim for areas beside the 18th tee, as Ernie Els is prone to do. A more common route is to aim for a spot to the right of the flag, parallel to the surface from where a par four is feasible.

The 17th

A Splash Shot of the Utmost Delicacy

The Road bunker on the 17th has probably ruined more cards than any other in the world and none more so than in the 1995 Open play-off between John Daly and Costantino Rocca. An hour earlier, Rocca had holed across the Valley of Sin to reach this position. Now joy turned to heartache. Rocca's ball lay well in the sand but the bunker is small, its face steep and the hole only a few yards beyond it. A splash shot of the utmost delicacy, one that would feather the ball over the lip and make it land softly, was demanded of him. But the instinct of most golfers in such a situation is for a swing that is short and hurried and Rocca proved another victim. He would need three strokes in all before emerging and the four hole play-off was over as a contest without the 18th needing to be played.

The Road bunker as it was. Now it has a deeper, flat floor and vertical face. The 17th was the hardest hole in the 2000 Open Championship.

to slice out-of-bounds at this point would be lunacy indeed. Only the Valley of Sin, a smooth bowl which gathers the timid approach, remains to be avoided and so on to Tom Morris's green. Always it seems there are people leaning from the windows and over the fences. Behind them rises the cloistered little city, grey, peaceful and so very old. This was the setting for the most dramatic last hole the Open has known in modern times.

When Doug Sanders, at the end of a torturous day of wind in 1970, hit a long drive up the last fairway, victory was there for the taking; he needed a four to beat Nicklaus. The task seemed only a formality but he took three putts, finally missing from a yard – and Nicklaus had enjoyed the escape of his lifetime. In the play-off the following day, Sanders bravely fought back from four behind to one as they stood on the last tee. Nicklaus, with an unconsciously masterful gesture, took off a sweater for greater freedom and unleashed a thunderous drive that almost hit the pin. It ran through the green into thick rough, from where he chipped to six feet. As the putt just curled in he flung his putter high in the air, a rare show of emotion for Nicklaus and a heartbreaking moment for Sanders.

In the 1995 Open the old green saw more drama, when Costantino Rocca holed a putt from in the Valley of Sin to force a four hole play-off against John Daly. Moments earlier, Rocca had fluffed a 50-yard chip and a lifetime of regret was staring him in the face. The putt negated the tears. He fell to his knees and then pummelled his fists into the turf in jubilation. Rocca would lose the play-off but the smile would not leave his face. He had lost with honour rather than humiliation and the difference became apparent in the years that followed, as he established himself among the finest players.

Hell bunker, which yawns so menacingly at the end of the Elysian Fields, forces the player to choose a right- or a left-hand line to the green and thereby court trouble of a different sort. The left side of the green is well protected by the Ginger Beer bunkers.

The 18th

To Pitch or Run?

Doug Sanders' approach shots at the 18th in the 1970 Open. In the final round Sanders chose to pitch over the grassy hollow of the Valley of Sin, which can be seen at the front left hand corner of the 18th green. His pitch shot (1) was hit with loft and landed, as he intended, close to the pin, but, despite the backspin, the ball failed to stop. The following day, from a similar position, Sanders hit a classic pitch-and-run shot with top-spin (2) through the Valley of Sin and up to the pin.

Perhaps no shot better illustrates the yawning difference between golf played on a traditional links and those lush venues to be found throughout the United States than the approach to the home hole at St Andrews. The tendency among the Americans is to pitch to the hole and try to impart enough spin to keep the ball near the flag. The danger is in going too long and leaving oneself the sort of putt which is easy to misjudge. Most British players prefer the classic method of the chip and run and unless the ground is heavy and slow this is usually the safer shot. The overwhelming concern in this situation is not to fall short in the insidious grassy hollow of the Valley of Sin, from where it is also simplicity itself to take three putts.

Which is the better method? There is no better method, rather depending instead on the skills of the player involved, the conditions of the day, and whether the flag is positioned towards the front or the back. But in mid-summer, when the ground is hard and baked and the pin to the front, there is no finer shot either to watch or to play than the chip and run executed with a true sense of feel. One such shot was played by Nick Faldo in 1990, when he won the Masters at Augusta and the Open at St Andrews by five shots. In the first round his drive down the 18th left him 40 yards of ground to cover. He selected a seven iron, and the ball crawled over the arid earth before dropping into the hole for an eagle two.

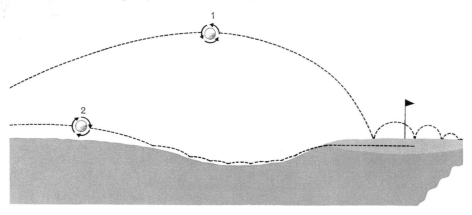

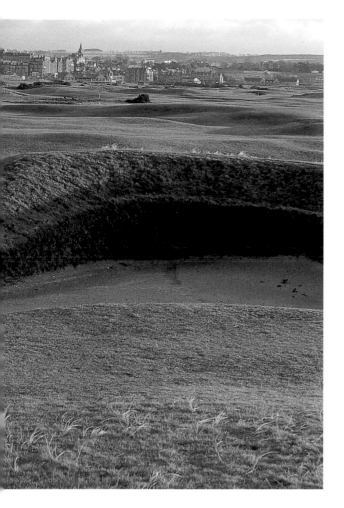

The Last Bastion
of Defence

Traditionally, the Old Course has three lines of defence: the weather, its greens, and its bunkers. In 2000 the weather was never a factor with hardly any wind all week and sun-baked fairways that were said to be playing faster than the greens. While the complexities of the greens continue to puzzle the handicap golfer they presented little difficulty to the Open competitors, the whole field averaging only 1.82 putts per green. The bunkers are another matter. In recent years the water table has been lowered at St Andrews which has enabled the bunkers to be dug deeper. At the same time certain key bunkers, such as the Road Bunker and Hell, were given flat floors and vertical, revetted faces. Escape was never easy, now it can be impossible. With the fairways running quickly and no wind to speak of, Hell Bunker was effectively taken out of play for an Open field which was driving an average distance of 285.7 yards throughout the championship. Everyone could drive so far down the Elysian Fields that the 14th yielded 6 eagles and 115 birdies during the four rounds. However, the Road Bunker proved disastrous for many. Sergio Garcia found himself so close to its face that he could neither get the ball out onto the green nor get a club to the ball to come out sideways. All he could do was swish dejectedly and hope to move the ball into some other part of the bunker. At the time he was not in contention. It was different for David Duval. With a hot streak down the front nine, he had been challenging Woods in the final round,

at one point getting to within three shots of him. He lost his momentum at the 12th, but second place still seemed assured – until he knocked his approach to the 17th into the Road Bunker. It took him four shots to get out, he ended up with a quadruple-bogey eight, and, by finishing in joint 11th, his week's wages were reduced by over £200,000. Clearly, Tiger Woods recognised the threat posed by the St Andrews bunkers from the outset. Playing some of the most intelligent golf ever witnessed, he plotted a safe route round the Old Course and so brilliant was his execution of this master plan that he never went in a single bunker during the 72 holes of that Open Championship!

Tiger Woods was in a class of his own during the summer of 2000. Having destroyed the cream of world golf in June to take the US Open at Pebble Beach with a record 15-stroke margin, he came to St Andrews in July hoping to join Gene Sarazen, Ben Hogan, Jack Nicklaus and Gary Player as the only men to have won all four Majors. That he succeeded at the age of 24 is remarkable enough, but the manner in which he achieved it was astonishing. He put together four sub-70 rounds to set a record low score of 269 for a St Andrews Open. Woods went on to equal Ben Hogan's record of three Majors in a season by taking the US PGA at Valhalla. By winning the Masters in the following April, Woods became the only man ever to hold all four Majors at the same time.

As much by skill
as by strength

Royal Troon GC

Record: 64,
Greg Norman,
The Open 1989

Hole	Yards	Par
1	364	4
2	391	4
3	379	4
4	557	5
5	210	3
6	577	5
7	402	4
8	126	3
9	423	4
10	438	4
11	463	4
12	431	4
13	465	4
14	179	3
15	457	4
16	542	5
17	223	3
18	452	4
Out	3,429	36
In	3,650	35
Total	**7,079**	**71**

Royal Troon is rarely acclaimed among the great Open Championship golf courses. It possesses neither the beauty of Turnberry, the dunes of Birkdale, the fairness of Muirfield or the reverence of St Andrews. But its place on the rota is deserved for all that and its motto, "Tam Arte Quam Morte" (As much by skill as by strength) was much in evidence at the 1997 Championship when the laurels were handed out not to the celebrated Tiger Woods but rather Justin Leonard, a short-hitting Texan who showed a greater awareness of its subtle demands.

Troon's most celebrated member is Colin Montgomerie, who has made his name with his accuracy and an acute sense of course management. One round over the fabled links of his home course is sufficient to understand where he learned his rudimentary knowledge of such skills. Without them, no-one can hope to prosper over this dour and forbidding stretch of Ayrshire coastline.

The first six holes, though, are wonderfully inviting, and Greg Norman demonstrated the possibilities for low scoring when, in the final round of the 1989 Open, he birdied them all. The last seven offer no such prospect, however. Back into the prevailing wind, it is as much as a golfer can do to hold on to par if the elements possess any ferocity. The links has more than its share of prized holes. For many years it could boast both the longest and the shortest holes on the present-day Open roster. The mantle of the longest hole passed from Troon's 6th to Carnoustie's 6th, then to the 14th at St Andrews. There are no imminent challengers for the distinction of shortest hole, Troon's 8th being world famous. It is the most celebrated of all short holes, the Postage Stamp, a magnificent testament to the belief that the game, indeed, is as much about skill as strength. Henry Leach described it perfectly when he wrote: "It is as full of wickedness as it is of beauty." Like many seaside courses that were formed in the closing years of the nineteenth century, Troon owed its

formation to a railway line, in this instance the main link between Glasgow and Ayr. For the citizens of Glasgow and Paisley a stretch of coastline offering sandy beaches and miles of duneland was now within their grasp. It was also perfect for golf and the developers seized upon the land like prospectors at a gold mine. Their legacy is a necklace of sublime links courses, stretching one after the other: Irvine, Glasgow Gailes, Western Gailes, Barassie, Troon, and Prestwick.

Troon was formed on March 16 1878, at the instigation of a Scot called James Dickie, who owned a summer house on Troon's South Beach and wanted to kindle the interest of some of the local people for a golf club of their own. Dickie approached the Duke of Portland, who gave permission to build a course on land between Craigend and Gyaws Burn. Craigend Burn is now piped under the road in front of the

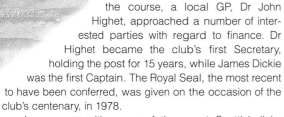

along the shoreline. The next six holes broadly form a loop, turning back and forth, rather like that at the Old Course at St Andrews. The last six all head homewards, towards a clubhouse steeped both in history and beauty.

Not even the opening hole at St Andrews can offer a more welcoming start to a round than the first at Troon. The fairway may run close to the edge of the shoreline but it is a poor shot that locates it. The driving area is inviting and the short second shot is to a generous green. The hole runs to 364 yards and in the summer months with a helpful wind a big hitter can open his shoulders and contemplate reaching the front apron. The 2nd is almost as straightforward although Darren Clarke might be tempted to disagree after finding the beach with his tee shot during the final round of the 1997 Open. Given that he only finished three shots behind the winner, to lose two here was wasteful in the extreme. Two fairway bunkers lie in wait to capture the big hitter but with length not a factor the player with an artful sense of course management will play short and still have a small iron to the green.

Similarly the 3rd, where the Gyaws Burn crosses the fairway at 300 yards, thus taking the green out of range. Another short iron approach, nonetheless. The 4th is a long par five which did not appear very long after Tiger Woods launched his drive during the first round of the 1997 Open. A yardage circle painted into the turf nearby indicated that, give or take a yard, he had struck his tee shot 435 yards. For more mortal players the hole plays as a dog-leg to the right. The 5th is the first of a quartet of splendid short holes. To the right are clear views of the Isle of Arran. With the wind blowing off the sea and the flag to the right the line can be the very edge that separates the green from the beach; a brave shot, to say the least.

The 5th is the one hole over the first six where a reasonable player in reasonable weather needs to be fully on

clubhouse but Gyaws Burn is still very much part of the layout, crossing both the 3rd and 16th holes. While Dickie was securing the land for the course, a local GP, Dr John Highet, approached a number of interested parties with regard to finance. Dr Highet became the club's first Secretary, holding the post for 15 years, while James Dickie was the first Captain. The Royal Seal, the most recent to have been conferred, was given on the occasion of the club's centenary, in 1978.

In common with many of the great Scottish links courses, no one architect was responsible. The initial six holes at Troon were laid out by the greenkeeper at Prestwick, Charles Hunter. As for the rest of the holes, which grew in number as more land was acquired, no-one is sure who designed them. The first man to carry out alterations was the 1883 Open Champion Willie Fernie, the Troon professional at the time. In turn he has been followed by James Braid, Dr Alister Mackenzie, and Frank Pennink. Between them they have fashioned an honest course that requires the utmost concentration and skill to unlock a score. Even Arnold Palmer, who won the Open there in 1962, once talked of his determination "not to get locked into a life and death struggle with the course."

Troon is laid out in the manner of a classic traditional links. The first six holes head away from the clubhouse,

The 6th hole was for many years the longest in Open Championship golf, an endless par five to a green surrounded on two sides by dunes.

The 11th

Tiger's Torment, Nicklaus's Nemesis

Not since Jack Nicklaus had any player come to his first Open as a professional with a bigger reputation than Tiger Woods. Coincidentally, both made their debuts at Troon. It is not coincidence, however, that both were humbled by the 11th. Arnold Palmer once said that he aimed to get the 11th before it got him but Woods and Nicklaus were not so fortunate. In their first encounters with the hole in serious competition, they played it in a combined total of 17 shots.

Nicklaus ran up no less than a ten on the hole and typically learned from the experience. "It taught me how much knowledge I needed to absorb before I could think of taking on the original form of golf," he would say. Woods's seven arose from hooking his tee shot into the whin bushes to the left of the tee. He donned his waterproofs for his recovery shot but when the ball moved but a few feet he had to concede defeat.

Palmer's strategy was clearly the correct one. Before the 1962 Open began he had identified the hole as the key one, based on where it came in the round and also its difficulty. The hole had recently been converted from a shortish par four into a par five and over the four days of the championship Palmer would birdie it three times and par it once. Thirty-five years later it was once more a par four, though, at 463 yards, not one that now lacked for length. Woods was hardly alone in suffering. The 11th was played in an average of 4.65 shots, thus easily securing its ranking as the most difficult hole on the course, and adding still further to its formidable reputation.

Tiger Woods's first Open as a professional saw him encounter difficulty with the daunting 11th hole.

his mettle. The 6th, therefore, continues the run of holes from which a golfer must make his score, a raking par five where, despite its length of 577 yards, accuracy is the prime requirement.

The 7th lies resplendent before the player standing on the tee. For the first time the wind is no longer in the same direction. Then, the wonderful 8th, its green tugging at a dune for protection from the sea breeze. Before they think of designing a course, all architects should stand on this tee to discover the true glory of the short par-three.

The distance is just 126 yards but into the wind it can feel more like 226. In such conditions it is not uncommon to see members taking a wooden club yet still fall short of the target. In more normal conditions it is just a seven iron or less, and the premium on hitting the green is high. To the left of the green is not only the dune but two deep bunkers. To the right are two more cavernous sand traps, while another lurks to the rear. In the 1997 Open there was a certain poetry when the man who had struck the ball 435 yards down the 6th ran up a triple bogey six on the shortest hole on the course. As much by skill as by strength, remember.

The 9th takes the golfer to the far end of the course, a par four of 423 yards that plays somewhat shorter than its yardage. The second shot is to a tricky two-tier green. The homeward nine begins with the one "blind" drive on the course, and is a foretaste of the sequence of difficult holes that follow. The second shot is invariably a long iron to another green that rejects any ball played towards its outer rim. After the 8th, the 11th is the most famous hole on the course and, since they changed the par at the 1997 Open from five to four, one of the hardest par fours in golf. From the fairway there appears little to aim at. The railway runs hard against its right hand side but to the left the whins make an equally troublesome prospect. Neither is there any let up with the second shot as the right hand side of the green snuggles cosily against the railway line.

The 12th hole was the scene of an extraordinary stroke of luck during the 1989 Open. Mark Calcavecchia was struggling to come to terms with Troon's ominous challenge and ready to concede defeat as he stood over his ball to the left of the green. He had already spilled several strokes and now was to lose at least one more, since

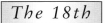

Brain Beats Braun

Greg Norman lost the 1989 Open because he forgot the motto that lies below the club's crest at Royal Troon. Coming to the home hole, the fourth in a four hole play-off, Norman was level with Mark Calcavecchia. The American, fearing his drive would catch the bunker down the right hand side of the fairway, fell off his tee shot and the ball sliced badly to the right. Yet when Norman took out a wood, Calcavecchia suddenly became less worried. He knew the bunker stood 310 yards from the tee but he also knew it was in reach for such a long hitter. Such thoughts never came into Norman's strategy. He wanted to intimidate his opponent, and punish him for his errant drive. Norman caught the drive perfectly. But when, on first bounce, it veered to the right, it was Calcavecchia who

was watching closely. Sure enough, the ball bounded for an age and finished in the trap. Norman was devastated. Once more, from the trap he went for brawn, and the ball smashed into the bunker's face, and limped into another bunker. This time Norman thinned his shot and the ball careered out of bounds.

Norman had started that last day by humiliating Royal Troon with six consecutive birdies. He eventually finished with an incredible 64, as good a score as the old course has ever seen. But at the end of the day it was Troon that had delivered its telling reminder that it is not a course with which to trifle.

there appeared no hope of getting down in two, save to hole a 45 feet putt. Such was the lie, he could not contemplate getting the ball any closer. He thrashed at the ball with his wedge and was happy enough to see the ball fly into the air, even though he knew he was going to be left with the long putt he had forecast in his best-case scenario. And then, just as he contemplated all this, the ball dropped from the sky and into the hole without a bounce. A bogey at best had become the unlikeliest of birdies and when he eventually collected the title after a four hole play-off he could not help but reflect on this moment of outrageous good fortune.

The 13th is a rarity, a par four without a bunker. For its protection it relies instead on an uneven fairway where the bounces can be capricious. In many ways it is an unfair means of defence. Golf was never meant to be a fair game and links golf is the unfairest form of all. But this crosses the boundary and the 13th has proven unlucky for many and unreasonably so. Accordingly, it is probably the least distinguished hole on the course. The 14th is another stoutly defended short hole, the premium again on a well-struck tee shot. And so to Troon's fierce finish, one to match the terrors at Carnoustie and Lytham. In poor weather the 15th and 16th can seem unremittingly bleak. Staring into the distance at the former, unable to see the green for his second shot, Lee Trevino once remarked: "I did not know the First World War was played out here." One of the difficulties common to both holes is there is little on the horizon a golfer can use for a line.

The 17th is a long par three with a vast apron and here a player must call upon all his skill to judge how far the ball will run upon landing. In the 1989 Open play-off Greg Norman misjudged it. His tee shot, a beauty from the tee, or so it appeared, ran through the back from where he chipped weakly and ran up a bogey.

The home hole is reminiscent of that at Lytham. A resplendent clubhouse stands guard in the distance. From the tee there are bunkers left and right to avoid. The green, too, is heavily protected by sand. From the tee the drive has to travel at least 230 yards to reach the fairway. From there, though, the player is faced with one of the nicest shots in golf, to a green that positively implores a good stroke.

Greg Norman thought his drive down the 18th in the play-off for the 1989 Open Championship was perfect. But it never stopped rolling until it fell into a fairway bunker and the error of judgement cost him the title.

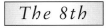

A Perfect Short Hole

Anyone who stands on the tee will not dwell to wonder why the hole is called the Postage Stamp. Even with a short iron in one's hands the green looks the very devil to hit. With the wind blowing off the sea it can prove as much although it did not to Gene Sarazen in a lovely interlude to the 1982 Open. Sarazen had been invited back, 50 years after winning the Championship and participated with two other former holders of yore, Max Faulkner and Fred Daly. The years might have robbed Sarazen of his length but his feel remained intact. In the first round he played a five iron which pitched short of the hole before rolling in. The following day, after finding a deep bunker to the right, the man who invented the sand wedge played the perfect shot with it, holing for a wonderful birdie two. Thus, in two rounds, Sarazen had played the hole in three strokes. If that was the sublime, the ridiculous came in the 1950 Open when a poor German amateur named Hermann Tissies one-putted for a 15.

Character to test a
champion

In common with most of the links courses of Scotland, the beginnings of golf at Carnoustie are a matter of legend and vague historical references. Early in the sixteenth century Sir Robert Maule, one of the first known golfers, delighted in exercising the "gowf" on the Barry links, adjoining Carnoustie on the northern shores of the Firth of Tay. The club was formed in 1842, in the early years of Victoria's reign, a prolific age for the birth of Scottish clubs; in 1867 the genius of Young Tom Morris first came to light there when, aged 16, he played against and defeated all comers. Almost ninety years later a golfer named Ben Hogan came to Carnoustie and confirmed, in a masterful act of supremacy, that he was the greatest player of the age. In 1975 Tom Watson, hitherto known as a player who buckled under pressure, ably demonstrated that competing in a melting pot is a talent not god-given but acquired. His victory in the Open proved the making of him, for he knew that if he could conquer Carnoustie then nowhere need hold any fears. His victory would lead to him dominating the game for eight years, during which time he won no fewer than eight Major championships. Sadly Watson's year was to prove the last Open at Carnoustie until its long overdue return in 1999. In the interim years the course was allowed to fall into neglect and for many years its unkempt appearance was a pitiful sight. Happily that has been corrected in the 1990s, its condition now in accordance with its status. Even the clubhouse, so long an eyesore and

comfortably the worst of any distinguished course in Britain, has been demolished as well.

Rarely can it be said of a course that it has few weaknesses, but this is true of Carnoustie. Every hole is different in character. Only three are short, and at no point during the round do more than two follow exactly the same direction. The problems set by the wind, therefore, are ever-changing and furthermore Carnoustie lies on the flatlands between the estuary and the low, distant hills, so that judgement of distance is critical. In every way it is a big course, and even from the ordinary competition tees it is a test of golf for good players. Most of the hazards, which include the sinuous menace of the Barry Burn at several holes, are placed to threaten the stroke that is slightly less than perfect, rather than one that is slightly better than awful.

The evolution from the ten-hole course made by Allan Robertson in the middle of the nineteenth century was a long one. Even after the extension to eighteen holes under the guidance of Tom Morris it knew many changes, until in 1926 James Braid made some new greens, tees and bunkers. The result was a superb course. Within its general confines is another, smaller, eighteen-hole course – the Burnside – and both are held in trust by the town council. Since the last years of the nineteenth century, almost 300 young men of Carnoustie have become professionals. A great number went to the United States and three of the most notable were the Smith brothers. The eldest, Willie won the US Open in 1899; Alex was twice champion thereafter, but poor Macdonald always failed. In twelve years from 1923 he was second, third and fourth twice each in the British Open, and was runner-up to Bobby Jones in both his victories in 1930. No more distinguished golfer ever failed to win an Open.

The early development of American golf owes much of its strength to the men of Carnoustie. It is written that, at various times, every State title had been held by one of them. Stuart Maiden, mentor of Jones, Archie Simpson and many another, sought fame and fortune far from the great links that

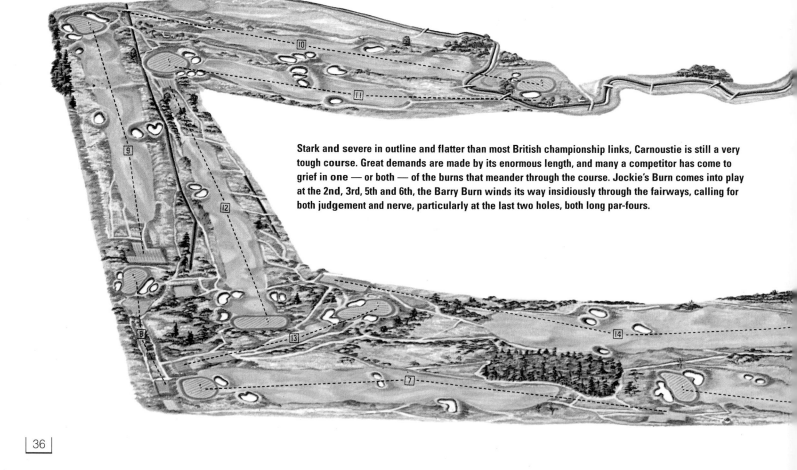

Stark and severe in outline and flatter than most British championship links, Carnoustie is still a very tough course. Great demands are made by its enormous length, and many a competitor has come to grief in one — or both — of the burns that meander through the course. Jockie's Burn comes into play at the 2nd, 3rd, 5th and 6th, the Barry Burn winds its way insidiously through the fairways, calling for both judgement and nerve, particularly at the last two holes, both long par-fours.

had brought forth their skills. There is no gentle introduction to the course. From the long rise of the first fairway a lengthy stroke is needed to reach a hidden basin of green. In his first round in the 1953 Open, Hogan used a 2-iron, searing into the wind. The next day he was home with a pitching club; each time the ball finished in the same place on the green. Controversy – particularly among professionals, many of whom seem to think that driving should be an unthinking process – has long centred upon Braid's bunker in the middle of the second fairway, where a good straight drive may finish. There is sufficient room to either side and why, occasionally, should the drive not have to be exactly lined?

The 3rd is a beautiful little hole, with its pitch over a stream to an awkward green, and then one turns again towards the prevailing wind for a finely shaped par-four with a long second over level ground. On the left-hand side is a thick wood of firs, a pleasing break in the bleak severity of the scene, and the 5th, again angled to the right, with its approach to a raised green, runs along the wood's far side.

Despite Hogan's feats the 6th is one of the great long holes in golf. Far down the fairway, which has a boundary fence the full length on the hooking side, are two bunkers which a good drive can reach. Again hard thought is called for on the tee: to play short or to either side? The right is the safer, and from there a long second must be placed on to the left of the fairway to avoid the mean little Jockie's Burn, which cuts in from the right. Then, and only then, is the 3rd to the green fairly straightforward. The 7th,

Jean Van de Velde wades into the Barry Burn during his disastrous skirmish with the 18th hole, when a modicum of conservatism would have handed him a comfortable victory in the 1999 Open Championship.

Tiger Woods struggling out of the rough during the 1999 Open Championship.

a good straight hole, moves to the farthest corner of the course and then, at last is the first short hole. The shot to a slightly raised plateau green is never easy to judge and here again a little spinney leavens the setting. The 9th is downhill – the only perceptible change in level on the whole course apart from the 12th, which ascends a parallel course with equal gentleness. Carnoustie, mercifully, does not hasten coronaries. Many have wondered why, in this Scottish fastness, the 10th should be called South America. Seemingly, a young citizen of Carnoustie, in the days when it produced more emigrant golfers than anywhere else on earth, had hopes of reaching that continent but celebrated his departure too freely and got no farther than the spinney by the 10th before succumbing to after-effects. The green here is within a loop on the Barry Burn, which cruelly snares the underhit shot as well as the one that is sliced. One drives across it from the next tee, but at no substantial range. The real menace of the water is yet to come.

The short 13th, tightly trapped though it is, brings some breathing space before what is probably the most exacting finish in Britain. The second shot from the long, curving 14th fairway must carry a hill in which have been carved the "Spectacle" bunkers. This shot deceived Hogan into underclubbing more than once and cost him the only five in his final round of 68, but it brought lasting fame to Gary Player when he held off the challenge of Nicklaus fifteen years later. The 15th swings along a hog's-back fairway into duneland and – except in a helping wind – is a demanding four.

By modern par standards the 16th is a short hole, but only by a yard or so from the back tee; by any standards it is ferociously difficult, with its tiny entrance between bunkers to a narrow shelf of green. And then the ghoulish fun of the finish begins in earnest. A solid drive in the right direction

A controversial restoration to the Open Championship roster

A gap of 24 years ensued between Tom Watson's victory in 1975 and the return of the Open Championship to Carnoustie. There was no gainsaying the potential of the course to test the greatest players in the world. Sadly the facilities for visitors and players, press and officials did not meet the demands of a modern championship. The condition of what was a mere municipal course began to deteriorate. Eventually the nettle was grasped, and the construction of a luxurious hotel overlooking the 18th green confirmed a new confidence in the return of Carnoustie to the highest division. The Royal and Ancient needed no convincing of the course's reputation as the sternest test of all Open venues. It was pencilled in for the last championship of the millennium.

Unfortunately this reputation, and a few exceptionally low-scoring rounds in recent championships, led the R&A to set up the course as something of a monster, with ridiculously narrow fairways and an impenetrable jungle of rough. An excuse was found in the wet spring and early summer which preceded the championship, but the plain fact was that great golfers were made to look like 28-handicap beginners as they hacked about trying in vain to escape, having missed the fairway by perhaps only a few inches. The casualty list of those who failed to make the cut after two days made morbid reading.

Eventually a leader emerged from the pack, a Frenchman called Jean Van de Velde. He played sound and, above all, intelligent golf to put himself five shots

clear of the field at the end of the third round. No one had surrendered such a substantial lead since the Argentinian Jose Jurado in 1931 – also at Carnoustie. Gradually the shots slipped away, the diminutive Australian Craig Parry gaining the lead briefly. But Van de Velde kept his head until he stood on the final tee with a three stroke lead needing only a double-bogey six to take the coveted claret jug back to France. The first priority was simply to find the fairway, which could be done with an iron. The gallery was dumbfounded as he reached for his driver. He flirted with the water but, miraculously, the ball found dry ground. Then the nightmare began.

Next he hit a slice which bounced off the grandstand into thick rough short of the Barry Burn. His wedge shot lumbered pathetically into the water. His shoes and socks came off and he paddled about for an eternity wondering if he could possibly play the ball as it lay, shin-deep beneath the surface. Accepting defeat he dropped out under penalty only to bungle his pitch into a greenside bunker. Now he needed to hole out from the sand for his victory. He did well to finish eight feet from the pin, bravely sinking the putt to get into a three-way play-off.

No one had really noticed Scotsman Paul Lawrie who had finished with a 67, the best round of the tournament by far. By playing par golf over the four hole play-off he became the first Scotsman to win the Open on native soil in 68 years, and the first qualifier to win since exemptions began in 1963.

from the 17th tee will carry the Barry Burn twice, but against a strong wind the tee shot must be placed on what is virtually an island amidst its wicked curves.

The drive to the last, haunted by the burn and out-of-bounds, is formidable. Then comes the last challenge of the burn, which is no mere stream but twenty feet or more across. Gene Sarazen tells of how, one evening during a championship, bets were made on the possibility of jumping it. The history of the Open is as much one of tragedy as of triumph and few would wish to match the fate of Jose Jurado of Argentina in 1931. Tommy Armour had set the pace with a closing 71, but Jurado could beat him by playing the last two holes in nine strokes. After a smothered drive had cost him six at the 17th Jurado (unaware of Armour's total, for score boards did not exist then) played short of the burn, took five and then learned that he could have tied with a four

when he had been within range to risk the carry. There was no talk of tragedy in 1937, when Henry Cotton achieved his finest hour. The whole American Ryder Cup team was competing and the weather was appalling. Cotton began his last round in a deluge and there was a danger that play might be abandoned, but he was round in 71, a tremendous performance. Al Laney, one of the finest and most perceptive of all American writers, was there and later described Cotton perfectly: "A strange, forbidding man in those days, but he could handle a golf club with his three-quarter swing more expertly than anyone I have seen since except Ben Hogan. When Cotton hit an iron to the green with chilling, humourless concentration it seemed magic. Like Hogan again, he gave the impression of coldness, but there was also the same feeling as with Hogan that the ball had been given no option, that there was nothing he could not achieve."

One Of The Great Championship Finishes

The 1968 0pen was in destiny's melting pot when Gary Player and Jack Nicklaus came to the 14th in the last round. Player was two ahead and had to wait on the fairway while Nicklaus, lucky to have a wooden club lie, extricated himself from the trees on the right. He smashed a 4-wood which finished just off the green and then, even before the excitement for Nicklaus had subsided, Player hit the shot of a lifetime. The 1975 Open was also decided by a great shot, by Tom Watson at the 18th.

The 14th to the 18th

In the 1968 0pen, Gary Player made a perfectly timed thrust at the then par-five 14th. He struck a magnificent four wood over the Spectacle bunkers to within two feet of the hole. Down went the putt for an eagle. The look of a champion was about Player that year; he was less tense, more relaxed and philosophical than usual. He had need to be, because from that point Nicklaus outgunned him from the last four tees with a series of thunderous strokes with a driver. When intent on a big drive Nicklaus always took the club away from the ball even more deliberately than usual, and never hurried the first movement. It helped to ensure that no suspicion of haste marred his swing's rhythm. His most remarkable shot was at the 17th. Everyone had been playing short of the Burn, but Nicklaus was two behind and the light breeze was helping. His massive hit, all of 340 yards, soared over the Burn and left him only a wedge. But he did not make a three and Player was almost safe.

In 1975 the 18th was reduced to a par-four 448 yards. This was done to emphasize the challenge of carrying the burn for the second shot instead of forcing the lay up short, as the longer hole often did. It also intensified the drama for the watching thousands. The decision certainly was justified as Tom Watson would agree. A golfer could ask for little more than to make a birdie on the last hole of

The 14th to the 18th _____ Player
 ------- Nicklaus

an Open aware that he needed to beat Nicklaus, who had just finished, and Johnny Miller, his companion, to win. Watson did just that with a perfect long pitch about ten feet from the hole. Then, in the play-off next day, after Jack Newton had bunkered his second shot and Watson knew that if he hit the green all the glory of victory and its manifold rewards would probably be his, he did it again. The hole was playing longer in relentless rain and Watson hit a two-iron. Later, being the honest golfer he is, he admitted that it was struck a shade heavy; nevertheless, it flew straight and far enough over the Burn to finish in the heart of the green. The merit of the shot was that Watson took enough club to allow for any slight striking error. It proved that his swing could withstand intense pressure, something of enormous importance to one who had failed in the two previous U.S. Opens.

Above: One of the great triumphs during Gary Player's illustrious career came in the 1968 Open at Carnoustie, when he held off the challenge of a rampant Jack Nicklaus.

Historic links and noble traditions

Northernmost of the world's great golf courses, Dornoch shares its latitude with the Bering Sea and Hudson Bay and its antecedents with those other places on the North Sea coast of Scotland, where golf had its beginnings. Among the early evidence of the antiquity of its links is a book, *The Earldom of Sutherland*, by Sir Robert Gordon, who was tutor to the family in the seventeenth century. Writing of Dornoch, he said: "About this town are the fairest and largest links of any part of Scotland, fitt for Archery, Golfing, Ryding, and all other exercises; they doe surpasse the fields of Montrose and St Andrews." The earliest written record of golf at Dornoch dates from 1616, putting it in third place behind St Andrews (1552) and Leith (1593) in the noble list of early Scottish links. The club was formed in the spring of 1877 by Alexander McHardy, pioneer of golf in the north of Scotland, and Dr Gunn, who learned the game at St Andrews.

For the first ten years of its life the course had only nine holes, but gradually more people were making the long pilgrimage beyond the Highlands and it was decided that old Tom Morris should be called upon to add another nine. He was charmed with the place from the outset, particularly with the presence of many natural plateaux which could serve for greens. From time to time alterations were made – notably by John Sutherland, a famous secretary – but for the most part the golf is wonderfully natural. The beautiful seaside turf, the dunes, hummocks, and undulating fairways owe little to the hand of man. Because of its remoteness, many golfers may not be aware of Dornoch's existence; others, aware of its fame, have never ventured so far in search of their game, for it is some sixty miles north of Inverness. Those who have speak of its glory with one voice. Dornoch stands comparison with all the finest in Britain. It curves along the shores of Embo Bay at the mouth of Dornoch Firth, a setting of wondrous isolation from the foulness of the cities – London is over 600 miles away – and a place of madly contrasting moods. The wind may be firm, bringing forth the golf at its splendid best; it can be a roaring gale, thundering down the valleys through the old western mountains, making the course a fear-

some test of all the strength, purpose and technique that a man can muster; or its voice may be stilled and the day alive with sunshine.

On such a day the golfer is reminded of the words of a man who visited Dornoch long ago and wrote: "Looking westward and, indeed, bounding the view from the Ord of Caithness on the northeast to the far away hills of Aberdeenshire, in the south, there is a grand circle of highlands before us, embracing all the finest 'Bens' in Sutherland, Ross and Inverness. On fine summer days the play of cloud shadows and sunlight gleam on these distant mountains is a very remarkable feature of the scenery." Let it not be thought that Dornoch is normally afflicted with tempest and extremes of climate. It can often be more temperate the farther north one travels – but how swiftly it can change, as the golfer discovers when enduring the challenge of the ferocious wind. This can be fun for the average golfer, except perhaps in competition, for rare pleasure can be had in improvising the strokes necessary to combat a wind.

The 1st, along a shallow rippling valley, and the 2nd, a pitch to a table green, are tricky rather than severe, especially if the turf is keen. From the 3rd tee the course falls away to the great curving basin of the links itself. Now follow two lovely holes of medium length, then a pitch to a long, narrow green high above the fairway and a beautiful short 6th, with its green a shelf hard against the flank of a heathery hillside. This must be climbed to the 7th tee, and for a moment the golf is that of open heathland. But the drive to the 8th plunges towards a green in a secret hollow.

To the golfer at one with his game, and helped perhaps by a prevailing breeze, the course thus far may not seem unduly difficult; but thence-forth his task begins in earnest with one of the most glorious stretches of seaside golf to be found anywhere in the world. From the 9th tee one turns for distant home and the next seven holes follow the gentle left-handed curve of the bay – a great scimitar of blue and silver and grey. This is true linksland golf, compelling not only strong, accurate driving but fine judgement of long approaches if par is to be achieved. Should the wind be against the golfer, or from either hand, control of flight and

Royal Dornoch is a links of splendid isolation rather than the bustle of championships, but two great golf architects, Pete Dye and Donald Ross, have bestowed on it the accolade of imitation. Dye's short par-four 5th at the Columbus Golf Club, Ohio, is patterned after Dornoch's 15th, while the basic character of Ross's famous No 2 course at Pinehurst, North Carolina, also derived from Dornoch — where Ross was born and learned his golf under Old Tom Morris, four times Open Champion, in the 1890s.

length will be examined to the utmost. There is respite of a kind at the short 10th and 13th, but their greens are far from generous targets and true strokes alone will prevail.

The one hole that does not instantly appeal is the 16th, with its steep, mounting fairway and no sight of the green unless the drive is very long; but the 17th is dangerously attractive with its drive to an unseen valley, whence the pitch must be truly struck or it will not reach the tableland of green. Two good shots will see one home at the last. The length of the second can be deceptive but the green stands free and open, inviting a good bold stroke. Analyse and examine the course as you will, the conclusion is inescapable that it is sufficient to test the most accomplished golfers in the world. There is little hope that it will, because of its remoteness. In 1984 the Amateur Championship did extend beyond its natural parameters and an Irish Walker Cup player Garth McGimpsey will always treasure, in particular, the decision to do so. Now Dornoch has returned to its blessed place in the game's roster, a place for pilgrims and the many distinguished golfers that have come to love it. Perhaps it is fitting that it remains in such splendid solitude, far removed from the turmoil and the excitement of championships.

Character for Export

The 14th is the greatest of all Dornoch's holes and the most demanding. Long known as 'Foxy', it measures 445 yards and requires two outstanding shots. The fairway swings to the left at about the range of a solid drive, then pursues its original direction before moving to the right again and rising to the plateau green. The beauty of the hole is its simplicity of design and the way in which the natural feature of a formidable hummock of dune on the right has made possible the two changes of direction. It has no need of artificial hazards and there is not a single bunker. Ideally, the drive should draw slightly with the tilt of fairway into a position from where a wood or long iron can be faded over the corner of the hill to the green. For those whose approaches fall short of the green there is the alternative of pitching their third shot or nursing it up the slope with a running shot. Although few modern links play as fast as they once did, the pitch and run is still essential to the successful golfer's armoury.

Undoubtedly the natural character and subtlety of Dornoch had a great influence on Donald Ross, who was professional and head greenkeeper there before going to America at the turn of the century and becoming one of the greatest architects. Numerous examples of his work there remain, including Pinehurst, the venue for the 1999 US Open. One of Ross's basic principles in designing a green was to raise its surface slightly – three or four feet _ above the level of the fairway and then fashion subtle undulations. This meant that the slightly erring shot would tend to roll off.

Above: Ben Crenshaw, preparing for the 1980 Open at Muirfield, played Dornoch. When asked about his visit on returning to Muirfield he said, "Let me put it this way, I nearly didn't come back". Tom Watson described Dornoch, "The most fun I have ever had playing golf". With the gorse in bloom it is easy to see why. This is the view from the tee on the 5th, one of Watson's favourite holes.

The Course Card

Royal Dornoch
Golf Club,
Dornoch,
Sutherland

Hole	Yards	Par
1	331	4
2	184	3
3	414	4
4	427	4
5	354	4
6	163	3
7	463	4
8	437	4
9	529	5
10	177	3
11	450	4
12	557	5
13	180	3
14	445	4
15	358	4
16	402	4
17	405	4
18	456	4

Out	3,302	35
In	3,430	35
Total	**6,732**	**70**

A punishing kind of
perfection

Tucked compactly away by the shores of the Firth of Forth, Muirfield is a beautifully simple and testing links, the fairest of all British championship courses. It has one of the most exacting finishing holes in golf, a wickedly bunkered 449-yard par-four. The front nine ends in an equally daunting par-five of 508 yards, protected on the right by bunkers and on the left by an out-of-bounds area. Muirfield has only three successive holes which are played in the same direction – a decided asset for a course that is almost always played in windy conditions.

To define the perfect golf course is well nigh impossible; so many factors of design, situation and personal taste are involved. Nevertheless, no course in the British Isles embraces more of the qualities one seeks in a great and fair challenge of skill than Muirfield, home of the Honourable Company of Edinburgh Golfers, the oldest club in the world with a continuous history. Royal Blackheath in London can claim to have existed in 1608 and is technically the oldest club, but the Honourable Company has its complete records from 1744 when it first held a competition on the links at Leith.

For almost half a century the Company played over the five holes there, but eventually encroachment caused difficulties and they went to Musselburgh. In time this links also became disagreeably crowded, and in 1891 the Company again moved east, down the Firth of Forth to Muirfield. At first the new course met with much abuse, partly because the club had taken the Open Championship with them. This championship had been started by the Prestwick club, and was played there for the first time on October 17, 1860. Willie Park of Musselburgh won the handsome red morocco challenge belt.

Ten years later Young Tom Morris, a supreme golfer, annexed it for himself by winning for the third successive year. There was no Open in 1871, and thereafter the

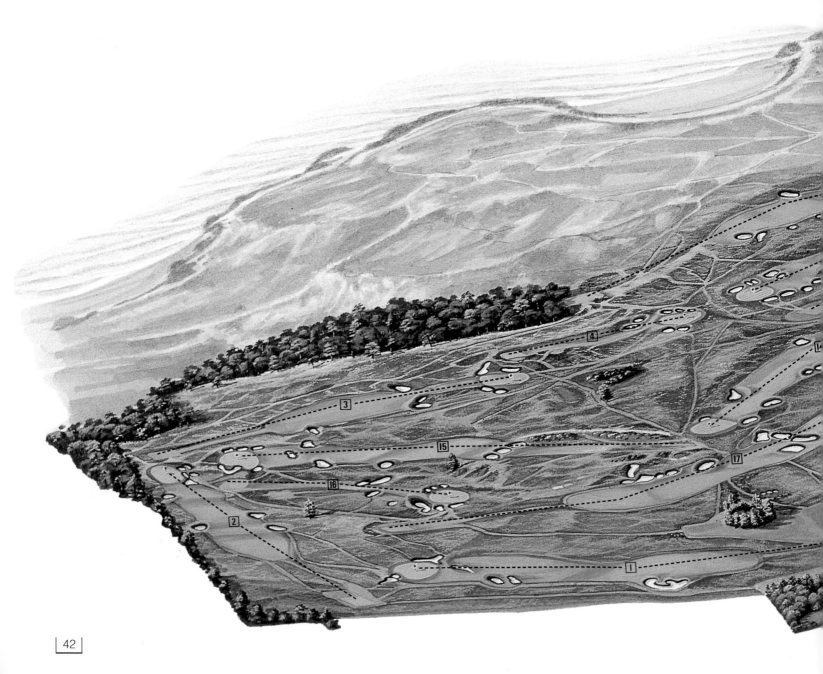

Honourable Company and the Royal and Ancient joined with Prestwick in subscribing for the present trophy and in managing the Championship. For the next 20 years it was played on each of their courses in turn. The disappointment of Musselburgh in losing the championship may have prompted unkind comment about its successor, for apparently it was neither long nor testing enough, albeit surrounded by a grey stone wall and with water. Andrew Kirkaldy, a famous professional of the time, notorious for his sharp tongue, was moved to dismiss Muirfield as an old water meadow. In spite of this the first championship to be played there in 1892 has a place in history. For the first time it was over 72 holes instead of 36, and was won by Harold Hilton, one of the great Hoylake amateurs. His score of 305 with the gutty ball was considered to be remarkably low; he won again five years later and since then no amateur, except Jones, has been Open Champion.

Thereafter the stature of Muirfield grew apace. Every few years down the generations it has been the setting for one or other of the great occasions. Harry Vardon won the first of his six Open titles there in 1896, after a play-off with J. H. Taylor. The third member of the great triumvirate, James Braid, also won his first victory at Muirfield and, just before World War I, the vast figure of Ted Ray bestrode the

links and the Championship. It is unlikely that he was afraid of the thick, clinging rough which, long before his time, had struck fear and fury into the hearts of golfers.

The first post-war champion to arise at Muirfield became one of the greatest amateurs of the period. Although the American challenge was not regarded by the British in the apprehensive light of nowadays, there must have been acute anxiety abroad the afternoon Cyril Tolley beat R. A. Gardner in the final. Tolley was three up and four to play, but the American squared the match on the last green. In 1920 the 1st was a short hole: Tolley followed Gardner's fine shot to the green with a better one, and eventually holed for a two and the Championship. After his first pilgrimage to Britain in 1921 Jones was only beaten once in three subsequent visits and five championships. This was in the quarter-finals of the Amateur in 1926. His conqueror was a young Scottish golfer, Andrew Jamieson, who, it is said, practised his putting for three hours on the eve of the match. Jones previously had beaten Robert Harris, the defending champion, an occasion in itself because never before had the champions of Britain and the United States met in either event. O. B. Keeler, who for so long played Boswell to Jones's Johnson, was certain that his hero would win this championship and his agony must have been considerable,

The Honourable Company of Edinburgh Golfers, Muirfield, East Lothian.

Record: 64, Rodger Davis, The Open, 1987

Hole	Yards	Par
1	448	4
2	351	4
3	378	4
4	213	3
5	560	5
6	468	4
7	185	3
8	443	4
9	508	5
10	475	4
11	389	4
12	381	4
13	191	3
14	448	4
15	415	4
16	186	3
17	546	5
18	449	4

Out	3,554	36
In	3,480	35
Total	**7,034**	**71**

Nick Faldo acknowledges the applause from the crowd after playing one of the great shots of his career, to the 18th at Muirfield in the 1987 Open Championship. Two putts meant an 18th consecutive par in that last round, good enough for a one stroke victory over the American Paul Azinger.

for he wrote later, "In all my life I have never heard anything as lonely as the cry of the peewit in that twilight on the rolling Muirfield course, nor was I ever so lonesome." The peewits and the curlews still cry over the links; it is a place that haunts the memory.

Walter Hagen's comprehensive victory in the 1929 Open Championship was a classic instance of a champion playing with great skill. While others, including most of the American Ryder Cup team, were blown to oblivion by a gale, Hagen shrewdly used less lofted clubs than previously, improvised all manner of shots under the wind and won by a street. The 8th hole at Muirfield is a big dog-leg to the right, and within its curve there is an alarming cluster of gathering bunkers. On the last day Hagen, instead of playing down the fairway and having a long second over a great cross-bunker to the green, drove far out into the rough on the right, scorning the architect's purpose and considerably shortening the hole. He was rewarded with two threes, but soon afterwards a spinney was planted to defeat such liberties.

Much of the greatness of Muirfield is in its test of driving. The fairways need not be menacingly narrow, but the rough (unlike the normal links grass) is consistently lush and tenacious. To be in it invariably means the loss of half a stroke or more. This is as it should be, for many British links do not penalize the errant stroke enough. However strong a man may be, he cannot score low without accu-

rate driving. When Henry Cotton won his third Open at Muirfield in 1948 he missed only four fairways in 72 holes. His second round of 66 was played in the presence of King George VI. The rough caused much speculation before the 1966 Open. It had been allowed to grow exceptionally thick, and Sanders was moved to say after finishing second that he wished he had the hay concession. Never was rough more punishing; but Jack Nicklaus approached the course with a finely preserved balance between attack and defence, frequently used an iron from the tees and was rewarded, one stroke ahead of Doug Sanders and David Thomas, with a total of 282. Their closest pursuers included the most accomplished golfers in the field, proof that the course was a fair, if severe, examination. In one round P. J. Butler returned a 65, which set the record. This victory was a climax in Nicklaus's career. At the age of 26 he had won the four Major titles of the world: so another illustrious name was added to the roll of Muirfield's champions.

Rough is not the only problem, for the bunkering reveals an imagination of design that would be cruel if it were not so fair. Rarely at Muirfield does a ball jump a bunker; if the shot is fading or drawing towards one then in it will go, for the bunkers have been fashioned with sleek, beautifully preserved surrounds to gather the slightly wayward stroke. This can be maddening, but always in one's heart there is the knowledge that the stroke was

Faldo Realizes a Famous Victory

The moment of truth in the career of Nick Faldo arrived on the 18th hole at Muirfield in 1987, and the player both recognized it and embraced it. Three years he had spent changing his swing in order to cope with pressure moments like the one he now faced and it is a measure of the confidence he had in his new method that he welcomed the opportunity to test it. The shot in front of him was almost 200 yards in length, with little margin for error. In short it was the sort of shot that defines champions, and why Muirfield was Faldo's favourite course long before he won there. Normally he would have struck a four iron given the distance but this was the last round of the Open, the trophy

was on the line, the adrenalin was flowing, and so he took a five. If Faldo lives to be 100 he will always remember what happened next. It was the shot of a lifetime, the ball emerging from the core of the sweetspot to never leave the flagstick for a second. In that moment all the pain and sacrifice had found their reward, and everything he achieved in his career thereafter flowed from that one life-affirming shot. It showed that he could play a perfect stroke when nothing else would do and players who reach that state of grace invariably go on to greater things. Five years later Faldo returned to Muirfield and won another Open, again with another telling blow on the home hole.

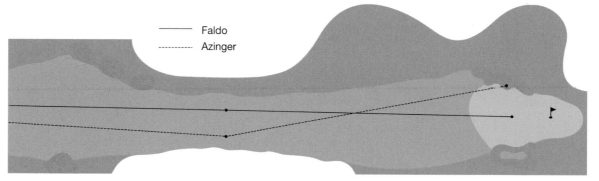

———— Faldo
----------- Azinger

imperfectly struck or aimed. The man playing good golf, or the man who knows his course and his limitations, need have no fear of Muirfield. It is a far-from-fearsome place: there are no trees, no water, no unduly strenuous carries, and only one blind stroke to play. The greens are not enormous (in fact some tend to be small), but this is another strength, for the influence of putting is kept within reasonable proportion. Those of the short holes, in particular, are sharply defined within their embracing bunkers. Always the golfer can see what is expected of him in the approach to the green: in this respect Muirfield is similar to Birkdale among the championship courses of the British Isles and for that reason likely to commend itself more readily to American eyes, used to golf on the target principle. A man gets what he hits and, what is more, can see it happen; no golfer could justly claim that the course took unfair advantage of ignorance.

All of this is contrary to the common conception of a seaside course and, in appearance, Muirfield resembles none of them. There is nothing of a long desolate sprawl of dunes and linksland, with holes that are subtle in their identity and not easily memorable for the casual visitor; there is nothing, either, of the sense of limitless freedom that one feels at Sandwich, or Carnoustie. It lies on the southern shores of the Forth and its boundaries are precise, for the grey wall patrols three sides. To the north are the dunes, protected by great banks of buckthorn, and

beyond is the great estuary – a magic stretch of water, whether dancing silver in sunshine and a brave wind, tranquil in the haze of summer or eerily haunted as ships, booming in the mist, steal upstream to Leith and Rosyth. Across the Forth spreads the graceful coast of Fife, ever-changing in its patterned hues as the cloud shadows glide by. Along the eastern side of the course the dark gnarled trees of Archerfield heel forever from the winds – the woods of Archerfield are called Graden Sea Wood in Robert Louis Stevenson's *Pavilion on the Links*. Away to the west stands Gullane Hill, commanding not only the two splendid courses on its flanks but also a view of rare majesty, from Bass Rock, sentinel of North Berwick, to "Auld Reekie" itself, smokily enchanted in the distance.

The immediate impression of Muirfield is of a place beautifully contained and private, but spacious in its policies. The eye can roam the course in a glance, and therein is one of its greatest charms. It was laid out in two approximate loops: the first nine holes form an outer ring in a clockwise path, the homeward half runs within but is less constant in its counter arc. The result is that no hole is more than a few minutes' walk from the clubhouse, and only once, from the 3rd to the 5th holes, do as many as three consecutive holes follow the same direction. The golfer thus is never bored by having the wind against or behind him for long spells as on many links of an older

hole demands the greatest care; the fairway leans from right to left and the drive must hold its lower side or the pitch to a wickedly sloping green will be uncommonly difficult. A well-placed drive to the 3rd leaves a tempting view of the green through a vale between the dunes, otherwise the distance of the approach is hard to judge. The first of the short holes is at once disturbing and beautiful, for the green is a plateau closely protected at the front and on either hand by deep bunkers, and if in fear of them the tee shot is too bold, it will leave a long downhill putt. This can easily happen in the prevailing westerly wind, and a slight criticism of the course is that three of the short holes play in the same direction, generally helped by the wind. For the 2002 Open Championship the 4th and 13th were both stretched by over 30 yards to remove any suspicion of target golf and to bring their bunkers back into contention. Tom Watson rates the 13th as his "favourite short hole in the whole world". It plays uphill to a long, narrow green which is slightly angled, emphasising the threat of its attendant bunkers. From an elevated tee, the 4th is played to a long, plateau green with a ridge running through the centre. The ground drops away on all sides and an errant tee shot which fails to hold the putting surface is certain to end up in one of the deep bunkers.

The story goes that Hagen deliberately played into one of the bunkers short of the green, preferring an uphill shot from sand to a long slippery downhill putt, but this was on a severe day. For the most part the holes offer absolutely fair targets. The remaining short hole, the 7th, faces west and also has a high plateau green exposed to all the moods of the wind. It was lengthened in preparation for the 1966 Open, and against any wind at all demands a stroke of unerring accuracy and power.

As already noted, Muirfield is a great test of driving. The long 5th curves from left to right with an obvious temptation to carry a shoulder of ground on the right and shorten the hole. Unless this tactic is resisted the drive almost certainly will vanish into one of a nest of bunkers designed to punish those who try to cheat the hole of its glory. A pull at the 6th can likewise be disastrous; the problems of the 8th have already been mentioned, and then comes one of the finest par-five holes in existence. From the far southeastern corner of the course, where Archerfield Wood comes to an end, one

The 17th hole at Muirfield is a mighty par five that extracted a costly mistake from Paul Azinger in 1987 and another from John Cook five years later, when he missed from no more than 18 inches. In both instances the beneficiary was Nick Faldo.

fashion, but always he must take heed of its changing angle of approach.

Straightaway the golfer at Muirfield is made aware that he is setting forth on a considerable exercise of his powers. The opening drive must be exact to find a narrowing waist of fairway between subtly placed bunkers on the left and rough on the right; as often as not the wind will be against it, and the approach, a lovely, straight long shot, may not get home. If the greens are fast the next drives to an ever-narrowing fairway with a large bunker defying those who try to play the hole absolutely straight; it was not designed for this. To have a clear third to an unusually open green, the second must be played to a broad expanse of rolling fairway, but this Elysian field ends abruptly against the wall that runs the length of the hole. Now one is by the clubhouse, and the long ribbon on the 10th, a superb two-shot hole stretches away in the distance. Here again cross bunkers challenge the second shot, yet somehow at Muirfield they do not seem old-fashioned but entirely fitting; and there are more to come. The drive to the 11th is blind but not unduly alarming; the 12th, with its falling fairway and long, narrow green, is a charming hole; the 14th needs a drive that must not be pulled, and keen judgement of distance for the second; the 15th fairway is invitingly wider than most, but the measure of these last three holes is a prevailing wind. If there is a wind, substantial second shots are needed. Even then the 14th may be out of range, but toil here-abouts will find recompense on the mighty 17th, which then can be reached with two good shots. With a helping

breeze behind him Nicklaus was home, using a three-iron and a five-iron, in the last round of his Open. Here again temptation to cut a corner must be sternly resisted. Innocent though the prospect may seem, a horrid waste-land of humps and bunkers awaits the pull. The round offers few more satisfying moments than the sight of a long second soaring over the great range of bunkers that traverse the fairway, but anyone unsure of his capacity to carry the bunkers is well advised to play short; rare is the third shot that reaches the green from their depths. The 18th has few peers as a finishing hole. The slightly angled tee shot must be kept from bunkers on the left and rough on the other side. Then a wonderfully challenging stroke remains to a green tightly embraced by bunkers, but with no trouble beyond.

This is a feature common to Muirfield: the straight, bold stroke rarely, if ever, is in any way seriously punished, but the timid, the gutless and the wayward rarely escape retribution. This surely is the mark of a great golf course.

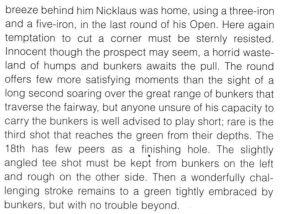

The 17th

A Crushing Blow for Jacklin

In the last round of the 1972 Open, Muirfield's 17th hole was the setting for one of the most dramatic turns of fortune in modern championship golf. Tony Jacklin and Lee Trevino were level on the tee needing, as events proved, two pars to beat Jack Nicklaus. Trevino pulled into the nearest bunker, exploded out, slashed a wood into the rough short and to the left of the green and walked after it looking a dejected and defeated man. Jacklin meanwhile had followed a fine, solid drive with another good shot into a perfect position for a chip.

When Trevino's fourth shot raced over the green into the fringe rough it seemed certain that he would fall at least one, if not two, behind. But, even before Jacklin had time to mark his ball on the green after chipping rather short, Trevino hurriedly played his chip as if heedless of the outcome. It was not an easy one against the grain of the grass on to the fast green, but all the gods were with him. It vanished into the hole, dealing a crushing blow to Jacklin, who then took three putts to fall behind.

Left: It is a hallmark of many of the great champions that not only are they very good players but they are blessed with good fortune as well. Of course the key is having the ability to capitalise on moments of good luck and no-one did that more than Lee Trevino, left, in winning the 1972 Open at Muirfield.

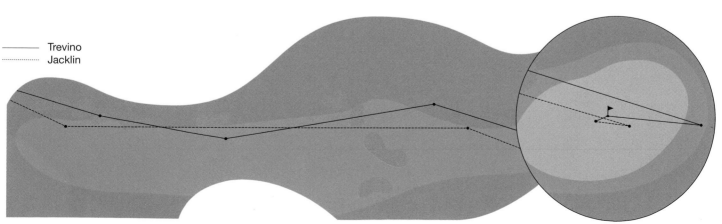

—————— Trevino
·················· Jacklin

Vision and faith
resurrect a compelling course

The sun sets on another golden day at Turnberry, the symbolic lighthouse that dominates part of the course framed here behind the 14th green. The rugged grandeur of its seaside holes is vividly illustrated on Pages 24 and 25.

No small part of the pleasure of golf is that the game is so often played in beautiful surroundings, which can soothe anger, console frustration and enhance joy. Such a place is Turnberry and, travel the world as he will, the golfer would be hard-pressed to find its like. As a course it stands high in any championship company and was endowed by nature with a background that none of the others can surpass. It lies on a curve of rock-bound coast, far from the anxious turmoil of everyday, in the southern reaches of Strathclyde where the river estuary spreads forth to the sea.

Across the waters the great mass of Arran's mountains, the long curves of the Mull of Kintyre and the lonely rock of Ailsa, rising like some primeval beast from their depths, make a scene of compelling majesty. Other courses may have sea and mountains for their setting, but none compares with those at Turnberry, which are forever changing with the whimsical moods of the weather. It can be transformed within the hour from a place haunted by mist, or savage in wind and rain, to one of entrancing beauty. On a fresh day, with the sea tranquil and deepening in its blueness as the sun rises higher, or at evening when the mountains turn black in the fading light and the sky is vivid with colour, Turnberry is incomparable.

There are two courses, the revamped Kintyre and the nobler Ailsa – scene of many championship events, but staging its first Open only in 1977. It may well be the most memorable too, a duel in the sun over the last 36 holes between the two great players of the age, Tom Watson and Jack Nicklaus. Here we had the greatest strokeplay tournament effectively turned into a matchplay event, so much so that Hubert Green, who finished third, remarked: "I won my tournament." Nine years later it was the turn of Greg

With eight of its first 11 holes played alongside – and often over – the ocean's edge the championship Ailsa course is no place for the golfer suffering from a hook. The outward half culminates in the spectacular Bruce's Castle, where the drive is from a spit of rock above the sea, with, for the brave, a carry of 200 yards over the sea and rocks towards a cairn on the horizon. Further inland, the second course, renamed Kintyre, has been completely updated by the renowned golf architect Donald Steel.

Norman to finally win his first Major championship. In 1994 Turnberry staged its third Open, another memorable event, this time won by Nick Price. Watson had his chances that year, 17 years on from his greatest performance. Time had not been kind to his putting stroke, however. He missed a crushing series of short putts and at the end those hands that had looked so sure and steady in 1977 were shaking as badly as an old man's.

Turnberry has changed considerably in recent years. The majestic old hotel, which surveys an unparalleled vista from a hill above both courses, was modernised at considerable cost and now stands among the best in the British Isles; a new clubhouse has been erected. But the cost has been passed on. Now, to get a tee-time in high summer at Turnberry one must stay a night in the hotel and while the pleasure is considerable so is the cost. Both courses date from the early 20th century and both have survived mutilation through their transformation into an airfield in two world wars. The extensive wartime levelling operations, laying of runways and building destroyed not only the courses themselves but also many natural features. Anyone seeing Turnberry in 1945 would have found it hard to imagine that a first-class course had once existed there, and harder still to believe that it ever would again. Within a few years it had been restored, involving vast movements of concrete and sand – to all intents, the creation of a new course. It remains a tribute to Mackenzie Ross, the architect, and to the vision of men like Frank Hole, who had faith in the future of its golf. The recent addition of the Colin Montgomerie Links Golf Academy leaves no excuse for rustiness on the visitor's part.

After a comparatively quiet beginning the course gathers momentum, so to speak. The 2nd and 3rd holes can be formidable, depending on the wind, and even if there is none they are still considerable. By then the coast has

The greatest Open Championship of all? When Tom Watson took on Jack Nicklaus for the title in 1977, everyone became wrapped up in two days of compelling golf.

been reached. The tee of the short 4th is hard by the lapping waves, the line is over the edge of a sandy bay, and the slightest pull to a green cradled in the dunes will find its way on to the beach. The hole, not inaptly, is called Woe-be-Tide. A long valley contains the great curve of the 5th and, whatever the weather conditions, the stroke to the 6th, one of the longest of short holes, is always a substantial hit, often with a driver.

As on all really fine courses accurate driving is essential and never more so than on the next three holes. The carry to the narrow 7th fairway, sharply angled across the line of flight, needs a powerful stroke and then follows a long second over rolling ground to a far green. The 8th fairway leans from left to right, and unless the drive is true it will fall towards bunkers; the green is a plateau, the shelf of rock behind it a hint of glories to come. There are few more spectacular or beautifully sited tees than the 9th on its pinnacle high above the rocks, and few more forbidding prospects to the frail in heart and swing. The carry is not

enormous, but the sight of the cliffs, the abyss below and the knowledge that a mishit will be lethal, is disturbing. The hog's-back fairway is by no means easy to hold nor, once one has arrived there, is the second shot easy to judge. This is a superb golf hole, marked for the viewer from afar by the slender white pencil of the Turnberry lighthouse. To stand on the 10th tee at the height of a summer morning is to know the full beauty of Turnberry. Past the remains of a castle, a base for some of Robert the Bruce's stirring deeds, the hole plunges down beside the rocky shore; there are few more satisfying moments than the sight of a drive arching away to the broad, crested fairway. Small wonder the golf hereabouts has stirred memories for many Americans of the great courses of Monterey.

Again on the 11th there is the feeling of being at one with the sea and the rocks, for here is another pulpit tee, though the hole is short and not overly taxing. As the course swings for home along the 12th traces can be seen of the airfield that Turnberry became on two occasions. The monument placed on the hill high above the green commemorates those who died in World War I.

The 13th, with an elusive plateau green, and the 14th, which can be reached only with two splendid shots, usually into wind, form a prong towards the hills and bring a welcome variety of direction to the long homeward trail. The 15th is a classic short hole, normally a long iron to a green with bunkers on its left to trap those who steer too safely away from a steep hollow on the right. At the 16th comes a hole decisive to the outcome of the Walker Cup match in 1963, when, but for the stream in front of the green, there might have been a British victory. After the long valley of the 17th, with its second to a green on the uplands, the last hole is not severe. The drive is testing with bunkers on the inside curve and great banks of gorse on the right, but the pitch to the broad green is inviting and a memorable round is done.

It will have tested the golfer to the limit of his skill – and beyond, if the wind was firm: its direction is of no consequence, because the holes are angled with subtlety and imagination. There is nothing of monotony. Every one is a challenge and every prospect a joy. The golfer, whether talented or humble – or simply in search of exercise and beauty – will find fulfilment in rich measure. Over the years Turnberry has had many great moments. The women golfers were the first to avail themselves of its beauty in 1912, and nine years later Cecil (Cecilia) Leitch, the strongest golfer of the period either side of World War I, beat Joyce Wethered (as she was then) in the final of the British Championship. In a sense this was a historic occasion; Miss Leitch avenged her defeat of the previous year in the English championship in which Miss Wethered achieved the remarkable performance of winning at the first time of entering. But the old order was changing. Miss Wethered had ascended her throne, there to remain supreme until her abdication in 1929.

J. H. Taylor said that the best way to win a championship was to win easily – a dictum that he himself observed on many occasions and which Norman followed in winning the 1986 Open at Turnberry by five strokes. But, in the history of the game, few have proved their right to a title in more emphatic fashion than Michael Bonallack in the 1961 Amateur championship. He won eight matches and only on the morning of the 36-hole final was he called upon to play the last two holes. This was a triumph of many qualities: rare devotion to the game, boundless perseverance and determination and a charming, natural, manner. After that Bonallack won many championships before settling down to oversee both The Amateur and The Open in his role as Secretary of the Royal and Ancient Golf Club of St Andrews. But this was the start and there could have been no more perfect setting for it.

Failure for the Faint-hearted

The sanctuary of the 16th green is only reached after a demanding approach over a deeply-sunken burn.

The very nature of British courses, where allowance for run after pitching often has to be made, encourages underclubbing. Usually the penalty for doing so is not severe because fairways flow into greens, but there are holes where the aerial route is essential. Just such a hole is the 16th at Turnberry, where a deep, steep-sided cleft in the land, containing a little stream known as Wee Burn, winds across the fairway immediately in front of the putting surface. There is nothing subtle about the hole. In most obvious terms it warns: take enough club for the second shot.

In the 1963 Walker Cup match several experienced British golfers signally failed to do so when an uphill green with banks behind and the wind against begged for a bold shot. Many of them stood on the 16th fairway dithering between a 3-and a 5-iron, usually choosing the more lofted club, often with dire results.

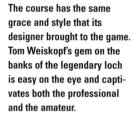

The modern masterpiece of
timeless beauty

The course has the same grace and style that its designer brought to the game. Tom Weiskopf's gem on the banks of the legendary loch is easy on the eye and captivates both the professional and the amateur.

Since golf has been played in Scotland for over 500 years it would be asking the impossible of an architect to come up with something entirely new in golf course construction. Wherever he goes he is standing in someone's footprints. Who could hope to create a links course that could compete with the mystique of St Andrews, the sheer terror of Carnoustie or the remote beauty of Dornoch?

Yet in the 1990s we saw something unique and magical created on the bonnie banks of legend that sit tight to the ethereal beauty of Loch Lomond. Not even Gleneagles is a rival when it comes to the majesty of its setting; none of its courses comes close to the perfection of Tom Weiskopf's design. The tall American was, of course, the most elegant of players. His swing was an exquisite study in technique and had he had a temperament to match he would have won

far more than his solitary Major championship success in the 1973 Open at Royal Troon. Weiskopf's foray into golf course design has been as impressive as any former champion in this business. Together with his partner Jay Morrish, he has created an intelligent portfolio that runs counter to the belief that modern architects have precious little to contribute. His version of Troon in Arizona, for example, is worthy of carrying the name while Loch Lomond is as good an inland course as one could hope to play. It will prove his legacy to a game he has graced with elegance and style.

Loch Lomond's passage to greatness, however, was fraught with difficulty. The original developer needed almost a decade to gain planning permission. When Weiskopf was approached he needed no second invitation, for no architect sane of mind would turn down such a site; yet it took three

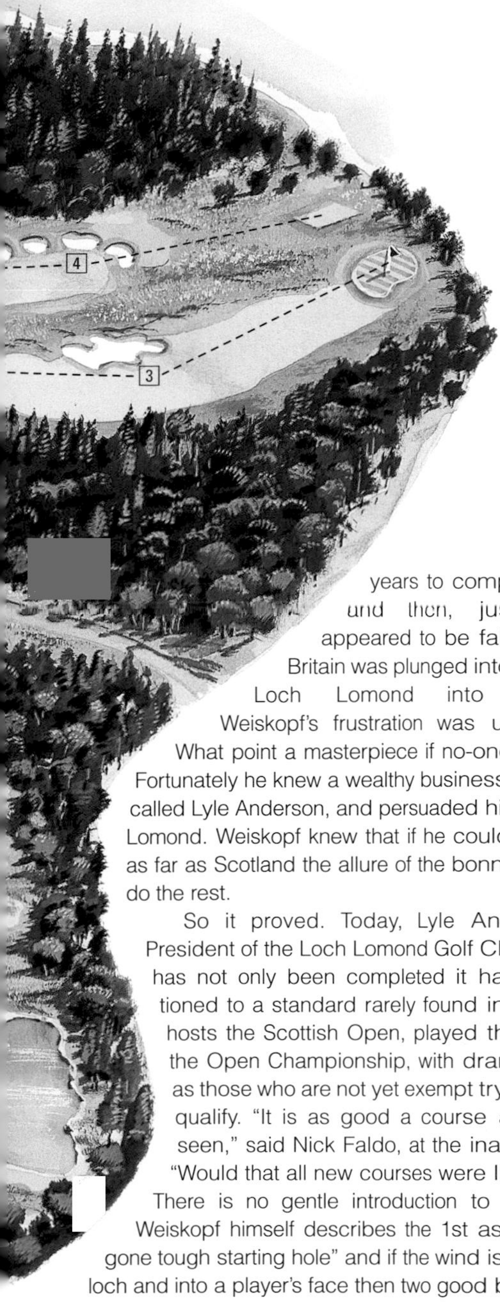

The 14th hole diagram with markers "4" and "3".

The 14th

Tom and Jay's Chance:

The tendency in modern course architecture is to forsake subtlety for force, to measure the strengths of a hole not in terms of the demands it makes on the power of the imagination but on power, full stop. The 10th at The Belfry is a welcome move away from such damaging schools of thought, a short par four that cleverly uses a natural enclosure of stream and trees to create a setting that positively dares the big hitter to seek out the green. The 14th at Loch Lomond is similar in many ways, hence its name. The conventional drive leaves a pitch over Arn Burn. For those with the ability to carry the ball 230 yards through the air, however, the temptation to try for the green is overwhelming. Sanctuary lies in the long apron to the front of the putting surface.

The Course Card

Loch Lomond Championship Tees

Hole	Yards	Par
1	425	4
2	455	4
3	505	5
4	385	4
5	190	3
6	625	5
7	440	4
8	155	3
9	340	4
10	455	4
11	235	3
12	415	4
13	560	5
14	345	4
15	415	4
16	480	4
17	205	3
18	430	4
Out	3,520	36
In	3,540	35
Total	**7,060**	**71**

years to complete the layout and then, just as things appeared to be falling into place, Britain was plunged into recession and Loch Lomond into receivership. Weiskopf's frustration was understandable. What point a masterpiece if no-one could play it? Fortunately he knew a wealthy businessman in Arizona called Lyle Anderson, and persuaded him to fly to Loch Lomond. Weiskopf knew that if he could get Anderson as far as Scotland the allure of the bonnie banks would do the rest.

So it proved. Today, Lyle Anderson is the President of the Loch Lomond Golf Club. The course has not only been completed it has been conditioned to a standard rarely found in Britain. It now hosts the Scottish Open, played the week before the Open Championship, with drama guaranteed as those who are not yet exempt try desperately to qualify. "It is as good a course as I have ever seen," said Nick Faldo, at the inaugural staging. "Would that all new courses were like this."

There is no gentle introduction to Loch Lomond. Weiskopf himself describes the 1st as a "pretty doggone tough starting hole" and if the wind is blowing off the loch and into a player's face then two good blows are needed simply to reach the green. The fairway is beautifully contoured. An old oak tree, perhaps standing in the grounds since the days when the Clan Colquhoun fought here against Robert the Bruce, provides a perfect sight line and opens up a small green that is well protected by bunkers both to the front and left hand side. The 2nd is played into the prevailing wind and features some of the delicate touches that make Weiskopf and Morrish's courses such a delight to play. A low wall runs across the fairway some 50 yards from the green and so is not really in play. When the architects were surveying the site the wall was a sorry site, just remnants remaining from the past. Most designers would have left it there. Weiskopf and Morrish rebuilt it, a small aesthetic that accentuates the hole.

The 3rd is a par five, complete with an architect's optical illusion. From the tee the bunker to the left of the fairway appears in play; in fact it is a carry of over 300 yards. Instead of being a hazard in the true sense of the word, therefore, it is more a sight line and helps to give the hole definition. For the long hitter the green remains reachable in two but there is marshland to avoid to the right of the putting surface. The hole is a beauty as is the 4th, played back towards Ben Lomond which frames it in a graceful idyll. The 5th plays back towards the water and is the first of Loch Lomond's four very good short holes. At 190 yards it does not lack for length, and can prove a wooden club even for a useful amateur. The key is to miss the bunkers on the left, for only a rare

touch with a sand iron will lead to a par from there.

The 6th is the longest hole in Scotland, a monstrous par five measuring 625 yards. The hole is saved from being simply a grotesque slog by its setting. For its entire length it runs alongside the loch, with the snow-tipped mountains in the distance lending an eerie sense of stillness. The 7th is a beautiful par-four, a dog-leg in the classic manner with a bunker on the angle at 190 yards signifying the change of direction. The short 8th is overlooked by Rossdhu House, an 18th century Georgian mansion that in the lingering years of the 20th century has become a positively palatial 19th hole. The front nine is completed by a short par-four, which is driveable for the professionals from the front tee, although the green, as one would anticipate, is heavily protected by the jagged bunkers which are a trademark of the course.

The loch disappears from view at the start of the back nine but not the sumptuous surroundings. The tee shot at the 10th is an inviting one, downhill towards the hills and mountains. The long approach is then played across the Arn Burn from which the hole takes its name. The par three 11th continues the forbidding start to the home half, 235 yards long and playing every inch of it. The 12th is Weiskopf's homage to Donald Ross, with a green that falls away sharply both to the front and right. The 13th is a fine, downhill par five, the 14th a splendid short par four with the green reachable for the professionals if the wind blows from a helpful direction.

And so we come to Loch Lomond's exceptional finish, beginning with a breathtaking tee shot from the 15th, the fairway flowing away from the plateau tee towards a narrow, deceptive green, where the yardage appears to be playing tricks with the mind's eye. The 16th is another sweeping, majestic par four before the golfer returns to the loch for the final two holes. The 17th is a daunting par three across marshland to a well protected green. A quietness pervades the setting here, a solace allied to the surroundings which led Weiskopf to select it as his favourite hole. Most people, however, prefer the last, a 430 yard par-four that sways gently around the loch. How much dare one take off the drive? Enough, certainly, to avoid crashing into the bunkers that sternly guard the right hand side of the fairway. The approach shot is enticing, the sort that characterises this splendid addition to the great Scottish courses. Behind the green lies the ruins of Rossdhu Castle, a gentle reminder of turbulent times past.

The 18th, below, sweeps around Loch Lomond and makes for a glorious finishing hole.

An exercise in fear

Hoylake is older than all but one of the English seaside golf courses (Westward Ho!, founded in 1864, is its senior by five years) and is considered among the foremost of all the links of northern England because of its traditions and infinite merits. It was responsible in 1885 for starting the Amateur Championship, the oldest event of its kind in the world. The first international of all, between England and Scotland, was played there in 1902. In the same year Alex Herd won the Open with a rubber-cored ball, and the gutty was dead for evermore. In 1921 the first men's match between the United States and Britain was played at Hoylake, inspiring George H. Walker to inaugurate his contest – the Walker Cup – the following year. In all, ten Open Championships were played there before the event grew beyond what Hoylake's confines could then accommodate.

rhythmical imaginable". He was a formidable competitor with an austere approach to the game but was, withal, a modest man. After he had retired to a home in the Welsh hills someone asked to see his medals; he had given them all away. In 1890 he was the first amateur and the first Englishman to win the Open; he was amateur Champion the same year, a feat equalled only by Bobby Jones in 1930. A measure of his enduring skill was that he competed in the Amateur championship of 1927, 49 years after his first Open appearance.

Remarkably, Ball's greatest amateur rival was also a Hoylake member. Not only did Harold Hilton win the Amateur four times and in 1911 the US Amateur Championship at Apawamis, but he was Open champion twice again, an achievement that only Jones among amateurs has surpassed. Hilton was said to be the most accurate wooden

Long before golfers came, Hoylake was a significant place. Late in the 17th century the broad Dee estuary, at the mouth of which Hoylake stands, sheltered a fleet which transported the army of William of Orange to Ireland for the battle of the Boyne. In time the estuary filled with silt and at low tide it looks as if one could walk across to Wales. The importance of Hoylake diminished with the gathering sands and Robert Browning, in his scholarly *History of Golf*, wrote that the waste of dunes and links, on which the course now lies, would not then have fetched £10. In 1911 the Royal Liverpool Club bought it for £30,000.

Until 1876 the golfers shared the links with a racecourse and it cannot have been amusing, even in those days when courses were not sleek and manicured, to find one's ball in a hoof mark. Now only faint traces of racing remain; a post or so, an old saddling bell and the names of the first and last holes, the Course and the Stand. The club soon became a lively spirit in English golf. In 1884 the honorary secretary, Thomas Owen Potter, suggested that an open amateur tournament be held the following year. At once the club was faced with the problem of what was an amateur; status was not defined in those days. An entry was received from Douglas Rolland, a Scottish stonemason who had won second prize in the previous Open championship. Rolland was ruled out – but what of Hoylake's greatest son, John Ball, who, as a boy of 15, had played in the Open some years before and had accepted a half-sovereign for finishing sixth? The decision in favour of him doubtless was delicate and possibly tinged with nepotism. In the years to come Ball was amateur champion eight times.

Comparison between the ages is fruitless, but Ball was supreme in his own time. Apparently his grip was unorthodox and his stance a little stiff, but the swing was described as the "true poetry of motion, the most perfectly smooth and

club player of his day, with a swing of great vigour. He also had a lively intelligence and love of experiment. He and Ball were great masters; another, Jack Graham, was almost so and it was small wonder that Hoylake worshipped these men. Hoylake is unique among British championship links because it is possible to be out-of-bounds within the confines of the course, and innumerable golfers have condemned it on this count. Until 1920 the penalty for out-of-bounds was loss of distance only and thus the golfers of old were not so harshly punished. Now, Hoylake can inflict the tortures of the damned. There is always an alternative to flirting with danger, but what an exercise in fear some of those holes can be.

The right angle of the 1st makes a forbidding opening hole. On the left from the tee is the clubhouse with its silken putting green; on the right, for the full length of the hole, is the sinister "cop", a bank no more than three feet high which encloses the practice ground. A good drive will finish past the corner, but a long shot remains with the haunting thought that a slice will be fatal if one aims for the green, which is hard against the cop. Many a player has been out-of-bounds with his drive and approach; many have run out of ammunition before completing the hole. Before the 3rd was changed, and a fine new short 4th created in readiness for the 1967 Open, the slightest pull would sail out-of-bounds over another cop. But now the golfer is free until the 6th. This is the famous Briars, where a long carry across an orchard is called for; against a strong prevailing wind the carry from the back tee is terrible to behold.

The 7th, named Dowie after Hoylake's founder, used to

be one of the most treacherous short holes in golf. A ball landing on the green could all too easily hop over an out-of-bounds bank within a few yards of the flag. In 1994 the nettle was grasped, the bank was removed, new moundwork and bunkers were introduced and a much fairer hole was the result. In the last round of the Open in 1930 Jones needed two fours to be out in 35. After two long shots over the 8th fairway he was no more than 15 yards from the green but, as he wrote later, he took seven for the hole "in the most reasonable manner possible". His torment of mind is only too easy to imagine; so too is the enormous effort of will and control that enabled him to finish just safe from pursuit. This was the second leg of the "quadrilateral".

From the 8th the golf is of the old, true seaside character, dipping and curving along the sandhills; Hilbre Island and its myriad birds and the quiet hills of Wales are in the distance. The 9th with its bowl of a green, the superb short 11th, the Alps, its green an oblong oasis in the dunes, the lovely sweep of the 12th, and the tightest of pitches to the 13th, with

its necklace of bunkers, make a splendid prelude to the long, long finish on the plain below.

The field comes into play again. It is possible to hit into it from the 15th tee, and again on the second shot, and its corner cuts across the direct line to the 16th. Then shorter, this hole was decisive in the last round of the 1967 Open when Jack Nicklaus and the sentimental favourite, Roberto de Vicenzo, fought a superbly entertaining duel. Nicklaus, playing ahead, scored a birdie-four, before Vicenzo struck his drive to the very edge of the field. From there he hit a soaring spoon to make sure of a birdie and the title. Of all the finishing holes at Hoylake the 17th can make the greatest play on courage and fear. Until recently its green was situated hard up against the fence. It was all too easy to hit the approach shot out-of-bounds onto Stanley Road and it was not unknown for players to putt out-of-bounds! When the wind blew from left to right it was a terrifying hole. As part of Donald Steel's alterations to make the course once more suitable to host Open Championships a new green has been constructed twenty yards to the left and forty yards further on, making the hole more of a dog-leg, at the same time improving spectator access and all-round safety. Other significant changes include a reshaping of the fairway and a new, angled green on the 3rd, tightening of the landing area for drives at the 10th and 12th, and a reworking of the final green so that the approach shot is now played to a putting surface angled away to the left and tightly bunkered.

Royal Liverpool
Golf Club,
Hoylake

Hole	Yards	Par
1	427	4
2	371	4
3	528	5
4	200	3
5	451	4
6	421	4
7	196	3
8	533	5
9	390	4
10	411	4
11	193	3
12	454	4
13	158	3
14	552	5
15	457	4
16	558	5
17	449	4
18	416	4
Out	3,517	36
In	3,648	36
Total	**7,165**	**72**

Few great courses combine such a searching trial of skill and courage as Royal Liverpool – or exact such a toll for loose play. In 1930 it was the scene of the second leg of Bobby Jones's unparalleled "Grand Slam." The recent acquisition of two neighbouring properties has given Royal Liverpool the extra space needed to house the tented village and media facilities of a modern Major. An arrangement has been made to use the municipal course over the road as a practice ground, and Donald Steel has made the few alterations to the course felt necessary to restore Hoylake to the Open Championship roster. It is likely, then, that Royal Liverpool will add to its tally of ten Open Championships in the second half of the decade, and that daunting finish, 2,432 yards for the last five holes, will once more provide a searching examination for the world's finest players.

Soft to the eye,

steel to the touch

Hole	Yards	Par
1	206	3
2	438	4
3	458	4
4	392	4
5	212	3
6	494	5
7	557	5
8	419	4
9	164	3
10	335	4
11	542	5
12	198	3
13	342	4
14	445	4
15	465	4
16	359	4
17	467	4
18	412	4
Out	3,340	35
In	3,565	36
Total	**6,905**	**71**

Unlike some of its peers among British links, the Lytham and St Annes course, founded in 1886, has no visual splendour. It has an urban setting, hedged about for much of the time by houses and with a railway forming one boundary. No noble sandhills mark its horizons, the ground does not move in dramatic fashion and the sea might be miles away. But let nobody be deceived by this apparent tranquillity and smoothness. The course is a test of golf many times proven to be among the finest in Britain. The clubhouse is serene, substantial and Victorian, similar to others in the northwest of England; it is at one with the links, which touches its very walls. There is, too, a dormy house – a rare facility at British clubs nowadays and about its grounds a garden atmosphere that makes a soothing background to the earnest pursuit of golf.

The club has a proud place in the championships of the past century. It was there in 1926 that Bobby Jones won the first of his three Opens in Britain. Soon afterwards he won the United States Open as well, becoming the first man to hold both titles in the same summer. After World War II an international parade of champions, Bobby Locke, Peter Thomson and Bob Charles, had their hours before Tony Jacklin arrested the tide of overseas domination. In 1974 Gary Player won one of the most emphatic victories of his generation before the course paid testament to the true genius of Severiano Ballesteros. Twice he won the Open at Lytham, firstly in 1979 and then in 1988 with a last round of 65 that will stand for the ages. In 1996 Tom Lehman created history by becoming the first American professional to win at Lytham, a popular triumph for a humble man. Another American, David Duval, triumphed in 2001, and the course, once again, received great praise from the players.

Lytham's tally of champions is an impressive tribute to the quality of the course, of which Bernard Darwin, the first golf writer of real distinction, wrote long ago: "If the day is calm and we are hitting fairly straight the golf seems rather easy than otherwise; and yet we must never allow ourselves to think so too pronouncedly or we shall straightaway find it becoming unpleasantly difficult." Many great golfers today would agree with him.

The short 1st hole, with its tee in a pleasing arbour, is comparatively placid, but the shots to the next two are haunted by the adjoining railway and in a flanking wind it is all too easy to slice or push out-of-bounds. Bunkers, too, are nicely set up to harass those who take an overly cautious line to the left. If a breeze helps on the opening holes it certainly does not on the 4th. It is a timely reminder of what may lie in wait on the homeward journey. Often the island of fairway between dunes and rough can seem disconcertingly remote and the green is angled to the left. An early birdie can easily be encountered here, and anything but a straight and truly judged shot to the short 5th is more likely than not to be punished. In normal summer conditions the next two holes quicken thoughts of birdie fours, given a fair stance on the crumpled 6th fairway from which to carry cross-bunkers and hold an exposed crown of green and a drive threaded down the long ribbon of the 7th. The green here is concealed by a bank between sentinel dunes, but in a helping breeze Tiger Woods and his like in power from the tees can be home with medium or even short irons.

Hereabouts the course has more the expected character of a links; the dunes are wild and owe nothing to the hand of man. High on a plateau among them is the 8th green, an exposed and deceptive target for the approach from the valley below. Many players take irons from the high tee because – with the railway taking its last look at the course – straightness is all. The 9th is a pure target shot down to a green nestling amid bunkers and is rather more taxing than it looks, though numerous golfers have made light of the outward half. As long ago as 1963 Peter Thomson and Tom Haliburton turned in 29 on the first day of the Open, a record for the championship, but few such starts have not been retarded by the demands of the closing holes.

The 10th is a relic of days past with its blind drive and tiny, tilted green. To reach the raised 11th green in two, a pair of cross-bunkers on the left must be carried – not too daunting a task.. The 12th is quite another matter: it is the only short hole on the inward half, and presents the most difficult and uncompromising shot to a green of the whole round. A wood shelters the tee from the prevailing left-hand wind and the shot – long iron or even wood – must

Though it lays no claim to be the most attractive course in Britain, Lytham and St Annes is certainly one of the most difficult, demanding both nerve and subtlety. It has become less of a links and more of a seaside course over the decades – softer and lusher – but nonetheless it remains essentially a testing layout and a premier championship venue.

be held against it if the raised green, with bunkers to the left and front right, is to be reached. If the shot slides away or is overhit, out-of-bounds is perilously close. The hole is as finely designed as any of its length on a British links and is the introduction, after a breather at the 13th, to a finish that rarely fails to influence the outcome of any event.

The 14th is straight enough, but even in a light cross-wind the fairway is hard to hit and hold and so, from the rough, is the green, which falls gently away from the striker. Revised bunkering and additional length have made the 15th even more demanding. A masterly 215-yard 6-iron from the rough to 15 feet put Duval in clear control of the 2001 Open. When the 15th is tough the 16th offers relief and likely birdies, but the blind tee shot must be placed to avoid bunkers, and to take advantage of the

opening to the guarded green, to which the strength of the short approach must be perfectly judged. For Ballesteros in 1979, placing the tee shot meant locating the temporary car park to the right of the fairway. He argued that it opened up the green, a line of thinking that did not hold court when judged alongside the three stentorian bunkers that guarded the side to which he took aim. But, Seve, being Seve, got his birdie three.

Then the course attacks once more. Three new bunkers have been added to the right of the 17th fairway, complementing the seven which lurk on the left, with four more set into a bank further on. The hole then swings to the left with an inviting shot to an open green with bunkers on either hand – but it is inviting only to the man who has driven far enough on the right line. Ideally, the shot should

The 18th

Ballesteros's Finest Hour

Only one man in the last 30 years has come close to matching Tony Jacklin for popularity with the British crowds and, oddly enough, he is Spanish. It was in Lancashire that his skills were first appreciated, at the 1976 Open at Birkdale, and 12 years on at Lytham they had matured to the point where Ballesteros' golf was an exquisite mix of talent and maturity. Two years earlier he had lost a Masters he should have won and had brooded upon his failure. Now he forgot the past to conjure an unforgettable final round of 65, one he would later describe as the sort "a player may complete only once or twice every 25 years." Pity Nick Price, the brave runner-up, who had lost out on the main prize as he had six years earlier at Royal Troon. But he took solace in the fact he could have done nothing else on this occasion. Six years more and his philosophy would gain its reward when he won the Open at Turnberry.

be as far as possible down the right side of the fairway. If short or to the left, the green is invisible.

It most certainly was for Bobby Jones in 1926, as he faced the shot which, down the ages, was to become a legend. Rarely has the destiny of a championship depended on one stroke and the balance between disaster and triumph been so sharply defined. Jones had come from behind in the last round and he and Al Watrous were level after 70 holes. Watrous hit a good drive into position for a clear shot to the green, but Jones pulled into one of the little bunkers just off the fairway. Between his ball and the flag, some 170 yards away, were all kinds of perdition – sandhills, thick scrub and rough. Watrous played to the edge of the green and his feelings can be imagined as he waited for Jones to play. He must have thought that he would lead by at least a stroke going to the last tee.

Jones must have been angry with himself for what seemed likely to be a fatal drive, but when he saw the ball lying clean, hope must have stirred anew. He had to go for the green; a safe recovery to the fairway would probably cost a stroke and leave Watrous with the psychological advantage and the lead. It was all or nothing. He took his mashie iron (which remains a precious reminder in the clubhouse) and struck the deathless stroke. It finished on the green inside Watrous.

The wonder of the stroke, now marked by a plaque on the side of the bunker, was that Jones had the control of nerve, rhythm and swing to strike the ball perfectly at such a moment; the margin of error was so slight. As later he wrote of this moment: "An eighth of an inch too deep with your blade, off dry sand, and the shot expires right in front of your eyes. And if your blade is a thought too high

... I will dismiss this harrowing reflection." The effect on Watrous must have been fearful. Suddenly all the pressure was upon him and who would condemn him for taking three putts ? He was bunkered by the last green and Jones was safe except from Walter Hagen, who eventually had to hole his second shot to tie. Hagen, with his love of the dramatic, had the flag removed. His ball very nearly pitched into the hole but it went over the green. Jones moved nearer to Olympus.

Crisis and the 17th seem almost inseparable. In 1963, Nicklaus stood on the 17th fairway in the last round, knowing that two fours would probably be good enough to win. They would have been, but a 2-iron was a club too much for the second shot. It ran through the green into heavy rough, from where he took three more. His last drive was pulled into the left hand of the seven bunkers that make the hole so testing from the tee and he took another five. This was one of the rare occasions when Nicklaus could be said to have cast away a major championship. A few minutes later Bob Charles and Phil Rodgers made their fours on the last hole to beat him. The next day Charles became the first left-hander to win one of the world's major championships.

There was no crisis for Jacklin in 1969. He could afford to take five at the 17th and still remain two ahead of Charles. With all the confidence in the world he played the last hole superbly and strode down the fairway towards a moment the like of which even Lytham, in all its long history, had never seen before.

In 1974 the large 1.68-in ball was made compulsory for the Open and the elements combined to make the golf a severe test of control and patience. It confirmed the

David Duval, whose technique and nerve held up well to give him his first Major over the supremely testing Royal Lytham course.

Heading here

Royal Lytham is not the longest course on the Open Championship roster, and with four of its par-fours under 400 yards – two under 350 – it would seem, on the face of it, to offer the professional golfer a gentle stroll. Nothing could be further from the truth. It has never failed to test seriously the finest golfers of every age and its list of Open Champions contains no fluke winners. David Duval came into the 2001 Open with the unenviable reputation of the best golfer not to have won a Major. Like Phil Mickleson and Colin Montgomerie, two others who have been given that dubious description, he had been close on several previous occasions. He started out on his final round as one of four co-leaders, following a fine 3rd round 65, but there were no fewer than twenty eight players within five shots of the lead. Anyone could have won. The Swede, Niclas Fasth, closed with a 67 two hours before the leaders, posting a total of 277. One by one the challengers fell away, Ian Woosnam in the most bizarre fashion when, on the 2nd tee, he found he was carrying 15 clubs, one too many, and was penalised two strokes. Fasth's name was still at the top of the leaderboard when Duval drove poorly at the 14th and 15th, finding the rough both times, but his recoveries at both holes were first rate. He must have known then that he would at last break his duck, and steady play over the last three holes saw him home in 67, to win the Open by three shots. His acceptance speech, in which he praised links golf – and the knowledgeable spectators in particular – won him many new supporters in Britain.

greatness of Gary Player. Of his eight major championship victories it was unarguably the most commanding, and his winning margin of four was less than he deserved.

The last two holes were responsible. Player was leading Peter Oosterhuis by six shots when he pulled his second into the menacingly deep rough to the left of the bunkers guarding the green. Several minutes' frantic search followed before the ball was found; he could hardly move it at his first attempt, but chipped dead for his five. His second to the 18th was too strong and overran the green to settle close to the wall beneath the clubhouse windows. From there, the Open champion played his last, dramatic approach – left-handed, with a putter.

In 1988 there was an equally memorable shot for the members to observe, this time a deft chip from the side of the green from Ballesteros to defeat a gallant Nick Price by a stroke. The Spaniard had confirmed his brilliance eight years earlier, collecting his first major championship at Lytham at the tender age of 22. Now a second triumph meant more because the years between had rendered a ceaseless flow of emotion.

Some are born great but Tom Lehman achieved greatness with his victory in 1996. His third round of 64 was not only a course record but he created the space he needed to parry the challenges of Nick Faldo and Ernie Els. In the last round he was paired with Faldo, and his six stroke advantage carried echoes, for some, of the similar deficit that the Englishman had wiped away three months earlier when defeating the challenge of Greg Norman at Augusta. Lehman held his nerve and the 18th green was bathed in a beautiful light as he collected his glittering reward.

The 18th

A Supreme Moment For Jacklin

In all British golf there has never been a moment to compare with that when Tony Jacklin walked on to the 18th tee in the last round of the Open at Lytham in 1969. He was two strokes ahead of Bob Charles, his partner and closest challenger, and the championship was his for the taking. It was to be the first British victory since Max Faulkner had won at Portrush in 1951, and the end of the longest span of overseas domination since Henry Cotton had arrested American supremacy at Sandwich in 1934. The vast amphitheatre of stands embracing the last green was packed with thousands and the flanks of the fairways were solid with people, tense, expectant and longing to explode with pride and acclaim for the young and popular champion. The greatness of the 18th hole, only 412 yards, lies in the tee shot. Across the fairway in the driving area are two diagonal lines of bunkers, seven in all. The farthest of these from the tee are on the left, threatening the drive pulled away from the wilderness of bushes on the right. It is the most demanding final tee shot on any British links. Watching Jacklin's swing for the drive was sufficient to know whether the shot was good because the pace of the takeaway was so smooth and deliberate. It proved to be a superb stroke far clear of any danger, and leaving him only a quiet 7-iron from the green. Tempo or rhythm had always been the key to Jacklin's best golf. In his younger years he would whip the club away from the ball too quickly, but as he pro-

gressed towards the heights he concentrated on making his backswing much slower and thereby smoother. Throughout that Open he preserved his finest tempo, concentrating his practice each day, mostly with a 7-iron, towards the point where he felt that the slow tempo was natural to him.

Rare is the golfer who would not profit greatly from striving to find the rhythm best suited to him. It can vary considerably according to individual temperaments, but once discovered it is worth preserving, so that in moments of pressure the swing is less likely to become a nervous snatch.

Tony Jacklin throws his golf ball into the crowd after winning the Open Golf title in 1969. He was the first British player in 18 years to win the title.

Much of Sunningdale's air of open innocence disappears when the golfer off the tee
arrives to play his second shot, with tricky pitches to raised greens and well-placed bunkers to
catch anything that rolls. The course starts off in
unusual fashion with a long hole, just short of 500
yards. The boundary is to the right, but the fairway is
comfortably wide. However, playing to the left and too
much safety can leave an awkward chip up the banked
side of the plateau green and, with bunkers set into it,
there is little room for error. With half the greens
placed on hills, Sunningdale rewards good chipping
and pitching.

The supreme
heathland course

Early golf in Britain was confined to links
beside the sea. Apart from a few courses in Scotland it
was not until the late 19th century that it was played to
any extent elsewhere. As the game increased in popularity, the eyes of golfers turned inland; courses were laid
out on public commons and in private parks and a new
conception of the game was in being. The most significant development was the discovery that even rough
heathland could swiftly be converted into ideal golfing
ground. The outcome was a proliferation of splendid
courses which, in their fashion, have become almost as
distinctive an expression of British golf as the ancient
links themselves.

The finest examples of heath courses lie on a stretch
of country west of London. All have common features of
pine, birch, heather and wonderfully firm, smooth turf
that, on account of the sandy subsoil, absorbs moisture
with rare speed. Of all these courses, Sunningdale
stands supreme.

The Old course owed its foundation to the enterprise
of two brothers, who conceived the idea of golf on the wild
heathland spreading away to Chobham Common. It was
owned by St John's College, Cambridge University, which
granted leaseholds for a course and the building of
houses nearby. This was one of the earliest instances in

England, if not the first, of property development in har-
ness with the creation of a golf course. Willie Park, son
of the first Open champion, was commissioned to lay it out
for £3,800, a sum that would not suffice for one of its
greens today.

The club was fortunate – or inspired – in its choice of
Park, for he was one of the pioneers of modern course
architecture. He had the experience from being a great
player, having won the Open twice, and was educated and
ambitious to a degree rare in professionals of those days.
In his appreciation of the classic features of the old courses, and his awareness of the changing needs of the time,
he set unusual standards that, doubtless, influenced many
of his successors.

Seeds were sown in the late summer of 1900 and a
year later the course was ready. It was an immediate success. The inaugural Club Secretary was Harry Colt, himself a most gifted golf course designer, and it was Colt
who rebuilt the course into its present day form in the
1920s.

The course is one of enchantment, rarely of menace;
its challenge is one of subtlety rather than length. When
the fairways are running in summer the longest holes, the
1st and 14th, can be reached in two shots. At no time is
the Old overpowering and it offers an appealing variety of

shots, not least at the short par-fours. The 3rd green can be driven, but the normal tee shot leaves an approach of rare delicacy to an away-sloping green. The 11th is a gem; the blind drive to a falling fairway must avoid a bunker on the left and a copse of pines on the right, but the greatness of the hole is in deciding how to play the little approach to the raised table of green.

Several tees command superb views and offer the exhilaration of driving from high places: from the 5th with its green beyond a shining pond, and the 6th mounting into the wooded distance from an island fairway; from the 10th where the driver looks down upon a promised land with, far beyond over the woods, a glimpse of the russet and white of the clubhouse; and the short 13th, with its deceptive shot from a pinnacle tee to a green part-embraced by an insidious little grassy trench.

The 15th, a taxing shot across the prevailing wind, is a noble short hole which begins a sternly beautiful finish. Unless the drive is long the approach to the 16th green must be flighted from a downhill lie over cross-bunkers on the far side of a shallow valley. Again, at the 17th – unless the drive flirts with a spinney lurking on the left – the approach must be played from a hanging stance. The gentle incline towards the home green, with a great spreading oak just beyond, makes for a fine drive and an approach that was improved by German bombs in 1940. One bomb made a crater to the right of the green which prompted the idea of converting it into bunkers. The shot can be demanding, the more so because a path marks out-of-bounds beyond bunkers flanking the left of the green and is more in play than the striker from the fairway might imagine.There never was a course that someone did not murder on occasion. In kindly weather, when the beautiful greens are at their best, the expert can readily enjoy himself. Shortly after World War II, Australian Norman Von Nida burned his way to victory with a 63 in the last round of the Dunlop Masters. Gary Player, in winning the first important event of his life in 1956, played the Old in 64. Ian Woosnam averaged 65 shots per round for 72 holes when winning the 1988 European Open. In the same event two years earlier, Nick Faldo went round in 62, the course record. In 1997, on her way to a commanding eight stroke victory in the women's British Open, the Australian Karrie Webb shot 63; but the most famous of all rounds were those of Bobby Jones when qualifying for the Open in 1926. The first, a 66, was often quoted as the perfect round; 33 putts, 33 other shots, every hole in three or four. The next day he did have one five and one two in a 68 and it was no wonder that he said later, "I wish I could take this golf course home with me." Other golfers must have thought likewise after playing one of the loveliest of all courses.The New course, designed by Colt in 1922, is quite different from its elegant sister. Where the Old might be feminine in its grace and wiles the New is sterner, more masculine. It is more exposed to the winds and bleaker in prospect but it has beauty in the emerald fairways curving through the heather, the broadness of the scene and the downs rolling away in the distance. And the challenge of the golf is undeniable.

The Course Card

Sunningdale Golf Club, Berkshire Old course

Record: 62, N. Faldo

Hole	Yards	Par
1	494	5
2	489	5
3	319	4
4	161	3
5	419	4
6	415	4
7	402	4
8	182	3
9	273	4
10	478	5
11	325	4
12	451	4
13	185	3
14	509	5
15	226	3
16	438	4
17	421	4
18	432	4
Out	3,154	36
In	3,465	36
Total	**6,619**	**72**

In the 1997 British Open at Sunningdale, the runaway winner Karrie Webb from Australia gave probably the finest exhibition of golf ever played by a woman in Britain. She is playing here from the 10th tee, one of the most inviting on a handsome course.

A young course worthy of the

100th Open

The Course Card

Royal Birkdale Golf Club, Southport, Merseyside

Record: 64,
Mark O'Meara

Hole	Yards	Par
1	449	4
2	421	4
3	407	4
4	203	3
5	344	4
6	480	4
7	177	3
8	457	4
9	411	4
10	403	4
11	408	4
12	183	3
13	498	4
14	198	3
15	544	5
16	416	4
17	547	5
18	472	4
Out	3,349	34
In	3,669	36
Total	**7,018**	**70**

Standing within a glorious expanse of dunes on the Lancashire coast, Royal Birkdale has been the setting for more championships and international matches than any other British course since the end of World War II – not even St Andrews has been as richly endowed. During that time it has tested the mighty and produced a number of champions of enduring stature.

Birkdale arose from the inspiration of a handful of visionaries who rented for a mere £5 a plot of land, so plentiful on the Lancashire coast where dunes tumble in wild profusion; the first clubhouse was a five-shillings-a-week room in a private house, and the first professional discharged his duties for only three times that sum. The club has been extremely fortunate in its professionals. Only three have been there this century: David McEwan, Robert Halsall, and the present incumbent, Richard Bradbeer.

The course, mainly designed by George Low, did not follow the principle, beloved by architects of old, that blind shots were essential. Instead, the holes were laid out in valleys between the towering sandhills and were not the adventurous exercise they might have been. A new clubhouse was built and pulled down again when it was found to be on someone else's land. The foundation of present eminence did not really begin until 1931, when Southport Corporation bought the land and gave the club a 99-year lease. Thenceforth all was progress. Fred Hawtree and J. H. Taylor redesigned the course and the clubhouse was built. Even then Birkdale was not a seaside course in the traditional sense. Many of the fairways are flat and pose no problems of stance, the greens mostly are outlined against the dunes, often in clefts between them, giving a perspective of distance to help the golfer and also some protection from the wind when putting. There is nothing of the typical old seaside green with its flag shimmering on some distant horizon, and all manner of folding ground to make the hole look shorter than it is.

More than any other British championship course, Birkdale offers golf of a target nature. But if problems of judging distance are not so acute, others are emphasized – notably the cardinal virtue of straightness. It is well enough to say that a green is a sharply defined target, like the 2nd, 10th or 17th, but it still has to be hit. To miss the greens at Birkdale, even narrowly, can leave an infernally difficult stroke, especially after the rebuild which followed the 1991 Open Championship, Martin Hawtree's greens re-contoured to perfection, cleverly borrowed. When the fairways are narrowed for a championship they make a fine test of driving, and should they happen to be fast as well, accuracy is crucial and power of little significance. The Open Championship in 1965 was a fine example; it brought victory to Peter Thomson, simply by virtue of his unerring straightness, and precious little reward to Arnold Palmer and Jack Nicklaus. In preparation for this memorable year in Birkdale's history – the Ryder Cup followed a few months after the Open – further alterations were made to the course. These involved a new 12th, a short hole cradled in the dunes, the elimination of the short 17th and the lengthening of the finish. Birkdale became possibly the only course in the world with four of the last six holes measuring over 500 yards. By the 1991 Open, however, the

The final six holes at Royal Birkdale extend across one and a half daunting miles, yet aspiring champions are rewarded more for accuracy than for power. The many well-placed fairway bunkers are a key feature, for wherever there is a stroke to be saved, by cutting a corner or stretching a fairway wood to the green, there is inevitably an abundance of traps through which the golfer must thread his way. The approach to the 13th is particularly demanding and the prevailing wind and intimidating cross-bunkers make the 15th daunting. But when pressure mounts at the finish, it is a brave player indeed who is prepared to open up among the ten bunkers of the 18th hole.

13th and the 18th had been slightly reduced to become fours, and Birkdale had a finish that was not only daunting in length but par too. In the 1954 Open, Birkdale's first, Peter Thomson's winning score of 284 was about strict par for the event; seven years later Arnold Palmer won with the same total but in dreadful conditions. The days were never free of wind, with a gale for the second round. Not since 1938, when wind almost wrecked an Open at Sandwich, had the golfers been as violently assaulted as that day at Birkdale. Before play began many tents were flat and the

fairways were heavy with casual water but Palmer, loving the challenge of it all, was inspired to attack.

Few had ever seen iron play such as his that fearful morning; his massive hands rifling the ball under the wind made the senses reel. He was three under par for the first five holes. A magnificent round was in the making, but it was not to be. The 7th tee is high, yet protected from a sea wind, and Palmer should have forced a low shot. Instead he used a 9-iron; the ball was swept away and when he pulled from the next tee the spell was broken.

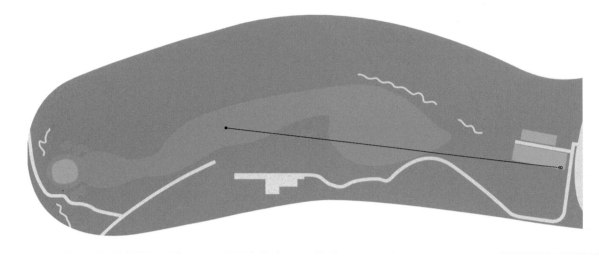

Severiano Ballesteros introduced himself to British audiences in 1976 with a drive that made a nonsense of the hole's pretensions to be a double dog-leg. Eschewing the caution exhibited by practically the rest of the field, the Spaniard drove over the bunker that guards the corner, leaving himself a short iron to the green.

The 1st and 18th

The Making of a Legend

It is only natural that when people think of the great times of Severiano Ballesteros they think of the courses associated with his victories: the young conquistador at Lytham in 1979; the vengeful champion of Augusta in 1980 and 1983, atoning for some hurtful remarks made by certain Americans; the smiling matador of St Andrews, saluting the crowds on all sides after winning over the Old course in 1984; the domineering captain of Valderrama, overseeing his charges to inspire an unforgettable win in the 1997 Ryder Cup.

There are many people, however, who cannot look back over the Spaniard's career without remembering the place where it all began, where he signed his name into the consciousness. That place was Birkdale in the 1976 Open. It began at the opening hole, a double dog-leg, where the perceived line from the tee in the year of that parched summer was an iron to the right of a dune to hold the fairway. Ballesteros was having none of it. He drew his driver and proceeded to carry the dune with yards to spare. The ball bounded miles down the fairway, turning a double dog-leg into nothing of the sort. Over the next 70 holes Ballesteros went from unknown to local hero; only Tony Jacklin had known such acclaim in these parts. When he walked down the last the cheers were deafening. He had led after the second and third rounds but experience had caught up with the 19-year-old on the final day; that and a golfer called Johnny Miller near the apex of his considerable talent.

Miller recognised the genius of the man close by. When it was clear he would win he encouraged Ballesteros not to give up, that second place was still within his grasp. As he accepted the thunderous acclaim, Ballesteros knew he had to get down in two shots from a seemingly impossible place to the left of the green to tie Jack Nicklaus. The pin was cut to the left as well and there were bunkers to negotiate. Ballesteros found the stroke for the occasion; it would invariably prove thus. He threaded the ball between the bunkers and it came to rest 4ft from the hole. Miller putted close and generously decided to tap in. He left the stage for Ballesteros and when he holed a bond had been established between the player and his people that lasts to this day.

The 9th is one of the more testing drives because the angled fairway is not quite visible from the tee. Birkdale tends to punish the hook rather than its opposite. The 10th and 11th certainly do so, but offer no great problem if the drive is straight. Woe betide the player who hooks on the latter, however, into the scrub, as Severiano Ballesteros discovered in 1976. This was the hole that effectively ended his chances of victory, for even his remarkable powers of recovery did not alleviate matters. He ended up with a seven to Johnny Miller's four, and the American was clear on his way to his solitary Open triumph. At the 12th there is a brief excursion into the lonely sandhills but wonderfully worthwhile for this is a short hole to rank with the finest, the green tucked intimidatingly away in the distance. The treacherous road for home has begun in earnest.

The 13th has a long diagonal carry from the tee to a fairway fringed with bunkers, and the last short hole, again from a high, sheltered tee, is over a valley to a closely trapped green. The 15th is a superb hole, compelling a drive in the fairway if a great gathering of bunkers is to be carried with the second shot. These are angled so that the player going for the green must attempt the longest carry. The 16th green, poised on a table of rising land, can be difficult to judge. From the 17th tee a platform in an ocean of willow scrub – the line is guarded by huge dunes, Scylla and Charybdis, on either side of the fairway's entrance; it is a forbidding shot under pressure. In 1971 Lee Trevino pulled into one of these in the last round and his struggling seven enabled Lu Liang Huan (Mr Lu) of Taiwan to challenge to the end. Trevino, however, held on to become one of six players to date who have won the British and American Opens in the same summer: the others were Bobby Jones, Gene Sarazen and Ben Hogan before him, and Tom Watson and Tiger Woods since.

Palmer, too, survived a savage break on this hole in 1961. Down the hard wind his second whistled through

the green into a small bunker. Normally recovery would have been easy, but the wind moved the ball as he struck. He skimmed it into bushes beyond the green and holed out in six. On reporting to officials that he had hit a moving ball he was automatically penalized another stroke. Nevertheless, if a player has to complete the last two holes in nine strokes to collect the title, he would hope to march on to the last tee with a birdie four on his card. The 18th is now one of the great par-four finishing holes, one that captured Tom Watson in his pomp in 1983, when he struck a two-iron second shot 213 yards to within 15ft of the hole to secure the fifth of his Open titles. He would later call it the best two-iron of his life, and with good reason.

One of the strangest Opens to have been staged was at Birkdale in 1991. The greens had succumbed to disease and infuriated many of the players but they seemingly did not bother a tall, dark Australian called Ian Baker-Finch. Reaching the turn in just 29 strokes on the final day, he won by a more comfortable margin than two strokes over Mike Harwood would suggest. But the club grasped the nettle, dug up the greens, and called in Martin Hawtree to re-contour them. When the Open returned in 1998 there were no complaints about the course, and it almost provided a fairy tale ending, with both the 17-year-old amateur, Justin Rose, and little-known American, Brian Watts, threatening to upstage the big names. Watts played a brilliant recovery shot at the last to force a play-off with Mark O'Meara, in which the recently-crowned Masters Champion calmly prevailed. As on other great links – such as Lytham, Turnberry and Westward Ho! – women were the pioneers in holding a championship at Birkdale. In 1909 Dorothy Campbell (later Mrs Hurd) won the trophy with "beautiful and deadly cleek play". She remains the only woman to have won the British and American titles more than once.

Some 50 years passed before Birkdale was host to an important men's championship. Then, in 1946, the prodigious recovery power of James Bruen was too much for Robert Sweeny's graceful golf in the final of the Amateur Championship. Bruen made light of the willow scrub, a feature of Birkdale and a fearsome hazard for ordinary mortals. He was the first of Birkdale's famous champions. Since then a host of great events have been held at Royal Birkdale, not least the 1969 Ryder Cup match, when the home side held the Americans to a tie. Remarkably, of the 32 games played, foursomes, four-ball and singles, no fewer than 16 were decided on the last green, and the last of all made an unforgettable climax. The countries were even when Jacklin, who had holed a monstrous putt on the 17th to square his game, and Nicklaus stood on the last tee in the final match – all to play for between the two finest golfers of the generation from their respective countries. The hole was halved, Nicklaus holing from four feet and immediately conceding Jacklin's short putt, which was by no means dead. It was a gesture totally in keeping with the man and it ensured that a proud day for Britain and Birkdale would pass into history.

The story of Birkdale came full circle in 1971 with the 100th Open Championship and victory for Lee Trevino, ultimate extrovert of golfers. This was the peak of a sustained spell of success that had rarely been matched in the game's history. Trevino played with formidable confidence, skill and attack; his command of the championship was absolute on the last day until he took a seven on the 71st hole, which enabled Lu Liang Huan to challenge until the last putt.

Tom Watson's second shot to the 18th at Royal Birkdale in the 1983 Open was one of the finest of his career, and deservedly led to tumultuous applause for a popular champion. It was his fifth Open win.

A monument to
technology

A map of the Sutton Coldfield area in the 1970s would have shown a potato field lying in the region now occupied by The Belfry, one of the most successful hotel and golf course establishments in Europe. The venue is a monument to the wonders of technology, to what can be achieved with massive investment and obstinate faith.

The original design was uncompromisingly American and marked a new departure in golf course architecture in Britain. This was going to be a course that took into account the changes in technology that allowed the players to hit the ball even farther distances. This was one venue where all the par fours would not be reduced to drive and pitch holes. More than £2 million was spent revising the course and its facilities in order to host an unprecedented fourth Ryder Cup in 2001 – no other course has ever staged more than two. But the events in New York of 11 September caused the postponement of the matches until October 2002. The changes have improved the front nine in particular. The third, hitherto a straight and tedious par four with little to relieve the

The story of the Belfry illustrates that with the help of machinery and courageous investment it is possible to create a silk purse out of a sow's ear. Once a potato field, the venue is now among the most successful golf establishments in Europe.

monotony, is now a dog-leg par five, with water coming into play for the shot to the green. The big hitters are encouraged by the sight of the putting surface within reach for their second shots but the penalties are plain. This man-made lake used to fall in front of the fourth tee and serve little purpose other than for drainage. Now it is a focal point of the front nine and the 3rd joins the other water holes, in particular the 9th, 10th, and 18th, for which The Belfry is deservedly famous. The 4th, previously a long, straight par five with little chance of reaching the green in two because of a ditch in front of the putting surface, now plays as a difficult par four. The ditch is more of a feature; instead of people pitching over it with a nine-iron or wedge, they have to tackle it with a long iron.

The first two holes are straightforward par fours, the second in particular a nice hole to play at less than 400 yards. The amended third gives the player a further chance to ease himself into the round before the course begins to extract its price. The 5th is often played directly into the wind and if it possesses any teeth then the ditch that runs across the fairway at the 180 yard mark can come into play.

The 6th has water patrolling both the left and right hand sides of the fairway. The architects, Dave Thomas and Peter Alliss, have created an illusion from the tee as the fairway is much wider than it appears. Nevertheless, most professionals take a long iron from the tee as insurance against finding the hazards. The Belfry's great weakness has always been its three short holes, none of which possesses much character. The first of them is the 7th, a mid to long iron shot to a green protected both fore and aft by an enormous bunker. The 8th is another good long hole which achieved a peculiar sort of fame during its early years. The right hand side has two bunkers to catch the pushed drive, an all too likely occurrence given the far greater hazard of water down the left. In 1979, Severiano Ballesteros, going for the big drive, turned in disgust almost at the moment of impact since he knew he had violently hooked the ball. The drive was not merely in danger of finishing in the hazard but likely to find the middle of the lake. Whereupon it struck a small boat advertising wares for the sponsor and bounced back on to the fairway. It hardly needs adding that the Spaniard went on to win the tournament, the English Open.

The 9th is the best hole on the outward half, a testing par four to a green shaped cleverly around the lake that also dictates play on the closing hole coming home. In the three Ryder Cups to have been played to date this area has become a splendid amphitheatre. Massive stands have been erected behind the greens allowing spectators to watch the action on both the 9th and 18th holes.

The 10th is the famous short par four, its features deservedly well known owing to the enormous influence of television. Originally designed to measure 310 yards, it was shortened to just 267 yards at the last two Ryder Cups in order to encourage more players to go for the green with their tee shots. It played to its best length at the 1985 Ryder Cup, when measuring 299 yards, and provoked an almighty row among the American players.

Lee Trevino, the US captain, stood on the tee in practice and declared the green, its sliver tucked behind trees and protected to the front and side by water, out of range. He ordered that whatever the state of the matches his players should take an iron and hope to make a birdie by getting their approach shots close. The strategy greatly upset attacking players. The unrest in the American camp was obvious, and played its part in the humbling five point margin of defeat that gave the Europeans their first victory in the Ryder Cup since the continentals were assimilated into the team in 1979.

The 11th is a dog-leg par four, the green opening up to the drive that misses two bunkers that guard the fairway's left and right sides. Alterations have been made to the long par three 12th, hitherto the worst hole on the course. Before, it offered no option but a mighty smash with a metal wood or one iron. Now the tee has been raised to establish some character and the ditch in front of the green has been widened.

The 13th is a par four that skirts the outer rim of the site and is a little too similar to the 11th to be rated highly. The 14th is the last of the short holes and in 1993 Nick Faldo holed in one against Paul Azinger in the singles matches.

So to one of the longest finishes in golf, the final four holes measuring just under 2,000 yards. The 15th is a 545 yard par five where the drive has to be threaded between two bunkers. A ditch that crosses the hole at the 390 yard mark becomes a problem for anyone who has strayed from the tee, or if the wind against has any velocity. For the straight hitter, a bunker that sits imposingly in the middle of the fairway, 50 yards from the front of a three-tier green, invariably dictates the strategy for the second shot, leaving a pitch that can be anything from a half swing to a full nine-iron depending upon where the pin is positioned. This is the first of the four big greens that are a feature of the Belfry's closing holes.

The green at the par four 16th falls away dramatically to the left, and with the flag invariably positioned on the top shelf this can mean the most difficult of putts for the iron shot that has narrowly missed its target. The 17th is another par five that dog-legs sharply to the right and, when downwind, is reachable in two shots. The drive, a forerunner to the strategy the player will have to adopt at the last, is one of the most intriguing on the course. Enough of the dog-leg needs to be cut off to avoid running into the bunker that sits on the angle but another bunker guards the right hand side to ward off any greedy golfer. The green is again massive at 39 yards and slopes gently from back to front. The 473-yard 18th has become one of the most famous finishing holes in British golf. Its reputation was made at the Ryder Cups in 1985 and 1989. The hole's difficulty comes in deciding how much of the severe left hand dog-leg to carry. Too little and the shot to the green, over a large expanse of water, becomes daunting; too much and the ball will not make it over the water. The green is of St Andrews proportions, measuring 59 yards from front to back, with three tiers. Locate the wrong tier and it is all too easy to three putt. It is the sort of hole that no golfer easily forgets. While the sum of all its parts might not lead to the conclusion that The Belfry is a great course, it undeniably has greatness contained within its boundaries.

The Course Card

The Belfry,
Brabazon Course,
Wishaw,
Warwickshire

Hole	Yards	Par
1	411	4
2	379	4
3	538	5
4	442	4
5	408	4
6	395	4
7	177	3
8	428	4
9	433	4
10	311	4
11	419	4
12	208	3
13	384	4
14	190	3
15	545	5
16	413	4
17	564	5
18	473	4
Out	3,611	36
In	3,507	36
Total	**7,118**	**72**

The 18th

The Perfect Finishing Hole

The Brabazon at The Belfry is not unique in having received critical press reviews in its early days. The same was true of the TPC at Sawgrass, Valhalla and Medinah No.3 when they staged their earliest big events. The plain fact cannot be denied, however, that The Brabazon has produced some scintillating Ryder Cup matchplay over the years. It has the merit of being able to handle large crowds and there are good public transport facilities within easy reach in this readily accessible part of the country. It also has the 18th, perhaps the most demanding finishing hole in golf.

It is the perfect matchplay hole. In the three Ryder Cups to date, no fewer than 25 of the 36 singles matches have finished there and they form an unforgettable memorial to the range of emotions that a great finishing hole can inspire. We have seen Sam Torrance stand in the middle of the green, his arms forming a V for victory salute after taming the 18th with a perfect drive and nine-iron; witnessed Christy O'Connor jnr, equally jubilant after a daring two iron approach over what must have appeared a cavernous expanse of water. Naturally there have been many failures too, many who have discovered the hole and the context in which it was framed beyond their capabilities. It will be the same always. One may argue with considerable justification that the Ryder Cup should not be going once more to The Belfry; but no-one can counsel against the 18th again providing scenes of unique drama.

The Course Card

Royal St George's
Golf Club,
Sandwich, Kent

Record: 64,
Tony Jacklin,
Dunlop Masters 1967;
Christy O'Connor
Jnr., The Open 1985

Hole	Yards	Par
1	441	4
2	376	4
3	210	3
4	468	4
5	421	4
6	172	3
7	530	5
8	418	4
9	389	4
10	413	4
11	216	3
12	365	4
13	443	4
14	551	5
15	478	4
16	163	3
17	425	4
18	468	4
Out	3,425	35
In	3,522	35
Total	**6,947**	**70**

A Kentish haven of history

No course is closer to the golfing heart of England than Royal St George's at Sandwich because of its association with the growth of championship golf and its distinctive character. No other English club moved so swiftly from a quiet and pleasant beginning to a lasting place in the chronicles of the game. Since Roman times Sandwich has been a harbour. More than 1,000 years ago Wilfred, Bishop of Northumberland, arrived "pleasantly and happily in Sandwich haven" – and a haven it remains. The town, with its quaint, mysterious little streets and ancient dwellings, is snug and peaceful, and the links are wild and lonely, free to the winds and the sky as they have been since the tides withdrew countless centuries since.

The setting has changed little since one Doctor Laidlaw Purves "spied the land with a golfer's eye" from the tower of a Sandwich church. The sight must have stirred his imagination, and that of others. A syndicate was formed and in 1887 the club was founded.

That was the age of mighty amateurs, whose stature surpassed that of all the English professionals with only one notable exception. The Scottish had commanded the scene until 1894 when J. H. Taylor, a sturdy young professional from Winchester, won the first Open Championship to be played outside Scotland. His score of 326 on the desolate and windswept links seems monumental by modern standards.

In those years there was no challenge to the supremacy of British golfers until in 1904 Walter J. Travis, described by one observer as "a little man in middle age with a black cigar and a centre-shafted putter", came to Sandwich from the United States to compete in the Amateur Championship. He was, it seems, a coldly determined, implacable person who played with great steadiness, winning match after match with accurate approach work and uncanny skill on the greens. His success was not popular, for the British were unaccustomed to defeat and American golf was hardly out of the embryonic stages. The chagrin that must have swept St George's when he beat Horace Hutchinson in the semi-final and the vast hitter Ted Blackwell in the final can be imagined. The centre-shafted putter was banned for years to come, but it was too late. Travis, who was born in Australia, was the first American citizen to win in Britain.

Soon after World War I, in 1922, another American came to Sandwich. He also had cigars and an enchanted putter – and more besides, for Walter Hagen was the most colourful personality that British golf had seen. He won the Open that year, the first in which native-born American supremacy was becoming established, and at its peak Hagen won again at Sandwich, in 1928. In 1930 Bobby Jones led his side to an overwhelming victory in the first Walker Cup match to be played in England. Then, four years later, the incomparable Henry Cotton stemmed the transatlantic tide not far from where King Canute had made his fruitless gesture a while earlier.

In 140 years of championships no golfer can have endured a greater agony of suspense than he did on the last day, when illness threatened to sabotage his triumph. In 1938 Cotton again played magnificently in one of the most ferocious gales that has ever beset an Open, but the yeoman figure R. A. Whitcombe just prevailed. After Bobby Locke had won the first of his four Opens at St George's in 1949 the championship came no more to Sandwich until 1981, when a young American with a genial smile walked off with the main prize. It was to be the highlight of Bill Rogers's career. He did return later that year to Walton Heath as part of the strongest American Ryder Cup side of all time but in the team photograph he was almost hiding in the back-

Soft-sprung rolling fairways and yawning duneside bunkers make Royal St George's a classic links course. A good score on the outward half – much improved by Frank Pennink's recent modifications – can lay the foundations for a winning total, but this can be so easily spoiled by the long par-four 13th, the daunting 14th alongside the boundary wall, and the heavily bunkered 15th. No matter what his score the golfer can take pleasure from the beauty and seclusion of verdant fairways that run along hollows between high dunes, making golf at Royal St George's a very private pastime.

ground and it proved pertinent. When the Open came back to Sandwich just four years later he was already harbouring thoughts of retirement and now he rests easy, the head professional at San Antonio Country Club in Texas with just the flag of the 18th hole at St George's to remind him of his daring deeds of yore. In 1985 it was Sandy Lyle's year, repeating the feat of Cotton long before in ending overseas dominance. It was the first home triumph since Tony Jacklin in 1969 and it was duly celebrated with raucous scenes. No British player since Jacklin had been more popular than Lyle, an easy-going character from the heart of Shropshire. It said everything about his unassuming demeanour that three hours after winning the Open he was washing the dishes at his rented home in Sandwich. The 1993 Open at St George's is a firm candidate for the greatest last day of all. The greens were hard, the fairways parched, and the leaderboard read like a who's who of the modern game: Norman, Faldo, Langer, Pavin. Norman It was who triumphed, returning a 64, the lowest final round in Open history. As he walked down the 18th the wise old denizen Gene Sarazen was standing by the 18th green, 92 years old and bright as a button. Later he said of Norman's achievement:"I never thought I would live to see golf played like this," a statement verified by Norman's generous playing partner Langer, who called it the finest round he had witnessed.

What a glorious place Sandwich is for golf. When sunlight is dancing on the waves of Pegwell Bay, the white cliffs of Ramsgate shining in the distance, the larks singing as they always seem to sing at Sandwich, and a sea wind

The Sandwich hall of fame includes such figures as, left to right, Walter Travis, Walter Hagen and Roger Wethered. It was there in 1904 that quiet American Travis became the first overseas player to win the British Amateur title, and where the great Hagen became America's first British Open champion in 1922. In 1930, Sandwich was the first English venue for a Walker Cup match with Wethered making the fourth of five British team appearances. But it was not enough and the Americans won for the sixth successive time.

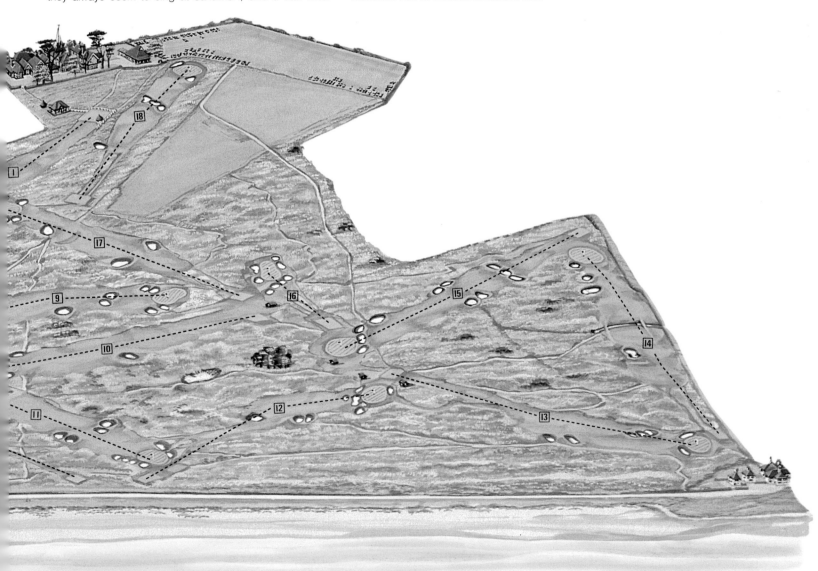

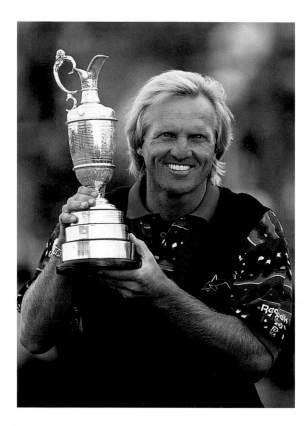

Henry Cotton's first big success at Royal St. George's was when he won the 1934 Open there, setting an Open record of 65. But his return there in 1938 was less happy when he lost in the gale-swept final round by going out-of-bounds at the 14th hole.

stirring in the sand grasses, the golfer may share the famous golf writer Bernard Darwin's view that it is "as nearly my idea of heaven as is to be attained on any earthly links".

As with many another historic course, St George's was admired in its earlier days more for its charm than the quality of its golf. It was a place of mighty dunes and blind carries, and there were those who claimed that the art of the game was not hitting a ball over a sandhill and running to the top to see where it had finished. But changes were made and the course is now a rich and varied examination of golf, owing little to guessing or fortune.

The 1st, its fairway like a stormy sea of green with a cross-bunker threatening the second shot, is a perfect opening hole; a mounting crest before the 2nd green makes the approach difficult to judge. Then comes a demanding new short hole, a long iron or more over wild country to a narrow shelf of green. This hole replaced a relic from gully days and was one of several changes by the architect Frank Pennink which came into play in 1975. Previously three short holes pursued the same direction. The 6th, alongside

The 14th

The Low Road Home in a High Wind

The ability to maintain balance and rhythm of swing and to flight the ball truly in a strong wind is not given to many. Among modern golfers few have mastered the art to a greater degree than Sandy Lyle. His stance is so solid that it seems immovable; his hands so powerful that he can drive the club through the ball, keeping it so low that its flight is hardly affected, even by strong wind. During the final round of the 1985 Open Championship at Sandwich Lyle had dropped a shot at the 13th hole and so when he came to the par five 14th he knew he

needed a birdie to maintain his dream of emulating Tony Jacklin's achievement in 1969. The drive at the 14th is the most difficult on the course and Lyle's was duly hooked away from the out of bounds and into wild rough. He had to play short of Suez Canal, thus leaving him over 200 yards to go for his third shot. A par not a birdie now appeared the limit of his achievements for the shot was far from easy to a green lavishly protected by sand. Yet into the wind Lyle flighted the ball beautifully, keeping it low as it raced over the ground to finish 35 ft from the

the Maiden, remains, as does the 16th. The 8th is now an appealing par-four with its drive to a plateau amid the crumpled land and approach down to a green in a dell of its own. It is replaced as a short hole by the 11th.

Early in the round the golfer will be aware of frequently changing levels and stances, such as the long rise of the 4th past a mountainous bunker to a sharply contoured green high on a folding hillside, and the drive from the next tee into a valley enclosed by dunes. Only if the drive is placed right is a sight of the distant green possible, for otherwise the approach is blind. This hole is typical of the course's beauty; so, too, is the 7th with its drive to a lovely, hidden expanse of fairway running clear to a green that may or may not be reached according to the wind.

Thereafter the mood of the course quietens somewhat except for the approach to the 10th high on an exposed plateau, a fiercely testing shot in a wind. Around the turn pars may not be too difficult, but the 13th is the first of a great trinity. The drive is diagonal over a long shoulder of rough country towards the clubhouse of the neighbouring Prince's, white and remote in the distance. The 14th can be the most fearsome tee shot on the course, with dunes to be carried and with out-of-bounds on the right all the way to the green. Then the golfer must decide whether or not he can carry the wide waters of the stream crossing the fairway.

A similar decision is often required at the 15th, unless the wind is helping or the fairway running fast. An array of cross-bunkers must be carried, and the narrow green is farther beyond them than it seems to be. The 16th is fringed with sand, a target shot. This is the hole that gave British television viewers their first sight of a tee shot being holed in important competition. On his way to winning the 1967 Dunlop Masters, Tony Jacklin holed out with a seven-iron. The 17th is a strong four and the approach to the 18th, from a downhill fairway, is a great finishing stroke, made by one beautifully placed greenside bunker.

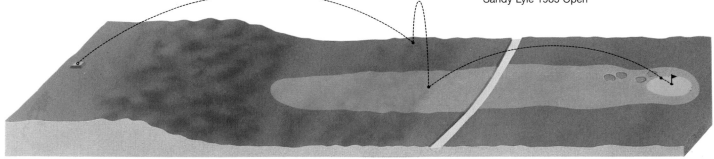

Sandy Lyle 1985 Open

flag. It gave him sustenance at the time he most needed it and the confidence to hole the putt for a birdie which changed the face of that Open. The 15th would yield a birdie as well and Lyle could afford the bogey that resulted from missing the green at the 18th and still claim the prize – though not before a 30 minute wait for others to finish that seemed to drag for an eternity. When asked about a turning point afterwards he had no hesitation in pointing to the two iron that set up the unlikeliest of birdies at the 14th.

Ganton

An inland course of seaside character

Yorkshire, England's largest county, possesses a long coastline, stretching from remote Spurn Head at the mouth of the Humber northwards to the heavy industry of the Tees Estuary. There is only one true links course to be found anywhere on this coast, the Cleveland at Redcar, Yorkshire's oldest club. Yet in many respects Yorkshire's noblest course, Ganton, is almost a links course, despite being some twelve miles inland from Scarborough. It does not come as a surprise, then, to learn that many thousands of years ago this spot had been an inlet from the North Sea. When the sea retreated it left behind a naturally sandy soil from which sea shells are still occasionally dug up. So, when golf was first played at Ganton in 1891 it was over very rough ground, covered in gorse and the many varieties of grasses and wild flowers characteristic of heathland. It is much the same today, its links qualities so abundant that Ganton is the only inland course ever to have been used for the Amateur Championship, which it has now done three times. The quality of the winners – Gordon Clark, Peter McEvoy and Gary Wolstenholme – speaks for itself. And when Ganton hosts the 39th Walker Cup Match in 2003 it will join Royal Birkdale and Muirfield as the only clubs to have staged each of the premier team cups played between Great Britain and Ireland and the USA, the Ryder, Curtis and Walker Cups. (When the Ryder Cup was played at Ganton in 1949 it was long before the advent of the continental Europeans in the team).

There is something soothing about turning off the busy A64 road by the church in Ganton village, down a lane which seems to lead to another world. Here in the peaceful Vale of Pickering, with wooded hills and patterned meadowland overlooking the course on either side, larks rise in song, emphasising an awareness of space. The 17th and 18th holes cross the lane amidst a great outbreak of gorse and some idea is given of the seriousness of the task ahead. A first glimpse might also be had of Ganton's bunkers: deep, sandy caverns in which a player may vanish from view. In an age when many bunkers are being made less penal, Ganton's are welcome. The player who is bunkered is surely punished for his error. In all England, Woodhall Spa in Lincolnshire is probably Ganton's only peer for the depth and expanse of its bunkers. Trees successfully screen the course from the outside world, but they are only occasionally a factor in play.

The opening holes are fine examples of the admirable play made of the contours of the land, the 1st rising smoothly. As early as the second shot it becomes immediately apparent that the bents and fescues growing on this free-draining, sandy subsoil provide a wonderfully crisp fairway turf. Good control is needed with the approach on the 2nd, played slightly downhill to a fast green menaced by encroaching gorse, which also threatens the drive at the 3rd. It is possible to drive this hole, but the green is narrow and well guarded by deep bunkers.

Many architects of the highest calibre have contributed to the evolution of Ganton since it was first laid out by Tom Chisholm of St Andrews and R. Bird, the club's first Professional: Tom Dunn, Harry Vardon (Professional at

Ganton is a course of considerable beauty, surrounded by miles of unspoiled countryside, but it punishes wayward golf mercilessly.

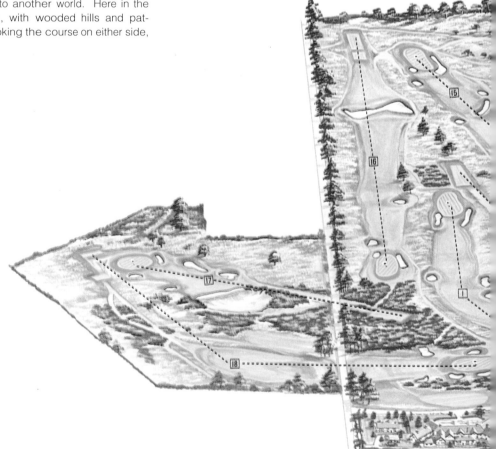

Ganton from 1896 to 1903), Ted Ray, J.H. Taylor, James Braid, Harry Colt, Alister Mackenzie, C.K. Cotton and Frank Pennink. Colt was responsible for the lovely 4th with its drive to the crest of a fairway and an approach shot played across a valley to a tricky green. After a short hole played downhill to a green encircled with sand, the handsome 6th strikes out along the edge of the course. Members play it as a par-5, but for championships it is a strong par-4, well bunkered on the approaches to the green. The 7th and 8th swing back and forth, the dog-leg of the 7th being filled with a host of bunkers, and the outward half ends with a shortish par-5, narrow between trees.

Played towards the village church, the short 10th is difficult to judge in a wind, and the 11th fairway is memorable for a line of cross-bunkers 100 yards short of the green. Trees are a factor on the 12th, a hole on which the strong are invited to cut the corner from the tee, while, appropriately, 13 bunkers must be avoided on the 13th. If the 14th is to be driven the tee shot must be threaded through the narrowest of gaps between a tree on the right and a number of bunkers. A long thin bunker must be carried from the 15th tee, and Ganton's tough finish has started in earnest. A monumental bunker crosses the 16th fairway, but it will be of little concern to the modern long hitter who will be anxious to get a good line on the approach shot to a green raised up in front of a sea of gorse.

Even played as a short par-4 (which it usually is) the 17th can be wicked with the lane and a quarry to be carried, bunkers on either side, and the green only 26 yards deep. As a one-shotter for championship play it is sternly punishing. There remains a classic 'cape' hole to end. Drive slightly left from the tee and it is clear why this is one of the most celebrated finishing holes in the country. The second shot is then blocked out by a stand of tall pines, posing a severe problem of combining height with length

if they are to be cleared. Err to the right from the tee and the ball will be lost in bushes and dense undergrowth. Play too conservatively and the second shot will be far from easy to the sloping, well-bunkered final green set amid the gorse bushes. The hole proved critical to the outcome of the Curtis Cup in June 2000. On the first day six of the nine matches came as far as the 18th, but the home side could gather only two half-points and the Americans ended the day 7-2 up. A spirited reply on the following day almost brought the match within reach but eventually Hilary Homeyer (the best American player with 3½ points out of 4) edged out Becky Brewerton on the 16th and the Americans recorded a second successive 10-8 victory.

Ganton held its first Yorkshire Championship in 1895 and it was soon followed by the Yorkshire Ladies'. Despite the physical challenges of the course, the ladies have returned many times. Ganton provided many British golfers with their only sight of the incomparable Babe Zaharias in 1951 when she led a team of six lady professionals from the United States in an international mixed foursomes match partnered by British men professionals. In recent years men professionals have played only rarely at Ganton, the last occasion being 1981, when Nick Faldo won his 3rd PGA Championship. But the most remarkable scoring spree at Ganton was by an amateur, albeit one of the finest amateurs to grace the British game, Michael Bonallack. In the final of the 1968 English Amateur Championship, Bonallack went in to lunch 11-up on an opponent, David Kelley, who had played to level par! Bonallack had gone round in 61, 32 out and 29 in. Ganton has known many proud and unforgettable moments. But its enduring place in English golf is in the pleasure it has given, and continues to give, to countless golfers from the humblest to the most accomplished who revel in the test it sets, its invariably flawless condition, the warm Yorkshire welcome, and its own incomparable Ganton cake.

The Course Card

Ganton Golf
Club,
Scarborough,
North Yorks

Hole	Yards	Par
1	373	4
2	445	4
3	334	4
4	406	4
5	157	3
6	470	4
7	435	4
8	414	4
9	504	5
10	168	3
11	417	4
12	363	4
13	524	5
14	282	4
15	461	4
16	448	4
17	249	3
18	434	4
Out	3,538	36
In	3,346	35
Total	**6,884**	**71**

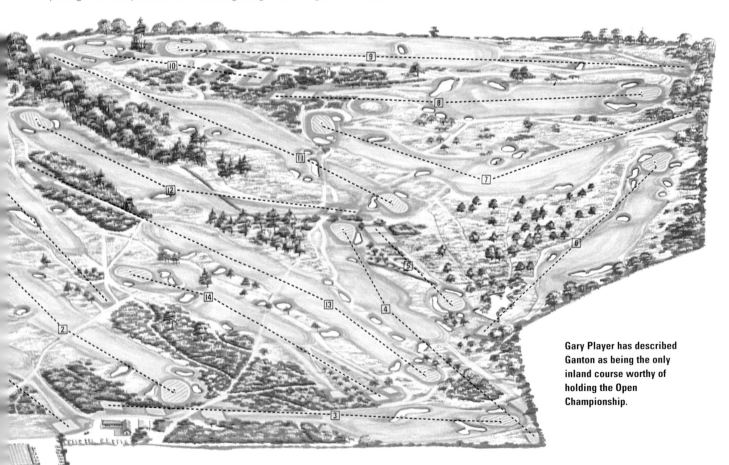

Gary Player has described Ganton as being the only inland course worthy of holding the Open Championship.

Intimacy that belies

quality

An odd characteristic of seaside golf in the British Isles is that many links courses permit little more than an occasional glimpse of the sea; it can be heard, but is usually invisible. A fine exception is Royal Porthcawl, on the rock-fringed southern shores of Wales.

In the strictest sense it is not a links. There are occasional sandhills, but gorse, hummocks, heather and deep bunkers are its principal features. The land hereabouts leans down to the rocks and the smooth shining sand and from every point the golfer can look across the Bristol Channel to the long dark line of the Somerset coast. At times when wind and rain sweep in from the Atlantic he might long for the shelter of dunes, for Porthcawl is exposed to every mood of the elements, but such days are exceptional. For most of the time there are few courses as agreeable to play.

The origins of golf in Wales are by no means as ancient as those in Scotland. Most of the early clubs were formed towards the end of the last century and Porthcawl is regarded as the senior, in stature if not age; the charming links at Tenby is credited with that honour. Porthcawl was founded in 1891 and started with nine holes laid out on common land near the sea. However, cattle on the greens, carriage wheels and camping were a constant nuisance and 18 holes were planned afresh. Many years passed before their quality was appreciated and even now a first sight of the intimate little clubhouse would not suggest the presence of a championship course. Nevertheless a more beautiful, princely beginning could hardly be imagined.

The opening holes follow the line of the coast and when surf is foaming on the rocks, and the sky fresh and clear, the urge to play is almost overwhelming. The 1st is not severe – a tempting drive into a valley and pitch to a subtle green. For the 1995 Walker Cup a tee situated between the clubhouse and the sea was used. Tiger Woods drove the green with a 3-wood every time he played the hole. The next two holes

are beautifully fashioned over gently falling ground, demanding substantial approaches to greens on the shore's edge. They are classic seaside holes. After a fine short hole the course swings inland, mounting the long 5th to a trough of green whose sides were once so steep – alas, no more – that many a wide shot would find its way unerringly and obligingly into the hole.

The golf on the uplands is more heathland in character. Great banks of broom and gorse, a glory in early summer, threaten, but not too unkindly, the 6th and 8th. Between them is a charming little hole for which strong players hardly have a club small enough. Anyone would settle for a four at the 8th with its long second uphill over cross-bunkers, and the 9th is harder than it looks. The drive must hold a leaning fairway and huge bunkers guard a sharply sloping green which positively invites three putts unless a player thinks carefully before approaching it. The golfer's task thus far may not have been too severe unless there is a firm wind and this proviso must be made for all British seaside courses; wind is as much a part of their character as the links turf, the dunes and the gorse. They can vary enormously in difficulty and Porthcawl is as good an example as any. During the 1995 Walker Cup the weather was turbulent causing problems for many players and, during his first day singles with Gary Wolstenholme, Tiger Woods struggled to keep the ball in play. His sand wedge approach to the 3rd went through the green and out of bounds. Two holes later he pulled his 8-iron second over the wall to the left of the green to go out of bounds once more. He dug deep and pushed the tenacious Wolstenholme all the way to the final green, only to drift out of bounds again with his approach shot, losing the match by a single hole.

From the turn the levels of the holes vary constantly. The 10th dips into a valley and offers a testing pitch to a narrow oblong of green. The short 11th is a target hole, while the

At Royal Porthcawl, as is often the case with British seaside courses, a high premium is placed on a golfer's ability to play accurately despite the elements. Finding the fairway from the tee is often only the beginning. At the 5th, for example, the player who manages to avoid the out-of-bounds and the pond on the left has to play hard up against the boundary again to find the green. At 124 yards, the 7th is one of the shortest holes in championship golf, but there are several long holes on the back nine.

ond shots of rare quality. The whole of the greens cannot be seen, but the distant, fluttering flags should be guide enough to the golfer who knows his course. Cross bunkers dictate the driving strategy on both holes. On the 15th they lie about 320 yards from the tee, effectively restricting the length of prodigious players. On the 16th, however, they need a carry of 305 yards. In his first day singles Woods cleared the bunkers with his drive, yet still lost the hole to Wolstenholme. And it was on the 16th green that Jody Fanagan had the honour of holing the putt that secured a home victory in that 1995 Walker Cup.

Whether by design or coincidence most of the famous British courses have 17th holes of great distinction. During practice for the Walker Cup Tiger Woods and Graham Rankin both achieved remarkable albatross twos with no more than a drive and wedge, the hole playing directly downwind.

The last hole can be most exacting, tumbling gently towards the sea and a slippery, falling green. The approach over hummocks, hollows and heather demands a delicate touch to finish within reasonable putting distance. And, when the sun is going down and the Bristol Channel gleams like polished pewter, the shot can be the very devil. Despite its perils, this hole provided birdies in 5 matches on the opening day's singles of the Walker Cup, with one of them halved in birdies.

12th mounts a somewhat forbidding hill. Few can reach its green with their seconds, but the effort is worthwhile. From the crest of the 13th fairway the prospect is superb. The green lies at the foot of a long slope with the sea shining beyond. All around, the great basin of the course can be seen; the golfers moving out on the early holes, climbing the 5th, approaching the 10th and 11th, toiling up the nearby 12th and – it is hoped – choosing the right club at the short 14th, where nothing but a true shot is rewarded.

The 15th and 16th are similar holes, pursuing opposite directions, with drives to island fairways far below and sec-

The Course Card

Royal Porthcawl
Golf Club,
Glamorgan

Hole	Yards	Par
1	327	4
2	454	4
3	421	4
4	196	3
5	515	5
6	389	4
7	124	3
8	475	5
9	384	4
10	336	4
11	186	3
12	468	5
13	441	4
14	150	3
15	464	4
16	433	4
17	511	5
18	411	4
Out	3,285	36
In	3,400	36
Total	6,685	72

The Rise and Rise of Welsh Golf

It was no coincidence that the Walker Cup was staged in Wales for the first time in 1995, for it was the centenary year of the Welsh Golf Union. Appropriately a Welsh captain was appointed, Clive Brown, who had himself represented Wales as an international player in the 1970s and 80s. Porthcawl stood up well to the atrocious weather conditions on the second day, with only the 1st green accumulating any water, so brilliantly did the course drain. The event's success, not least the fact that it was a home win, surely helped to influence the decision to bring the Ryder Cup to Wales in 2010. It will be going to Celtic Manor, a spectacular development outside Newport, a few miles to the east along the M4 motorway. At last Wales will see the sort of professional play of which it has long been starved, despite producing such world-class players as Dai Rees, Brian Huggett (a Porthcawl native), and Ian Woosnam. And, if it opens the eyes of a wider public to the glories of courses such as Aberdovey, Conwy, Pyle & Kenfig, Royal St David's, Southerndown, and dozens of others, it will have been a priceless investment.

Sweden's Helen Alfredsson who won the 2001 WPGA Championship of Europe at Porthcawl.

A breathtaking backdrop of mountains and sea is reward in itself at **Royal County Down**, but the golfer who strays can pay devastating penalties in the fierce rough and bewildering frequency of traps that make the championship course one of Ireland's best. It is an added hazard, too, that the 2nd, 5th, 6th, 9th and 15th holes all call for blind tee shots, and others, such as the 13th, offer only markers to guide approach shots to unseen greens.

Emerald fairways
by a sapphire sea

The lasting appeal of the finest British courses is their variety. County Down bears little resemblance to its great Irish companions, Portrush, Portmarnock and Ballybunion; an occasional valley hole might stir memories of Birkdale or Turnberry, but not strongly. At County Down one is, as so often, on a course with such individual character that it is among the hardest, yet most rewarding, to play anywhere in the British Isles.

It lies on a curve of Dundrum Bay, with the Mourne mountains in the background. It can be a paradise for the golfer in early summer, when sunshine turns the sea to sapphire and brings forth the golden glory of the gorse and the richness of emerald fairways, and greens with cloud shadows playing on the mountains and the quiet green hills to the west.

The club came into being in 1889 and minutes of an early meeting reveal the remarkable fact that Tom Morris was to lay out a course for a sum not exceeding £4. How far this princely sum availed the old man is not known, but within a decade the links were written of as the finest in Ireland. It was reconstructed later; Vardon gave it high praise in 1908 and the same year King Edward VII

bestowed the Royal title on the club. Since then the golf has changed but little. Purists might claim that there are too many blind shots – five from the tees and others where the green is all or partially concealed – but somehow they are so in keeping with the nature of the course that they cannot with any justice be condemned.

The opening holes head northwards along the shores of the bay, which is screened by ranges of dunes. The long 1st resembles a trough from the tee – an inviting prospect for the straight driver – but the next tee shot is the very reverse. A high ridge must be carried and against the wind it can seem insurmountable; the second shot must be steered through a divide in another ridge to a well-guarded plateau green – not a long hole, but one that can be fierce indeed. The drive down the valley of the 3rd should be held to the left, for bunkers in a spur of dunes on the right protect the straight line to the flag.

The short 4th, a medium shot over a waste of rough heather, is followed by a great 5th. The drive must be aimed to carry as much as the striker dares of a heathery outcrop of land, around which the hole swings to the right. The approach is a fine shot to a green backed against sandhills.

The 6th is a lovely hole, blind from the tee but not harassingly so, and the 7th a tricky little pitch over a gully; part of the green is behind a hummock and its sides are closely bunkered. In the Irish Open amateur final in 1933 Eric Fiddian, playing Jack McLean, holed his tee shot there in the morning round.

In the afternoon he did likewise at the 14th, a feat without parallel on an important occasion but one that still failed to give him victory. Into a prevailing wind, the approach to the 8th green between its embracing hills can be a taxing stroke. This is the highest point. As one drives from the next tee into a valley far below, leading to a distant plateau green, the mass of Slieve Donard, highest of the Mourne mountains, can seem menacingly

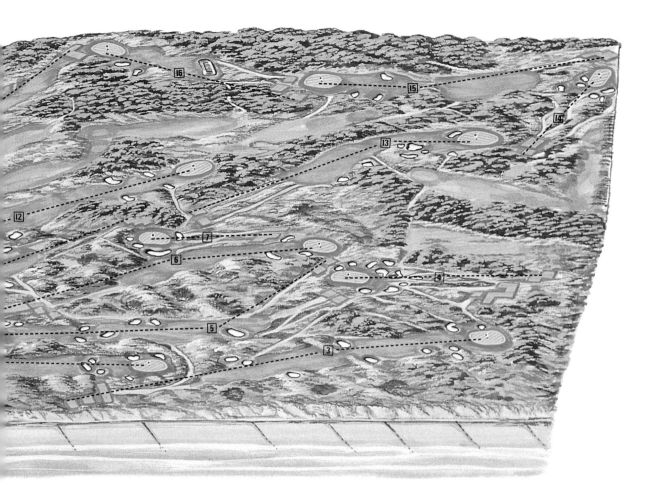

The Course Card

Royal County Down Golf Club, Newcastle, Down No 1 course

Record: 66,
James Bruen, Irish
Open 1939

Hole	Yards	Par
1	506	5
2	421	4
3	474	4
4	212	3
5	438	4
6	396	4
7	145	3
8	429	4
9	486	4
10	197	3
11	438	4
12	525	5
13	443	4
14	213	3
15	464	4
16	276	4
17	427	4
18	547	5
Out	3,507	35
In	3,530	36
Total	**7,037**	**71**

close, and the spires and roofs of the town at its foot almost alpine in appearance.

The turn is by the clubhouse, blessed virtue of design, and the 10th, although short, is another characteristic hole, from a raised tee along a valley to a green where bunkers abound. The 11th leads to more open country and after the falling sweep of the 12th comes a gracefully curving hole in a valley all its own. The second shot is blind and the one swinging in over the hill has the best chance of finding the green. This is a splendid hole to watch from on high, where its secrets are visible to the spectator but not to the player.

After the challenge of the 14th, a downhill shot over sand and gorse to a well-bunkered green, the course heads for home. The 15th demands two substantial strokes of anyone's game, and maybe more, but the 16th is fun. The strong can drive the green, but to threaten the frail a charming little pool with an island lies in the fairway below. The finish on the landward side of the big dune country is not typical of the rest but a pond, just out of driving range, must be carried at the 17th, and the last hole is the longest of all.

Newcastle is an examination for any golfer whatever the elements, and how swiftly these can change. Once during an international meeting the seas were a tossing, angry turmoil and the wind so violent that eight holes could not be reached with two wooden club shots. So low were the clouds that one young golfer, forgetting that the sea was at his feet, asked, "How high are we here?" Mercifully such days are rare.

Many of the most memorable moments at County Down have involved women golfers, not least three from France. In 1927 the tiny Simone Thion de la Chaume became the first Frenchwoman to win the British championship. Her daughter Catherine succeeded her, remarkably also in Northern Ireland, at Portrush in 1969. The dark, lithe grace of the Vicomtesse de Saint-Sauveur prevailed in 1950, and Brigitte Varangot, one of the most accomplished woman players of her time, succeeded in 1963.

The first Amateur Championship to be played there was in 1970 when Michael Bonallack won for a third successive year. This was a record and also his fifth victory, a tally surpassed only by John Ball long ago. The Amateur Championship returned to Newcastle in 1999, Graeme Storm from the north-east of England emerging victorious, his enormous bag carried by his petite mother, Jane!

The sweep of the Mountains of Mourne provides players with a diversion so magnificent as to make concentration difficult at the 4th. The hole measures 212 yards, almost all of it carry across gorse and heavy rough. The green, much longer than it is wide, is protected by no fewer than ten bunkers, most of them positioned to catch the underhit or the sliced tee shot.

Ulster's

green leagues of links

The informed golfer in search of the game in Northern Ireland may head south from Belfast to Newcastle in County Down, or north to Portrush; if he is wise he will make both journeys. When Portrush is the first choice, and there is no particular haste, he should take the Antrim coast road, not only because it is one of the most beautiful in Britain but because, as an approach to a links, it has few parallels. Soon after the road passes the ancient ruins of Dunluce Castle it turns a corner, and there below, with enchanting abruptness, the whole spread of the course can be seen in a sweeping glance: green leagues of tumbling, broken links falling away to cliffs of sand – the highest near any golf course – and the shining seas. The course, much changed since it was established in 1888, winds and climbs and falls over a profusion of green hills, and within their grasses are primrose, bluebell and dog-rose. To the east and west the dark headlands of Benbane and Inishowen rise from the sea, and not far off shore the long, low sprawl of the Skerries stand patient against the tide. Well distant, the faint shadows of Islay and the Paps of Jura, remote outposts of Scotland, can be seen when the air is clear, and a few miles away lies the Giant's Causeway.

The modern version of the main course, named Dunluce after the ancestral home of the Lords of Antrim, evolved from the work and imagination of many men, from one McNeill, a greenkeeper who laid the greens, to the architect, Colt, who was responsible for most of the improvements. From a purely golfing point of view the most distinctive feature is the severe driving. There are few great courses where the erratic driver can consistently escape all consequences of waywardness; at Portrush he has less chance of

doing so than on almost any other championship course, not because of particularly savage roughs or hazards but by the design of the holes. The first and last alone are straight; all the others curve, usually more than 200 yards from the tee. When the rough is allowed to grow inwards for an important occasion, and the fairways are no more than the width of a street, uncommon accuracy is essential for any golfer, let alone the long hitter who tries to carry the corners.

Another unusual aspect is the comparative absence of bunkers about the greens. Mostly these are protected by natural hills and mounds, hollows and runners, and holding the greens can be difficult unless the drive has been rightly placed. If they are missed then the little shots can be a real test of touch. Neither are the greens enormous, and this accounted for Max Faulkner having so few putts when he won the Open in 1951: few champions have had less over four rounds. The number was said to be 108; even allowing for exaggeration it was an astonishingly low proportion of a winning total of 285.

The opening holes move along the uplands of the course. After a rise to the plateau of the 1st green, the 2nd winds down a long path through the dunes. The 4th is a lovely hole with its drive over a stream, out-of-bounds on the right and a green nestling in the sandhills, and from the next tee the whole glory of the links can be seen. The 5th fairway cascades to a green by the sea, and an inadvertent step backwards would bring a long tumble down a precipice of sand to the beach. The 6th is a beautiful short hole calling for a long fade into the green; and now the stern stuff has begun.

The middle holes of the round swing back and forth, but in no way monotonously, for the angles of their approaches are alternately inclined, never unduly favouring the slice or hook. After a picturesque dropping shot to the 11th, the course takes a turn towards the sea again; and soon one stands on the tee of the 14th, as famous a short hole as there is in Ireland, with the singularly appropriate name of Calamity Corner. Between tee and green, 200 yards away, is a chasm of rough, and the prevailing wind does not help; often enough the stroke calls for wood. The merest slice can mean disaster, just as a pull from the next tee is a most unhelpful

Spread out over tumbling dune country on a beautiful stretch of the Ulster coast, Portrush offers a unique kind of links golf. All but the first and last holes curve and it is this rather than tough hazards which proves challenging. Bunkers are few, and natural mounds and hollows guard the greens. In the 1951 Open (the only British Open held in Ireland) only two players managed to beat 70 in testing, blustery conditions.

stroke. The 16th fairway leans left towards a grassy bank, and it was there, in the last round of the 1951 Open, that Tony Cerda's drive finished and, as it proved, his challenge to Faulkner expired. Nine years later the hole saw a memorable stroke in a semi-final of the Amateur Championship. Robert Cochran, an American of middle years, was two down to Gordon Huddy when he struck a three wood shot low under the wind to within only 12 feet of the flag to win the hole.

The last two holes, lengthy and flat, are not entirely in character, but they favour the strong as they did Joe Carr in the other semi-final against James Walker. Rarely had Carr been so pressed, though he was a different golfer the next day. All the anxiety, the straining at the leash and the tendency to steer had vanished. He drove vast distances, usually to the heart of the winding fairways; the mood of conquest was upon him and Cochran could muster no lasting response. As a beautiful May afternoon reached its zenith, Carr became ten up and ten to play. Life could hold little more for a golfer and soon he was champion a third time.

The Amateur Championship returned to Portrush in 1993 when the Yorkshireman, Iain Pyman, defeated his fellow Englishman in a final described by Michael Bonallack as the best he could remember. It finished on the 37th and represented a considerable conquest over nerve for Pyman since on the home green he had missed from barely 2ft for victory. A number of memorable women's championships have also been staged over the Dunluce links. In 1895, Lady Margaret Scott, a handsome figure with skirts trailing the turf, won her third successive victory in the British championship. She could hardly have done more; the championship where Scott's family had their enduring hour, and in 1969 Catherine Lacoste, one of the greatest of all women golfers, won the British title on the way to conquering all her worlds. Another Hezlet – Charles – was an Olympian amateur golfer during the years astride World War I, years in which a young caddy at Portrush, Fred Daly, was learning to become one of the longest straight drivers of his time. Daly, a great competitor, won the Open – the only Irishman ever to do so – in 1947.

Why No Open Since 1951?

It is a question that has often been posed, not least by the Irish, and the sad answer lies in the fact that the Open Championship has long outgrown some of the courses with which it grew up. No-one doubts that the venue is challenging enough at Portrush, just as it is at Royal Liverpool. But it is the infrastructure that goes with an Open, from trying to accommodate upwards of 40,000 people a day to ensuring their safety as they line each fairway, to housing the exhibition and hospitality tents, that causes problems. The Royal and Ancient took the Senior British Open to Portrush in 1995 to see how the event would cope with 10,000 people a day and the answer was that it was very difficult to find a spare hotel bedroom within 30 miles of the course; it was also hard to watch several of the matches that drew sizeable crowds. Imagine the problems for four times that number? Of course the years of the troubles have sadly had their effect too. Would all the top Americans still make the effort to come over if the Open was at Portrush, knowing the event would be a security nightmare? One thing that is beyond dispute is the success of the Senior British Open, which was held there for a fourth successive summer in 1998. The first was singularly memorable. One week after the recovering alcoholic John Daly won the Open Championship at St Andrews, his senior equivalent, Brian Barnes, triumphed at Portrush, and over the course where his father-in-law Max Faulkner had won the Open. With Faulkner among the gallery, celebrating his 79th birthday, it was a most dramatic occasion as Barnes triumphed on the third extra hole of a sudden death play-off, the 17th, by holing an eagle putt from 25 yards. His winning prize, incidentally, was £58,330. Faulkner's was £300.

The Course Card

Royal Portrush
Golf Club,
Antrim
Dunluce Links

Record:
66, Jack Hargreaves,
The Open 1951

Hole	Yards	Par
1	392	4
2	505	5
3	155	3
4	457	4
5	384	4
6	189	3
7	431	4
8	384	4
9	475	5
10	478	5
11	170	3
12	392	4
13	386	4
14	210	3
15	365	4
16	428	4
17	548	5
18	469	4
Out	3,372	36
In	3,446	36
Total	**6,818**	**72**

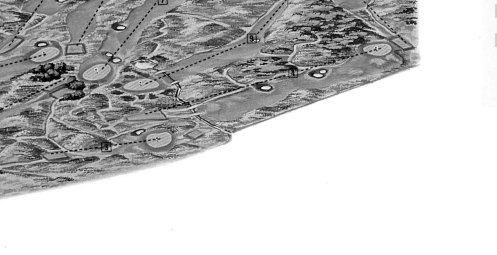

The very Irish hazard of
Maggie Leonard's cow

**The
Course
Card**

Portmarnock Golf
Club, County
Dublin

Record: 64, Sandy
Lyle 1989

Hole	Yards	Par
1	388	4
2	378	4
3	384	4
4	441	4
5	398	4
6	601	5
7	184	3
8	398	4
9	437	4
10	373	4
11	429	4
12	152	3
13	564	5
14	383	4
15	189	3
16	525	5
17	469	4
18	412	4
Out	3,609	36
In	3,496	36
Total	**7,105**	**72**

In a land where beauty, poetry, conflict and passionate belief in the individual are constantly intermingled, the Irish have found golf to be a ready expression of their character and flair for games. The enthusiasm of the players, the variety of styles and the quality of courses is remarkable. Ireland is not large, but it has several of the finest tests of golf to be found anywhere in Europe.

Except in the country itself, where local feelings might influence judgement, one would be hard-pressed to find agreement as to which was the greatest course – Portrush, Portmarnock or County Down on the coast to the east and north; or Ballybunion on the far Atlantic shore. Killarney, serene on its lakeside amid the mountains; Waterville, and Rosses Point also have elements of majesty. Of all courses, few are blessed with the natural magnificence of Portmarnock. Within the fine sweep of coastline curving to an end at Howth Hill, the northern guardian of Dublin Bay, there is a long tongue of linksland between the Irish Sea and an inland tidal bay. It is thus almost enclosed by water, a private place where a man is alone with the turf, the sea, the sky and the challenge of the wind. It is brave, splendid golfing country. Portmarnock's moods can vary from a sternness, that can be savage, to wondrous peace. In summer, with a fresh breeze sparkling the bay and stirring the dune grasses, Ireland's Eye and Lambay rising sharp from the sea, there are few more tempting places for a golfer to be. On such a day, long ago, Sam Snead was at practice, pouring a stream of flawless strokes with a one-iron into the morning distance. Watching golf could offer little more.

Like its great Irish rivals, Portmarnock often changes direction, somewhat after the fashion of Muirfield, with two distinctive and separate trails finishing by the clubhouse, a graceful white landmark from afar. The spectacular quality and unexpectedness of County Down are absent, but Portmarnock's problems are straightforward, even if considerable and often severe. There are no blind shots to the greens and few from the tees, no sharp changes of level yet no monotonous flatness, either. Several holes follow shallow valleys, but they are never as pronounced as they are at Birkdale. They might suggest, but certainly do not afford, protection from the wind.

The design of the course is natural rather than contrived. The 3rd, along a strath of turf, narrow and slightly convex between sandhills on one side and the marshy fringes of the bay on the other, is an example. So, too, is the one bunker guarding the pin at the 5th. The approaches to the shorter par-fours such as the 2nd and 8th, are beautifully shaped. There are only three short holes – the 7th, into a dell, the 12th, high in the dunes, and the 15th, which can be fearsome with a wind from the sea on the right. To hold the narrow table of green, it may be necessary to swing the shot over the beach – which is out-of-bounds – and back again. Even in still air the green, shelving away on either hand, is difficult to hold. Only a true stroke here will prevail.

The three par-fives can be immense. At times the 6th, along its dimpled fairway and valleys, can be three-woods for the strongest, yet the second shot can be as little as a medium iron when the course is running fast. The 13th has a long carry from the tee, behind which the waves pound, and there are bunkers to attract and destroy the second

shot. The 16th is of similar shape, down from the sea with the approaches swinging in from the left.

These two noble holes are part of a challenging finish, for the 14th, too, is a great hole although less than 400 yards. According to the wind, the second from a rolling fairway can be anything from a wood to a pitch and must carry huge bunkers in front of a long plateau of green in the dunes. Legend has it that Joe Carr, greatest of Irish amateurs, drove the green, the ball somehow escaping the bunkers; fact in its turn states that Henry Cotton once took seven strokes there – and lost an Irish Open in the process.

Surrounded by the sea on three sides, Portmarnock offers a genuine links course comparable with any of the great British championship links; indeed, Bobby Locke rated it among the finest in Europe. It never lacks challenge, and many of the less demanding holes become severe tests of skill and control when the wind comes in off the sea. Two in particular – the 14th and 15th – can wreck a card.

As a strong par-four, the 17th takes a deal of beating. Bunkers flanking the straight fairway are cause for thought on the tee and the second demands a long, accurate shot to a closely guarded green. The 18th, a fine hole, owes less to fortune than it did when the home green was hard by the clubhouse. The hole has been shortened and the green moved to a position offering less of a threat to the constantly peppered building.

Portmarnock has been the setting for many great occasions, played in the wildest extremes of weather. When a tempest assailed the last round of the Irish Open in 1927, George Duncan one of the greatest of inspirational golfers – was round in 74, the only player to break 80. The weather was such that, even with this historic round, his winning score was 312. Christy O'Connor took 36 strokes fewer when he won the Dunlop Masters at Portmarnock 32 years later. The inexorable march of improvement reached its apex with Bernhard Langer's winning score of 269 in the 1987 Irish Open, an achievement that still provokes open-mouthed awe in in the vicinity of the links. Langer's victory was the second of five consecutive Irish Opens to be staged at Portmarnock. The roll call of winners reads like a Who's Who of European golf: Ballesteros, Langer, Woosnam (twice) and Olazabal. The oft-heard cliché, to judge a course on the quality of its champions, leaves Portmarnock

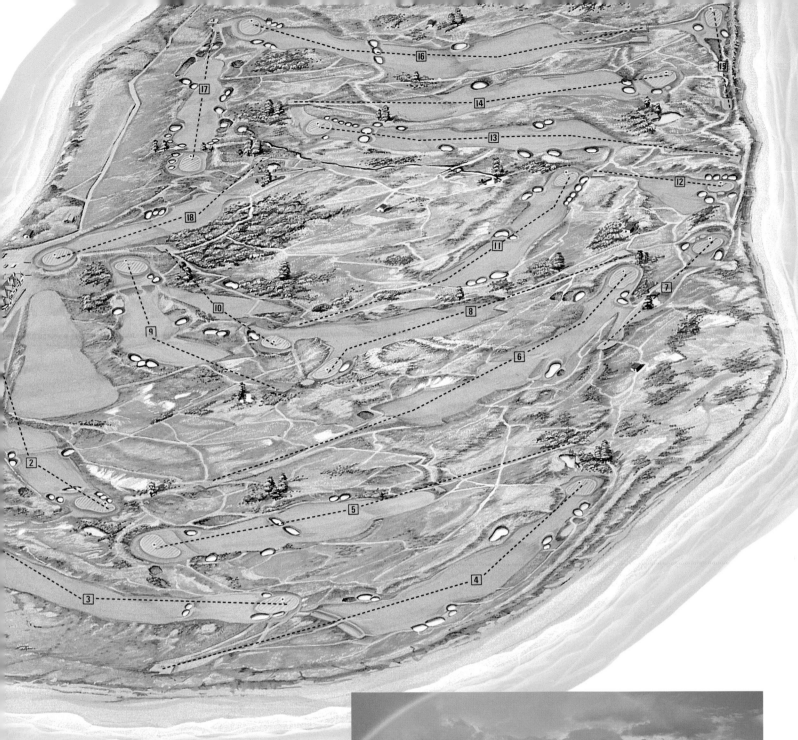

to puff out its chest with justifiable pride, although more than one or two of the locals would have been happy for Woosnam to have settled for just the first of his titles. His successful defence, you see, was achieved in a play-off against Philip Walton who hails from the town of Malahide, a matter of miles away from the links. Woosnam's birdie on the first play-off hole, the 18th, doused the anticipated hoolie.

In 1991 the first Walker Cup to be staged in Ireland took place at Portmarnock, won by America. The only time the Amateur Championship has been played in Eire, in 1949, it was won by Max McCready. His golf had power, authority and great confidence and it disposed of the two most formidable Americans in the field, Frank Stranahan, the defending champion, in the semi-final, and Willie Turnesa in the final.

None of this might have happened but for the inspiration in 1893 that impelled two men, J. W. Pickeman and George Ross, to row across the mouth of the estuary from the point where the Sutton clubhouse now stands. By some blessing of the imagination they visualized a golf course on what was then a wilderness of dune and bracken inhabited only by a remote and self-sufficient community of farming and fish folk, yet only ten miles from Dublin.

The first clubhouse was only a shack and the greatest hazard Maggie Leonard's Cow, which devoured hundreds of balls. Golfers reached the course by crossing the estuary at low tide in a horse-drawn cart, at other times by boat. There is a road now and this delightful and very Irish way of reaching the 1st tee has gone the way of Maggie Leonard's Cow.

Portmarnock is a spectacular links course within ten miles of Dublin. Like all seaside courses, how it plays is dependent on the weather and wind, and can change almost hourly.

At the K Club there is hardly a hole on which water does not come into play. A stroll on the banks of the River Liffey might be idyllic for hotel guests after dinner, but for the golfer its limpid waters present a nagging threat over the closing holes.

Palmer's jewel on Liffey's banks

The Course Card

The Kildare Hotel and Country Club Straffan, Co.Kildare

Hole	Yards	Par
1	418	4
2	413	4
3	170	3
4	568	5
5	440	4
6	478	4
7	395	4
8	173	3
9	461	4
10	584	5
11	415	4
12	173	3
13	423	4
14	213	3
15	446	4
16	606	5
17	365	4
18	537	5
Out	3,516	35
In	3,762	37
Total	7,278	72

The richly fertile soils of County Kildare produce some of the best grass in the world. Not for nothing is it the home of Irish racing, with dozens of world famous studs all within a gentle canter of The Curragh. It is a county of big estates and old families with lengthy pedigrees, not least the Dukes of Leinster, whose ancestors the Fitzgeralds were granted lands at Straffan as long ago as 550 AD. Fourteen centuries later a wealthy Irish businessman, Dr. Michael Smurfit, called in Arnold Palmer to lay out a golf course in the parkland surrounding Straffan House which was soon to become Ireland's first 5-star hotel. Opening in 1991, the K Club became the regular home of the Smurfit European Open tour event in 1995, and in 2006 it will host the first Ryder Cup Matches to be played in the Emerald Isle. Palmer has also designed a second course here, ready for play from July 2003, but more open in character.

Away from the bustle of tournament time the K Club is a place of considerable tranquillity. The grounds slope down to the banks of the River Liffey, embryonic Guinness as its waters wend their way towards Dublin and the famous brewery. But here it is a clear liquid occasionally revealing to the keen-eyed fisherman the trout and salmon which form an enticing part of the country sports on offer to guests. (There is something particularly satisfying about catching your own supper). Palmer has contrived to create a grandstand finish along its banks, for the climax of many heroic Ryder Cup tussles occurs on the 16th and 17th holes, and these two are well equipped to provide nail-biting action.

The estate was already blessed with abundant specimen trees before Palmer began construction. Many have been incorporated strategically into the design. They also mean that the K Club looks as though it has been here in this form for generations, with none of that barren artificiality of so many contemporary courses which resemble more the aftermath of a First World War battle. In truth nature has been supplemented with the planting of mature trees, some 50 years old, weighing four or five tons, the Irish climate ensuring rapid establishment. The plentiful bunkers are filled with fine seaside sand imported from County Wicklow. Fish ponds, stocked variously with rainbow and brown trout, carp, bream and tench, punctuate golfing proceedings frequently, while the one proper lake of the round makes for a great finishing hole.

It is alongside this lake that the round begins, though it should be of no concern to the good player whose line must be close to the trees on the right in order to set up the best approach to the green. Palmer himself is commemorated on the 4th, the first of the par-5s, Arnold's Pick, an appropriately cavalier hole on which the brave drive out over a bunker-festooned hill in an attempt to open up the raised green, between trees and beyond a pond on the banks of which is a vast expanse of sand, more beach than bunker. Running down the hill in parallel, the 6th is a sterling par-4 with an all-carry approach to a green on a narrow spit of land with water on both sides. For the average player the prospect on the 7th tee is terrifying, and it has been suggested that blinkers should be obtained from the nearest stables before attempting to drive, with a stretch of water to be cleared to reach a fairway narrowed by trees. Then a mid-iron must be inch-perfect to find the shallow green on the far side of a pond, with another on the right, and the Liffey itself just through the back. For the professionals, who hit the ball so much further, it is far less intimidating, though a visit to the water began Darren Clarke's downfall while leading in the last round of the 1999 European Open. Push the tee shot at the short 8th

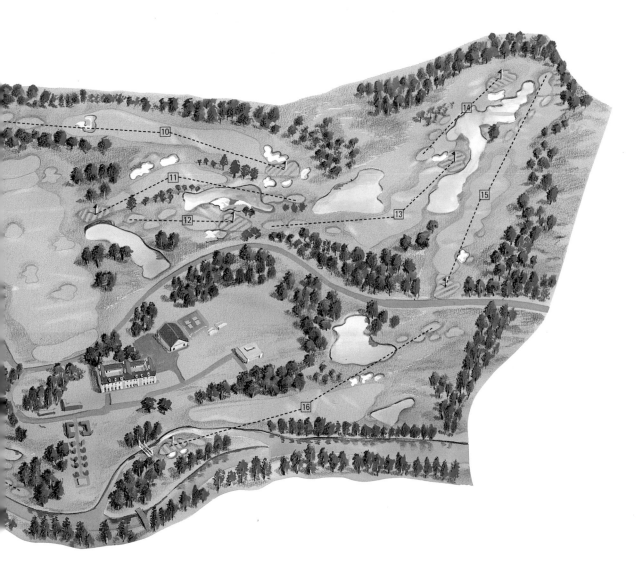

and the Liffey awaits again, while a chestnut tree in mid fairway dictates that the best line from the 9th tee is down the right.

For day-to-day play the order of holes is usually switched so that the round begins at the tournament 10th, a tough start, to be followed by a tricky downhill approach to the 11th, the green set just above a pond. When the short 12th was being built an underground tunnel was discovered leading from the house to the church, a safe escape route in times of old when religious persecution was rife. After an excursion to the far end of the park and back you stand on the tee of what is bound to be one of the keynote holes of the Ryder Cup, the 16th. It is believed that Tiger Woods, on a private visit to the club, is the only person to have reached this green set on an island in the Liffey in two shots from the very back plates. Even he needed a 5-wood to cover the pin after a monumental drive, but he was playing into the teeth of a gale!

For the Ryder Cup a new 17th tee has been built out into the Liffey, giving a compulsory carry of 210 yards over the river to a narrow curving fairway, from which it is obvious how the hole gets its name, Half Moon. (Coincidentally, this tee, overlooking a dark pool, now provides one of the best spots from which to cast for trout.) It was on the 17th green in the second round of the 1999 European Open that Darren Clarke had a 9-foot putt to set a new European record of nine consecutive birdies, and if he could birdie the last, too, he would record a 59, never achieved on the European tour. The green leans towards the Liffey. Clarke allowed 4-inches of break. It broke about 3¾-inches, agonisingly close, and Clarke had to settle for 60, still one of the great rounds of golf, smashing the course record by 4 shots. But by the final round Clarke's fortunes had turned for the worse and the battle was now

one between his great friend and rival Lee Westwood and the Australian Peter O'Malley. Because it is not too long and professionals expect to reach it in two, the 18th at the K Club is a great finishing hole. The problem is that the lake eats into the fairway on the left, the green jutting out into it. As the entrance is cut off from the right by a succession of bunkers, only a full carry will find the putting surface. Westwood drove about 310 yards up over the outbreak of pot bunkers which litter the hill in front of the tee. He then did the sensible thing, smashing a 3-wood 230 yards to the back of the green, well clear of trouble. Two putts later he was the champion. This hole was also decisive in deciding the outcome of the first European Open here when that master of the dramatic situation, Bernhard Langer, had to eagle the hole to catch Barry Lane, which he did, duly winning the playoff. 2001 saw Darren Clarke make up for his disappointment in 1999, winning by three-shots from a quality field.

The charm and challenge of the K Club is summed up in its pretty ponds and majestic trees, both fundamental to the playing strategy of Arnold Palmer's challenging layout.

Ballybunion, situated in a remote corner of Kerry on Ireland's west coast, rewards all who make the long trek to get there, for its ocean holes are among the best of their kind to be found anywhere in the world. Three tame holes from the 3rd may lead to some initial scepticism but no-one would dispute the quality of golf on offer from the 6th onwards. There are fairer links courses, and more daunting ones too, but few can compete with the sheer pleasure that playing Ballybunion offers.

Man made beauty

at the ocean's edge

Hole	Yards	Par
1	392	4
2	445	4
3	220	3
4	498	5
5	508	5
6	364	4
7	423	4
8	153	3
9	454	4
10	359	4
11	449	4
12	192	3
13	484	5
14	131	3
15	216	3
16	490	5
17	385	4
18	379	4
Out	3,457	36
In	3,085	35
Total	**6,542**	**71**

Few golf courses can compete with Ballybunion when it comes to the naturalness of its setting. Located against the Atlantic shore in a remote region of County Kerry, the first surprise is that it was designed by man not evolution. Tom Watson considers it a course that all architects should live and play before they practise their art and certainly one would be hard pushed to find another venue so perfectly in tune with its surroundings.

Ballybunion is a traditional links in every sense of the word. Its configuration is delightfully eccentric with back-to-back par fives on the front nine followed by consecutive short holes on the inward half. It has several blind shots and its hard, crumpled fairways can lead to difficult stances and undeserved moments of ill fortune. But there's a rewarding feeling for a good shot perfectly executed that one rarely finds elsewhere and the sea views are extraordinary.

In common with most links courses, Ballybunion can seem straightforward on a calm day. It possesses no great length and its small greens appear inviting targets with short irons. A zephyr is enough to change the examination and on doleful days, when the Atlantic closes in, the course can be completely merciless.

Ballybunion was founded on March 4, 1886 but it quickly ran into financial problems and for eight years lumbered in oblivion. It might never have emerged but for Colonel Bartholomew, an Indian army man who retired to the area. He formed the present club in 1906 and contracted Lionel Hewson, for many years the editor of Irish Golf, to lay out nine new holes. The course was extended to 18 in 1926 by a Mr Smyth.

Smyth did such a fine job that when the English architect Tom Simpson was called in 11 years later to make changes he suggested just three minor ones, the most famous being a sand hazard on what is now the first that has become known as "Mrs Simpson's bunker". The reasons for the name remain shrouded in mystery, thereby adding to the mischievous possibilities that countless clubhouse wits have

suggested. Owing partly to the remoteness of its location, Ballybunion has staged few tournaments of note. However, a strong international field contested the 2000 Murphy's Irish Open, with Patrik Sjöland of Sweden emerging victorious.

It is only in more recent times that Ballybunion has gained the recognition it deserves, for which ease of travel is but one explanation. Two further factors were responsible: the first, the decision to relocate the clubhouse and change the numbering of the holes. Hitherto the closing two holes had been a pair of mundane par fives. Now these holes are the 4th and 5th. They are still not great holes but tucked away on the front nine they occupy the less pivotal place they deserve.

The second factor was the patronage of Tom Watson when at the height of his powers. Watson fell in love with links golf from the moment he made his first trip to Britain, for the 1975 Open Championship at Carnoustie, which he would go on to win. It whetted his appetite. Before each Open he would come a week early and discover new gems. In 1981 he made his first trip to Ballybunion and was startled by the beauty of the surroundings and the challenging nature of the links. For many years it became an annual pilgrimage. "The contours on the fairways and greens are what make it a great golf course," he explained. "There are uphill, downhill, and sidehill shots, uphill and downhill par threes. You must play accurate iron shots into the greens, usually to a small target with not a lot of margin for error. But there is room to roll the ball on to the greens in the true links manner and I like that style of golf best of all."

Ballybunion is not a links course that immediately captivates the player. The first six holes are modest, played against an austere background. Like Turnberry, which starts out equally slowly, it then opens out and its spectacular ocean holes again invite comparison with the Ailsa course in Ayrshire.

The opening hole is a par four of medium length, the chief feature the unusual hazard that captures stray golf

balls to the right; and yes, the graveyard, for that is what it is, is out of bounds. The 2nd can be a difficult par four, with bunkers patrolling both sides of the fairway followed by a second shot to a raised green that needs to be threaded through two enormous dunes. At 220 yards the 3rd is no easy short hole, but we are impatient for the glories to come and must contain ourselves until we pitch to the 6th green. Now the course asserts itself. The 7th winds its way along the cliff top, a magnificent par four that any player is happy to walk off recording a regulation figure.

The next three holes loop inland in a triangle; the pick of them is the 8th, a lovely short par three where the penalty for missing the green is severe indeed. Watson said it was one of the most demanding tee shots he had faced, and it is the severity of the punishment that makes it so intimidating. The three bunkers towards the front are huge and the hollows and mounds that surround them are equally penal.

The 9th measures 454 yards and anything less than a well-struck, arrow-straight drive leaves a player glumly confronting a green he cannot but hope to reach in two. The first hole coming home is a dog-leg par four of unassuming length with a green that sits on the cliff top and on sunny days the urge to look west is irresistible. The pleasures are only starting to unfold. The 11th would feature in many people's list of the world's best 18 holes, a dramatic par four that once more runs along the cliff top.

The short 12th and the 484-yard par-five 13th offer respite and the chance for a player to recover his score before the tribulations to come. First the back-to-back par threes, both of which are wonderful. The 14th is just 131 yards and presents torment over club selection. The 15th, at 216 yards, is less problematic in that area but presents other difficulties. It is probably the hardest of the five par threes.

The 16th and 17th holes are dog-legs of quite breathtaking severity. The first bends to the left, a par-five where the drive is away from the sea to a small target area; at the par-four 17th the tee shot is back towards the Atlantic, leaving a short iron to one of the more accessible greens

on the course. So to the 18th, described by one critic as merely a device to get from the 17th green to the 19th hole. The cause of the ire is the appropriately named Sahara bunker that sits grotesquely in the middle of the fairway and allows little strategy.

Blind shots have always caused controversy on links courses yet they are a feature of the traditional venues. They stem from a time when it was not possible to move huge amounts of earth as it is today. Nowhere is this more apparent than at Ballybunion where the huge dunes that punctuate the course both straddle it and dominate it. On a younger links like Birkdale they are used to create amphitheatres; at Ballybunion you play around them, over them, on top of them.

This is a course that scores highly on all counts: it lingers in the mind and long after the day's play is done, a player can mull over his score and play and recall all 18 holes with little difficulty.

Tumbling links amidst the
Dutch sandhills

The Course Card

Kennemer Golf &
Country Club,
Zandvoort
B/C Course

Record: 65, Sid Brews,
Dutch Open 1935;
David Thomas,
Severiano Ballesteros,
Wayne Grady,
Glenn Ralph, José-
Maria Canizares,
Gordon Brand.

Hole	Yards	Par
1	452	4
2	165	3
3	524	5
4	330	4
5	346	4
6	476	5
7	371	4
8	187	3
9	425	4
10	361	4
11	460	4
12	546	5
13	373	4
14	385	4
15	163	3
16	480	5
17	168	3
18	398	4
Out	3,276	36
In	3,334	36
Total	**6,610**	**72**

There is no finer example of seaside links on the continental mainland than the Kennemer club at Zandvoort, half an hour by car from Amsterdam. Despite the popular conception that Holland is a land of unwavering flatness, this coastal stretch is a place of wild tumbling dunes to stir the heart of any golfing architect. It must have inspired H. S. Colt when he came to create the present course in the late 1920s. The club was founded in 1910 and started elsewhere with nine holes on flat meadowland; no greater contrast to it could be imagined than this links with its glorious fairways, towering sandhills and spinneys of pine. It has no parallel in America but, at first sight, brings thoughts of problems of stance – not in a severe or arduous sense, but sufficient to test balance and control and to compel thought before striking.

One essential feature of a good course is that its attraction should be immediate. There are few more inviting prospects than the tees of the 1st and 10th holes at Kennemer; the course runs in two loops of nine, beginning and ending by the handsome thatched clubhouse poised high with a commanding view of the whole golfing scene. The 1st hole falls away to a spreading fairway, flanked by dunes with pines on their crests, the kind of drive that would appeal to the most humble performer. After an exciting short hole over a valley to a huge sloping plateau green one stands again on a high tee looking down upon another expanse fairway, gently curving to the left around a wood: a splendid hole. Even if you have not started 4, 3, 4 – none too difficult down a prevailing south-westerly wind – a sense of pleasure to come and beauty all around is inescapable.

There are all the pastel shades of quiet fawns and golds and greens, and in the summertime the rough, often uncommonly tenacious, is alive with wild flowers. Buckthorn, with its savage spikes piercing the thickest trousers and vivid orange berries in the autumn is another occasional menace and delight. Pheasants nest in the long grasses and twice a year or so shoots are rewarding. Only the wild driver need fear the rough. For all normal purposes the fairways are of a generous width, but they could be narrowed, as could the entrances to the greens, to an extent that would challenge a championship field of the highest quality.

The 4th begins a fine stretch of golf. Colt considered this the one weak spot in his design and it has been converted from a par-three into a par-four. This hole apart, the course is little changed from his original concept, although it is some 400 yards longer and has a par two strokes lower. The drive from the new championship tee at the 4th through a cluster of trees, together with a tightly trapped green, makes a challenging hole. The 5th is a challenge, too, with its fairway all swales and mounds, out-of-bounds threatening the slice, and a valley before the green to confuse estimates of distance. Most of the greens are fairly large, offering a variety of pin positions; happily their undulations are slight and subtle and the surfaces of fine fescue putt swiftly and true. The carry to the next fairway, the longest outward hole, is deceptively far and the golf hereabouts can be sterner than the card suggests; the wind, more often than not, will be leaning against the line of flight. Blind shots can be a tiresome affliction, but an occasional drive to an invisible fairway is effective for contrast. The one to the 7th is welcome, for the sight from the fairway's peak is splendid with the green set against tree-crested dunes and protected by a considerable cross-bunker. The 8th presents no great problem if a long iron is hit straight. It is followed by another tempting drive to a slightly angled, crumpled fairway, and an approach to a green in a basin below the clubhouse. Here, as on many holes, the placing of the drive determines the difficulty of the second shot as much from the question

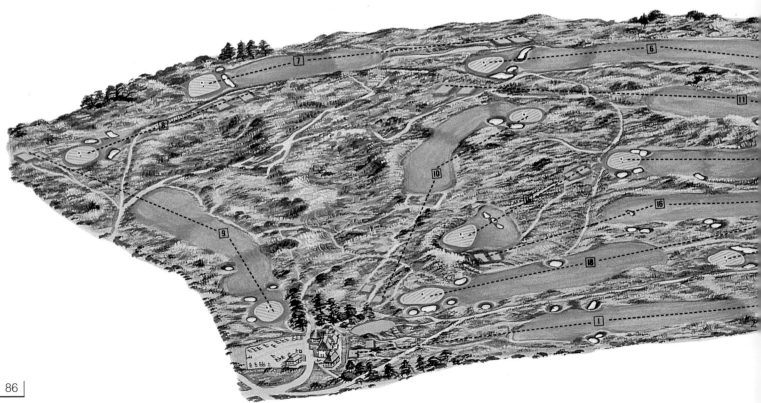

of stance as of line. In this respect Colt made memorable use of the terrain's natural features.

The drive to the 10th over a wild valley to a distant unseen fairway can be infinitely satisfying or disastrous, according to contact with the ball. The course then swings away to more open country, past the tunnel entrance to the 11th green, down the long, straight 12th, turning again for a lovely 13th with its green on rising ground, outlined against a dark cluster of pines. The long hitter may reach the deep hollow of the 14th fairway and find his view of the green obscured, but not if he holds the left side of the fairway.

At first glance the tee shot to the short 15th looks formidable, for the green is on the summit of a smooth, grassy cliff, down which the underhit or underclub will roll relentlessly into one of three traps at its foot. The high ground by the green makes a superb vantage point from which to watch the play of the last five holes – the long second away to the 16th cradled in the dunes; the last turn for home with the shot over wilderness to the short 17th, and the gradual rise of a fine finishing hole, its green between two large guardian bunkers.

Perhaps the most memorable contest at Kennemer was for the 1976 Dutch Open, since it marked the first victory of a young 19-year-old Spaniard called Severiano Ballesteros. Three weeks earlier he had competed strongly for the Open Championship at Birkdale, conquering its parched fairways and winning over its galleries with the sort of swashbuckling play that was his trademark. At Kennemer he showed he could win. Thirteen years later, his protégé, Jose-Maria Olazabal, would win the same title over the same course. Well, parts of the same course anyway. By then nine new holes had been built and they were incorporated into the championship design. But it is Colt's original 18 that is described here.

The most shining moment in the club's history did not occur in competition but when a Canadian colonel – presumably a golfer – agreed to demolish the anti-tank wall built across the course during World War II. The area had been a defence zone, and the course virtually vanished under the concrete. By 1947 golf was again being played at Kennemer and now all recognizable traces of a massive stupidity have gone from a beautiful course.

Dutch Links and the Origin of Golf

There has long been a school of thought that golf evolved from the ancient Dutch game of het Kolven, but the evidence is far from conclusive. Down the centuries many games have shared the aim of hitting a ball with a club towards a target, but learned researchers have failed to discover a definite link between any pursuit of the Middle Ages and the game of golf as mentioned by James II of Scotland in his famous decree of 1457. This demanded that "the fute-ball and golfe be utterly cryed downe and not to be used"; presumably the citizenry were neglecting the practice of archery and military training in those troubled times when England was a bitter enemy.

The precise origin of golf probably will never be known but the paintings by van der Velde, Avercamp and others of kolven on ice, and not its normal form on indoor courts, stirred the imagination of historians. The indoor game was played in a walled space or court with a club and ball and involved the striking of posts at either end, but both club and ball were larger than those used for golf, as were those used on ice. The attitude of the players about to strike was the main resemblance to golf. The ancient Flemish game of chore has also been suggested as an origin because of its cross-country nature. It was played to targets often miles away but both sides used the same ball. It had little similarity to golf save in the act of striking a ball with a club. This simply fulfils a fundamental human instinct from which various games have evolved. The likelihood is that golf was the form peculiar, in the beginning, to Scotland.

The continental challenge to Scotland's outstanding claims as the birthplace of golf is led by the Dutch. This painting by Adriaen van de Velde shows 17th-century Dutchmen adapting their game of kolven, normally played on an enclosed area of sand and clay with posts as targets, to winter conditions.

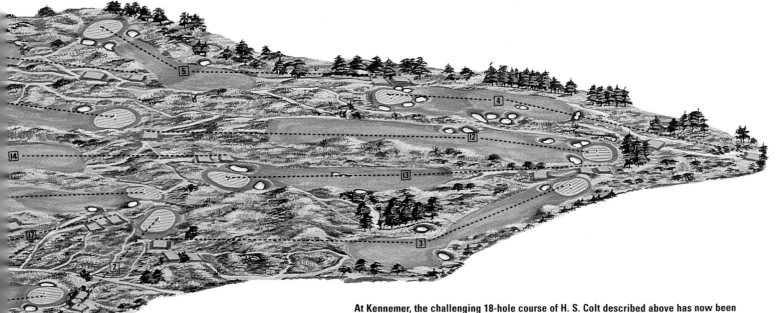

At Kennemer, the challenging 18-hole course of H. S. Colt described above has now been extended by a further nine holes, and it is possible to play three variations on the 27 holes: A/B, B/C and A/C. The old course illustrated here is the B/C course.

A Royal course

that has few peers

Belgium is not one of the world's great powers in golf, but it has made a notable contribution to the European game. Nonetheless, among its courses are several of outstanding quality: Waterloo, where Henry Cotton was professional between the wars; the Royal Club de Belgique at Ravenstein, the birthplace of Flory Van Donck, one of the finest European players; the Royal Zoute, a splendid links by the sea; the Royal Club des Fagnes at Spa, a beautiful examination of golf; and Royal Antwerp at Kapellenbos, which comes close to being a masterpiece of its kind.

All those clubs are distinguished by the Royal title, bestowed upon them by Belgian kings. The choice of a single course from this excellent company is difficult but Royal Antwerp, 12 miles from the seaport, makes so favourable an impression that it takes pride of place. It is also the oldest club in the country, founded in 1888 – the year that the St Andrews club in New York became the first in the United States. Like most of the older continental courses (only Pau is its senior on the continental mainland) Antwerp was formed by a few members of the local British settlement there. The course at first was laid out on an army training ground. It cannot have been a particularly sympathetic site and soon after the turn of the century an area of woodland

was bought some seventeen miles north of the city. Willie Park was called upon to make the new course and it was in play several years before World War I. It remained as Park designed it until, in the late 1920s, Tom Simpson created what became the 10 middle holes of the course. Within its confines nine shorter holes, including some of Park's original work, remain for those seeking relief from sterner pursuits.

In all Europe Antwerp has few peers for the type of course that wends its way through woods of pine and silver birch, heather and shrubs. Its level changes hardly more than a yard or so; rarely do the trees threaten peace of mind, even that of a golfer. Yet its very flatness calls for fine judgement of distance, and the unusual disposition of some 6,700 yards makes the strict par of 73 severe even for the good player. Few courses anywhere have so high a proportion of good long par-fours. Only the 1st, with its uncommonly billowing fairway, and the 4th, where the drive must be placed for a clear shot to the pin, are drive and pitch holes. On most, even the first-class golfer will be using longish irons to the greens – or occasionally wood, depending on the strength of the wind and the pace of the fairways. For the driver of average length the course is a great test of iron play, because the greens are not large and only that of the 16th, which is the shortest hole, is in any way set up as a target.

If there is a criticism it is that all the par-fives are of a similar length and short of their kind. Each must be viewed as a realistic birdie proposition. The 3rd is a lovely hole with the fairway angling away to the left, a heathery crest to threaten the second shot, and a long, narrow green. Finely placed bunkers encourage accuracy on the parallel 5th and 15th, and good players get home with an iron on the dog-leg 11th, one of the finest holes of all. The drive must hold the left centre of the fairway and, unless the second is similarly placed, it will probably break from a shoulder of ground towards a bunker well short of the green.

The course is notable for its economy of bunkering – an admirable precept of the architects of old. The 7th, with a smooth hump protecting the line to the pin and ground falling towards a single right-hand bunker, is a beautiful short hole. The 12th has an extra bunker, threatening the safe way home, but the 2nd is the stiffest of the short holes. It is a big shot, with a fold of ground making it look less than it is.

Several holes are compellingly beautiful. The 6th curves around an elbow of woods and narrows like an hour-glass where a long drive finishes. The fairway of the 8th is almost an island of heather, from where a medium iron shot should flight to the heart of a green set against a shining stand of birch. From the back tee of the 13th the carry is considerable, and the drive must be right to open up the hole round trees to a green that is for once beset by bunkers. The 14th is a real dog-leg, swinging sharp left with cross-rough challenging the approach. The finish is testing enough to keep hope alive in the breast of anyone who is trailing. The 15th needs two long shots, and, though it is not a particularly long hole, the 17th gives food for thought. Two big bunkers emphatically suggest that the approach should come in from the right, especially as a smaller bunker lies concealed beyond. This was the inspiration of a secretary wise in the ways of golf. At first it was known as Beatty's Bath, but its victims were so plentiful that it is now called Bloody Bidet.

The professionals have rarely graced these fairways, but for one glorious moment in 1980 a star studded field was assembled to contest the Trophée Laurent Perrier. Only four players finished under par after four rounds, with Curtis Strange holding the lead from the very start following a course record 62.

The 9th, 10th and 14th

Tackling The Dog-legs

Tom Simpson, the architect of Royal Antwerp, was a great believer in the dog-leg hole and seventy years ago was something of a pioneer in this form of design. It is a conspicuous feature on the course's middle holes, seven of those between the 6th and the 14th curving markedly. Five swing to the left, favouring the right-to-left player.

Dog-legs provide variety and avoid the monotony of a sequence of straightaway holes. As at the 10th, with its narrow-waisted fairway, they stress the importance of placing from the tees. Occasionally, as at the 14th, the dog-leg is used to restrict the length of the drive, but the player with power and skill can bend his shot around the curve.

Such holes can be a snare in that they may tempt the player into attempting over much in order to cheat the corner, either by trying to clear it or by bending his shot around it, despite the ease with which an intentional draw can become a hook and a fade become a slice. Architects often place bunkers within the inside of the curve, as at the 9th, and where position rather than length is essential one can visualize Faldo, for instance, aiming at the hazard and fading the shot gently away from it. In this way, when the shot's power is expiring, the ball is moving away from and not towards trouble, as the shots of humbler mortals are prone to do.

The Course Card

Royal Antwerp
Golf Club,
Kapellenbos

Record:
62, Curtis Strange

Hole	Yards	Par
1	331	4
2	203	3
3	480	5
4	381	4
5	512	5
6	424	4
7	185	3
8	418	4
9	449	4
10	416	4
11	500	5
12	183	3
13	398	4
14	478	5
15	492	5
16	147	3
17	377	4
18	394	4
Out	3,383	36
In	3,385	37
Total	6,768	73

Classic links
in a remote northern landscape

Hole	Yards	Par
1	449	4
2	191	3
3	558	5
4	416	4
5	405	4
6	170	3
7	317	4
8	197	3
9	421	4
10	383	4
11	159	3
12	405	4
13	563	5
14	230	3
15	514	5
16	388	4
17	377	4
18	481	5
Out	3,124	34
In	3,500	37
Total	6,624	71

True links courses are rare outside the British Isles. There is one at Le Touquet and a few nestle amongst the sandhills of the Low Countries, but one of the finest examples on the mainland of Europe is at Falsterbo in Sweden. It is not the oldest of Swedish courses – Hovas, near Gothenburg, came into being a few years earlier – but its very nature and its spectacular setting give Falsterbo pride of place. The course is laid out on the tip of a tiny peninsula that all but drops off the southernmost corner of Sweden – Stockholm is more than 300 miles away to the northeast, Copenhagen a mere 30, and easily accessible across the new Ôresundsbron bridge.

In Sweden, golf's beginnings around the turn of the century were at best hesitant – the first 18-hole course was not built until 1929, and as recently as 1945 there were only 22 clubs. Now there are more than 420 golf clubs and 540,000 players. The explosion in recent years stems from the commendable policy to encourage junior golfers. Unlike many countries in Europe, golf in Sweden is not just for the bourgeoisie and the reward has been a string of fine players, both men and women, who have contributed hugely to the world game over the past 20 years.

From its start, in 1909, Falsterbo has been a pace-setter. In the year it was opened it staged Sweden's first inter-national match between clubs (against its near neighbour, the Copenhagen Golf Club) and it became, in 1930, one of the country's first 18-hole courses. Falsterbo incorporates all the links qualities of turf, natural hazards and changes of wind – now from the mainland, now from the Baltic – which can present a totally different test within a matter of hours. Such is its strength that it has been altered little over the years. It is an obvious setting for a golf course. The holes blend beautifully into natural surroundings which no amount of money could ever copy or create. The vast stretch of water that gives the 4th, 5th and 11th their menace and charm is to a measure reminiscent of the marsh holes at England's Royal West Norfolk, although only at the short 11th hole does very much of it have to be crossed.

At the excellent 4th, however, a stiff second has to skirt the water dangerously and it preys on the mind in the way that only water can. It is a feature by which players remember this links.

Falsterbo is invigorating rather than oppressively daunting, but like all good courses it commands respect, calling for unrelenting concentration, confidence and sound technique. From the moment the golfer encounters the dog-leg at the demanding 1st hole, with out-of-bounds on the right, he is confronted with the severity of Falsterbo's challenge.

The next four holes form a narrow offshoot out to the end of the marsh and back and, because of their low-lying position, they have more of an inland character than the rest. The high, marshy reed grasses readily identify the edges of water hazards – which add flavour to the short 2nd, with its well-bunkered green, divide the 3rd and 4th holes and completely surround the 5th. The 3rd is the only par-five in the outward half. It has all the hallmarks of a long hole, offering little alternative to a good drive, a good sec-ond and a good pitch. But it is probably the 4th, with its green tucked into a little alcove by the water's edge, and the 5th, where there is no margin for error with the drive, which most players will be pleased to pass without a skir-mish with the water that haunts the slice. Not that the short 6th offers any respite. It has more water in front of the tee, and is now almost encircled by the trees which have grown taller and thicker over the years. However, the 7th, a dog-leg to the left, offers the chance of a birdie and heralds the start of what the British would recognize instantly as true links golf. With the odd exception, bunkers now take the place of water and at the 8th, the third short hole, two, which are particularly well sited, have to be avoided from the tee. The two medium par-fours which follow do not pre-sent too much difficulty, but when the wind is against, the short 11th can only be reached with what is perhaps the most spectacular shot on the course. Although only 159 yards, it is death or glory, all or nothing, with water on all

Since this map was drawn there have been revisions to the bunkering on every hole and the greens have been redesigned, but the basic layout and playing strategy remain unaltered. Although an irrigation system has been installed and the drainage improved, the customary links qualities of fast-running fairways and firm, speedy greens have been preserved rigorously.

A Finish Fit for a King

sides and the green nestling on a peninsula which looks minute from the tee.

The 12th has its fairway split into two by bunkers and the green is generously encircled by sand, but it can be child's play compared with the 563-yard 13th, known as Tipperary. Both fairway and green are closely guarded with bunkers and a substantial carry is necessary from the tee, the drive again being threatened by out-of-bounds on the right.

The 14th is the last and longest of the five short holes. The tee shot is threatened by a large cross-bunker, but it is the setting which makes this hole memorable. Beyond the green stands the old Falsterbo lighthouse, a reminder of the remoteness of the setting and the nearness of the sea. Golf's rich variety of settings provides a powerful reason for playing and at Falsterbo there is the added delight of a vast, uninhabited stretch of shoreline, a haven for migratory birds in spring and autumn. Birds and golfers have chosen well at Falsterbo, and it is fitting that the true character of the course finds appealing expression in its finish. Shaped rather like the head of a fish, the 15th and 16th run out to the tiny peninsula's tip, where the sound and the Baltic meet, and the 17th and 18th return along the line of dunes.

The 15th and 18th are par-fives and, with the 16th and 17th among the best of the par-fours, Falsterbo certainly does not use up its ammunition in its opening salvoes. Since 1995 the course has undergone a modernisation programme strengthening its traditional links qualities. The greens have been redesigned by Peter Nordwall and the former head professional at Falsterbo, Peter Chamberlain. The bunkering has been revised, and attention has been given to the areas immediately surrounding the greens, calling for a great variety of recovery shots. These amendments have been designed to reward good positional play, tempting the player to flirt with many of the course's natural hazards in order to reach the best approach positions. Good examples are the 5th, 12th, 15th and 16th holes.

The uncertainty and drama of matchplay often makes it more enjoyable than strokeplay. There is something fundamentally appealing about two men duelling their way round a golf course and it is through such encounters that many courses have become legendary.

Professionals of world class or even amateurs of international standing rarely play at Falsterbo, but in 1963 the European Team Championships brought it to the notice of golfers of many countries, and one of the matches produced a dramatic finale which can seldom have been repeated anywhere. Appropriately, the scene – as in all good matchplay plots – was the 18th. From a tee in the sand-dunes, the hole dog-legs to the right between fairway bunkers to a deeply bunkered green some 481 yards away. On the day on which Sweden played Italy it was reachable in two. Italy's Angelo Croce was just on the fringe at the back of the green, but Sweden's Rune Karlfeldt was short and much less likely to make the four it seemed he would need to halve the match, in which he had the support of a few hundred Swedes, including King Gustav.

The celebration, the cheering and stampeding which followed the chip with a 6-iron which Karlfeldt holed for his three is therefore not hard to imagine. Victory seemed assured, the King shook his hand and Croce, who had yet to play, somehow managed to convey that he, too, was pleased. After order had been restored, Croce stepped up to a putt which, to a man having only one shot in which to save the match, must have seemed an impossibility. But Croce duly holed it for as unlikely a half as anyone could remember. Happily he too was hailed by the Swedes and the celebrations and the handshakes were resumed.

For many golfers their first glimpse of Falsterbo is from the air, for the course lies just across the water from Copenhagen Airport. The sea and beach views from the course are superb.

Sweden's
answer to Wentworth

History was made in 1993 when Joakim Haeggman became the first Swede to play for Europe in the Ryder Cup. Nowadays a team without a Swede would be unthinkable, and the exploits of Jesper Parnevik, Per-Ulrik Johansson, Anders Forsbrand and others on the world golfing stage have been more than matched by their female counterparts, with Annika Sörenstam, Helen Alfredsson, and Liselotte Neumann heading a distinguished company on account of their impressive victories in Majors. The Swedes take their golf seriously, their juniors encouraged to take up the game in great numbers, being coached in a manner which suggests that there will be no shortage of future stars. For many, especially in the north of the country, winter practice can only take place indoors, the compensation coming in the summer months when it is perfectly possible to play 24 hours a day on courses far beyond the Arctic Circle. But the winter climate in the south west is milder, tempered by the waters of the Kattegat. Here are to be found many of Sweden's finest courses, the two best, Halmstad and Falsterbo, consistently ranking in the top 10 in continental Europe. Strangely, neither course has been much used for professional tournaments despite the fact that both are within easy reach of sizeable centres of population, and it is even possible to catch a bus direct from Copenhagen Airport to Halmstad! But significant international amateur tournaments have been played here, Scotland beating the home side into second place in the 1985 European Amateur Team Championship, and the Ladies of Europe easily defeating those of Great Britain and Ireland for the 1997 Vagliano Trophy. The coming of the Chrysler Open to Halmstad in 1999 and Challenge Tour events in 2000 and 2002 augurs well.

The course itself is situated at Tylösand, a pretty little seaside village famous for its miles of golden beaches and Miniland, a representation of Sweden in miniature. There is nothing miniature about Stockholm architect Rafael Sundblom's course which opened in 1938. It is within earshot of the sea, though the woods through which the fairways wind a narrow course keep it well out of sight, woods so dense that there is little need for rough in the traditional manner. The underlying soil is sandy, almost heathland in nature, and it is entirely fitting that Halmstad is often described as the Swedish Wentworth, for Sundblom studied the great Surrey course in the company of its designer, Harry Colt, before embarking on his own masterpiece. The similarity of both courses extends also to the sparing use of fairway bunkering,

Pia Nilsson, head coach to the Swedish Golf Federation, talks of educating her charges, "in the game of life and in the game of golf." Another of Pia Nilsson's beliefs is, "To play 18 holes in 54 strokes is possible." Perhaps it is possible, but it is unlikely round the 6,900 yards of Halmstad's Norra banan, North Course.

Outright length is less of an issue on the back nine, shorter by some 200 yards, with only one par-4 exceeding 400 yards. From the 10th tee the emphasis is again on finding the ideal line, a perfectly placed fairway bunker indicating that this is the better side to be in order to see past the trees to the tightly bunkered green. On the 11th, the easiest hole on the course, there are good prospects of a birdie provided the drive can be threaded past the fairway bunkers. Far fewer birdies are yielded up, however, on the much sterner 12th, with its fairway leaning to the left, and a brook to be cleared with what for most handicap players will be an uncomfortably long club. A short hole to a two-level, raised green offers a moment's respite before the rigours of the 14th, a particularly narrow par-5 on which the fairway is split by a gully about 350 yards out - of consideration for the average player, though it is cleared easily enough by the professional who is more concerned with shaping the second shot to hold the angled green. Problems are fewer on the 15th which has, unusually for Halmstad, no greenside bunker.

The outcome of many matches is decided on the 16th, on which the obvious hazards are a snaking stream and a pair of bunkers at the back of the green. A diagonal ridge is the main factor on the 17th. With out-of-bounds close on the right and a cross-wind off the sea this becomes a stronger hole than mere yardage suggests. Laura Davies made light work of the 18th in her closing round, a 30-foot putt for birdie giving her a 67, to add to her course record 66 on the day before. Between the two rounds she had taken only 53 putts. "I really believe that we will never see her like again," said runner-up Alison Nicholas, whose 7-under-par total was hardly a disgrace over this sterling course.

The Course Card

Halmstad Golfklubb, Tylosand

Hole	Yards	Par
1	434	4
2	544	5
3	383	4
4	166	3
5	600	5
6	356	4
7	213	3
8	423	4
9	455	4
10	394	4
11	510	5
12	439	4
13	172	3
14	558	5
15	337	4
16	179	3
17	353	4
18	395	4
Out	3,574	36
In	3,337	36
Total	**6,911**	**72**

driving here governed very much by the angles at which the fairways are cut through the woodland. Nine further holes were added by Nils Sköld in 1967, and Frank Pennink completed this charming second course with another nine in 1979.

From the back tees the 1st is a testing opener, the drive needing to find the right side of the fairway to open up the green. In the final round of the 1999 Chrysler Open Britain's Laura Davies hit her approach to three feet to post the first birdie of a brilliant round, the hole measuring 352 yards for the ladies. She followed that with a majestic 242-yard 3-iron past the green-front bunkers at the 2nd to set up her next birdie and the foundation of an eight shot win over Alison Nicholas. With Catrin Nilsmark and Helen Alfredsson in close pursuit, here was clear proof of the adage that the cream rises to the top on the best courses.

To succeed at Halmstad it is necessary to be able to move the ball both ways, most of the outward holes swinging to the left. On the huge 5th the drive needs to pierce a gap in the trees, ideally holding the left of the fairway, before continuing down that side to give the best angle of approach to the green, long and narrow between bunkers and trees. Of no great length, the 6th is, none the less, a fine hole, all about accurate positioning from the tee, the green, once again, long and narrow. The correct line is imperative from the 8th tee, with trees encroaching from the left, effectively increasing the angle of this already sharp dog-leg. Then, on the 9th, the dog-leg swings the other way, a solid drive essential if there is to be any sight of the green far round to the right. It is raised up somewhat so that only the most soundly struck long-range approach shot will hold it.

Dog-leg holes abound at Halmstad, putting a premium on accuracy from the tee and the ability to shape shots.

The heavily forested 220 acres of the Club Zur Vahr holds one of the most difficult layouts in Europe. The length (well over 7,000 yards including six par-fives) undulating fairways narrowing at strategic points great patches of heather and comparatively small greens all combine to produce a real challenge. Any wayward shots are punished by dense rough.

The 5th hole at Club Zur Vahr is a short par four that offers a reasonable chance of a birdie.

A forest
where even the caddies get lost

The end of the 19th century was a halcyon time for golf. Adherents to the game were growing in number, especially among city dwellers seeking exercise in the open air. Cities were expanding rapidly, but not yet to such a degree that put the availability and cost of land at a premium – as, for example, in Japan today, where enthusiasm for the game, which almost amounts to a national obsession, is stymied by shortage of space in which to indulge it.

Bremen Golf Club, one of the oldest in Germany, was founded in the last years of the 19th century as the Hanseatic town was beginning its years of growth. It began with a nine-hole layout and the present course is the result of a decision by the Club Zur Vahr, which embraces a number of sports and social activities, to build a course suitable for major championships. The site chosen for the new course was the Garlstedter Heath, a setting with all the natural attributes needed to echo, in the mind of the club's president, August Weyhausen, those virtues he had found when playing the great Scottish and English courses. He sought a course where players of all standards would be forced to think, to accept their personal limitations and negotiate a tough test according to their abilities. The course planned by Weyhausen and architect Bernard von Limburger occupies 220 acres in thickly forested, undulating countryside. On the premise

that nature itself is the best architect, the Bremen course was constructed with minimum change to the existing landscape. It is dominated by pine trees, tall and dense, crowding in from tee to green, controlling play on holes which bend narrowly to generally small targets. The strategic effect of the forest was such that it was necessary to construct only 24 bunkers. From the championship tees, the course measures 7,147 yards, with six holes of more than 500 yards.

Since its completion, the Garlstedter course has commanded respect from all who have played there and appreciated its disciplines. From the fine, modern clubhouse, three holes – the 1st, 7th and 9th – run over fairly level, pastoral parkland. Most of the others make their way through the forest, narrow and with sharp dog-legs which call for clear tactical thinking, since most fairways offer a choice of routes to the green. Among the trees there is thick undergrowth, with its risk of an unplayable lie and almost certainly a lost stroke.

The pressure of the natural hazards is compounded by the fact that, to reach the ideal driving area, shots must be long as well as straight. When he was competing in the 1971 German Open, Roberto de Vicenzo was asked if it would help to have more fore-caddies. "No," he replied, "for then the fore-caddie is lost also."

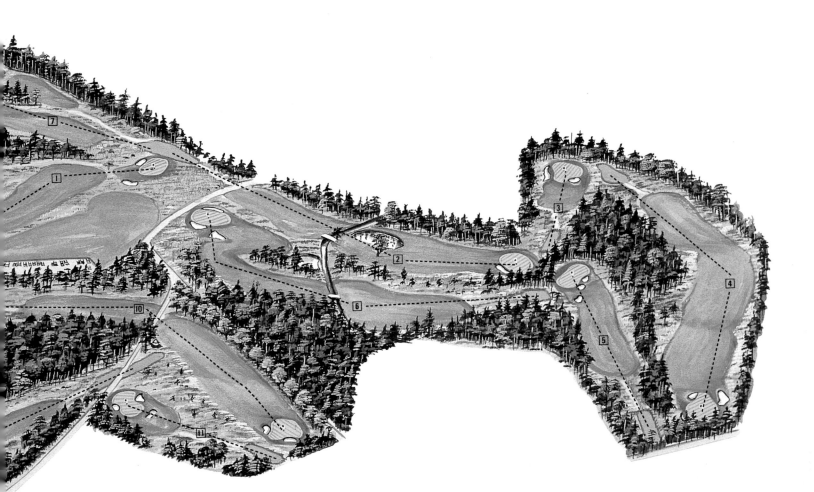

The 7th hole is a good example of Bremen's thoughtful design, a 410-yard par-four with two completely separate routes to the green. Here the player has to weigh up the risks and make a clear choice. The good golfer drives out to the right to a fairway that begins only after a carry of 220 yards. Accuracy is essential, since there is out-of-bounds close by and the approach can be easily blocked by a copse just before the green. The second shot would normally be a 6- or 7-iron. A much wider fairway is open to the left, following a curving route around the copse. It is an easier choice, longer and over trees, but better for the handicap player.

Bremen has been an infrequent host to the German Open, perhaps owing to the fact that the city is less accessible than Munich or Frankfurt. The last occasion was in 1985 and the tournament was something of a disaster, owing to continual rain. Eventually it was reduced to 54 holes and, with parts of the course flooded, a kilometre was trimmed from its original length. At least the name of the winner – Bernhard Langer – bore the stamp of authenticity. Probably the best tournament to have been staged there was the 1971 German Open which attracted a fine field from 23 different countries, including Peter Thomson, Roberto de Vicenzo and Peter Oosterhuis. The winner was Neil Coles, who remembers the course well. "I would rate it as one of the best championship courses I have played in Europe," he said. "One could compare it to Augusta – it is a course with a big feel about it. The construction is very natural; there are not a lot of fairway bunkers off the tee, because they are not needed. The big thing about Club Zur Vahr is that it is a very good driving course, the penalties are tough if you are off line. Once you are among the trees which come right up to the edge of the fairway, you can only hope to come out sideways – assuming you find a playable lie.

"I think the par-fives are the outstanding holes. The 2nd and 6th, both of which have two routes, are particu- larly good. To reach the green in two, you have to take a chance off the tee and drive very close to the trees. The 10th, 568 yards and almost a right-angled dog-leg, is probably the best hole of all. You drive from the apex of a V, with tremendously tall trees on both sides. You must take a driver because you cannot play safe – you need the length, but with tall pines either side, it's quite a drive. "The main thing about the course is that it is not only tight but long – on most holes in a tournament, you need that driver to avoid being blocked off by the dog-legs. The 12th hole – 509 yards, par-five – is one of the narrowest, and is a good example. Even after a long drive you are still left with another long, narrow shot to the green over marshy rough and scrub. It is an easy five, but to get a four you have to take a chance.

"Another good hole is the 15th – a snaking, double dog-leg of 548 yards, lined with tall trees all the way. Again you have to keep close to the left to get the best shot in for your second. If you go right, playing safe, you really are shut out.

"Like all good courses, the finish is tough. The 16th is good, with a single, large tree plumb in the way of your drive, leaving a narrow entrance on to the fairway. The 215-yard 17th is probably the best short hole on the course. You play through a narrow avenue of tall pines to an elevated green with one large bunker front left. There is out-of-bounds just on the left; if you hit the bank, you can very easily go out. Altogether, an excellent championship test – forcing you right to the limit all the way."

Brian Huggett, another Ryder Cup player and a former German Open champion, agrees: "It is like Champions at Houston, the best course that I have played in America. If you don't drive on the correct side of the fairways, you have to hook or cut your next. There is probably no harder course in Europe, not just because of length but because there are so many holes which call for skill as well."

The Course Card

Club Zur Vahr,
Bremen
Garlstedter Heide
Course

Record: 68, Neil
Coles, Peter Thomson,
German Open 1971

Hole	Yards	Par
1	366	4
2	529	5
3	206	3
4	547	5
5	320	4
6	555	5
7	410	4
8	165	3
9	420	4
10	568	5
11	183	3
12	509	5
13	401	4
14	348	4
15	548	5
16	445	4
17	215	3
18	412	4
Out	3,518	37
In	3,629	37
Total	**7,147**	**74**

Europe's first
Stadium course

Golf may have been introduced to France (continental Europe, too, for that matter) at Pau in 1856, but its subsequent development was pitifully slow. The main problem was that it was the preserve of the wealthy and the aristocracy. Around Paris Harry Colt and Tom Simpson laid out or developed a number of distinguished courses in the years either side of the First World War, with Chantilly, Fontainebleau, St. Cloud, St. Germain and Morfontaine leading the way, following the initial success of La Boulie. But then stagnation set in. The members of these exclusive clubs kept their jewels very much to themselves, and hardly a Parisian course was built between Morfontaine in 1925 and St. Nom-la-Bretêche in 1959. The consequence was a dearth of good French players, and out of those only a few turned to course design. That situation changed dramatically as the commercial potential of golf was recognised by the entrepreneurs of the seventies. A pioneering generation of French golf architects emerged, constructing new courses at an astonishing rate. Prominent among these were Jean Garaialde, Michel Gayon, Olivier Brizon, Robert Berthet, Alain Prat and Hubert Chesneau. And it was Chesneau – in consultation with Robert von Hagge – who designed the course which has become the permanent home of the French Open Championship, L'Albatros at Le Golf National, the first stadium course in Europe.

In appearance L'Albatros could not be more unlike Chantilly or Morfontaine. While they are gentle parkland, L'Albatros is rather akin to a Scottish links with its lack of trees, exposure to the wind, endless mounds, prolific bunkering and grasping rough. To these traditional defences are added 270,000 cubic metres of lakes, and length – over 7,100 yards of it from the back tees. 1.6 million cubic metres of earth were moved to transform this desolate waste into a challenging golf course. While the hopes of many championship contenders have been dashed in the waters it is a course which has earned the respect of the professionals who have played it. "Fantastico campo de golf," was the opinion of Severiano Ballesteros who went on to describe how you have to use every single club in the bag during the course of a round. "All the shots you have to play offer multiple choices." It is in this respect that L'Albatros so closely resembles a traditional links.

A lake to the left of the 1st fairway threatens the opening tee shot, though the ideal drive is down the right, given the orientation of the green and its extraordinary length, all of 68 yards from front to back! Only the supremely confident attack the pin on the 2nd when the hole is cut close to the lake. Birdie chances are offered to those who drive down the left on the 3rd, and once the ditch has been cleared there will be no more water until the turn. Instead, bunkers appear in quantity, that separating the 4th and 5th fairways well over 100 yards long. Around the greens they are seaside in nature, deep pots, although the most links-like hole, the 6th, has no bunker at all, relying for defence instead on

a semi-blind approach to a long, thin green hard up against the out-of-bounds. Out-of-bounds also looms to the right of the 7th, one of the toughest holes against par, and there is trouble in the mounds and swales to the right of the 9th fairway.

When South African Retief Goosen took the 1997 French Open title he led from start to finish, having begun on the first day at the 10th which he eagled by sinking a 126-yard wedge shot. Goosen's only real challenge came from the relatively unheralded Martin Gates who took advantage of the comparative simplicity of the holes around the turn by birdying four out of six of them in the final round. For lesser players the 12th is far from easy, the fairway being particularly narrow between bunkers, the green elevated and receptive only to a high-flighted approach. On the 13th the left-hand side of the fairway is the place to be in order to open up the green on the far side of a lake. Coming to the 14th with a slender one-shot lead in the 2000 French Open, Colin Montgomerie drove imperiously, and then powered his second shot exactly 262 yards with a three-wood, the ball finishing a mere nine inches from the pin. His tap-in eagle gave him the cushion he needed when he subsequently went through the back of the 15th green into the lake, being fortunate to end up with nothing worse than a bogey five. The threat of water on the right of the fairway is sufficient to push many drives to the left on this superbly testing hole, leaving a much longer and hazardous approach over the lake to the island green.

Bernhard Langer came to the 16th in the final round of the 1998 French Open looking for a birdie to give him a share of the lead with his Ryder Cup colleague, Sam Torrance. His tee shot finished ten feet from the hole, but the putt would not drop. It is not an easy green to read. On the lengthy par-4 17th Langer's second shot finished fifteen feet from the hole, but once again the putt missed by a fraction of an inch. Torrance, aware that Langer could still catch him,

The auld alliance – a very Scottish scene translated to France, the profuse bunkers and dune-like mounds suggesting more the Ayrshire coast than a Parisian suburb.

The Course Card

Le Golf National, Guyancourt

Hole	Yards	Par
1	415	4
2	202	3
3	530	5
4	439	4
5	404	4
6	377	4
7	443	4
8	207	3
9	563	5
10	377	4
11	191	3
12	437	4
13	410	4
14	552	5
15	421	4
16	175	3
17	470	4
18	514	5
Out	3,580	36
In	3,547	36
Total	**7,127**	**72**

took out his 7-wood for his approach to
the 17th. It finished two feet from the
hole and Torrance's birdie meant that
Langer now had to eagle the last, a
par-5 short enough to tempt all professionals to go for glory. Langer finished
12 feet from the cup and yet again just failed to hole the putt.
His birdie meant that he could only win if Torrance failed.
Langer might have been aware of Goosen's tribulations on
this hole in the previous year. Standing on the 18th tee
Goosen had five shots in hand and decided to play safe. He
ducked the challenge of reaching the green in two, laying
up short of the water. There were only 66 yards left to go
and, like a 24-handicapper, Goosen topped the ball into the
water and ended up with a seven. Despite this he still had

three shots to spare for victory.
Torrance, for his part, needed a regulation five, but after a fine drive he was left in two
minds: 8-iron or 9-iron? Opting for the 8-iron he easily
cleared the water, and all but cleared the green, too.
However, two putts comfortably saw him home. Two years
later, in May 2000, Colin Montgomerie was still under pressure standing on the 18th tee. He had not won in Europe all
year and by this hole his lead was only a single stroke. A
majestic drive left him a shot of 178 yards to the pin. His six-
iron finished a foot away, his second eagle of the day was a
formality, and Montgomerie was back on the winner's ros-
trum. Drama of this kind is almost guaranteed at L'Albatros.

Hole	Yards	Par
1	454	4
2	394	4
3	153	3
4	375	4
5	410	4
6	217	3
7	439	4
8	480	5
9	576	5
10	465	4
11	427	4
12	402	4
13	457	4
14	219	3
15	417	4
16	219	3
17	429	4
18	596	5
Out	3,498	36
In	3,631	35
Total	**7,129**	**71**

"... Nor the slightest glimpse of
an alien world"

Situated in beautiful woodland in one of Europe's greatest horse-racing areas, Chantilly is an outstanding course that has hosted several French Open championships. It is a pleasure to play there – not merely because of its serene forest setting but also because of its demanding qualities. Two series of holes in particular – the 9th to 11th and the 13th to 15th – provide a stern test of power and accuracy.

Around a century and a half has passed since golf was first played in France. In 1856, when the Duke of Hamilton and a few of his friends formed a club at Pau, in the foothills of the Pyrenees, golf was hardly known outside Scotland; there were but few courses in England and no others on the Continent of Europe. In the last years of the 19th century clubs appeared in Biarritz, Cannes and the hinterland of Paris; now, the game's influence is growing and numerous beautiful courses have been created.

Few would dispute that the course in the forest of Chantilly, 25 miles north of Paris, stands high if not paramount in France. The club was founded in 1908 under the presidency of Prince Murat, and five years later the French Open championship was played there after seven years at La Boulie, the golf course of the Racing Club de France. Few clubs other than Chantilly have longer enjoyed the blessing of two courses. In the early 1920s Tom Simpson was commissioned to lay out a new 18 holes, and to redesign those which form the present championship course, known as the Vineuil. Much of his work was damaged during World War II and nine of the new holes were abandoned, but there is little doubt that Simpson's work on the main course, which included reducing the number of bunkers, was the foundation of its greatness. A first sight of Chantilly gives an impression of dignity, peace and space. Nothing is confined or cramped; there is always ample room around the greens and tees and

between the holes. The course falls quietly away from the clubhouse, rather as it does at the Augusta National: all around is the great forest and nowhere is there the slightest glimpse of an alien modern world. At once the impulse to play is strong; the awareness of a beautiful and demanding course immediate. After the opening drive over a valley, a long second must avoid bunkers staggered to the right and slice traps by the green. A pull from the 2nd tee is disaster; a fade may be engulfed by a long bunker but a good shot leaves a pitch to a raised target of green. A long, flat bunker acts as a false lighthouse on the short 3rd, and the view from the 4th tee is like looking down a gun barrel. The hole is not long but the entrance to the green is tight with bunkers across and flanking the approach.

The French Open returned to Chantilly for a hat-trick of titles from 1988. The first two were won by Nick Faldo, the third by the Irishman Philip Walton but all three championships emphasised that the course had withstood the test of the new technological age. The respective 72 hole winning scores were 274, 273, and 275. The 5th is a fine hole, turning at a point from where the approach must be played through a neck of woods, with a cluster of pines by the green threatening the golfer who has driven too far to the left. Every instinct suggests a faded tee shot to the short 6th, but if it is played too safely pines again come into the reckoning. Although it might not appear so, there is room

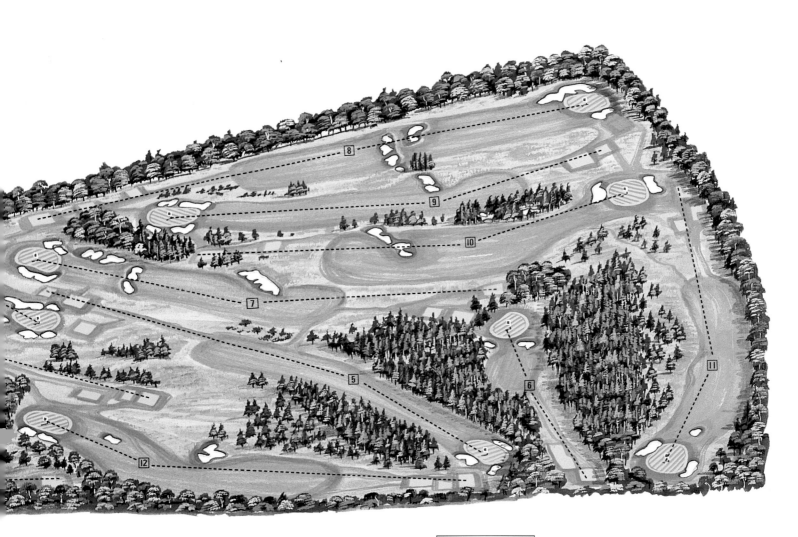

enough to pitch and hold after carrying the bunker guarding the green. A compelling feature of Chantilly is its constantly changing character and, for that matter, direction as well. The holes around the turn swing back and forth across more open country. The woods may flank – as for the full length of the 8th and the 11th, curving away from the dark forest towards a green set against a backdrop of ivy-clustered trees – but they never enclose. A whole series of bunkers, quickening memories of Muirfield, await the sliced second to the 7th. The angled curves of the 9th and 10th run parallel, but each drive and approach poses different problems. The importance of placing the tee shot is emphasized at almost every hole and is particularly true of the 12th, where no player would wish to come into the green from the right and towards the steeply falling ground beyond. At its foot lies the 14th green in a secret dell, and a golfer can enjoy a brief, if imaginary, feeling of superiority watching those putting far below. For the next three holes the golf is spectacular and testing.

A good drive to the 13th leaves a lovely second shot over a deep, grassy chasm to a green set against a fringe of trees. The 14th is the longest of the short holes, the green an oasis in its basin. Then comes a formidable drive. The championship tee is high in woods which snare the slightest hook and, on the right-hand peak of the deep valley – which must be carried to reach the fairway – is a tall spinney of oak and lime trees. The second shot is straight to a twin-level green.

The closing holes are sternly orthodox. Another target tee shot, to a green ringed with sand, is followed by a perfect-length 17th. A diagonal of hazards is meant to challenge the second shot. The green, like so many of Simpson's, has bunkers for the man who does not stay with his shot. The 18th, plunging and rising through a valley, makes a compelling climax to a noble course.

A Test of Stamina to the End

When Nick Faldo stood on the 18th tee in the last round of the 1989 French Open he knew that he needed a birdie four to retain the title he had won over the same course a year earlier. A par five would have presented the unpalatable prospect of a sudden death play-off with three other players: Bernhard Langer, Hugh Baiocchi, and Mark Roe. At 596 yards a four is not an open invitation. Furthermore the green is well protected with two bunkers either side and when Faldo's second shot trickled into one of them, a play-off appeared likely.

This possibility was compounded by the lie. The ball was perched so near the front of the bunker on the upslope that Faldo's left foot was outside the sand. It is difficult to judge the yardage with such a shot; the temptation is not to hit the sand hard, consequently the ball flies vertically and comes up short of the target. Faldo was not fooled. The ball finished a yard from the flag and he knocked it in to complete his defence.

Unlike Faldo, Peter Oosterhuis had room to manoeuvre in needing a par five on the hole to win the 1974 French Open. The beauty of the hole is that the green encourages an attacking stroke because there is no trouble beyond and the ground slopes gently upwards. Oosterhuis's beautiful three wood approach located the middle of the green to secure a two stroke victory over Peter Townsend.

Chantilly is perhaps the most highly regarded of all French courses, a sublime experience for amateurs and a consummate test for professionals.

The intelligent routing of El Saler ensures that players enjoy the contrast of pine forest and sand dunes on both nines, the 17th and 18th classic links holes which would not be out of place in Scotland.

Langer
reveals Arana's genius

Until an astonishing round of 62 by
Bernhard Langer on the final day of the 1984 Spanish Open few outside Spain had heard of El Saler or its architect Javier Arana. Arana had been a fine amateur player before turning to golf course design, but because he never worked outside his native country his genius was largely unrecognised internationally until the explosion in golf tourism hit Spain in the 70s and 80s. Even so, El Saler remained undiscovered mainly because of its location, on the coast a few kilometres from Valencia, an important commercial and industrial city, spiritual home of paella, but hardly a holiday centre. Langer's ten-under-par round put El Saler belatedly on the map, though some of his fellow competitors wondered if he had forgotten to play a couple of holes given the considerable challenge of this unforgiving course. No, Langer had played all eighteen. The truth was that he was cross, having been fined for slow play earlier in the tournament and having had his briefcase and all its contents stolen. His golf in the first three rounds had been undistinguished and he had up to that point rather lost interest in this tournament. Not a man to show aggression in public, Langer took it out instead on his golf ball! Naturally such a round catapulted him ahead of the field, he won the tournament and, as if to prove that he bore no grudges against the course itself, he repeated his triumph five years later when the Spanish Open returned to El Saler, though in a rather less dramatic fashion.

There is not much genuine linksland to be found anywhere on the Mediterranean's European coast, which makes El Saler's allocation all the more precious. Arana saw to it that both front and back nines visit the sand hills, the remainder of the course running through a rather more typically Spanish pine forest replete with its glorious scents. The greens are big, undulating, and difficult to read, there are almost 100 bunkers, the rough is vicious, and the wind can blow as fiercely as on any Scottish links, though on the whole a wind off the sea is more than welcome once temperatures soar in the blazing sun of a Spanish summer.

The trees may offer a little shade over the first few holes, though they are a distinct threat to the wayward on the solid 1st, a strategic dog-leg. One of the beauties of El

Saler is its frequent change of pace, the 2nd being a mid-length par-4 to a mischievously borrowed green with a narrow entrance through trees and bunkers. There are occasional blind shots, the drive at the 3rd for instance, where the good player must clear a scrub-covered hillock on the inside of the dog-leg if trying to attack the hole. Andrew Coltart came to grief here in the last round of the 1996 Turespaña Masters when seriously challenging for the lead. Having lost a ball and playing an air shot in a bush he ran up a ten. El Saler has a wicked bite!

After the short 4th, through the trees to a two-tiered green, the character of the course changes, with a drive over the brow of a hill before sweeping down the other side to a well-bunkered green in front of the sparkling Mediterranean, the first of the links holes. In 1989 Langer nearly wrecked his chances after a skirmish with a bush on this par-5. By any reckoning the 6th is a stirring hole, needing a long drive back over the summit of the hill to give a sight of the sloping green on the far side of a depression beyond gaping bunkers. There is an opportunity to retrench on the 7th, provided the fairway bunkers are avoided, but the 8th is a seaside special with the beach

A typically defended Arana green, the slopes throwing the weak approach into the swale or bunker low to the right, bunkers left penalising caution.

out-of-bounds on the left and a two-level green nestling below a giant sand dune. Mark McNulty solved the problems of the short, well-bunkered 9th in 1989 by holing his tee shot.

Then it is back into the woods at the 10th, a hole on which it is all too easy to become blocked out by trees on the right. Immediately the course opens out a little with the plainer 11th, and the short 12th is almost heathland in character, on the flat past stunted bushes. In contrast the 13th is one of the prettiest holes on the course, the shortest of the par-4s but requiring accurate placement from the tee, the green cleverly angled and raised up behind bunkers, with trees effectively blocking out the approach from the left. Leaving the forest once more the 14th beats off into the scrub, the drive slightly uphill with a bunker to be cleared on the right and bushes in wait if the approach should stray the least bit. Trees return as the main threat on the long 15th, and there is an out-of-bounds on the 16th as it makes its way to the edge of the sand hills.

One of Javier Arana's personal touches was to contrive that his 17th holes were par-3s and the 17th at El Saler is a fine example. It is a full carry over scrawny rough to a narrow, heavily contoured green, raised up between deep bunkers, and backed by a huge mesembryanthe-mum-clad sand dune keeping the Mediterranean at a manageable distance. This hole provided the climax to the 1996 Turespaña Masters when 24-year-old Diego Borrego from Marbella and Tony Johnstone of Zimbabwe were involved in a sudden-death play-off. The pair tied the first two play-off holes, but on the 17th green the borrows proved too much for Johnstone who three-putted giving Borrego his first European Tour title.

The final tee is fully exposed to the wind, up on top of the dunes, the seriousness of the challenge ahead plainly visible. There is a substantial carry to the none too gener-ous fairway with awful trouble in the rough on either side, and bunkers where the fairway bends left. More bunkers must be avoided on what is for ordinary golfers a very long approach to the green beneath the Parador Luis Vives.

El Saler was the first championship course in the Valencia region, opened in 1968. Others followed slowly, Escorpión designed by Ron Kirby with a number of extra-ordinary dog-legs amongst the orange trees, lovely Mediterraneo further up the coast at Castellón de la Plana, and El Bosque an American-style course by Trent Jones, giving the region plenty of variety. Then in 1992 Severiano Ballesteros entered the frame with his Oliva Nova layout to the south, and Bernhard Langer, whose 62 had first brought golfing attention to the region, returned to design Panorámica. Happily for the visitor green fees in this part of Spain are relatively inexpensive.

The Course Card

Campo de golf El Saler, Valencia

Hole	Yards	Par
1	428	4
2	376	4
3	531	5
4	189	3
5	515	5
6	442	4
7	358	4
8	359	4
9	156	3
10	399	4
11	568	5
12	198	3
13	348	4
14	418	4
15	564	5
16	427	4
17	213	3
18	466	4
Out	3354	36
In	3596	36
Total	**6950**	**72**

Water and sand on the
grand scale

The peak of La Concha provides a vivid backdrop to golf at Las Brisas.

One of the finest of the first generation of Spanish resort courses is Las Brisas. Designed by Robert Trent Jones and opened in 1968, it is part of vast 2,700-acre residential and holiday complex that includes, for the Hemingways among its golfers, a bullring. The course has been used for a number of major competitions, including three Spanish Opens, the World Cup of 1973, won by Jack Nicklaus and Johnny Miller for the United States, and the rain-affected 1989 World Cup.

Las Brisas is a fairly typical example of Trent Jones's work. It is dramatic, difficult and controversial, attracting praise, respect – and some criticism. One of the most prolific and successful architects in the history of the game, Trent Jones believed that a course should always provide

an easy alternative route for the Sunday golfer, but a tough test for the par shooter. Large, sculptured and strategically placed sandtraps, mammoth water hazards often pinching into narrow driving areas, undulating greens with variable pin position – these are the Trent Jones hallmarks which turn what is simply a difficult course into one of true championship quality.

At Las Brisas, the course follows a valley leading towards the sea from the Sierra Blanca mountains. Set on high ground and framed by a stand of pines, the clubhouse looks out across the entire course with its series of attractive but critical water hazards excavated from the valley floor. Inevitably, in a country where green turf is uncommon – and, where it exists, the product of great care and even greater expense – the course is essentially artificial, with exotic trees planted to enhance its beauty and increase its difficulty. At its far end, a grove of mature olive trees has been used to create a number of tight dog-leg holes, contrasting with the more open, undulating holes of the higher ground.

By clever use of the rolling land and the placement of hazards, Trent Jones avoided the need for virtually any rough at all. Unless a drive is placed correctly on the sloping fairways and pitched right into the large holding greens, the ball will most certainly be in sand, water, or out-of-bounds. The penalties are visible, clear – and total.

Las Brisas is both a stern and unusually testing course, combining an examination of playing skill with the distractions of beauty. It is liberally sprinkled with pine and eucalyptus, palm and almond trees, Indian figs and sugar cane and acres of orange orchards that scent the air at dusk. Vivid shades of green contrast with the crushed white marble of the bunkers, and dominating it all is the stark peak of La Concha, the white mountain which towers over the course.

With the improvement in performance of golf balls and clubs over the last ten years, Las Brisas would now be too short to seriously test the modern professional, with only two par-fours exceeding 400 yards. For its wealthy members and a few lucky visitors, however, it remains one of the best-presented courses in Spain.

The qualities that make a course a great playing test, even in perfect weather, are best seen at those holes which expose the skills or limitations of a golfer, which force him to elect to play perfect nominated shots (often at full stretch) or else settle for safety and second best. Arguably, the best holes on this demanding layout are the 2nd, 12th and the finish from the 15th.

The second hole is a 421-yard par-four with a narrow, sloped driving area between two traps and water hazard among trees; there is also out-of-bounds all along the right. The green, which is well protected on a high plateau, tilts sharply towards the front and can leave an almost impossible downhill putt, on the pin position. Another good hole in the first nine is the 8th, 530 yards with two clear routes of approach. The main feature is water, following the right-hand side of the fairway all along the hole and crossing in front of the green. The safe second is played away to the right, across the water to a fairway area leaving a simple pitch to a small green between two sandtraps. To reach the green in two, the shot must be perfectly struck, avoiding the hazards and the water which hugs the steep slope of the elevated green. Johnny Miller had an eagle there during his record round of 65.

One of the toughest and most beautiful of the short holes is the 208-yard 11th, played from a slightly elevated tee to a small green, bunkered on both sides, with water stretching across the front and completely around the left-hand edge. A long iron, possibly even a wood, is needed in wind for there is no room for error here.

The 15th, at 427 yards dog-legging sharply right through the grove of mature olive trees, is not the toughest hole on the course, but it does require careful negotiation. It is also notable for having been the setting for one of the greatest nominated tee shots of all time. The hole runs straight for more than half its length, through a narrow avenue of olives, with two fairway traps on the left-hand side at the corner. An out-of-bounds fence follows the hole. During the World Cup, Jack Nicklaus aimed right and calmly knocked his drive over the olives and the out-of-bounds, completely over the corner – a full 270- yards of carry, to leave a simple approach to the small, angled green. The hole following, a 224-yard par-three, has claimed many victims and probably aroused more controversy than any other hole on the course. The steeply sloping green has two bunkers biting deeply into its surface from either side and a large water hazard across its front.

It is always a long shot and often barely reachable from the back tee into a wind. Finishing above the hole, the golfer can putt straight back off the green.

The 17th is a short two-shotter of 323 yards, requiring discretion off the tee followed by an accurate pitch to a small oasis encircled by water on three sides, date palms and olives. Two large bunkers guarding the entrance and steep slopes down to the water demand a positive, accurate shot. The caddie's regular cry here is "agua" (water).

Now comes the last hole, a moderate par-four, where placement of the drive between out-of-bounds and a large, gathering water hazard is vital. The elevated green, two tiered and well bunkered, is a good deal farther away than it looks.

The greens were treacherously glassy for the 1987 Spanish Open and it took all of Nick Faldo's courage and experience to hold on for victory. In 1989 Australia won the second World Cup to be played here in a tournament seriously truncated through flooding, and the rains returned to spoil the inaugural Mediterranean Open the following year when Ian Woosnam triumphed over 54 holes.

The 12th
A Birdie for the Brave

Las Brisas' 520-yard 12th combines to perfection the ideal characteristics of a championship par-five. Played strictly as a three-shot hole, it offers ample room and the prospect of an easy par. However, for the player seeking a birdie and striving to reach the green in two, the margin for error is minute and the penalties for a slightly mishit shot severe.

To reach the green in two, the player must play down the left-hand side to a fairway which slopes left and gathers the over-ambitious shot to cause substantial problems. The water hazard continues menacingly all the way along the left side of the fairway until it crosses in front of the green.

If he aims to be up in two a handicap player will have to hit two of the best golf shots of his life.

The
Course
Card

Las Brisas,
Nueva Andalucia

Hole	Yards	Par
1	399	4
2	421	4
3	503	5
4	202	3
5	580	5
6	383	4
7	170	3
8	530	5
9	355	4
10	394	4
11	208	3
12	520	5
13	383	4
14	394	4
15	427	4
16	224	3
17	323	4
18	399	4
Out	3,543	37
In	3,272	35
Total	**6,815**	**72**

The pursuit of
perfection

Valderrama stands testament to one man's dream to recreate the immaculate precision of Augusta in the Andalusian region of Spain. He has succeeded to the extent that you almost feel inclined to remove your golf shoes while walking the fairways for fear of damaging the grass. Tom Kite believes the greens to be among the best he has ever putted on, and the setting is idyllic too. From the highest point, on the 11th green, Gibraltar's imposing rock slips easily into view, as does the faint outline of the coast of North Africa.

At 6,734 yards Valderrama is a short course by today's standards but the bald facts do not take into account the capricious winds that swirl and bedevil club selection. Valderrama has not one prevailing wind but two: the Poniente that blows warm breezes in from the west and the Levante which brings cooler air from the east. Occasionally the two appear to mingle; the weather vane perched next to the 11th green can be flapping furiously one minute and resting the next. The confusion is often a reflection of the mind of the poor golfer who has to make sense of it all.

When Kite, the American captain at the 1997 Ryder Cup made his first reconnaissance visit to Valderrama the winds caused him more concern than anything else. He knew the Europeans were familiar with the course, since it was then the annual venue for the Volvo Masters. His players would have no such luxury. Kite practised on the course one day and was confronted by the Levante; the next by the Poniente. After America had lost he would remember those practice days and look back with regret that he had not been stronger with his team in persuading them to visit the course in advance of the match to experience Valderrama's moods.

The man whose dream it was to create this celestial setting was a Bolivian tin magnate called Jaime Patino, who had retired to the area. When he moved to Spain's Costa del Sol the courses were filling up and he was fed up with it. So he bought the second course at Sotogrande, a Robert Trent Jones layout called Las Aves, and renamed it Valderrama.

Jones was commissioned for a redesign but the course possesses as many Patino hallmarks as those of the great American architect. The waterfall protecting the 4th green is one example of his pursuit of perfection and the 17th has had more facelifts than a Hollywood actress.

It is said that he spends £5 million a year maintenance. Average American courses need around 600 sprinkler heads to maintain pristine condition. Valderrama has 4,600.

The 1st hole sets out the challenge of Valderrama. The fairway is narrow and lined with cork trees. It is a fairly modest par four at 389 yards but the reward of a short iron to a green that often lies in shadow will only follow a straight drive. The 2nd is one of several controversial holes, owing to the cork tree that splits the fairway. It stands 264 yards from the tee and many a player has strode to his ball after his drive only to be disappointed when he arrives at it, the green blocked from view by the imposing cork. Valderrama's four par-threes are fine holes, and the third is the first of them, requiring a mid-iron to a green where the punishment is severe if missed either long or to the left.

The 4th is a gorgeous par-five, the drive an inviting one from an elevated tee. The second shot provoked some early excitement in the Ryder Cup since it is clearly in range for the long hitters. The waterfall proved a diligent guardian and few players found the putting surface in two. The fifth is a dogleg par-four to the left, a drive over the angle setting up a birdie opportunity to a contoured green that possesses many subtle breaks. The 6th resembles the 6th hole at Augusta, a wonderful par-three from a raised tee to a green surrounded by six dazzling bunkers. The effect is intimidating, the club selection difficult as the tee is sheltered by a cluster of trees. To add to the difficulty, the green is tiered and three putts is a likely consequence of finding the wrong shelf.

The 7th is one of the hardest holes on the course, particularly if the Levante is blowing into a player's face. At 461 yards it has plenty of length anyway, but bunkers and cork trees at 260 yards place the emphasis on a long, straight drive to have any prospect of reaching the green in regulation. The 8th runs parallel, a fine short par-four with a deceptive bunker that guards its front edge. The 9th is a par-four straight into the teeth of the Levante, and if it possesses any ferocity the green can be unreachable in two.

The inward half opens with two holes where a professional has birdie opportunities. The par-four 10th requires a short iron to the green off a drive that reaches beyond the angle of the dog-leg. The 11th is a par-five that is reachable in two on less windy days. The 12th might well be the hardest hole, a par-three that never plays less than a long iron. The green tilts from front to rear and is hemmed in by cork trees which also offer protection down the par-four 13th.

Enhancing the pleasure of Patino's beautiful course is the profusion of wildlife that garlands the course. Fluttering between the cork oaks and olive trees that line almost every fairway are 22 species of butterfly; when someone asked Patino whether the lake that guards the 10th green was dyed blue, as they sometimes are at Augusta, he replied haughtily: "We don't put dye in our water because it would harm the otters."

The controversial 17th pictured on the final morning of the 1997 Ryder Cup.

A feature of the par-four 14th is the raised green that requires one iron more than usual and the 15th tee makes use of the same high ground to create a long, plunging par-three to an angled putting surface. The 16th is called 'Very Difficult,' not without reason. The hole dog-legs to the right and the tee shot has to be bold, towards the right side of a sloping fairway that will throw it to the left. The 17th seeks to recreate the 15th at Augusta but controversy has dogged its various recreations. In two recent American Express Championships at Valderrama several players repeatedly found the water when perfectly struck short approach shots spun back unpredictably, generating anger and fierce criticism. So the hole was re-modelled, becoming more akin to Trent Jones's initial design, although without the band of rough which once inhibited driving.

The 18th is a fine finishing hole. The drive has to be kept away from the trees on its right side but not so far that a player runs out of fairway to the left. Even so the second shot is still a long iron to a well-protected green.

At the 1997 Ryder Cup the match went to this final hole, where Colin Montgomerie proved equal to the task and Scott Hoch did not. The 18th, therefore, had shown itself to be cherished ground where the difficulties were severe enough to sort out the confident from the ill at ease. Indeed Valderrama did this as a whole, easily justifying its reputation as the Augusta of Europe. One man's dream has become reality.

The 17th

Seve's Focal Point

When it was announced that Valderrama would have the honour of being the first course to host a Ryder Cup in mainland Europe, attention immediately turned to the 17th hole. Redesigned by the European Captain, Severiano Ballesteros, his team were divided as to its merits. Colin Montgomerie, somewhat hurtfully, referred to it as the worst hole in Europe. What cannot be denied is that it became the focal point of that Ryder Cup, its vast bank behind the green turned into an amphitheatre where swathes of supporters gathered each day to watch what was invariably a critical hole of action. Some of the deeds witnessed there were incredible, and none more so than Ignacio Garrido's recovery from a back bunker to get down in two to force a remarkable half in his fourballs match with Jose-Maria Olazabal against Phil Mickelson and Tom Lehman. For all the fuss about the unfairness of certain aspects of the hole, there were a number of instances where players showed that the green was receptive to the perfectly struck second shot, thereby negating much of the criticism. Why should anything less than precision succeed when it is a second shot to a par five?

The Course Card

Valderrama
Sotogrande,
Cadiz, Spain

Hole	Yards	Par
1	389	4
2	399	4
3	173	3
4	535	5
5	381	4
6	163	3
7	461	4
8	345	4
9	441	4
10	364	4
11	547	5
12	197	3
13	402	4
14	370	4
15	200	3
16	422	4
17	511	5
18	434	4
Out	3,287	35
In	3,447	36
Total	6,734	71

An extravagant
American entry
into Europe

The courses at Sotogrande, on the Spanish Costa del Sol, lie twenty-two miles from Gibraltar, a massive silhouette on the western horizon. Designed by Robert Trent Jones, the Old course, completed in 1965, was his first venture in Europe. The second course is now even more famous, and known as Valderrama.

American influence is clear in every aspect of the design of the Old course. The tees are long, sleek quadrangles of turf allowing great variation in the length of the holes. The greens are large – perhaps excessively so – but they allow for a variety of pin positions, and as putting surfaces their contours are subtly fashioned. The bunkers and traps gleam white, made of crushed marble from Andalusian quarries because the local sand was not considered good enough. No spectre of economy haunted the architect's plans.

The turf itself is probably the strongest reminder of America. This was the first time Bermuda grass was used on a European course, and two sacks of seed from Tifton in Georgia proved sufficient for a nursery from which all the fairways were sown. These are superb to the tread and for the lie of the ball: there is no such thing as a bad lie on these fairways. At first the Bermuda was used on several greens, but eventually all were sown with Pencross bent, and beautiful putting surfaces they are.

The golfer fresh from the courses of Britain has to accustom himself to pitching approaches right up to the flag in the true target manner, otherwise he will forever be short. All the greens hold; so, too, do the fairways, for an automatic electric system feeds almost 500 watering points. For a course to survive throughout the long, dry summers constant watering is essential, but unlike the desert courses in America and elsewhere one has no impression of playing in an oasis. The dark green of the cork trees, the fertile valley of the Guadiaro River, the Mediterranean itself, all serve the cause of richly contrasting colours, but the long savage outlines of the sierras beyond the foothills on which the course lies quicken memories of Nevada.

The sea does not enter the golfer's reckoning at Sotogrande except as a background. The graceful clubhouse and its clusters of neighbouring villas stand a little way inland and the course flows quietly away towards the

Sotogrande's difficulties are evenly spread throughout the round, with a welcome variety to individual hole lengths. Rough hardly occurs, the strategic challenges of trees, bunkers and water being considered quite sufficient.

hills. The 1st hole runs parallel to a splendid practice ground, with its sentinel palm trees, so there is no excuse – especially in a land where haste is not part of civilized life – to start the round cold: a good drive and a medium iron will suffice. The 2nd calls for much more. It is a beautiful, long hole, rising and curving to the left with bunkers to trap those who would cut the corner, little spinneys to threaten the erring second, and a raised green to tax the final pitch.

Contrast is immediate, for the 3rd and 5th holes each offer hope of threes, given a well-placed drive and an accurate pitch. If the pin is placed on any of the petals at the 3rd the approach must be most delicately judged, but this is fair because the hole is only 339 yards. Meanwhile, the short 4th has demanded a long, straight stroke over a valley to a green above the level of the tee – few twos are scored at this hole – and as one stands on the 6th tee there is the feeling that henceforth the tasks will be real and earnest. The hole swings uphill to the right, and only a long drive to the left centre of a dimpled fairway will give a sight of the green: except for the strong, this is a fine par-five.

Most people will settle happily for their pars at the 7th, a spectacular hole. The drive plunges into a valley cleared from a forest of cork trees, and the second from a downhill stance looks alarmingly narrow. The green is a shelf sloping from woods on the left towards a lake and, even with merely pitching club in hand, the shot would give anyone cause for apprehension. The green of the short 8th, another hole across a valley, is typical of hundreds on the other side of the Atlantic. Its fall from back to front is considerable, and an overhit from the tee probably means three putts. At the 9th the drive is tight between trees to a ribbon of fairway, and now the highest point of the course has been reached, without awareness of effort.

As if in celebration, the ground falls away from the 10th tee, leaving a tempting carry over woods for those who wish to shorten the hole, and a line for others content to play it safe. The 11th green is another of the pulpit tar-get variety and is followed by the first of two fascinating loops. The 12th pursues the side of a large lake, which looks far more natural than it is. Those who try to get home in two court danger, for the green is tucked away behind a far corner of the lake, which further threatens on both sides of the par-3 13th, a beautiful short hole. From any tee the 14th is the hardest five of all. However much the lake's edge is trimmed only a second of tremendous order, shaped to draw into a tree-cloistered green angled against a hillside, has any chance of getting home.

A long drive should give a sight of the 15th green, otherwise the second over a crest on the fairway is the one blind shot of the round. A slice from the tee will descend into a stone-walled paddock. A similar stroke to the 16th is threatened by another artificial lake, which enables the next green to be sited on a little peninsula similar to that at the 13th. The tee shot, although shorter, is more testing: if aimed at the flag most of its flight must be over water. These short holes, an instance of the imaginative use of water in which American architects are so skilled, contrast pleasantly with those on the outward half. The gentle rise of the last hole is an invitation for two satisfying long shots towards a finely bunkered, crested green, and for the cool drinks beyond. As the relaxing golfer looks out across the broad acres to the green hills, and the mountains turn black against the fading light, there is a sense of peace and beauty and fulfilment that few other golf courses in Europe can match.

Despite the development of Valderrama into a top notch tournament venue Sotogrande's Old Course has remained firmly ranked in the top ten in Continental Europe, very much the cultured home of social golf for its well-heeled members and discerning visitors. Only once did it witness comparative humiliation at the hands of the professionals, back in 1966 when Roberto de Vicenzo used his enormous power to bring the course to its knees. His course record 66, despite three-putting the final green, on the second day gave him a commanding early lead which the wily old campaigner never relinquished.

The Course Card

Club de Golf
Sotogrande, Cadiz

Hole	Yards	Par
1	394	4
2	527	5
3	339	4
4	235	3
5	361	4
6	517	5
7	422	4
8	199	3
9	363	4
10	453	4
11	373	4
12	582	5
13	214	3
14	503	5
15	426	4
16	388	4
17	174	3
18	440	4
Out	3,357	36
In	3,553	36
Total	**6,910**	**72**

Peaceful golf beside the

Ria Formosa

The final green at San Lorenzo, set out into the water, is one of the great finishing holes in Iberian golf.

One of the oldest international friendship agreements still honoured is that between Portugal and Britain, who have remained allies since the Treaty of Windsor was signed over six hundred years ago in 1386. For centuries the British have been very much involved in the port wine trade and it is hardly surprising, then, that it was at Oporto back in 1890 that they introduced golf to Portugal. It was a genteel pastime and by the outbreak of the Second World War there were still only six courses in the whole of the country, the number managing to creep into double figures during the 1960s. Penina, opened in 1966, was the first resort course as such, and, once again, it involved a Briton, Henry Cotton, whose vision, creating a magnificent golf course out of an unpromising, flat, wet, rice field, revealed the huge golfing potential of this fecund land. It sparked a golfing revolution, so that by the turn of the century fifty courses were in play, and it is said that a hundred will be opened by the year 2005. Of those fifty courses no fewer than ten were ranked in Golf World's Top 100 in Continental Europe as the Millennium closed, and the highest ranked was San Lorenzo.

What lifts San Lorenzo into top spot is not only the design of American architect Joe Lee but also its incomparable situation with rolling Bermuda fairways sweeping through umbrella pines, past reeded freshwater lagoons, and down to the shores of the Ria Formosa Estuary. Here, in a mere fraction of the vast Quinta do Lago estate, golf is a peaceful occupation, shared with all manner of exotic birdlife - hoopoe, stork, stilt and gallinule. Lee's design is sympathetic to the surroundings, a hand laid on only gently. San Lorenzo opened in 1988, the actual construction work having been carried out by another of the prominent Americans working in the Algarve, Rocky Roquemore.

At a little over 6,800 yards from the back tees San Lorenzo is not unduly long, but it calls for courage often enough if attack is the order of the day. Whatever the level of play, wisdom is of the essence, with accurate placement required from the tee and a canny touch with approach work. Right from the start thought is required despite the encouragement of a downhill opening drive. If there is to be any chance of reaching this green in two the tee shot must defy a bunker in the angle of the dog-leg. A well-bunkered short hole and a pair of comparatively benign par-4s continue through the pines taking play to the first of

the holes setting San Lorenzo apart, the par-3 5th. It is only short but it plays across a valley towards the Atlantic Ocean, the views distracting, accuracy all important, the green set up on a rise. Suddenly the golf gets harder, the 6th fairway curling as it tumbles past an inhospitable hillside on the left, the waters of the Ria Formosa on the right. It is much the same on the 7th, again tempting the unwary to play cautiously down the left, keeping the drive away from the marshes, a temptation which should, never the less, be avoided. When the tide is high and waves lap at the edge of this green only an inch-perfect approach will suffice. Good though these holes may be there is better still to come, the 8th needing thoughtful course management with its fairway snaking left and right along the shores of the largest of the inland lagoons. To attack the green, set out into the waters, after a good, long drive needs bravery allied to supreme skill, the carry perhaps 240 yards. Almost as much skill is required by the lesser player to work out how to lay up safely given the twists and turns of the fairway and frequent incursions of water from the right. Holes such as this have caused San Lorenzo to be criticised occasionally in the golfing press because it can be so unforgiving to the high-handicapper, but did anyone tell George Crump or Henry Fownes that they had to flatter the beginner at Pine Valley or Oakmont? Only a long drive to the crest of a hill reveals the 9th green in front of the clubhouse.

Typical of the strategic challenge of San Lorenzo is the 10th, a par-5 playing up to a plateau fairway. A thoughtful second shot to the far end of the high ground gives sight of the green down below, beyond a central bunker. Given the constant curve to the left and abundant trouble on that side, big hitters seeking to shorten the route need extreme accuracy. Danger also lurks on the left of the 12th, the longest of the par-4s with a treacherous ravine lurking below the ledge fairway. The charm of these inland holes is their variety. So where the 11th is principally a second-shot hole, the green not one to overshoot, it is the drive on the 13th which is the key to success with the need to avoid bunkers on the left of the dog-leg. Similarly the first of the short holes on the back nine, the 14th, can be severely punishing on the left, whereas that is the better side to be on the 16th, the longest of the par-3s which very often plays into the wind adding a club or two to its length.

When San Lorenzo opened for play in 1988 it was immediately apparent that here was an unbeatable combination of a brilliant Joe Lee design and an idyllic setting. It is still ranked No.1 in Portugal despite the abundant merits of many of its neighbours.

The Course Card

San Lorenzo,
Almancil, Algarve

Hole	Yards	Par
1	540	5
2	177	3
3	366	4
4	371	4
5	141	3
6	422	4
7	377	4
8	574	5
9	400	4
10	567	5
11	383	4
12	432	4
13	393	4
14	172	3
15	517	5
16	208	3
17	376	4
18	406	4
Out	3,368	6
In	3,454	36
Total	**6,822**	**72**

Between them, the 15th flows downhill, inviting a big drive, but there are ten bunkers judiciously placed throughout the length of the hole giving golfers of all abilities plenty to think about.

Lee had not used all his trump cards in that stunning run of holes from the 6th to the 8th. He still had a couple of winners in hand for the end. Like all great courses, San Lorenzo finishes in dramatic fashion, the 17th returning to the lagoon, this time on the bank opposite the 8th. Its waters prey on the mind on each shot, though the hole is not especially long and its fairway generous enough despite the bunkers on the right. Again the green is set out into the lagoon and there is no margin for error on the approach shot. Simply brilliant, the 18th calls for daring

and precise execution. The closer the drive can be held to the lagoon on the left the easier the approach shot to the island green, the water this time on the right. There is room of a sort on the right of the fairway for the tee shot, but then, of course, the approach will be longer and more hazardous over water to the shallow, tightly-bunkered green, and it is all too easy to end up blocked out behind one of the umbrella pines lining the right of the fairway.

After a visit to San Lorenzo Solheim Cup captain, Mickey Walker, said of it, "It's a very tranquil course, in a totally different sense to what we are used to in Britain. It is magical." Perhaps it is in keeping with that tranquillity that San Lorenzo has not been subjected to the hubbub of a modern tour event.

A test of finesse
high above the Atlantic

The Course Card

Vilamoura Golf
Club, Algarve

Record: 67,
Des Smyth, 1979

Hole	Yards	Par
1	339	4
2	476	5
3	354	4
4	178	3
5	531	5
6	232	3
7	430	4
8	458	4
9	290	4
10	167	3
11	427	4
12	533	5
13	381	4
14	481	5
15	164	3
16	562	5
17	386	4
18	452	4
Out	3,288	36
In	3,553	37
Total	**6,841**	**73**

Until the mid-1960s, the sunny Algarve coast in the south of Portugal – a beautiful stretch of white beaches, rugged, red cliffs and tessellated villages – was a well-kept holiday secret enjoyed by only the few: a place apart, rich in orange, olive and fig trees, fish and flowers. There was not a golf course to be seen. Even now, despite its popularity as a high-class resort, the Algarve retains the essential charm and character that are the legacy of its history, its situation and its climate. It also now offers some outstanding golf.

All the early courses, although scenic and kept in immaculate condition, were of high championship quality and, even off the forward tees, much too difficult for the average golfer. Not that golfers have been deterred, relishing as they do a really stout challenge. And on all the Algarve coast, few courses offer that challenge more surely than Vilamoura.

The Algarve climate, temperate in winter, and not too hot in summer (temperatures moderated by cooling Atlantic breezes) makes Vilamoura a practical holiday destination all year round. A recent restoration programme has greatly improved the condition of the course and the bunkering has been slightly revised.

Designed by Frank Pennink on and around a ridge of high ground as part of a 4,000-acre development, it opened in January 1969. Pennink's original brief was to create a course resembling the beautiful but testing courses of England's Berkshire, and this is what he achieved. Using the steeply sloping land as well as the more level areas, and judiciously siting his fairways through mature umbrella pines, he produced a flowing succession of fine golf holes that are reminiscent of Swinley Forest or of the Berkshire Club itself. From the outset he planned it as a championship course, but in the event it turned out to be tougher than he intended.

Although basically a holiday centre, Vilamoura has staged its share of professional events, the 1970 Algarve Open, and the 1973 and 1979 Portuguese Opens, the 1973 event shared with Penina. Big hitting Brian Barnes won the 1979 Portuguese Open on a score of 287, a high score reflecting the testing nature of the layout. From the beautifully appointed clubhouse at one end of the ridge, the course spills down either side in green ribbons between the attractive but punishing umbrella pines. Four holes occupy the high-level ground, from where there are fine views out over the rolling Algarve countryside. Vilamoura is an attractive course, with no blind shots and much variety in the holes and in the recently relaid greens. The strength of the par-threes registers immediately. Each is different, each intensely visual and attractive; all require careful club selection and con-

trol for a par. For the rest, a crucial role is played by the trees which line the fairways and often encroach strategically to block off a long approach. There is little or no rough under the umbrella pines – merely sand and rocky ground. But try to play a golf shot up through one of the trees and you discover why they are such an effective hazard – the pine needles clutch at the ball and kill its flight immediately. In the trees, a player must accept the fact that the only sensible shot is a chip out sideways back to the fairway.

Despite its situation at the centre of a popular coastal resort, Vilamoura has a unique feeling of quiet isolation. This is partly due to its setting, high on one of the few pieces of elevated ground on this part of the coast. With holes rising, curving and dipping down through a billowing green sea of bushy-topped pines, the course has 18 quite separate holes presenting widely varying problems. On the long holes, bunkering is minimal and strategic – the main hazards are the trees which line the narrow fairways. There is no need for semi-rough; a shot under the trees is a stroke lost.

Vilamoura is memorable for the umbrella pines which line each hole, providing a beautiful backdrop and creating an atmosphere of seclusion. Its taxing par-threes are well known, but Vilamoura also has five par-fives, three of them more than 500 yards long. Even here judiciously sited single bunkers, inconvenient trees or the fierce dog-leg of the 12th put the premium on accuracy, not length.

The best long holes come in the tough back nine, a

Vilamoura's main defence is the umbrella pines lining each hole, but a duck-festooned water hazard presents a further dilemma.

rugged, 3,553-yard par 37. The 12th is 533 yards from the back tee and curves sharply to the right around a large hill. It is an excellent hole, since a player cannot bite off too much from the tee – there are trees on the right coming into play, and he has no view of the green wherever he reaches the fairway. The hole narrows for the second shot, which is all uphill with concealed bunkers waiting to catch the errant approach. A tilted, elevated green has out-of-bounds immediately behind. The course's longest hole is the 562-yard 16th, a great driving hole with the ideal landing area between a large bunker and some trees on the right. The hole follows a gentle curve to the right, partly downhill, requiring exact placement of each stroke and – like all good par-fives – it leaves no room at all for error to the birdie-shooter. Tall trees and a bunker on the outside of the dog-leg at 265 yards narrow the driving area; the kidney-shaped green is well bunkered, offering a narrow target, with steep fallaway on all sides. Bunkers on the left of the dog-leg 17th can be cleared with a solid drive, but trees beyond can still thwart the over-ambitious. The round ends with another lengthy par-four on which even a mildly misdirected tee shot is easily blocked out by the lone trees either side of the fairway, and the green is long and narrow with bunkers either side guarding the entrance. Bernard Hunt, veteran of eight Ryder Cups and a former winner of the Algarve Open, has great respect for the layout. "It is one of the hardest courses in Portugal because there is no let-up," he contends. "It is a very tight driving course, demanding mastery of all the shots in the bag, and it is the sort of course that the longer you go on the more certain you are that you will have a disaster somewhere. For me, the three short holes are outstanding. I believe a good short hole should be a test of finesse. I would criticize any course or any par-three hole where you have to fire a wood to a large green with big bunkers. The modern, American style of golf tends towards this. But I think the short 4th, 10th and 15th at Vilamoura, which are all mid irons or less, yet still very difficult par-threes, represent the ideal test. They also happen to be the most attractive holes at Vilamoura. One of the big problems at these holes is picking the correct club. The greens are not very big anywhere on the course, but this is particularly so on the short holes.

"Two of the short par-fours, the 1st and 9th, are almost reachable off the tee and you are very tempted to go for a birdie because you know that somewhere out on the course you are going to drop a shot or two, so the temptation is to gamble. But they are par-fours where, in going for a three, you can well end up with a six. Although they are short, they are still good holes. Two other really good holes are the 11th and 12th. I think Frank Pennink did a great job when he laid out this course – it is a very tough test indeed."

Few who have marvelled at Vilamoura's beauty or tangled with its ubiquitous umbrella pines would disagree.

North America

Golf in North America is statistically overpowering. Since the emergence of Tiger Woods in the autumn of 1996 courses are being built at a rate of 450 a year in order to cope with the game's new status as the trendiest sport on the block. In the last 20 years the numbers have practically doubled and most of the 20 million who express an interest in the game try to play at least once a month – a feast of golfing indulgence that far exceeds that of all other countries put together. There is a breathtaking diversity of settings for the game, from the Monterey Peninsula on the west coast, where cypresses weep over the shot that is sliced into the Pacific, to the nation's capital, Washington, and the Congressional Club which stands just a short helicopter ride from the White House. The science of agronomy has made golf possible in deserts where previously grass could never grow; and shrewd businessmen, together with brilliant architects, have bulldozed forests and drained swamps to create resort golf in the islands of the Caribbean and elsewhere. Linksland courses in the manner of the Old Country do not exist, but other true tests of golf are there in profusion. The game in America had its tentative beginnings in the old colonial states of the Atlantic seaboard during the latter years of the eighteenth century, but records are fragmented and discontinuous. The first authenticated club was St Andrews at Yonkers, New York, founded in 1838 (here, the United States must give precedence to Canada, where the Royal Montreal began life fifteen years earlier). Within twelve years the United States had more then 1,000 courses – including the first outside Britain for public use, at Van Cortlandt Park in New York City (1895). From that time on, golf in America passed through well-defined phases. There was an early period in which the Scots still dominated all things to do with the game, from course design to the winning of championships. The free-spending, freewheeling 1920s saw considerable growth, much of it due to the luminous talents of Bobby Jones. The next dramatic boom coincided with the rise of Arnold Palmer, one of the most compelling of all sporting heroes. Now we are living in the most extraordinary period of all – the era of Tiger Woods.

1. Shinnecock Hills 2. Augusta 3. Cypress Point 4. Oakmont 5. Baltusrol 6. The Country Club
7. Olympic 8. Harbour Town 9. Winged Foot 10. Pinehurst 11. Merion 12. Seminole
13. TPC Sawgrass 14. Valhalla 15. Oak Hill 16. Muirfield Village 17. Inverness 18. The National
19. Pine Valley 20. Firestone 21. Southern Hills 22. Medinah 23. Oakland Hills 24. Champions
25. Pebble Beach 26. Dorado Beach 27. Banff 28. Capilano 29. Royal Montreal 30. Mid Ocean
31. Club de Golf Mexico

Shinnecock Hills is the American course closest in style and spirit to the ancient links of Britain. Interestingly, the construction supervisor on the 1931 reconstruction was the young Dick Wilson, who, himself, went on to an illustrious career as a golf architect.

Golf takes root

among the burial mounds

The Course Card

Shinnecock Hills Golf Club, New York

Record: 65, Raymond Floyd and Mark Calcavecchia US Open, 1986

Hole	Yards	Par
1	394	4
2	226	3
3	453	4
4	408	4
5	535	5
6	471	4
7	188	3
8	367	4
9	447	4
10	409	4
11	158	3
12	472	4
13	377	4
14	444	4
15	415	4
16	544	5
17	186	3
18	450	4
Out	3,489	35
In	3,455	35
Total	6,944	70

More's the pity, but it is next to impossible to find in America the kind of pristine golfing conditions that exist on the historic seaside links of Great Britain. There are a few approximations along the north-eastern seaboard facing the Atlantic Ocean, and of these nothing of finer quality exists than Shinnecock Hills, which has a claim to being the first "formalized" golf club in the United States and the first eighteen-hole course. Part of the stylish summer resort of Southampton at the eastern end of Long Island, Shinnecock's qualities have been overshadowed by the exclusive "social" panache that was attached to it over the years.

Because of the club's seniority, the genesis of Shinnecock Hills is of considerably more interest than that of most other clubs, for it epitomizes the almost casual manner in which golf started in the United States. During the winter of 1889-90 William K. Vanderbilt, the prominent sportsman and son of the founder of the Vanderbilt dynasty, was travelling through southern France with a couple of his friends. At Biarritz they came across Willie Dunn, one of the early Scottish professionals who were then beginning to export their native game to foreign countries. Dunn was building a course at Biarritz, so he staged an impromptu exhibition of his skills for the visiting Americans. Within a few months, the Americans were back home and excitedly discussing the possibility of building a golf course at Southampton. Two of Vanderbilt's companions in Biarritz, Edward Meade and Duncan Cryder, began the search for a suitable location for their proposed golf course. Eventually, they settled on some low-lying sandhills a couple of miles from the seashore and within a few minutes' drive of a small summer colony. Equally important, the land adjoined the railroad line from New York City, giving those golfers who made the journey from the city in future years easy access to the club.

Willie Davis from the Royal Montreal Club was brought down to lay out the course. He had 12 holes ready for play in late summer 1891. Davis is rarely given the credit for his work because in 1894 Willie Dunn arrived as professional. Dunn certainly added the six holes which made the course up to a full 18, but he left Shinnecock in 1895. Then at some time in the 1930s Dunn made up a story about building the

course with Indian labour, turning Indian burial mounds into bunkers and finding discarded firewater flasks when playing explosion shots from them. He told it to a gullible author who never checked out the details, and the whole fabrication found its way into golf folklore.

When the first twelve holes were ready to play there is little argument that this was then the most sophisticated golfing facility in the country. Forty-four members had already been enrolled at $100 apiece, and the eighty acres on which the course had been laid out were purchased for $2,500, a sum that would today scarcely buy a piece of turf on the same property. Stanford White, the most fashionable architect of the day, was commissioned to build a clubhouse in the shingled style of the region, with such modern appurtenances as a grill-room, lockers and shower-baths. Although there have been additions in subsequent years, White's original building, which was ready for use by the summer of 1892 has essentially remained intact. Golf quickly became a fad among the wealthy and prominent figures who summered at Southampton, and the club became a thriving vortex of the social whirl, the members adding to the splendour of it all with their red blazers, monogrammed brass buttons and white flannel trousers.

In 1894, an attempt was made to conduct a national championship (for amateurs, of course) at Newport, Rhode Island. It ended in unhappy bickering, but an open championship that was appended to the Newport event was won by Shinnecock's Willie Dunn, giving him the unofficial claim to having been the first US Open champion. Due to the sniping, the United States Golf Association was formed with Shinnecock Hills as one of the five founding clubs.

The USGA's first official championship was held at Newport in 1895, and the following July the championship was brought to Shinnecock Hills. In the Open championship that was played over 36 holes on the day after the Amateur championship was completed, so many of the professionals broke 80 – not a commonplace feat in championship golf until the introduction of the rubber-cored ball a decade later – that some second thoughts were prevalent regarding the quality of the course. At less than 5,000 yards, it was not of

Only the Good Shotmaker Will Succeed

championship calibre, and so the first of a long series of alterations and improvements was undertaken.

Eventually William Flynn of Toomey and Flynn in Philadelphia was engaged to turn Shinnecock into a top flight test of golf. His design was shown to the distinguished English architect Hugh Alison for a second opinion. Alison approved strongly. It opened for play in 1931. Flynn's course measured 6,740 yards and the only alterations made thereafter (even in preparation for two recent US Opens) have been the lengthening of the course by some 200 yards by adding new tees. Shinnecock fully utilizes the outstanding features of the area – the strong prevailing winds off the Atlantic to the south-west, the sandy and rolling terrain and the thick, reed-like grasses that border the fairways. While not truly linksland – the grass is of an inland texture – the windy bleakness of Shinnecock Hills on an average day evokes feelings of the British seaside links.

At 6,944 yards Shinnecock Hills has been lengthened to cope with the improvements made in club and ball technology and it remains a course that brings one's long and middle irons out of the bag quite often enough. Virtually all the shorter par-fours play into the wind, and the longer ones with it. The true playing qualities of the course are never more evident than on the parallel closing holes of the front and back nines, both dog-legs with the wind blowing strongly from the right and the long roughs on either side that are bound to cost a stroke or two, if the ball can be found at all. The fairways are undulating, in the Scottish tradition, so the placing of the drive is half the battle. The second shots off a good drive are in each case entirely reasonable, yet the price of a misplay is very high indeed. In fact, that might be said to be the predominant nature of Shinnecock Hills.

Ben Hogan remarked after playing it in the early 1960s: "Each hole is different and requires a great amount of skill to play properly. You know exactly where to shoot and the distance is easy to read. All in all, I think Shinnecock is one of the finest courses I have played." His sentiments were echoed by many when Shinnecock hosted the 1986 US Open, won by Ray Floyd. Lee Trevino, who finished three shots back, said, "I wish all our courses were like this."

It goes without saying that any great course (Augusta may be the only exception) is a strong test of driving. This is conspicuously true of Shinnecock. Whatever one's standard may be, to drive indifferently from either the members' or the back tees is to court unavailing struggle for the remainder of the hole; but drive solidly and the rich rewards of a glorious course are there for the playing. In one sense, although certainly not in setting, Shinnecock is reminiscent of Augusta in that the ability to carry crests on the fairways sets up the approach nicely. Otherwise, it can be most demanding. In this respect holes like the 9th, where it is essential to carry a great mound in the fairway (or the second to an uphill semi-blind green is most taxing), and the 15th come immediately to mind. If the drive from the 15th tee, poised high in a wilderness of scrub, can carry into a valley the next shot to an island target of green is comparatively easy.

But Shinnecock is far from being only a driver's course, as Corey Pavin, one of the game's shortest hitters, so splendidly proved in the centenary US Open in 1995. Pavin's main rival for the title was Greg Norman, who met all the pre-tournament criteria predicting the winner would be someone who drove the ball long and straight. Pavin, however, demonstrated that, ultimately, Shinnecock is a shotmaker's course, as he shaped his strokes around the hazards and never more so than at the 72nd hole where he rapped a four wood up and over the mound at the front of the green, the ball eventually coming to rest no more than 5ft from the hole. Pavin was the only player in the 156-man field to match par over 72 holes; a testament not only to his own shotmaking skills but to a consummate test of golf.

The heavily bunkered, 415-yard 15th is typical of Shinnecock's short but difficult par-fours. The US Open returns to Shinnecock in 2004.

Augusta National is one of the most idyllic of golf courses. It is at its best in the spring, when flowering shrubs are a blaze of colour among the trees that bring seclusion to almost every hole. Few changes have been made to the course since this map was drawn: the bunker on the left of the 3rd is now four traps, the greenside bunkers have been removed on the 8th and a bunker removed at the 11th.

Dream course
in a dream setting

Needing three birdies in the last four holes to tie the Masters, Gene Sarazen sank his 4-wood second at the 15th, then a 520-yard par-five, for a double-eagle. This remarkable shot brought Augusta National and the Masters Tournament instant fame.

It was characteristic of the uncommon grace, the high intelligence and ordinary horse sense which had marked his too-brief career that, when it came time for Bobby Jones to build his dream course, he employed a wisdom far beyond his years by enlisting the aid of a professional architect.

After all, he was certainly well qualified in his own right to build any kind of course he wanted and people would have bowed to it. In eight Olympian years he had won more than 60 per cent of the national championships he had entered, winning thirteen national titles in all. And he had won them on some of the most hallowed fields in golf – St Andrews, Merion, Hoylake, Oakmont, Winged Foot. At the age of twenty-eight, he retired from competition. He played every note there is to play in the symphony of golf, capping it all with a Beethovenian burst by winning the Open and Amateur championships of both the United States and Great Britain in the single triumphant year of 1930. It was a feat so far beyond the imagination of the public that people did not even have a name for it until months after, when a New York newspaperman tagged it the "Grand Slam", picking up the parlance of the day when contract bridge was the great indoor pastime.

Having performed his masterpiece, Jones walked off the stage of competitive golf for ever. He had decided never to play professional golf, and that was that. Naturally, there was a call for an encore by the genius from Georgia, for his audience reached to every continent where grass will grow. Jones refused to leave the wings, but he did leave a legacy. This is the Augusta National Golf Club – easily the most famous American course, quite possibly the best and, for a certain period each year at least, simply the most beautiful golf acreage anywhere in

the world. Jones could not have made the course more universally appealing, and it remains so today as it has since its inception some seventy years ago – and as it undoubtedly will do a century from now. It is one of the few courses anywhere which even the tweediest of professionals will play tight-lipped and then go home and rave about. Despite the force of his personality, his golfing background, his intelligence, Bobby Jones's 365 acres did not come into being in a final, perfected form. The Augusta National as it is now is far different from the course he had visualized and – as Jones would have been the first to admit – it is far better today. The architect he chose and with whom he worked side by side was Alister Mackenzie, a Scottish-born physician who had recently emigrated to America and who abandoned medicine in order to concentrate on his first love – golf.

In Mackenzie, Jones could not have picked a more adept partner for the venture, particularly for the venue he had chosen for the course of his dreams. The site was on rolling hills ablaze with fruit-bearing trees and flowers – the kind of scene any lesser architect might have ruined by building a good golf hole at the sacrifice of its beauty, or else a bad hole in order to maintain it. Mackenzie best showed his self-discipline in this respect at the spectacular Cypress Point in California. So an architect who had an artistic bent for hewing a golf course out of exciting terrain joined forces with a designer who knew more about shot values than anyone in the history of championship golf since the great Harry Vardon.

Like many of America's great courses, Augusta National is not exactly at the centre of things. The city of Augusta is hardly the crossroads of the United States or even of the south-eastern part of it – or, for that matter, of

Georgia. Its history had been that of an ante-bellum resort which Jones, as an Atlantan, often visited. He married an Atlanta beauty named Mary Malone and it was at Augusta that he made the acquaintance of a well-to-do New Yorker, Clifford Roberts, who often wintered there. Soon after his retirement from golf, Jones had expressed to Roberts his desire to found a very private golf club which his many friends throughout the world could join, or just visit to revel in – a course that he himself would design with the master's touch clear down to the roots.

Roberts, who always had a knack for knowing when to buy and sell things, had got wind of a famous nursery in Augusta, named Fruitlands, that was for sale. It had been owned for three-quarters of a century by the family of a Belgian baron, Louis Mathieu Edouard Berckmans, whose son Prosper became a renowned horticulturist. Almost single-handedly, Prosper had popularised the azalea, now so common all over the south-eastern stretches of the United States. The setting was practically perfect for Jones's wishes. It had the gentle hills he wanted for his inland "links", which would capture the spirit – but not imitate the characteristics – of the British seaside courses he loved so much. What with its almost endless flora, the property would be ablaze with the colours of so many flowers that it later became no problem at all to name each hole after a different one – dogwood, redbud, magnolia, and so on. Furthermore, it seemed to have just the right cluster of trees through which Jones would want his fairways to meander. To top it all off, the highest point on the property was dominated by a pre-Civil War mansion that could form the nucleus of a clubhouse. Bobby Jones looked no further.

Bobby Jones, one of the truly great figures of golf, achieved a unique combination of old Southern charm and pure golfing challenge at Augusta National.

The Course Card

Augusta National Golf Club, Augusta, Georgia

Record: 63, Nick Price, 1986

Hole	Name	Yards	Par
1	Tea Olive	435	4
2	Pink Dogwood	575	5
3	Flowering Peach	350	4
4	Flowering Crab Apple	205	3
5	Maglia	435	4
6	Juniper	180	3
7	Pampas	410	4
8	Yellow Jasmine	570	5
9	Carolina Cherry	460	4
10	Camellia	495	4
11	White Dogwood	490	4
12	Golden Bell	155	3
13	Azalea	510	5
14	Chinese Fir	440	4
15	Firethorn	500	5
16	Redbud	170	3
17	Nandina	425	4
18	Holly	465	4
Out		3,620	36
In		3,650	36
Total		**7,270**	**72**

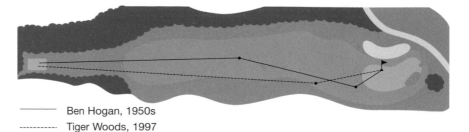

The 11th

Strategy For Winners

———— Ben Hogan, 1950s

----------- Tiger Woods, 1997

No golfer can win the Masters without a carefully planned strategy for every hole. At the 11th Ben Hogan used to say that if he was ever on the green in two it meant he had hooked his second shot; he used to play for the right hand side of the green to avoid any prospect of finishing in the water to the left. By 2001 the likes of Woods and Mickelson were driving so far down the hill that they only needed a sand wedge for the approach shot. For them the 11th held no terror. A significant change made for the 2002 Masters was to re-grade the fairway landing area, levelling the downslope to reduce run on the drive. The tee was also moved back 35 yards, effectively restoring the approach shot to a mid-iron. Many golfers, even Woods in the final round, did not risk attacking the green, so dangerously close to the pond, but reverted instead to Hogan's tactic, hoping for a good chip and single putt.

Amen Corner –
Where Even Golfing Gods Pray

The Masters has been won or lost so often between the 11th and the 13th that this three-hole stretch, menaced by the waters of Rae's Creek, has become known as Amen Corner. The term was first coined by Herbert Warren Wind in a 1958 *Sports Illustrated* article and years later the American professional Dave Marr took up the theme when he quipped: "It's called that because if you get around it in par you believe a little bit more in God." When Byron Nelson won in 1937 and 1942 it was mainly because of his sub-par barrages at Amen Corner, where possibly his most memorable shot was a gently chipped 3-iron for a fifty-foot eagle-three at the 13th in 1937. Five years later he birdied all three holes to defeat Ben Hogan in a play-off. Hogan did the same thing many years later when, at the age of 54, in one of the most emotional moments in golf, he tamed Augusta's back nine in a remarkable thirty shots. In 1954, a little-known amateur, Billy Joe Patton, muffed his chance to beat the great Hogan and Snead when, after making up a five-shot deficit, he hit into the creek at the 13th and wound up with a disastrous seven. Greg Norman, six shots clear of Nick Faldo going into the final round in 1996, three putted the 11th and then pushed an eight iron into Rae's Creek at the 12th to finally torpedo his chances.

Jack Nicklaus sinks his birdie putt on the 71st hole at the 1986 Masters. The look of triumph says it all. Supposedly all washed up, he was about to become, at 46, the oldest winner of a green jacket.

Fruitlands would be his Augusta National. In essence, the course Jones and Mackenzie finished in 1933 – with Jones playing thousands of experimental shots off every potential tee and to every possible green site – is almost the same today. The original front nine is now the back nine; Jones reversed them in 1935 because he thought that the original 9th was a far more demanding finishing hole than the old, shortish 18th, which could not be lengthened without giving the player an unconscionably difficult shot off a downhill lie to an elevated green. One thing Jones wanted Augusta National to have was flexibility, to be a course that would not overpower his 90-shooting members or be a push-over for his par-busting visitors. It remains so to this day.

By and large Augusta National remains as Bobby Jones planned it. He was not afraid to make alterations and the one big change, the construction of a completely new 16th hole, was made during his lifetime. Improvements in club and ball technology meant that by 2001 the longer hitters rarely needed more than a sand wedge to approach the par-fours, so the architect Tom Fazio was brought in to toughen up the course. By adding almost 300 yards to the length and repositioning several tees he achieved the goal simply but very effectively.

So what makes it so great? It is great because Augusta National is a thinking man's golf course, the least obvious championship layout in America, perhaps matched nowhere in the world except by the Old Course at St Andrews. Like all great courses, it must be played mentally from the green back to the tee before a single shot is hit. Since the greens are so fast, three-putting is a very real hazard, no matter where the flagstick is placed. A shot to the green must be finely gauged and truly struck, else it will bounce and roll unimpeded across yards of green, making three-putting a staggering reality. The pin positions traditionally employed throughout Masters week put enormous pressure on the golfer who needs to attack the course. For many years the fairways were generously wide, but Tom Fazio's alterations have tightened many drives especially that on the 18th. Here the tee has been moved back 60 yards, the fairway bunkers enlarged and trees added on the left. Most players are now forced to take a driver to get enough distance to see round the dog-leg and the uphill approach is now made with a mid-iron, not the sand wedge of the past. So stringent has the 18th become that it is now the hardest hole against par with a stroke average of 4.321, making it a worthy championship finisher. Yet Augusta might easily have remained one of the great but rarely tested championship courses in America – such as Quaker

No Place to Gamble

No man is better qualified to assess the problems of Amen Corner than Jack Nicklaus, who has won a record six Masters titles. In his estimation the short 12th, only 155 yards long, is "the most demanding tournament hole in the world". The target is a mere sliver, with bunkers both fore and aft. The problem comes in trying to judge the wind from a sheltered tee. In the final round in 1992 Fred Couples got it wrong. His tee shot pitched into the sharply sloping bank in front of the green and 99 times out of 100 that translates into the ball rolling back into Rae's Creek. But this was the one time that fate put an arm around Couples's shoulder. The ball stopped before the water and Couples was able to make par. A certain five became a three and he won by two shots. Amen indeed.

Strengthening the Defences

Statistically, the 13th is one of the easiest holes on the course and, until recently, measured a mere 485 yards. Strong players could hit far enough round the corner to be left with a straightforward mid-iron to the green. For 2002 the club purchased a plot of land from the adjoining Augusta Country Club which enabled the tee to be moved back some 25 yards. Now the margin for error on the drive is minimal and the approach with a long iron over the creek from a sloping lie is at best daunting, at worst reckless. Els, pursuing Woods in the 2002 Masters, knew he needed an eagle here to get back in the hunt, but his drawn drive turned into a hook, tangling with the trees, he found Rae's Creek twice and his challenge had ended.

---------- short hitter
———— long hitter

Ridge or Prairie Dunes – had it not been for the almost incidental invention of the Masters Tournament.

Soon after the course was finished, Jones decided to hold an informal get-together, a tournament of sorts, with all his amateur and professional friends. He agreed to play himself, but only under the condition that he was participating as host. Even though he had lost his amateur standing, he refused to accept any prize money: that, he said, belonged to the "pros". Despite the fact that for eight years he had handled them on the course like yo-yos, off the course he deeply admired them. And they, in turn, revered him. Bobby Jones was probably the most genuinely loved golfer who ever lived.

This get together would be by invitation only, he decided, and without anyone giving it much thought it was tagged the Augusta National Invitation. The title did not last past the four days it took to play it. Newspapermen almost immediately began calling it the Masters. Among all the reasons behind the evergreen success of the Masters as a golfing saga, none approaches that of its gift for supplying the unexpected. Like all larger-than-life stories, the history of the Masters has always been strong on character. from the improbable sixth triumph of Jack Nicklaus at the age of 46 in 1986 to the stirring first victory for Tiger Woods in his first appearance in a major championship as a professional in 1997. But its greatest strength lies in its plot, in its unique ability to supply each year another chapter of almost unen-

durable suspense, bordering on the impossible and stopping just short of the implausible. Each year it is invariably the most dramatic of the four Major championships; even when a relative journeyman such as Larry Mize triumphs it is in the most incredible circumstances imaginable, holing a 30 yard chip on the 11th in a play-off against Greg Norman that he could not hole again if he had 100 chances.

Since the tournament began in 1934, there remains not a single hole that hasn't been eagled. The course record is 63, set by Nick Price in 1986 and equalled by Greg Norman ten years later. Even Fazio's toughened course of 2002 has seen a round of 65 from Vijay Singh, but there have also been some horrendous scores. Indeed Singh went on to record a quadruple-bogey nine on the 15th in the last round, but it was as nothing compared with the thirteen run up by Tommy Nakajima at the 13th in 1978 and equalled by Tom Weiskopf at the 12th in 1980 when he put five balls in the water. No one has yet played four rounds at Augusta under 70, not even Woods in his record breaking year of 1997, although several players have managed three.

In 1935 Craig Wood was in the clubhouse, the apparent winner. Out on the par-five 15th Gene Sarazen gambled on carrying across the water which fronts the green. He knew he needed three birdies to catch Wood and he hadn't much to lose. He chose a 4-wood for the 220-yard shot he had left, caught the ball flush and watched it soar over the

Top: Most people know only the Augusta of the Masters, with its vast crowds. Then the 12th green, so peaceful in this view, becomes the focus of world attention as the heart of Amen Corner, the scene of so much drama.

The 16th
Lovely but Lethal

In Mackenzie's original design the key to the 16th hole – then 150 yards, now 170 – was a tall pine at the edge of a narrow creek. The green lay directly to the left of it and had two steeply terraced levels. It was approached from two different tees, one to the left and one to the right of the 15th green. In 1947 the hole was completely redesigned by Robert Trent Jones. He kept the tee on the left but, along with the original green, abandoned the other. He then turned the innocuous creek into a lake that runs virtually the entire length of the hole, thus forming a classic hazard. A new green, to the right of the pine and about twenty-five yards beyond the original, was constructed.

Trent Jones made the green kidney shaped, the length of it facing the player. To the right front he placed a smallish bunker, a large one along the right side, and a strip trap back on the left. The green has no distinct terrace, but it slopes sharply from right to left and from front to back, the lowest points being the left front and left rear. As a final bit of dash, he placed two grassy mounds directly behind the green.

"All these revisions", says Trent Jones, "give the

tee-markers set forward of the more usual position, since the hole was playing into the teeth of the near-gale. At the instant Middlecoff struck the ball, the wind died. His ball was a hundred feet in the air when it reached the green, carried clear over the gallery standing behind it and sailed off the confines of the golf course.

The lovely 16th hole, set in a verdant glen epitomises the elegant tranquillity of Augusta. The tee is set back in the shadows of tall pines and in April, at the time of the Masters, pink azaleas bloom amongst the trees and-sunlight sparkles on the long lake. Finding the green from the tee is no guarantee of a par. Three putts here sealed Ben Hogan's fate when he went down to Sam Snead In the 1954 play-off.

water. To the astonishment of Walter Hagen, his playing partner, and Bobby Jones, who had wandered down from the clubhouse to see what was going on, the ball rolled slowly on to the putting surface and trickled into the hole for what is known in America as a double-eagle. In one shot he had caught Wood, and he won the play-off the next day. It remains one of the most famous golf shots of all time. It is difficult to name a hole at Augusta on which something spectacular hasn't happened. Take the 435-yard 1st hole, a slight dog-leg to the right. (There are eleven dog-legs at Augusta National, but only the first and the last bend to the right.) In 1968, after a booming tee shot, Roberto de Vicenzo holed a 9-iron for an eagle to catch the lead – which he later tragically lost by signing an incorrect scorecard.

In 1966 Jack Nicklaus engaged in a play-off with Tommy Jacobs and Gay Brewer. On the 2nd hole a curving downhill par-five, neither Jacobs nor Brewer could reach the green with their drivers and their best fairway woods. Nicklaus hit a 3-wood off the tee to give himself a level lie. Then, again using his 3-wood, he hit the flagstick on the fly! He won the play-off handily for his third Masters. The second shot to the par four third can be a devil if the pin is back on the left. It helps, however, if your name is Tiger Woods and you drive the ball to the brink of the putting surface.

During one particularly windy tournament, Cary Middlecoff elected to use a driver on the par-three 4th, the

The 5th hole – a 435 yard par-four, with an uphill second shot – has a two-level green which is lightning fast. Sam Snead once left himself on the lower level fifty-five feet from the flagstick, which was on the upper level. His approach putt just barely made the crest of the upper level, turned left, and then rolled down the crest leaving him sixty-five feet away from the hole. He then proceeded to sink that one!

In 1991 Jose-Maria Olazabal finished one shot off Ian Woosnam's winning score and while the immediate temptation was to critically analyse his bogey at the last, what about the quadruple bogey seven he had run up at the par-three sixth, the highest score ever recorded on that hole? And so it goes through the gorgeous 10th – 495 yards, par-four – where Severiano Ballesteros once cried his way back up the hill after falling out of the 1987 play-off with Norman and Mize at the first extra hole Then there is Amen Corner – the deviously treacherous 11th, 12th and 13th holes. And finally the exciting finishing holes where all sorts of drama has taken place. Art Wall won in 1959 by making birdies on six of the last seven holes. On the 18th, in 1961, Arnold Palmer needed a par for his second successive title and a bogey to play-off against Gary Player. As he was walking up the hill to play his approach a member of his gallery cried out and Palmer walked over. "Congratulations on winning the title again," came the hole more definition. It now has a more receptive landing area for the shots required to carry the water." He might have added that his revisions gave the 16th infinitely more beauty, the spectators a million new thrills, and some of the contestants cause for a heart attack.

Yet the 16th is symptomatic of Augusta, a perfect example of a hole that can be relatively straightforward or terrifying depending simply on where the greenkeeper happens to have placed the flag that day. Even though the experienced competitors who return year after year know where the pins will be placed they still struggle for an answer to at least two of the options. Easily the most difficult is the one perched almost on the fringe of the green in the back right quarter. It is possible to be 8ft beyond the flag here and, if too aggressive, be putting for par from 35ft away, as Tom Watson was in 1996. Watson, incidentally, went on to five putt. It will come as no surprise to learn that this is often the pin position for the final round, although another is back left, tucked behind the bunker. Although it sounds perilous, it is the easier of the back pin positions, since the green's natural contours will shape a well-struck tee shot towards the target. The easiest pin position of all is the one to the front and right, and usually offers up a number of birdies.

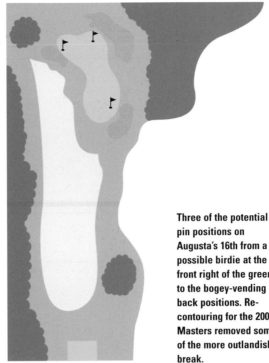

Three of the potential pin positions on Augusta's 16th from a possible birdie at the front right of the green to the bogey-vending back positions. Re-contouring for the 2000 Masters removed some of the more outlandish break.

words of wisdom. "Thank-you," said Palmer. Moments later he hit his second shot into a bunker, took two to get out and lost by a shot to the South African.

Doug Ford won in 1957 by holing out of a bunker at the last, a stroke that was equalled for drama and quality by Sandy Lyle in 1988 when he plucked a fairway sand shot with a seven iron to 10ft from the flag and holed the putt to defeat Mark Calcavecchia by one.

In 1956 Jack Burke won over Ken Venturi by picking up a clear nine strokes in the last round. In 1997 Tiger Woods had nine shots to spare coming into the final day. It led some to believe that perhaps the course had become too easy, but Woods's effort fitted effortlessly into the philosophy espoused by Bobby Jones, who once declared: "I have always said that this can be a very easy course or a very tough one. There isn't a hole out there that can't be birdied if you just think. But there isn't one that can't be double-bogeyed if you stop thinking. A lot of the difference has to do with the weather."

Proof of this had been established in 1965 and 1966, when Nicklaus first shot the tournament record of 271 (which stood until Woods broke it in 1997), winning by nine strokes from Palmer in near-perfect weather. The following year he ballooned to 288, even par, under less than ideal conditions. He still won. That 1966 victory made Nicklaus the first player to win back-to-back Masters. Nick Faldo achieved the same distinction in 1989 and 1990 and by winning in 2001 and 2002 Tiger Woods has now joined this elite band. At the end of the third day Fazio's revamped course had produced a leader board of the highest quality. On Sunday, yet again, Augusta identified the best player amongst them, technically, physically and mentally.

Tiger Woods, right, on the final green at the 1997 Masters. He had not only become the youngest winner of the event but had achieved it by a record 12 stroke margin.

The terrain of Cypress Point on the Monterey Peninsula varies in the most exciting way. The 8th and 9th are typically inland in character; the 5th, 6th, 7th and 10th are of the wooded hillside type; the 1st, 12th, 13th, 14th and 18th are seaside holes; and the 15th, 16th and 17th are grand examples of the spectacular oceanside, clifftop hole.

The Course Card

Cypress Point Club, Pebble Beach, California

Hole	Yards	Par
1	421	4
2	548	5
3	162	3
4	384	4
5	493	5
6	518	5
7	168	3
8	363	4
9	292	4
10	480	5
11	437	4
12	404	4
13	365	4
14	388	4
15	143	3
16	219	3
17	393	4
18	346	4
Out	3,349	37
In	3,175	35
Total	**6,524**	**72**

The best
seventeen-hole course in the world

Cypress Point, it has often been claimed, is perhaps the loveliest golf course ever built. If anything, that is an understatement. Cypress Point is not just lovely; it is dazzling. Situated on the palisades of the Pacific at the tip of the Monterey Peninsula, it is 100 miles or so south of San Francisco and barely a mile from its more famous neighbour, Pebble Beach. "Pebble", Julius Boros once claimed, "has six great holes – all those that lie on the coastline. Cypress has eighteen of them, whether they lie on the coast or not."

For a championship course, and nobody would deny that it is, Cypress Point has several anachronisms. For one thing it has never staged a Major championship, indeed it does not hold any event of national prominence at all these days, since it backed down from hosting the US Tour event, the AT&T pro-am. For another, it has two par-threes and two par-fives back to back, an architectural anomaly it shares with Ballybunion. To top everything off, the course is only 6,536 yards long, the length you would expect of a public links. Cypress Point, however, is anything but: its clubhouse, one of the most conservative in America, is barred to all but its small number of members, even during tournaments.

One thing the great architects have all understood is the dictum best expressed by "Nipper" Campbell, the pioneering Scottish architect who helped establish golf in America: "The best golf course is built into the landscape you've got." Consider, then, the landscape Alister Mackenzie, Cypress Point's architect, got when given the job by the promoter, Marion Hollins, the 1921 Women's Amateur Champion.

Cypress Point sits at the foothills of the Santa Lucia mountains where, when the tide is out, the land drops sixty feet or more straight down into the Pacific. When the seas are high they batter the edge of the course with the immense waves and awesome roar you would expect to see or hear only in the North Atlantic. Just offshore, sealions bask in the sun atop gigantic rocks. The ocean is dotted with fishing smacks plying between the nearby fishing grounds and the canneries of Monterey. And the course itself is set within the Del Monte Forest, 5,200 acres of private land developed by the late Samuel Morse into one of the world's most stunning seaside resorts – complete with deer that roam freely across the course.

The turf at Cypress Point is rather special – springy and sparkling. In the dusk or in the light of dawn, when the deer

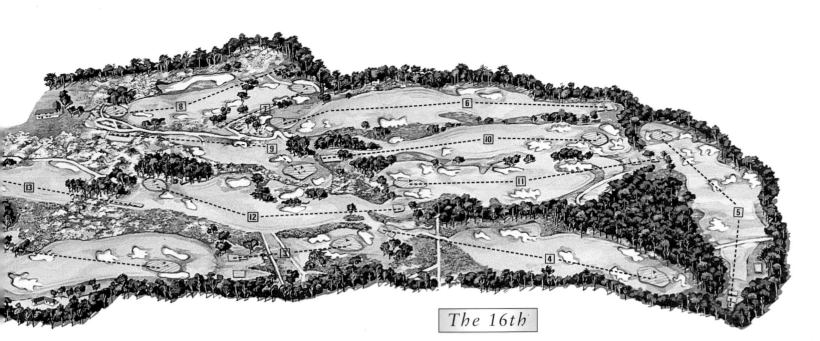

come out of the woods to romp upon the fairways, the dew gives the grass an emerald brilliance that contrasts vividly with the chalky sand of the dunes and bunkers. Bordering the fairways and many of the greens are Monterey cypress, bewilderingly picturesque trees. To O. B. Keeler, the Atlanta newspaperman who was Bobby Jones's Boswell, they were "the crystallisation of the dream of an artist who had been drinking gin and sobering up on absinthe". The real wonder of Cypress Point is how anybody can keep his mind on golf.

Given the spectacular site, Dr Mackenzie's design at Cypress Point was a monumental work of conservatism. There are a hundred places where he might have sacrificed the principles of sound golf course architecture to show off the natural beauties of the property – to make a hole badly in order to make it look good. The miracle is that not once did he succumb to such a temptation, although it usually takes several rounds to realise that you are playing a traditional, marvellously strategic course as well as a thrilling one, and not just moving within a playground of the gods.

The 1st hole at Cypress Point starts from atop a hill and drops into a valley with a turn to the right that cannot truly be called a dog-leg; you can see the green quite easily from the tee. The hole goes inland, so there is no sight of the sea. Just a glimpse of it comes into view on the magnificent 2nd – a par-five that is 548 yards long – and over the next three holes. From there on, the course winds its way through eight holes of sandy dunes and sylvan glades and past Fanshell Beach until, at the 15th, it reaches the point from which it derives its name. Now the golfer faces the first of the back-to-back par-threes. It is a mere niblick shot across the booming surf of a deep rocky inlet; a lovelier 9-iron has never been called upon. Then comes the 16th, 219 yards long from the championship tee. The carry is again across the water, but this time it holds real menace and a large bunker may temper the pleasure of those relieved at just making it across.

The 17th is the hole most admired by the professionals. It measures a mere 393 yards. The drive from the elevated tee high above the steep cliffs behind the 16th green carries across the Pacific to a wide fairway. This is only the beginning. The second shot must bypass a strategic pine to the right front of the green, not in itself the least tricky but backed and flanked by massive bunkers and a tangle of cypresses.

If there is a weak hole at Cypress Point it is the 18th, which should be the strongest hole on any golf course. It is a par-four dog-leg going right and uphill to a green where it is hard to know where the flagstick is, leaving grave doubts as to what kind of putt must be faced. However, a long iron off the tee will still leave only a nine iron. Over this hole alone Jimmy Demaret takes issue with Julius Boros's assessment of Cypress Point. In Demaret's view, "Cypress Point is the best seventeen-hole course in the world".

The 16th

The Ultimate in Water Hazards

The 16th at Cypress Point is quite possibly the most beautiful golf hole in the world. Both tee and green are perched above the ocean and the roar of the surf drowns all other sounds. The green is lush and circled by sprawling traps of white sand and beyond to the horizon, is the blue Pacific.

Officially, the 16th has a par of three. But everybody who has ever made a par feels he has made a birdie. It should be a par-four, it can be a par-eight. In the 70 years since it was designed, only a few holes in one have been made on it. Amazingly one of them was by Bing Crosby, a long-time member and mentor of the National Pro-Amateur, that used to be played annually over Cypress Point and neighbouring Pebble Beach and Spyglass Hill (the tournament is now sponsored by AT&T and Cypress, of its own volition, has been replaced by Poppy Hills).

This hole stretches 219 yards from the blue tee. Every inch of that distance is complete carry. Fall short means disaster. The dangers of the hole are obvious and members and even some of the professionals use the alternative route to the left settling for a drive and a pitch for a bogey-four. In this way they avoid the possibility of picking up. Against the wind – and it usually is – the hole calls for a full driver. Even with the wind, only hitters with the power of a professional would use an iron. To compound the problems of this devilish hole, going over the green can present worse trouble – more rocks, or the ultimate in water hazards, the swift tides of the Pacific.

For the powerful player the 16th green is an elusive target found only after a full carry over the ocean. However, there is a bale-out area to allow the less muscular golfer to play it as a bogey-4.

The toughest
golf course in the world?

Oakmont is torn in two by highway and railroad and scarred by nearly 200 bunkers. It can be a cruelly punishing course, boasting as it does such fearsome hazards as the mammoth Church Pews bunker separating the vast 3rd and 4th fairways. For those who succeed off the tee, torment and anguish can be found on the lightning-fast greens. The strength of any golfer will be sapped by the 12th, a huge par-five of 602 yards which ends in a typically treacherous green.

The Pennsylvania Turnpike is America's oldest super-highway. It wends its way westwards from Philadelphia, connecting the heavily industrialised eastern coast with Pittsburgh, the coal and steel capital of the nation. It bends across the northern section of the city and through the suburb of Oakmont, a lovely stretch of flatlands that lies at the foothills of the Alleghenies.

When the turnpike was being constructed it had to go directly across a dream of a golf course that had been fathered by a steel magnate, Henry C. Fownes, in 1904. Luckily for Fownes and the rest of the golfing world the course had already been sliced in two by a railroad whose tracks formed a gorge. The Pennsylvania Turnpike was also laid through the gorge, leaving the Oakmont Country Club course practically intact. Bobby Jones, Tommy Armour, Sam Parks, Ben Hogan, Jack Nicklaus, Johnny Miller, and Larry Nelson might have given their heartfelt

thanks, for it was there that all seven wrote some of the finest chapters in America's golf history. But perhaps no professional expressed more gratitude than Arnold Palmer, who was brought up in the same state at Latrobe and who has been a member at Oakmont for nigh on half a century. The courses's eminence was further recognized in 1987 when designated a National Historic Landmark.

Oakmont might well be the toughest golf course in the world, barring the weather as a factor. It is a course that will humble a golfer like no other, even on a lazy day in May. Bobby Jones played there in the 1927 US Open and never broke 76. That year Armour won over 898 entries, without even breaking par. In 1935 Sam Parks – who knew every blade of grass on the course was the only player to break 300 on the way to his surprising US Open victory. Hogan won the US Open there in 1953 with ridiculous ease by breaking par – by one stroke. Nine years later, Nicklaus tied Arnold Palmer with an identical score – 283 – and then won the play-off simply by matching the scorecard.

In contrast Johnny Miller won the Open at Oakmont in 1973 by playing the last round in 63. It has been said

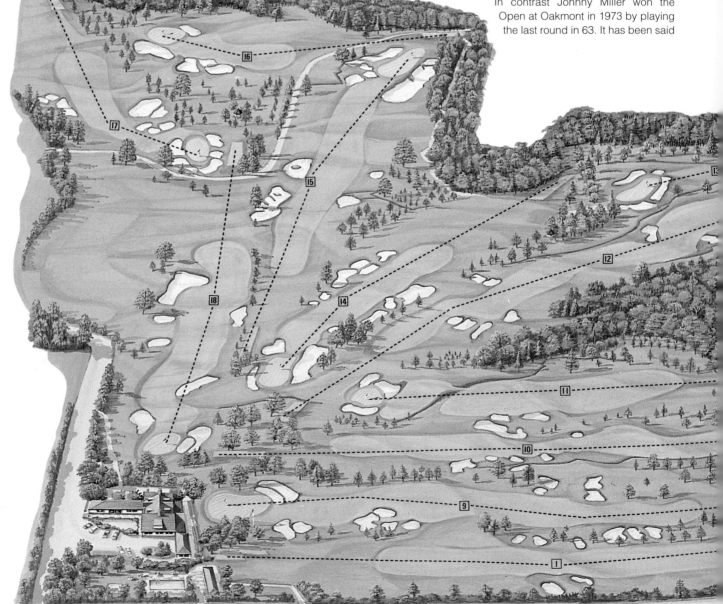

that it was the finest round of golf ever played. A decade later, Nelson won with 280, rallying from four strokes back. Even in the 90s, a decade where architecture has strayed towards the machismo, the course retains its reputation. On the eve of the 1994 US Open Nick Faldo declared it the toughest course he had seen. The event was won by Ernie Els after a play-off that went to 20 holes. After recording totals of 279, five under par, Els, Loren Roberts and Colin Montgomerie went out the next day for a scheduled 18 holes. Montgomerie ballooned to a 78 and even Els and Roberts could do no better than 74, three over par. Els eventually prevailed with a par at the second extra hole.

What makes Oakmont so tough? To begin with, it once had 220 bunkers (it now has some thirty fewer, five times more than Augusta National). Each was raked in furrows two inches deep and two inches apart, a process carried out with a rake specially designed by Henry Fownes. "You could have combed North Africa with it," the 1950s golfing wit Jimmy Demaret used to say, "and Rommel wouldn't have got past Casablanca."

Then there are the greens, originally rolled with barrels of sand weighing a quarter of a ton each. After that was done, they were cut to a sixteenth of an inch and an area within six feet of the cup to one thirty-second of an inch. They were not watered in any way, by sprinklers or otherwise, during the early years. In 1935 Jimmy Thomson drove, on the fly, the par-four 17th. Thomson was then justifiably known as America's longest hitter, though not as one of its best putters. Tied with Sam Parks at that point, he proceeded to four-putt the green. Thomson recalls, "I could have six-putted. When the ball got to two feet from the hole, I thought I had an eagle.

The famous Church Pews bunker, which will catch any hooked drive at the 3rd and 4th holes, has come to epitomise the terrors of Oakmont. The tapering trap, almost 40 yards wide at its broadest point, takes its name from the seven grassy ridges that run across its 60-yard length.

Then it took off again. I had to hole a three-footer for my bogey. On the 5th green I had spotted my ball with a dime so Parks could putt out. When I got back to the ball, the dime was gone. It had slid off the green!"

Under championship play no other course has bigger greens or narrower fairways than Oakmont. "I only had six three putts in nine holes," Tom Watson said ruefully during practice for the 1994 US Open. "If this course were a woman it would never say 'I do.'"

The Course Card

Oakmont
Country Club,
Oakmont,
Pennsylvania

Record: 63, Johnny
Miller, US Open 1973

Hole	Yards	Par
1	467	4
2	346	4
3	425	4
4	564	5
5	382	4
6	199	3
7	435	4
8	253	3
9	478	5
10	462	4
11	382	4
12	602	5
13	185	3
14	360	4
15	471	4
16	232	3
17	319	4
18	456	4
Out	3,549	36
In	3,469	35
Total	**7,018**	**71**

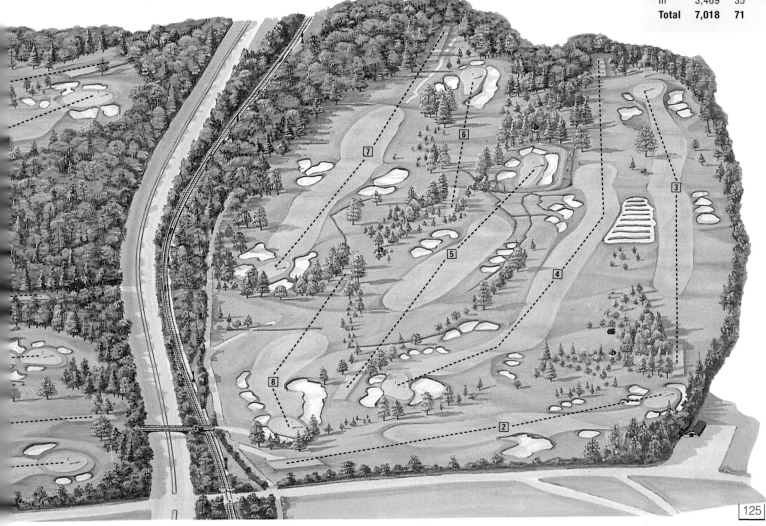

Above: The 16th green. Here in the 1952 US Open Hogan played a memorable 4-wood to the very centre, 25 feet from the pin, which was placed on the extreme right. For the 1973 Open a bunker was added to the front right-hand corner and this has made the flighting of a high fade over the left corner even more crucial than it was for Hogan.

Above: At 382 yards the 5th is, for Oakmont, a relatively short par-four. The three fairway traps, positioned to catch the hooked drive, are matched by a series of four on the right side. But, like the ditches running diagonally across the front of the green, they should not present too much of a problem. The real difficulty in this hole is in mastering the heavily trapped and severely undulating green. In the final of the 1951 PGA championship Sam Snead managed to circumvent any putting problems by sinking his wedge shot from the hillside rough above the green. His birdie-three gave him the hole and helped him defeat Walter Burkemo.

All that has been said about Oakmont might seem as though it were some sort of tricked-up golf course. The opposite is true. Oakmont has character, the quality that separates the men from the boys, the players from the ball-hitters. A player can have the time of his life – or hours of torture. The par-five 9th is so short that a professional can easily reach the green in two shots. The problem is that he might have a putt more than one hundred feet long. The 9th green is not the biggest in the world but it comes mighty close. In 1919 Bobby Jones, then a lad of 17, lost to an Oakmont member named Davey Herron by the lopsided margin of 5 and 4. Six years later he returned for the US Amateur and won his matches 11 and 10, 6 and 5, 7 and 6, and in the final, 8 up. All this was done with hickory shafts, iron heads that were drop-forged, a driver that had a hole in the centre of the sweet spot, and a putter – later to become famous as "Calamity Jane" – that looked like a toy. Now, as the years have passed, the tools of golf have improved immeasurably. Had Jones played out the last four holes of the 1925 Amateur final against a better match, he would probably have gone round Oakmont in 66, hickory clubs and all. It was a performance to be surpassed only by Johnny Miller's in 1973.

Palmer's Paradise

It all began for Arnold Palmer at Oakmont in 1953 and, as far as the US Open was concerned, it ended there as well in 1994. The local member had come home to hang up his spikes. It was one of the most emotional occasions that golf has seen. The fact he missed the cut mattered not; his was still the biggest gallery by miles and when he walked up the 18th that Friday afternoon half of Pennsylvania appeared to have turned up to watch. Palmer first played at Oakmont when he was just 12 years old. "I came with a member called Harry Saxman and it was one of the great thrills of my life," he recalled. "I thought the locker room was just the most elegant thing I had ever seen. The wooden lockers are the same as they are today." In his press conference that day 52 years on, Palmer was asked one question but for a long while did not answer, his face buried in a white towel. Eventually he composed his thoughts sufficiently to speak in sentences fractured by a catch in his voice. He said: "I have not won all that much… I have won a few Majors I suppose… the most important thing is the fact that it has been as good as it has to me… " The silence in the room was complete as Palmer tried to come to terms with his feelings, to speak further. Eventually he gave up and wizened old hacks who thought they had seen everything stood as one and applauded him as he made his gentle farewell through a small gap at the back of the tent.

Oakmont's Finish Fails to Humble Hogan

All great courses have great finishing holes. Sometimes it may only be the last, sometimes the last two. Oakmont has four and they are positively heroic, The 15th – a par-four – is a back breaking 471 yards. There are two key bunkers, the first lying to the right of the landing area to catch the errant drive, the other guarding the left side of the green. The par-three 16th is 232 yards, which is just about as long as a par-three can be without becoming ridiculous. The 17th is a short par-four of 319 yards – but every inch of it goes uphill and bunkers are everywhere, the key one guarding the right front of the green. The 18th is a 456-yard par-four. The tee is elevated, but the second shot plays uphill. How these four holes play is best illustrated by the way they were tackled by Ben Hogan in 1953, the year he won the Masters, the Open at Carnoustie, and the United States Open at Oakmont. Hogan's closing round 71 gave him a winning margin of six strokes.

During the last round Hogan came to Oakmont's 15th tee with a slender lead over Sam Snead, playing a few holes behind him. Hogan, who often played an intentional fade to offset an earlier tendency to hook, this time let his fade get away from him. The ball bounded into that key fairway bunker. He had to choose between pitching out sideways into the fairway, or going backwards into the rough, which was not a very exciting prospect. He shook his head, plucked out his wedge, and then almost nonchalantly played a light sandshot on to the fairway. He then hit a soaring long iron twenty feet from the flag, and holed the putt.

On the 16th he elected to use his 4-wood. He wanted height on the shot so the ball would drop, which it did – about 25 feet to the left of the flagstick. Two putts. The 17th in those days was 30 yards shorter than it is now. Hogan slashed a drive that landed a few yards short of the green and bounded on, leaving him about 35 feet away. Two more putts, this time for a birdie three. At the 18th he hit a towering drive that left him with only a 6-iron to the flagstick, which was situated towards the rear of the putting surface. Hogan struck the shot six feet to the right of the hole. The championship was over, because in the meantime Snead had faltered badly and, as it turned out, Hogan could have taken five putts and still won. He took one, for his third straight three.

Above: Curtis Strange said of Ernie Els after partnering him in the early rounds of the 1994 US Open: "I've just played with the next golfing god." They were to prove prophetic words. Above, Els is on the 72nd hole after securing his place in the following day's play-off against Loren Roberts and Colin Montgomerie. It was one he would win to collect his first major championship at the age of 24.

The 15th to the 18th

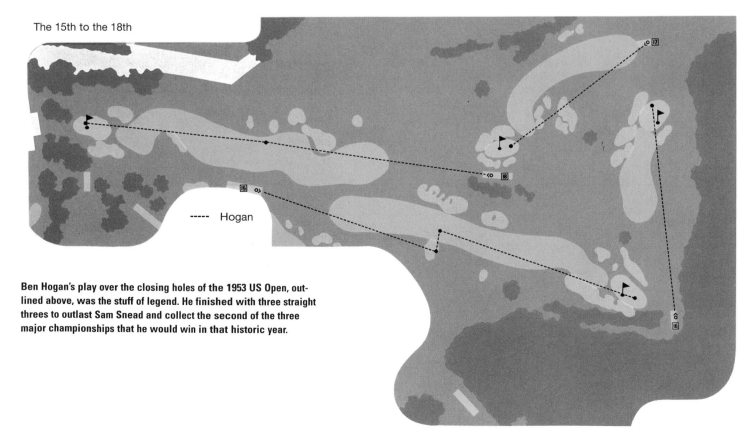

----- Hogan

Ben Hogan's play over the closing holes of the 1953 US Open, outlined above, was the stuff of legend. He finished with three straight threes to outlast Sam Snead and collect the second of the three major championships that he would win in that historic year.

The reluctant legacy of

Mr Baltus Roll

The Course Card

Baltusrol Golf Club, Springfield, New Jersey

Record: 63, Jack Nicklaus and Tom Weiskopf US Open 1980

Hole	Yards	Par
1	478	4
2	381	4
3	466	4
4	194	3
5	413	4
6	480	4
7	494	4
8	384	4
9	205	3
10	454	4
11	416	4
12	218	3
13	423	4
14	428	4
15	430	4
16	233	3
17	630	5
18	542	5
Out	3,495	34
In	3,774	36
Total	**7,269**	**70**

The curious distinction of having won a major championship – the US Open – by playing two different courses in his winning round belongs to Ed Furgol, a consistent if until then not markedly successful competitor on the American circuit. Furgol's never-to-be-forgotten year was 1954, the course – or courses – Baltusrol, located just 40 minutes south of New York City in New Jersey. Named oddly after a local farmer, one Baltus Roll, whose life was brought to an untimely end by a murderer in 1831, Baltusrol has two courses, the Upper and Lower. The Lower course was chosen for the 1954 championship and for, the most part, was used by Furgol.

At the end of the third round Furgol was four under par, leading Dick Mayer by a stroke. Not far behind were Lloyd Mangrum and Gene Littler, at that time the boy wonder of the American circuit. Baltusrol is an architectural oddity in that the last two holes are both par-fives. The 17th is a 630-yard monstrosity that is half sand – a lot of which is left unraked – and with a green as high as a house. The 18th is much shorter – 542 yards – with a downhill tee shot that can be hit so far that reaching the green in two is foremost in the mind of any professional player as he stands on the tee.

Playing in front of Furgol, Mayer hit himself out of the championship with a wild push to the right into some Jersey jungle to finish with a horrendous eight. Furgol, in his turn, hit a darting hook off the tee into the woods which line the fairway to the bottom of the hill where he had hoped to land. He had a nasty lie with no possible access back to the fairway. Looking to his left, he found an opening, no bigger than a doorway, to a patch of fairway on the Upper course. He

called for an official, and asked if he could play to it. Baffled, the official called another official, who in turn called for another. Finally, they decided that, since the fairway of the Upper course had not been staked off as out-of-bounds, Furgol could play there if he wished. He took his 8-iron, punched the ball through the doorway, used the same club to leave the ball short, chipped to 6 feet and made the putt.

Golf first came to Baltusrol when the land once owned by the ill-fated Baltus Roll eventually found its way into the hands of a New York socialite, Louis Keller, the owner and publisher of the *New York Social Register*. He had been one of the first enthusiastic golfers when the game hit America in the 1890s, playing it in Newport and Southampton, where the rich spent their summers. In the early nineties he laid out a nine-hole course of his own and formed a club of friends that was soon 200-strong. Keller then added on another nine holes and gained 200 more members. For a professional he hired a transplanted Scotsman, Willie Anderson, the first man to win four US Opens (a record since matched only by Bobby Jones and Ben Hogan).

The courses today bear no resemblance to the original. They were both laid out by the ubiquitous A. W. Tillinghast during the Roaring Twenties, when everybody was getting rich and when Bobby Jones and Walter Hagen were converting golfers out of fast-talking opportunists who didn't know the difference between a bunker and a brassie. The Lower course has a great deal of variety, playing to what would seem a monotonously long 7,269 yards and a par of just 70 for the US Open, 72 for members. The 1st hole is a very short par-five, only 470 yards (for the Open it

Fifteen national championships have been staged at Baltusrol where every hole presents a unique challenge. For championship play on the Lower course, the par-five 1st and 7th are played as long par-fours, leaving only two par-fives, both at the finish. The shorter holes offer no refuge; the difficult 4th is well protected by water and at the 12th the tee shot is aimed towards a semi-blind green sheltering behind an expanse of sand.

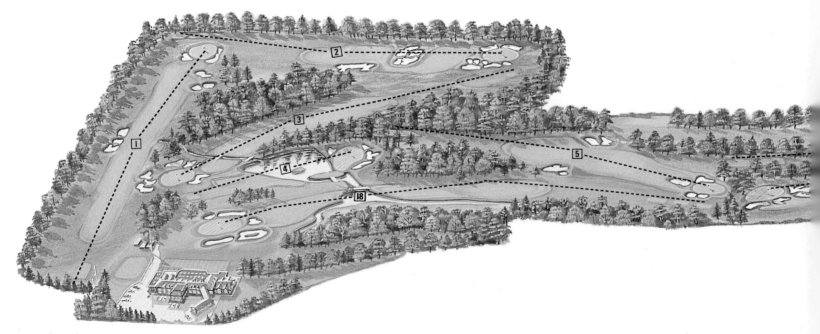

is played as a par four). It is followed by a slightly uphill par-four 381 yards long and out-of-bounds guards the left of both holes. Now there is another fairly sharp right turn to face a longer par-four of 466 yards, downhill off the tee.

Then all hell breaks loose. The 4th is 194 yards long, every inch over water, to one of the most diabolical greens

The 630-yard 17th, the longest par-five in the history of the US Open. The drive has to be threaded between two towering banks of trees; should a player find trouble off the tee he may not be able to carry the Sahara Desert, which splits the fairway at the 375-yard mark.

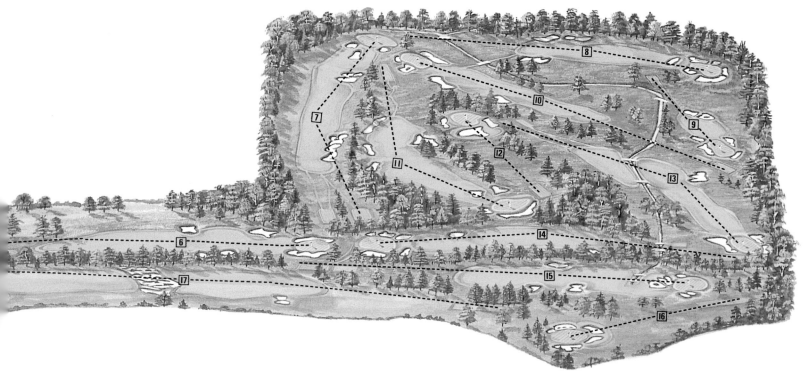

ever made. The 5th is a relatively short par-four, but requires a very exacting drive. Then comes a long par-four followed by a short par-five (both played in the Open as monstrously long par-fours, 480 and 494 yards respectively), a short par-four and a long par-three.

The course varies as much on the back nine as on the front nine: a teasingly short hole here, an agonisingly long one there. The cloth of the course has been so cut that it seems to have no pattern at all, which may account for a golfer wanting to come back again and again. Like the whole course itself, the bunkers have the variety of shapes and sizes, flatness and depth that can put a frown on a brow or a smile on a face. Tillinghast did some of his finest bunkering at Baltusrol. There are not too many and each one seems always to be in just the right place.

The contours of his greens were masterpieces of restraint. There are no steep terraces to drive a putt up to or, on the other hand, feather a putt down from. There are no ninety-foot putts across half an acre of putting surface and no six-footers with three feet of break. To be sure, a player has to borrow something here and something there, for the greens are not just eighteen pancakes. But they are, in a word, subtle.

In keeping with the greens and bunkers, Tillinghast's fairways are just as decorous. They do not bend in those ridiculous right-angled dog-legs to which contemporary architects are so prone, thus creating more home sites for the real estate developers who underwrite them. There are no downhill lies where the right foot is as high as the left knee. Nor are there sidehill lies where the ball seems to be up to the waist, or a yard below the feet. Tillinghast's fairways just roll along, like miniature Mississippis, with just a slight bend every now and then. Baltusrol, in the final analysis, is simply aristocratic.

Nicklaus's Finest Moment

It seems ridiculous with hindsight but when the US Open returned to Baltusrol in 1980 Jack Nicklaus was not so much considered an outsider but written off altogether. He was 39 and the previous year had been his first without a victory since he began his professional career. "Forget Nicklaus," opined one newspaperman, who better remain nameless. To say that Nicklaus was a Golden Bear with a sore paw when he read these press cuttings is not putting too fine a point on it. He was also returning to the course where he won the 1967 US Open, when he smashed Ben Hogan's 19-year-old record 72 hole total. Then he had been imperious but still unloved, the thuggish usurper to Arnold Palmer's matinee idol. In 1980 it was a completely different matter. In the first round he matched Tom Weiskopf's new course record of 63; and that despite not birdying either of the last two par fives. The final round was an emotional cliffhanger with Isao Aoki trying to become the first Japanese to win a Major. The 17th was the crucial hole. Aoki, two adrift, was certain of a birdie; Nicklaus, 20ft away in three was not, and desperately did not want to go down the last clinging to a one stroke lead.

Consequently, he took an age over that 20ft birdie putt but, as so often during his illustrious career when it really mattered, he found a way of willing it into the hole. The 18th duly became a lap of honour as the New Yorkers saluted the man they had derided 13 years earlier. Years later, Nicklaus would declare it his finest moment, unlike the aforementioned newspaperman.

Right: The 4th hole at Baltusrol was redesigned for the 1954 US Open by Robert Trent Jones and is now considered one of the finest on the course.

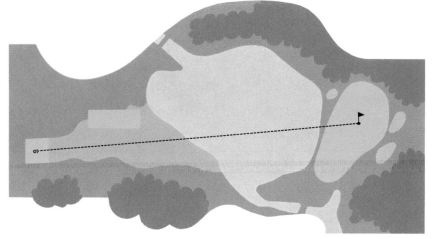

The 4th

An Heroic Hole Made by an Ace

When golfers start choosing the greatest holes they have ever played, their minds invariably turn to par-threes and, in America, almost inevitably to the 4th at Baltusrol. It is not a strategic hole in the sense that there are a dozen different ways to play it. It is more along heroic lines, meaning that it takes one good shot to get anywhere near the flagstick and then the courage to try to do it. It also means that if a player does not bring the shot off, he just has to grit his teeth and reload.

The 4th at Baltusrol is simply a water hole, water hazards being almost a trademark of American courses for a variety of reasons, not the least of which is that they feed the sprinkler systems when Artesian wells cannot be found or when piped water is simply too expensive. The shot to the green can be anywhere from 150 yards to almost 200, depending upon where the tee markers are set. It must be all carry, because the entire front edge of the putting surface is faced with a stone wall. The green itself is about four times wider than it is deep. It slopes down from left to right and from back to front. To the left, guarding the high side, is a fair-sized bunker guarding the entire rear are three other bunkers side by side. Thus if you over-club you end up in one of those, thereby facing a delicate sand shot to that down slope which might well take you back into the very water you were trying to avoid.

The hole was redesigned over Tillinghast's original by Robert Trent Jones for the 1954 US Open. When Jones got through with the job, the members protested that it was too tough. Jones disagreed. He offered to pay for any necessary changes out of his own pocket and to settle the issue he, Johnny Farrell, the club's famous pro, the club president and the chairman of the Open Committee went to play the 4th. Jones stood by while each of the others played their shots. Now it was his turn. He struck a lovely shot that hit short of the flagstick, bit the green, and gently rolled into the cup for a hole-in-one. Jones shrugged. "As you can see, gentlemen," he said, "this hole is eminently fair."

The 4th, a 194-yard par three is a daunting prospect for the amateur golfer: the water awaits the less powerful, the bunkers the overambitious, and trees and more water await any slice or hook. The shot must be from tee to green with no detours. In the background is the clubhouse which has admirably lived up to the aims of its founders who, in Article II of their original constitution, declared: "The object of this club shall be the playing, cultivation and advancement of the royal and ancient game of golf."

The definite article

despite its extra hole

W. C. Fownes Jr, the son of the man who made Oakmont so awesome, won the US Amateur title at Brookline in 1910.

The schisms that were to split the United States into the warring factions of North and South were appearing when The Country Club, in the Boston, Massachusetts, suburb of Brookline, was chartered in 1860. In the definite article of its title, The Country Club stresses its ascendancy over all other country clubs; it was the first of its kind, as befits a city whose links with the founding fathers are impeccable.

Golf was a long way from the minds of its first members, who bought the land merely to exercise their horses and take the air, *en famille*, in their carriages, "free from the annoyance of horse railroads". It was 22 years before the club put the site to the use for which it was purchased, and 30 years before it laid out some of its spare land for six holes of golf. Nevertheless, on the basis of this somewhat fragile start, the club was one of the five to form the American Golf Association, later to be renamed the United States Golf Association.

The original six holes were extended in 1910 to eighteen, setting the stage for an event three years later that was to prove a watershed in American golf – the victory of a young unknown, Francis Ouimet, in a play-off for the US Open title. The 20-year-old former caddie at The Country Club beat two British immortals, Harry Vardon and Ted Ray.

The manner of Ouimet's victory over Vardon and Ray – his steady game waited for them to make mistakes, which they duly did – is enshrined in the histories of golf. Ouimet's subsequent career as one of golf's outstanding amateurs and best-loved characters received unique recognition in 1951, when he became the first non-Briton to be elected Captain of the Royal and Ancient.

The value to American golf of his win was inestimable. It marked the first real loosening of the grip which players from the British Isles had seized upon the game in the New World. More, it showed Americans that success was not limited to those with a high and esoteric talent, or to those with deep pockets.

Francis Ouimet is not the only champion that The Country Club has produced. The club has an ice rink, and six members – one of them Tenley Albright, an Olympic gold medallist – have won a total of 41 United States figure-skating championships. Its world-class tennis players have included Hazel Wightman, winner of 53 national tennis titles and donor of the now disbanded Wightman Cup.

The golf course over which Ouimet played and won was later the scene of a US Women's Amateur Championship, and three Men's championships. In 1927, a third nine holes was added "for ladies, children and beginners".The championship course now draws holes from all three nines, one of them, the 11th, is composed of two holes ordinarily used by members – a short par-four and a par-three over water. Combined, they make a brute

of a par-four, particularly since the golfer must drive through an avenue of oaks and maples.

There are probably 300 golf courses in America that are tougher to play than The Country Club and perhaps fifty that are more artistically designed. Neither is it excessively bunkered nor severely dog-legged and its greens average about 6,000 square feet, about half that of most modern greens. Wind is only an occasional factor and while there are a number of trees, the course was certainly not hacked from a forest; all in all, playing it is rather like playing through a park.

If these seem modest credentials, they are deceptive. When the US Open was played there in 1963 to commemorate the fiftieth anniversary of Ouimet's famous victory, it produced the highest winning score for eighteen years, Julius Boros's nine-over-par 293. The previous highest was Sam Parks's eleven-over-par 299 at Oakmont, which was then more of an obstacle course than a golf course. The Country Club's greens are of bent grass and are feathery-fast. If the golfer misses them he is bound to chip – or, more likely, pitch – out of ankle-deep rough of rye grass. At tournament time the fairways are like ribbons in a schoolgirl's hair and the 19 holes that are chosen from the 27 available (remembering that two holes form one for championship purposes) are certainly not the easiest. It proved an inspired choice to host the 1999 Ryder Cup, producing exciting match-play, though the boorishness of some spectators ruined the spirit of the event.

Already drenched in tradition as the first-ever country club, Brookline became even more famous with tantalizing finishes in the three US Opens held there and an extraordinary American recovery at the climax of the 1999 Ryder Cup. Narrow, tree-lined fairways and exceptionally small greens make accuracy off the tees and fine chipping essential for a low score.

The 1988 US Open, with hindsight, could almost be seen as a dry run for those matches. Oddly enough, another Championship at Brookline ended in a play-off, this time between the best American player of the day, Curtis Strange, and the leading European, Nick Faldo, who had tied on a 72 hole score of 278. It was Strange who prevailed in the 18 hole play-off the following day, 71 to 75, to become the first player since Ben Hogan in 1950-51 to successfully defend the US Open.

The 1st hole runs straightaway down an old polo field with a stretch of The Country Club's old racecourse on the right. It is a routine par-four of 452 yards; the 2nd, an uphill par-three of 185 yards to an ample green, is also unremarkable. The 3rd becomes demanding, for the rough intrudes on the fairway at about 260 yards, leaving a long iron to a green overshadowed by ancient oaks and guarded from every conceivable angle by sand.

From the 3rd to the 8th, the course is again nondescript – no more demanding than a thousand other holes in the USA: the 9th is where the golfer really has to start to play. If he is not under par at that point his chances of finishing in par are remote. The 9th measures 510 yards, nothing to speak of as par-fives go. Drives from the elevated tee must be hit comfortably short to avoid rolling into a stone-filled cliff, or hit hugely long to carry it. It is a do-or-die hole – an easy par or a muscular birdie. One of the most spectacular shots played in the 1999 Ryder Cup was during the Saturday morning four-ball. From the top of the rocks, Davis Love hit a magnificent long-iron no more than a foot from the pin. The eagle three was readily conceded. His descent from the cliffs was rather another matter!

Now the course narrows. The 10th, 11th and 12th are long and hazardous par-fours, 439, 453, and 450 yards in turn – and the 12th is one of the most rugged par-fours anywhere. Even a long hitter must use a long iron to reach the green, which is not only elevated but hidden from view. Access to the green is cut off by five bunkers in front, and too much club lands the ball in either of two bunkers behind.

The remainder of the course is deceptively simple, even the 18th, which is straightaway to an elevated green guarded by an enormous bunker and shadowed by a similarly imposing oak that was something to be avoided even in Ouimet's day. In its lifetime, The Country Club has been host to more than a dozen international events, including the Walker Cup (twice); its members, too, have a special international distinction – their annual contest with Royal Montreal, first played in 1898, was the world's first golf match between teams from different countries. Having had the course set up in the English manner, Crenshaw inflicted a poignant victory over the Europeans in Brookline's crowning international moment. Added to Ouimet's famous victory, they give The Country Club a pedigree of which it is justly proud.

The Ryder Cup 1999. Partisan behaviour at these matches is nothing new. At The Belfry in 1985 cheers went up from the home crowd when an American missed a decisive putt. This was nothing compared with the baying of 10,000 at the 1929 match at Moortown, Leeds, when something more akin to a football crowd lent vocal support to the home team.

The Hole That Influenced Three US Opens

Quite apart from the geography of the course itself there were quite a number of reasons for the stratospherically high scores of the 1963 US Open, played at The Country Club to commemorate Francis Ouimet's famous victory there fifty years earlier. They were so high that even Jack Nicklaus failed to qualify for the last 36 holes.

The championship was staged, as usual, in June, but the weather was unseasonably cold — so cold that two sweaters were the order of the day and, for those who had the uncommon foresight to bring them, windbreakers. The cause of all this was a freakish storm blowing from the north-east off the North Atlantic, and the winds made the greens like slate. Sitting as it does so far inland and protected by its numerous ancient trees, the course is not ordinarily a windy one. But that week it was more like the Open in Britain than the Open in America.

However, the wind brought into the reckoning two holes in particular – the 1st and the 17th, which had been redesigned by the New England architect Geoffrey Cornish. The 1st hole, already 452 yards, now played in to the teeth of the wind. But it was the 17th, regarded for years as one of the pushover holes, which had the decisive influence. It turned out to be the most difficult hole to par. The 17th, then 365 yards long and slightly dog-legged to the left, had already influenced the result of one Open. In the crook of that dog-leg was a small but deep bunker – the key hazard to the hole – and it was there that the 1913 Open was effectively won by Francis Ouimet or, more accurately, lost by Harry Vardon. In the fourth round, Ouimet hit a fine drive safely to the right of that bunker, hit a jigger 20 feet past the hole on a green that is long and extremely narrow, and made the birdie-putt that enabled him to tie with Vardon and Ted Ray. In the play-of the next day Ouimet came to that same hole with only a stroke advantage over the seemingly invincible Vardon who, realising he had to make a birdie quickly, bit off too much of the dog-leg and landed in the bunker. He took a bogey-five. Ouimet played the hole precisely as he had the day before, including another downhill putt for a birdie. Fifty years later Geoffrey Cornish enlarged that bunker, added two more to the left of the green and re-contoured the putting sur-

Francis Ouimet and caddie Eddie Lowry in the 1913 US Open at The Country Club. A former caddie himself, the 20-year-old Ouimet snatched the title from Vardon and Ray.

face, giving it multitudinous breaks. The hole still required no more than a three wood off the tee (as against Ouimet's hickory-shafted driver) and a niblick pitch to the green (against Ouimet's jigger) but, half a century later, it was still baffling. The late Tony Lema bogeyed it to lose the chance of a tie and Arnold Palmer's bogey cost him the opportunity to win the championship outright. And Jacky Cupit, needing only a par and a bogey to win, took a double-bogey six. Julius Boros took only one putt at the 17th to join Cupit and Palmer in a play-off. He won handily with a one-under-par 70.

In 1988 it was Rees Jones who was called in by the USGA to look at the course and he added nearly 300 yards to its length, taking it above the 7,000 mark that now seems to be mandatory for most Major championships. At the 17th during scheduled play Curtis Strange three putted to fall back into a tie with Nick Faldo. Then, in the play-off the following day, Faldo overshot the green and the resultant bogey cost him any prospect of winning the title. Once again the 17th had been instrumental in deciding a US Open.

The 17th: 381 yards par 4

Old

The old 17th showing Vardon's bunker shot and Ouimet's precision.
Right: How the hole has been changed since then.

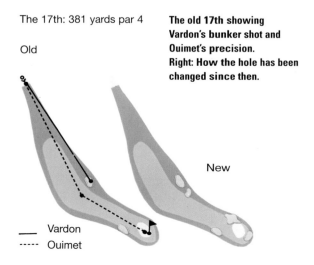

New

——— Vardon

----- Ouimet

The nursery of
future champions

The Course Card

The Olympic
Club,
San Francisco,
California
Lake Course

Hole	Yards	Par
1	533	5
2	394	4
3	223	3
4	438	4
5	457	4
6	437	4
7	288	4
8	137	3
9	433	4
10	422	4
11	430	4
12	416	4
13	186	3
14	422	4
15	157	3
16	609	5
17	468	4
18	347	4

Out	3,340	35
In	3,457	35
Total	**6,797**	**70**

San Francisco's reputation for beauty and charm is so widespread one tends to forget many of its less celebrated assets: the great University of California just across the Bay; the influence it has had on the literature of the Far West; and, by no means least, the fine sportsmen and athletes who have been sent out from time to time to spread fame in foreign lands. The first of the international-class golfers was Lawson Little, and a generation later came Harvie Ward, winner of US and British amateur titles in the 1950s, and Ken Venturi, the 1964 US Open champ-ion. Remarkably, that year the club could boast three USGA champions, with the young Johnny Miller winning the US Junior Amateur and Bill Higgins the US Senior Amateur. Like Venturi, Miller also went on to claim the US Open (in 1973).

Almost all American cities of any size contain some organisation akin to San Francisco's Olympic Club. These are athletic clubs with a membership numbering many hundreds, and their facilities usually include a sizeable clubhouse in the downtown area with a swimming pool, gymnasium, squash and handball courts, Turkish baths and pleasant common rooms in which to dine and drink or just read and relax. The Olympic Club, founded in 1860, is the oldest athletic club in the United States. It fosters teams in almost every sport that Americans enjoy, and just after World War I it expanded into golf.

In 1918, the Olympic Club bought a golf course on the western edge of San Francisco alongside the Pacific Ocean. The course had been built by the then floundering Lakeside Country Club and, as its name implied, it bordered a lake – Lake Merced. In 1924 the club replaced the existing 18-hole course with two courses, the Lake and the Ocean. Both were designed by Willie Watson and constructed by Sam Whiting. Only three years later Whiting

redesigned and rebuilt the courses. The Ocean Course went on to be remodelled several times until in 2000 an entirely new course was designed and built by Tom Weiskopf. The Lake Course, however, has stood the test of time. Its most significant alterations came in 1953 when Robert Trent Jones prepared it for the US Open two years later. He raised the length from 6,433 yards to 6,700, added the only fairway bunker (on the 6th) and tightened the entrances to many greens by wrapping the bunkers round.

Towering trees (planted by the club years ago) and sloping fairways are all that is needed to make this a real test of skill. The golfer must play the slopes and contours, which may very well be contrary to the routing of the hole. The nearby Pacific and its enormous dunes play no part in the personality of the Lake Course except for the prevailing wind that blows off the sea most afternoons throughout the year and the fog that comes rolling in from the ocean most evenings to wrap the course in its silent, cottony moisture, keeping it soft and damp and green even during the hot, dry months of early autumn. When the winter rains begin around December, the Lake Course tends to become much too heavy for real enjoyment, and it stays that way during the wetter winters until the early springtime of northern California begins to dry it out in March and April.

By June, the course is almost always in its ideal playing condition, a lovely and noble-looking arboreal parkland. It is not surprising that the USGA has four times chosen the Lake Course as the site of its Open (including the summer of 1998), always a mid-June affair, and so made it one of the only three courses in all of sports-minded California ever to play host to its premier championship, Riviera and Pebble Beach being the others.

The Lake Course plays long – very long. During the

1955 Open, with the 17th hole reduced from a par-five to a par-four only seven rounds were played in sub-par figures, the lowest being Jack Fleck's closing 67 that brought him a 72-hole tie with Ben Hogan. The second Open to be played at Olympic was 11 years later and this also resulted in a tie and a horrendous turn of fortune for Arnold Palmer: he lost a seven-stroke lead in nine holes to Billy Casper, who then beat him in the play-off by four strokes. In the 1987 Open, only winner Scott Simpson and runner-up Tom Watson broke par.

Except for the short holes there is no such thing as a straight line at the Lake Course. The course winds and bends its way through the trees in such a way that the second shot on at least half its holes is dictated entirely by the terrain and little, if any, advantage is to be gained by the big drive. It is, in addition, a course that plays havoc with the player who likes to draw big, long drives from right to left for added roll. Those who would take a shortcut on the bent and crooked holes find their route frustrated by the towering trees that close in on both sides of every fairway. Off many of the tees, the shot must be played as out of a chute because of overhanging branches at the front edge of the tee or just beyond, thus further confining the leeway available on the drive. Finally, the Lake Course's use of the sloping fairways and the dog-leg has been so artfully contrived that the very shot designed to defeat the purpose of the hole will bring on the most severe penalty; for example, if a golfer tries to cut the corner on the right with a fade and misses the trees, he will probably find his shot slipping downhill off the fairway and into the scrubby rough, with his next shot a rather humiliating little recovery into a playable area.

The course starts out docilely enough with a par-five that can be reached comfortably in two shots by the modern professional. The 2nd hole, however, abruptly indicates the sort of trouble ahead. The hole feels as if it moves leftwards, and the fairway slopes sharply to the left towards the lake, yet the two big shots must be moved from left to right – against the contour of the land. The 3rd is a longish par-

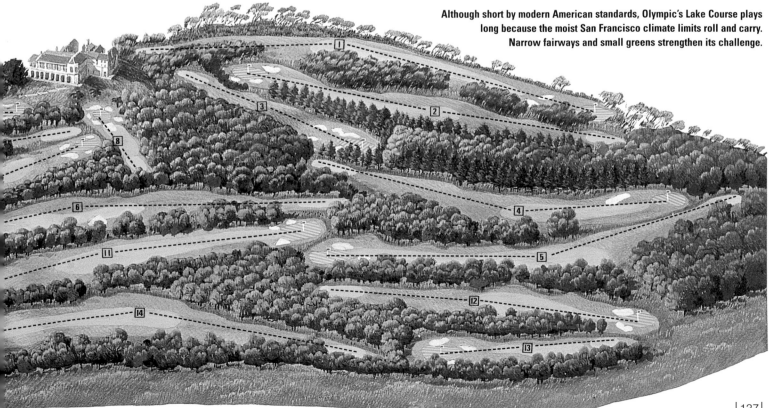

Although short by modern American standards, Olympic's Lake Course plays long because the moist San Francisco climate limits roll and carry. Narrow fairways and small greens strengthen its challenge.

three, with bunkering that is typical of the Lake Course. There may be only one fairway bunker, but the Lake greens are small (averaging only 4,500 square feet in area) and irregular with, for the most part, tiny openings. On the three very short holes, the 8th, 13th and 15th, there is no opening to the green at all. Only the 1st and 4th have no greenside bunkers, so Olympic is very much a course to test the approach shot played full to the green at a great variety of lengths and elevations.

In the San Francisco climate the trees planted many years ago by the club have grown luxuriantly. There has had to be some trimming and removal of them to prevent the course becoming choked. From the 4th tee they are less of a constriction than they once were – they are no longer overhanging the tee, for instance – and the biggest difficulty is that of keeping the ball on the fairway which slopes unhelpfully down to the right. As is so often the case on this course the trouble is on the high side of the fairway, forcing one to favour the side that will bounce the ball into the rough and the trees. This same problem exists in reverse on the 5th hole, where the trouble is on the right, and the fairway slopes to the left.

The 6th hole, a slight dog-leg left, is notable because it provides the only fairway bunker on the entire course – a large sandtrap in the left rough, usually carried by today's professionals. In typical Olympic fashion, the fairway slopes down to the left. The 7th is an unusually short par-four; with

a drive out of a chute to a small fairway from which there is just a little flip of a pitch shot to a green that falls away if one plays the shot too boldly to the back portion. The 8th would be a rather easy par-three were it not for the branches overhanging the entrance to the green on the right.

The 9th through the 12th are all longish par-fours affected by the prevailing wind. It cuts across the second shot on the 10th, while the 11th and 12th play directly into it. In and in all of them there is the problem of the precisely hit drive between the trees and the carefully hit second shot into greens that offer only a minimum target. The turn for home really begins at the 13th, where two par-threes and a par-four now border a deep culvert on the left that is played as out-of-bounds, except in major tournaments such as the Open. However, anything hit into the impenetrable foliage of this culvert is virtually unplayable and might just as well be out-of-bounds.

The 16th is extremely long – more than 600 yards – and played with the prevailing wind at one's back. Despite this, few players have putted for eagle, although Bobby Jones was one of them. The trees on the left were smaller then and no doubt he took a shortcut over them, for the hole bends in a seemingly endless crescent to the left. The drive needs to be played to the centre of the fairway, with a long iron for the second shot to the right side, avoiding a large tree on the left. Then a short iron is needed for the approach.

The 15th to the 18th
——— Palmer
- - - - Casper
······ Hogan

The 15th to the 18th

Hogan, Palmer, and Watson Fail

Late one June afternoon in 1955 all the world was convinced that Ben Hogan was assured of a record fifth Open victory; Gene Sarazen even announced it prematurely on NBC television. But as a weary Hogan waited in the locker-room, his task complete, the news came that Jack Fleck, hitherto quite unknown, needed a birdie-three on the last hole to tie. Hogan dreaded the prospect of a play-off. Since the accident which nearly destroyed him in 1949, he had to husband his resources with great care.

His strategy for a championship was confined to 72 holes and as he waited he said that he hoped Fleck would make two or four. Fleck did neither. He holed from seven feet for the tie. Even then nobody dreamed that he could beat the almost invincible Hogan the following day. But Fleck was in an exalted state of

Olympic members play the 17th as a 522-yard par-five. In 1998, US Open competitors played it as a 469-yard par-four (40 yards longer than for the 1987 Open). The deep greenside bunkers and the severe slopes of the putting surface (from left to right and front to back) put considerable pressure on the long, uphill second shot, hit into the prevailing wind. It is a critical championship hole and was ranked as the most difficult on the course in both the 1987 and 1998 Opens. The 18th hole, a very short par-four at 347 yards, is a driving problem. The trouble is on the left, but again the fairway slopes so sharply to the right that one is always tempted to flirt with the left rough. On the other hand, if the ball carries to the right side of the fairway, the pine trees and their overhanging branches cut off any entrance to the green, which leans steeply forwards and seldom offers a simple, straight putt. Hogan had to sink a 30-foot putt for a six here in his play-off with Jack Fleck for the 1955 Open, and that was the *coup de grace* to any chance he had for an unprecedented five US Open championships. Despite its catalogue of unexpected outcomes, the Lake Course remains one of the most stringent tests on the US Open roster because it requires the player to hit the ball straight, left-to-right and right-to-left, to be able to counter the slopes and contours or else to use them to profit.

Lake Course's Upset Finish

Rarely in the history of championship golf has expectation been as thoroughly confounded as in the first three US Opens to be staged at Olympic's Lake Course. All three ended in startlingly similar fashion. Each time they had apparently been won by the emotional crowd favourite – Ben Hogan in 1955, Arnold Palmer in 1966, and Tom Watson in 1987 – when a sudden change of fortune let in the unfancied outsider. The first two produced play-off wins for, respectively, Jack Fleck and Billy Casper with the third claimed by Scott Simpson for his only Major championship success.

The climax of two great chases, and ties, in US Opens – Jack Fleck after Ben Hogan in 1955 and Billy Casper after Arnold Palmer in 1966 – the short par-four 18th at Olympic has tempted many players to flirt with the rough on the left. Most wish they had gone for accuracy and safety – the golden rule of the course.

confidence, seemingly unafraid of the implacable presence beside him or of the prospect of victory, and he was playing the golf of his life.

After 17 holes he was one ahead. Then, on the last tee, Hogan's foot slipped, he hooked into a patch of vicious rough from which he needed three strokes to recover and Fleck had achieved the seemingly impossible. If ever there was an instance of a golfer being betrayed by the very qualities that made him the most compelling sporting figure of his time it was Arnold Palmer's failure to win the 1966 Open. For all that Billy Casper played one of the great last rounds, Palmer should never have allowed him to tie. On the 10th tee he was seven strokes ahead and surging to victory. Casper was forgotten and Palmer was intent on beating Hogan's record score of 276, but Casper was playing superb golf and he had regained two strokes by the time they reached the short 15th. The flag was close to a bunker which Palmer's shot, just failing to hold the green, found. He took four while Casper holed for a two. On the huge 16th Palmer drove into heavy rough and "the finest six I ever made" was of no avail. Casper's flawless

birdie had gained him two more strokes. Palmer pulled his drive from the next tee and Casper had drawn level. One of the greatest of attacking golfers had attacked when it seemed that prudence decreed a conservative approach, but had Palmer been a prudent golfer he would never have been the idol of millions. Again in the play-off Casper came from behind, two strokes at the turn, and even Palmer's resistance was spent.

When Tom Watson rolled in a 20ft putt at the 14th on the final day in 1988 to draw level with Scott Simpson, once more convention dictated a win for the favourite; in this case a ninth Major championship. How could Simpson hope to compete against the dominant player of the age? He found a way, just like Fleck and Casper before him, to stifle a legend. From the 14th he managed three birdies in a row, a credible achievement at Olympic, and then surpassed each of them with a save from a greenside bunker at the 17th that can scarcely have been bettered by anyone who has ever played the hole. When Watson misjudged his second shot to the 18th, the Lake Course had maintained its reputation for the unexpected.

Behind the 18th green the lighthouse at Harbour Town makes for a picturesque backdrop.

Only a week after Harbour Town Golf Links was opened its name was known around the world. Before even a round had been played there, it was chosen as the site for the 1969 Heritage Classic. That tournament was won by Arnold Palmer, his first victory in fourteen months, and all the world heard the news.

Harbour Town's fame has proved to be lasting. The course is spread out among the trees and along the inland coast of Hilton Head Island, in South Carolina. The nearest city is Savannah, Georgia, which is 25 miles away. It is one of the most beautiful golf courses in America, but it owes its reputation not so much to its undoubted scenic attractions as to its genuine quality. Each year the Heritage falls after the Masters and usually the week following a major championship is a tough one to attract the top players. It proves no such problem in this instance, the allure of the venue and an alluringly docile part of the southern states weaving its charm. Harbour Town measures 6,973 yards from its extreme back tees and possesses a par of 71. The course has only fifty-six bunkers, eight of which are off the fairways. Every bunker lies absolutely flat; not one is banked, so it is almost impossible to get a buried ball. Fully a third of the bunkers are set up behind or to one side of a green, simply to make the green a better target. There are a dozen bunkers at Harbour Town that hardly anybody has ever been in. The greens are small and so lacking in undulations that three-putting is more a matter of incompetence than a geographic survey that went awry. For every long par-four there is a short par-four. For every dog-leg left there is one to the right, and only two of them are so bent that you cannot see the green from the tee. There are no uphill or downhill lies on the course because of the nature of the land, which is so flat that the highest point on the course is only six feet above the lowest.

The course was bulldozed and chain-sawed through sub-tropical vegetation, but Pete Dye, the designer, and Jack Nicklaus, Dye's consultant, went to extraordinary pains to leave trees just where they could come into play: palmettos, towering pines, magnificent magnolias and oaks draped in Spanish moss, thick as tinsel on a Christmas tree. Where the trees stand in groves, they encroach upon the fairways so closely that they make the landing areas look much smaller than they really are.

The 1st hole is a straightforward par-four, calling for a mid-iron to the green. The 2nd is typical of the par-fives, short but reachable only by two very exacting shots. It calls for a drive down the extreme left side of the fairway, flirting with a bunker on the way. Only from this position is it possible to hit the green with the second shot, for a long bunker and a gigantic oak stand sentinel over the right side.

The 3rd is like the 1st, a drive and mid-iron. Although the fairway is wide, the green is very small. The 4th is one of the most diabolically beautiful par-threes a golfer is ever likely to face. It is 200 yards of pure carry, because water fronts the green and lies to the left and to the rear. A flurry of pampas grass lies to the right and, to make matters

America's oldest club
finds a fine new home

worse, the green is banked right to the edges with railroad ties between the pampas grass and the water. It is impossible to roll the ball on to the green. Like the 2nd, the par-five 5th can also be reached in two, and again both shots have to be played down the left-hand side to bypass trees near the green – which, to make the second shot even tougher, banks from left to right. Two of the more interesting holes on the front nine are the 7th and the 9th. At the 7th, a 195-yard par-three, the green is surrounded by sand except for a spit of land to the rear which provides access. The 9th is one of the shortest of par-fours, a mere 337 yards. A long bunker protects the front of the horseshoe-shaped green, which is wrapped around yet another bunker; land on the wrong side and the golfer will have to three-putt purposely to find a way around it.

The 10th and the 11th bend to the left away from the clubhouse, and the 12th makes a quick dog-leg to the right with, unusually on an American course, a double green. It is impossible for any golfer to putt from one part to the other in two without holing at least a 30-footer for his second.

The 13th is a fascinating hole. It is not a long par four and it is wise to leave the driver in the bag. Unless the narrow fairway is hit, there is no shot to the green because oak trees narrow the approach. The green itself is Y-shaped, with the stem protected by a bunker that seems to be half an acre in size. More, the elevated green is banked with boards.

The 192-yard 14th, like the 4th, is a par-three that is water from tee to green – all of it banked with railroad ties and sawn-off telegraph poles. The four finishing holes then present some of the most thoughtful shotmaking a golfer will ever be asked to countenance. The par-five 15th is the-longest hole on the course. Although the tee shot is straightaway, close to the tiny green the fairway dog-legs around a small lake. Consequently, even touring pros often lay up with their second shots.

The 16th is a shortish par-four, sharply dog-legged to the left. The tee shot must avoid three lonesome pines scattered down the middle of the fairway and the start of a mammoth bunker, fully 130 yards long, on the left. The narrow 17th green widens to the rear, but a strip-trap about 80 yards long skirts the left side and becomes, at the rear, a huge basket trap. For two-thirds of its flight the tee shot must carry water, which continues close along the left side all the way to the green. A par-four of 452 yards, the 18th is unforgettable. Both shots must carry the tidal saltmarsh along the shores of Calibogue Sound. Played bravely the hole is absolutely straight, with the tee, the fairway landing area and the green jutting out into the marsh. It is one of the great finishing holes in golf, as events in the Heritage have proved.

This tournament was so named in recognition of the fact that the South Carolina Golf Club – whose home Harbour Town became – is the oldest golf club in North America, having been founded in 1786 at Charleston. In turn the Heritage has been won by some truly gifted golfers, testimony to the worthiness of the course over which it is played. Among the victors have been Johnny Miller, Hale Irwin, Arnold Palmer, Tom Watson, Greg Norman, Nick Faldo, and Jack Nicklaus, who calls it "a thinking man's golf course".

The Course Card

Harbour Town Golf Links, Hilton Head Island. South Carolina

Record: 63, Jack Nicklaus, 1975; Dennis Watson, 1984

Hole	Yards	Par
1	410	4
2	502	5
3	437	4
4	200	3
5	530	5
6	419	4
7	195	3
8	470	4
9	332	4
10	444	4
11	436	4
12	430	4
13	373	4
14	192	3
15	571	5
16	395	4
17	185	3
18	452	4
Out	3,495	36
In	3,478	35
Total	**6,973**	**71**

At a time when the trend in American course design was very definitely towards length and large greens, architect Pete Dye, working closely with Jack Nicklaus, created a refreshingly different course at Harbour Town. Very few alterations have been made to the course since it was first built, with the lengthening of the 14th by almost 30 yards the only significant change.

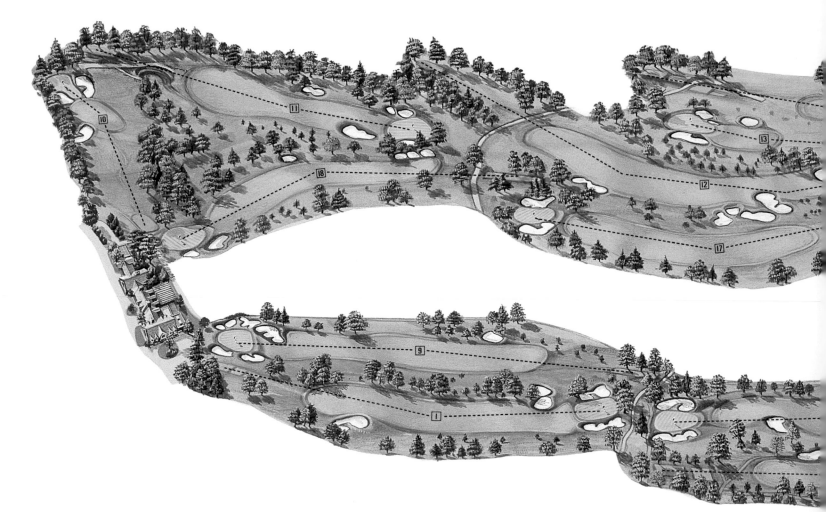

"Give us a man-sized course..."

In the vast Manhattan bedroom known as Westchester County, golf courses are almost as numerous as car service stations and, like them, they frequently lie side by side. Many of them are undeniably of championship calibre, like Westchester itself and Quaker Ridge. But Winged Foot, across the street from the latter in the town of Mamaroneck, is undoubtedly the best. It has two courses, the East and the West, both designed in 1923 by an eccentric but highly imaginative architect named A. W. Tillinghast. He was one of America's truly great designers, whose creations include Baltusrol, San Francisco Golf Club, the aforementioned Quaker Ridge, Ridgewood, Five Farms and Fresh Meadow. The winged foot from which the club takes its name is from the emblem of the New York Athletic Club, Manhattan, a number of whose members banded together

to form the suburban golf club. Later, the affiliation between the two was severed but the emblem stayed.

It has long been a locker-room debate among the members as to which course is the better. But most professionals who have played both would probably agree on the longer, somewhat more treacherous West, particularly since in 1972-3 it was toughened up in some places for the 1974 US Open. Normally, par for a tournament is dropped from 72 to 70 as it was for that Open, which Hale Irwin won with 287, seven over par. In 1959 Billy Casper had won the same championship with 282, one-putting 31 greens in the process. And way back in 1929 Bobby Jones and Al Espinosa tied at fourteen over, Jones winning a 36-hole play-off by the humiliating margin of 23 strokes. It is not difficult to see why these scores came close to being stratospheric even by US Open standards. The reason lies in the par-fours, as everybody learns to their dismay when they first play the course. There are 12 of them, fully ten measuring more than 400 yards. This means that even the good amateur club player capable of hitting a drive 220 yards straight down the middle of the fairway is faced with a second wood shot on all ten, on seven of which he won't be able to reach the green at all. And even the other three are doubtful, for all the greens are elevated and each is protected by bunkers that are not only big but very deep. Tillinghast once explained his design philosophy on bunkers: "I think that I always will adhere to my old theory that a controlled shot to a closely guarded green is the surest test of any man's golf."

In all, Winged Foot has 60 bunkers and every one of its greens has at least two of those deep bunkers carved

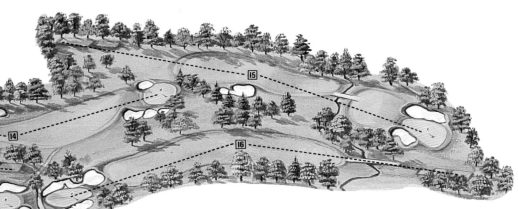

Tillinghast's stunningly tight West course unfolds along two distinct, parallel arms. The lower front nine includes a deceptively easy looking, long par-three, the 3rd, which caused so much trouble in the 1959 US Open. The inward half starts with another impressive short hole, the 10th, which precedes a succession of seven dog-legs and concludes with the infamous 18th, where the narrow fairway leads into a fiendishly undulating green.

The Course Card

Winged Foot Golf Club, Mamaroneck, New York West course

Record: 64, Jug McSpaden, Goodall Tournament 1946

Hole	Yards	Par
1	446	4
2	411	4
3	216	3
4	453	4
5	515	5
6	324	4
7	166	3
8	442	4
9	471	4
10	190	3
11	386	4
12	535	5
13	212	3
14	418	4
15	417	4
16	457	4
17	449	4
18	448	4
Out	3,444	35
In	3,512	35
Total	**6,956**	**70**

out about as close to the putting surface as you can get without actually being on it. Claude Harmon, an astute teacher who was a professional there for over 30 years, once claimed there was not a low-handicap member there who was not an excellent bunker player. It is impossible to chip from them or even to pitch out. A sand iron must be used with a finely timed swing for an explosion shot or, if one has the nerve, a semi-explosion. Alternatively, if the ball is buried in the sand, an outright blast with plenty of muscle is called for.

Many of the finer players among the members have learned from Harmon and other professionals a good way of dealing with a ball buried in sand. They leave their sand-iron in their bag and instead use a pitching wedge or even a 9-iron. The flange on the sand-iron more often than not will not permit the clubhead to cut through the sand. The club just bounces off, thereby moving the ball only a few feet. The thinner flange of the pitching wedge or 9-iron will cut through the sand like a knife. One thing more: they suggest closing the face slightly, for the force of the blow will almost surely open it out to a square position at impact.

The Winged Foot membership list has always been something to talk about, as have the professionals who have worked there. At one time the club had both the Open and Amateur champions of America. Member Dick Chapman won the Amateur in the autumn of 1940 and the following spring the head professional, Craig Wood, won the Open. Harmon, who became head professional six years later, won the Masters in 1948 and three years later member Joe Gagliardi (later Judge Gagliardi) was runner-up in the Amateur. Among the former assistants to Harmon were Jack Burke, who won both the Masters and the PGA Championship in 1956, Dave Marr, winner of the PGA in 1965, and Mike Souchak, a star on the tournament circuit who long-shared the record for the low round on tour at 61. Dick Mayer, who won the US Open in 1957, was a member at Winged Foot before turning professional. Harmon's son Butch, a former assistant pro at Winged Foot, has become one of the game's most renowned teachers, his pupils including Greg Norman and Tiger Woods. It is certainly no accident that so many fine exponents have emerged from Winged Foot or have chosen to work there. The course perfectly exemplifies the design philosophy of Tillinghast, which he himself succinctly sums up this way: "In planning holes there are thousands of combinations, each offering a mute appeal for recognition. It is necessary to decide on the collection which will work out economically and satisfactorily from many angles. But this is sure: every hole must have individuality and must be sound. Often it is necessary to get from one section to another over ground which is not suited to easy construction, but that troublesome hole must be made to stand right up with the others. If it has not got anything about it that might make it respectable, it has got to have quality knocked into it until it can hold its head up in polite society."

There can be no doubts about Winged Foot's social standing or of Tillinghast's confidence in his own workmanship, as his assessment of the course shows: "As the

various holes came to life they were of a sturdy breed. The contouring of the greens places a premium on the placement of the drives, but never is there the necessity of facing a prodigious carry of the sink-or-swim sort. It is only the knowledge that the next shot must be played with rifle accuracy that brings the realisation that the drive must be placed. The holes are like men, all rather similar from foot to neck, but with the greens showing the same varying characters as human faces."

Looking at those lush, velvet greens and emerald fairways, it is difficult to believe that Tillinghast had to move 7,200 tons of rock and cut down 7,800 trees to create them. The magnitude of his task was in stark contrast to the brevity of the instructions he received from the gentlemen of the New York Athletic Club: "Give us a man-sized course," they said. Tillinghast's response was a Herculean achievement.

The beautifully manicured fairways are a feature of Winged Foot, one of the most difficult tests of golf in America.

Love Conquers All

It was the sort of performance that the hugely talented Davis Love had threatened throughout his career and, for a true traditionalist, it could not have come at a better place than Winged Foot.

Love's father was a teaching professional whose best finish in the USPGA Championship was 55th in 1967. In 1988 he died in a plane crash and for two years or more Love would find his mind wandering when he should have been concentrating on his golf. Thirty years after his father's career-best in the USPGA, however, he put together the sort of performance in the same tournament that players can only think of achieving once of twice in a career. His winning score of 11 under was scarcely believable around a course so penal; in three of the four rounds he shot 66, including the last two, which gave him a five shot winning margin over Justin Leonard, who had won the Open Championship at Royal Troon a month previously. One of the more unusual occurrences in a Major championship also happened at Winged Foot in the 1984 US Open. The protagonists were Fuzzy Zoeller and Greg Norman, who were level playing the final hole. Norman, one group in front, holed from 45ft on the home green and set off after the ball with a jubilant spring to his stride. Back in the fairway, Zoeller waved a white towel in mock surrender. What Zoeller did not know was that Norman's putt was for a par not birdie, the Australian having missed the green with his approach. Someone in the crowd alerted him and he made the par which secured a play-off. They were the only players under par that year and the following day, only Zoeller could manage the feat, shooting 67 to Norman's 75. They walked off the last green arm in arm.

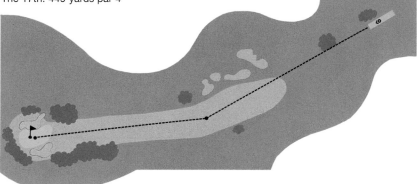

The 17th: 449 yards par 4

The 10th and 17th

Tillinghast's Finest

Two holes, the 10th and the 17th, stand out at Winged Foot. Jack Nicklaus describes the 449-yard 17th as "one of those text-book tests of golf – a hole that really pits the player against the designer". The hole is a slight dogleg to the right, the crook of which contains four huge bunkers. On either side of a slim, curving green are long, well-like bunkers. In Nicklaus's words: "A straight tee shot is a definite necessity. The second shot requires a long iron, which again must be hit with great accuracy to a well-trapped, extremely narrow green."

Two of Winged Foot's four short holes are at least two club lengths longer than the 10th, but it is a superior hole. Seen from the tee, the hole is not all that imposing. At 190 yards it cannot be called short. The broad, deep green tilts invitingly towards the tee. Directly in front is an opening between the two flanking kidney-shaped bunkers. The third bunker, on the left centre of the fairway, is so short of the green as to be practically out of play, although the handicap golfer must be conscious that it has to be carried.

It is only at the green itself that the hole becomes imposing. One look at its smooth, subtle undulations brings worries not of two-putting but of three-putting. With the flagstick at the front of the green and the ball well behind it, comes the possibility of a chip back or, worse, playing from one of those bunkers, both of which are deeper than a man is tall. A shot out of either of these, played not quite tenderly enough, can easily see the ball back into the other one. When the flagstick is to the rear of the green, a club too many could result in hitting into the out-of-bounds area, which is no more than thirty feet behind the putting surface. The hooked shot will land in a pack of trees on the left.

The hole requires precise judgement in club selection, the shot must be hit truly after that and then the putt must be stroked, not jabbed. All the hazards and other trouble are in plain view from the tee. There is nothing tricky about the 10th. The greatest endorsement the hole ever received came from A. W. Tillinghast himself. He considered it the finest par-three he had ever built.

Pinehurst was the first resort to offer 72 holes of golf, but it was Donald Ross's No 2 course that brought it world renown. Ross created a masterpiece, blending visual harmony with a balanced array of hazards: mounds guarding the greens, wire grass and pine needles waiting off the fairways, and greens falling away on all sides. As Sam Snead put it after one North and South Open: "You've got to hit every shot on old No 2. "

Donald Ross creates his

masterpiece

There is no resort in America that is quite so saturated with golf as Pinehurst, a charming little New England-style village located in North Carolina some three hours east of Augusta. Quite fortuitously, and long before anyone had golf in mind, a pharmacist from Boston named James W. Tufts conceived the notion of starting a modest winter resort in the South so that other New Englanders of modest means and advancing years could escape the bitter winter weather. He finally chose the Sandhills of North Carolina because of the mild climate and the reasonable price of $1 an acre then being asked for this rather barren, cutover timberland. Nobody but an incorrigible optimist or an oaken-hearted New Englander would ever have had the temerity to think he could create anything habitable and attractive on such desolate land.

The North Carolina Sandhills are a geological phenomenon dating back to some ice age. They reach a hundred miles inland from the Atlantic and, except for the thick stands of pine forest, they provide much the same sort of terrain as is found on the linksland of Great Britain. Thus, when James W. Tufts and his pioneering neighbours of Pinehurst suddenly found themselves intrigued by this peculiar new game of golf somewhere around 1897/98, they had the ideal landscape on which to build an experimental course.

The year 1900, however, provided the two events that shaped Pinehurst's future. In March Harry Vardon stopped by and played four rounds over the rather primitive eighteen holes of Pinehurst Country Club's No 1 course. Just watching the great Vardon was enough to whet the appetites of the locals for this game. In December Donald J. Ross arrived in Pinehurst to assume the duties of resident professional. At the time of his arrival in Pinehurst, Donald Ross was a young man, a Scot from Dornoch who had taken his apprenticeship under Old Tom Morris at St Andrews and then served a few years as professional and greenkeeper at Royal Dornoch. His youthful enthusiasm and natural gift for the "feel" of the game were just what the budding new resort needed. Within his first year at Pinehurst, Ross started to build the first nine holes of what is now the justly famous Pinehurst No 2 course, and he completed the original eighteen holes in 1907. So great was the artistic triumph of Pinehurst No 2, even in those Paleolithic times of sand greens, scruffy fairways and only 5,860 yards, that Ross eventually became the doyen of American golf architecture. It was a matter of lasting regret that Pinehurst's location, far from a major centre of population, militated against its hosting a modern major championship. When eventually the USGA brought the US Open in 1999, Pinehurst proved more than a match for the

best in the world. Through the years, Ross was continually altering and improving Pinehurst No 2 as equipment and technique required until he arrived at the course we know today, one of the masterpieces of golfing architecture of its particular genre. That is to say, Pinehurst No 2 is a kind of idealisation of the old-fashioned parkland courses that characterised American golf architecture until World War II – tree-lined, following the natural terrain, with small greens and ample but not profligate use of bunkers. It is the kind of course that puts the emphasis on the planning and precision of the golf shot rather than the great strength that the more recent courses demand, although, as it stands today, No 2 measures an imposing 7,175 yards and calls forth the use of every club in the bag during the progress of a round. In addition to these qualities, No 2 has the added advantage of being located on the Sandhills, thus giving it something of the playing qualities of a linksland course.

In the 100 years since James W. Tufts first began to develop his resort, the timberlands of Pinehurst have grown back to their full maturity. As a result, nearly every one of the eighteen holes of No 2 is a separate aesthetic entity unto itself, completely surrounded by the tall pines and shut off from the rest of the course. Except for those who may be engaged on the same hole, a player has the feeling of being entirely isolated from the rest of the world, golfing or otherwise. Aside from whatever one's problems may be on the golf course and at No 2 they can often be most humiliating – there is an atmosphere of peace and solitude that is seldom found in golf or any other social game. The course opens with a rather uncomplicated hole of 404 yards, which places no great premium on distance and with plenty of fairway space on which to unlimber. The only really serious trouble is the boundary fence that runs the length of the 1st and 2nd holes on the left but not unduly close to the line of play. At the 2nd the distance begins to build, and here is a hole requiring a strong second shot. At the 3rd, a shortish two-shotter, finesse suddenly comes into play, and the emphasis is on strategy, with a birdie awaiting those who have their shots under control. The 4th

A superb hole, lined with trees and with a green falling away to bunkers at the sides and back, the 191-yard 17th is typical of Pinehurst No 2.

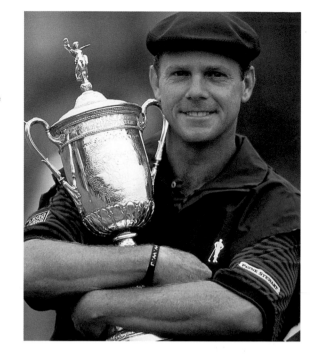

In June 1999 Payne Stewart rolled in a 15-foot putt on the final green to win the U.S. Open at Pinehurst by a single stroke from Phil Mickelson. It was his third major victory, and he was shortly to play a key role in the Ryder Cup. In October he perished in a plane crash.

Fairest of the Fair

Although the 482-yard 5th is not the longest par-four on the course, the player is probably more aware of distance there than at the longer 8th, and it is certainly more demanding. The drive, over a quietly rising crest of fairway towards a gentle valley beyond, is the only blind one on the course, but is in no way distracting because of it. According to the length of the tee shot the second can be anything from wood to medium iron and is a most exacting stroke. The green, which leans towards the player, is angled away to the left on rising ground with large bunkers on either hand. Unless the approach is played from the right side of the fairway there is no clear entrance to the green, and the shot must carry the forward of the left-hand bunkers. The 5th is a truly beautiful hole, as indeed are all the par-fours, not one of which is similar to the others.

The 8th hole, a par-four of 485 yards from the championship tee, plunges into a long valley from where the fairway rises smoothly to a green which, because of

Very much in the Tuft spirit, Pinehurst has been expanded over the last century into a resort now encompassing eight courses, and all exploiting the sand hills and pines in similar fashion. This is the par-3 8th hole on No 8 course, designed by Tom Fazio.

and 5th are played over the only hilly portion of the course, the 4th providing one of only two par-fives as the course was set up for the 1999 US Open. It can be reached in two by most modern professionals, but the immensely long 10th is another matter. In fact Pinehurst's considerable length is found not in the par-fives, nor in its short holes, but in its two-shot holes, three of them over 480 yards long. They call for a big drive and powerful second, with precious little margin for error. Unlike so many of the better American parkland courses, Pinehurst is virtually without water. The only water hole is the 16th, where a small pond

in front of the tee requires a carry of no more than 180 yards on the proper line of play, yet the water does serve to fashion the tee shot and increase the problems of mound and bunker beyond. This is the second of a stretch of four closing holes that make No 2 one of the most exciting courses for tournament play that exists in America.

Probably because it is somewhat off the beaten path it has not entertained nearly the amount of national championship and international golf that it deserves. The 1999 US Open was only its second Major championship – the first was the 1936 USPGA, which was a matchplay event

Left: The fifth hole at Pinehurst No 2 is a truly wonderful par four, where a drive to a tilting fairway needs to be followed by a raking long iron to an extravagantly protected green. Par is always a good score on this hole.

its slight elevation above the surrounding land, will only hold a truly struck shot. Such greens are a notable feature of Donald Ross's design. His intention was that a good shot should always be rewarded but that the fractionally erring one, leaking a little either way, would tend to slip off the putting surface. Punishment for missing his greens usually is not too severe but recovery can involve a variety of shots and decisions as to the most effective one to use – chips, little throw-up pitches, even

bumbles with a putter. Ross had no call to protect his greens with thick fringes, common to many American courses, which can harshly penalize a good shot that is no more than a matter of inches too strong or too wide.

Pinehurst Number 2 is a monument to the genius of Ross, who spoke of it as being "the fairest test of championship golf I have ever designed". Even the most carping of professional golfers could hardly disagree, and the 5th and 8th holes are striking examples of Ross's skill.

in those days – to be played at Pinehurst. The Ryder Cup matches brought international golf in 1951, and in 1962 the US Amateur championship was played there for the first time.

Since 1901, however, the North and South championship, an amateur tournament ranking in prestige only just below the national Amateur championship itself, has been played annually at Pinehurst, first on the rather short No 1 course but since 1909 on No 2. In 1903, the North and South Open was inaugurated there, too, but as the purses and galleries of professional golf became the paramount concern following World War II, the latter event was abandoned. It will be remembered in the record books largely for the 1940 renewal, which was the first professional tournament won by Ben Hogan at the start of his fabulous string of victories that were to extend for the succeeding fourteen years.

The World Open was played there for the first time in 1973 and for it the par-five 8th hole was shortened by some twenty yards to make it a par-four of 464 yards. Gibby Gilbert set the record of 62 for this par 71 course. His score was equalled by Tom Watson, the eventual winner. The Tour Championship, the annual end of season extravaganza for the leading 30 players on the PGA Tour, was played in consecutive years at Pinehurst in 1991 and 1992, the winners being two noted shotmakers, Craig Stadler and Paul Azinger. In 1994 the US Senior Open was played there and won by the South African Simon Hobday. Nerves of steel were required during the 1999 U.S. Open in which Pinehurst's raised putting sur-

faces proved elusive to many, protected as they were with traditional Open rough and their own lightning pace.

Nowadays the golf at Pinehurst is largely social. Particularly in the fall and spring when the Carolina climate is propitious, groups of friends will travel to Pinehurst from all over the eastern and southern part of the country to spend a few days in the soothing environs of Pinehurst's peaceful little village, living quietly in one of the numerous little inns or the large and stately Pinehurst Hotel, playing golf by day and talking golf well into the evening. For aside from the splendid testing qualities of No 2, there are currently seven other excellent eighteen-hole courses of considerably less rigour fanning out from the pleasant clubhouse on the hill. Since James W. Tufts first conceived this semi-paradisical retreat for winter-bound New Englanders, four generations of the Tufts family have taken an active part in the development of the community. To the world of golf, the best-known of these is James W's grandson, Richard S. Tufts, a man who served the USGA selflessly for several decades in numerous capacities, including the presidency. Among his many great services to amateur golf was his contribution to the unification and standardization of the USGA and Royal and Ancient versions of the Rules of Golf and the inauguration of the World Amateur Team Championship, known as the Eisenhower Trophy. In 1948 the Pinehurst Resort was purchased by the Club Corporation of America, a large company that is the owner and operator of private country clubs, city clubs, and athletic clubs.

When the World Golf Hall of Fame was opened at Pinehurst in 1974 Walter Hagen was an automatic choice by the Golf Writers of America as one of the thirteen initial members. Winner of four British Opens two US Opens and five USPGA titles, the extrovert Hagen was without peer in the ranks of professional golf in the 1920s.

There could be no more enduring tribute to the quality of his design than the United States Open at Merion in 1971. After 72 holes Jack Nicklaus and Lee Trevino, two of the greatest of all golfers, alone had matched the par of 280 in conditions that were uniformly fair throughout. For that Open, Merion measured 6,482 yards, only 12 yards longer than the shortest course used for the championship since World War I, and hundreds shorter than most of the others. Out of that length, 1,136 yards were contained in the only two par-fives, the 2nd and the 4th. It is this lack of length with seemingly no way of remedying it, that has prevented the United States Golf Association from returning to the course since David Graham's victory in 1981. It is an acute loss.

At 6,482 yards Merion is the shortest course used for the US Open since World War II. Yet the leading scores – Hogan's 287 in 1950 and the even-par 280 of Trevino and Nicklaus in 1971 – reflect just how difficult Hugh Wilson's course is to master. Narrow par-fours, 120 telling bunkers and tight, fast greens make it one of America's great golfing trials. It was ironic that it took a virtual unknown, Lee Mackey, to humble Merion with a record 64, including seven birdies and one bogey, in the opening round of the 1950 Open.

A flawless setting for
high drama

Tommy Armour, the "Silver Scot ", is one of many pros to have suffered at Merion. He sliced his tee shot out-of-bounds on the 6th in every round of the 1934 Open, ending with 314.

Some years ago an informal poll was taken among three of America's leading golf architects: Robert Trent Jones, Pete Dye, and George Fazio. They were asked to pick the finest examples of United States course design in which they had not themselves been involved. Between them they named some two dozen courses, but agreed unanimously on only six: Pine Valley, Augusta National, Seminole, Pebble Beach, Pinehurst Number 2 and Merion.

Ironically enough, four of those six had been designed by complete architectural amateurs. Fourteen of Pine Valley's 18 holes were designed by a Philadelphia businessman called George Crump; Augusta National was Bobby Jones's first try at architecture (although with the inestimable counsel of Alister Mackenzie); Pebble Beach was designed by Jack Neville and Douglas Grant, two amateur players from California; and Merion was the first effort of a transplanted Scot, Hugh Wilson, a member of the old West course when it was affiliated to the Merion Cricket Club, whose members at the time wanted a championship layout. They dispatched young Wilson to Scotland and England to take a post-graduate course in British linksland before transforming a section of Philadelphia's Main Line – the long stretch of the city's socially elite suburbs – into a "golf links" no proper Philadelphian would be ashamed of. It remains the only complete course that Wilson was to write his name to, for he died at the relatively young age of 46 and was never able to pursue his newly found vocation.

Bobby Jones played in his first Amateur championship at Merion, leading the field after the first of the two qualifying rounds. This happened in the autumn of 1916 when Jones was a lad of 14 standing all of five feet four inches but weighing a chunky 165 pounds (in contrast to the spindly, sickly boy who had been practically pushed on to his neighbourhood golf course – East Lake near Atlanta). He shot a 74, ridiculously high by today's standards, but it was good enough. He was playing speedy bent grass greens, not the coarse and harsh Bermuda green of his native south, for the first time in his life.

The 6th of the West was a short par-four, which Jones hit with a drive and a mere pitch with his wedge. The ball ended 30 feet past the flagstick. Forgetting that he was no longer playing on his home greens, Jones hit a horrifying putt that sailed back past the cup, over the green, and into a brook in front of it. That afternoon, the "Kid from Dixie" had to play the newer East course. Suffering from stage-fright, he shot 89, with every golf fan in Philadelphia and every sports-writer in America peering over his shoulder at every stroke. But he still qualified, eventually going out of the competition to Bob Gardner, the defending champion, in the quarter-final. Eight years later, again at Merion, he won the first of his record five US Amateur titles and in 1930 the last of them, achieving the Grand Slam in the process. If the years of Jones were enough for any course to achieve immortality, 1950 brought a new drama when an unknown, Lee Mackey, broke the US Open record with a first round of 64. But a colossus, Ben Hogan, was to bestride the stage that year like some golfing Caesar, casting Mackey's moment of glory into deep shadow.

Little more than a year before, Hogan had been badly hurt when the car in which he and his wife were travelling collided head-on with a bus. Only a man of indomitable fortitude could have returned to golf as quickly as Hogan did and he was still in considerable pain when the Open began at Merion in 1950.

He played through the competition in great discomfort, at one time stopping the car taking him back to the hotel because he felt so ill. On the final day, the Open reached its climax and Hogan

reached for his astonishing reserves of courage. There were two rounds left, thirty-six holes. Hogan managed the first round with a 72, suffering no ill effects. As a precautionary measure during the afternoon round, he had his caddie pick the ball out of the cup for him so he would not have to aggravate the pain in his legs by bending over.

He made the turn in 36; par on the back nine would give him a winning score of 282, four under the 286 which he had anticipated would be enough to triumph. As he started the final nine he was seized by an extreme cramp in his left leg. By the time he reached the 18th green near the clubhouse, the pain had become so acute that he thought about withdrawing – not because he did not think he could win, but because he didn't think he could walk, much less play.

That he did not withdraw is now history, and he stumbled home with a total of 287, level with George Fazio and Lloyd Mangrum. When he won the play-off next day it was an anticlimax, the denouement taking place on the 16th green when Mangrum was penalised two strokes for blowing a bug off his ball. Hogan then scored a birdie-two on the 230-yard par-three 17th with a 4-wood and a 60-foot putt, for the second and greatest of his four Open wins.

Ten years later Jack Nicklaus, then a young amateur, shot 269 for four rounds, eighteen strokes better than Hogan had scored in 1950. American golf history has marched on at Merion.

In a sense the course is old-fashioned. It covers no more than 110 acres, compared with the 250 acres most American courses take in order to accommodate the trappings now needed to back a golf course project financially. There are 120 bunkers, which may seem a lot until compared with the 280 that Oakmont once had and to those on the Old course at St Andrews. Hugh Wilson placed each

Merion Golf Club, Ardmore East course

Hole	Yards	Par
1	362	4
2	536	5
3	181	3
4	600	5
5	418	4
6	420	4
7	350	4
8	360	4
9	193	3
10	310	4
11	369	4
12	371	4
13	127	3
14	408	4
15	366	4
16	428	4
17	220	3
18	463	4
Out	3,420	36
In	3,062	34
Total	**6,482**	**70**

Olin Dutra (left) made up eight shots over the last 36 holes to win the 1934 Open at Merion.

Right: The 9th is typical of Wilson's tight greens guarded by a brook, lagoon and several bunkers.

one exactly where it ought to be. When Chick Evans won the US Amateur there in 1916, he nicknamed them the "white faces of Merion" after the glaring sand from a nearby quarry with which they had been filled.

Merion straddles Ardmore Avenue, and the 1st hole goes directly towards it. Eleven holes – the 2nd to the 12th – lie on the other side. There are only two holes at Merion, the 2nd and the 4th, which play to a par of five. On the back nine there are none – hence the par of 70. The first hole is a short par-four – as an opening hole should be – bending slightly to the right but not quite enough to be classified as a dog-leg. The green is clearly visible from the tee, but so are nine bunkers, most of them on the right side of the fairway to snare a slice. Once they are bypassed only a pitch to the green is left. Across Ardmore Avenue there is a completely different style of hole: a skinny, 536-yard par-five uphill, with out-of-bounds all the way along the right side. Then follows a fairly long par-three – not quite 200 yards – to a large green that is hard to miss. This, in turn, is followed by the longest hole on the course, a par-five of 600 yards. It is straight and bunkered only for the most errant shot – two pleasant, straight woods followed by a 6- or 7-iron across a thin stream to a very deep green. It is guarded to the rear and on both sides by six bunkers to trap the foolhardy who try to reach the green in two. Four par-fours follow. All are of medium length, the longest being the 6th, 420 yards but with very little bunkering, and the shortest the 7th, a mere 350 yards. The 6th and 7th present no sand problems off the tee, but they are very strategically trapped around the greens. Hugh Wilson never put a single extraneous bunker into Merion; despite the fact that there are 120 of them, every single one is for play, not display.

The 8th hole is a perfect example of his use of sand-traps. There is a bunker short to the right of the fairway for the slicer and another far to the left for the hooker. In other words, the short hitter has to be aware of the first trap and the long hitter, ignoring the first, has to be aware of the second. If both are avoided only a short iron is left, since the hole is just 360 yards long. Here, Wilson formed a snake-like trap to protect the entire front of the panhandle green, the handle of which faces the player. If the pin is on the handle, it is one of the most challenging and nerve-racking par-fours to be found anywhere. The par-three 9th is some 193 yards long, but the tee shot is from a hill to a green in a small valley so it requires less club than that distance usually calls for. A brook, and a lagoon which spurs off it, have to be carried; but they lie well short of the huge green, which is guarded by six bunkers to the left, right and rear.

From the 9th green there is a walk up a hill to the 10th tee. At 310 yards and a par of four, it falls just short of being a joke until played. Big hitters have often driven nearly hole-high, only to find themselves with a pitch as delicate as picking up a teacup filled to the brim. Both sides of the green are edged by sand, and the oblong green has a dozen varieties of pin positions.

The golfer now faces the 11th, which is played in the opposite direction and, at 369 yards, is really not much longer than the 10th. The tee shot is into a slight valley and the pitch, although not overly long, is across a creek to a green banked with rocks. In 1930 Bobby Jones – having won the British Amateur at St Andrews, the British Open at Hoylake and the US Open at Interlachen – then stood dormie-eight on Eugene Homans, needing only a niblick shot to the green to be the first and only man to have won all four championships in a single season. He flicked the ball upon the green, took two putts to halve with Homans and so won, 8 and 7, to ensure himself a place in golf history. It took a body of marines to protect him from the slaps on the back and the handshakes of the immense gallery.

The 11th was also the scene of a moment of comedy during the US Open four years later. Bobby Cruickshank – the "Wee Scot", as he affectionately came to be known in America – was very much in contention. After a good drive into the valley he had to carry the brook in front of the green. He hit his approach to the green a little "fat"; the ball plopped into the water.

To everyone's astonishment it hit a rock in the brook and bounded on to the green. Cruickshank was so elated that he threw his niblick into the air and turned to the gallery in disbelief. As everybody cheered the club fell and hit him squarely on the head, knocking him to his knees. "Aye," said Bobby as he rubbed his head, "that's the first time I've made a par hitting two rocks on the same hole." The 12th is again a drive off a high tee, with no drastic situations for the moderately straight driver. There are bunkers to the left but they are of no concern to the long hitter – mainly because they serve as hazards for the short hitter off the parallel 11th. The hole is a dog-leg to the right where there are trees which cannot be carried and which therefore dictate the placing of the drive. The second shot is uphill, thus compensating for the downhill tee shot, and the long green

now facing the golfer is bounded everywhere except in front by bunkers, all of which drop off quickly into rough.

The green sits alongside Ardmore Avenue and may be unique in that it is probably the only putting surface that lies not two feet from out-of-bounds. Walter Hagen, one of the most delicate putters who ever lived, once overhit his putt and rolled it into the street – thus leaving him with another improbable record: the first important player in a major contest to hit a putt out-of-bounds! Next to the 7th at Pebble Beach, where the wind is always a major consideration, the 13th at Merion – only 127 yards long – may be the most stringent par-three in America. It is a mere pitch to the green, but it has to be perfect because there is no margin for error whatsoever. Directly in front of the green is one of those "white faces" and to the left and behind it are three more, staring like ghosts. The putting surface is wide but not deep, and a misjudged shot or mishit is certain to find one of them. Since the first is deep and the others slanted, getting out and on to the green presents an even more tender shot than that which has to be played off the tee.

The next two holes, both par-fours, are tightened by a road down the left side which is out-of-bounds. For the 1971 US Open the 14th played at 408 yards, some thirty yards shorter than its full length. The hole dog-legs left and from the back of the tee the trees on the left emphasise the need to draw the ball round the corner and clear of the traps on the right. The second shot requires only a mid iron to an oval green, protected by three sprawling traps. The 15th is another drive and a mid iron. It dog-legs to the right and the well-placed drive has to carry two traps on that side to open up the green, which is angled diagonally across the line. Two traps flank the left side and a large bunker eats into the front, making it very difficult to go for the pin when it is placed anywhere on the right side.

The last three holes at Merion provide a great championship finish. The "quarry hole" – the 16th – is 428 yards long off an elevated tee through a valley which stops at an old overgrown quarry which, fortunately, cannot be reached with the drive; the second is the worrying shot with anything from a 4-iron to a 4-wood needed and the golfer has to succeed in carrying the green on the fly.

The 17th, played in the reverse direction, is the 220-yard par-three where Hogan made a momentous two in the play-off for the 1950 US Open. The quarry lies at the foot of the tee, but does not have to be taken into account any more than it does at the 18th, which again comes back across it. The 18th is 463 yards long, calling for a wood shot – or at least a long iron – to the green. It is immortalised in a photograph of Hogan making his second shot to the green with a 1-iron. It was the last time he used the club, for as he signed his card it was carried off by a souvenir hunter. One of the men Hogan beat in 1950 was George Fazio, later a golf architect and adviser to the United States Golf Association. Nobody was more qualified than he to assess Merion, which he rated alongside Pine Valley as the kind of course he most admired. Why? "It has character," he said. "It is challenging, without being backbreaking."

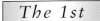
The 1st

The 1st: 362 yards par 4

0 yds   100 yds

An Elusive Touch of Poetry

Almost anyone can design a par-five or a par-four that can only be reached in regulation figures by the supremely long hitters and seldom by the average player. The same holds true for a par-three that will accept only one shot. But it takes a touch of the poet to lay out a short par-four like the 1st at Merion, a mere 362 yards long but one of the great opening holes in golf.

It is a dog-leg to the right, in which the only problem for the average golfer lies in his tendency to slice. The hole has no fewer than nine bunkers, only three of which are on the left, two alongside the fairway and one beside the green. A solitary trap lies in the middle of the fairway, but it is far out of reach of the amateur. All the others line the right side of the fairway clear to the green, which is so exquisitely contoured that it contains half a dozen different pin positions. The putting surface is pear shaped and slopes gently from right to left and from the front to the back, where there is a tiny, shallow trap. Thus, while the second shot may be nothing more than a mere pitch, it must be very exact. For the professional the problems from the tee are somewhat different. He must see that he does not drive into the two bunkers on the left, since he is more prone to hook, or right through the very broad fairway into the rough, which contains a series of mounds from which it is a near impossibility to pitch anywhere near the flagstick. Many of the holes at Merion have more instant appeal but the golfer who plays there regularly finds that he appreciates more and more the subtleties of the 1st. It combines the two most difficult objectives sought by a master architect: a great opening hole, and a great short par-four. That achievement alone shows why Hugh Wilson was able to build such intricate poetry into the design of the Merion course.

Touches that Mould Tradition

In his determination to make Merion East a course apart, Hugh Wilson concerned himself with the kind of detail that so many other architects ignore. Over the years these touches have conspired with momentous golfing events to create a tradition at Merion that is rare among American courses. One of Wilson's ideas, which he picked up from Sunningdale in Berkshire during his long pilgrimage to Britain, was to do away with flags and to mark the holes with wicker baskets atop the usual flagsticks. For many years the baskets were woven in the maintenance shop at Merion.

Although now out of favour elsewhere, wicker baskets were once widely used in Britain because they could be seen from any angle and did not aid a player in judging wind direction and strength. In the unlikely, but not entirely inconceivable, event of a ball lodging in a basket, the Rules of Golf permitted a player to remove the ball and, without penalty, place it on the edge of the hole.

The deepest south

gets its first great course

The Course Card

Seminole Golf Club, North Palm Beach, Florida

Record: 60, Claude Harmon, 1948

Hole	Yards	Par
1	370	4
2	387	4
3	501	5
4	450	4
5	195	3
6	383	4
7	432	4
8	235	3
9	494	5
10	382	4
11	403	4
12	367	4
13	168	3
14	499	5
15	495	5
16	399	4
17	175	3
18	417	4
Out	3,447	36
In	3,305	36
Total	**6,752**	**72**

Golf in the tropical climate of southern Florida is a seasonal thing except to those stalwarts who will forsake their air-conditioning for the Turkish-bath atmosphere of the months from May through October. During the dead months, when their members are in the northern states or the spas of Europe, clubs like Seminole tend their courses only just enough to prevent them from running to seed. It is, then, something of a miracle that the best of these courses – and there is none better than Seminole – can be brought to such a peak of perfection during the winter.

For many years, Seminole was so pampered by a singularly devoted golfer, Christopher J. Dunphy, who had been a close friend of and uncompromising competitor against just about all the leading amateurs and professionals of his time. In fact, when one thought of Seminole, one thought of Chris Dunphy. Dunphy's love affair with golf began in earnest soon after World War I. He was employed at the time by Mr Edward B. McLean, a wealthy Cincinnati newspaper publisher who was himself a golfing enthusiast, so in his younger days Dunphy was able to spend a good deal of his leisure on the famous courses of America and Europe in company with his employer. After McLean's death, Dunphy and his wife settled down in Palm Beach, and Dunphy began to spend more and more of his time playing at Seminole.

The club had been built in the 1920s during that prosperous period in American life. The course was laid out by Donald Ross, who was the architect for so many of the outstanding courses on the East Coast of the United States. With assistance from a former Tennessee mountaineer, T. Claiborn Watson, Ross designed a true linksland course over the Florida sand ridges adjacent to the Atlantic Ocean some fifteen miles north of the exclusive Palm Beach winter colony. At the time, the club was no more than a half-hour's drive from the colony over an uncrowded highway. Ross and Watson's course was the first truly fine test of golf in that southernmost part of America, but the exclusive and expensive nature of the club meant only a few of the very rich ever had a chance to play it. From the back tees it was a long course, but its principal feature was its profligate use of large bunkers covered with snow-white sand. Even today, the bunkers, which have grown to more than 200 in number, are the most conspicuous feature of the course. As was the case with so many of the enterprises of America's wealthy businessmen, the fortunes of Seminole declined during the great Depression, but the club survived through the attention of a few deeply devoted members. When World War II left it with virtually no patronage, there was some question whether it would survive. It was at the end of this bleak period that Dunphy arrived and restored the Seminole course and club to its former glory.

The war over, members began to drift back to Palm Beach, and a new generation of the rich discovered the area as a winter playground. It was then that Dunphy

assumed the role of Seminole's *ex officio* ringmaster. He spent countless hours with Watson, who had remained on as greenkeeper ever since the course was first built, restoring and improving Seminole. New hybrid grasses of the Bermuda strain were added to the fairways and greens to give them firmness and depth and to keep them in first-class playing condition during the latter part of the season when the less hardy grasses begin to die out. As a result, the ball sits up on the Seminole fairways as if it had been ever so gently placed on a soft cushion. The greens, with their Bermuda base, are large with subtle borrows, averaging around 7,500 to 8,000 square feet, and they are as true as any greens can be in that humid region with its constant spray of salty mist from the ocean. The club's annual professional-amateur tournament was discontinued in 1960 and had the largest pool connected to any American tournament during its time, reaching several hundred thousand dollars. It was always interesting, however, to see the professionals struggling with Seminole's complex design of sand and water, and it should be noted that few of them ever dominated it. None the less, Claude Harmon, who was for many years the distinguished resident professional at Seminole in the winter months, once scored a course record 60. A map of his remarkable round hangs on the clubhouse wall. The sight of the Seminole course on a balmy day with a brisk wind blowing in off the Atlantic is one to be cherished. The sweep of the rolling green fairways, punctuated by the multitude of dazzling white bunkers and the tall palms leaning with the breeze, is one of the most spectacular vistas to be found in this flat, tropical country, the highest point of which is only 65 feet above sea-level. It is a wide open course with little of the scrubby underbrush that characterises so many Florida courses.

Finally, there is an unforgettable pair of closing holes running alongside the dunes that separate the course from the sea. The 17th, a par-three, plays almost always into the wind from an elevated tee to an elevated green with a vast amount of sand falling away on three sides and the thick tangle of sea-grape bushes on the ocean side. As Dunphy once put it, "It is a rare sight to see all four balls of a match on the green at once." The 18th is a very long shot from an elevated tee to the elbow of the fairway below, and then a long iron or fairway wood uphill to a splendid green nestling against the sea-grapes atop the dune. A par is dearly bought here, too. The strength of Seminole and its fascination to dedicated golfers was summed up by Ben Hogan when he said: "If you can play well there, you can play well anywhere." Every golfer finds that kind of challenge irresistible.

Dominated by 200-odd bunkers and traps, a large central lake and swaying palms, Seminole is one of the most attractive of America's courses. It is also one of the most exclusive and it is unfortunate that the claims made for it by regular visitors like Armour and Hogan have never been really tested in tournament conditions.

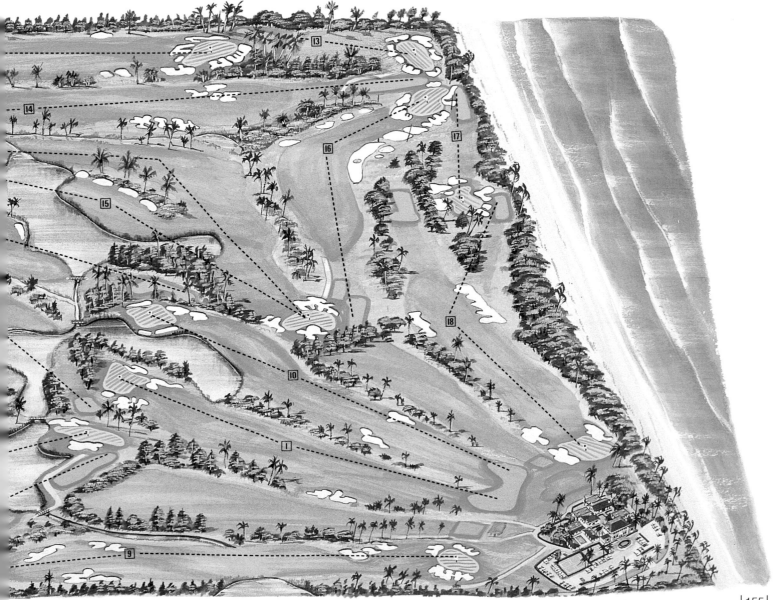

90% horse manure
and 10% luck

The most famous island green of them all, reproduced on computer games the world over, the 17th at Sawgrass.

One of the strongest fields of the year is assembled each March at Sawgrass for the PGA Tour's own Players Championship. At stake is one of the biggest purses of the year, the winner taking home over $1million. For some it is the last chance to engineer an invitation to the Masters. For Tiger Woods in 2001 it was the moment to silence the press in his build up to making history at Augusta. They said he had been in a slump. He proved them wrong – very wrong – by lifting the Bay Hill Invitational, Players Championship and the Masters in successive appearances. That the Masters turned out to be the last leg of his Grand Slam, holding all four Majors at the same time, is glorious history. However, many would say that he held five Majors, not four, because it is not only the press that frequently dubs the Players Championship 'The Fifth Major'. Vijay Singh, Colin Montgomerie and Hal Sutton (the winner in 2000) were among a number of players calling for official recognition of the championship as a Major following Woods's victory. It is, after all, the players' course, the one they agreed to have built at their tour headquarters when the idea was first suggested in 1978.

It was really Tour Commissioner Deane Beman's brainchild. He had appreciated just what could be done to make every aspect of a tournament's play visible to the maximum number of spectators at such innovative courses as Jack Nicklaus's Muirfield Village. At Sawgrass Beman would build the first true stadium course. 415 acres of Florida wasteland were purchased for the grand sum of $1. Pete Dye, the former insurance salesman, now the most adventurous of golf course architects – some might say the *enfant terrible* – was engaged to design this stadium course. His earliest layouts had been low-budget affairs in the Midwest – hardly high profile – but, after a study tour of the great Scottish courses, Dye had evolved a distinctive style of small greens, pot bunkers and railroad ties. He already had a track record in Florida, having

The Moorings, Amelia Island Plantation and John's Island Club to his name, he had been part of the team at Harbour Town, and his stunning "Teeth of the Dog" course at Cajuiles in the Dominican Republic was widely acknowledged as world class.

The chosen site was flat. No part of it was more than five feet above sea level. So, 850,000 cubic feet of soil had to be excavated to build the massive spectator mounds that line most fairways. That left behind a number of hollows that soon became a network of intimidating water hazards. The route plan was cleverly devised to bring several holes close to the clubhouse allowing spectators easy access to most parts of the course. But the players hated it. When it was first used for the Players Championship in 1982, Ben Crenshaw denounced it as "Star Wars golf designed by Darth Vader". Jack Nicklaus said, "I've never been very good at stopping a 5-iron on the hood of a car," while J.C. Snead summed it up as "90% horse manure and 10% luck." Hardly surprisingly, Jerry Pate, who won that year, was less condemnatory. "It's too early to rate this course. It's like trying to rate girls when they're born. They get better with age."

However, Dye and Beman were not prepared to live through a long and difficult adolescence. All aspects of the course had been criticized, the narrow fairways, horrendous rough, exceptionally penal placing of the bunkers, constricting trees and, worst of all, the viciously contoured greens. Dye worked with an advisory group of players to rework the greens, alter some of the bunkers and make a number of fairways more receptive to a decently struck drive. It is still not easy but it is undoubtedly fairer, and soon the previously critical Crenshaw was describing it as a "darn good course with no weak holes."

Dye encourages bravery from the start, calling for a drive that defies the bunkers and trees to set up an easier approach to the narrow green. By keeping the par-5 2nd at a reasonable length, the good player is encouraged to go for the green in two, but there are trees on both sides plus a lateral water hazard in wait if the drive is the slightest bit off line. Birdies are not uncommon on the short 3rd, but Paul Azinger has described the 4th as the sort of hole on which "you can make double- or triple-bogey in a heartbeat." Hal Sutton twice holed his second shot for an eagle during the course of his winning performance in 2000. Length is more at a premium on the 5th, a 466-yard par-4 on which a generous landing area persuades many to reach for the driver, but the green is well protected. Dreadful problems confront players who only just miss the 6th green.

Everything at the TPC is on the grand scale, with the bunker on the left of the 7th fairway running almost the entire length of the hole, along with a water hazard. It is

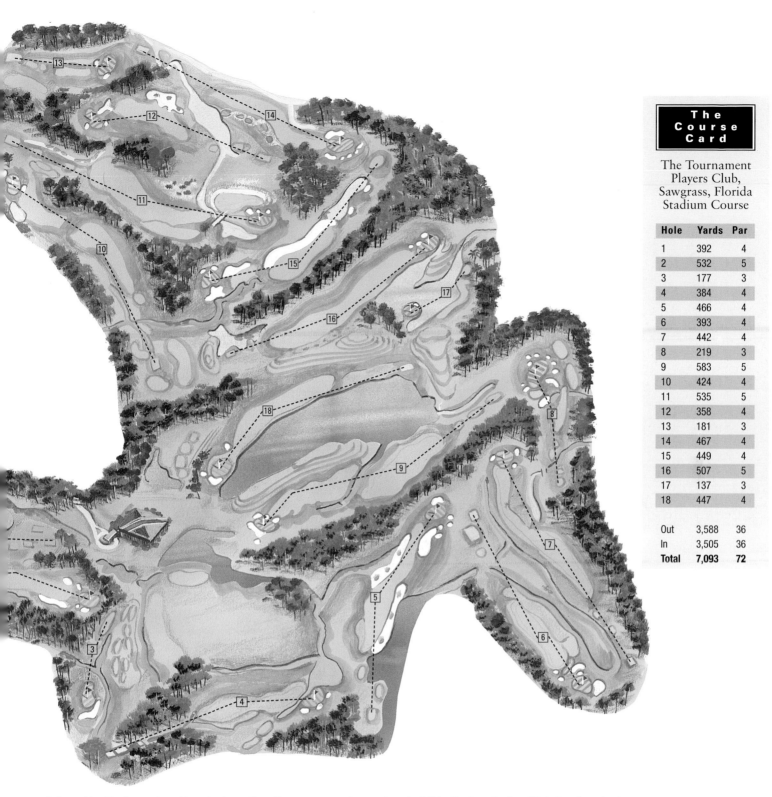

The Course Card

The Tournament
Players Club,
Sawgrass, Florida
Stadium Course

Hole	Yards	Par
1	392	4
2	532	5
3	177	3
4	384	4
5	466	4
6	393	4
7	442	4
8	219	3
9	583	5
10	424	4
11	535	5
12	358	4
13	181	3
14	467	4
15	449	4
16	507	5
17	137	3
18	447	4
Out	3,588	36
In	3,505	36
Total	**7,093**	**72**

followed by the longest and toughest par-3 on the course and one of the most demanding par-5s in America. Indeed, the 9th proved to be the toughest par-5 on the entire tour back in 1984.

As the alternative starting point, the 10th is almost a mirror image of the 1st. Bernhard Langer birdied the 11th and 12th holes to mount a challenge to Woods in 2001, the 11th a cleverly contrived par-5 offering various combinations of routes. (Langer eventually finished two shots behind Woods). The 14th has usually been one of the hardest holes to play against par under tournament conditions. Vijay Singh ran up a triple-bogey 7 here while in hot pursuit of Woods. He caught up again with an eagle on the 16th and birdie on the 17th. Tiger Woods knows the course intimately, having won the first of his three US Amateur titles at Sawgrass back in 1994. He nearly came to grief on the 17th in that final. The hole is world famous, the best-known island hole of them all. It is not long, but club selection is critical. In 1994 Woods, who had never

been ahead of Trip Kuehne in the 34 holes they had played so far, came to the 17th all square for the first time since the very start. He played first, hitting a pitching wedge over the flag, landing in the fringe at the far side of the green, stopping only a foot short of dropping into the water. Woods had a difficult, curving putt, but he read it correctly and his birdie took him into the lead for the first time. A solid par-4 on the 18th was then enough for Woods to take the title. In the last round of the 2001 Players Championship Woods hit a 9-iron to the 17th. It spun vigorously on landing and would have finished up in the water, except that the course had been drenched in rain. Miraculously the ball stayed above ground and Woods made his par. This time a bogey-five on the 18th was sufficient for a one-stroke victory over Singh. It is a hole that makes for a brilliant finish to the round with water running the length of the hole on the left and just enough curve on the fairway to call for perfect line to be allied to good length.

Kentucky battleground of

Odin's warriors

Valhalla has become a favourite with the PGA of America. They like the course, they like the welcome they get from the club and spectators alike, and they have vowed to return there: it is already confirmed as the venue for the 2008 Ryder Cup Matches. The Ryder Cup is head-to-head matchplay. The PGA Championship used to be, only becoming a strokeplay tournament in 1958. For one glorious day in August 2000 the championship effectively reverted to matchplay with one of the great last day duels being fought out by the giant of the age, Tiger Woods, and an American better known in Europe than at home, Bob May. They tussled for the championship neck and neck all the way to the 72nd hole and on into a playoff. So captivating was the struggle that few spectators noticed that the Valhalla course itself had almost capitulated to the players. Records were being set almost every minute.

On the Saturday 53 players broke par, a US PGA record, with José Maria Olazábal setting a course record 63. Woods and May needed only 270 strokes to complete their regulation 72 holes, 18-under being a PGA record. Woods had used a mere 15 putts over his final 12 holes, while May fired a back-nine 31 to give him his third successive 66. Would the course be criticized as harshly as it was when the PGA came to Valhalla in 1996, with Mark Brooks defeating Kenny Perry, also in a playoff? The answer was no. The players loved the course and the praise flooded in. Phil Mickleson described it, "The fairways are some of the best I've ever seen. They are immaculate." Ernie Els said, "It's a very good golf course to play a major championship on."

Valhalla was first laid out in 1986 by Jack Nicklaus. Following the initial criticism, twelve holes were altered in some way or other, the course was extended to 7,167 yards and, as in 1996, the 12th and 16th confirmed their status as the hardest holes of the tournament. On the last day, however, it was the 1st that turned out to be the toughest despite its lack of bunkers. The hole had been lengthened to force the majority of players to have to take wood off the tee to find the angle of the dog-leg from which the approach is made past a deep, green-front swale. In contrast, the 2nd is the easiest hole, yielding up 180 birdies and 11 eagles in the 2000 PGA. The 3rd can be made one of the most demanding of all simply by placing the flagstick in one of the four corners when to attack is dangerous to say the least.

A bunker 250 yards out on the left of the 4th fairway tempts strong players to drive over it, leaving only a lob wedge to the green. Although there is no fairway bunkering, the 5th is a strong hole, with thick rough on either side of the fairway in the landing zone. It yields few birdies. A sharp dog-leg characterizes the 6th, a hole that is straightforward only if the correct part of the fairway (left-centre) is found from the tee.

Valhalla's longest hole is the 7th – at least it is if the main fairway is taken. But for long hitters there is a strip of fairway on the straight line to the green, which reduces the overall length to around 530 yards. For the professionals it is one of the easiest holes. The short holes, on the other hand, are by no means simple, with each of them averaging above par during the PGA. There is certainly trouble aplenty lurking just off the 8th green in the shape of bunkers, deep rough and a slope leaning towards Floyd's Fork. Returning to the clubhouse, the 9th has been narrowed in the landing area, encouraging players to carry the right-hand fairway bunker with their drives.

At the turn on the Sunday afternoon of the 2000 PGA only two strokes covered seven players in contention. On Saturday, the 10th had been a turning point for the Dane, Thomas Bjorn, his eagle-3 moving him up the leaderboard. He went on to finish the championship in third place. The 10th also proved crucial for Woods and May in the final round, their birdies giving them their first daylight

In capturing the 2000 US PGA at Valhalla Tiger Woods equalled Ben Hogan's record of winning three Majors in the same year.

over the pursuing pack. May moved further ahead with an 8-iron birdie on the short 11th. In the third round Woods had pulled his 3-wood tee shot deep into the trees at the difficult 12th to run up a double-bogey 6. It was very different on Sunday, May hitting an 8-iron stone dead, but Woods, who was further away, sank a nail-biting birdie putt to keep May's lead to a single shot. The 13th is a pretty hole, with the green set up on boulders, surrounded by water. It makes an attractive target from the fairway, but the green is much less easy to find from the treacherous rough.

As the final round built to a climax, May and Woods both hit 4-irons to the 14th, May's ball finishing about six feet away. Woods had run his ball round behind the flag, cleverly using the slopes on the left of the green. He was putting like a demon and sank a testing birdie putt to put the pressure on May. May's cross-handed putting stroke held up solidly and he matched Woods's birdie to retain his one-shot lead. The approach to the 15th is one of the most daunting of the round, with water on the right of the green and two deep collection areas on the left. May almost hit his 7-iron into the hole. Woods was fifteen feet away in three. His long putt for par went safely into the hole. For the first time May's putting let him down, an obvious birdie turning into a routine par. But he still retained his one-shot advantage. It was a brilliant wedge-approach at the 17th that saw Woods draw level with May for the first time since the second hole. They made the 18th look simple, both able to reach the green in two shots. May was a

long way from the pin, though, and hit his first putt into the fringe 18 feet from the hole. Woods got his first putt much closer, some 6 feet away. May made his long and difficult putt for birdie to put the pressure back on Tiger, who calmly sank his putt to tie, before punching the air in characteristic fashion.

The 3-hole playoff began at the 16th, which has a bunkerless fairway but trees threaten the pulled shot. With May in trouble off the tee and unable to reach the green in two and Woods safely on with a 2-iron and 7-iron, it looked as if the playoff might be anticlimactic. But May played a brilliant recovery shot to save par, whereupon Woods sank a magnificent curling 25-foot putt for birdie and a one stroke lead. Neither made the 17th green in regulation, but a superb bunker shot by May and a long putt from behind the green by Woods set up their pars, maintaining the margin. While they had played the 18th easily in the last round, both made something of a hash of it in the playoff, pulling their drives into trouble on the left. In fact neither player was ever on the fairway as they hacked their way towards the green. Woods was bunkered in three while May hit his third with a wedge to 25 feet. Tiger's bunker shot was stunning. He was certain of par. May had to hole his long putt to remain in the match. It was a hard one, up over a ridge, then breaking sharply to the left. It missed by inches. It was a brilliant attempt, but Woods had retained the PGA Championship (the first golfer to do so since Denny Shute in 1937). He had done so after an epic battle worthy of Odin's warriors.

The Course Card

Valhalla Golf Club, Louisville, Kentucky

Record: 63,
José Maria Olazábal

Hole	Yards	Par
1	446	4
2	535	5
3	208	3
4	350	4
5	465	4
6	421	4
7	597	5
8	166	3
9	418	4
10	551	5
11	168	3
12	467	4
13	348	4
14	217	3
15	402	4
16	444	4
17	422	4
18	542	5
Out	3,606	36
In	3,561	36
Total	**7,167**	**72**

Oak Hill Country Club, Rochester, East Course

Hole	Yards	Par
1	460	4
2	401	4
3	211	3
4	570	5
5	436	4
6	177	3
7	460	4
8	430	4
9	454	4
10	342	4
11	222	3
12	372	4
13	594	5
14	323	4
15	177	3
16	439	4
17	460	4
18	480	4
Out	3,599	35
In	3,499	35
Total	**7,098**	**70**

Oak Hill could hardly be more appropriately named, for there are some 80,000 trees, the great majority of them oaks, lining the East and West Courses. Oddly enough, when the club moved to this site in 1924, the 6,000 shrubs initially planted shrivelled up miserably. The landscaping committee, some of whom were nurserymen, had failed. They passed the problem over to one of their most renowned members, Dr. John R. Williams, Sr. His reputation, however, was founded not with plants but in medicine. He had pioneered refrigeration for the safe preservation of food, revolutionised home milk deliveries and had helped to establish the country's first laboratory for the study of diabetes. "It was then that I discovered the Almighty was the greatest landscape architect of all. It was His plan to have oaks at Oak Hill." Williams set about locating acorns from some of the world's historic trees and he propagated enormous numbers of them in his Munroe Avenue backyard, soon becoming an expert in all facets of arboriculture. Happily, Williams is commemorated by a bronze plaque affixed to one of the English oaks on the Hill of Fame crowning the amphitheatre around the 13th green.

The club had begun in 1901 when twenty-five golfers from the Rochester area set up a simple 9-hole course on the banks of the Genesee River. Golf flourished, the course was expanded to 18 holes and a proper clubhouse erected. But, a few years later, the neighbouring University of Rochester decided that it would like to purchase the site for expansion. In exchange for the land the University was prepared to finance the construction of two new courses and a substantial clubhouse on 355 acres of barren farmland in suburban Pittsford. There may have

been few trees, but when Donald Ross was consulted on the potential of this land he could see straight away that it could be made into "one of the finest golf courses in the United States." He began construction in 1924 and after two years' work the East and West Courses were ready for play and the planting of Williams's saplings.

For the next twenty years golf at Oak Hill was principally of the social kind, although Snead, Hogan and Sarazen took part in tournaments there in the 1940s. Then in 1948 USGA director Joe Dey made a visit. "Where have you been for the last twenty years?" he asked. "There's nothing like this in the whole of America." A year later

Great Oaks

from little acorns grow

Almost all of Donald Ross's 1924 design at Oak Hill survives, continuing to challenge the modern golfer with its combination of narrow, tree-lined fairways and subtly borrowed, tightly defended greens. Around 80,000 trees have matured to make this one of the most attractive of all Major venues.

Charlie Coe took the first of his US Amateur titles at Oak Hill, and the course was set to make its US Open debut in 1956. Robert Trent Jones was brought in to make a few adjustments to the course, which he knew well having lived locally. The length was increased by some 350 yards and par was dropped from 72 to 70. Jones added over twenty bunkers and altered the design of others, but it was still very much Donald Ross's course which stood up well to the best that Hogan, Snead, Demaret and the rest could throw at it. No one broke par during the first round, and Cary Middlecoff's winning score was a one-over 281. But it was not the same story in 1968 when victor Lee Trevino became the first man to shoot all four rounds in the sixties,

tying the US Open record with 275. Changes had to be made.

The most significant of the alterations made in the 1970s by George and Tom Fazio were the elimination of a weak hole, modification of the old 6th, now played as the 5th, the creation of a new par-3 6th, the digging of a pond on the 15th, and substantial alterations to the 18th. These were sufficient to ensure that in the 1980 US PGA Jack Nicklaus was the only player under par, finishing at six-under. Nine years later, Curtis Strange became the first man since Hogan to win back-to-back US Opens with a score of 278, two-under.

Oak Hill played very long in the cold and wet condi-

Oak Hill's 13th with its hazards of Allen's Creek, mature trees and plentiful bunkers rarely yields a birdie even to the top professionals.

tions prevailing when the 1995 Ryder Cup came to Rochester. The Europeans were still smarting from their defeats in the last two contests at Kiawah Island and The Belfry but they held their form in the last day's singles to claim a 14½–13½ victory. The US Amateur Championship returned in 1998, and preparations then began for the 85th US PGA Championship to be held over the East Course in August 2003. Par has remained at 70, but the length has crept up to almost 7,100 yards and, with fairways averaging only 23 yards in width, Oak Hill calls for immaculate driving.

Ben Hogan called Oak Hill's 1st "the toughest starting hole in golf." An out-of-bounds on the right and the narrowness of the fairway between tall trees can ruin a card from the very outset. Those who combine length with straightness can benefit from a downslope at the 260-yard mark. Similarly, driving on the 2nd is like hitting down the barrel of a rifle. Cary Middlecoff, during the 1956 US Open, let a drive slip into the right-hand fairway bunker. From there he hit a majestic recovery to four feet, a key moment on his road to success. Ross built the 3rd green on what is said to be a 25,000 year-old glacial drumlin. It is not a green to miss and regularly proves one of the hardest holes on the course. In contrast, the 4th yields 50% more birdies than any other hole. The key to success is the drive which must be played as a high fade carrying over two deep fairway bunkers.

The Fazios' revised 5th is one of the toughest holes at Oak Hill, with Allen's Creek only just off the fairway in the landing area. It crosses in front of the green threatening the approach shots of those who drove into the grasping rough on the left, trying to avoid the water from the tee. The creek also lurks on the left and in front of the 6th green. In

the 1989 US Open it yielded four aces in the first 90 minutes of play, but has proved treacherous to the careless, none the less. Once again the creek must be avoided from the 7th tee and this recently lengthened hole has one of the narrowest fairways, only 22 yards across.

The first hole visitors to the course see as they drive in is the 8th. Being absolutely straight, this 'welcome mat' encourages the big hitters. An extra 35 yards have been added to the 9th, another tough driving hole, with a testing uphill approach to the green. Oak Hill's oldest oak, a native dating back to the mid-1800s, stands on the left of the fairway.

The back nine then starts with an encouraging downhill drive onto an early Indian site, where meetings to promote peace took place as long ago as 1570 between the Senecas, Mowhawks, Oneidas, Ondongas and Cayugas, known as 'The Five Nations', the ancient League of the Iroquois. Nearly 400 years later, in 1968, Lee Trevino blitzed the 11th with three birdies and a par on the way to his first US Open triumph. Now the hole is 30 yards longer with the possibility of testing pin positions in the customary left-to-right wind.

Oak Hill's professional Craig Harmon reckons that longer hitters can reasonably expect to get within 50 yards of the green on the 12th, with its gentle downhill fairway, but that the smarter option is to take an iron from the tee to leave a 150-yard approach shot which can be hit more accurately to the green, especially when the pin is in the rear, left part of the green. He also anticipates that the 13th will be reached in two by someone during the 2003 PGA. It has not been achieved to date. The reason is that the ubiquitous Allen's Creek crosses the fairway at about the 300 yard mark, so most players opt for a fairway wood off the tee. Bunkers and trees give the fairway a double-dog-leg effect and the green is set in a natural bowl surrounded by bunkers. This is the Hill of Fame where the great and good of golf's history are commemorated.

The shortest par-4 is the 14th and, again, the art is to place the tee shot to leave a full wedge in to the correct part of the two-tier green. During the 19th century there was a sulphur spring complete with bath house to the right of this fairway, attracting visitors from far and wide to drink and bathe in the waters. The Fazios introduced water to the 15th, making it one of the handsomest holes on the course, but the prevalent left-to-right wind tends to push the tee shot towards that pond. Big hitters have an advantage on the 16th if they can find the downslope on the fairway which adds 30 or more yards of extra roll. But there is also a slope on the left which guides many tee shots into the deep rough.

Oak Hill's finish is tough, with the 17th traditionally yielding the fewest birdies in championship play. The uphill drive must be shaped from left to right and it is imperative to find the fairway, with heavy rough and pines on the left and further trees on the right which block many second shots. It was on this undulating green in the 1956 US Open that Ben Hogan missed a 2½-foot putt which ended his chances of a fifth title. In the last two majors played on the East Course the 18th has come out statistically as the 2nd and 3rd hardest hole on the course. Now it is over 30 yards longer, putting an even greater premium on the drive, ideally shaped left-to-right to follow the dog-leg. With a depression running through the fairway just short of the shallow green and a steep slope up to the putting surface, the approach must be played with absolute precision.

When, 75 years ago, Dr. Williams collected his famous acorns he had them sent from such prestigious specimens as the Shakespeare Oak at Stratford-on-Avon and the Great Oak at Ravenswood in Sherwood Forest. Williams was present when the members of the 1949

British Walker Cup team – the event had just been played at Winged Foot – came to Oak Hill to try their luck in the US Amateur. None of them succeeded, but they were popular visitors and a Pin Oak, native to Oak Hill, was selected to receive a plaque to commemorate the visit. Two years later the oak fruited for the first time. Williams collected a sack of acorns and had them sent to England in the diplomatic bag to avoid Ministry of Agriculture regulations! They were distributed to the home clubs of each of the members of that British team with full instructions on how to grow them. Sadly, there is no happy ending to this tale of 'acorn diplomacy', for the Pin Oak does not thrive in Britain and only two have survived to this day, one at Sandy Lodge in Middlesex, the other at Wildernesse in Kent.

Not only did the University of Rochester give Oak Hill 355 acres on which to build two 18-hole courses but also it financed the building of a vast, Tudor-style clubhouse.

During the 1995 Ryder Cup Matches Sam Torrance and Colin Montgomerie struggle to keep their fourball match with Brad Faxon and Fred Couples alive on the 15th. They lost the next hole to go down 4 & 2. Both won their singles on the following day, contributing importantly to the Europeans' narrow one point victory.

The course

that Jack built

The
Course
Card

Muirfield Village
Golf Club,
Columbus, Ohio

Hole	Yards	Par
1	451	4
2	455	4
3	401	4
4	200	3
5	527	5
6	447	4
7	563	5
8	182	3
9	407	4
10	441	4
11	567	5
12	166	3
13	455	4
14	363	4
15	503	5
16	215	3
17	437	4
18	444	4
Out	3,633	36
In	3,591	36
Total	**7,224**	**72**

It was almost inevitable that when Jack Nicklaus, the greatest golfer of the age, decided to try his hand at course design he should start at the very top. In 1974 he was at the height of his playing powers, having four Masters, three US Opens, three US PGAs and two Open Championships already to his name, and he would go on to win a further six Majors before that particular golden age came to a close. Yet he made space in his busy playing schedule at that time to lay out a remarkable course. Many say it is his finest, not least because he put so much of himself into it. For a start, it is located near his hometown of Columbus. He named it after Muirfield, where he won his first Open Championship. He incorporated design features from some of his favourite courses, not least Augusta. The course favours a long, high fade, Nicklaus's trademark shot. Above all, it requires intelligent golf, at which Nicklaus always excelled.

The property was blessed with gently rolling land, streams and mature trees and Nicklaus was assisted by the experienced Desmond Muirhead in the routing and land planning of the course. Nicklaus has always held strong views about good course design – he does not like having to play uphill blind over a brow, for instance. He and Muirhead contrived to make the course as fair as possible in that the golfer can always see what he is required to do. They also considered the spectator from the very outset, setting many of the tees and greens in amphitheatres of moundwork to provide unrivalled viewing. In this respect it was the prototype for the many stadium courses built around the world since then.

It was envisaged from the start that Muirfield Village would host one of the premier events on the professional stage, and every May since 1976 a world class field has been assembled for the Memorial Tournament, so called because the tournament is dedicated to an individual who has 'played golf with conspicuous honor'. The first honourand was Nicklaus's hero, Bobby Jones, and they have since ranged from Tom Morris (Old and Young) to Glenna Collett Vare, Walter Hagen to Payne Stewart. Its list of champions is equally distinguished with Irwin, Watson, Floyd and Nicklaus himself among early victors, while more recently Tiger Woods has almost taken personal possession of the event with a hat-trick of wins from 1999 to 2001. As Greg Norman (also a Memorial champion)

**Jack Nicklaus planned
Muirfield Village in great
detail, often incorporating
features of other great
courses around the world.
He has continued to develop
the course, just as Bobby
Jones did at Augusta.**

Streams are used strategically on many holes at Muirfield Village. Two water crossings are required to reach the 11th green.

The handsome 12th reproduces many of the problems encountered on the 12th at Augusta.

From the beginning, Jack Nicklaus designed Muirfield Village to give huge galleries unimpeded views of the action.

says, 'Muirfield Village is the type of course that inspires great players to play their best golf.'

Muirfield Village played host to the 1987 Ryder Cup. Nicklaus was Captain of the American team, Tony Jacklin of the Europeans. European confidence was high. They had won at the Belfry two years previously, they had the reigning Open champion in Nick Faldo, and Severiano Ballesteros and Bernhard Langer had both won at Augusta during the past few years. Their confidence was well-founded and they entered the last day with a healthy 10½-5½ lead. The Americans fought back doggedly and very nearly snatched the cup from the visitors, but in the end the Europeans prevailed with a 15-13 win for the first time on American soil. It was exciting and the course proved to be excellent for matchplay, but the match was also memorable for the gentlemanly sportsmanship of the two captains. Nicklaus has always known how to win emphatically, but there are few more gracious or generous in defeat.

Over the years Nicklaus has made minor alterations to the course, adjusting the bunkering here, putting in new tees there or further improving the spectator facilities. The Tour professionals love and respect the course, and have rated it the best conditioned course on the tour. Despite the amendments, the course plays today much as it was designed to do back in 1974. The round starts with a challenging par-four, a dog-leg left to right with the fairway sloping right to left. Trees and bunkers punish the wayward drive and further sand surrounds the green. The creek which runs down the left of the 1st hole now crosses to become a serious threat on the right of the 2nd,

another tough hole. Water again lurks on the 3rd, awaiting a pulled drive or weak approach shot. It may not be entirely coincidental that the first short hole is the 4th, as at Augusta. It plays downhill to a green cut into a bank and well bunkered, and is one of the hardest holes against par on the course.

In the final round of the 2001 Memorial Tournament Tiger Woods came to the 5th tee one shot behind the overnight leader, Paul Azinger. Both found the fairway comfortably. The air was damp and Azinger's 3-wood shot to the green hung in the air agonisingly before dropping into the pond in front of the green. He finished up with a bogey-6. Woods, however, sent a 2-iron shot soaring 250 yards over the water, landing it on the green about 6 feet from the pin. His eagle gave him a three shot swing and he never looked back. Yet again water is a danger on the 6th, especially if the approach to the green is made from the wrong angle when overhanging trees complicate matters. By today's standards none of the par-fives is unduly long, and the 7th can be reached in two, but only if the angles of the double dog-leg are correctly negotiated. In his four rounds in 2001 Tiger Woods played the par-fives in 66 shots, 14-under par! Played through dogwood, beech and hickory, the 8th is the easiest of the short holes, and trees compel a straight drive on the 9th before the approach shot is played over a creek to a sloping green on the far side.

Bunkers constrict the landing zone on the 10th, while a stream restricts the length of the drive on the 11th, a particularly handsome hole running through a wooded valley. Augusta is again brought to mind at the 12th, with a short-iron shot across water to a kidney-shaped green. Some years ago this hole turned out to be the hardest par-three on the entire US tour. The wind is not likely to be so treacherous as at Augusta, but it is a far more difficult putting surface to read. After another dog-legged par-four, on which position from the tee is paramount, comes the shortest two-shotter on the course. It may be only 363 yards long but it can be the very devil, with the drive is restricted for length by the creek which crosses the fairway. The real problem comes with the next shot, for the green is long and narrow, set on a hillside with bunkers on the left and the stream on the right. Escape from one of the bunkers is nerve wracking with the probability of the ball running through the green and down the hill into the water.

At 503 yards the 15th is a par-five reachable in two by all today's professionals, its main protection being the narrowness of its rolling, tree-lined fairway. The last short hole has been lengthened by some ten yards and is nowadays the longest of the par-threes and it leads to a fine 17th. On the left of the fairway lies a vast expanse of sand, beyond which the fairway bends to the right, passing through a valley before rising steeply to the green which is protected by seriously deep bunkers. Much drama has been witnessed through the years on this hole during the Memorial Tournament. In a great many Memorials the 18th has turned out to be the hardest hole of the tournament. The drive is governed by a dog-leg with trees and sand in the angle and the green is an elusive target set above bunkers on a hillside which accommodates 20,000 or more spectators every day of the Memorial Tournament. In the first eighteen years of the tournament's history there were many tight finishes, with eight one-stroke victories and four playoffs, including a particularly memorable one in 1984 when the playoff winner turned out to be Nicklaus himself.

The free-form nature of the tee gives a variety of angles and lengths of shot to the 12th (above).

Severiano Ballesteros and José Maria Olazábal formed an outstandingly successful partnership during the 1987 Ryder Cup Matches. Jack Nicklaus, the American Captain, displayed exemplary sportsmanship and dignity throughout, always ready to congratulate players of both sides warmly.

Measuring men
by what they are

In an age when the top golfers earn more than the President of the USA and are treated like royalty, it is chastening to realise that until 1920 they were not even allowed inside the clubhouse at a national championship, changing their shoes in the back of the golf shop or on the running board of somebody's car. When the Inverness Club was invited to host its first major event, the 1920 US Open, the Club's president, S.P. Jermain, decided that Inverness would be remembered for its hospitality. The professionals were welcomed cordially, every part of the clubhouse was open to them, they were allocated individual lockers, and the dining room was reserved exclusively for their meals. In addition, accommodation was arranged at five downtown hotels, and transport to the club was laid on. Their treatment was so splendid that the professionals clubbed together to buy an ornate chiming clock, which they presented to the club, inscribed with the words:

God measures men by what they are
Not what they in wealth possess
That vibrant message chimes afar
The voice of Inverness.

The Course Card

The Inverness
Club, Toledo,
Ohio

Hole	Yards	Par
1	395	4
2	385	4
3	200	3
4	466	4
5	450	4
6	231	3
7	481	4
8	569	5
9	468	4
10	363	4
11	378	4
12	172	3
13	516	5
14	480	4
15	468	4
16	409	4
17	470	4
18	354	4
Out	3,645	35
In	3,610	36
Total	**7,255**	**71**

During Major championships Inverness has always proved notably resistant to scoring. Its narrow fairways and small greens demand pin-point accuracy from aspiring champions.

When next the US Open was pencilled in for Inverness, steel-shafted clubs had radically changed the way in which golf was played. A.W. Tillinghast, a former resident of Toledo, was brought in to toughen the course up. He designed four new greens, added a number of bunkers and lengthened the course by about 300 yards to 6,529 yards. The weather was ferociously hot for what turned out to be an extraordinary tournament. At the end of normal play on Saturday, Billy Burke and George Von Elm were tied on eight-over at 292. They came back for a 36-hole play-off on Sunday, but both of them shot 149, so they had to return again on Monday for another 36 holes. This time Burke managed a 148, to win by a single shot. Burke had effectively played two Opens to win one.

There was a long gap before the US Open returned to Inverness in 1957. To prepare the course for this Dick Wilson was engaged. He added a few more bunkers and a bit of length, bringing it up to 6,919 yards. His alterations were effective enough to ensure that, as with the previous two Opens at Inverness, the winning score was above par, and again there was a play off, Dick Mayer disposing of Cary Middlecoff. A casualty at the half-way stage that year was a stout 17-year-old amateur, Jack Nicklaus, who carded a pair of 80s. Wilson's bunkers were subsequently taken out in an attempt to restore the course to Ross's design, but there were more sweeping changes around the corner.

For the 1979 US Open, George and Tom Fazio were called in to do something about the 17th green. By the time they left they had also built three totally new holes (the present 3rd, 5th and 6th), knocked the old 6th, 7th and 8th into the present par-5 8th, disposed at last of the "forgotten hole" (the old 13th) and lengthened the charming 18th. Hale Irwin won that year, hanging on despite a closing 75, but the tournament is as much remembered for the invention of a man who finished tied for 53rd, Lon Hinckle. Standing on the 8th tee on the first day, Hinckle took out a 1-iron, knocking it through a gap in the trees onto the 17th fairway, from which he only needed a 3-iron to find the 8th green. He two-putted for an imaginative birdie. News soon got round and others followed him down the 17th. Next day players arrived on the 8th tee to find that, overnight, the USGA had planted a 25-foot Black Hills spruce tree near the tee box to prevent any further short-cuts. The tree lives on in legend as the "Hinckleberry."

That 1920 Open was won by Ted Ray, the big-hitting, pipe-smoking 43-year-old from Jersey. It was to be fifty years before another Briton would take the title – Tony Jacklin at Hazeltine in 1970. Ray and his fellow competitors (which included Bobby Jones and Gene Sarazen, taking part in their first Opens) were playing a new course laid out the previous year by Donald Ross. The club had been in existence since 1903, when its first course had been constructed by a good player, Bernard Nichols, competent enough, no doubt, with brassie and niblick, but hardly a distinguished mathematician. When the course was almost finished someone realised that Nichols had only built 8 holes! Another hole was hastily added and this 'forgotten hole' lasted for many years. Ross had initially been commissioned simply to make the existing nine holes up to 18, but he took the opportunity to remodel the Nichols holes at the same time, giving the whole course his distinctive stamp and a consistency of style. Much of his work survives even today, which is more than can be said for the original clubhouse. Two were destroyed by fire, the present one dating from 1919. A photograph of the present clubhouse hangs in the grill with the inscription, "Not burned yet!"

At first many of the senior players were unimpressed with the new holes. "I personally like to see the old courses left alone," said Jack Nicklaus, while Tom Weiskopf asked, "Why change the course? You can't measure what the players of the past were shooting." Both are now distinguished architects themselves. What might their views be today? The club has continued to use the Fazio course, hosting two dramatic US PGA Championships in 1986 and 1993. In the former, a brilliant bunker shot straight into the hole on the 18th gave Bob Tway victory, while the 1993 title was decided in a play off, Paul Azinger coming out on top. On both occasions the unlucky runner up was Greg Norman. A programme of restoration was undertaken in 1999 under the direction of Arthur Hills, the well-known course designer and Inverness member. It will be tested in 2003 by the field of the United States Senior Open.

Inverness is renowned for its greens, with tiny putting surfaces and mysterious contours. None is as deep as 30 yards and the 1st is the shallowest, only 21 yards from front to back. It is a relatively straightforward hole provided the ten bunkers separating this fairway from that of the 10th are avoided from the tee. Accurate placing of the drive is essential to survive at Inverness. Overhanging branches close out many approaches from the right on the 2nd, the classic, undulating Ross green giving a number of testing pin positions. The first of the Fazio holes, the 3rd, features a pond which guards the right side of the 3-level green.

For some years the 4th was the longest par-4 on the course. It remains one of the toughest, with no mercy shown on the drive. Pine trees, bunkers and deep rough smother inaccurate drives, and the green is elevated enough to have a devilish slope down from the left side which must be avoided. The 5th has been lengthened by about 50 yards since it was constructed by the Fazios, and the trees have grown tall enough to block out any drive hit left, while a stream lurks in the trees on the right, before swinging in to guard the right front of the hog's back green.

Bob Tway drives from the 7th tee in the final round of the US PGA Championship in 1986. He carded a score of 276, the first time the winner had finished under par in a Major at Inverness.

The Fourball Invitationals

For twenty years, starting in 1935, with a short break during the war, the Inverness Invitational brought the finest players to Toledo, attracting huge galleries to watch them. The club paid all the expenses for the golfers and their families and the list of winners is impressive. Most prominent on that list are Ben Hogan and Jimmy Demaret, who took the title four times between 1941 and 1948. There could hardly have been a greater contrast between them, Hogan reserved and calculating, Demaret the brightly-clothed extrovert. Demaret loved Toledo's night clubs where he could often be found running the floor show or singing the latest hits in a more than passable crooner's voice. One morning, a journalist spotted Demaret's car outside a night club as he was on his way to report on the tournament. He went inside, found Demaret fast asleep, splashed water on his face to wake him up, and pointed him in the direction of the Inverness Club. When Hogan spotted that Demaret had neither shaved nor changed his clothes since the previous day he was furious. Demaret birdied the 1st, 3rd, 4th and 6th, then turned to Hogan with the remark, "I think I've carried you as far as I can. I'm tired. Your turn."

There are only three short holes at Inverness and the 6th is the longest, although it often plays downwind. Three bunkers guard the angled green. No sand bunker is necessary on the 7th, one of golf's great par 4s. A new back tee has stretched the hole to 481 yards, thereby demanding a carry of over 250 yards to clear the creek which cuts in from the right just where a series of mounds lurks on the left. The green is protected by a steep fall into trouble on the right and a grass bunker on the left, and three putts are not uncommon.

Since Lon Hinkle's day, the trees separating the 8th and 17th have grown considerably and the 8th must, today, be played by the conventional route. With bunkers and tall trees guarding the inside of the dog-leg, the drive must be lined perfectly if there is to be any chance of finding the green in two (a much harder task now, as the hole is 40 yards longer than it used to be). In contrast, the 9th is these days a par-4, when it was actually built as a par-5. From the back tees it plays to a very full 468 yards, but the members play it at 369 yards, a difference of almost 100 yards. The green is mischievously sloped and ridged. Few putts are conceded here.

A downhill drive is welcome on the 10th, almost a mirror image of the 1st. The green is attractively sited in an amphitheatre, guarded in front by a stream and to either side by bunkers. Length is not at a premium here, nor is it at the 11th, but the 11th fairway is narrow and so is its green. A ridge runs through the centre of the 12th green, the only remaining Ross short hole, a little gem ringed by bunkers.

The second par-5 at Inverness is not unduly long and easily reachable in two shots by modern professionals, but only provided they find the fairway off the tee. The landing area at the 13th is narrow between bunkers and there is a series of undulations about 250 yards out. The green is quite elevated and those who do not reach it in two may find their third shot, the approach, partially blind. Two solid par-4s follow, the fairway of the 480-yard 14th defended by a 50-yard horseshoe-shaped bunker in driving range on

The 'Hinkleberry' planted beside the 8th tee during the 1979 US Open to prevent players taking a shortcut down the 17th fairway. Since then the trees have grown taller and thicker and that route is no longer an option.

A great, if outrageous, bunker shot

the left, with another, simpler bunker some 30 yards beyond to trap the really long hitter. A mid- or long-iron will be needed to find the tiny, rippled green which is reckoned to be the hardest of all to read at Inverness. From a tee set far back in a chute of trees, the professionals should drive well beyond the horseshoe-shaped bunker which reappears to the left of the 15th fairway. The approach shot is played downhill to another tricky green guarded by five bunkers. Those who par these two holes usually gain ground on the rest of the field.

Although the 16th is somewhat shorter, the landing areas is tight, bordered by trees and three prominent bunkers. A big bunker on the right of the green deceives the eye, the greater danger lying in the bunker along the left of the putting surface. Then comes another huge par-4 on which length off the tee is rewarded. Short drives leave a long, blind downhill second shot. An extravagantly shaped bunker guards the left of the green which slopes from back to front steeply enough to make a downhill putt something best avoided. One of the shortest finishing holes in championship golf remains, with most players taking an iron from the tee to ensure the best position for the pitch. This is not a green to miss, with four bunkers in close attendance and "Death Valley" just off the putting surface to the right. Set in a natural amphitheatre this green has seen more than a few men measured for what they are.

1986 should have been Greg Norman's annus mirabilis. He had led the Masters by a stroke going into the last day, but came up against Nicklaus in imperious form to miss out by a stroke. Norman should also have taken the US Open at Shinnecock Hills having, again, started the final day with a one-stroke lead. Raymond Floyd took that one, with Norman fading away. The Australian did manage to hang on to claim the Open Championship that year at Turnberry, so he knew he could, at last, win a Major. Surely there would be no slip up at the PGA, leading by four strokes going into the final round. But Norman let his lead slip, coming to the last hole tied for the lead with Bob Tway. A fiercely spinning approach shot from the middle of the fairway left Norman just off the green in two, though perfectly safe. Tway, however, had bungled his approach from a poor lie in the rough into a bunker below the green. Up in the television commentary box, Jack Nicklaus commented, prophetically, "If Tway was going to miss this green, that is the best place to do it." Tway holed his bunker shot, Norman missed his chip, and Tway's name, not Norman's, went into the record books.

Bob Tway celebrates the brilliant bunker shot that won him the 1986 US PGA.

The features of traditional Scottish links golf that Macdonald reproduced at the National have stood up impressively to the test of time.

Charles Blair Macdonald's
Ultimate design

The National Golf Links of America, Southampton, New York

Hole	Yards	Par
1	327	4
2	330	4
3	426	4
4	195	3
5	478	5
6	141	3
7	478	5
8	424	4
9	540	5
10	450	4
11	432	4
12	435	4
13	174	3
14	365	4
15	397	4
16	404	4
17	375	4
18	502	5
Out	3,339	37
In	3,534	36
Total	6,873	73

On the eastern seaboard of the United States, National Golf Links, known simply as the National, has attained something of the status of an institution of golf, comparable in its way with Pine Valley in New Jersey and the Augusta National in Georgia. Some such destiny must have been in the mind of its founder, the late Charles B. Macdonald, to have given the club such an imposing, almost presumptuous, name.

Macdonald was a most complex and controversial figure. Although his home was in Chicago, he attended the University of St Andrews in his youth, and there he grew enamoured of the great Scottish pastime. Returning to the American Middle West, he was easily the outstanding player of a game that was just beginning to take root among the well-to-do. In the year 1905, he travelled east to Rhode Island and won the first National championship, then an amateur event.

In the course of time, Macdonald became obsessed with the notion of building the ultimate golf course in his native land. Starting in 1902, he made an annual visit to Britain, taking meticulous notes on all the greatest links and measuring what he considered to be the best holes in England and Scotland. It was a labour that lasted through five summers.

A great many sites along the Atlantic coast were carefully considered by Macdonald as a possible location for his golf course and rejected for a variety of reasons, not least among them being the cost of the real estate. He finally settled for a parcel of some 250 acres of gently rolling landscape on the shore of Peconic Bay in eastern Long Island, a mere three miles from the Southampton railroad station and one hundred miles from New York City. Construction began on the course in 1907, and it was first played two years later. As originally laid out, the National was relatively short at 6,100 yards, but subsequent changes and modifications have stretched it to its present moderate length of 6,873 yards from the back tees.

Distance, however, is not the yardstick by which one measures the quality of the National. There is scarcely a day, even in midsummer, when the air is thin and the fairways hardened by the sun, when either the outbound nine or the incoming holes are not stretched formidably by the winds blowing off the Atlantic from the south or from Long Island Sound on the north. It is these elements that bring out the ingenuity and forethought of Macdonald's design, for virtually every two-shot and three-shot hole offers an alternative route or two to suit the elements as well as the strength and nerve of the player, and there is seldom any agreement on the best line to a hole in any given wind.

Of the five holes at the National which are close imitations of celebrated holes in Britain, three are encountered almost at the start of a round. The 2nd is modelled after the old 3rd at Royal St George's, a short par-four with the direct route from the tee requiring a carry of 200 yards over a wide, deep bunker that presents a bold choice at a moment when one is not yet sure of one's strength and timing on a given day. The 3rd reproduces the problems of the Alps at Prestwick. It is a 426-yard hole with a blind second shot hit over a sharply rising hill to a very wide and steeply contoured green, protected from end to end by a bunker front. Only a strong, well-placed drive leaves any hope of reaching this harrowing green in two. The 4th is a copy of North Berwick's Redan, a middle iron par-three with a long green falling off diagonally to the left. Here the direct shot to the green flirts with a deep bunker on the left that can destroy any chance of a par. The more cautious shot to the right will leave a long and delicate downhill chip or putt.

Two remaining holes, the 7th and 13th, were both designed to recreate something of two classic moments on the Old course at St Andrews. The former is more suggested by than modelled after the famous Road Hole, where so many championship hopes have died. However, the absence of the railroad sheds, which are represented

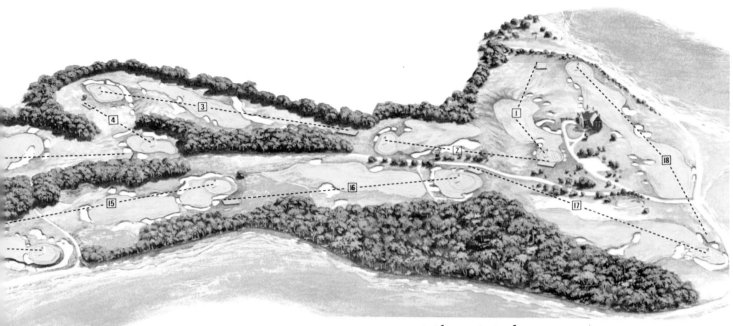

The 14th:
A rare penal touch

only by a large expanse of scrub-filled bunkers, removes a great deal of the terror once implicit in the tee shot at St Andrews. Yet the plan of attack remains much the same, and third shot into the green asks for a most delicate touch if it is not played from a perfect position. It can impose some grievious mental hardship when it must carry the pot bunker at front left towards the gaping deep bunker that runs half the length of the green to the right rear. The 13th is a splendid hole of medium iron length across a pond with deep bunkers protecting the green to both right and left. While by no means a copy, it is very much reminiscent of the 11th at the Old course, where the green lies alongside the River Eden. So there would be no mistaking its origins, Macdonald even named the 13th after the famous St Andrews river.

Although the National has so many features reminiscent of the finest British seaside links, it is not strictly a links course in the British sense. The soil on which it is built is of inland texture, and the fairways and greens are of the softer inland quality. Only the great sprawling bunkers, some 500 in number, and stretches of sandy hazards filled with huckleberry bush and other cloying scrub reproduce the playing characteristics of linksland, and the frustrations involved in extricating oneself from their grasp.

Despite the character and diversity of the National, the first Walker Cup match, played in 1922, was the only occasion when an event of international interest has taken place there.

The splendid days of the National, when members arrived by private yacht, are long gone-although the telescope on the front porch by which arriving members' yachts were identified, still stands as a reminder. But the club itself and its magnificent course continue to serve a generation of prominent, if less pretentious, golfing enthusiasts with a taste for perfection.

It is a rare golfer who completes his first experience of the National without commenting on the large and sharply contoured greens. Through the years they have acquired a deep matting of grass and the subtle little borrows that come only with age. But their original undulations, as conceived by Charles Blair Macdonald, supply their true personality, so it is worth pausing to hear his explanation of how he designed them. "I take", he said, "a number of pebbles in my hand and drop them on a miniature space representing a putting green on a small scale, and as they drop on the diagram, place the undulations according to where they fall."

For some years after the National was opened for play in 1909, Macdonald was busy altering the holes, both in length and bunkering. "I am not confident", he said once in a rare moment of self-doubt, "that the course is perfect and beyond criticism today."

On another occasion Macdonald expressed at greater length some of the philosophy behind his most notable creation: "It is", he said, "to endeavour to make the hazards as natural as possible. I try not to make the course any harder but to make it more interesting, never forgetting that 80 per cent of the members of any golf club cannot on average drive more than 175 yards, so I always study to give them their way out... by taking a course much as a yachtsman does against an adverse wind, by tacking."

Macdonald certainly was the first American architect to appreciate the subtleties of design, for instance the difference between penal and strategic. Mostly he used the latter but the 14th is a rare example of a hole where the player has no alternative but to hit a reasonably straight shot. The carry over the water is not too formidable but it must be made, and having found the fairway options are negligible. The approaches form a narrow waist of fairway flanked by water and bunkers and the green itself has a wide collar of sand around its back and sides.

George Crump's
184-acre bunker

Pine Valley is the perfect example of penal architecture, the ultimate test for the giants of golf. It lies on the New Jersey side of Philadelphia and it is hard to believe that what is reputed to be the toughest course in the world could be located in such nondescript countryside: desolate enough in itself, and a wasteland of filling stations and billboards, dusty and tawdry and almost treeless – an environmentalist's nightmare. Pine Valley may not be as tough to play as some British championship courses in a forty-knot wind, nor tougher than Pebble Beach in the near-gales which so often sweep that seaside course in winter. Yet it is assuredly the world's most challenging inland course – perhaps inevitably, when it was fashioned from such a landscape as this.

Each hole is a separate and distinct entity. No hole parallels another, and each is protected by huge tracts of pines, bushes, shrubs and jungle-like undergrowth. During the 1936 Walker Cup a member of the British squad – P. B. "Laddie" Lucas, then only 21 years old – hit a wild slice directly into the woods.

"Watch it! Watch it!" he yelled at his caddie.

"You don't have to watch 'em here," the caddie replied. "Just listen for 'em."

Few championships are played at Pine Valley, because it cannot accommodate spectators, but the Walker Cup did return in 1985, resulting in the then customary victory for the home side, although, at 13–11, not the normal one-sided affair.

Uniquely, Pine Valley has no fairways, no rough, no chipping surfaces, and no sandtraps in the accepted sense. The course itself is in effect one huge, 184-acre bunker. Since the whole Chinese Army couldn't keep it raked – even if it was available for a task of such capitalist decadence nobody bothers to. On it are 18 tees and 18 greens, the more distant sets reached via islands of immaculate fair-green. Once off these verdant oases the player is either in the trees or inside a part of that apparently endless sand that has been designated a trap. The par-threes have nothing between the tees and the greens; the greens are hit on the fly – or else. Surrounding the greens and running right up against the putting surfaces are countless little potholes of sand, some so steeply faced that it is often necessary to play away from the green in order eventually to get on to it. Pine Valley took seven years to build. It was the brainchild of a Philadelphia hotelier, George Crump, who died in 1918 with only 14 holes finished and the remaining four only roughly sketched out. It was completed in 1919. Notwithstanding its appalling penalties, Pine Valley has occasionally been tamed. The course record stood at 67 for many years, but one pro who shot it twice in 66 did not report this to the members for fear of not being invited back. What then did the members make of Robert Lewis's remarkable 64?

The chief reason most golfers fail at Pine Valley to score within ten or even twenty strokes of their regular game is psychological – the course simply terrifies them. For years they have heard of its fiendish hazards. After a few holes they discover they are even more frightening than they had been led to believe and desperation enters their play – backswings became as fast as a snap of the fingers, and follow-throughs do not pass the hip. One story

Pine Valley's reputation as the toughest inland course in the world has not often been tested in a major professional tournament, since there is virtually no room for spectators. But the evidence of visiting players is there: all testify to the constant pressure, the severe penalties, the unique challenge of every hole. One pro after a disastrous encounter in its sandy soil, called it "a 184-acre bunker".

which Pine Valley members have been telling for years illustrates how easy, and yet how terrifying, the course can be. The late Woody Platt, a gifted local amateur who knew Pine Valley well, started off the 1st hole with a birdie-three, no easy task since the hole bends sharply to the right after the tee shot to a green that drops steeply into trouble on both sides and to the rear. Platt had hit a 4-iron for his second stroke.

The 2nd hole, which changes direction sharply to the left, is not long – only 367 yards. But the tee shot – no topped shots here – must carry over 180 yards of sand peppered with flash traps completely along its right side. The green is highly elevated and, being almost completely surrounded by a wasteland of sand, it resembles a miniature Mount Suribachi. Platt hit a 7-iron into the hole for an eagle two.

The par-three 3rd is, like all the short holes at Pine Valley, strictly a one shotter. There is nothing between the player and the green but sand. The green lies below the level of the tee and tilts sharply from right to left downhill. Missing the green may mean six more shots to get back on to it. Platt solved the problem by the simple expedient of a hole in one.

The 4th hole is very long for a par-four: 444 yards. The tee shot is blind and the hole swerves slightly to the right. Sand is everywhere, as on every hole at Pine Valley, but it is not much of a factor here, lying just in front of the tee and way short of the green. Platt hit a driver and a 4-wood, and then holed a 30-footer for a birdie. He was now six under par after only four holes of the roughest test of golf in the world.

The first four holes make a full circle back to the clubhouse. Platt now faced the prospect of playing the 5th, which juts out from behind the clubhouse and is easily one of the most stringent par-threes in golf. A huge bunker lies well short of the green, falling steeply to the right into saplings and undergrowth. If Platt's ball had bounced there, his main problem would have been in trying to find

it. Since the hole is 232 yards long, the problem was compounded by the fact that he would have had to play a wood – probably a driver – off the tee.

Before facing the task, he decided to bolster his spirit with a drink in the clubhouse while he contemplated the dual problem of maintaining a pace of six under par and tackling the devilish 5th.

He never came out of the clubhouse.

At Pine Valley, golfers find their games falling apart with absolutely nothing at stake. People who are used to playing golf for hundreds of dollars find at Pine Valley that they cannot get their games in gear playing for matchsticks. The pines and oaks, firs and birches – which are actually well away from the trajectory of anything but a completely uncontrolled shot – now seem to form a corridor. The patches of fair-green, which will accept any moderately hit drive, now look as though they could not contain a 9-iron. And the greens, most of which cover a third of an acre, begin to look like watch crystals.

On precisely which hole this terror begins to strike the heart nobody ever knows. But it happens, almost invariably. Knowing this so well, the members at Pine Valley have a standing bet that nobody can break 80 on his first try at the course. One man who did was Arnold Palmer, in 1954, when he was US Amateur Champion. "I was desperate for money at the time," Palmer recalls. "I was about to be married. So I collected all the bets I could find. I don't know what I would have done if I had lost – it was far more money than I could afford. But everything turned out all right. I shot a 68." One more record for the spectacular Palmer. But there are few Arnold Palmers. Not many really good players can get around the course without a few triple-bogeys, or worse. Many rounds that might have otherwise been under par have been marred along the line by a nine or a ten – or worse. For this reason, Pine Valley is in a class by itself as a test of matchplay. A golfer can be three down and four to play and win easily, simply by watching his opponent suddenly discover that he has

Pine Valley Golf Club, Clementon, New Jersey

**Record: 64,
Robert Lewis, Jr., 1981**

Hole	Yards	Par
1	427	4
2	367	4
3	181	3
4	444	4
5	232	3
6	388	4
7	567	5
8	319	4
9	427	4
10	146	3
11	392	4
12	344	4
13	448	4
14	184	3
15	591	5
16	433	4
17	338	4
18	428	4
Out	3,352	35
In	3,304	35
Total	**6,656**	**70**

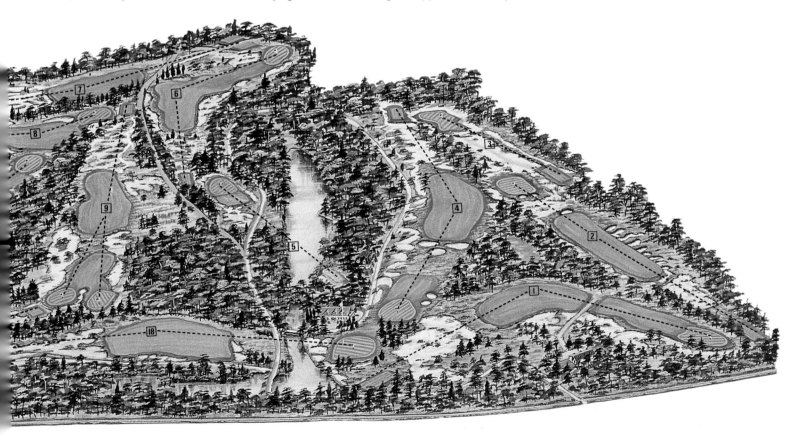

The 7th: 567 yards par 5

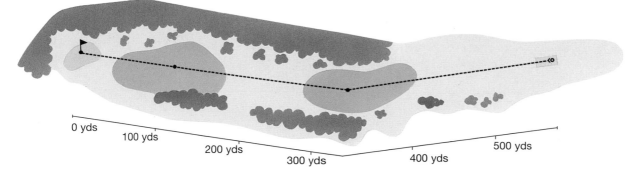

The 7th

The Evils of Hell's Half-Acre

George Crump was not the only architect to work on Pine Valley, for he had had the experienced guidance of the British architect H. S. Colt, whose most famous course in England was Sunningdale, near London. But it was Crump who drew up the first basic outline and the master plan, not to mention pouring $250,000 of his own money into it. Colt simply added the final touches that made it into a masterpiece of the macabre. When he died, Crump had not finished his outlines for the 10th to the 15th holes; that was done by Hugh Wilson – whose own masterpiece had been Merion – with the help of his brother Allen.

Nobody can be sure if there is even one hole which was Crump's work alone, but there is little doubt that the 7th is the hole of which he would be most proud. It may be the most exacting par-five in the world. Absolutely no mistakes may be made if that par is to be equalled, and it takes a minor miracle to score a birdie. At 567 yards, there are plenty of par-fives that are much longer. There are many that are much trickier. But there

is none that requires the three shots of the difficulty of those needed to reach Pine Valley's 7th green in regulation figures. The length of the drive is limited by an area of sand and scrub so diabolical in nature and of such frightening dimension that it is known as Hell's Half-Acre. It begins some 285 yards from the tee and does not end for more than a hundred yards. This means that the drive and the second shot must travel at least 385 yards, the last hundred yards on the fly, just to be clear of trouble. In other words, if the tee shot is missed it leaves the golfer with no choice but to play short of Hell's Half-Acre. If he hits a good drive and a poor second shot, he is in it. Nobody can make a par from there. Even after two perfect wood shots the golfer is faced with an equally difficult problem for his third shot, which could very easily be a mid iron. The fairway comes to an end some twenty yards short of the green, which virtually sits in a huge bunker. The green, not overly large and crowded by trees on both sides, falls away steeply at the rear.

Is it any wonder nobody hits that green in two?

The 18th hole at Pine Valley, below, is perhaps not as heroic as some that have gone before. Nevertheless, an iron shot will need to be truly struck to clear both the brook and the greenside bunkers.

been walking on water. Woody Platt made his discovery at the 5th, but Pine Valley offers no respite and even if he had completed the 5th in respectable fashion he would then have been faced with a crucial decision on the tee of the 6th. This hole is a medium-length par-four, 388 yards. The pay-off shot is the drive, for an enormous bank of sand runs along the bias of the fairway as it turns right. The player is therefore faced with deciding how much of the sand he wants to bite off. Just the right amount and he will have only a pitch to the green, but too much and he will be shooting uphill off a mountainside of sand. Now comes the "Sahara", a horror of sand all along its 567 yards, with much lying around the green. It is practically impossible to smite in two shots because of the huge belt of sand (from which the hole derives its name) which crosses the fairway and stifles all hope of a really long drive.

By contrast, the 8th is only a drive and a pitch, being a mere 319 yards downhill. But what a pitch! Many a player has hit what he thought was a perfect wedge to within a foot of the flagstick, only to watch in disbelief as the back-spin on the ball started it creeping down the steep slope to end up in the deep bunker in front of the putting surface.

The 9th is a long par-four – 427 yards – with two greens. Behind the left one is a cliff, not just a slope. The man brave enough to even attempt finding a ball down there would need to climb down a rope to do so. The 10th

Where a Par is a Triumph

The 13th, a par-four, is one of the four holes finished off by Hugh and Allen Wilson after George Crump's death. It follows his basic plan and may very well have exceeded his grand ideas of what a hole at Pine Valley ought to be. The 13th is the epitome of the heroic hole in golf, though it also incorporates elements of the penal and strategic styles of architecture.

It takes the heart of a heavyweight to play the hole successfully. It can be punishing to the point where a player might not be able to finish it. And yet, it can be played strategically if it is viewed as a par-four-and-a-half.

At 448 yards it is, by the card, a par-four. It is a single dog-leg to the left if it is played bravely. It is a double dog-leg if the player is content to seek only a bogey. There are two tees, but the difficulty of the drive and the length of the hole remain the same from both. A forest of pines obscures all view of the green from the tee. But

the patch of fairway you are supposed to hit is in plain view. It begins about 175 yards from the tee. Providing the drive is not short and to the right, the green can be seen from the fairway. However, also in full view is a bunker lining the entire left side of a second patch of fairway which leads into the green from the right.

The second shot, most certainly a wood, must carry the full length of that bunker, hit the green on the fly, and hold. Running downhill to the left of the bunker is that forest of pines, and behind the green lies yet another bunker. Those who prefer discretion to valour can play the second shot short and to the right of the green with an iron. From there it is a simple pitch and, with two putts, a bogey-five.

Of course, there is always the possibility of a par. Most players are more than content to complete the 13th in the regulation four.

The 13th: 448 yards par 4

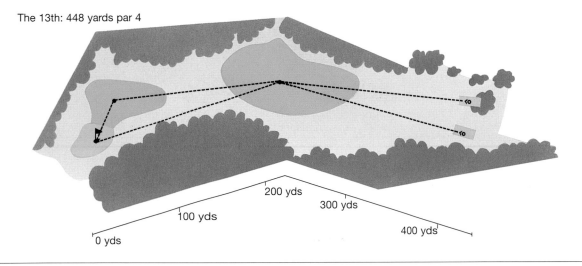

200 yds

300 yds

100 yds

400 yds

0 yds

is just an 8 or possibly a 7-iron, but the green is protected all round with what can best be described as sandpits, one of which is cone shaped and has been nicknamed after an unprintable part of the Devil's anatomy. The 11th is a fine two-shotter, at 392 yards one of those rarities in golf architecture: a great short par-four. It is followed by another four, so short that the player can drive hole-high then pitch to the green from the fairway as it turns sharply to the left.

The par-four 13th is another story altogether. It requires a tremendous drive and, because the 448-yard hole is a dog-leg, almost certainly another wood, all of it sheer carry, to get home. At 184 yards, the par-three 14th does not play that long because the green lies well below the tee. But, again, it is a hit-or-miss one-shotter. Fifty feet of water lies directly in front of the green and a bunker to the left of it.

The 15th hole, which sits at right angles to the 14th green, carries over this same body of water, but any fair tee shot will easily carry it. At 591 yards it is the longest hole at Pine Valley and, to make matters worse, it goes straight uphill into a narrowing fairway. Like the 7th, nobody hits this green in two shots. The par-four 16th – 433 yards – plays long although it travels downhill. It has a tiny patch of fairway, guarded in front by a minor desert, and then plays over more sandy wasteland to a green strategically bunkered on the left and guarded by water on

the right. The 17th is a shortish par-four, only 338 yards, but it is uphill all the way. By Pine Valley standards the green is small but it is protected all around by sandtraps, which begin a full fifty yards in front of it. Oddly, the final hole is not as heroic as might be expected at the Pine Valley finish. At 428 yards it is not short, but a drive off the high tee will have no problems carrying the 180 yards or so of sand which lies in front of it, and this to a very wide patch of fairway. The second shot readily clears a brook lying well short of the green, provided it can be truly struck from a downhill lie. But the green is mammoth and the key here lies in the choice of the correct club for the approach. The route is uphill, so it is difficult to see where the cup is, and if the wrong club is chosen avoiding three putts presents a real problem.

Despite its unprepossessing environs, Pine Valley is one of the most beautiful golf courses in the world. It has no backdrop of mountains, no craggy coastlines with waves lapping at its shores. It is simply gorgeous in its own right. Trent Jones likes to tell the story of Lowell Thomas, an avid golfer and traveller for many years. After playing his tee shot safely across the water at the 15th, he turned to admire the scenery around him. "In all my travels", he said to Jones, "I do not think I have seen a more beautiful landscape. This is as thrilling as Versailles or Fontainebleau."

Completely redesigned by Robert Trent Jones for the 1960 USPGA tournament, Firestone is familiar to many through some 40 years of television broadcasts. It is especially notable for its succession of tough par-fours (particularly the 4th and 9th, which proved the most testing over eleven years of World Series play) and for the 625-yard 16th, named "The Monster" by Arnold Palmer after his triple-bogey eight there in the 1960 USPGA competition

A rubber man's
long,
long,
stretch

The Course Card

Firestone Country Club, Akron, Ohio
South course
Record: 61, Jose-Maria Olazabal, 1990

Hole	Yards	Par
1	400	4
2	500	5
3	450	4
4	465	4
5	200	3
6	465	4
7	225	3
8	450	4
9	465	4
10	405	4
11	365	4
12	180	3
13	460	4
14	410	4
15	230	3
16	625	5
17	390	4
18	465	4
Out	3,620	35
In	3,530	35
Total	**7,150**	**70**

They are fortunate sportsmen indeed whose employer provides that ultimate in off-duty amenities – a golf course for their own use. Firestone Country Club, at Akron, Ohio, began in this way, the gift to his workforce in 1928 of Harvey Firestone, the millionaire industrialist. In the 70 years that have passed since it has become much more than an amenity for Firestone people; it is a challenge to the best in golf, rating as one of the toughest courses on the American tour.

The first of the club's two courses, Firestone South now bears little resemblance to its original plan, having been altered beyond all recognition by Robert Trent Jones in 1959. When Trent Jones had reworked it, Firestone was one of the longest championship courses anywhere, although many others have now caught up with it. Firestone is also a golf course with which American enthusiasts are most familiar; it has been the site of more televised tournaments than perhaps any other course. Its television exposure began with the 1960 USPGA Championship, for which Trent Jones carried out his drastic surgery – to say merely that he redesigned it would be an understatement. He added 50 bunkers, two ponds and two greens; the remaining sixteen greens were vastly enlarged. Although always formidable, the greens were redesigned in 1985 by a Jack Nicklaus company to make them even more challenging.

This is never more typified than at the 17th – at 390 yards one of the shortest par-fours on the course where there is a ripple running right through the spine of the green. Getting down in two putts is never easy. Bobby Nichols, once Firestone's head professional and a former winner of the USPGA title believes it takes a subtle blend of strength and accuracy to win at Firestone. "You don't use 9-irons and 8-irons out here, as a pro can expect on at least a few courses on the tour. At Firestone almost all your approaches to the par-fours and par-threes call for long irons." It is a measure of technological and physical progress in golf that Nichols's remarks might now apply more to good amateurs.

Even so, Firestone has been humbled, most notably by Jose-Maria Olazabal when he won the 1990 World Series of Golf, the annual tour event played there. In the first round Olazabal was simply in what the professionals refer to as "the zone," that blessed state when fairways appear the size of football fields and the hole a bucket. Olazabal shot 61, eventually finishing 12 shots clear of the field. Only three players broke par that year; one of them, Olazabal, was 18 under. Next to winning the Masters four years later, the Spaniard regards it as his finest achievement to date.

The 1st is a modest opening par-four of 400 yards to a narrow fairway. It is followed by one which has been described as a "gambler's hole", a 500-yard par-five uphill, with deep woods on the left and a heavily bunkered green. Two woods will give the chance of a birdie, but those who want to play safe will hit short and wedge it into the green.

Now begins the first of the lengthy par-fours, one of five on the front nine and measuring 450 yards. After a 270-yard drive, the second must carry 180 yards on the fly over a pond in front of the green. The 4th is a par-four dropping just short of a par-five. There are only three bunkers: one to the right of the fairway, the others on either side of the green. Despite a prosaically easy green to putt, the 4th remains the most bogeyed hole on the course. Olazabal, meanwhile, during his round of rounds, was five under par to this point having started birdie-eagle-birdie-birdie. The 5th – a 200-yard par-three – is particularly well protected at its front by one large and one small bunker. There follows a 465-yard par-four, bunkered only around the green; a 225-yard par-three, bunkered broadly to both the right and left; the downhill 450-yard par-four 8th, severely trapped around the green; and the magnificently bunkered 9th, first downhill and then uphill for 465 yards to the green. It is considered by many to be the second-toughest hole on the course and tournament statistics back them.

The 10th is a bit of a breather. Only 405 yards, it nevertheless calls for a well-nigh perfect tee shot to split the

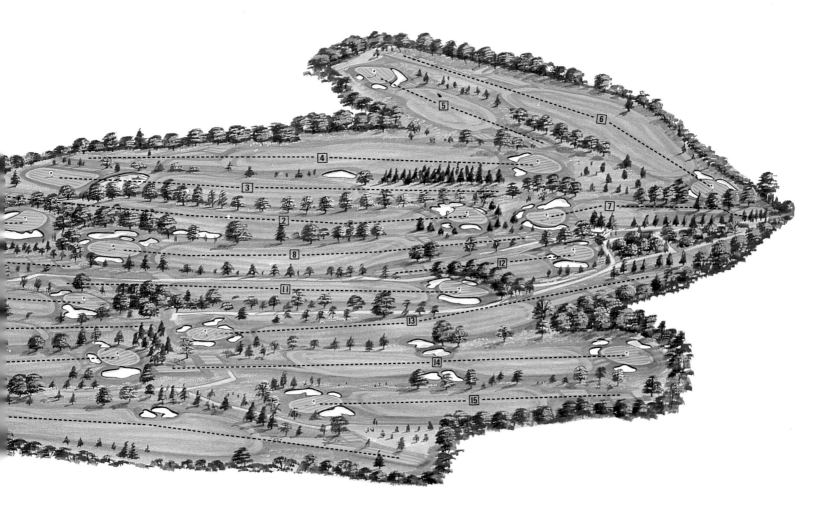

fairway between two finely placed bunkers. The 11th is perhaps the easiest hole on the course, a good drive to a trapless fairway and a pitch to a well bunkered but broad green.

The 12th is the shortest par-three on the course, 180 yards and nothing to speak of by Trent Jones's standards. Yet it is, as has been pointed out, "fickle". The green is elevated, guarded to the front and on both sides by big bunkers and with lots of trees, the most intrusive of which is a gigantic oak to the rear. The 13th is another 460-yard hole, but Tommy Bolt once scored an eagle-two on it – using a 3-wood for his second shot.

Television has made the last five holes at Firestone the most familiar. The 14th is just 410 yards, but the tee shot is made difficult by two deep bunkers on the right and another on the left which very much tighten the landing area. Most pros choose to lay up off the tee and then play a mid iron for their second shot, which is slightly uphill, to a relatively flat green. If there are such things as birdie holes at Firestone, the 14th is one. But that is the last.

The 15th does not look an exciting hole, because although it is the highest on the course it is long and flat. Club selection is all important because of the winds which swirl off the flatlands of Ohio and around the elevated green, from which the ground drops away sharply on both sides. The two large bunkers on both the left and right and a much smaller one to the front-right help to make this the most disturbing one-shotter on the course. Many tournaments played at Firestone have been won with a birdie at the 15th.

The 16th is not the longest par-five in the world, though it is all of 625 yards. That length seems impossible in print but the hole is entirely downhill. The second shot is the crucial one, because in all probability the left foot will be below the right for a shot into a spit of fairway. The pitch from there is into a wide green directly fronted by a pond. Only a very limited number of players have carried that pond in two shots and hit the green. Even Nicklaus, not trying to reach the green in two, has found his third shot in the

water. This happened during the World Series one year, but, ever the great competitor, Nicklaus calmly removed a shoe and played his fourth where it lay. He found the green and sank his putt for a miraculous par. The 17th, only 390 yards, is the last of the shortish par-fours, but it is uphill and four bunkers – two of them on either side – dictate such a tight tee shot that most long-hitters use an iron off the tee. This leaves them with a medium iron shot to the green with its notorious rippled surface.

The 18th is the signature hole for the entire Firestone layout – long and tough, but truly great. It is 465 yards long from an elevated tee, from which you must play to the right of the fairway to open up the tightly bunkered green. The drive is threatened on the left by a thick grove of trees and on the right by two huge bunkers that will catch any slice or push. The second shot is yet another long iron to a huge green virtually surrounded by bunkers. Three putts are not unusual here.

The reshaped 18th green has four pin positions of varying difficulty, the central one being the easiest, the front one the toughest.

Southern Hills remains essentially the same as it was when this map was drawn. However, there has been extensive reworking of the bunkering.

Rough like steel wool,

sand like talcum powder

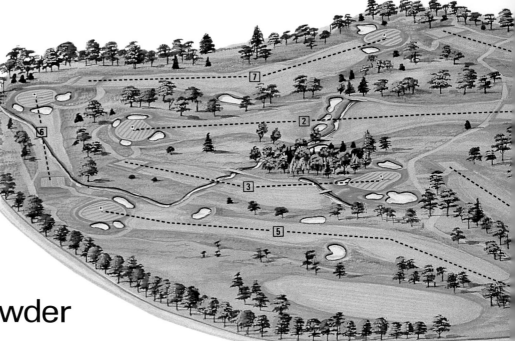

Southern Hills
Country Club,
Tulsa, Oklahoma

Hole	Yards	Par
1	460	4
2	471	4
3	405	4
4	372	4
5	655	5
6	178	3
7	384	4
8	228	3
9	374	4
10	369	4
11	173	3
12	458	4
13	537	5
14	223	3
15	405	4
16	491	4
17	352	4
18	465	4
Out	3,527	35
In	3,487	35
Total	**7,014**	**70**

Southern Hills Country Club, at Tulsa, Oklahoma, was built in 1935. It was an act of enlightened self-interest by a group of wealthy Tulsans at a time when one in five of the nation's workforce was unemployed.

Tulsa had made its money from oil, and its better-off citizens put up the money for a club of which the state could be proud – and one which, in its construction, would provide employment. In the event, course and clubhouse cost no more than a new locker room at today's prices. For their architect Southern Hills chose Perry Maxwell, and their choice could not have been wiser. Although he lived in Oklahoma his golf knowledge was universal: examples of his work are to be found all over the mid-west. The excellence of his work has been carried on by his son, J. Press Maxwell.

Southern Hills is fundamentally a driver's course and thus the key to it is the tee shot. While an accurate drive is a necessity for any course with championship pretensions, it is absolutely crucial at Southern Hills. Nobody ever won anything there who did not drive the ball with extreme accuracy and plenty of length. The reason is that Southern Hills, which now stretches to more than 7,000 yards for major championships, plays every inch of that measurement and more. Most of the holes are flat – the club's name is misleading, for there is no help from nature, such as a downhill roll, in driving. The only holes with any real elevation are the 9th and the 18th, and they go uphill to the clubhouse sitting majestically at the top of a hill that is, on the plains of Oklahoma, a minor mountain.

Adding to these difficulties is the tough Bermuda grass with which the entire course is planted; any other type of grass could not survive the sizzling heat in which matches at Tulsa are often played. When the USGA holds one of its championships at Southern Hills – there have been a number, including the US Open for a third time in 2001 (the course has also hosted two USPGA Championships, the most recent in 1994) – the Bermuda grass is allowed to grow in the rough to an ankle-height of almost three inches. It is like playing from a surface of steel wool so tough that Ben Hogan had to withdraw from the 1958 US Open after hurting his wrist trying to extricate a ball from it. Because of the baking sun and long dry periods, the sprinkler system at Southern Hills works night and day in the summer, and even while a tournament is in progress. In the course of one day Southern Hills may use up to 400,000 gallons of water. Its greens (most of them are steeply banked from back to front and are rife with undulations) often have to be syringed twice a day. All this works back to the tee, for without an excellent drive through Southern Hills' thick trees it is impossible to get in position for a second shot that leaves any kind of putt.

The bunkers add yet another premium to the drives. While they are numerous, they are not over-abundant along the fairways. They are filled with a sand called "Number Six Wash" culled from the nearby Arkansas River. It is not unlike talcum powder, and buried lies are common enough.

The first truly significant championship ever held at Southern Hills was the 1958 US Open. It was played in heat that would have made a camel faint and was won by Tommy Bolt, a temperamental man famed more for throwing clubs. Bolt won by a comfortable four strokes from Gary Player, who admitted afterwards that he had played some of the best golf of his career. Bolt missed only thirteen of the 72 greens in regulation figures, yet he was three over par; Player was seven over. Asked what had won the Championship for him, Bolt just pointed to his driver.

For the 1994 USPGA Championship the weather was far more clement, and Nick Price turned in his career best performance to win a second successive Major championship. The winning margin was six strokes as Price compiled a new record PGA Championship winning total of 269, 11 under par. Southern Hills has an extremely long opening hole, a par-four of 460 yards. It is off an elevated tee near the clubhouse and dog-legs to the left with deep bunkers either

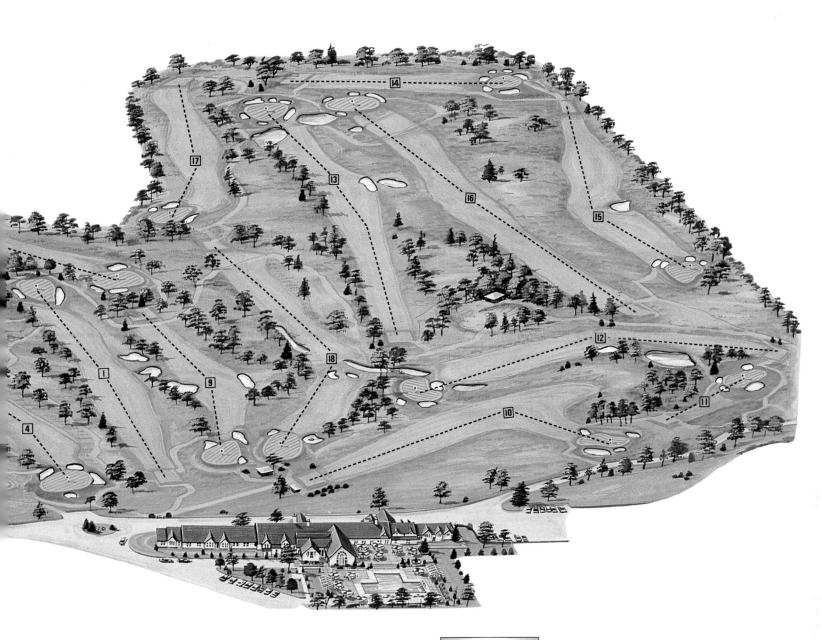

side of the green. At the next two holes, both par-fours, a stream must be carried. Along with two bunkers across the fairway it affects the drive at the 471-yard 2nd, demanding a full 225-yard carry, but presents no real problem for the approach at the shorter 3rd. The 4th, a shortish par-four of 372 yards to a slightly elevated green, provides some respite before the rigours of the long par-five 5th – a monstrous 655 yards with a heavily bunkered green backed by trees as thick as they are high. The 6th is a fairly easy par-three and the 7th little more than a 3-wood, for position, and a short iron. The 8th can be unnerving. At 228 yards it is a long par-three with two large bunkers protecting the green. The uphill 9th features a heavily sloping green with the potential for some particularly tough pin positions.

From the elevated tee of the 10th the course descends, playing through flatlands until it hits the 16th tee, just about the lowest point on the course. In that stretch are two particularly tough holes – the 12th, once described by Ben Hogan as the "greatest par-four 12th hole in the United States", and the 13th. Trees, rough and a big bunker strategically placed in the crook of the dog-leg make the tee shot especially demanding at the 12th. The long second shot is complicated by a blind water hazard in front of the green and down its right side, and by bunkers and trees to the back and along the left side. The 13th is the only par five on the inward nine, measuring 537 yards over two lakes to a smallish green surrounded by five bunkers. A late dog-leg to a green heavily trapped in front imparts difficulty to the 17th, at 358 yards the shortest par-four on the course. The 18th is one of the great finishing holes in world golf.

The 18th

A Tough One to Finish

The final hole is the most difficult par-4 on the course, and the hardest against par with a stroke average of 4.506. It has the trees, the curves, the bunkers and the clinging rough which make par difficult to break anywhere at Southern Hills. From the championship tees the hole measures 465 yards, the drive going down a slight slope through an avenue of trees, which are particularly thick on the right. There is a narrow pond at the crook of the dog-leg, three fairway bunkers lie just around the corner, and there is more water on the left which means that overambition is punished. Assuming a safe landing, the approach is made uphill, between bunkers, to a wide green full of borrows. Such is the mischief of this green that no player has ever made par on the final hole at Southern Hills to win a major. As the 4th round of the 2001 US Open drew to a close the vast gallery could only gasp as the players in contention bungled their chances. First Mark Brooks, the 1996 US PGA Champion, three-putted from 40 feet. Then Stewart Cink rushed his putt of 18 inches, and missed. Retief Goosen was 12 feet away with two putts for the title. He left his first putt two feet from the hole, and promptly missed that. Brooks and Goosen had to endure an 18-hole play-off, which Goosen won mainly because he found more fairways from the tee than Brooks. Once again Southern Hills rewarded the better driver on the day.

Nick Price, in his imperishable year of 1994, when he won both the Open Championship and, above, the USPGA at Southern Hills. In 2001 Retief Goosen became the third South African golfer to win the US Open, the others being Gary Player and Ernie Els.

Originally built as a private course for members of the Shriner organization, Medinah has been the venue for the US Opens of 1949, 1975 and 1990. It has violent dog-legs and dense woods, crowding right to the fairway edge, border every hole and make the course seem narrower than it really is. Of all the US Open courses, Medinah probably inspires most controversy. The 17th green shown here was constructed for the 1990 US Open. It was heavily criticised and was subsequently rebuilt, with more bunkers, higher up the hill.

Chicago's controversial

golfing shrine

Medinah, twenty miles from downtown Chicago, is an American country club in the most dramatic sense of the term. Its clubhouse, built by the Shriners – members of the Ancient Arabic Order of Nobles of the Mystic Shrine, an association not unlike Freemasonry – is a mock-Moorish structure at once imposing and lavish. Today, its Number 3 course is considered by many golfers to be the finest in the Chicago area and by its more dogmatic partisans to be the finest in America. It is not known how Bendelow came to serve the big-spending Shriners. He had arrived in America to work as a compositor for the old *New York Herald*, but in 1895 joined Spaldings as an architectural consultant. From then on, he laid out some of the most abominable examples of golf landscaping ever seen, some of which he designed in a day for twenty-five dollars.

Medinah Number 3 has been changed out of all recognition from Bendelow's original conception. The process of change was sparked off by Harry Cooper, who shot the course record, 63, on his way to winning the 1930 Medinah Open. Five new holes were built immediately and in 1935 Cooper won there again, this time with a less spectacular 289. Since that time, the course has been revamped many times, including by George Fazio in time for the 1975 United States Open. This contest was won by Lou Graham with 287, three over par, which for the Open was 71, a stroke less than usual. For the 1990 US Open, there was another extensive redesign. Two new holes were added to the course and another was rebuilt. The course became the longest ever for a US Open – a mammoth 7,195 yards – and the par reverted to 72. For the 1999 US PGA No.3 was again lengthened, measuring an imposing 7,401 yards, with three par-fives

over 580 yards and only one par-three under 200. It suited the exceptional gifts of Tiger Woods who lifted his second major title at 11-under, though pushed all the way by the young Spaniard Sergio Garcia.

Much of the course is in sight of Lake Kadijah (named after Mohammed's wife) and four holes, the 2nd, the 13th, the 14th, and the 17th, are played across it. For the rest, the course has nine dog-legs, two of which swing through a full 90 degrees.

The first hole is dead straight and on the short side, as an opening par-four ought to be. There then follows a first trip across the Lake, a 188-yard par-three, followed by the slight dog-leg of the 3rd, to an elevated green protected on both sides by bunkers. Like the 3rd, the trees on both sides of the 4th fairway are the principal difficulties, although its contoured green is not easy. At 530 yards, the par-five 5th is a birdie hole, although there are two fairway traps, one to the right for the slicers and the other of consideration for members only. The second shot must then carry over two gaping traps on both sides of the green. What might have been gained on the 5th could very well be lost on the 449-yard 6th, which has five bunkers, one of which lies to the left-middle of the fairway, in the landing area. Out of bounds is behind the green. Then comes the formidable 7th, a dog-leg par five playing to just under 600 yards. Since the hole bends right, the tee shot should stay left but it must be carefully positioned to avoid an inconveniently placed bunker. The second must carry through groves of trees on both sides and miss another bunker on the left. The third goes to a pear-shaped green, heavily bunkered, with an almost infinite number of pin positions.

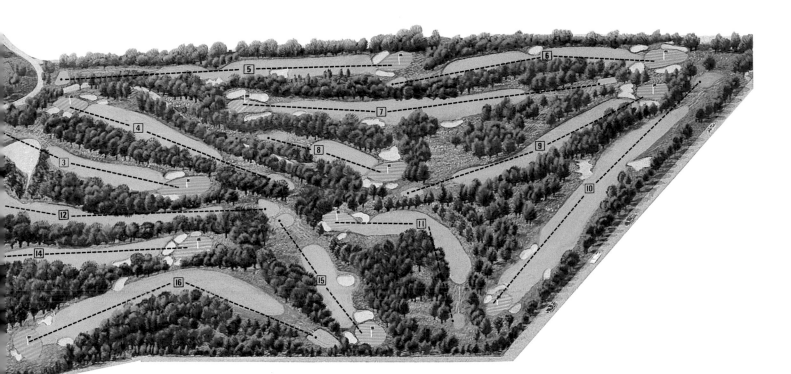

At this stage the golfer begins to wonder when Medinah is going to show any mercy. As he makes the turn – from the 8th to the 11th – he finds out that it doesn't. The 468 yard 12th is considered by some to be the most difficult hole on the course and then comes the famous par three 13th over Lake Kadijah, a hole that has caused heartbreak to many and cost Sam Snead a US Open.

At the 14th the players drive back over the lake, a par five of 583 yards to a green heavily bunkered to ward off any big hitter trying to find it in two. The 15th offers some respite; at a mere 389 yards it is reckoned to be the second easiest on the course. The 16th is where Hale Irwin began his move in the 1990 US Open play-off. He trailed Mike Donald by two but a birdie here enabled him to put pressure on his less experienced opponent.

The 17th, built specially for the 1990 US Open, was heavily criticised, so a new sloping green, further back up the hill was constructed for the PGA, making it a longer and fairer hole. Swiftly on to the 18th, a sweeping dog-leg to the left that plays its full 445 yards. In 1990 Nick Faldo, the winner of that year's Masters, needed a birdie here to get into the play-off and keep alive his Grand Slam hopes. A wonderful four-iron approach, to 18ft, appeared to have given him his chance. The putt looked in the hole all the way, but at the last it dived to the right and lipped out, finishing 18 inches away. Faldo grimaced in agony; by such fine margins are Major championships frequently won and lost. Medinah is already scheduled to host the 2006 US PGA Championship and 2012 Ryder Cup Matches.

Sergio Garcia who, still only 19 years old, challenged Tiger Woods all the way over this enormous course in the 1999 USPGA.

The 18th

Irwin's Moment of Glory

Hale Irwin was always considered among the most austere of professionals. He did not kill them with length but with formidably straight hitting and imperious course management. It was hardly a coincidence that his favourite tournament was the US Open, one that most lends itself to such strategically sound players. However, in 1990, a new Irwin presented himself. The glasses were gone, replaced by contact lenses. And then came the extraordinary scenes at the 72nd hole of that year's US Open at Medinah.

In truth, Irwin had not played the hole well, given that this was a man who needed to be aggressive for a birdie. His second shot pulled up 45ft from the hole. However, the putt that followed made up for any deficiencies. It travelled for fully seven seconds, borrowing this way and that before dropping into the hole. Pandemonium followed and the roar would have shaken elephants. What did Irwin do? If Irwin had followed the habits of a lifetime he would have raised a hand into the air, tugged at his visor, and thanked spectators for their reaction to his good fortune. What did this Irwin do? For a start there was no visor. He set off on a run that brought back reminders that here was a man who was a good college footballer. But he did not stop his run at the green; he then went along the front row of spectators and high-fived them each in turn; he high-fived the stewards and then he high-fived his caddie.

When he returned the following day one had the feeling that fate was on his side, although not when he walked to the 16th tee, trailing Donald by two shots. A birdie at the 16th, though, halved the deficit and then the 18th once more came to his rescue, Donald missing the green with his approach and recording a bogey.

Irwin needed no more invitations. He birdied the first sudden death play-off hole for the most dramatic of his three US Open titles. At 45 he was the oldest winner in the history of the Championship. Given his shenannigans on the 18th it would appear one of the sprightliest, too.

The Course Card

Medinah Country Club, Medinah, Illinois Number 3

Hole	Yards	Par
1	388	4
2	188	3
3	415	4
4	447	4
5	530	5
6	449	4
7	588	5
8	206	3
9	439	4
10	582	5
11	407	4
12	468	4
13	219	3
14	583	5
15	389	4
16	452	4
17	206	3
18	445	4
Out	3,650	36
In	3,751	36
Total	**7,401**	**72**

A course more
mellow than monstrous

Oakland Hills
Country Club,
Birmingham.
Michigan
South course

Hole	Yards	Par
1	433	4
2	523	5
3	194	3
4	430	4
5	455	4
6	356	4
7	405	4
8	440	4
9	220	3
10	450	4
11	399	4
12	560	5
13	170	3
14	471	4
15	400	4
16	403	4
17	200	3
18	465	4
Out	3,456	35
In	3,518	35
Total	**6,974**	**70**

The most overworked nickname for an American golf course is "The Monster". Press agents use it weekly (and weakly) to describe any course where the touring professionals happen to be setting up their nomadic camp, and more often than not it is applied to some harmless sequence of eighteen holes that are as drab as they are undistinguished. The original and authentic "Monster", however, is Oakland Hills, so christened by Ben Hogan after winning the US Open there in 1951.

Prior to that Championship, Oakland Hills had twice before played host to the tournament – in 1924, when it was won by an obscure little golfer named Cyril Walker, and again in 1937, when Ralph Guldahl was a surprise winner over Sam Snead. That was quite a different course, though, than the one on which Hogan scored his third US Open victory. It had been designed in 1917 by Donald Ross, the George Washington of American golf architecture, who said of the rolling woodland when he first saw it, "The Lord intended this for a golf course."

When the time for the 1951 Open approached, the USGA hired Robert Trent Jones to modernise the work of the Lord and Donald Ross. "The game had outrun architecture," Jones has since explained in describing his work at Oakland Hills, and he set out to give the world's best players what he called "the shock treatment". The philoso-

phy behind his rebuilding programme was to create two target areas on each of the par-four and par-five holes, one on the fairway for the tee shot and another at the green. The result was a series of wasp-waisted fairways, formed by bunkers on either side, and greens surrounded by wide and deep bunkers and overhanging lips – a total of 120 bunkers in all containing some 400 tons of so-called medium-sharp sand. On his first round of the 1951 Open, Hogan spent a great deal of his time in this sand, and bogeyed five of the first nine holes to bring in a 76 that apparently spoiled any chance he might have had to win the Championship twice in a row. The next day was a slight improvement – a 73 that left him five shots behind Bobby Locke, the leader at the half-way point. Despite three bogeys and a double-bogey in his morning round on Saturday, Hogan was able to wring four birdies out of the course for a one-over-par 71, leaving him two strokes behind Locke and Jimmy Demaret, who were now tied for the lead.

There are those who still call Hogan's final round on Saturday afternoon "the finest eighteen holes of golf ever played by anyone". To escape the trouble on the fairways that had bothered him so much in his early round, Hogan often used his three wood off the tee and once even his four wood. He played the first nine holes in an even par

English-born Cyril Walker held off defending champion Bobby Jones to win the US Open at Oakland Hills in 1924 – the first championship in which steel-shafted putters were permitted.

35. At the undulating 10th, Hogan hit a 2-iron to the green, a shot that travelled more than 200 yards and stopped five feet from the pin."It was one shot that went exactly as I played it every inch of the way," Hogan said afterwards. He sank the putt for his birdie-three and a few minutes later a fifteen-foot putt for a birdie-two at the 13th hole. A bogey-five at the long 14th cost him a stroke when his second went over the green, but he got it back with a birdie-three at the 15th. Standing on the 18th tee, Hogan knew he had at least a two-stroke lead over the field, but he still refused to play safe. He hit a drive that even today is held in wonder by those who saw it – well over the bunkers guarding the elbow of this fearsome dog-leg right, leaving him only a 6-iron uphill to the green. He played his second shot perfectly to within four feet of the hole and sank the putt for his fourth birdie in the final nine holes and at that time a competitive course record of 67. "I'm glad that I brought this course, this monster, to its knees," he is said to have remarked at the presentation ceremony. Thus, the Monster was born. Locke, incidentally, finished with a 73 to drop into third place behind Clayton Heafner, whose closing 69 was the only other sub-par round of the entire tournament.

The US Open returned to Oakland Hills ten years later to be won by smooth swinging Gene Littler, but the Monster had lost a great deal of its bite. "The course has matured," explained Al Watrous, the club professional. But the USGA had mellowed too. The rough was not nearly as severe as it had been during the Hogan victory, and architect Jones had even removed seven of the 1951 bunkers while preparing the course for the Championship. Still, the large, undulating greens were there and are today, somewhat reminiscent of the North Atlantic during a mid-winter storm. Littler's winning score was 281, and eleven players finished with 287 or better, the score that had won for Hogan. There were a number of sub-par rounds during the tournament, and on the second day three players tied Hogan's. During the first Carling World championship in 1964, much the same kind of field scored even better. Even so, and taking into account the understandable pride of the designer, it is only a slight exaggeration when Jones calls it "the greatest test of professional tournament championship golf in the world. The player with the best shots, swing and nerve control has the best chance to win."For all that, Oakland Hills has produced a bizarre set of US Open Champions. In 1985 it was Andy North, who only won three tournaments during his career but two of them happened to be US Opens. However the tournament is remembered as much for the joint runners-up as North, belying the old belief that the man who finishes second is quickly forgotten. One of them was the South African Denis Watson who made an error in the opening round that probably still haunts him. At the 8th his putt stopped on the brim of the hole – and he waited 25 seconds before it toppled in, so contravening the rules of golf. He was penalised two strokes for unduly delaying play. He lost by one to North. Even more poignant was TC Chen's story. He was trying to become the first Asian to win a Major championship and with 14 holes to play he had a four stroke lead. In attempting a delicate chip from beside

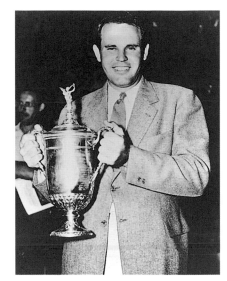

In winning the first of his two consecutive US Open titles at Oakland Hills in 1937, Ralph Guldahl became the first player never to go over par in any round of the championship.

Though no longer the frightening spectre it was for the famous Open in 1951, when Ben Hogan battled with Robert Trent Jones's changes, Oakland Hills remains a stern test with awkward dog-legs, plentiful bunkers and notoriously undulating greens. Gary Player, who won the PGA title there in 1972, claims only Carnoustie rivals it as the world's toughest.

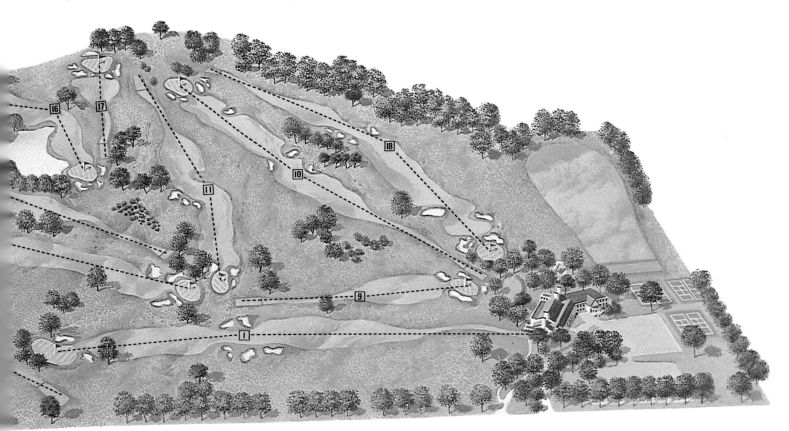

the 5th green the clubface got caught in the thick grass and then, when it freed itself, struck the ball while it was in flight. The double chip meant a one stroke penalty and an eight on his card. Greatly disturbed, he bogeyed each of the next three holes. He would finish with a 77 and again, one stroke adrift of the winning score.

When the championship returned in 1996 it was a qualifier of all people who prevailed. At the start of the week the extent of Steve Jones's ambitions lay in making the cut. But he showed tremendous courage on the closing hole to emerge a winner from the company of such skilled protagonists as Tom Lehman and Davis Love. Lying as it does in a Detroit suburb and less than an hour's drive from the heart of that great city, it is fitting that Oakland Hills should be an offspring of the motor industry. The property belonged originally to a printer and an accountant who were connected with the Ford Motor Co. They played golf together at the nearby Bloomfield Hills Country Club, which even then was a gathering-place for car makers, and eventually decided to see if Ross could fashion an exciting course on their land. They opened for business in a modest way during the summer of 1918, and Walter Hagen, who lived near by, was their first professional.

In due course, it was decided to build a clubhouse for the rather impressive sum of $275,000. The result was the huge neo-colonial structure that now dominates the entire course from the crest of the hill overlooking the 1st, 9th, 10th and 18th holes, certainly one of the most spacious clubhouses to be found anywhere and a marvellous spot from which to watch the golf unfold at the start and finish of each nine holes. The clubhouse presented only one problem at the time it was built, however: due to innumerable changes and modifications during its construction, it cost $650,000 instead of the anything-but-modest amount which was originally budgeted for it.

Oakland Hills maintained a long relationship with Robert Trent Jones, who as a consultant kept the basic character of the course intact during his 1951 Open revamp. Although its yardage is not excessive by modern standards Oakland Hills

concentrates a great deal of its more hazardous yards and more trying problems in the closing holes where they test the nerves as well as the ability. The 14th at 471 yards requires two very long shots. The 15th, all 400 yards, is uphill all the way with a large bunker in the middle of the fairway just where it turns left towards the green. The second shot at the 16th is a medium iron across a large pond that cuts right into the middle of the green. The 17th, with the deeply undulating green in a plateau some 30 feet above the tee, allows no margin for error since the green is completely surrounded by yawning bunkers. The 18th hole, the aforementioned dog-leg, with its bunkers to the right to guard against the shortcut and rough to the left to inhibit the long approach and a hump-backed green that has only the smallest entrance between protecting bunkers in front, is the kind of hole where tournaments are far more often lost than won – as many know to their cost.

Two of these are Love and Lehman who both came to the 18th tied with Steve Jones in 1996. Love was first, finding the green with two wonderful shots. The putt he had left however, from 18ft, was downhill and exceedingly slippery. He did the one thing he did not want to do – he left it 30 inches short. Moments later he had completed the saddest of three putts. Lehman's undoing was the left hand bunker that guards the far angle of the dog-leg. His drive was too straight, running into it and from there he had no hope of reaching the green.

Oakland Hills has undergone some drastic changes in character. It started out merely as a good course, falling short of greatness. It was then transformed by Trent Jones into a course too severe even for the elite among professional golfers. It has now mellowed with age into one of America's finest and fairest tests of golf.

The 16th

Player Goes for Glory

Every great champion has had the capacity to make a telling stroke in the heart of crisis, but few more so than Gary Player. Three instances come to mind. There was the four wood shot to within two feet of the 14th hole at Carnoustie in the last round of the 1968 Open. The superb eagle stayed the challenge of Jack Nicklaus who, strive as he did, could not catch the little man.

Then there was a 9-iron shot stone dead on the 71st hole at Augusta which well-nigh ensured his second Masters victory in 1974, and two years earlier he played an even more remarkable stroke with the same club at Oakland Hills. Player was pursuing his second USPGA Championship with all his intense tenacity and with three holes to play was level with Jim Jamieson, who was on the 18th. The 16th curves elegantly but sharply to the right around a long lake with the green set so close to it that any approach has to cross it. Weeping willows on the near side discourage those who think of trying to cut the corner, as Player discovered when he sliced from the tee. His ball lay well in rough trampled by spectators, but he faced a blind shot of 150 yards, the willows and the lake between him and the flag. The carry was huge for a 9-iron but Player felt he needed that much loft to clear the trees. A seat stick left on the ground under the trees helped him decide the line. It was a carefully calculated death-or-glory shot; the slightest mishit, or if the 9-iron were not enough club, and he would probably take five or even six. He struck it perfectly and the ball came to rest only four feet from the hole. Down went the putt and, as Jamieson had missed a short one on the last green, Player had an insurance stroke in hand. He did not need it, thanks to a consummate blow delivered under pressure.

The 16th: 403 yards par 4

----- Player

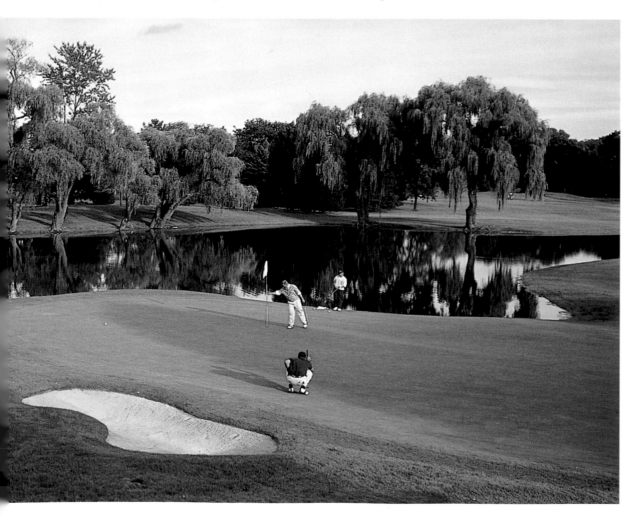

The par four 16th hole curves elegantly around a lake, which is a factor for the approach shot.

The brainchild of two of America's finest golfers, Jimmy Demaret and Jackie Burke, Champions can claim to be one of the best courses in Texas. More than 70,000 trees dominate Ralph Plummer's layout, which has quickly become a regular venue for major events.

The largest and finest –

of course!

Right: There was no sand at the Champions club when the course opened but that has changed and shallow sand traps are now prevalent. The course was an impressive host to the Tour Championship in 1997, so much so that the tournament returned in 1999, with Tiger Woods once again unstoppable. In 2001 it was the turn of the Canadian, Mike Weir, after a 4-way play-off. This is the green of the highly rated 14th.

A golf club like Champions could really only be found in the State of Texas, where superlatives are not only commonplace but also, as often as not, quite justified as well. It has not just one but two championship courses, Cypress Creek and Jack Rabbit, a clubhouse that has almost every amenity imaginable, and a membership roll that even includes several astronauts.

The men responsible for the idea were champions, too. Jimmy Demaret, winner of more than 50 tournaments, was the first to conquer the US Masters three times. When he died, in 1983, his partner, Jackie Burke operated the club. He took the Masters and the USPGA Championship in 1956, two years after being the first to take four consecutive PGA Tour events.

Slighter qualifications might not have sufficed for Houston, where, it is claimed, millionaires are more numerous than policemen. Many Texans have made their mark in golf. Apart from Demaret and Burke, Texas has produced Ben Hogan, Byron Nelson, Lloyd Mangrum, Ralph Guldahl, Babe Didrikson Zaharias, Harry Cooper, Lee Trevino, Mickey Wright, Don January, Charles Coody, Miller Barber, Ben Crenshaw, Tom Kite, Justin Leonard … the roll of honour is seemingly endless. Considering the size of Texas (it is twice as big as the British Isles, for instance) and the number of great golfers it has produced, it is surprising that it should have so few really memorable golf courses. Texas does, of course, have a number of good courses, among them Colonial at Fort Worth, Pecan Valley, Preston Trail at Dallas and the Dallas Athletic Club. But none has the charisma of Champions, as those who have played in tournaments there – the 1967 Ryder Cup was one, the 1969 US Open another – will readily testify. Today its merits have been brought to an

appreciative new audience as it held the season-ending PGA Tour event, the Tour Championship, in 1997, 1999 and 2001.

When Demaret and Burke decided to build Champions in 1957, they not uncharacteristically announced that it would be "the world's largest and finest" course. "When you do something in this town, you have to do it on a grand scale," said Demaret. "So we decided to model our holes after the world's classics. We weren't going to imitate them; rather, we were going to blend their characteristics into the terrain we had. We wanted a golf club right here in our home town that would become to Houston and Texas what Augusta National is to Georgia, or Pinehurst to North Carolina, or St Andrews to Scotland."

Burke added: "While we wanted an ample clubhouse, we wanted it strictly for golfers. We didn't want to build some barn of a place and then put the course on what was left over, meanwhile going broke with a lot of idle waiters standing around an empty ballroom. Furthermore, Jimmy and I decided we would run the club our way. You can't run a club smoothly through a board of directors, however brilliant each member may be in his own field. One wants a swimming pool, one some tennis courts, while another wants to fix up a couple of holes. So everything suffers.

"The only concession they made was to construct a swimming pool, because most of Champions' members were successful men in their thirties and forties, with children. The site Demaret and Burke decided to buy was 500 acres, heavily wooded with oaks, pines and sweet-gums in an otherwise threadbare northern section of the town. Later, members bought a further 1,500 acres around the course for future home sites. Although the course is 20 miles from downtown Houston, it can be reached by one of the city's network of freeways in 20 minutes. Knowing their architectural limitations (as few professional golfers do), Demaret and Burke hired Ralph Plummer to lay out a master plan. Two of Plummer's most successful previous efforts had been the Dallas Athletic Club course and Shady Oaks, near Fort Worth, where Ben Hogan had localized his golf activities after retiring. After Plummer had finished, he would indicate the possible location of a tee or green to Demaret and Burke, who would then hit hundreds of balls to make sure the shots would play as projected.

At first, no bunkers were built. Instead, grass-covered mounds were bulldozed into shapes that could eventually be removed if unwanted or converted into carefully shaped bunkers. Most bunkers are on the shallow side, especially those on the fairways. "We felt", Burke explained, "that if a player hits into a bunker, he should still be able to scramble his way to a par if necessary. There is no prettier shot in golf than a well-executed stroke out of sand, particularly a long shot."

While the Jack Rabbit course, designed later by George Fazio, is just as stringent as the Cypress Creek, it is utterly different. It has narrower fairways, smaller greens and deeper and more numerous bunkers. Cypress Creek, on the other hand, has wide fairways, tremendous greens and bunkers that are more strategically placed. Both are about the same length, around 7,200 yards. Choosing the best hole at Cypress Creek is not easy, but two stretches of holes have impressed the professionals particularly: the 6th through the 8th, and the 12th through the 14th

The 6th and 7th are both medium-length par-fours with big, inviting greens. Gay Brewer said of the 424-yard 6th that "the drive is the key shot. The hole is wooded both right and left. Under normal conditions, I'll play a 6 or 7-iron at the

big green, which is guarded on the left by a sandtrap. The great fear and problem on this hole is hooking the drive, for then the player is going to have to try to recover by hooking his ball out over the big lake which guards the right side of the green. It can turn into a disastrous hole." The 7th, only a few yards longer, can be difficult if the wind is against because hugging the right side of the fairway can be dangerous and aiming to the left makes the hole play longer. The green is large and has a big dip, and this invites three-putting. If you don't select the right club for your second shot, you can leave yourself a 100ft putt. The 8th, a par-three of 186 yards, resembles the 12th at Augusta National.

The second group of holes makes no great demands on length but they come at a vital time in a round. Scoring well here can give the lift that every golfer needs to finish in style. The three-hole stretch starts with a par-three and a par-five back to back. The 12th is 213 yards long and, believed Jackie Burke, "a good player will use anything from a 3-iron to a 4-wood, depending on the wind. The green is rather large, well guarded on the right by sand and in front by a lake that runs practically from tee to green. We call it Bob Hope Lake because he was the first person to hit a ball into it. He's hit a whole lot more since then." The 13th, a par five of 540 yards, proved pivotal for David Duval in the 1997 Tour Championship. The American hit a drive and three-iron here to 50ft and holed the putt for an eagle. Five pars to finish game him his one stroke victory over Jim Furyk.

The 14th is a par-four of 431 yards. "This is the hole that has been consistently the toughest to par," says Jack Nicklaus. "The oddly shaped green is bunkered tightly to the left, right and rear, and a small lake directly in front of the green must be carried. Arnie Palmer says this is the finest 14th hole he has ever played. I'm inclined to agree with him."

After everything has been said about Champions, what gave it its special character were the two ebullient men who founded it. During his time on the tour the good-humoured Jackie Burke was one of the most popular players amongst his fellow professionals and Bob Hope, adhering to the principle that only a superlative is adequate to describe a Texan, called Demaret the funniest amateur comedian he had met.

The Course Card

Champions Golf Club, Houston, Texas Cypress Creek course

Record: 63, Wayne Levy, 1990

Hole	Yards	Par
1	455	4
2	450	4
3	416	4
4	230	3
5	514	5
6	424	4
7	431	4
8	186	3
9	512	5
10	453	4
11	460	4
12	213	3
13	540	5
14	431	4
15	416	4
16	181	3
17	448	4
18	440	4
Out	3,618	36
In	3,582	35
Total	**7,200**	**71**

Where the old-fashioned still
reigns supreme

The Course Card

Pebble Beach Golf Links, Pebble Beach, California

Hole	Yards	Par
1	373	4
2	502	5
3	388	4
4	327	4
5	166	3
6	516	5
7	107	3
8	431	4
9	464	4
10	426	4
11	384	4
12	202	3
13	392	4
14	565	5
15	397	4
16	402	4
17	209	3
18	548	5
Out	3,274	36
In	3,525	36
Total	**6,799**	**72**

Without any argument, the supreme golf course in the western United States is Pebble Beach, four times the site of the US Open, and very much in the record books following the astonishing achievements of Tiger Woods in winning the 2000 US Open. Stretching for several miles alongside the rocky shore and steep cliffs of Carmel Bay, some 120 miles south of San Francisco, Pebble Beach has gained, thanks to television, a fame – indeed, even a notoriety – far beyond the immediate world of golf. Each January it is the remarkable scene of the closing round of the AT&T Pro-Am, a tournament that attracts a larger television audience than virtually any other event on the golfing calendar. It is almost axiomatic that once it goes on the air, the climate of the Monterey Peninsula goes into a frenzy, and Pebble Beach becomes a ruffian that intimidates and manhandles the world's finest professional golfers. Not in 1997, mind. Then Tiger Woods closed with three successive birdies for a 64 and the world learned that a special talent was about to emerge.

Tiger Woods opened with a 65 to dominate the 2000 US Open at Pebble Beach.

By American standards Pebble Beach is an old-fashioned course. At only just under 6,800 yards it is not particularly long; nor is it heavily bunkered. But the greens are small by present-day standards; many of them are well contoured, and when the course is in its best playing condition they can be as slick as any in the world – including the notoriously speedy Oakmont. The unique quality of Pebble Beach, however, is to be found on its stretch of seaside holes. Beginning at the 4th, the shortest of the par-fours, and continuing through the 10th, it presents one of the loveliest and probably the most severe succession of seaside holes to be found on any American course of championship calibre. The vista of these holes, particularly as viewed from the upper part of the 6th fairway and looking down the shoreline to the 10th green, is one of the loveliest sights of a sport that is by no means short of beauty. More than that, the last three of these holes, even on the balmiest of days, are enough to unsettle the strongest players and take the momentum from a round that seems on its way to something memorable. Gil Morgan certainly discovered this at the 1992 US Open. One minute, during the third round, he had created history and become the first man to reach double digits under par at any stage in any US Open. The birdies kept coming; he reached a scarcely credible 12-under. Then he stepped on the 8th tee. He played the next three holes in five over par; indeed he went on to play the last 29 holes in 17 over. Clearly Pebble Beach was not happy with its earlier humbling.

The 8th, the first of the vicious triumvirate, is 431 yards on the card and begins with a blind drive from a slightly depressed tee perched on the side of a cliff that falls away some fifty feet to the sea below. The amateur's uphill drive of some 200 yards to the middle of the fairway leaves an awesome shot across an elbow of the bay that

Jack Neville was hired by Sam Morse in 1918 to lay out Pebble Beach (right), and with Douglas Grant and H. Chandler Egan as consultants, he produced one of the most magnificent and testing of all courses. Pebble Beach was honoured to host the 100th US Open in 2000, and for this event Jack Nicklaus constructed an entirely new 5th hole along the cliff edge. The event was distinguished by the magnificent play of Tiger Woods who set a new record for the largest winning margin ever achieved in a Major – 15 strokes. He was the only player to finish under par (at 12-under) with second-placed Ernie Els and Miguel Angel Jimenez far distant at 3-over.

Bing Crosby started his pro-am tournament at Pebble Beach in 1936. It is now sponsored by AT&T and continues to attract both the best players of the day and the glamour of Hollywood. Here, Crosby is with Bob Hope and Frank Sinatra.

cuts into the fairway approximately 250 yards from the tee. There is an absolute carry of 180 yards across the bay to a small green that is liberally trapped on three sides. A scrubby bank rises up on the left side of the green to catch the overhit shot, and one would prefer not to be there either. Probably half the pars achieved here during a major tournament are made with one putt. The 9th has been described by more than one tournament professional as the toughest par-four in golf. The hole runs downhill all the way to the green, and the fairway slopes towards the sea, so the tendency is to keep the ball to the left and thus

lengthen the hole beyond the 464 yards it measures on a straight line. With the wind blowing in from the sea, as it so often does, even the very strongest hitters sometimes struggle to reach this green in two. The 10th, although a little shorter at 426 yards, still poses the same forbidding problems – the sea on the right and the green tucked up against the side of the cliff. On a day when the winds are on the rampage, anyone who can go par-par-par along this stretch is playing virtually perfect golf.

Pebble Beach turns inland from there, but it returns to the sea at the 17th and 18th, two holes where tournaments are frequently won and lost. It was at the 17th, a 209-yard tee shot – usually into the wind – to a large, two-level green with the sea to the left and behind, that Tom Watson produced one of the greatest shots of his illustrious career. It was like the Open Championship at Turnberry all over again as he and Jack Nicklaus duelled for supremacy over the closing holes in the 1982 US Open. When Watson missed the green on the left at the 17th, it appeared that Nicklaus would triumph this time. Watson's chip was from clinging rough and he appeared to have no chance of stopping the ball close to the pin, which had been positioned on the left side of the green. Unless, of course, he hit the pin. "I'm going to hole this," he said to his sceptical caddie. But hole it he did, in one of the great prophecies the game has witnessed. Watson birdied the last for good measure, to win by two shots. As he came out of the scorer's tent there to greet him was the great sportsman himself, Nicklaus. He put an arm around Watson's shoulders and said: "You son of a bitch, you're something else. I'm very proud of you."

Until 1966, Pebble Beach was, to all intents and purposes, a public golf course designed for the use of visitors to the Lodge at Pebble Beach, the large resort hotel overlooking the 18th green and the sea. It was built during 1919 as part of the Del Monte Properties (now Pebble Beach Co.), which undertook to develop a remote and exclusive resort community in the wild pine forests of the Monterey Peninsula. Until World War II few but the very rich were attracted to the Pebble Beach area. For the most part it was the weekend and summer playground of the corporation presidents and their wives from Los Angeles and San Francisco, with a sprinkling of just enough Middle Westerners and Easterners to give the area and its expensive houses an aura of eastern sophistication. The Pebble Beach course was too splendid to go unnoticed, however. California state championships were played there, and its reputation grew to the point where the USGA finally brought the Amateur championship there in 1929 – the first national championship ever played west of the Mississippi. The tournament is remembered nowadays largely because it was the only Amateur championship during the last seven years of his active career in which Bobby

Jones failed to reach the final round. On five of the other six occasions he was the winner, but at Pebble Beach he lost his first-round match to unknown Johnny Goodman, probably the biggest sports upset of the entire year. The impact on American golfers can be imagined. As an amateur Jones was supreme to an extent that no other has ever been, and who on earth was Goodman? Although he lost to Lawson Little later in that championship, he was soon to make an enduring mark. He was the last amateur to win either the US or Open Championships – in 1933 – but that morning at Pebble Beach the great crowd was stunned. The words Pebble Beach are engraved on the heart of Nicklaus, and not just for what happened in the 1982 US Open. He has often said it is his favourite golf course and it must be quite a thrill for him to have designed a totally new short 5th hole for the 100th US Open. Previously it had been little more than a means of getting from the 4th green to the 6th tee. Now it is another of the course's clifftop beauties. As for his on-course exploits, in 1961 progress to his second US Amateur title was little short of a massacre. Eleven years later he walked in triumph up the last long fairway by the ocean

Right and below: At 107 yards Pebble Beach's 7th is one of the shortest holes in golf but one of the most difficult, particularly in a wind, when it may take as much as a 3-iron to hit the tiny green only eight yards wide and tightly trapped. After a punched 7-iron Nicklaus holed a birdie putt of 25 feet here in the final round of the 1972 Open.

The 7th: 107 yards par 3

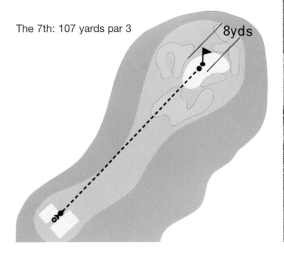

The 7th

An Eloquent Plea for Delicacy

When, in the 1973 Open, Gene Sarazen holed his tee shot at Troon's 13th hole, the famous Postage Stamp, only 126 yards long, it was seen by millions and commanded welcome attention to the virtues of the short short hole. There is no finer, or more beautiful, example of this than the 7th at Pebble Beach. After mounting the crest of the 6th the golfer turns towards the ocean. There below him on a promontory, bounded with rocks where the surf spills silver, lies a tiny green of 2,000 square feet embraced by sand. The hole measures only 107 yards and is downhill. In calm air a wedge of one sort or another is the club, but when the wind is strong from the Pacific golfers may be fingering medium irons to keep the ball low on line. Normally the

shot offers no problem to the expert, but the distance is not all that easy to judge and there are no marks for being too bold. The heaving tumult of the waves awaits. Short the hole may be, but the shot requires the utmost precision because the green lies directly along the line of approach and offers a target of no more than eight yards in width. In the 1992 US Open, the 7th proved pivotal for the eventual winner Tom Kite. Having overshot the green in the wild and windy conditions with his six iron, Kite then chipped in from a seemingly impossible position to turn a bogey into a birdie – a momentum builder if ever there was one.

The 7th is the shortest hole on any Major Championship course, but nobody scorns it because of towards his third US Open victory. In all golf there can be no more beautiful walk for a champion about to be crowned. His victory was assured when a magnificent 1-iron shot, drawn into the strong breeze, almost went into the 17th hole, gently hitting the pin and finishing inches away. He became the first and most probably the last, American golfer to have won both US Open and Amateur championships on the same course. In Britain, Jones alone has accomplished the feat with his victories at St Andrews in 1927 and 1930.

In addition to his Amateur and Open, Nicklaus had won the Pro-Am tournament three times and a fourth seemed likely in 1976 when he was sharing the lead after the last turn. Then suddenly it was revealed that Nicklaus could be as human a golfer as any humble hacker. On the 13th, after a big drive, he hit an inexcusably bad iron shot and made seven on the par-four hole. A good tee shot to the 17th was harshly bunkered and led to another triple-bogey and, in trying to get home in two at the last, he pulled into what Bing Crosby nicknamed the "mollusc country" and took seven. Nicklaus, smiling disbelief, was back in 45 for an 82 and golfers everywhere were comforted by the thought that even the mightiest of the age, if not of all the ages, could be as vulnerable as they.

The post-World War II prosperity and the jet age drastically changed the character of the Monterey Peninsula and, in turn, brought Pebble Beach to its present fame. The new-rich built houses in the area by the hundreds, and the nation's growing population of golfers could afford to fly there from anywhere on the continent in a matter of hours. Almost adjacent to Pebble Beach was the small and exclusive Cypress Point Club with its lovely links-like course built in 1930, and it was there that most of the better-connected golfers played, if they could arrange it, leaving Pebble Beach to the general public and the visitors at The Lodge. Bing Crosby moved the National Pro-Am tournament (now sponsored by AT&T) to the area in 1947, and as it grew in size he used not only Pebble Beach and Cypress Point but a third course farther along the beach belonging to the Monterey Peninsula Country Club. By 1966, a fourth course called Spyglass Hill, designed by the eminent Robert Trent Jones, was in operation, assuming the burden of the public play; and Pebble Beach became private, yet still available to the guests at the Lodge.

No description of Pebble Beach would be complete without some mention of the professional who ran the course with as autocratic a hand as any medieval monarch's. A Scotsman whose powerful voice and style seemed never to have left the heath and heather, Peter Hay was as much a part of Pebble Beach as the misty rain that blows in from the Pacific. Some claimed they built the course around him. Peter Hay may be long gone but his stern commands remain as relevant as ever, not the least of which was "Play your shots quickly and don't complain." If only it was the clarion call of all golfers.

The 9th And 10th

A Classic Test of Technique

Never were golf architects more richly blessed in a setting than were Jack Neville and Douglas Grant when they came to create Pebble Beach. With scarcely a second glance they must have visualized the great sequence of holes along the coast. By right of its place in the round the 18th is the most famous; the 7th is the most beautiful and the 8th the most spectacular but, in pure golfing terms, there cannot be two successive par-fours anywhere of greater quality than the 9th and 10th. Both are classics of their kind, rolling along the jagged coast, their greens hard against it and the land leaning  towards the ocean all the way. If ever holes reward, indeed demand, true striking these do. Few shots test a golfer's technique more precisely than those which compel him to hold a true line when the elements are from left to right, whether they be wind or, as on these holes, falling ground. The man who fears the slice or push towards the ocean and holds his shot overmuch to the left may be bunkered or, at best, face a fearsomely long approach to the green with all the perils that lie beyond. In the final round of the 1972 US Open Jack Nicklaus twice found the beach at the 10th to wind up with a six that almost cost him the title.

The 9th hole at Pebble Beach is not only one of the most picturesque of par fours but demanding as well.

that. For the player seeking a birdie it demands a more sensitive touch than most shots of similar length from the fairway. Rightly, therefore, it commands its place in the heart of the most compelling stretch of seaside golf in the world. Pebble Beach has become the yardstick against which all new seaside courses are measured. It is a matter of regret that more architects have not been inspired by this short but memorable 7th hole.

Sadly, though, such holes are rare. The increased power of golfers in recent decades has led to short holes being made longer and longer. Often the average player is blinding away with wood or long iron, concerned mainly with making the distance and not finessing the shot to the most favourable part of the green. Every course should have at least one truly short hole, where delicacy rather than strength is of the essence. No architectural genius is needed to make it extremely testing – and hugely enjoyable.

The Course Card

Dorado Beach
Hotel Golf and
Tennis Club,
Puerto Rico
East course

Record: 64, John
Buczek, International
Pro-Am 1975

Hole	Yards	Par
1	360	4
2	530	5
3	175	3
4	370	4
5	570	5
6	370	4
7	410	4
8	195	3
9	440	4
10	520	5
11	215	3
12	390	4
13	540	5
14	205	3
15	430	4
16	455	4
17	415	4
18	415	4
Out	3,420	36
In	3,585	36
Total	**7,005**	**72**

The luxurious sprawl of Dorado Beach, its hotels and golf courses conjured out of fruit plantations and mangrove swamps on the Puerto Rican seashore, offers the apparent incongruity of a resort only the wealthiest can afford in a place where it can do some good for a poor society.

Dorado Beach was built in the late 1950s and early 1960s by Laurance Rockefeller, who retained Robert Trent Jones to design the four golf courses that it now has. His singular talent for creating resort golf could not have found a better canvas on which to work, nor one which would require more landscape engineering. Tens of thousands of tons of earth and rock were shifted to create lagoons, well stocked with fish – and, by the same token, to drain the swampy ground. The spoil was used to contour the course.

Dorado Beach is well away from the mainstream of golf and as a consequence has not staged many important contests. It has, however, staged the World Cup on two occasions, the first in 1961 when it was called the Canada Cup. This was won by Sam Snead and Jimmy Demaret, whose combined ages were then 99 years. These matches were staged over a composite course, for only nine holes of the East course had then been completed. Major events are now played over the East course, which is considered tougher. Not tough enough for Davis Love and Fred Couples in the 1994 World Cup, who took advantage of humid conditions and little wind. In perhaps the greatest performance in the tournament's long history, the American pair finished a mind-boggling 40 under par to win by no fewer than 14 shots. Couples won the individual honours with a total of 265.

The first four holes are pleasantly challenging, the sea sparkling away to the golfer's left as he drives from the first tee. The par-five 5th, 570 yards, is the longest hole on the

course. Trees flank either side of the hole from tee to green and the tee shot is threatened by a glaring trio of bunkers and one large mango tree. The second is no easier, with three more bunkers standing sentinel on the left and a fourth on the right. The third shot is to an elevated green, from the rear of which the player is faced with a harrowing putt. One bunker lies to the left of the green, another directly in front.

There follow two par-fours moderate length and then the 195-yard par-three 8th, where the chief difficulty lies not in hitting its immense green but in getting down in two putts. The 9th is another matter; it is the most demanding par-four on the course, although at 440 yards its length is not back-breaking. Three bunkers demand accuracy from the tee and the second shot is menaced by trees on either side. It is almost certain to be a long iron and the green, which is hemmed in by two giant bunkers, is deep and narrow.

The 10th is a shortish par-five, the beach keeping it company on the left. The 11th is only 215 yards long, but it is moated about by water and the green is not one to miss. The short par-four 12th plays longer than it looks because the prevailing wind is in the player's teeth and the two lakes of the 13th, 540 yards, pose a fascinating dilemma for both long and short hitters. The 14th, a par-three going away from the ocean, presents no special problem if the golfer does not slice or push his tee shot. Four bunkers embrace the green and water comes into the reckoning on the right.

The last four holes are all par-fours, only the long 16th calling for real power hitting. The 15th requires extreme authority off the tee and in the approach to the green. The fairway is narrow and the elevated green has two tiers, with traps lying to the left, right and front. At 455 yards the 16th is the longest par-four on the course, but the wind is now

Trent Jones transforms
a swamp

Over a million cubic yards of earth were moved to fashion the East course at Dorado Beach, the best of five fine courses situated just east of San Juan. Shortly after it opened it was host to the 1961 World Cup, when Sam Snead won the individual title with a sixteen-under-par 272.

following. The long, narrow green rises to the rear and is surrounded by bunkers. The dog-leg 17th is made more difficult by two bunkers just beyond the corner. Double bunkers guard the front of the green. The finishing hole provides a challenging finale, with two large fairway traps to be sidestepped and two more barricading the green. A strong breeze gusting in from the ocean stiffens the challenge.

When the late Ed Dudley first went to Dorado Beach as head professional in 1958, from the Augusta National, he called the original eighteen holes "the toughest test for the top professionals of any course I have played". On paper, as Couples and Love so eloquently proved, the course is more attractive than tough. The secret of Dorado Beach lies in the Atlantic winds. Thus it is a perfect resort course, offering a tough challenge to the handicap player and, at the same time, giving little away to the professional.

The 13th

Trent Jones Explains His Strategy

Robert Trent Jones likes to design a golf hole that is not only beautiful but can be played at least two different ways, and preferably more – ten, if he can manage it. He wants the hole to play heroically for the professional who is going for a birdie, daringly for the low-handicap amateur who must go all out for his par with the possibility of a birdie, safely for the high handicapper to whom par is a victory, and not overly long for the ladies.

In this respect, the 13th at Dorado Beach is one of his favourites. It is a double dog-leg par-five that twice bends sharply around a wafer hazard, first to the left and then, near the green, to the right. The green is elevated and, in addition to the protection of the seventy-five-yard-wide lake, is surrounded by traps. Behind the green, about thirty yards away, is the Atlantic. The courageous and capable golfer can reach the green, but he will have made two thoroughly superb shots. The hole embraces four possibilities. The confident golfer can hit over both lakes to reach the green in two strokes, thereby cutting off a hundred yards of the hole's 540-yard length through the fairway. Or he can elect to play to the right of the first lake and to the left of the second, leaving himself a short pitch to the length of the

Left and above: The 13th hole on the East Course at Dorado Beach, left, with the characteristic palm tress swaying in the breeze.

green. The handicap golfer also has two choices. He may drive safely to the right of the first lake and follow this with a straight second before deciding on whether to gamble by going for the green with his third or settling for the fourth alternative, the safe four-shot route to the green. The ladies have the same options. In the words of its designer, the hole is "fair to all, demanding to be sure, but it demonstrates clearly the rewards and penalties that should be innate to all great golf holes".

Mind the bunkers

and the bear cubs!

If the greatness of golf courses were determined by their setting then Banff Springs, nestling a mile up in the Canadian Rockies, would certainly make the world's top ten. Though not a venue for major championships, it is a first-rate course where the towering mountains make distances seem shorter causing many players to under-club. The most famous holes are the 8th (Devil's Cauldron), the taxing 16th (Big Bow) and the 18th (Wampum), which harbours 28 of Banff's 144 bunkers.

It was once suggested to no less qualified a judge of golf course beauty than Bobby Locke that Banff Springs occupied one of the most spectacular settings in the world. To which Locke replied: "Not really. It's out of this world." So striking is the setting of Banff Springs, in the Canadian Rockies, that few visitors can concentrate only on their golf.

Banff's first course, of only nine holes, was created by the Canadian Pacific Railway Company in 1911 as an added attraction for its huge, turreted Banff Springs Hotel. During World War I a further nine holes were built by German prisoners of war. Stanley Thompson, the Canadian architect with whom Robert Trent Jones served his apprenticeship, was commissioned to redesign the course in 1927. He was assisted by Casper McCullough, a turf expert who became the course superintendent for the next 44 years.

Maintenance problems remain legion. Golf course greenmasters in southern Alberta wage an endless battle with the ravages of alternate freezing and thawing, caused by sub-zero temperatures and mild Chinook winds of winter, and by the warm, sunny days and sub-zero nights of spring.

Measured against the exacting standards of today's top players, Banff Springs remains a true championship test. Yet its 6,729-yard challenge has never been used for a major competition, perhaps because of its remoteness. The course is a maze of bunkers – 144 in all. Twenty-eight of them come into play at the 18th, an imperious finishing hole running parallel to the Bow River and only a few hundred feet from thundering Bow Falls.

The 1st tee, immediately below the clubhouse pavilion overlooking the often torrential confluence of the Bow and Spray rivers, presents a breathtaking vista. A precipice drops to the Spray tributary directly in front of the tee and, although the carry across it is less than a hun-

The imposing sight of the Banff Springs Hotel would look over-the-top in a less sublime setting.

dred yards, the churning river has been known to unnerve the most composed of scratch players. The green opens up after a mound on the right, but accuracy is essential for a safe par, as six narrow traps crowd around the sides and rear. The 2nd and 3rd are both short, undemanding par-fours. They contrast sharply with the 4th, the course's longest hole, where mounds and bunkers are neatly stacked on the fairway. The drive must clear a cavernous bunker snaking from the left; a sound second, across a nest of mounds and traps, leaves a fairly open avenue home. From a straightforward par four of undemanding length, the route swings south towards the steep face of Mount Rundle, which so dominates the course. The short 6th is conventional, requiring an iron shot to a raised green imprisoned by traps, but the par five 7th, aptly named Gibraltar, is unusual. The tee gazes out on a rather lean strip of greensward, bounded on the right by the rising cliffs of Mount Rundle and on the left by a series of traps. A precise shot is required to reach the green in two, for it is tucked away to the right, partially hidden, and the approach must thread between the precipice on the right and the sand that lies to the left. An easy climb to a high lookout affords a heart-stopping view of the par three 8th, known as the Devil's

Cauldron. This famous hole calls for a most difficult shot, complicated by swirling wind, from an elevated tee across a lake to a tiny, heavily bunkered green. The 9th, a dog-leg par-four is sliced out of dense woods. The fairway curves and slopes left, guiding hooked shots into bunkers which lie beyond an awkward trough. A prodigious second shot is required to reach the green, trapped heavily to the right. The relatively routine 10th, straight but to an elevated and well-trapped green, leaves one at the farthest point from the club-house as the course angles north towards the Bow River and a cliffs beyond, webbed with pillars of clay, sand and gravel known as the Hoodoos. A network of bunkers surrounds the green on the downhill par five 11th, which, if the two cross-bunkers are avoided, offers birdie chances.

The course now turns back along the Bow River towards the distant battlements of the hotel. The drive at the tree sheltered 12th, the 138-yard Papoose, carries a long strip of tee and a backwash of the river. The 13th green, hidden from the tee, is accessible in two with an exacting drive that will stand some pull out of a chute of trees to the more elevated left side of the fairway.

An arm of the river severs the 14th, which is lengthy for a par-three: the temptation is to use a wood to reach the green, but the fairway banks sharply in the direction of the water and any slight fade or short shot is doomed. It makes the 14th a score wrecking-hole. Two cross-bunkers and nine greenside traps make the 15th tough, yet it is the 16th, another par-four, which boasts the toughest rating at Banff. It is a slight dog-leg to the right with a series of bunkers off the tee and a fairway that rolls and heaves, pinching in to the right and trees and sand to the left. The green is long and narrow. Accuracy with the middle irons is vital.

The shadow of nearby Tunnel Mountain looms directly above the 17th, a flat, long par-three with severe traps flanking the green. The 18th, another slight dog-leg right, has two massive clusters of bunkers, one of which must be carried. The fairway traps, which stretch to 185 yards off the tee, can only be avoided by courting the trees down the narrow right side, but this only makes for an extremely difficult shot across the second nest of traps.

The Banff Springs course lies within a National Park; deer and even the odd bear cub can be seen from time to time. Banff Springs calls for thoughtfulness and accuracy and is indeed out of this world.

The Course Card

Banff Springs Hotel, Alberta

Hole	Name	Yardage	Par
1	Spray	479	4
2	Goat	382	4
3	Sarcee	376	4
4	Windy	570	5
5	Prettie	438	4
6	Rundle	178	3
7	Gibraltar	513	5
8	Devil's Cauldron	175	3
9	Trough	432	4
10	Fairholm	349	4
11	Hoodoo	525	5
12	Papoose	138	3
13	Jinx	484	5
14	Little Bow	210	3
15	Magpie	400	4
16	Big Bow	430	4
17	Sulphur	225	3
18	Wampum	425	4
Out		3,543	36
In		3,186	35
Total		**6,729**	**71**

The 8th

Devil's Cauldron

Famous the world over for its splendid situation in an amphitheatre beneath a soaring rock face of the massive Mount Rundle, Banff's 8th hole, known as the Devil's Cauldron, is universally recognised as one of the great holes of golf. It is a par-three which calls for the drop-shot which was so popular amongst golfers in the 1920s and 1930s. A natural miniature glacial lake is the hole's chief hazard, but there are others – notably scattered bunkers encircling a green set on an oval terrace sloping slightly towards the water. The green is separated from the lake by a narrow ribbon of lower terrace and rimmed on three sides by more pronounced grass slopes, which rise through trees to the base of cliffs. The mountain wall had to be blasted to clear the site when the course was reconstructed in 1927.

Accuracy from the tee is vital and it is a matter of precision – an ideal example of Stanley Thompson's uncanny knack for producing marvellous holes in rugged terrain.

A course worthy of its
glorious setting

The Course Card

Capilano Golf and Country Club, British Columbia

Hole	Yards	Par
1	482	5
2	400	4
3	467	5
4	172	3
5	520	5
6	394	4
7	426	4
8	381	4
9	176	3
10	434	4
11	165	3
12	368	4
13	400	4
14	130	3
15	430	4
16	247	3
17	425	4
18	557	5
Out	3,418	37
In	3,156	35
Total	**6,574**	**72**

The visitor's first impression of Capilano is of its almost Olympian setting. Buttressed to the north and east by the coastal mountains of British Columbia, it overlooks the not unpleasing sprawl of urban Vancouver with Mount Baker beyond, south of the 49th Parallel; to the west is a misty Vancouver Island, across the Strait of Georgia. It is a vista decidedly distracting to the concentration of the visiting golfer and even to those club members most used to it.

A glorious setting does not in itself make a great golf course. But while the views at Capilano may distract, they do not detract from the course's true golfing qualities. This course, in which no two holes are remotely similar, would be outstanding wherever it were set down. Capilano is exceptional in this part of the world as one of the few courses – if not the only one – which has not been drastically remodelled since it was opened. It was designed and constructed in 1937 by Stanley Thompson, the well-known Canadian golf course architect and creator of many other exquisite courses, among them Banff Springs. The course was part of a huge project embarked upon in the early 1930s by Guinness Estates. The scheme was for a high-class residential development and golf course at West Vancouver, isolated from the city proper by the Burrard Inlet but to be linked to it by a mile long bridge. It was a huge undertaking by anybody's standards, not least in the construction of the course itself.

Capilano had to be shaped from a hillside tangled with the stumps of Douglas firs, cedar and hemlock, a forest of second-growth trees and massive outcrops of rock. The result, nevertheless, is a gem. It is not difficult for the player of average ability who keeps his drives in the fairways. The championship course measures 6,574 yards but it can be stretched by more than 300 yards for special events.

The 1st is downhill all the way – 482 yards, but closer to 500 from a seldom used championship tee, within a whisper of the men's bar. It is a hole where the par of five feels more like a bogey to the scratch player. The par four 2nd, a drive and medium iron, is followed by a blind uphill tee shot at the 467-yard 3rd, a par-five that is littered with bunkers. Sprayed wood shots here create problems in reaching the relatively small and well-guarded green in regulation figures. A mid-iron will suffice to carry a pond safely to the double-tiered green of the par-three 4th, though insufficient club leaves a nasty putt if the pin placement is on the upper level.

Then comes yet another par-five, a dog-leg right over more water which, from one of the upper tees, demands a flush and perfectly placed drive. The second shot, hit downhill towards the city, must also be accurate to the vicinity of an undulating, treacherously fast green. The stroll down the 6th is a divine pleasure; the spectacle below of the Lions Gate Bridge, linking Vancouver with the North Shore across the sparkling waters of Burrard Inlet, is simply entrancing. By the time the golfer is putting on the 6th green he has descended almost 300 feet from the 1st tee, 672 feet above sea-level. Many handicap players have negotiated these first six holes well under par figures. But there are pitfalls ahead, for now the course flattens out and Capilano begins to catch up on the careless golfer. The next two holes are both fine par fours. The climb back towards clubhouse level begins from the 9th tee. The hole is a troublesome, 176-yard par-three on which club selection varies according to the weather. It usually requires a low iron or spoon to reach the elongated green guarded by gaping bunkers, from which only the top of the flagstick is visible.

The beginning of the second nine offers a possible birdie at the par five 10th. It is just over 430 yards long, a dog-leg left calling for accuracy with the second shot to

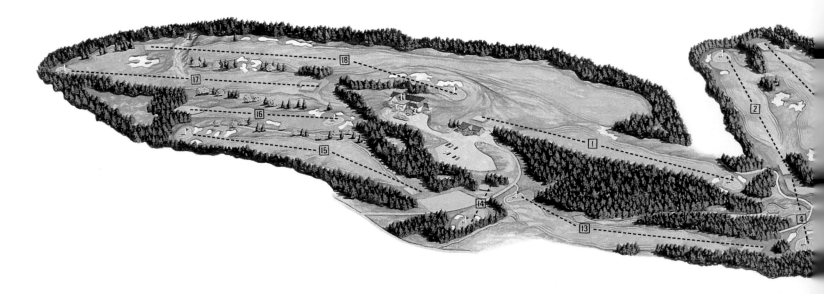

an elevated, narrow-necked entrance to the green. The next hole is quite simply a sheer delight. From the elevated tee it is nothing more than a 6 or 7 iron over a man-made pond, but the slick green undulates like an oily sea in a swell. On the last seven holes birdies are all too rare and pars require considerably more finesse and thought than has previously been necessary. The exception, perhaps, is the short 14th, a pitch over the main driveway from another elevated tee. The 12th and 13th, both par-fours, call for well placed drives followed by precise shots over a stream at the 12th and a gully at the longer 13th.

The 15th, like the 7th, cannot be manipulated without two exceptional shots. It is an ominous 430-yarder, directly into the face of the mountains and slightly uphill to the green. The best that short hitters can hope to do is chip and single putt to achieve a well-earned par here. At the 16th a par three, even on the calmest of days, is a sheer victory. From the back tee it is 247 yards to the green, which sits immediately beneath the clubhouse.

At the 17th, slightly over 400 yards long, the main difficulties lie in club selection and in avoiding an awkward lie among the fairway mounds while steering clear of a long bunker and the obtrusive trees on the left. The green is in a beautiful setting, softened by the shadows of tall trees and the mountains.

The home hole is a classic, 557 yards long and uphill all the way to a green set on the side of a hill scattered with a network of bunkers. The safe way to approach this monster is to lay up short of the three diagonal bunkers fronting the green, leaving a mid-iron approach over the inviting sand to the elevated but reasonably flat green. Few long hitters have ever reached this green in two. It is a feat requiring a "Sunday best" drive and a gambling three wood over the narrow, upper portion of the fairway, which is flanked by the bunkers and out of bounds stakes. Really big events have been few and far between at Capilano, so it was a rare treat to welcome the cream of amateur golf in June 1992 when the World Amateur Team Championship was played for the Eisenhower Trophy. On this occasion New Zealand beat the USA into second place with what has proved to be the lowest aggregate score to date, 823.

The 4th and 11th

Thompson At His Fiercest

Stanley Thompson, Capilano's Scottish-born architect, made something of a speciality of creating fascinating short holes. Among the more celebrated are the Devil's Cauldron at Banff Springs and, at nearby Jasper, the 150 yard Bad Baby and the slightly longer Colin's Clout. At Capilano Thompson maintained his tradition of colourfully named, tough par-threes.

Two of them, the 4th and 11th, are across stretches of water after which they have been named. Paradoxically these names imply a certain ease and benevolence on the part of the architect. Indeed, the water at the 4th, known as Lily Pond, is intimidating only to the handicap golfer who might otherwise find the hole relatively easy. It is only from the extended championship tees, which can stretch the hole to almost 200 yards, that the 4th becomes in any way fierce. Then, because of three huge traps which guard the front half of the smallish, two-tiered green, the drive must be absolutely accurate, particularly when the pin is on the farther, upper level.

The 11th, called Wishing Well, is an entirely different proposition. It embodies all the characteristics that have made Thompson's short holes so feared. Typically, it is only 165 yards long but the green, wonderfully sited amongst stately pine trees, is fast and heavily undulated and tightly enclosed by hazards. Immediately in front is a small lake and around the back and sides are four long, sprawling bunkers. Anything other than the most precise medium iron shot will find severe trouble. Fittingly, this beautiful hole became the architect's favourite.

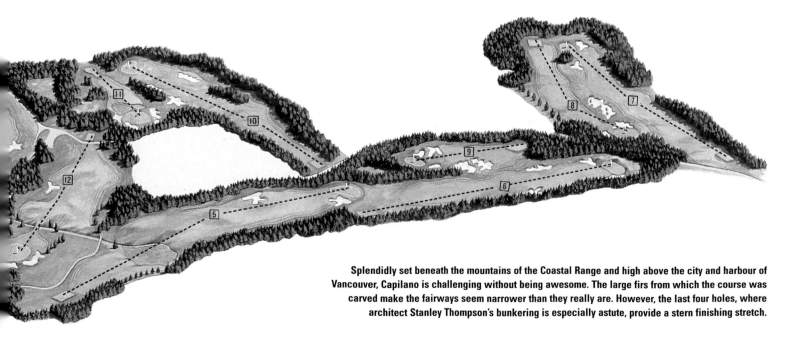

Splendidly set beneath the mountains of the Coastal Range and high above the city and harbour of Vancouver, Capilano is challenging without being awesome. The large firs from which the course was carved make the fairways seem narrower than they really are. However, the last four holes, where architect Stanley Thompson's bunkering is especially astute, provide a stern finishing stretch.

Fit for the next
fifty years

The Course Card

The Royal
Montreal Golf
Club, Ile Bizard,
Quebec
Blue course

Hole	Yards	Par
1	434	4
2	375	4
3	390	4
4	440	4
5	179	3
6	570	5
7	154	3
8	397	4
9	429	4
10	452	4
11	438	4
12	197	3
13	533	5
14	361	4
15	420	4
16	433	4
17	156	3
18	444	4
Out	3,368	35
In	3,434	35
Total	6,802	70

Whatever insubstantial traces of golf there are to be found in the history of North America before the late 19th century, pride of place in seniority must go to Canada and in particular to the Royal Montreal Club, which celebrated its centenary in 1973. It was the first properly constituted club on the continent, predating the first in the United States – St Andrews at Yonkers, New York – by 15 years.

Golf in Canada is older than in the United States probably because Canada attracted the larger proportion of Scottish immigrants. Toronto Golf Club, Royal Quebec and Brantford Golf and Country Club, Ontario, though marginally younger than Montreal, are older than any of their counterparts across the border.

Royal Montreal's beginnings were similar to those of countless clubs throughout the world – a group of Scots men getting together to recreate, in alien surroundings, their national sport. They were led by a bearded giant, Alexander Dennistoun, whose name was proof enough of his antecedents. The medal he gave for competition (upon which, by means of a little Scottish finagling, he managed to have his name the first to be engraved) is still played for to this day as the symbol of the club's championship.

Fletcher's Field, a public park on the slopes of Mount Royal, was the club's first site. The joining fee was five dollars, the annual dues half as much; a wooden club would set a member back two dollars. The site was adequate to begin with, but in time the game attracted more players and, moreover, Montreal was growing rapidly. In 1896 a new site was found at Dixie, ten miles to the west of the city, and here the club was to remain for the next 63 years.

The par four 15th hole at Royal Montreal, once the scene of a memorable play-off victory in the Canadian Open for Tom Weiskopf over Jack Nicklaus.

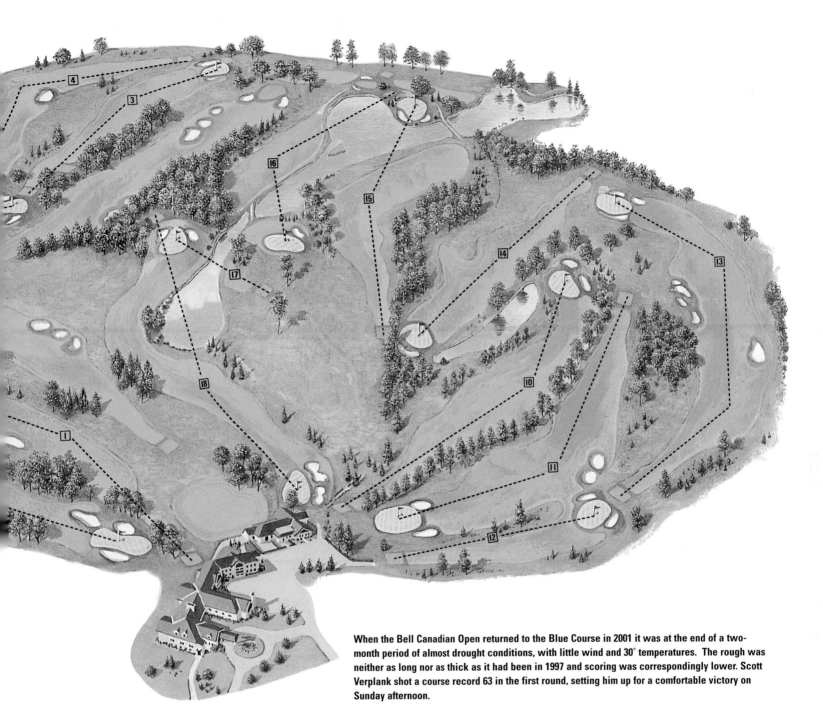

The numbers visible on the course map: 4, 3, 16, 15, 14, 13, 17, 10, 11, 18, 1, 12

When the Bell Canadian Open returned to the Blue Course in 2001 it was at the end of a two-month period of almost drought conditions, with little wind and 30° temperatures. The rough was neither as long nor as thick as it had been in 1997 and scoring was correspondingly lower. Scott Verplank shot a course record 63 in the first round, setting him up for a comfortable victory on Sunday afternoon.

The Dixie course saw the first Canadian national championships, the women's amateur in 1901 and the men's a year later. The club also staged the world's first "international", the first of an annual series between Royal Montreal and The Country Club of Brookline, Massachusetts. The contest predates by four years the England-Scotland series, which began in 1902, and is still played.

Dixie was to be the venue for five Canadian Opens, won by J. H. Oke (1904), Albert Murray (1908 and 1913), Macdonald Smith (1926) and Jim Ferrier (1950). It was played by those legends of the links Harry Vardon and Ted Ray; and by the Prince of Wales (later King Edward VIII) and Lloyd George. The tentacles of the urban octopus that had squeezed the club from its first home reached out again in the 1950s. A site was found on Ile Bizard in the Lake of Two Mountains, and Dick Wilson was fetched from Florida to design the course.

Wilson, an outstanding golf architect, was the second choice. The Royal Montreal had first sought the services of Robert Trent Jones but he was otherwise committed. Trent Jones and Wilson made much of their professional rivalry and were never slow to damn each other's work with faint praise. The two were as different as a driver and a sand-iron. Trent Jones brings to his work a background that is almost academically perfect for the job of golf course design. At Cornell he successively studied engineering, architecture and agriculture, taking in the essential disciplines of surveying, hydraulics and landscape architecture, among other things. He is an urbane man and his courses reflect this.

Dick Wilson, a down-to-earth, blunt-spoken man, was a fully fledged civil engineer who went to college on a football scholarship. To him, a Jones course was too contrived, paying too little attention to the nature of the land on which it was built; he believed that it took a better man to build a course than to lay one out. Trent Jones is equally succinct: the heart of a good golf course is its design, he believes – any good engineer can do the rest. How Royal Montreal's Ile Bizard courses – two of 18 holes, the Red and the Blue, and a nine hole – would have differed had Jones and not Wilson designed them is mere speculation. Wilson engaged Joe Lee as his site supervisor. Although now in his eighties, Lee is still an active course designer and has returned to Royal Montreal over a number of years to make improvements and adjustments, including reconstructing the bunkers to Wilson's original designs.

The par four 18th hole, complete with its dominating features: the sand protecting its left side, and the magnificent and imposing clubhouse in the background.

All 45 holes were completed for play in just over two years, finishing in May 1959. Wilson was proud of his creation. On a visit to the club before his untimely death he remarked: "There is a sweep and dimension to this layout which can only be described as exciting. That vista of the Lake of Two Mountains is the perfect backdrop to these courses. Don't ever shut off the view with too many trees."I have designed these courses for the present and the future. With the improvement in players' abilities and training and with better equipment, older courses will become old-fashioned and inadequate in the next 15 years. The Red and the Blue courses will remain modern and can be made even more challenging for the next 50 years."

Wilson's words have held true. In 1997 the Canadian Open returned to Royal Montreal after an absence of many years. It developed into an exciting duel over the Blue course between Steve Jones and Greg Norman, with the latter claiming the title by just a stroke on a five under par total of 275. In all, only seven players managed to break par for 72 holes and one of them, Davis Love, said: "It is a very trying course, just like a Major Championship venue. The rough is very penalising and the greens are fast. It is a tough course to score on." The event achieved one other small historical footnote: it was the first tournament since he turned professional at which Tiger Woods missed the 36-hole cut.

Both Red and Blue courses are formidable assignments and are distinctive in that they are among the few in

Quebec which, for handicap purposes, are rated higher than their par. Both courses have a par of 70 but are rated at 72 (Red) and 73 (Blue). It is accepted that a Royal player can play to his handicap anywhere.

The greens – to which Dick Wilson paid particular attention – are enormous, averaging 12,000 square feet in size, nearly double the conventional size in North America. It means that from the same patch of fairway, under comparable wind conditions, the approach might call for anything from a three-iron to a five-iron, depending on where the pin is placed.

Putts of extraordinary length are often called for, up to 120 feet in extreme cases. Pat Fletcher, who was for many years the professional at Montreal said: "The secret is to hit your approaches a little longer rather than a little shorter. While some of the entrances are narrow, they all widen out considerably towards the back. The greens also putt deceptively."

Unlike many challenging courses, Royal Montreal is not renowned for its fairway bunkering; there are only 11 on the Blue course. But closer to the scoring areas, no fewer than 48 traps – deep gouges filled with heavy sand and with diabolical contours – guard the greens themselves.

The thoughtfully placed and artistically moulded bunkers are typical of Dick Wilson's design. Indeed, Royal Montreal could well be described as the archetypal Wilson course. It has the bunkers, the gently contoured greens

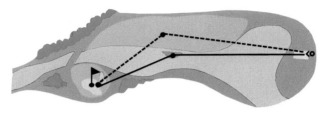

The 16th

Determination Gains Immortality

The 16th on the Blue course at Royal Montreal is one of the most intimidating par fours in Canada. At about 415 yards from the regular tee markers and slightly over 430 yards from the very back, it is not inordinately long. It has only one sand trap – but that is all it needs.

The challenge is that the normal flight of the ball between tee end green is almost wholly over water. The drive is across a lake which the approach has to recross to reach an elevated pear-shaped green. The wind is almost always against and the second shot is invariably a long iron shot or even a wood hit low.

The lake is contoured so that the safer the line a player takes from the tee – in other words the farther to the right – the more difficult his approach becomes, because the carry over the water in front of the green is lengthened.

It is not uncommon for a proficient player to pump two or even three balls into the lake from the tee and then follow them with two or three more negotiating the approach. Scores in the low 20s have been recorded on the hole. In one tournament played by Canada's premier senior players flooding made the hole unplayable and it was assigned an arbitrary rating of 5.5, the figure being added to everybody's card.

The hole was also the setting for a memorable par four by an intense young tour regular named Pat Fitzsimons in the 1975 Canadian Open. In the second round his drive was struck off line to the left, straight towards the water. Fitzsimons was preparing to reload when the ball came down on a raft-sized island some 10 yards from the shore. The ball was plainly visible but seemingly inaccessible. Or was it?

Nobody had ever tried it before, but there was nothing in the rules of golf to stop Fitzsimons from attempting to reach the island. He climbed on to his caddie's back but proved to be too much of a load and the two of them tottered and nearly went under. Fitzsimons then ventured out alone. The water turned out to be no more than waist deep.

He completed the crossing, lofted a four iron to the green, made the return trip without incident, partially dried himself and two-putted from 30 feet for his par. The inconsequential island has since been named after Fitzsimons.

and the winding fairways, softly mounded to blend superbly with their surroundings. The hand of man is unobtrusive, the beauty of the course is muted and, despite the changes in the landscape wrought by Wilson, there is not jarring artificiality, only a serene naturalness.

Regular players regard the Red course with more respect as a test of all-round golfing skills. The "Blue Monster" is far more celebrated, largely because of the four finishing holes that throw out a direct challenge to the player, daring him to take on their vast expanses of water. Nobody in tournament play was able to peel more than two strokes from par before the 1975 Canadian Open, when both Nicklaus and Weiskopf opened with 65s. Nicklaus let the title slip from his grasp when he hooked his tee shot into the water on the dog-leg of the finishing hole, and was forced into a play-off.

The tie-breaker started on the 15th, then a 410-yarder distinguished by a lake that bites into the fairway and protects the green. Because of the water, both Nicklaus and Weiskopf had to hold back off the tee, but both were left with only seven iron approaches. Weiskopf's stopped two feet from the pin, Nicklaus's almost hit his rival's ball, but was carried back eight feet by the backspin. Nicklaus missed the putt, Weiskopf did not.

Nicklaus had come face to face with the realities of the philosophy espoused by both Trent Jones and Dick Wilson: "A golf hole should be a hard par and an easy bogey." At Royal Montreal that is true of all the holes.

Golf with a
mid-Atlantic
accent

**The
Course
Card**

The Mid Ocean
Club, Bermuda

Hole	Yards	Par
1	404	4
2	465	5
3	190	3
4	350	4
5	433	4
6	360	4
7	164	3
8	339	4
9	406	4
10	404	4
11	487	5
12	437	4
13	238	3
14	357	4
15	496	5
16	376	4
17	220	3
18	421	4
Out	3,111	35
In	3,436	36
Total	**6,547**	**71**

The name of Mid Ocean has a faraway, compelling sound. It is one of the remotest of all the Commonwealth of Nations courses in the northern hemisphere, yet it is still a very famous course. It lies on the southern shores of Bermuda, that entrancing island in the western reaches of the Atlantic, and has become familiar to legions of Americans; New York is only 90 minutes away by plane.

Mid Ocean has no close parallel; in some aspects it might resemble Cypress Point, because while the ocean plays little part in its design, it provides a glorious background to the beginning and the end. The greater part of the course is laid over beautiful inland country of rolling hills and crests, gentle vales and valleys, coursing through deep woods of casuarina and innumerable flowering shrubs. One might be miles from the sea, but no point is more than a few substantial golf shots from the coast.

The course was designed in 1924 by the great pioneer of American golf Charles Blair Macdonald, who had matriculated at St Andrews yet it bears no resemblance to any course in Scotland. In 1953 the course was revised in some measure by Robert Trent Jones.

The impact of a wondrous setting does not diminish respect for the quality of the golf. It begins with a magnificent par four, curving to the left and rightly called Atlantic; it is simple enough to pull the second away from the raised green down to the rocks below. The 2nd swings down into the woods and up again to make a hole that is harder the longer one looks at it. From tee to green the short 3rd is a perfectly straight offering; it seems no greater problem than a thousand others of its length, until suddenly one is aware of the long fall to the ocean on the left and the garden on the right.

The 4th is another plunge-and-rise affair, narrow between trees and not altogether appealing. But what rewards await the climb; the 5th is one of the world's unforgettable holes. Far beneath a gun platform of a tee spreads the shining expanse of Mangrove Lake and, in a manner of

speaking, one sips as much of it as one can swallow. There is a way to the right for the frail of heart, but any carry over the water is considerable. The next three holes are a quiet interlude before the stern tasks really begin. Solid drives to the 6th and 8th leave only pitches, but these are to greens above eye level. This is a feature of Mid Ocean, making distances – even of little shots – difficult to judge precisely. The greens are not too small, but the slopes protecting them are often steep and recovery of an erring approach can be difficult. The greens are not watered artificially, but the ample rain and sunshine permit two growths each year – Bermuda in the summer, rye and bent for the winter. Thus, the greens are good the year around, although their pace and contours need knowing.

The 7th is a medium pitch over a pool and so far par has not been too exacting; the golfer, on his first visit, may wonder whether the course is as demanding as he has been led to expect. But the hard part is at hand. From the back tee of the 9th the carry is disturbingly long, with no easy alternative, over a wilderness of rushes that would not be out of place at Westward Ho! on the north Devon coast. The drive down the 10th, after ice has tinkled in glasses at the turn, seems spacious enough, but only one of exact placing will leave a clear shot to the green. A huge bunker guards its right side, and usually the pin. This is a splendid hole except that the over-bold shot is likely to be punished too severely. After a drive over a crest the 11th is a fair par five, the 12th nobody's easy four with the tee shot across a leaning shoulder of hillside, and the 13th a long short hole to a green ringed with traps. The bunkers on the left of the 14th are suggestive of Muirfield in their clustered insistence on trapping a pull to the fairway that tilts in their direction. Two good hits to the 15th should leave an easy pitch over rising ground to the green. Then follows a menacing uphill drive between trouble on the left and a great green basin, into which anything but the truly struck drive will roll. From there the second, naturally enough, is blind; but even from the fairway – and

The Atlantic plays little part in the design of Mid Ocean, but it provides a magnificent backdrop to a course which is given something of a cathedral-like atmosphere by tall, elegant pines. Although length is important at Mid Ocean (the par-three 13th is 238 yards long, and six of the par-fours measure more than 400 yards), there is some compensation in the size of the greens. The course is the best of four excellent ones on an island 21 miles long.

the hole is not long – the green on its high place, free to all the wind's force, can be elusive. And now the ocean is in sight again and a splendid 17th awaits. It was named Redan – presumably after the famous 15th at North Berwick, although there the similarity ceases. The shot is downhill, but into wind many golfers will be feeling for a wooden club.

The 18th pursues the line of the beach and the tee is situated high above it. Behind are the cliffs with pink and white houses clustered about their edges; ahead the handsome white mass of the clubhouse, where Churchill and Eisenhower once conversed of matters other than golf. The long driver must beware here because the fairway narrows abruptly. But the hole is beautifully shaped, and as one holes out there is a feeling that an enduring memory has been made. Beyond the green is the little practice ground where Archie Compston, so long the professional at Mid Ocean, gave his lessons; a memorial to him stands near by.

Golf in Bermuda is not confined to Mid Ocean; far from it. There are four other 18 hole courses, two of nine holes and a par-three – remarkable riches for an island of only some 22 square miles. Castle Harbour, with the most beautiful 1st tee imaginable, and an abundance of hills and valleys, is quite an experience to play. Belmont Manor is of a quieter undulating kind, and Riddell's Bay is charming. It flows along a green tongue of land with inlets of the Great Sound, where the ships glide by to Hamilton, testing the golfers from time to time. It is all gentle and appealing after the splendours of Mid Ocean. Finally, Port Royal (see gazetteer) is another Trent Jones creation. It makes fine strategic use of water and sand; the land is sharply contoured and some 200,000 trees and shrubs were planted over a period of about seven years. There are also some challenging holes, not least the 16th, hard by the ocean. Everywhere there is stunning beauty, that precious part of the golfer's legacy; and the island, a minute speck in the northern Sargasso Sea, makes a background for the game that very few places on earth can match.

The 5th

A Play Upon Courage, Fear And Greed

Feel for a shot is vital, as any golfer standing on Mid Ocean's 5th tee preparing to play across Mangrove Lake will tell you. The hole, 433 yards long, is a perfect example of how an architect can play upon courage, fear and greed. The fairway curves around a lake which is at its widest on the direct line to the green. The timid can play safely to the right, from where there is little or no hope of reaching the green with the next shot; the alternative is to attempt to drive over as much of the lake as he can or dares. The longer the carry made, the shorter and easier the approach. From the tee high above the lake the distance across to the fairway looks shorter than it is, as distances invariably do over water. And so, until the golfer knows the limits of his skill and nerve, usually from the chastening experience of seeing a well-struck drive splash from sight forever, short of where he thought it would finish, discretion is the better part.

The principle of being invited to bite off as much as one can reasonably hope to do is a basic of good design, and not by any means confined to water holes. The drive to the 6th at Pine Valley, where a wilderness slants across the line to the fairway, has deceived many into thinking they were stronger than they were, or has taught them not to be greedy. But then water is the classic hazard for such purposes. It has a dreadful finality.

The 5th hole at Mid Ocean. Even when the Mangrove Lake has been successfully negotiated there remains this demanding approach to the well-bunkered green.

High-altitude golf

amongst the cedars

Golf is a long, long way from replacing the *fiesta brava* or *futbol* in the hearts of the Latin Americans, but it is making good progress as a sport for the privileged minority. This is especially true in Mexico, which affords a great many more opportunities to play than most of its Pan-American neighbours to the south. It was not until the late 1940s that the Club de Golf Mexico was formed, giving the country its first course of international calibre. Since its fairways were opened in 1951, the club has played host to many of the world's leading golfers and several international events, including the World Cup in 1958 and 1967 and the World Amateur Team Championship in 1966. Perhaps the most memorable of these was the first of the two World Cups, which featured a splendid win for Christy O'Connor and Harry Bradshaw. Their winning score of 579 illustrates the course's difficulties; indeed, only one winning score in the 45-year history of the World Cup has ever been higher.

Club de Golf Mexico emerged from the imagination and

determination of Percy J. Clifford, six times amateur champion of Mexico and six times runner-up. With the sponsorship of President Aleman, Clifford found just the terrain he wanted at a place called El Cedtal, a lovely grove of cedar, pine, eucalyptus and cypress trees on the outskirts of the town of Tlalpan, an hour's drive south of Mexico City. Through the heart of the grove runs a deep, usually dry, creek that comes into play in varying ways on nearly half the holes.

Designed by Clifford and American architect Laurence Hughes, Club de Golf has a par of 72 and plays at an imposing 7,250 yards from the back tees. However, Mexico City's altitude of 7,500 feet lends a great deal of distance to the longer shots. A drive of 230 to 250 yards at sea-level will travel anywhere from 10 to 20 per cent farther in this rarefied atmosphere depending on the temperature and climatic conditions, a circumstance that makes the proper selection of clubs a distinct problem to the golfer who plays here for the first time. While he may be agreeably surprised at the new distance he has acquired off the tee, he may similarly find that his well-hit seven-iron to the green ends up in serious trouble ten or twenty yards past the target.

Due largely to the thousands of trees guarding its fairways, Club de Golf Mexico is principally a driving course with a secondary premium on long irons and fairway woods. While not heavily bunkered like so many of the newer courses north of the border, the target areas off the tees are generally narrowed and confined by at least one strategically placed sandtrap. The real punishment for the stray drive is, however, the trees themselves. From amongst them, it is seldom possible to do more than nudge the ball back to the centre of the fairway. Even the sides of the fairways are apt to cost a stroke now and then, for the overhanging branches will quite often block a straight route to the green.

The second shot problem is easily grasped by a glance at the yardage figures for the individual holes. Only four of the par fours measure less than 425 yards, and one of them is a full 470 yards. All four of the par fives extend over more than 550 yards, and two – the 11th and the 15th – offer but a minimal entrance to the green for even the finest second shot. Only one of the short holes is less than 200 yards and all four are extremely tight, due to the crowding trees, the enclosing bunkers or the confining boundary of the club property. Of medium size in terms of the newer golf courses, the greens have only the subtlest borrows, but they are well protected by bunkers without being unduly surrounded. In short, Club de Golf is a course where the straight golfer will be rewarded by pars, while the birdies are bought at peril.

As with all fine courses of championship quality, Club de Golf offers an imposing sequence of finishing holes that test not only the skill but the nerves of a player. The 15th is a dauntingly long par-five down an avenue of trees to a green protected by two bunkers. The 16th is either a long iron or a wood off the tee with no margin for error; the 17th, and 18th are both par-fours, the latter featuring a creek that plays a fundamental part in both holes that close the front and back nines. Considering it has been played often by the best professionals, the record of 66 indicates how difficult it is to bring this course to its knees.

The Course Card

Club de Golf
Mexico,
Mexico City

Hole	Yards	Par
1	390	4
2	563	5
3	175	3
4	470	4
5	230	3
6	580	5
7	376	4
8	425	4
9	437	4
10	431	4
11	573	5
12	427	4
13	377	4
14	200	3
15	442	4
16	225	3
17	570	5
18	359	4
Out	3,646	36
In	3,604	36
Total	**7,250**	**72**

The 6th to the 8th

High Drama in Thin Air

At the 6th hole at Club de Golf Mexico, the advantage of extra distance that the atmosphere of this mile-high city adds to a shot is suddenly taken away. Out-of-bounds to the right is a feature on all the four finishing holes to the outward half, and the trees that so effectively screen out the wind line the left. The golfer can forget about those 20-odd extra yards and concentrate on accuracy. Thus Latin Americans, who glorify length, learn that the second shot is just as important as the first.

The 6th, a par-four, is very demanding off the tee. The 7th offers no room for error all the way from tee to green. And then comes the 8th. Stretching 562 yards, it is a mighty par five even in this rarefied atmosphere. For once the golfer finds a bonus in a thick grove of trees – they prevent him from hitting out of bounds.

Topographically, the hole is a lot more difficult than it looks. A cluster of traps lies just short of the green to catch those who drive to the right of the fairway, but what makes the hole really tough is that the second shot is entirely uphill. Rarefied atmosphere or not, you must bust the second shot in order to reach the green.

In the 1967 World Cup, the American team of Arnold Palmer and Jack Nicklaus was so far in front of the rest of the field (at 19 under par) that the championship looked a formality. They won by 13 strokes over New Zealand. Palmer won the individual title with a 12 under par score of 276, and Nicklaus, driving poorly for once, ended up seven under. But together they played that 8th hole (then the 17th, for the two nines were the other way around) for four rounds in a total score of five under par.

Asia

Golf arrived in Asia in the early 19th century, its vectors the garrisons and administrators of the British Empire. Far and away the oldest golf club in the world outside the British Isles – far older, even, than most of them there – is the Royal Calcutta, founded in 1829. In course of time golf spread to all the countries of the East where the European presence was strong – even into China, where there were courses adjoining the now-vanished European cantonments. For more than a century, golf was essentially a game for the representatives of Colonial power, and a club of any standing rigorously excluded even the most important locals from membership. Colonialism and its trappings have now vanished, but the game has survived. It flourishes in India and south east Asia generally, in the Philippines and Taiwan (thanks to American influence), and countries like Thailand where the sport has been boosted by the emergence of Tiger Woods, whose mother is Thai. The Omega Asian Tour did not begin life until 1994 but just three years later encompassed more than 23 events in 16 different countries.

It is in Japan, however – ironically the one country that did not come under the Colonial influence – where the game has taken hold to an astonishing degree. The number of golfers there so outstrips capacity that there are six times more Japanese wanting to play the game than there are registered golfers in the whole of Europe. There are 12 million actual golfers in Japan (playing on 1,800 courses), 16 million who use the driving ranges, and it is estimated that a further eight million would like to do either or both if they had the time. New courses continue to be built despite the fact that land is at a premium, and strong opposition has grown against the use of what land there is for the pleasure of a few. Entrepreneurs and course designers have been literally driven to the hills in order to find sites for which permission will be granted – some so hilly that players travel by escalator from one hole to another. Near the cities, a player may have to give six months' notice to play a round, and even then consider himself lucky. Fees to play an average public course are over £200. And still the obsession goes on. The game is wholeheartedly embraced in the continent where it first took tenuous root so long ago.

1. Hirono 2. Kasumigaseki 3. Fujioka 4. Royal Calcutta 5. Hong Kong 6. Singapore Island
7. Royal Selangor 8. Bali Handara

With subtle bunkering and a delightfully varied use of water, Charles Alison created Japan's best test of golf at Hirono. The pine trees which flank the fairways do not intrude into play but provide instead a decorous frame for the rolling terrain broken by strategically placed natural gullies. The water comes effectively into play at the short holes – the 5th, 13th, and 17th – and at the long 12th, a 550-yard par-five where the drive must carry an awesome combination of rough and water to gain the safety of the fairway.

Alison's restrained but

inspired architecture

Hole	Yards	Par
1	505	5
2	430	4
3	440	4
4	425	4
5	155	3
6	430	4
7	195	3
8	355	4
9	525	5
10	355	4
11	440	4
12	550	5
13	180	3
14	380	4
15	565	5
16	395	4
17	230	3
18	460	4
Out	3,460	36
In	3,555	36
Total	**7,015**	**72**

The Westernization of Japan, a breakneck process during the early decades of the 20th century, was most marked in and around the great maritime cities like Tokyo and – farther west on the island of Honshu – the port of Kobe. It was within these cosmopolitan communities that the game of golf first took root and at Kobe, Japan was to acquire one of the world's great courses – Hirono. It set the standard by which oriental courses are measured.

The site chosen for Hirono was in every way ideal. Twelve miles to the north-west of the port it was, in a contemporary description, "dotted with many pretty ponds, winding streams, running rivulets, pine woodlands, ravines and gentle undulations". The materials were at hand for an architectural artist, the Englishman Charles Alison. The course he designed in 1930 remains basically unaltered to this day.

At Hirono Alison took advantage of the terrain to arrange, as at Sunningdale and St George's Hill (where he had worked with Harry Colt), several splendid carries from the tees. He planned intriguing greens at the end of generous fairways and sprinkled the course with bunkers of the type that in Japan bear his name to this day. There are no fewer than 104 bunkers awaiting the errant shot. In every way it was a piece of Berkshire transplanted to the Orient.

Charles Alison was a skilful draughtsman. The holes, hazards and greens in Alison's drawings were produced with amazing accuracy after he departed, a tribute to his skill in designing and to the high quality of the construction work and the painstaking supervision required to achieve such impressive results.

Hirono measures 7,015 yards from the championship tees and 6,395 from the regular ones. From the outset it has had all the length a championship course needs. Subtle changes are being made to the course for the 2005 Japan Open in line with advances in equipment and ball performance that Alison could not have envisioned. Yet his basic principles – his shot values – are not compromised. Hirono

was designed for all levels of golfers and will remain thus.

Few courses outside Britain have the striking difference and variety in each hole that Hirono possesses. Each is named after its peculiarity – Lake End, Fiord, Wee-Wood, Devil's Divot, Boulevard and Quo Vadis? We can assume that Alison had a hand in the naming, which is thoroughly appropriate. In playing or just walking the course, the titles immediately strike home. Devil's Divot, for example, is a par three across a huge gouge in the earth, in the shape of a giant divot. Fiord is another par three, across an inlet of a lake resembling a small Norwegian harbour. Some of the names commemorate people associated with the club's founding, but most announce a hole's feature or situation.

At first the greens were all of creeping bent grass but it was soon found that the ten times more virile Japanese Bermuda grass encroached and took over, in spite of all efforts to stem its advance. A fine variety of korai grass – of the same family as the fairways – was substituted, but it had a wiry texture affecting putting, and it browned off in winter. In 1988 another effort was made to put in bent grass greens and they are holding up in fine form. With this change several of the greens were reconstructed to add undulations that would increase the test of putting. The surrounding indigenous pines form a perfect dark backcloth to the stunning brilliance of flowering cherries and azaleas.

The whole is a vista of beauty and naturalness that changes colour through the seasons. In summer it is a rich green with only the sandtraps offering a contrast to the softness mirrored in the lakes and ponds, while in autumn and winter it changes to the light brown of hibernation. At all times it is an inviting golf course of outstanding dignity and class.

Like Sunningdale, which in many ways it resembles, Hirono starts off with a par-five hole. It is straight, narrow and flat and clear of obstacles all the way to the flagstick, which can be clearly seen from the tee though 505 yards away. Two shallow depressions cross the fairway at the 100-yard and 400-yard marks. Alison placed his traps for the wayward

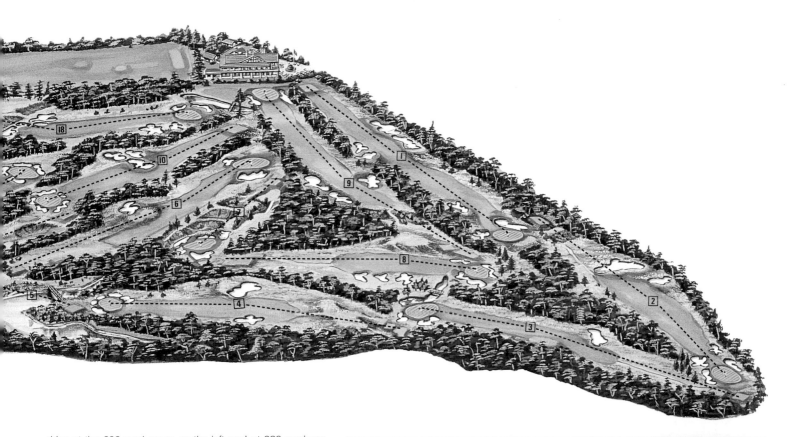

drive at the 200-yard range on the left and at 220 yards on the right, a pattern that has been almost universally adopted by all students of his work in Japan. Two bunkers guard the entrance to the green, which inclines enough to drain itself. Here, as throughout the course, natural features are used to their best effect. Two man-sized par-fours follow, the blank spots of which are filled with large-scale moundwork that suggests something of a linksland course. The 4th hole requires a spectacularly long tee shot and the green is raised high above typical Alison sandtraps. The 5th hole is a picture postcard par three of outstanding merit high across a large lake. Fearsome-looking sandtraps guard a modest-sized green so that even at 155 yards length the hole is a difficult one for golfers of all classes and experience.

The course turns inland via a tough par-four and an excellent 195-yard par-three. A natural, well-cleared ravine courses diagonally across it and, against a wind, it is farther than some golfers can hit, but the regular tee is set at 175 yards so that from this distance it is a pleasure for all golfers to play. The 8th hole uses a small pond by the green to effect. The second shot must skirt or carry the pond to an interestingly shaped green. For club golfers it is fun and a terror, the choice of shod never easy.

The 9th takes the route straight to the clubhouse. A par-five of 525 yards, the tee shot is all carry across brush and pathways to a generous fairway that disappears into a natural grassed and cut hollow in front of the green. The 10th and 11th holes are two pleasant fours that take the golfer out to the lake again. The 12th hole is one of the course's best – and also one of the best par-fives in Japan. Its tee shot is across an inlet of the lake, beyond which there is a small natural ditch, reminiscent of Carnoustie, to worry about. The shot is fearsome for lesser players, and difficult enough for professionals. To all except the very longest and straightest hitters the green is still two shots away. The tee shots at the 13th and 14th holes both have to carry water, although it would be an embarrassingly awful topped shot which failed to clear the water from the 14th tee! These two shorter holes lead to another outstanding par-five in the 15th, at 565 yards, Alison's longest hole. The 16th climbs farther away from the lake to a high plateau green seemingly set against the sky. From the back tee, the 17th is a 230-yard par three across the margin of another lake with plenty of open space

to be aimed at by those who are not ambitious or strong enough. Here Alison could have made the mistake of duplicating his 5th and 13th holes but sensibly he offered something different; water plays a lesser part but sheer length is used to compensate.

The 460-yard 18th is in every way a rewarding final hole. First there is the carry across a gully to the fairway. Then the fairway turns left for the long slog to the green. Again there is an area of mounds and hollows and sandtraps off to the right, more to distract than to impede, but the greenside traps have been sited in earnest. Eighteenth greens are almost always given the best attention, by constructor and maintainer alike, and this one is no exception. Alison never even dreamed of television but made a marvellously spectacular finish.

Hirono hosted the first of its ten Japan Amateur Championships in 1933. The Japan Open was first played there in 1939, and when it returns in 2005, it will be the fifth opportunity for the professionals to test their skills against the wiles of one of the master architects of Japanese golf, Charles Hugh Alison.

Hirono is the course of the straight-hitter. Nearly every hole is tree-lined with mainly conifers to catch the wayward shot.

Bunkers gain an Englishman

immortality in Japan

A Charles Alison course, marked by restrained bunkering and superb grooming, Kasumigaseki came to the fore in 1957 when the World Cup was played there. Japan's success in team and individual competitions sparked off an astonishing golf boom there. It later spread through much of Asia.

As a game that has more than its share of ritual and etiquette, golf might be expected to appeal to the Japanese. There has been an explosion of interest in recent years – too big an explosion, in fact, for the good of the Japanese themselves, for there are far too few courses for the army of enthusiasts who would dearly love to play 18 holes or any number of holes, for that matter – on a real course. There may well be many a Nipponese Nicklaus condemned to play out a lifetime of golf on one of Japan's proliferating practice ranges. And for those who are club members fees are hideously high.

Tokyo, one of the world's greatest conurbations, has a number of the country's principal clubs within its immediate area. One is Kasumigaseki, the country's most famous club. The course was built in a matter of months by a group of enthusiasts and opened in October 1929. The design was by a talented local player, Kinya Fujita, but it soon became clear that the possibilities of the site had not been exploited to the full. The English architect Charles Alison was called in and in his subsequent work at Kasumigaseki he was to achieve a curious immortality.

Alison was drawn particularly to the par-three 10th, a medium-length pitch across a deep ravine. He introduced several deep sandtraps into the side of a steep slope leading up to the green, and their depth was an innovation to the Japanese. Since that time, every deep sandtrap on a Japanese course has been known as an Alison – or "Arison".

The English architect stamped his personality on other holes also, and although some innovations have since been added the championship course is fundamentally his work. Alison was an outstanding golf course designer and his ideas place him amongst the giants of the profession. His simple principle was that hazards should be offset to catch the wayward stroke and that the path to the hole along the straight and narrow should be smooth and unencumbered. Alison's pattern of design has been adopted almost everywhere in Japan, but it has also given birth to some very dull and stereotyped reproduction.

The climate of Japan is one of extremes and at Kasumigaseki, as elsewhere in Japan, the soft English bent grasses recommended for putting greens could not survive the heat and oppressive humidity of summer; the grass just expired. The Japanese solution was to build two greens, one sown with conventional bents regrown each year, and the other with the hardiest grass they could find – a species from Korea called, appropriately enough, *korai*. It survives harsh winter conditions and although it turns light brown in its dormancy, it revives to a rich greenness in the spring. Finely developed strains make adequate putting greens, while the stouter grades make fairways of firm bristle.

The use of korai as a second green inevitably distorted the architecture by adding a considerable space to the green area. It also influenced the bunkering round the greens, the standard pattern being to have one trap to the extreme left, one to the right and another at the rear. This arrangement became the safe method of design and few local planners dared depart from it.

Kasumigaseki has the well-kept, well-prepared look about it that has become customary in Japan. A ground staff of more than 200, many of them women, ensure that no weeds grow anywhere and not a dead leaf can be seen. Trees are wrapped in hessian and twine to protect them from the cold of winter; many have stays or cables to hold them upright in the wind. Paths and bridges are guttered and well drained, like miniature avenues. Flower beds around the clubhouse would do justice to the Chelsea Flower Show. On course, the flora and the grasses receive the same meticulous attention, with the same impressive results. The expen-

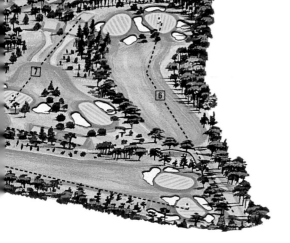

Kasumigaseki
Country Club,
Kasahata,
Saitama
East course

Hole	Yards	Par
1	400	4
2	379	4
3	424	4
4	155	3
5	535	5
6	378	4
7	211	3
8	466	4
9	554	5
10	177	3
11	436	4
12	464	4
13	379	4
14	595	5
15	424	4
16	174	3
17	356	4
18	472	5
Out	3,502	36
In	3,477	36
Total	**6,979**	**72**

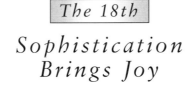

The 18th

Sophistication Brings Joy

Kasumigaseki's planner arranged a layout of outstanding variety, a feature of which is a sterling finish in the modern manner. A par-five of sporting length with enough dog-leg to make the best of golfers draw on his brain and brawn, the 18th makes a perfect finale to an exciting round. The drive is straight forward enough, sensibly trapped and yet wide enough to invite over-stretching. There is, of course, every temptation to do so, for the green, some 472 yards away, can be reached in two shots. Thus when Sam Snead, Roberto de Vicenzo and others of the same power stood on this last tee in the 1957 World Cup with an eagle in mind, it made for enthralling viewing.

The second shot, though, is the spectacular one. From the perfect drive, the direct line is across the deepest part of a valley and over the large, deep traps which guard the entrance from that angle. If the traps were not smoothed with a toothless rake, the whole exercise

sive white river sand of the bunkers, prepared to an exemplary smoothness, as elsewhere in Japan, with toothless wooden rakes, have a tidiness which defeats their purpose. This fact first came to light in the 1957 Canada Cup (now the World Cup), when the Japanese winners demonstrated a hitherto unknown skill at escaping from the sand after poor shots had trapped them. Torakichi "Pete" Nakamura, individual winner by a convincing seven shot margin, proved particularly adept. In the four days of the event he holed out from the sand four times, and never failed to get down in two when he was caught – as he often was.

The success of Nakamura and his partner, Koichi Ono, sparked the golf boom in Japan that shows no sign yet of collapse. At that time there were 79 courses in Japan. Today there are about 1,800, with applications before the authorities for many more.

Because the demand for courses quickly outstripped the availability of suitable land, golf took to the mountains. Consequently most modern Japanese courses are hilly, even mountainous. Some border on the absurd. Fairways shoot up one hill to tumble down the next. Greens are often placed out of sight over the brow so that only the flagstick is visible, and fairways are sometimes laid through ridiculously narrow cuts on the hillside. Yet such courses are popular because in Japan sport, and golf in particular, is a physical exercise. Kasumigaseki has no such architectural absurdities. Its standing in Japan was assured by Alison's masterly creation and consolidated by Fujita and Seichi Inoue, who collaborated on a second excellent course, opened in 1932. They faithfully followed Alison's lead.

Inoue, who was himself a member of Kasumigaseki, went on to design 39 courses in Japan, many still ranking amongst the country's best championship venues. Indeed, his 6,887-yard West Course at Kasumigaseki has already been selected to host the Japan Open in 2006. Like the East Course it is magnificently groomed, combining something of the ruggedness of a Surrey heathland course with the beauty of a Japanese garden. Both courses set a standard few can match.

would take even more courage. The same sand left foot marked and unraked would make for an extremely punitive hazard of real championship calibre but unfortunately only Pine Valley amongst the world's great courses maintains this principle. This last hole at Kasumigaseki would be fearsome indeed if the penalty for falling into one of the traps was two or even three strokes. At present, because of the invariably immaculate condition of the greenside bunkers, the penalty is most often only one, and, in a significant percentage of cases, none at all. Nevertheless, this hole is a marvellous example of sophisticated architecture and a joy to play.

The 18th hole on the East course at Kasumigaseki, above, provides the perfect finale to an exciting round.

Golfing innovations in
a land of
traditions

Fujioka came into being in 1971 and is one of the more successful manifestations of the golf fever that reached plague proportions throughout the country – a plague that eventually resulted in legislation to check the rape of open land by speculative golfing developments.

Fujioka was the brainchild of Mr Furukawa, the owner of land to the north of Nagoya. He set out to build a course in the established traditions of Kasumigaseki and Hirono, of modern design and to international standards, but with its membership strictly limited to a manageable 520.

The great Australian, Peter Thomson, was invited to become the course's architect, which was built by Tameshi Yamada. The practice of having a player of international repute associated with a new course had become commonplace in Japan – lucrative enough, but not without its risks for the player's reputation if the course should prove a failure.

The site was 180 acres of moderately hilly land made up of tea plantations, a large lake and a pine forest. The layout used all the lower-lying land and valleys, leaving the higher pines intact. Drainage to and from the lake and beneath the fairways was used with great imagination by Yamada. Pipes beneath the fairways were of one-metre diameter, an extravagant size that was to prove its worth a year after the course was completed: a typhoon devastated and flooded the region, but the course was left intact.

A feature of Fujioka is its lakes, reminiscent of those at Augusta National. At the time they were a radical departure in Japan, where, on the whole, water had been used more as an ornament than a hazard. A decade after Fujioka Robert Trent Jones Jnr was building challenging Japanese courses featuring heroic water holes such as Golden Valley, Springfield and Pine Lake.

A double green was made for the 4th, a long climbing par-four, and the 7th, a par-three played at right angles to it. This was the first double green in Japan. At Fujioka it was not built simply to be distinctive, but to solve a construction problem and conserve valuable space in a tight corner.

At one point there was some disagreement over whether the 12th green should be flush against a small lake or higher up and well away from the water. In the end a compromise was reached: both were built. The one beside the lake, which makes the hole into a dog-leg, resembles the 11th at Augusta in its setting, and the other is straight ahead. The lakeside green sits slightly below the fairway driving spot, from which the flag placement and the water surrounding the green can be seen. The alternative is blind; only the top of the flagstick and surrounding traps can be seen.

Alison-type bunkers were included at various holes, although Yamada modified their depths, knowing from experience that amongst his countrymen deep bunkers with straight faces are not universally popular. The sandtraps are flexible in their depth – for ordinary club play they can be shallow and not particularly penal, but they can be deepened to suit the more prestigious occasion. Thus Fujioka, like all great courses, is flexible enough to be enjoyed not only by champions but by golfers of all abilities.

The course has a one green system along modern lines, with modern trappings. The greens were originally laid in korai, but they were converted to bent grass for the club's 30th anniversary in October 2001, to give superior putting surfaces. The fairways are of a coarser and tougher variety of korai, grown on turf farms and transported to Fujioka in two-foot squares, the standard method of turf culture in the southern and western parts of Japan. The squares are laid and pegged in with small bamboo stakes to frustrate the crows which otherwise lift them, looking for worms, before they settle down. The turfing of Fujioka took about five months and kept almost 6,000 workers fully employed during that time.

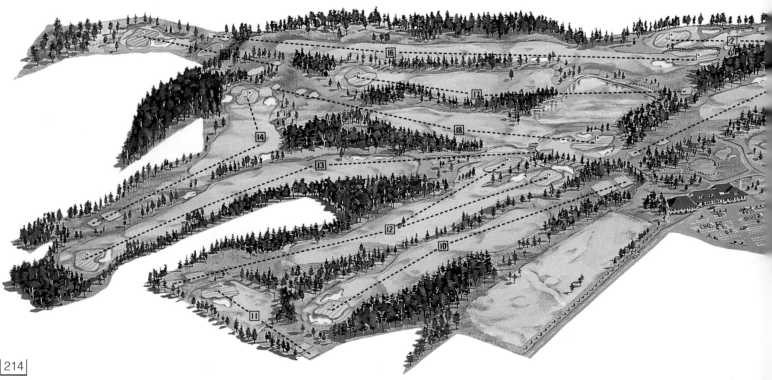

The 16th

A Man-Sized Par-Five

The huge par-five 16th is a real monster, playing every inch of its 620 yard length. The back tee is never used in club golf because the first shot involves a drive uphill – always a difficult task for a golfer of little experience. Although the fairway is not generously wide, every encouragement is left for the sliced drive to hit the bank on the right side and bounce back to the fairway, even though this cuts length from the shot. The left side plunges down to an out-of-bounds fence and hooking is something to be avoided. From the top of the hill, where a good drive will finish, it is still not possible to see the green, though the second shot is framed by some pines on either side and the V-shaped fairway makes the direction unmistakable.

It is really only with the third shot that the hole's true worth is revealed, for the task before the player is below him in the shape of a massive green curving along the side of a small lake, with a steep forested hill as a backdrop. A large sandtrap guards the entrance without blocking it off, but such is the large scale of everything, including green and trap, that the distance is deceptively long. When the flag is cut in the championship position at the far back of the green, a player can be faced with a putt of some 35 yards. The green becomes progressively narrower as it recedes and there are two smaller traps at the back to catch those who – mindful

of the water on the left – overshoot. The shot into the green varies according to the wind; when there is none, and when play is from the back tee, the third shot must be a seven iron at best for most people. The 16th is a man-sized par five.

The 16th hole at Fujioka is still one of the relatively few par fives in the world to measure over 600 yards.

The whole construction took less than a year and most of it was completed in only nine months. Fujioka Country Club is now acknowledged as one of Japan's outstanding courses, modern but nevertheless reflecting architectural links with older more venerable courses. Other modern courses in Japan are following the same lines and Japanese golfers are learning to enjoy what are to them wholly new challenges in the way they play their game.

As befitted a course that looked to Japan's golfing future, Fujioka's last three holes were designed with television in mind. Each is spectacular and in the way in which they bring into play a large, attractive lake they rival even the famous water holes of Augusta, both in their beauty and in their difficulty. For the members, many good scores are ruined over this final run-in, yet there is much pride in their existence, just as there is in the way that Fujioka pioneered a golfing challenge that was new to Japan.

Fujioka, with its gently hilly fairways, is one of the finer courses to emerge from the almost frenzied Japanese interest in golf. The course, unusually for Japan, is rarely busy, the club membership being strictly limited. Water is the dominant feature of a layout that winds sedately through groves of pine trees.

The Course Card

Fujioka
Country Club,
Nagoya

Hole	Yards	Par
1	400	4
2	190	3
3	540	5
4	420	4
5	350	4
6	445	4
7	180	3
8	500	5
9	385	4
10	400	4
11	160	3
12	440	4
13	550	5
14	370	4
15	200	3
16	620	5
17	405	4
18	430	4
Out	3,410	36
In	3,575	36
Total	**6,985**	**72**

The Course Card

Royal Calcutta Golf Club, Calcutta

Hole	Name	Yardage	Par
1	Island	366	4
2	Tank Ahead	436	4
3	Bull's Eye	156	3
4	The Long One	525	5
5	Madras Thorns	415	4
6	The Fields	418	4
7	The Jheels	455	4
8	Ditchers	401	4
9	Dhobi Ghat	404	4
10	Long Pal	448	4
11	The Nullahs	508	5
12	Dog-Leg	359	4
13	Chota	187	3
14	Right of Way	431	4
15	Far and Sure	493	5
16	Mutt and Jeff	364	4
17	Thomson's Tank	374	4
18	Pimples	437	4
Out		3,576	36
In		3,601	37
Total		**7,177**	**73**

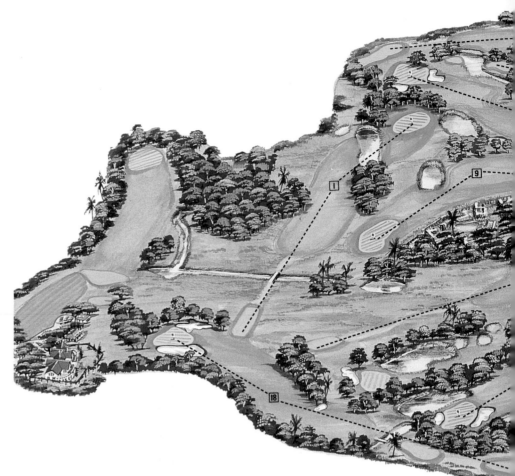

Vintage legacy

of the British Raj

Right: The clubhouse at Royal Calcutta, the oldest club in the world outside the British Isles.

Older than any club in the world beyond the British Isles – older, indeed, than most of those in Britain itself – the Royal Calcutta has antecedents stretching back to the days when the power of the British Raj was gaining strength, beyond the beginnings of Victoria's reign. The Royal Calcutta was founded in 1829 and first used a site at Dum Dum, where the city's international airport now stands. After a series of moves the Dum Dum Golfing Club, as the Royal Calcutta was originally called, settled finally towards the end of the century in the southern suburbs.

The 18 holes making up the present course are all that survive of the 36 the club once possessed but could not afford to keep up. The land farthest from the clubhouse was sold to the Bengal government to provide some much-needed recreational space for the refugees who have crowded the club's boundaries since the partition of Bengal in 1947.

The refugees still invade the confines of the course, giving it a colour and atmosphere found nowhere else in the world. They walk single-file along the well-worn track that crosses the course. The women wash their saris and their children in the ponds formed where fill was taken to build the tees and greens, which are the highest points on a course that is never more than six feet above the level of the River Ganges. Small boys swim in each pond and wait for a wayward ball, for which they will dive to hand back to the owner in return for a few coins. The golfers are often clad in white shorts and frequently in colourful turbans. They pause under umbrellas held by caddies dressed in khaki. And above everything are the birds – squawking ravens, buzzards gliding in the hot air and the vultures,

circling monotonously or peering balefully down from their nests in the trees by the 3rd.

Despite the distractions, golf continues to thrive in Calcutta. Some of the more august clubs died with the Raj, others have been created, enjoying a particular popularity among members of the armed forces, where the affectations of the old English – particularly their phraseology – linger in an odd post-colonial twilight.

Almost until independence, Indians were rigorously excluded from membership of Calcutta. A Sikh, Sardar I. S. Malik, was the first, and the first Indian to play in the all-India Amateur Championship. Years later, his son Ashok won the title five times and with his partner, P. G. Sethi, represented India in every Eisenhower Trophy event from 1958 to 1968. "Billoo" Sethi, the outstanding Indian golfer of his generation, made history when he won the Indian Open in 1956, twice equalling his own course record of 68 in the process.

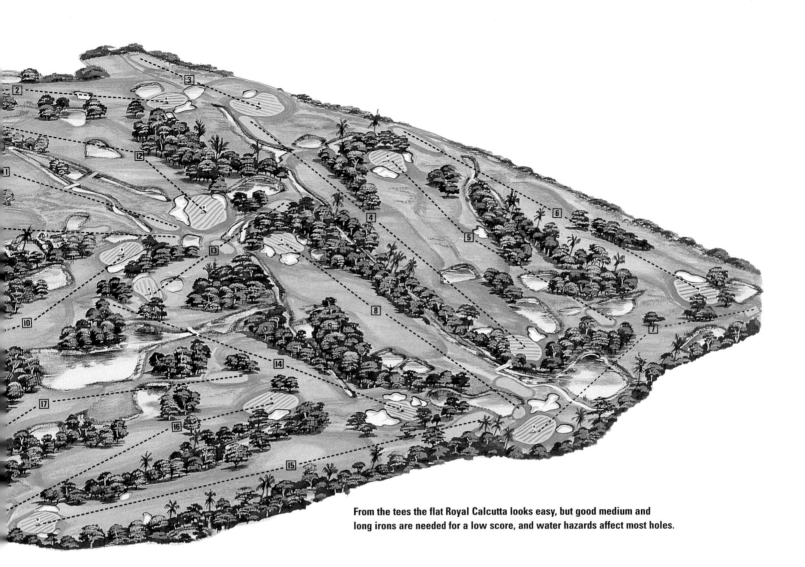

From the tees the flat Royal Calcutta looks easy, but good medium and long irons are needed for a low score, and water hazards affect most holes.

Royal Calcutta is immensely proud of its origins, its connections with the Royal and Ancient and with its influence on the game in India, where, until lately, it was the champion of the rules and etiquette of golf. Perhaps more importantly, there is another way in which this ancient club has exercised an influence on the game. Golf as a worldwide sport and, particularly as a game played in tropical and subtropical climes, owes a debt to Royal Calcutta for a special reason. It was the first course to be built in the tropics and as such had to make use of whatever indigenous grasses there were available. The most suitable, if not indeed the only one, was dhoob.

Dhoob grass covered Calcutta's first fairways, and golf on grass became a reality in the tropics. Since then, in all probability because of the Indian experience, dhoob and related grasses such as hariali, Bermuda, Australian couch and creeping dog's-tooth, have become the standard grasses, in pure, dwarfed or hybrid form, on thousands of golf courses all over the world. Without it, golf in all but the temperate zones would be played on sand.

The 18 holes that now make up the championship course are each a solid par of modern length and difficulty, in a flat parkland setting, with gorgeous trees and innumerable lakes or ponds (known, because they are used to store water, as tanks), drainage channels and gutters. The course can justifiably claim to be the best in the subcontinent.

The profusion of water hazards removes the need for many bunkers and, since they are below ground-level, the course at first glance gives the impression of being easy and wide open. Nothing is farther from the truth.

Its best holes are the 2nd and 14th, neither of which has a sandtrap. The stiff 2nd is a gentle dog-leg of 436 yards, curving around huge trees of thick, shady foliage. The boundary wall runs along the left side and against it,

at the 230 yard mark, is a lotus-filled tank that acts like a magnet. A drive that strays too far to the right lands behind the trees and so the placement of the tee shot is critical. The 14th follows the same pattern, but in reverse. It is a little shorter at 431 yards, but requires big hitting when the fairways are soft after the monsoon.

The 448-yard 10th is also a testing hole. Two large tanks split the fairway, and an out-of-bounds wall lines the entire left side. From the tee the bold line is straight over the first tank, a shot that must carry a full 230 yards. The safe shot down the right side leaves a long second over the other tank, which is all of a 100 yards wide, to a small, heavily trapped green. Other first-class holes are the par-three 3rd and 13th, both of which are entirely flexible in length: they can be played from 230 yards down to 150 yards. On both there are daunting water hazards, worrying to the golfer but a never-ending source of fun and funds for the small boys.

The Calcutta club has always enjoyed close ties with the Royal and Ancient, thanks no doubt to the many Scots who served in the Indian Army and Civil Service. In 1882, a group of members presented the Royal and Ancient with what is known as the Cashmere Cup, as a gesture of goodwill. To take advantage of their handsome new silver trophy, the Royal and Ancient introduced a new form of competition, the world's first handicap event. It was one which was to revolutionise club golf everywhere, although the first Silver Cashmere Cup (now known as the Calcutta Cup) tournament stayed with the traditional form of play, matchplay, with the handicaps in the form of "hole" starts.

In return for their new trophy the Royal and Ancient gave a silver tankard to the Calcutta club. This is still played for and it provides a reminder of the club's origins and, now that the gospel of golf has been spread worldwide, Royal Calcutta's status as the first mission established overseas.

Fairways haunted by Chinese ancestors

The Course Card

Hong Kong Golf Club, Fanling Championship course

Hole	Yards	Par
1	468	4
2	149	3
3	526	5
4	288	4
5	192	3
6	415	4
7	381	4
8	188	3
9	493	5
10	367	4
11	466	4
12	529	5
13	395	4
14	426	4
15	187	3
16	411	4
17	406	4
18	410	4
Out	3,100	35
In	3,597	36
Total	**6,697**	**71**

The only survivor of the six pre-First World War Chinese clubs is Hong Kong, or Royal Hong Kong as it was known until the recent return of the Colony to Chinese rule. It has three full-size courses sharing the same clubhouse at Fanling, close to the frontier with mainland China, as well as a nine-hole course at Happy Valley, on Hong Kong Island, where the club began in 1889. Here a handful of enthusiasts were forced to share the only flat and open space with other sports, including polo, with the result that the course's architect, Captain H. N. Dumbleton of the Royal Engineers, was not allowed to construct bunkers or holes. Instead, at such times as golfers had the run of the land, close mesh netting was used for bunkers and small granite setts as holes – they had to be hit by the ball to "hole out".

It was effective enough, and popular. In May 1890, a six-a-side match was played between the club and the Argyll and Sutherland Highlanders, which the club won easily. The match attracted a number of spectators and the membership reached 100 the following year.

The first course that was more or less for the exclusive use of golfers was sited at Deep Water Bay on the eastern side of Hong Kong Island, where a tiny 16½ acre triangle of flat land by a beach became available. It was reached from the city by circumnavigating the island in a launch, and had only to be shared with some occasional cricketers.

The links was a criss-cross affair, but enough to serve the membership. A modest single-storey clubhouse was built and, five years later, another storey was added. In time, the popularity of the game and a growing membership led to further expansion and the acquisition of a piece of land large enough to accommodate a full-size course, or even two. It was found at Fanling, on the mainland near the Chinese border. Fanling and its neighbouring villages were at the time beyond the reach of the Kowloon railway, and the journey to the course entailed a two-man rickshaw ride into the hills

above Kowloon and then a walk down the other side to Shatin, where a police launch could take you to the other end of the bay at Taipo. From Taipo to Fanling the journey was completed by pony, chair or rickshaw, depending on the weather. Mercifully the railway was completed to the border in 1911. The first course at Fanling, now the Old, sufficed until 1923, when the membership reached 800. Permission was sought to build the second course, but the members rejected this and voted instead for a bigger clubhouse.

Whether the clubhouse or the courses should be improved is a debate that has raged in most clubs at one time or another. In the case of the Hong Kong, the committee blandly ignored the rank and file and went ahead with the New course. It was opened in November, 1931, by the Governor of the Colony, Sir William Peel. In time it was to become the more popular of the two and a credit to its designer and supervisor, L. S. Greenhill.

The courses suffered from general neglect and dilapidation during the Japanese occupation from 1941 to 1945, and it required a huge effort and an equally large overdraft to put them back into working order. It was not until 1953 that all the holes of the Old and New courses and the club's third course, the Relief, were restored. Early in the 1960s it again became apparent that the two larger courses at Fanling were bursting at the seams. The answer was to upgrade the Relief course and add more land, to turn it into a course of modern dimensions and difficulty.

Land was acquired from the Royal Hong Kong Jockey Club and, under the creative supervision of Michael Wolveridge – who, along with John Harris, conceived the design – began to take shape. Numerous lakes and other water hazards were constructed to drain areas subject to flooding, and these became such strong features of the course that it could quite felicitously be called "The Lake" – as one entrant in the naming competition suggested.

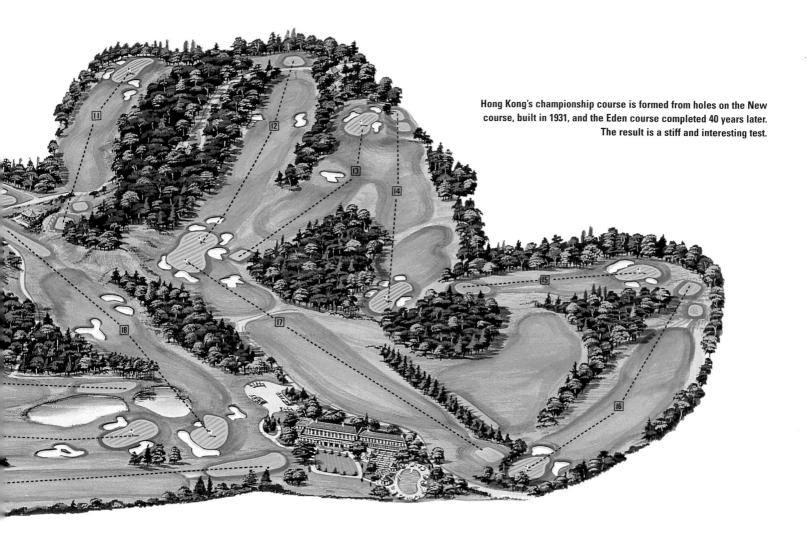

The 3rd

A Par-Five that is a Revelation

Rare is the par five that reveals all its secrets from the tee. The 3rd hole on Hong Kong's championship course does, and it is a gem. At the 250 yard range, still short of the foot of the slope, is a large white expanse of sand with a high, thin tree standing sentinel beside it. This is the first obstacle to avoid and it dominates the scene. But there is more trouble on both sides. Down the left flank is a dense wood, on the right a pond and open ditches. Driving from a high tee is exhilarating but, because curved shots have considerably farther to fly before they hit the ground, fairway widths are effectively reduced.

The second shot runs a gauntlet of sand and water. The sand is on the right, a large lake beckons on the left. Shirking the challenge and playing short leaves a near-impossible third shot because the green is small and angled to the right. Because the green is built up in table-top style the difficulty of the pitch is increased. Avoidance of traps is achieved by approaching from the right at an angle of some 45 degrees, which is possible with the second shot.

For its entire length this hole is carefully carved out and constructed to be of championship calibre. Sixes and sevens are not uncommon and a par is well earned.

As with the construction of earlier courses at Fanling, numerous old and forgotten Chinese graves were unearthed and compensation had to be paid to the families whose ancestors were disturbed. Ancestors continue to lurk in the hillsides around the course and on Ancestor Worship Day the golf course is crowded with people of all ages visiting their now long-departed forebears.

On completion, the new course was named the Eden – the name of the third course at St Andrews. Of necessity it was squeezed into the corners of the last available land, which gives it some tightness. But this limitation comes where it serves a good purpose – when holes are unavoidably short for par-fours. This applies to the 10th and 11th holes, which are at the point farthest from the clubhouse. The rest of the course rolls smoothly, with adequate width and stretch, and includes some holes of undoubted world class, notably the 3rd and 18th. To counter the severe monsoon rains the greens are mostly built up off the

ground. Hitting to these raised targets is an additional test of enterprise and skill, making the Eden course quite different from the other two courses.

The Hong Kong Open and other championships are played on a composite course of the New and Eden, choosing the convenient best of each to form a course that provides very nearly the ultimate in challenge for the competitors of many nations. One who certainly likes it is the German, Bernhard Langer, who won the 1996 Asian Masters there; it was a victory that saw him emerge from a wilderness of bad form, and his first win achieved with the long putter that ever since has been his salvation.

The weather was wet at Hong Kong during the Far East qualifier for the 1992 Alfred Dunhill Cup.

The Course Card

Singapore Island
Country Club,
Singapore
Bukit course

Hole	Yards	Par
1	407	4
2	205	3
3	408	4
4	537	5
5	175	3
6	449	4
7	450	4
8	366	4
9	364	4
10	380	4
11	426	4
12	223	3
13	563	5
14	191	3
15	501	5
16	429	4
17	132	3
18	488	5
Out	3,361	35
In	3,333	36
Total	**6,694**	**71**

A cool
oasis
of peace

There is no more cosmopolitan meeting place, outside the United Nations building in New York, than the Singapore Island Golf Club. Once the exclusive preserve of colonial administrators – the city was founded by a giant among empire builders, Sir Stamford Raffles – the club now reflects the island-state itself, an international entrepôt set at the heart of all eastern trade.

There are four courses: the Bukit (6,694 yards); the Island (6,365 yards); the New (6,874 yards) and the Sime (6,314 yards). They are grouped attractively around the Pierce and MacRitchie reservoirs, which help, in a humid climate, to generate refreshing breezes. All four courses are exceptionally beautiful, by any standards. The green fairways twist and turn their way across the hills and dales of the catchment slopes, between the huge native trees that were left in place when the course was made. In the background are the reservoirs and beyond them the jungle.

Each of the four courses has its own personality and qualities. Bukit is the parent course, built by the Royal Singapore club in 1924 after 33 years at a site on the old racecourse. It is the most popular, as well as the most important, of the present four courses. It is an undeniably hilly course, so some of its holes either plunge awkwardly downhill or else climb steeply. Yet each hole is a worthy challenge; the par-threes are especially difficult, even for champions. The fours are all strong, featuring either length, narrowness or canny trapping, and sometimes all three. The par-fives are an invitation to disaster, two of them being near the end of the round when the legs are apt to be wobbly.

The greens, built on local clay, are hard for the approach shot and fast for the putt, a combination that provides the most difficult of all championship conditions. The Bermuda grass in use can reduce the most stolid of golfers to a nervous wreck.

The Bukit course was chosen as the venue for the World Cup when it was first played in South-east Asia in 1969. Improvements were made by the English architect, Frank Pennink. The United States team of Lee Trevino and Orville Moody predictably won the team prize. Trevino just pipped the smallest of the competitors, Sukree Oncham of Thailand, for the individual honours although Oncham won the popularity contest. In 1993 the course again had a chance to show it could cope with the best, staging a Johnnie Walker Classic that is still talked about at the club. It featured Nick

holes across the valley below the clubhouse. It is a frightening prospect when results of matches – and a lot of money – depend on the final effort.

The merger of the two clubs in 1963 brought a boom in membership and resulted in the building of the fourth course, the New, starting from the old Island clubhouse and taking the last space along the shores of the reservoirs. It was originally designed by the English partnership of John Harris and Frank Pennink and is a massive and imaginative layout, with many fine and memorable holes on modern length lines. It makes a splendid course for the professionals who follow the Asian circuit through March and April.

The original layout was adjusted to accommodate changes in the lake level, but little was lost and the New course, with its tiny clubhouse, is outstanding in its own right. The Sime course is the shortest and hence is regarded as being the most appropriate for women, although it is not theirs exclusively. It occupies a section of the Bukit, using up, as it were, the ground the bigger course does not need. The first nine holes rush over hilly ground, while the second nine is a longer excursion with even more ups and downs, following more or less in tandem with the inward nine of the Bukit.

The Sime is an enjoyable and more than usually scenic club course. Nothing more is claimed for it. But the Singapore Island Club's members are proud of the strength of their championship course, the Bukit – and they have every reason to be.

Faldo at his finest, putting together four rounds in the sixties to defeat Colin Montgomerie by a stroke.

The Island course was that originally occupied by the old Royal Island Club, whose membership took in those golfers excluded by the Royal Singapore. It was built in 1927, three years after the Bukit course, and gathered the cosmopolitan membership enjoyed by the present club, which was formed when the two clubs merged in 1963.

The Island course is on the short side and some of its fairways are rather hilly on the transverse, making driving extremely difficult in dry weather. Its first nine holes wander around the reservoir shore and return to the foot of the clubhouse. The inward half is farther inland and uphill, but it is wider and longer. Both nines finish with attractive par-three

The 18th

Faldo Reigns Supreme

The best of finishing holes are made to provide drama and the ultimate hurdle. The Bukit course's 18th hole has few equals in that respect. It is a par-five, but it makes an excellent end to a round because it has awkwardness and, at 488 yards, length. The well-struck tee shot carries across a huge valley into a fairly steep uphill slope. It is from this slope that the most awkward of second shots – with wooden club if shooting at the green – must be executed. When swinging hard on a steep slope it is all too easy to forget about balance while altering the plane of the swing to a flatter one. The ball is considerably higher than the feet and this means that full power in the execution of the stroke is not possible because the club's full length must be curtailed to accommodate the lie.

Yet the target of the green seems tantalizingly within range and, given the golfer's usual optimism, it is tempting to have a go. A line of massive trees blocks out the left side so that more often than not the shot must be bent around them with a long draw. The slope actually helps this but disaster is always possible. At the green are deep traps and a small out-of-bounds wall, over which

most tour regulars have sailed at one time or another. A slice of any magnitude can end in the locker-room. It was on this hole that Nick Faldo completed his supreme performance in the Johnnie Walker Asian Classic in 1993. Having watched Colin Montgomerie two putt from 20ft, Faldo knew he had to hole from 12ft to prevent a play-off. This was a day when Faldo had every confidence in his putter. He knew the ball was in the hole almost as soon as it left the putter head.

The New Zealander Simon Owen putts out on the final green during the 1990 qualifying rounds for the Alfred Dunhill Cup.

Rescued and revitalised after the war, during which time it had been used for growing crops and as an army training school, Royal Selangor has become the regular venue of the Malaysian Open. Toughened and improved recently by the English architect Frank Pennink, it is now one of the best courses in Asia.

Grave problems in a
burial ground

The Course Card

The Royal
Selangor Golf
Club, Kuala
Lumpur
Old course

Record: 64, T. Kono,
Malaysian Open 1971

Hole	Yards	Par
1	428	4
2	405	4
3	512	5
4	164	3
5	346	4
6	463	4
7	187	3
8	388	4
9	493	5
10	467	4
11	422	4
12	391	4
13	488	5
14	207	3
15	579	5
16	351	4
17	147	3
18	435	4
Out	3,386	36
In	3,487	36
Total	**6,873**	**72**

The founder members of Malaysia's second oldest club, the Royal Selangor, must have been a singularly phlegmatic species of golfer. Sonorously, their early rules stated: "You cannot ground your club in addressing the ball, or move anything, however loose or dead it may be, when you find yourself in a grave."

For graves, on a course that included an old Chinese burial ground, were declared to be a hazard. No special mention was made of the long grass, despite the fact that to this day it is hung with bloodsucking leeches when the weather is humid. Unlike most Asian clubs of long standing, Selangor, which serves the Malaysian capital of Kuala Lumpur, has had only one change of address in its 80 years of existence. And this was not painful as the Govern-ment, in acquiring the site of the first course after World War I, provided a more convenient and attractive alternative.

For four years during World War II the club served as the headquarters for the Japanese Army of Occupation. During that time the clubhouse suffered no real structural damage, but the two golf courses reverted back to jungle, except for patches of tapioca and a small airstrip. "The first impression on inspecting the property", reported a member in 1946, "was that golf would never again be played there."

He reckoned without the club's professional, Yorkshireman Tom Verity, and the members. After months of backbreaking work the main course was reopened for play by the end of the year. By mid-1947 a third nine was cleared and by March 1948 both full courses were in play. Verity, an outstanding character, was appointed professional in 1937 and he was to hold the post for 27 years, leaving only to build new courses and to teach up-country. Some intangible quality departed from the club when he left.

The Royal Selangor Golf Club today is a hive of sporting activity. Besides its 36 holes, there are grass tennis courts, an Olympic-size swimming pool, a squash court, restaurant and entertainment facilities for hundreds of people. It is something of a diplomatic listening post; the ambassadors of the U.S. and, most unexpectedly, the Soviet Union battled for the honours of lowest handicap, and two kings have graced the premises with regular attendance.

Thirty members founded the club at Petaling Hills, outside the city area, in 1893. No clubhouse was available for the first handicap competition, and notice was sent from a refreshment tent that "St Andrews Rules, of course," would be used – a reminder that in 1893 golf had no set of standard rules. Leading clubs in Britain and elsewhere drew up their own until 1897, when it was agreed that those made by the Rules Committee of The Royal and Ancient Golf Club at St Andrews would be applied universally.

In 1918 Selangor State took over Petaling Hills and paid for the construction of a new course and clubhouse. Few clubs have ever been blessed with such official help. Work began on the new site in 1920 and within a year nine holes of the main course were ready, together with the clubhouse. In the next year four grass and two hard tennis courts were laid down; the swimming pool did not appear until 1937.

The greens on both the Old and New courses were at first laid with an indigenous growth known derisively as "cow grass", a dwarf species that proved suitable for animals but which left much to be desired when used on greens.

Bermuda was used for the greens of the Old course for 11 years in the 1920s and 1930s, but the strain was never satisfactory and was replaced in 1935 by serangoon, successful in Singapore. A hybrid Bermuda strain, a world away from the original "cow grass", has now been put to use.

Maintenance difficulties are enormous in a country that, apart from its heat, has an annual rainfall of 160 inches. Green surfaces have the shape of upturned saucers – a characteristic of courses in the monsoon regions – to drain off the immense quantities of water that will flood a course in a matter of minutes.

Golf events in Malaysia are often held up or cancelled because of rain, but one way to ensure protection is to hire a "Bumu", a specialist in keeping rain away – sometimes apparently with good effect. During the 1975 Malaysian Open Championship at Kuala Lumpur, heavy rain was forecast and arrived on schedule. The Asian hockey championships, held in a stadium less than a mile away, suffered badly and finished three weeks behind schedule. The golf championship had its Bumu. He came just after dawn on

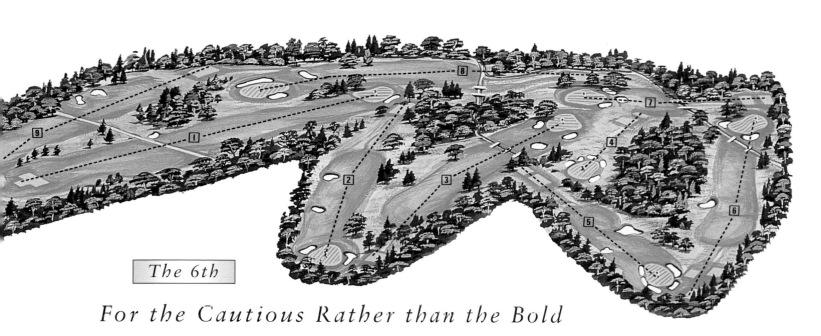

For the Cautious Rather than the Bold

At 463 yards the 6th at Royal Selangor is really neither par-four nor par-five. Of course in championships this does not matter, since par has no meaning in a stroke-play scratch event except perhaps to rate the total score. The hole is barely reachable in two shots into a wind unless the fairway is dry and hard, which it seldom is. Downwind, of course, it is not the same problem. During the Malaysian Open, played each March, it is usually a drive and a three or four-iron hole. But it is advisable to approach timidly: it is easy enough to get down in two from just short, but less likely from beyond.

The green is unusually narrow, being no more than 10 paces wide. This makes a tiny target, especially when fired at from 200 or more yards. It is guarded by a trap on either side, the right-hand one being a little shorter than the left. The green is elevated and of two levels, rising quite high at the back. It has gained something of a reputation because of the grain of its grass, which makes putting a chancy business. Knowledge of this makes the tee shot somehow

more difficult, since the player feels the need to gain as much length as possible in order to shorten the second shot. This has destroyed thousands of drives.

The tee shot is aimed at slightly higher ground and there is one yawning trap on the left which is not particularly threatening unless the shot is hooked violently. On the right side is a line of thin trees, under which the broad-stemmed indigenous grass grows lush and thick. Running diagonally across the fairway about 30 yards from the green is the course's main storm drain, which catches plenty of over-ambitious second shots. Its stone and concrete lining can sometimes be spectacularly beneficial and many a second shot nose-diving to destruction has rammed the hard rock and rebounded high in the air to safety. However, for most it means a certain one-stroke penalty, which often leads to more as desperate recovery attempts overshoot the green in the effort to get too close. Sanely played, though, it is a hole of immense challenge and, once parred, great satisfaction.

each of the four mornings and set up his stand beneath a simple shelter behind the 17th tee. No one spoke to him, nor he to them. He burned a few sticks, chanting all the while in an undertone, except when he ate or took a short sleep. No rain fell for four days, until the Malaysian Prime Minister presented the first prize to Australia's Graham Marsh. Then the heavens opened. In a matter of minutes the course and clubhouse precincts were awash. Had it fallen an hour earlier it would have been impossible to complete the event.

Royal Selangor is almost dead flat, which makes for easy walking, and the golf is pleasant when the sun is not high. But giant trees provide shade and the small stream which runs through the course adds its own freshness.

One gets the feeling that it is an easy course. This may be because each hole is a birdie proposition, or seems so. In the course of a championship the fortunes tend to fluctuate unpredictably and the explanation is often found in the grass on the fairways and greens.

Fairways are well grassed and when freshly cut provide excellent lies. Greens require special preparation because of the rain, but at their best rival anything other than the softest bent grass. Despite the flatness of the fairways, the thick-bladed local grass gives a wide variation in lies. The way the ball sits very often determines its flight and destination, the influence of the grass overriding the skill and planning of the striker. For all that, championship golf at Selangor calls for special skills at the short end of the game, as a list of winners of the Malaysian Open shows.

Most holes dog-leg around the massive trees. Numerous bunkers, strategically placed, provide the obstacles. In all, the Royal Selangor is a course in the highest category. In terms of architecture it is as the best-designed courses should be – all things to all golfers. It is a fearsome test from the back tees for the champions who come around frequently for the Malaysian Open, and at the same time real fun and pleasure for those with lesser gifts.

The 17th hole at Royal Selangor is a lovely par three over water.

Bali Handara
Country Club,
Bali

Hole	Yards	Par
1	500	5
2	180	3
3	450	4
4	180	3
5	400	4
6	410	4
7	400	4
8	411	4
9	527	5
10	412	4
11	180	3
12	410	4
13	410	4
14	180	3
15	540	5
16	432	4
17	442	4
18	560	5
Out	3,458	36
In	3,566	36
Total	**7,024**	**72**

Constructed almost entirely by hand labour under the supervision of the itinerant professional Guy Wolstenholme, Bali Handara is a fine reflection of, and response to, the golf boom in the Far East. The main problem in building a course on this beautiful island was the rainfall: up to an inch can fall every day during the two wet seasons.

The golf boom reaches
an idyllic island

Even if it were possible to uphold the dubious claim that the Dutch invented golf, there is no evidence that they took it with them to the outposts of empire, as did the British. Rather, the game arrived in Indonesia – then under Dutch suzerainty – as an appendage to the tea and rubber plantations owned by British commercial interests.

Until after World War II there were fewer than a dozen courses throughout the 2,500-mile chain of islands that make up Indonesia – all but two belonged to the plantations. The Djakarta club, in the capital, was the most successful. Its 18 holes were spread comfortably over 150 acres or more of park-like grounds not far from the city centre.

After the war the club suffered a cruel blow. Half its property, nine holes beyond a road, was compulsorily acquired for a new university and the club is now confined to the 75 acres which originally contained only nine holes. Its holes are crowded in more ways than one and the total length of the course barely reaches 6,000 yards.

The election to President of General Suharto brought to power an enthusiastic golfer and many of his ministers and senior army officers have dutifully followed his example. This growing interest in the game led, as it has done elsewhere in the world, to the need for a course of truly international quality and design. Djakarta Golf Club could never be that, because of its limited land space.

The choice for the site – and there could not have been a happier one – was Bali, at the eastern end of the Indonesian archipelago. Bali is an island of legendary beauty, little more than an hour's flying time from Djakarta, a volcanic structure sloping down through green forests and palm groves to the white sand of reef-protected beaches. It is the home of two and a half million Balinese who lead a peaceful, carefree life in an idyllic environment.

General Ibnu Sutowo, the moving spirit behind the scheme, found his site high in the mountains where, at 4,000 feet, the weather is cool and the rainfall adequate for growing the best golf grass. The land included a dairy farm, on a gently sloping tract between two large and splendid lakes near the small town of Bedugal.

Thomson Wolveridge Fream and Storm were engaged as architects and Guy Wolstenholme, the expatriate English professional, took on the task of supervising the construction.

He arrived in a downpour of rain in September, 1973. The only earth-moving machinery that Wolstenholme had at his disposal was an old-fashioned Russian steam-roller, converted into a bulldozer that crept along at less than walking pace. There was no other machinery available on the island, but there was something better – the wholehearted co-operation of the entire local population.

Altogether, 1,500 people, many of them women, worked on the course construction. The fairways were staked out, cleared up by the villagers and finally hand-sown. Under Wolstenholme's careful supervision greens were built entirely with hand labour, frequently in heavy rain.

Bali has two wet seasons. During February – March and September – October rains fall almost every day, in the higher altitudes, arriving punctually at one o'clock in the afternoon and continuing until four, during which time an inch might fall. The natural patterns of water drainage on the site were carefully noted, and the course now has a drainage system second to none. It is possible to play less than half an hour after the afternoon rain has finished, or to get at least a few holes in before the sun disappears at six o'clock.

The course took its final shape in six months. Ron Fream of California selected the grasses, flown in from the USA, and an elaborate watering system arrived from Australia. The clubhouse is a beautiful building in the Indonesian style and all about it are small cottages in the same style to complete the setting. In every way the course fits in with its surrounding environment. From the clubhouse there is a view over the course and beyond it to the lake, its far side lost in the distance. Everything is a rich green except for the red tile roofs of the far village and the blue sky reflected in the lake.

From the course, the clubhouse is dwarfed by a forest-clad mountain, its heights wispy with cloud. Monkeys, deer and pigs descend occasionally from the forest to cross the course, or to stop and feed before racing for cover at the approach of man.

The fairways, a superb blend of imported Kentucky blue-grass and the local Bermuda strain, roll out like an expensive carpet at every hole. Bluegrass, as its name implies, has a gentle hue distinguishing it from other vegetation. When close clipped it is crisp and firm, ideal for iron play or long wood shots. In truth, fairways so perfect take something from the play. To handle the infinite variety of lies and stances on a seaside links, by contrast, is a much more of a challenging task.

At Bali Handara the ball bounces and rolls truly, with a variation in proportion to the amount of rain that has fallen beforehand. The greens stand out as inspiring targets emphasized by the white sand of the bunkers, though these have not been overdone. Craters of sand would look extraordinarily inappropriate in a mountain setting; Bali Handara, like other courses in similar situations, is not a seaside links and should not be made to look like one. Golf is playable anywhere. It is one of an architect's jobs to arrange an arena for golfing in whatever natural circumstances there are and to get the best from them without destroying their character.

The trees, the flowers, the streams and lakes at Bali Handara are unique to the course and are its real features, with the golf holes running over and between them. Bali Handara turned out even better than its designers' dreams.

Bali Handara is a wonderful sub-tropical course that makes fine use of the wooded areas that line a number of holes.

The 3rd

Beauty Sweetens the Challenge

The 3rd hole at Bali Handara was the toughest to build, but in the end proved to be the most rewarding, It is a 450-yard par four, dog-legging left, its fairway divided by a stream that rushes off the mountain behind. From a high teeing ground, the drive is over a garden of wild shrubs and flowers into a wide, safe field of fairway. The stream winds its way along the right of the 1st fairway, cutting it off from the shorter 2nd fairway, which is offset to the right. The second shot must then be hit across the water to the long green, which is well beyond. An imposing trap of white sand cuts in to the green on the right side. When the flag is set on this side its base is hidden by the sand because a gentle dividing ridge spurs out from the trap.

This is a hole of beauty and pleasure, presenting a basic challenge to players of all standards. To tempt the long hitter there is a short stretch of fairway, partially obscured by trees. This is the direct line to the green, but the penalties of failure are severe. There is the stream to consider and thick trees and undergrowth to trap the slice.

From the charming single-file track that leads to the tee, to the little wooden bridge across the stream and the walk away from the green through the trees, this hole epitomizes the magic and the fascination of Bali Handara.

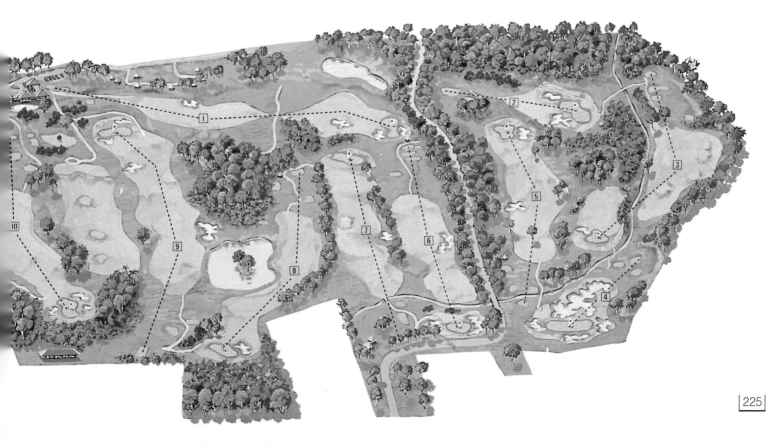

Australasia

Sport is king in Australia, a land where top-class tennis players are taken for granted and an endless succession of pubescent Olympic hopes cleave the water like dolphins. In such a climate, golf – a game that can be played from youth to near-dotage – was bound to find enthusiastic support. The number of Australians who play golf ranges from 750,000 to twice that number, with the lower figure representing at least the solid nucleus of devotees. Either way, support for golf in Australia is every bit as great as in the United States and twice as great, *per capita*, as in Britain, which despatched to the southern continent its first exemplars of golf during early Colonial days. There are now rather more than 1,600 courses in Australia, most of them concentrated in the populous south-east corner of the continent where the nation's first settlements were established. The antecedents of the earliest clubs are a little confused, for there were a number of false starts in Adelaide and Sydney. The Royal Melbourne, slipping through where others were stumbling, is the club with the longest unbroken existence, since 1891. The Royal Sydney and the Royal Adelaide soon followed and by 1895 there were clubs in Perth and Tasmania. The best of Australia's courses are among the best in the world. There is a particular quality about those in the neighbourhood of Melbourne, where the soil of the Sand Belt and the talents of architects like Alister Mackenzie and Dick Wilson have shaped testing golf in surroundings of great character. They have played their part in the breeding of great players who have made their mark around the world – Norman Von Nida, Peter Thomson (five times winner of the British Open), Kel Nagle, Bruce Devlin, Bruce Crampton, Steve Elkington, Greg Norman, and others. In New Zealand, where the game got off to a start – albeit in a limited manner – about the same time as in Australia, golf has made great strides in recent years. With 500 courses it has rather more than Ireland, where the population is about the same.

1. Royal Melbourne 2. Royal Adelaide 3. Royal Sydney 4. Warakei 5. Paraparaumu

A course to humble even the
giants

The Course Card		
The Royal Melbourne Golf Club, Victoria Composite Course		
Record: 62 Richard Lee (2002 Heineken Classic)		
Hole	**Yards**	**Par**
1	354	4
2	498	5
3	176	3
4	450	4
5	332	4
6	439	4
7	382	4
8	201	3
9	557	5
10	483	5
11	147	3
12	304	4
13	454	4
14	464	4
15	438	4
16	432	4
17	428	4
18	442	4
Out	3,389	36
In	3,592	36
Total	**6,981**	**72**

Something outstanding and exceptional was bound to emerge from the formation of the Royal Melbourne club. There was, to begin with, a dedication to the traditions of the game that stemmed through its earliest members and officers directly from St Andrews. Later, after two changes of location to the site it now occupies, it was fashioned from a duneland setting akin to the old Scottish links. And finally the inspired architecture of its East and the West courses.

Championship events are now played over a composite eighteen holes, a beneficial expedient forced upon the organisers of the 1959 Canada Cup (now the World Cup) to avoid busy roads which cross both courses. It has been the venue for most of the prestigious Australian tournaments and several more besides, including three World Cups. When the Presidents Cup, the biennial encounter between the United States and the Rest of the World, was looking for a venue for its first match outside America in December 1998, Royal Melbourne was the logical choice.

The necessary acreage of sandy dune left behind by a retreating sea, studded with native she-oaks and tea-trees, dwarf reed, heather and bracken, was acquired by 1924, when it was decided to secure "the best expert advice". The choice of adviser was Dr Alister Mackenzie, the celebrated architect of Scottish descent. Mackenzie arrived in October 1926 and started work immediately with Alex Russell, Australian Open champion of 1924. Mackenzie was a designer of the highest skill, and the Royal Melbourne is one of his masterpieces. This is not to overlook Russell's contribution – evinced by the quality of the East course, which he designed and built after Mackenzie's departure.

As significant as the layout and overall design of the course is the scale and speed of its greens, the credit for which belongs to the former head greenkeeper Claude Crockford, who joined the staff in 1934. In many ways the course is as much his as it is Mackenzie's or Russell's.

Crockford himself undertook to rebuild the short, uphill 11th hole to the concept of the then best player of

The best of Alex Russell and Alister Mackenzie, designers of the East and West courses respectively are taken to produce the composite Melbourne championship course. A feature of both men's work is their skill in bunker placement and green contouring. The 5th is Russell's creation – 332 yards long, dipping into a hollow and up to a tiered green that falls to the left. In contrast, the 1st is Mackenzie's hole, a slightly longer par-four that ends with the ball being played to a triangular green that falls away at the back.

Surrounded by sand, heather and bracken, the sloping 3rd provides a perfect example of a Royal Melbourne green. The bunkers, too, are worthy of study. Nick Faldo, in Australia to compete in the 2002 Heineken Classic, described how he had come to Royal Melbourne a few years earlier to do just that: "I videoed the bunkers, and it is great stuff. Royal Melbourne is one of the classic golf courses of the world, especially for a budding architect like me. It's very Augusta-ish. We all have our preferences in terms of where we rank them, but Royal Melbourne is definitely one of the greats."

the club, Ivo Whitton, after the original Mackenzie hole proved unsatisfactory. Crockford's 147-yard 11th is a rare gem of planning and construction. It was built on the sandy hill by horse and scoop like the rest of the course. It slopes in an intriguing line from back to front although there is adequate flat, or nearly flat, territory for the flagstick in one or two spots – a deception not always discovered until it is too late. It is surrounded by traps of good depth and formidable sides, with a foreground like a miniature natural park of small indigenous flora to add to its rugged appearance.

The greens are basically dry and firm and the grass sparse compared with the dense growth of most other courses. In 1996 the process of restoring the greens began using seed grown from the original Suttons greens. Ernie Els, who won the 2002 Heineken Classic, said of them, "The tour won't putt on better greens than these all year. This course is a second-shot course, like Augusta, but this is a lot tougher and there's more fire in the greens."

The order of play of the holes making up the compos-

ite course used for championship events has been varied over the years. For the 2002 Heineken Classic a novel sequence was employed which culminated in a demanding run of tough par-fours from the 14th to the end, the shortest of them measuring 428 yards. This routing also contrived to bring the climactic holes close to the clubhouse. So now the round opens with a clever drive and pitch hole of 354 yards played to a triangular green in which the apex points towards the striker and the slope falls gently away to the back. This 'falling away' technique was used again by Mackenzie at the 3rd at Augusta National.

Like many historic courses, Royal Melbourne is succumbing to today's advances in ball and club technology. New Zealander Michael Campbell played the course in 1996. When he returned in 2002 he said, 'I was looking at my old yardage books and am now hitting one, sometimes two clubs less than I was then. I am about 20 yards longer, which makes a heck of a difference around here.' The professionals now expect to reach the 2nd green in two as a matter of course. For the handicap player, however, it remains one of the toughest challenges, with an intimidating drive over a bunker-encrusted hill and a shot to the green over a valley of sand and scrub. Then comes the first of those ingenious par-threes which make this course so distinctive. It is a 176-yard shot across low ground to a green that forms a step on the farther slope. A sea of sand, heather and bracken awaits the errant shot, and the slope before the green is so steep and 'shaved' that a shot just feeble enough to land on the bevelled front edge invariably trickles back down to the foot of the slope. The green is deceptively fast and sloped from the back; holing out in two putts requires a keen eye and a steady hand.

The 4th is one of the world's best and a thriller to watch during championship play. Starting from a high tee, the fairway turns right at almost right angles around a wide

area of perfectly natural ground scrub and sand, which can be crossed with sufficient power and direction. The invitation is to bite off more than can be chewed. From the fairway there is a gentle slope up to a green set in a natural amphitheatre that is guarded by a massive, deep trap on the left side. The shot looks easy and

receptive, but there is a major problem of getting down in two from the back edge – which is usually the putt left when played into a stiff breeze and the second shot is a long iron. Putting across the line is no less examining, because the 'line' is apt to turn almost the length of the putt. In the 1987 Australian Open this green became infamous as it provoked what may be the first 'walk-out' ever staged by professional golfers. Sandy Lyle, that most genial of men, led the protest about a flag that had been placed on what he considered an impossible slope. He was supported by, among others, Greg Norman, who labelled it 'completely unfair'. The upshot was that the final round was postponed until the following day when the pin was placed in a vaguely puttable position. Norman went on to win that year with a record winning margin of ten strokes.

Another hole which is rendered impotent by the advances in technology is the 332-yard 5th, a Russell creation which used to require a tee shot into the wide spaces on the left, followed by a downhill pitch over a hollow to a two-tiered green – a shot requiring great delicacy of touch. Many of today's professionals drive the green or, if they find the greenside bunkers, such is their sand technique that they expect to be up and down in two. There follows a dog-leg par-four, again by Russell, that climbs uphill to a green, two-tiered on the crown, jealously guarded by a cluster of bunkers. Lined along the right side with trees, the 7th is a dog-leg sliding to the right towards a green of fiendish undulations. There are no bunkers to restrict the tee shot, but the fairway narrows between trees and bushes about 250 yards out. The 8th is a Russell par-three of 201 yards up a gentle hill. The back of the green, to the left, is more like

---

The 12th

The Ultimate in Temptation

Above and below: The 12th hole at Royal Melbourne, above, is only 304 yards long – but woe betide any player who trifles with it.

It is a stiff test of a golf architect's skill to ask him to make something out of a hole of only 304 yards; few holes on earth of this length can be reckoned to be anything more than stop-gaps. The par-four 12th hole on the Royal Melbourne championship course is an exception. Granted the designers, Alister Mackenzie and Alex Russell, had a perfect piece of land to work with but the result nevertheless is unique. It makes the sternest demands on good and bad players alike, and no matter what the weather conditions scores here can vary from two to ten.

In golf course design two interesting themes run counter to each other. The one rather standard principle, that the farther one hits and the nearer one approaches the target the finer becomes the margin of error, is cleverly offset by the axiom that the more finely judged second shot gets progressively more difficult the farther one falls short of the green. Architects often attempt to incorporate these two themes into their design, but few succeed.

The sporting length of the 12th offers the ultimate in temptation – that of driving on to the green and perhaps holing the putt for an eagle. But the very real likelihood and the dire consequences of failure on a shot of that particular line and length are apt to inhibit the free swing and bring disaster. The hole crosses a pleasant valley from one crest to the next. Ordinarily, this would present no problems to the modern professional, except that on the direct line to the flag is a cavernous bunker. However, the designers have cleverly led the player towards the right where they offer a safe shot, provided it is not too long. Failure to reach the top of the crest leaves a shot to the flagstick which is mostly blind and, should the green be firm and fast, as it usually is, the pitch requires the utmost accuracy to hold the green. All around there is sand, except for a tiny apron in the form of a hollow, the excavation of which helped form the green.

The main feature of the hole is the enormous chasm of bunker which must be carried by the brave player who goes for the green. A man feels small indeed standing in there trying to get out.

The 12th: 304 yards par 4

—— Bold line
----- Safe line

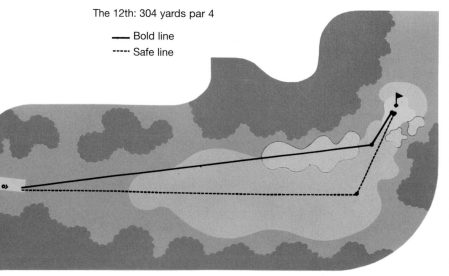

200 yards distant, a factor to remember when selecting clubs. Australia's Bruce Crampton ran up a six here just when he and Bill Dunk looked to have the World Cup won in 1972, eventually losing out to the Taiwanese. At 557 yards the 9th is Royal Melbourne's longest hole, once the sort of length that only the most powerful players such as Sam Snead might aspire to reaching in two, with a line of bunkers crossing the fairway over the last 85 yards. With no bunkers restricting driving length, this is now a birdie-must for aspiring champions.

The back nine starts with the last and shortest of the par-fives, an especially good hole when the wind is from south of west. The tee shot must clear a vast bunker – a carry of some 220 yards – to a fairway angled to the right, snaking through the trees towards the green. The second shot runs past craters of sand on either side towards a none too generous green, which can prove to be a holy terror when putting from a distance. Following Crockford's 11th, which offers no margin for error, comes one of Royal Melbourne's jewels. The 12th is only 304 yards long, but devilishly difficult. The green can be driven – and often is – but in this lie the seeds of destruction. The fairway crosses a large valley and winds its way by circuitous route to the right until, having reached the hilltop, it turns back left to the small green surrounded by a wilderness. Playing safe is no guarantee of a four because, even after a curtailed tee shot, the pitch from below the hill is blind and therefore risky. It remains a fine example of old-fashioned adventure.

Now the searching run in begins, six holes averaging 443 yards in length. The 13th hole is a substantial par-four which dog-legs to the left to the horizon and a green of

alarming undulation and wicked speed. Then the 14th runs a lengthy course up towards Cheltenham Road, a hole which may well have started its life as a par-five because, instead of a straightforward fairway and green, the route winds away to the right and a higher level, drawing the play with it and so adding to the length and interest. The tee shot carries some large-scale Melbourne traps and the second shot must avoid a green-front bunker and an expanse of rugged native rough from which escape is an uncertain business.

Another fine par-four is the 15th. The drive fires out onto a level area backdropped by a forest of tea trees, and there is no hint of what lies ahead until a hill is breasted at the 250-yard mark to reveal a spectacular target some 200 yards away across a shallow valley. The 16th (the final hole on the West Course) leads back to the clubhouse. Again it is a par-four of some merit, presenting a drive over a hill that is characterised by typical Mackenzie sand and a sharp dog-leg turn to the right where the green is viewed, framed by a host of ominous white sandtraps. For its 17th hole the composite course then strikes out along the 1st hole of the West Course. It makes a good opener, with a wide, bunkerless fairway to get play flowing. It is deceptive, however, for a bunker guarding the right of the green swallows many an approach made from the wrong angle.

The 18th is also the closing hole of the East Course, which was still the championship layout in 1963 when Gary Player won the Australian Open. It is often played into the wind, when it makes a great finisher. As at the 17th, there are no fairway bunkers troubling the drive, but the green is simply an island in a sea of sand, full of undulation and always testing to putt.

The 2nd: 498 yards par 5

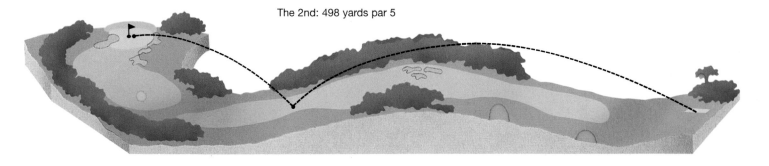

The 2nd

Fairways that Wander to Deceive

When this book first appeared in 1976, the 2nd (then played as the 14th hole of the composite course) was described as the most difficult hole on the Royal Melbourne layout, and for many it still is. But for the modern professional any par-five of 498 yards is a clear birdie opportunity. With their superior modern equipment and prodigious talent they have no difficulty in taking the first of Mackenzie's designed hazards out of play. For the rest of us, however, it is still a big thump to clear the three bunkers which occupy the sky-line as viewed from the tee. They require a carry of some 220 yards to clear them from the back tee. Aim out to the left to avoid them and the hole plays well over 500 yards. However, for those who can smash the ball far beyond the bunkers it is not all plain sailing. For them the drive is blind, and the fairway slopes downwards in the landing area, giving great assistance when the drive is straight, but sending the misdirected shot off into the

daunting rough. At about 300 yards from the tee the fairway is beginning its long curve to the right. It is not unknown to run out of fairway here.

The sloping fairway also complicates the stance for the second shot, and the clear view of the various obstacles between ball and green confirms that there is no margin for error. There is rough to carry for the first part, and then the fairway twists and turns through huge, deep bunkers that can bring disaster. Lee Trevino was caught in the heather overhanging the trap on the left in the 1974 Chrysler Classic and ended up with a nine. He vowed never to return. Eleven years later, in 1985, the winds blew savagely as Tom Watson tried manfully to defend his Australian Open title. Scores rocketed. In the end, it was the immense power of Greg Norman which helped him to eagle this hole into the teeth of the gale. It set up a best-of-the-day round of 74, good enough to win by two.

Royal Adelaide, vulnerable to winds, is a searching test combining the best of classic architecture with modern demands for length and accuracy. The nearest to a genuine links in Australia, its critical run home from the difficult 226-yard 12th is through narrow, thoughtfully bunkered fairways.

The Course Card

Royal Adelaide Golf Club, South Australia

Hole	Yards	Par
1	382	4
2	547	5
3	295	4
4	448	4
5	459	4
6	459	4
7	183	3
8	392	4
9	548	5
10	374	4
11	382	4
12	226	3
13	432	4
14	487	4
15	499	5
16	180	3
17	517	5
18	419	4
Out	3,713	37
In	3,516	36
Total	**7,229**	**73**

Taking on the teetotallers –

and the bishop

Golf came to Adelaide in 1869, among the steam-er trunks of South Australia's new governor, the Scotsman Sir James Fergusson. There were Scots enough already in residence (the administration of empire was a talent in which they were particularly distinguished) to help him establish the club with a small membership within a year of his arrival.

The early years were, at best, chequered. The golfing governor departed, having completed his term of office, and six years after it had been opened the first nine hole course now lost beneath the Victoria Park racecourse was abandoned as unsuitable. The club remained in limbo for 16 years. A new course was found, but it was an expedient, replaced in 1896 when the club merged with the palindromic Glenelg, in the southern suburbs of the city.

The new club was still called Adelaide but used the Glenelg course, nine holes were extended to 18 with the advice of Scots golfer, Francis Maxwell, whose brother Robert won the British Amateur Championship in 1903.

In 1904, the club moved to its present site at Seaton, 25 minutes by train from the city centre. The single-track railway line is still there but the station, beside which the clubhouse was built in the centre of the 204 acre property, has been closed.

Soon after it acquired the Seaton course, Adelaide appointed its first professional – not surprisingly a Scotsman, Jack Scott, from Carnoustie. The appointment of a talented professional was critical to a young club, particularly one so far from Scotland, source and inspiration of all golfing mores. He made and repaired clubs, not the least of his functions in a climate which played havoc with woodwork; he taught, and in teaching laid the groundwork for the club's reputation; and he was the final arbiter on the game's rules and etiquette.

Scott remained at Adelaide for nearly 20 years and had the pleasure of seeing one of his protégés, Rufus Stewart, become the first South Australian to win the Australian Open in 1927.

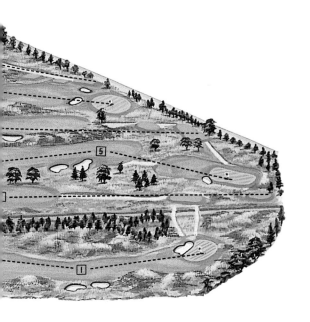

An Echo of Scotland's Best

When the property at Seaton was chosen as the permanent site of the Adelaide Golf Club, much of it was white sand left stranded by the receding sea. There was little change of level and nothing to protect the golfer from exposure to the winds, which must be tackled from each quarter. This is especially true of the back nine which twists and turns through every direction to provide a brilliant examination of a player's technique and temperament.

At 382 yards the 11th is not long for a par-4 yet it remains a fine hole even with today's high-performance clubs and balls. A great sandy waste must be crossed with the second shot, and there is little margin for error. If the wind helped on this hole it will surely hinder on the 12th, a lengthy par-3. The long curve of the 13th brings play back towards the clubhouse before the difficulties of the 14th must be overcome. This, the longest of Adelaide's two-shot holes, would not be out of place on Scotland's Ayrshire coast with its long, narrow putting surface protected by serious green-side bunkers. Four further changes of direction ensure a constantly varying challenge right to the very end.

Two exceptional shots are required to reach Royal Adelaide's 14th green in regulation.

The hazards of golf are not always just those of the sandtrap and the water. The Adelaide club had to contend with the prim city fathers – led by a bishop – who deplored the club's use of youngsters as caddies on the Sabbath. It drove off an attempt by two of its members to stop the sale of alcohol at the club, and itself banished one of its member's free-range turkeys from the course.

To make worthwhile all their strenuous efforts to keep going, Alister Mackenzie arrived in 1926 to advise on modifications to the course. The work he carried out forms the basis of the present championship route, although in subsequent years the holes were constantly improved. Among Mackenzie's innovations was the removal of the need to play across the railway line, and the introduction of the sand-dunes as features of the championship course.

Royal Adelaide (it acquired its Royal appendage in 1923) is perhaps the nearest course to a links that Australia has among its top championship venues. Its sand is in many places the natural hazard and rough. The 1st, 6th, 13th, 17th and 18th holes were upgraded in the 1970s to give them more of the "seaside" character than they formerly had.

The whole layout has the flat appearance of a links, except for a rise in the centre of the site where two tees, the 8th and 12th, are placed. Two huge craters of sand have been preserved to enhance the course's character.

Royal Adelaide has been host to the Australian Open plus a succession of other professional and amateur tournaments. It was also home to one of the most extraordinary incidents ever to take place on a golf course, concerning a shot played by Kevin Simmonds in a national amateur event. Simmonds hooked his drive at the second into the carriage of a passing train. Whereupon a passenger threw it back as the train approached the green, the ball finishing a yard or so from the hole. Sadly, we have to report that Simmonds missed what would have been golf's most astonishing albatross. Not a bad eagle three though.

Jim Ferrier, who attained world fame first as runner-up in the British Amateur in 1939 and the PGA Championship in 1947, won the double crown of Open and Amateur national titles at Royal Adelaide in 1938. Gary Player won the second of his seven Australian Open championships there in 1962 (an event in which Jack Nicklaus made his first appearance in Australia, finishing fifth). Player won with 278, five less than Ferrier's score 24 years earlier, but Ferrier was under no

pressure for he won by the enormous margin of 14 strokes from his contemporary, Norman Von Nida.

The final of the Australian Amateur in 1932 provided the most exciting contest in the championship's history. The defending champion, a 17-year-old left-handed prodigy, Harry Williams, was opposed by Dr Reg Bettington, a triple Oxford Blue and captain of the New South Wales cricket team. Williams appeared to have his title safely in keeping when, two up, he hit his tee shot to six feet at the par-three 12th, the 30th hole of the contest. Bettington followed to 20 feet and courageously holed the putt before stepping back to watch Williams miss. Bettington took the lead by birdieing the next two holes. He stymied Williams on the 33rd green and birdied the 34th. A half in par-fives down the long 35th gave Bettington an incredible victory; Williams shot pars through the last seven holes, yet lost four of them.

Scoring of this kind was unknown in Australia in 1932. Both players were of the highest standard and Williams was recognised as the best player Australia had produced until then. He played little if any golf after 1939 and died suddenly at the age of 46. Bettington left Australia shortly afterwards to settle in New Zealand and died in a car accident.

Although the match between Williams and Bettington was one of the most remarkable in the club's history, Royal Adelaide has seen much other quality golf and will continue to do so; in 1998 the Australian Open returned to the course for the eighth time.

Royal Sydney
Golf Club,
New South Wales

Hole	Yards	Par
1	277	4
2	549	5
3	182	3
4	427	4
5	415	4
6	154	3
7	563	5
8	302	4
9	359	4
10	419	4
11	438	4
12	384	4
13	514	5
14	194	3
15	443	4
16	563	5
17	210	3
18	402	4
Out	3,228	36
In	3,567	36
Total	**6,795**	**72**

Seaside golf in a
city saucer

A city whose premier golf course is little more than a ten-minute drive from its commercial and social heart is one where a dedicated golfer might be glad to live. The Royal Sydney is such a course, retaining the rugged look of a true links and set about by fashionable suburban houses.

In a land where sporting and athletic distinction is a matter of pride, the club is as much a feature of its city's life as the famous bridge and the billowing Opera House. Its membership roll reads like a Who's Who of New South Wales. Although formed as a men-only golf club in 1893, it is now an all-embracing golf, tennis, bowls, croquet, squash and social club with more than 5,000 members.

The whole of the property is in the shape of a huge saucer. The layout has peculiarities not found elsewhere. Many tees are sited against the club boundary on the higher grade with the fairways spread below and the greens in full view in the distance. During the 1980s the fairways were changed from kikuyu grass to pure wintergreen couch and extensive drainage work was carried out, giving the course an enviable reputation for remaining dry even after heavy rain.

In its formative years the course was of nine holes and "rooms were taken at Mrs Ebsworth's cottage for the use of members". In 1896 James Scott joined the club as its professional, his arrival coinciding with the extension of the course to 18 holes, taking in some of the lower-lying area, and in 1897 the club received the title Royal. It went from strength to strength as the course improved in quality and it soon became host to the Australian Open, hitherto held only at the Royal Melbourne Golf Club.

Royal Sydney is at its best on those clear, blue, hazy days that are characteristic of Sydney. The couch grass browns off a little during winter dormancy, but a plentiful supply of water from the club's own boreholes ensures admirable conditioning for the rest of the year. Like most courses by the sea, there is rarely a day when the wind is absent. This is a precious commodity for golfers as it adds that extra dimension to the course, enhancing its adventure.

Weather may just have been a factor in the eventual result of the 1969 Australian Open. Gary Player was struggling desperately to keep a narrow lead over Guy Wolstenholme. The skies to the south darkened in the late afternoon when Player was six slow holes from home. Lightning could be seen some miles away and amid the turbulence of the wind and the first shower Player and Bruce Devlin took shelter; they stayed there until ordered to resume. Wolstenholme played through it and lost by one stroke. Devlin and Lee Trevino finished close behind.

In 1988 Australia celebrated its bicentennial year and the Australian Open returned to Royal Sydney. The course was upgraded for the championship, the most significant change being the enlarging of several greens. This time an American prevailed, Mark Calcavecchia winning by six shots from his compatriot Mark McCumber. Calcavecchia called himself

The elegance of Royal Sydney 's layout diminishes the severity of its hazards in the eyes of less observant golfers. But its fairways are narrow, its rough fierce and its bunkers numerous. The judging of distances too, can cause problems, and at holes such as the 13th, with its cross-bunkers some 280 yards from the tee, this can be crucial.

"lucky" but no-one can enjoy so much fortune to win by such a margin without playing some superior golf as well.

Perhaps he was lucky in that for once the wind did not blow and he was able to amass a staggering total of 19 under the card. More typically no-one does well at Royal Sydney without a knowledge and command of the low, wind-escaping shot.

Except for five holes the course runs north and south, so that the shots called for have a repetition that can be destroying if the golfer is not particularly adept at playing into, or half across, a stout breeze. Most greens are surrounded by large bunkers inspired by Alister Mackenzie and cut deep into the bare sand underneath. The round begins with a drive-and-pitch hole starting from a tee by the clubhouse door. Then the course turns along the rim of the saucer with a well-bunkered par-five and a par-three played from an elevated tee, with a plentiful selection of bunkers awaiting the weak shot. During the course of the round there are many shots to the greens that have to carry all the way. Two splendid par-fours follow, arguably the best holes on the front nine. By today's standards they are not unduly long but, when the wind is against, many amateurs still have to reach for wood for the second shot to the green. On both holes the tee is higher than the fairway, magnifying any directional inaccuracy with the drive, and the approach shot is played uphill. The course changes direction again with another short hole, the 6th. It is a hole of no great length but from a high tee the ball is vulnerable to the wind during its flight. A long par-five and a couple of short par-fours complete the front nine, which is quite short – very short when the wind is from the north – but it is full of interest.

From the 10th tee the course descends into the lower area and only rises again at the last green in the shadow of the clubhouse. These holes are plainer than the outward ones, but because most of them are straight they become a hard test of a golfer's technique. A variety of indigenous trees separate these fairways and provide a savage penalty for waywardness.

The best holes inward are the long, par-five 13th, the 14th and the final hole, which is aptly one of Australia's best. The 14th is a 194-yard par-three. The green is surrounded by sand and, depending on ability, the prospect is either inspiring or wholly terrifying. A few years ago a tournament offered $100,000 to anyone who could make a hole in one but the professionals had a total of 440 shots without success. Then along came a club member, ID Magney, who swung mightily the very next day with a four wood and watched from the elevated tee as the ball hopped into the hole for an ace. Alas, the prize was now no longer available.

The 1999 Australian Open provided a fairy tale ending with the 18-year-old Australian amateur, Aaron Baddeley, holding off the challenges of Greg Norman and Colin Montgomerie to become the youngest ever winner.

The 18th

No Place for the Nervous

The moment of truth in golf comes when a match is all square on the last tee. Every golfer is affected by the situation, the more so when he knows the 18th will test his stamina and nerve in the manner of Royal Sydney's closing hole. It is one of the best finishing holes in Australia. It is a par-four of good length, dog-legging to the left around a small copse of trees. The well-trapped green is set above the fairway on a kind of Redan below the giant clubhouse. It slopes gently forwards and, like the home hole on the Old Course at St Andrews, has just enough subtlety to make putting a performance that is always worth watching.

The dog-leg puts the slicer at a disadvantage since his shot curls away from the hole. However, the hooker can gain ground if he can hit the 235 yards to the corner. There is a temptation to bite off too much, which, in matches, can lead to over-caution if the second player to hit is intent on avoiding at all costs the mistake of his opponent. The approach presents an invitation to mishit in an instinctive effort to hit the shot high so that the green will receive it sympathetically. There is seldom the need. The green is large and usually soft enough to hold most shots.

During 2002 the greens were relaid and the opportunity taken to make a number of alterations to the course, with subtle changes to the outline of several fairways, adjustments to the bunkering and reshaping of greens.

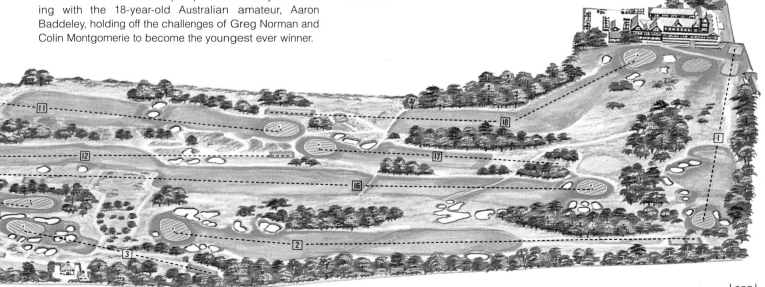

Golf among
the geysers

Wairakei is among the more modern of New Zealand's major golf courses, implanted by the government's Tourist Hotel Corporation in the heart of lovely countryside, bubbling with geothermal activity, midway between Auckland and Wellington. It is not in fact a club at all, but a green fee facility open to all who spend their holidays in the neighbourhood of the huge, trout-filled Lake Taupo and the hot thermal springs of Rotorua.

The popularity of the game in New Zealand was not reflected in the quality of courses available until Wairakei was built. In 1953 the NZGA met to approve courses for the New Zealand championships and only four were of international standards – Titirangi, Belmont, Paraparaumu and Shirley. Architects were called in and courses were lengthened (there was nothing, until Wairakei, approaching 7,000 yards), bunkering was modernized and the game as a whole was tightened up. Finally, H. T. (Dooley) Coxhead, an accomplished golfer and a member of the Tourist Hotel Corporation, persuaded his colleagues that what their hotel at Wairakei needed was a championship golf course, after the manner of Gleneagles or White Sulphur Springs.

The man he found to do the job was Commander John Harris, a civil engineer and England's leading and most travelled golf course architect, whose father had constructed Moor Park, Wentworth and Sunningdale in Britain. The possibilities of Wairakei must have appealed to him.

The course is set in gently rolling countryside with a few majestic spurs and a lattice of gullies and creeks.

Whoever plays golf at Wairakei, above, is conscious of a living earth.

Since the map, right, was drawn water has been added alongside the 8th and 12th holes and some revisions to the bunkering have been made.

Harris's layout made excellent use of the natural features and his sympathetic handling of the terrain made all but a little earth-moving unnecessary, apart from green-building and general fairway preparation. The construction was supervised by Michael Wolveridge, an Englishman whose keen appreciation of the subtleties of golf architecture had been enriched by a spell on the US professional tour. When completed, Wairakei lacked only a fairway watering scheme, a benefit excluded until later by the budget.

In its first year Wairakei came under heavy fire from the New Zealand Conference of Greenkeepers, who were "appalled" at the subsidence of the greens – which, like the rest of the course, were built on pumice, the "froth" of ancient volcanic lava. The subsidence was soon cured.

Wairakei makes few physical demands on the player. Walking is easy and mostly on the flat, with an occasional climb to the higher tees. The variety of holes, however, calls for a high degree of skill to match par – a skill beyond the reach of an average player. Many small creeks have to be cleared along the front nine and open-shouldered hitting is needed on the run in, making the course, from the championship tees at least, a handicap contest.

Whoever plays at Wairakei is conscious at all times of a living earth, for above the enclosing pine forests there rises the endless vapours of the Karapiti and Rogue bore holes. The Rogue is particularly awesome, its clouds of steam and spray rising to heights of 300 feet and more. It has given its name to Wairakei's most impressive hole, the 14th, 566 yards long from the back tee. The building of this hole exemplifies the importance of the construction supervisor's role in the creation of a golf course. Wolveridge improvised considerably as Wairakei was taking shape and for the end of the monster he dreamed up a banana-shaped green which is naturally set into a steep hill above the long, dog-legged fairway. It poses permanently for brochure photographers.

The Rogue with a Reputation

Flanked by soft hills and forestland, the long par-five 14th aims directly up a narrow valley towards a natural rogue borehole which belches forth clouds of sulphurous steam. Aptly named The Rogue, the hole has a reputation as the chief wrecker at Wairakei and it is an undoubted test of strength as well as skill. Its fairways wind past well placed bunkers and beneath a tall pine tree towards an unusual green some 566 yards distant.

The main interest lies in the third shot to the green, which is large, elevated and horseshoe-shaped; its left side is fraught with bunkers and hollows. The tougher pin spots are to the left and centre and they demand a fairly lofted approach. This means, of course, that if a par-five is to be attained in the usual manner, two mighty wood shots are needed before the final approach.

The Rogue is a special hole, vociferously attacked and defended with equal passion, but always memorable.

Wairakei, a splendidly natural course set amidst a spectacular thermal region of the North Island, was built in response to the growing clamour of the early 1950s for a true championship course in New Zealand. It is long – but not too long – and imaginative in the siting and construction of its greens and traps.

The Course Card			

Wairakei Resort International Golf Course, North Island

Hole	Name	Yardage	Par
1	Wairakei	519	5
2	Pines	235	3
3	Karapiti	554	5
4	The Oak	372	4
5	High Pitch	181	3
6	Glen	475	4
7	Huka	368	4
8	Challenge	383	4
9	Hillside	431	4
10	Terrace	193	3
11	Ruapehu	348	4
12	Tongariro	307	4
13	The Plains	438	4
14	The Rogue	566	5
15	Flyover	210	3
16	Tauhara	399	4
17	Gap	430	4
18	Home	567	5
Out		3,518	36
In		3,458	36
Total		**6,976**	**72**

Man conspires with nature to create

adventure

Hole	Yards	Par
1	403	4
2	202	3
3	464	4
4	446	4
5	162	3
6	326	4
7	500	5
8	371	4
9	393	4
10	311	4
11	427	4
12	544	5
13	446	4
14	146	3
15	372	4
16	138	3
17	442	4
18	550	5
Out	3,267	35
In	3,376	36
Total	**6,643**	**71**

Paraparaumu Beach is an antipodean phenomenon – a real seaside links. Thirty-five miles north of Wellington in New Zealand's North Island, it is reached by a winding, circuitous route overlooking the Tasman Sea and the sentinel off-shore island of Kapiti.

The founder of the club, Stronach Patterson, and his colleague, D. O. Whyte, were attracted to Paraparaumu Beach and its linksland because in the 1920s no course of its kind existed in New Zealand or, for that matter, anywhere beyond the British Isles and the western fringes of mainland Europe. By 1930, Patterson, Whyte and their colleagues had the support necessary to build their ideal links and Alex Russell, co-architect with Alister Mackenzie of Royal Melbourne, was chosen to design it.

Only a bare minimum of land could be afforded, but it was enough for Russell. Within its 130 acres he filled every square yard, either with natural, undulating fairways and carefully constructed tees and sandtraps, or with rough he left on the high dune tops. It says much for Russell's flair for architecture that the course bears no similarity at all to his work at Melbourne. The temptation was to duplicate the wide fairways and huge rolling greens that make Royal Melbourne such a distinctive course, but here they would have been out of place and Russell must have known it. Instead he drew upon his own experiences and observations in Britain, where he had travelled and played. The result must rank with Carnoustie or one of those happy courses along the Strathclyde coast, like Troon or Western Gailes. It is, nevertheless, different again from each of them – more a clever mixture of old and new, nature's sculpture and man's talent. Paraparaumu looks the way Troon would probably look if it had been built recently instead of 120 years ago.

To play the course in calm and sunny weather, or to battle gales from one quarter or another, is a satisfying and exciting adventure but it is best when the wind blows with moderate strength from the west. This is the prevailing wind, helping or hindering every stroke to some extent.

Bunkering is on a small scale – a sharp contrast to Russell's other courses, but here appropriate and sensible. There is a certain practicality in the creation of pot bunkers instead of the larger beach type. On some holes there are no artificial traps at all for the steep, close-cut slopes of the dunes serve as hazard enough.

The 1st hole, a 403-yard par-four, heads off towards the mountains that form a distant backdrop. There is a 100-yard carry through a gap in the dunes leading to a large arena of fairway, with a gentle downslope giving a clear view of the green formed by low mounds and soft gathering undulations. The 1st green is typical of Paraparaumu: its small undulations, their crests only a yard or two apart, make putting a chancy business from a long way off. The small depressions tend to be lusher than the higher spots, creating variations in speed, and if a hole is cut on the crest of a bump, putting becomes an exceedingly difficult proposition.

The 2nd hole is difficult, a par-three cleverly placed on the dune tops, the green having been made by ironing one into a suitable flatness. The target is not large, shyly hiding its shape behind a bump left judiciously on the apron: Tiger Woods, competing in the 2002 New Zealand Open, contrived to four-putt from 30 feet in the final round, sinking his chances of victory.

The 3rd fairway is reminiscent of the crumpled links of St Andrews. The green is at eye-level with a sunken bunker hidden at the left front corner. Inevitably, it catches most pulled shots. A new tee, put in recently, has added 45 yards to this hole. The danger used to be in overshooting the green. Now, in a northerly, it takes two big shots to get home.

The 4th is a 446-yard par-four which runs along the foot of the highest ridge of the course. The 5th is a gem. Only 162 yards long, it rivals the famous Postage Stamp at Troon and Russell must have enjoyed creating it.

On the fairway of the 326-yard 6th, massive undulations can throw a straight drive off to right or left, adding to the adventure of such a short shot. The 7th is a par-five of quality. At the 8th penalty, in the form of strong rough, awaits on either side of the plateau green. The second shot

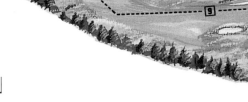

invites an inspired iron shot through a gap in the sandhills to a green nestling at the foot of the clubhouse hill; a large wild water channel runs alongside the left. Then follow three par fours and a par five reachable in two powerful shots. It was at this point that Craig Parry, Stephen Leaney, Michael Campbell and Steve Alker began piling on the birdies to turn up the heat in the 2002 Open.

At 446 yards the par-four 13th is one of the best holes in this part of the world. Nothing less than two perfect shots will get to the green. Of all holes the 13th, unique and thrilling, is the one that epitomises Paraparaumu Beach. It caused Leaney and Alker to drop back out of contention. Tantalizingly short, the 14th is a little drop shot par-three made trickier by even a moderate wind. The 15th is a lovely par-four, traversing between dunes up to a step-like green which is difficult to hit from any line except the straight one.

The 16th is a gem of a three. It is cut into the side of a small hill with no bunker to guard it, but plenty of slope. The 17th, like the 13th, is enchanting. It has a split fairway on two levels offering a choice of routes. The lower, more direct route is easier for the first shot but fiendish for the second. The upper level is by far the best from which to approach, but it is necessarily more difficult to get there. From it, the passage is open to the green, still some 200 yards off and a daunting target. There is a steep and shaven slope off the left side, and the right is all traps and depressions; into a westerly wind it is often out of the reach of even the best players. It was the pivotal hole in 2002. Michael Campbell, who won here in 2000, came to the hole in the lead. He had just birdied the 15th and 16th. But he hit his approach shot into the gallery and then three-putted. That let in Craig Parry, the Australian, for his first tour victory in two years. New tees have lengthened the final hole by almost 60 yards.

The 13th

Nature's Thrilling Invitation

As at many other holes at Paraparaumu, nature has played a great part in the creation of the 13th. Just like the very oldest courses on which the game of golf was born, it has many humps and hollows – some of them massive. It is most spectacular, for on a sunny day the view from the tee ground has few rivals in golf. The rough is splashed with the green and yellow of broom and the green can be seen against a backdrop of distant snow-capped mountains. The invitation is there to enjoy it and thrill to its stout golfing challenge.

The appeal of this hole can depend on a golfer's skills or, more pertinently perhaps, the distance he can

strike the ball. It is 446 yards long and it takes a massive drive from the back tee to reach the plateau halfway to the green. This is the ideal spot, offering a wonderful view of the slightly elevated green, about a three iron's carry across a huge hollow of fairway. Originally the green was a prepared saddle on the ridge without the back wall which members had demanded. Its addition has taken something away from the hole's uncompromising challenge but enough remains to make the 13th unique.

The 13th hole at Paraparumu offers an uncompromising challenge.

History was made at Paraparaumu Beach in the 2002 New Zealand Open when a 13-year old Rotorua schoolboy, Jae An, won the qualifying competition to ensure a place in the 144-strong field, becoming the youngest player ever to qualify for a national open. He made the cut, only two shots behind Tiger Woods.

Africa

Most of Africa is a golfing void: the terrain alone sees to that. Beyond a sprinkling of courses in countries bordering the Mediterranean, such as Morocco (with its royal jewel at Rabat) and Tunisia, golf in Africa has thrived where the British influence was at one time strong – in Kenya, Zimbabwe and, above all, in South Africa. The outstanding performances of South African golfers over the last 50 years bears witness enough to the quality of golf in their homeland and the attractive and testing courses on which they can hone their game. South Africa ranks about eighth in the world in the number of its golfers, but is amongst the van in their quality, with men like Bobby Locke, Gary Player and Ernie Els. Within the boundaries of the Republic there are courses of all types, ranging from true linksland challenges on the coastline of Natal to the many high veldt courses (there are at least 80 within a 60-mile radius of Johannesburg) where, in the thin air, the ball flies like a space shot and every man is a superman when he drives from the tee. Golf travelled to Africa by troopship in the confused and unhappy decades before the Boer Wars. A six-hole course was laid out by a Scottish regiment near Cape Town in 1832 and the Cape Golf Club, the senior in South Africa, was born a few years later with a Scottish general as the midwife. Scotsmen, both professional and amateur, were in almost total charge of South African golf trophies for 30 years. Conditions in those early days were far removed from those of Scotland. Greens were more often than not compacted sand, and grass was a luxury only a few clubs could boast. Modern strains of grass and year-round automatic watering systems have long since overcome the drawbacks of an unreliable rainy season and, with courses of the calibre of Durban Country Club on the Indian Ocean coast and Royal Johannesburg, thousands of feet up in the Transvaal, South Africa can now lay claim to some of the most challenging layouts in the world.

1. Royal Rabat 2. Royal Johannesburg 3. Durban Country Club

The thrill of
anticipation
and uncertainty

The Course Card

Durban Country Club, Natal

Record: 62, John Bland

Hole	Yards	Par
1	391	4
2	188	3
3	512	5
4	180	3
5	459	4
6	352	4
7	372	4
8	502	5
9	434	4
10	560	5
11	480	4
12	156	3
13	339	4
14	527	5
15	195	3
16	417	4
17	401	4
18	274	4
Out	3,390	36
In	3,349	36
Total	**6,739**	**72**

Since the time it was first shaped from the bush and dunes of the KwaZulu-Natal coast during the early years of the 1920s, the Durban Country Club course has achieved and maintained an excellence that keeps it at the forefront of South Africa's 250-odd courses.

The decision to build it grew largely from the misfortunes of the old Royal Durban Golf Club, which was host to the 1919 national championships: the course became so water-logged that the winner took 320 squelching strokes to finish. There was no guarantee that the low-lying course would not flood again and so Durban, one of the great cities of South Africa, was in danger of losing its place on the national tournament circuit.

There was already a need for a new course at Durban and pressure mounted after the 1919 debacle. A site was found and in 1920 the appropriately named George Waterman and Laurie Waters, four times winner of the South African Open, began its design. The course was opened in 1922 and two years later Durban Country Club staged the first of its many South African Opens. Much of the history of the game in South Africa has been enacted there, and most of the great players have made their pilgrimage to it. Sid Brews, Bobby Locke and Gary Player have had some of their greatest moments at the Country Club – and others they will want to forget. In 1998 Ernie Els won his third South African Open there, opening with a 64 that left him in a position of dominance he was not to relinquish.

The course saw Gary Player's first South African Open success in 1956, with 286. He returned in 1969 (having won the title another five times in the intervening 13 years) to score 273, which included a then record round of 64 (the record now is 62, held by John Bland).

The Country Club is not long at 6,739 yards, and this was Arnold Palmer's only criticism of it after his first experience there in 1963: "It would", he said, back in the days when the smaller, British ball was still legal, "be a much better course with the big ball." Palmer, with 71, lost his encounter to Player that time by a stroke, after Player had been out in 34 and Palmer had returned 34 for the second half.

To see the Country Club course at its best, it must be experienced in all its moods – especially in the wind, which blows often and puts a green out of reach of two shots when it could have been hit with a 7-iron only a matter of hours before. Suddenly all the bunkers then begin to make sense. The course has been updated on occasions – by Bob Grimsdell in 1959, and before him by the English architect, Colonel S. V. Hotchkin, the creator of Woodhall Spa, whose suggestions were adopted in 1928. Several tees have been resited and some holes have been renumbered, but basically the Durban Country Club has remained unchanged since 1922.

From the outset there was very little interference with the natural terrain but rather an accentuating of some of the site's original features. Grimsdell said: "The player is not shown everything at a glance, but is given the thrill of anticipation and uncertainty."

There are two distinct features – the holes on the dunes where either tee or green is elevated and surrounded by the natural bush, and those on the flatland, where trees still help shape the fairways but where the chances of a hanging lie are minimal – typically at the 6th, 7th, 10th, 11th, 14th and 15th. They are no easier, but are not likely to cause so much apprehension.

The course's difficulties commence at the very first hole, where the golfer who flinches from the out-of-bounds on his right hand risks a hanging lie on the hump to his left. From it he can be out of sight of the green, set into a huge tree-covered dune. From the plateau green at the 1st there is a climb to the tee on the 2nd, where the shot is played from one ridge to another, over a deep, grassed hollow.

One of the largest memberships in the world enjoys the trials of the Durban Country Club course, automatic choice when the South African Open is held in Natal. At first sight it seems undemanding but many hazards are apparent only when the wind gusts off the ocean – across the sandhills which support the elevated tees and greens, and over the undulating fairways on the lowland part of the course.

The 18th at Durban Country Club, left, is driveable in favourable weather conditions. In winning the 1998 South African Open, Ernie Els equalled Player's 1969 score of 273 on a course which has remained entirely unaltered in the intervening years (1969 was the year Els was born!).

The 3rd is rated one of the best par-fives in the world, played from an elevated tee at the highest point of the course into a valley. The ground rises again through a series of mounds, reaching like fingers on to the valley floor, to a green in the shadow of a tree-covered dune. Two shots are possible, but getting home with the second depends on the perfect placement of the first – and an ability to shut out the hazards lurking in the bush on both sides.

At the short 4th the golfer is coming off the dunes on to flatland, with the green, surrounded by slopes and mounds, looking deceptively small from the elevated tee. The 5th, 6th and 7th take the corner on the flat, taxing neither the golfer's endurance nor his talents to any great extent, provided he is placing his shots well from the tee.

The 8th journeys back alongside the 3rd, playing in the opposite direction and with the high ground now causing more than a little concern: a three-wood might not get the distance nor the height to hold the conical green, which is only partly visible. On the same level, the 9th tee looks down at a broad expanse of fairway – the green is somewhere to the right, out of sight. But for a time the pressure lifts.

The 10th and 11th are again on the flat, and length is the greatest prerequisite. There is a climb to the short 12th and the biggest concern again is to hold the green, as it is a long way back up the dune in the event of failure. Here Edward, Prince of Wales cut a ball down the bank and legend has it that he took 16 shots before he finally holed out.

Still on the parkland, the 13th tee is elevated – a pitch with the wedge for most players. A big second is required at the 14th and the 15th demands another mid-iron. None of the three is a really memorable hole. Now the player is back in the dunes, close to the sea. The 16th is a dog-leg to the right where danger lurks on the right of the fairway along which runs a road bordered by dense bush. The 17th is a spectacular hole requiring a carefully placed drive to the rim of the valley on the right, for otherwise there is no sight of the green from the bottom of a deep basin in the fairway.

One can drive the 274-yard 18th in favourable weather. Whatever the conditions, the severe temptation to hit beyond one's capacity is always there and this makes it a fine finishing hole, demanding accuracy even from the faint-hearted. The way into the green is left, but a big pull finishes below the level of the fairway; a quick hook is dead in dense bush and a slice is invariably headed down a steep bank to the practice area below. Durban's 18th is amongst the shortest finishing holes anywhere in championship golf, but this in no way makes it easy to play.

The South African Open returned to Durban in 2002, an event co-sanctioned between the European Tour and South African Sunshine Tour. With so many star players automatically in the field, local boy Tim Clark had to pre-qualify. He did, and won the tournament with a fine closing 65.

The joy of golf on
the high Veldt

The Course Card

Royal Johannesburg Golf Club, Transvaal East course

Hole	Yards	Par
1	517	5
2	249	3
3	457	4
4	486	4
5	159	3
6	580	5
7	420	4
8	535	5
9	400	4
10	513	4
11	511	4
12	203	3
13	393	4
14	435	4
15	218	3
16	490	4
17	387	4
18	512	5
Out	3,803	37
In	3,662	35
Total	**7,465**	**72**

To most golfers any mention of South Africa brings to mind Gary Player and Ernie Els, who have borne their country's standard in almost every land where the game is played. Since Player emerged as a player of outstanding skill in the late 1950s they have together preserved the name of South Africa as a nation capable of producing golfers of world class.

Compared with the United States, Britain and Australia, the most powerful golfing nations, South Africa is small, but the fact that so many good players have emerged is a measure of their quality of the golf courses. In common with most countries the gospel of golf reached South Africa in the closing years of the last century, and as usual the missionaries were Scotsmen. The first appearance of the game, in an organised fashion was on a six hole course, laid out by the Royal Scots Regiment on rough and stony ground at Wynberg in 1882. Thereafter golf spread in fairly swift succession to the principal cities, but the South African Golf Union was not formed until 1910.

Johannesburg was only a mining camp when the first course was laid in 1890. It was rough and windswept, enthusiasm soon waned, and within the next few years the course was moved several times. This was not as great a problem as might be imagined; the ground was cleared for fairways, leaving all the natural hazards, of which rocks were a feature, and a tin was sunk wherever a hole was required; the sand greens followed later.

Meanwhile Johannesburg was expanding so swiftly that not until 1906 was the club able to find land free from the covetous reach of builders. Money was advanced by Sir George Farrar and Sir Abe Bailey for the purchase of a site, part of which is still in use. The construction of grass greens and tees, the first in Johannesburg, was a great step forward; a mule bus carried the members to and from the terminus of the trams into the city, and the

club settled to a generation of steady progress. As golf gained in popularity, and the membership increased, it was decided to have two courses, East and West. In 1933 more land was bought and construction began under the guidance of Bob Grimsdell, a golf architect of rare skill. There were many problems, not least ridding the ground of the coarse kikuyu grass which threatened the fairways and greens.

The East was recognised as the more difficult, but a gradual improvement in scoring, notably by Harold Henning in the Transvaal Open in 1955, prompted changes. These included the reshaping of fairways; the creation of new tees on many holes so that fairway bunkers would threaten the long driver; and new bunkers and hollows tightening some of the approaches. Now the course was a true championship test; Gary Player ranks it as one of the very best.

The course wanders quietly over wooded parkland. After the great sweep of the 1st, and a long short hole to a green plentifully trapped on the fade side, one is soon aware that this is a driver's course. The fairway bunkering at times is tight at around 250 yards, but one shrewdly placed bunker on the right side of the 3rd fairway is enough to make the golfer think on the tee. The 4th, the first of seven holes that curve to the right, and the 8th are outstanding driving holes, demanding length and exact placing for approaches to tightly guarded greens.

The short holes are of a high quality and vary in their demands; the 5th is a pitch which must carry to a slightly raised green embraced by bunkers, and so must the long iron to the 12th – beautifully set against a backdrop of willows – because the entrance to the green is angled to the line of flight. The 15th is possibly the most testing, for the plateau green makes the distance hard to judge.

Length is not the only criterion in the difficulty of a hole, and the 13th is a fine example. It swings to the left and a

Needing big drives through a verdant valley, Royal Johannesburg's East course offers sheer golfing enjoyment tempered only by the abundant trees and strategic bunkers which narrow the fairways.

the tee. It can quicken fear in the mind of the golfer prone to hook because, as he stands on the 16th tee, he is aware that it follows the line of the hole too closely for comfort. Then at the last comes the challenging finish.

The design of the holes is not necessarily the greatest problem. The greens demand most careful reading because often the nap will more than counter the natural breaks of the ground. For a man to become a successful golfer in South Africa he must develop a firm putting stroke and a courageous attitude – and be a diligent observer of the greens.

good drive means only a pitch home, though the entrance is narrow between bunkers; a spinney on the right threatens the approach from that side, and a mishit to the left may be caught by a pool that cuts into the line. Of the par-fours only the 17th is shorter but the drive must carry a steep crest. Elsewhere the ground is gentle in its undulations, like the falling fairway of the splendid 11th hole. The drive must be placed as near as possible to a lone wattle tree, guarding the inside curve of the right-handed dog-leg, for the most favourable position from which to carry a stream in front of the green. The stream that winds its way across the northern part of the course also comes into play at the 7th, where it slants across the fairway and must be carried from

Regardless of whether the visitor to Royal Johannesburg can manage this, he is sure to agree that the East course has few peers as a challenging and beautiful place to play golf.

The par four 11th at Royal Johannesburg is the club's signature hole.

The 11th

Cole's Gamble Pays Off

The 11th, 511 yards long, is perhaps Royal Johannesburg's best hole. It is a gentle dog-leg to the right, with a long carry from the tee but without fairway bunkers to inhibit the drive. At a strategic distance in front of the green a stream crosses the fairway diagonally. Closer to the green the fairway narrows considerably and towards the bank on the left side is a solitary bunker. The hole demands placement as opposed to the length so often required on many of the other holes. Yet, curiously, one of the best shots ever made there was also the longest – Bobby Cole's second from the rough in the second round of the 1974 South African Open, which Cole started in fourth place.

Played by a lesser player it would have been a desperation shot, a careless gamble in pursuit of a cause already lost. It was undeniably adventurous but it was the only shot with which Cole could be sure of a four after his drive had leaked left into the rough. His approach to the green was blocked by the stream and by some willows, some 220 yards distant. Cole knew that to reach the green from there his approach would have to be long and high enough to clear them.

Using wood, he hit the perfect shot to make his four. He was on his way to a 65 and a new record total of 272.

Bravura Golf –
Close to the Casbah

The strong participating interest of King Hassan II and the need to attract tourists means that Morocco has over a dozen courses. By far the best is Royal Rabat a long and demanding layout by Robert Trent Jones in a superb setting near the capital.

As a broad generalisation, golf course architec-ture falls into two schools, the "natural" and the "artificial". Like most labels, these words, with their emotive overtones, must be heavily qualified in each individual case. The designer whose instinctive approach is to leave the landscape looking as nearly undisturbed as possible must compromise when he works with terrain which is alien to the golfing ideal. Compromise is always at the designer's elbow raising insuperable objections: "The client insists … the budget does not permit … the land does not allow … "

Compromise is the last word to be applied to the work of Robert Trent Jones, the founder of the "artificial" school of architecture. Jones shapes his landscape and does not undertake a commission unless he is guaranteed the batteries of earth-moving machinery, the train-loads of topsoil and the torrents of water needed to execute his bravura designs. His courses are stamped with a personality as distinctively as a signature. The vast tees, the sadistically moulded greens, the extravagantly shaped bunkers and torture by water are the flourishes by which his name is inscribed.

The specification for Royal Rabat exactly matched his style. It was to be a course fit for a king – Hassan II of Morocco, the most enthusiastic golfer among contemporary royals at the time. The championship layout, the Red course, was completed in 1971 and was the first of three courses at the club to come into play.

The drive to the clubhouse makes its way through the stands of cork oak from which Jones carved the course. and the visitor's first feeling of anticipation is tinged by a more guarded feeling, almost of trepidation; he will come to an intimate familiarity with the cork oak, with its drab, olive-green leaves, gnarled branches and trunks that are stripped annually of their outer layer of bark, leaving them smooth, pink and bare.

Between the trunks of these trees the visitor catches glimpses of brilliant green fairways and seemingly excessive blue expanses of water. The colours are exaggerated by the sombre tints of the cork oak foliage and the twinge of fear that has attacked the visitor is soon confirmed by the view from the first, and subsequent, tees. Trent Jones clearly has a high regard for the cork oak, since he spared far too many of them in cutting out his avenues of fairways.

Every golfing instinct screams for an iron – or at most a three-wood – off the tee, but the mathematical reality of the yardage demands that courage and driver be taken in both hands. What is more, the driving must be of high quality. The standard, unthinking boom straight down the middle may come to grief, for Jones slopes his fairways cunningly to deflect the ball towards his hungry bunkers. On nearly every hole the drive must be shaped, with draw or fade, if the ball is to finish in the prime position for an attack on the green.

Deception is the key to Jones's design and if he has failed to outwit the golfer with the demanding nature of the drive he has another trick in store for the approach. It looks fairly simple. His greens are invitingly large and will hold a well-struck shot. How can such targets be missed? To ask the question is to provide the answer, for any suspicion of complacency can send the ball away on a wayward course. But the cunning of the trick is that even if the ball finds the green it is by no means a formality to get down in two putts.

The two-putt zone on a Jones green is usually a small area and anything in the nature of an "outer" will need exceptional skill, or luck if the ball is to be caressed over those glassy undulations to within holing-out range.

And so it goes for eighteen tormenting holes. Some of them appear superficially to relax the challenge as the course moves into more open country, but it is an illusion. Artificial lakes are brought into play and, where they do not actually impinge on the target areas, their threatening proximity often induces the golfer to choose a "safe" line which turns out to be the road to some hazard from which his eye has been decoyed by the harmless water.

It is small wonder that the world's most skilled professionals have failed to master it. Although the Moroccan Open, a European Tour event, is frequently held there no-one has managed to better the 66 that Howard Clark shot in 1987. Swede Peter Hedblom, almost equalled Clark's feat, opening 68-67 in the 1996 Moroccan Open. The field subsequently closed on him, but he hung on to win by one shot. As on all Trent Jones courses, it is the easiest thing in the world to drop a stroke at every hole without the suspicion of a mishit. Without showing some dazzle, the player will fail.

For lesser players, even off the extreme forward tees, Rabat provides a humbling if unforgettable experience.

The 9th

A Drug to Make you Hook

Water is the most powerful hallucinatory drug known to golf. The sight of it anywhere near the target area causes an involuntary tightening of the grip, a slight acceleration of the normal speed of swing and, as often as not, a premature raising of the head in anxiety to see the ball pitch safely on dry land. Few holes in the world dispense this drug in such a powerful dosage as the 9th at Royal Rabat.

It is also one of the most picturesque holes to be found anywhere. The tee is set on the bank of a large lake with duck, geese and flamingos in noisy regatta. Far across the lake – some 189 yards, but seemingly farther since water deceives the eye – the island green assumes minute proportions. It is connected to the mainland by two hump-backed wooden bridges irresistibly reminiscent of a willow pattern plate. The golfer who is in serious action may be excused if he does not absorb the beauty of the scene.

Only a mid-iron for the tour professional, it can be a desperate business for the high handicap amateur. The urge to make certain of the carry often results in a forcing of the shot and consequently a hook. The ball may splash into the water left of the island or, more worryingly, pitch short on the upslope and roll back into the water. One contestant in the annual Moroccan Grand Prix, a professional with a notable tournament record, doggedly persevered with his idea of how the shot should be played and hit six balls into the lake before finally getting down in fourteen strokes.

Royal Rabat offers few more rewarding satisfactions then retracing one's footsteps across the wooden bridge with a three safely marked on the card – not that the golfer can afford to relax his concentration, for there are four more water holes still awaiting him.

The 9th hole may be Rabat's shortest but it is water all the way to an island green. Nothing but the most accurate iron will suffice.

There are, however, rewarding compensations for the eights and nines which blemish the scorecard, for this is golf at its most exotic. Where most clubs manage with a staff of a dozen, and often fewer, to maintain the course, here 500 men are kept busy grooming the fairways, raking the bunkers and cosseting the greens. Their labours have produced a herbaceous wonderland of flowering shrubs as a foil to the cork oak and eucalyptus background. Walter Hagen's famous advice of "Never hurry, never worry and always take time to smell the flowers" might have been coined for Rabat. Mimosa, Bougainvillaea,

fuchsia and orange blossom provide splashes of colour as dazzling as an impressionist's palette.

Geographically, the casbah seething with poverty and all manner of social deprivation is just down the road, but in every other sense it is a million miles away – another world, albeit still a Moroccan world. It would be a soulless golfer who could shrug off this juxtaposition with untroubled conscience, but in the narrow and unashamedly selfish context of golf, Royal Rabat represents an ideal which few inland courses can hope to achieve.

South America

South American golfers – players of the stature of Roberto de Vicenzo and Eduardo Romero – are better known to the world of golf than golf is in the continent where they learned their game. Of all the continents, South America has the slenderest golfing resources and most of them are concentrated in Argentina and Brazil. A scattering of courses have been built or are under construction in countries on the Caribbean shore like Venezuela, where Dick Wilson and Joe Lee laid out the taxing course at Lagunita Country Club as part of the sunlit circle of resort golf that now loops through the islands of the Spanish Main. But away from these areas, golf fades away almost to nothing. There is a handful of clubs in the Andean capital of Colombia (where the El Rincon course is a Trent Jones design), in Chile, Bolivia and in Peru where, high in the thin air of the Andes, the visiting golfer from less dramatic altitudes is likely to exhaust himself merely teeing up. Golf arrived by railway in South America; to be exact, by railways in the making. The English and Scottish engineers who went to Argentina and Brazil to lay down the tracks at the turn of the century also laid down the first golf courses, in the neighbourhood of Buenos Aires in Argentina and São Paulo in Brazil. Since that time the game has enjoyed steady rather than spectacular growth in popularity, although the facilities that there are – mostly for the better-off citizenry – possess outstanding qualities. The Jockey Club at Buenos Aires is a typical example. It has two courses dating from 1936, designed by the redoubtable Alister Mackenzie; the better known of the two, the Colorado (Red) course, was the venue for the World Cup in 1962 and 1970. It was fitting that, in the 1970 competition, the individual prize was won by Argentina's greatest golfing son, Roberto de Vicenzo, a man who had won his first Argentine Open in 1944 and gone on to add as much lustre to the game as any of its finest champions.

1. The Jockey Club
2. Lagunita

A superbly groomed

playground for the rich

Although, as its name suggests, the Jockey Club's main interest is racing – the racetrack (and polo fields) adjoin the golf courses – it hosted the World Cup in 1970 when only nineteen players finished under par after 72 holes on the Red Course.

The Course Card

Jockey Club, San Isidro Red course

Hole	Yards	Par
1	428	4
2	356	4
3	146	3
4	486	5
5	342	4
6	370	4
7	420	4
8	210	3
9	444	4
10	467	5
11	525	5
12	170	3
13	440	4
14	394	4
15	508	5
16	431	4
17	181	3
18	350	4
Out	3,202	35
In	3,466	37
Total	**6,668**	**72**

Golf is a sport for the well-to-do in Argentina and at the best known of its courses, the Jockey Club at Buenos Aires, it is merely an additional attraction to horse racing and polo. Its two courses at San Isidro are, however, none the worse for that; they were designed by Alister Mackenzie, whose imaginative flair has stamped the hallmark of greatness on golf courses worldwide.

The exclusive nature of golf in South America makes it hardly surprising that few golfers from the continent should have impressed themselves on the world stage but one who certainly did was Roberto de Vicenzo.

Vicenzo is a folk hero among the golfers of Argentina and something of a demi-god at the Jockey Club. When he first went to America at the age of twenty-four, he could not speak a word of English. He did not have to; his driver spoke for him. His length astounded even Sam Snead and Ben Hogan, and he achieved it without even bothering to tee the ball up. He simply dropped the ball to the ground, pushed it

with the clubhead of his driver on to a tuft of turf, and then smashed the ball into the atmosphere with a hook that was under complete control.

Born of poor parents, Vicenzo learned the game at a golf course in Buenos Aires – not the Jockey Club – where he caddied with his four brothers (who all became professionals), and turned professional at the age of 18. By the time he retired at the age of 52, he had won more than 140 tournaments, a record not even the evergreen Sam Snead has been able to approach. Among them have been more than 20 national championships won in 14 different countries, an unapproachable record.

The 1970 World Cup was staged at the Jockey Club. (Among his many other records, Vicenzo has played in more of these matches than any other man.) Now he won the individual title for the second time, winning by a stroke over Australia's young David Graham, and Argentina finished second, 10 strokes behind Australia. It was a fitting climax to

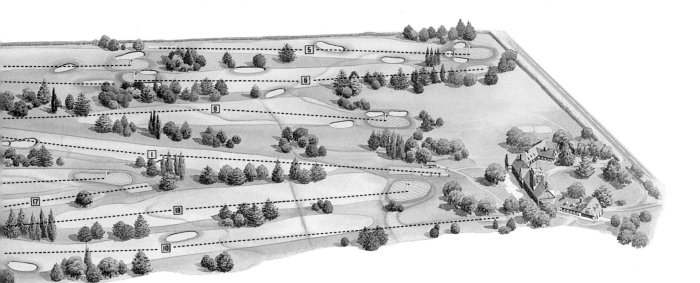

a career whose course was not yet run. In 1976, Vicenzo was invited to become an honorary member of the Royal and Ancient Golf Club of St Andrews.

The Red course of the Jockey Club, which was used for the 1970 World Cup, is not really suited for a game of Vicenzo's immense strength. At 6,668 yards, it has not nearly the length with which he can ordinarily overpower his opponents. Yet it is in superb condition all year round, for Buenos Aires has no harsh winters or summers – sitting as it does about as far south of the equator as Atlanta is north of it and, being a port, it lies practically at sea level.

The 1st hole shoots directly away from the rear of the stately, U-shaped clubhouse and belies what is yet to come. At 428 yards it is substantial by the standards of any opening hole. Starting at about 150 yards from the tee and running nearly to the green on both sides of the fairway is what the members refer to as a pared de pinos, or a wall of pines. Approximately 260 yards from the tee, on the left – very strategically placed for professionals – is a large, banked bunker. This must be avoided at all costs, for it is well-nigh impossible to reach the green from out of it. Thus, it is wise to favour the right-hand side of the fairway off the tee. There is still another reason for doing so. All the trouble about the green lies on the left-hand side. First comes a cross-bunker lying slightly short of the green to the left, making any successful recovery from the fairway bunker all the more improbable. And running the length of the long, green are two more thin bunkers, recovery from which is made more difficult by the undulating putting surface.

At 356 yards, the 2nd is more in keeping with the cunning of the course. A gigantic eucalyptus, not one hundred yards to the right of the tee, makes the hole half-blind. A cross-bunker lies to the left at the landing area and another lies to the right just short of the green – which is small, as it should be, for the hole calls for nothing more than a three wood and a wedge. The 3rd, a 146-yard par-three, is largely a matter of proper club selection. The green bends from right to left around a bunker. Another trap sits slightly short of the putting surface to the right, but this can easily be cleared. The one in the crook of the green must be avoided – and can be by using the proper club to carry the pin position.

At 486 yards, the 4th is short by the laws of any par-five, but the entire left side of the fairway is out of bounds. There are five bunkers on the hole, four of them scattered along the right-hand side of the fairway. The fifth protects the left side of the green. None of them presents a problem for three soft shots or two hard ones. This is the place for an early birdie. The 5th hole is one of those rare holes that only an architect of Mackenzie's imagination could bring off: a good, short par four. Only 342 yards long – a mere drive and a niblick or wedge – the hole must nevertheless be treated with respect. The entire left side is out of bounds and the tee shot must

carry a cross-bunker jutting into the fairway at the 220 yard mark. A sliced drive finds itself in another pared de pinos, ending with an ombú tree, a foliage typical of Argentina's pampas. The second shot, though short, must be precise, because the green is tightly guarded in front with three bunkers; the green is slickly undulated. The 6th, at 370 yards, lacks length and despite the small green is another promising birdie hole. The 7th is something else again, a full 420 yards and tightly bunkered off the tee. Two cross-bunkers intrude upon both sides of the fairway a good 230 yards off the tee and another lies to the right some forty yards beyond them. The green is large and has a pot bunker which bites into its left side. To the right lies a mound covered with shrubs and trees that can leave an all but unplayable lie.

The par-three 8th is most notable for its beauty and its length – 210 yards. The green is very deep, widening considerably at the rear. As it widens, two bunkers lie to the left and right, along the slants it takes. There is no birdie here.

Next comes the swing – the crucial 9th and 10th holes which can make or break a round. The first is a very long par-four, the second a short par-five. After the 10th green the course makes an abrupt turn to the left. The 11th is another par-five, but much more severe. For one thing, it is 50 yards longer than the 10th and, for another, it presents a much more severe dog-leg, this time to the left. Bunkers to the right and left of the green are the main problems once the bend in the fairway has been cleared.

The 12th, at 170 yards, is a one-shotter to a very wide green full of curves, and any shot not reasonably close to the cup makes three-putting a distinct reality. At 436 yards, the 13th hole is one of the longer and more demanding par-fours on the course. The fairway is narrow, as is the green. This, together with the fact that it rises sharply to the rear, makes it difficult to hit and hold. Two bunkers to the left and another to the right mean that the second shot is not only long but must be accurate. The 14th is a straight-forward par four just under 400 yards long. The 15th, a 508-yard par five, is much stiffer. Out of bounds lies along the entire left side of the hole and the right side is well bunkered. Three more traps flank the green. The 16th is an oddity in that it has only one bunker, lying right across the fairway, slightly beyond the 200-yard mark. The 17th presents a similar problem with its raised green and, although only 181 yards it is a tough par-three. In the final round of the 1997 Argentine Open, American Jim Furyk stood over a three-footer on the 18th green believing he would join Argentinian, Eduardo Romero, in a play-off if he sank his putt. What he did not know was that Romero and his partner, compatriot Vincente Fernandez, had forgotten to exchange cards. That unfortunate incident at Augusta in 1968 when Roberto de Vicenzo incorrectly signed his card came to mind. Reality was worse. Both Argentinians were disqualified, and Furyk found he had won by three strokes.

South America's
busiest course

There are a number of outstanding country clubs in the vicinity of Caracas, a sprawling oil-rich city of more than two and a half million people. The Caracas Country Club is one, for the Venezuelan upper crust; another is Valle Arriba, with a membership of American businessmen and foreign diplomats; and a third is the Lagunita Country Club, in the suburb of El Hatillo, and its membership is a combination of the other two, mainly Spanish-speaking but with a high percentage of English-speakers, too.

The Lagunita golf club is part of a real estate development which includes expensive housing and covers more than one and a half square miles. It was bought by a group of local businessmen in 1956. The club now has 1,100 members, of which 700 are active golfers with handicaps – a high number by South American standards. Although the club is strictly private it is, nevertheless, the "buzziest" golf course on that continent, according to Freddy Alcántara, an authority throughout the Americas both as player and official.

"Lagunita is not a very long course by British or American standards," Alcántara reckoned. "It is only 6,895 yards at its extreme back tees. But, despite this, it is a tough course and it is beautifully designed. It is a true and fair test for championship players. For example, there is not a blind shot on the entire course, so you always know where you are going. Furthermore, the greens are very big, slick and fast-breaking. I would say the lack of length in its par-fours is more than compensated by its par-threes. They are long and very difficult and there are five of them. Hence the total par of only 70. They are the key holes on the course."

Lagunita was designed by Dick Wilson during the latter part of his career and was for the most part constructed under the supervision of Joe Lee, then Wilson's assistant. It was completed in 1962.

Lagunita has been host to the Venezuela National Amateur Championship on a number of occasions, and fields of international amateurs have been assembled from time to time for the prestigious Simon Bolivar International Trophy founded by Alcántara. 1986 saw not only the world's top amateur men contest the Eisenhower Trophy (with Canada beating the USA into second place) but also the ladies of Spain triumph for the first time in the Espirito Santo Trophy. Lagunita can also claim to have brought the world's finest professionals to their knees: during the 1974 World Cup only three players – Bobby Cole of South Africa, Hale Irwin of the United States and Japan's "Jumbo" Osaki – managed to finish under par at the end of 72 holes, with South Africa the team winners and Cole taking the individual honours.

The course at Lagunita is dominated by a large, modernistic clubhouse complete with ballroom and mandatory swimming pool. From its position on a hill, five holes can be seen, together with the practice range. The course fans out both to the left and to the right of the clubhouse, bending back on itself at the 2nd and 3rd and again at the 13th and 14th.

The 1st hole starts away from the left of the clubhouse and is a bit of an oddity in that it is a par-five of 535 yards. Out of bounds lies along the left side – which is just as well, since the land has been turned into a quarry pit from which nobody could possibly play. The hole is a double dog-leg with two cross-bunkers at the 220-yard mark, after which the fairway bends left for an easy second if the player chooses not to go for the green. Few players do, for the green is completely cut off in front and on both sides by bunkers. The quarry is avoided by laying up and playing into the green from the second dog-leg. The 2nd is the first of those five treacherous par-threes. It is 205 yards to the large, deep green, and that quarry still lies on the left. In a delightful understatement, the course notes describe the 2nd as "dangerous". The most difficult thing about the 3rd hole is its length: it is 470 yards, the maximum for a par four hole. Again, out of bounds lurks ominously on the left.

The 4th is one of the most interesting par fours on the course. It is 455 yards and demands a good drive to get past a dog-leg that turns a complete ninety degrees and which cannot be cut because of three fairway bunkers and trees to the right. The green is shaped like a frying pan, with the handle protruding in front and guarded on either side by bunkers, with a flash trap to the rear. The 4th is not an easy par and no place to try to pick up a birdie.

The green of the 5th, a par-three of 190 yards, is beautifully bunkered all around and to the left is another gravel pit. The 6th and 7th holes, both shortish comparatively uninteresting par-fours, are followed by the longest par three on the course, the 220-yard 8th. It is the green which makes the hole, for it sharply inclines towards the approach and is well protected to the front and on both sides by bunkers. The prevailing wind at Lagunita blows across this hole from right to left. The 9th is a par-five of 590 yards, the last third of which is uphill. There are no fairway bunkers and the hole needs none. The second shot must be played around a slight dog-leg and requires something of a gargantuan effort to get anywhere near the green, which has two bunkers on either side. It is a truly fine par-five.

The 10th tee, which sits just below the clubhouse, takes a long iron to carry 210 yards across a dip in the

Lagunita is not particularly long by modern standards, yet only two of its par-fours measure less than 400 yards and three of its short holes are over 200 yards in length.

Below right: At Lagunita the natural defences of hilly ground and abundant trees are complemented by Dick Wilson's strategic bunkering.

ground to the green, which slopes severely towards the tee. The fairway of the 510-yard par-five 11th is very wide, but out of bounds runs the entire length of the right side. The green is very narrow, long and extremely fast. A cross-bunker sits just short of it for a lazy second shot and three more skirt the edges of the green. The 12th is one of the most treacherous holes on the course. A par-four, 445 yards long, it is a sharp dog-leg to the right with out of bounds all the way from tee to green. Three little bunkers and a copse at the angle of the dog-leg make cutting it unfeasible. There are no bunkers around the huge green, but it is protected in front by a lake which runs clear to the putting surface. The second shot must carry the lake all the way.

The 13th and 14th, both medium-length par-fours, are beautifully bunkered. At 435 yards, the 14th has plenty of length and no fewer than eight traps, three of them on the left side of the fairway in the landing area, where it bends slightly to the left. The ever-present out of bounds lies the complete length of the hole on the right. The elevated green is full of slopes and is practically encircled by five bunkers. The 15th – a favourite among the members – marches directly towards the clubhouse, as do the remaining holes. It is 425 yards, par-four and has three fairway bunkers to the left and close to the landing area. However, a gulley crosses the fairway and is played as a hazard. Out of bounds lies to the right of the fairway but can easily be avoided off the tee. A lateral water hazard, almost hidden, lies to the left of the green, which has but a single bunker directly in front of it. Also to the left of the green is another drainage ditch which is played as a hazard. All in all, it is a devious par four.

At only 170 yards, the 16th is the shortest hole on the course. However, the green is very large although fast and all but surrounded by bunkers. The 17th is short as par-fours go, only 390 yards, but it dog-legs to the right with two fairway bunkers lying short of the bend.

Three more, front, right and left, stand sentinel over every possible approach to the green. The 18th is a strong finishing hole, as it should be, 440 yards uphill to the clubhouse and against the prevailing wind. The fairway is wide, but bunkers lie on both sides of the landing area off the tee. The pear-shaped green is heavily bordered with rough and bunkers lie on both sides of its narrow entrance.

Lagunita, then, is a testing course and one that breeds a high degree of skill among those who play it regularly: the club is proud of the fact that over the years their membership has always included more than its fair share of scratch players.

Gazetteer

UK and Eire

1 Nairn
2 Gullane
3 Gleneagles
4 Prestwick
5 Royal St David's
6 Southport and Ainsdale
7 Little Aston
8 Formby
9 Saunton
10 Burnham and Berrow
11 Royal Cinque Ports
12 Berkshire
13 Hunstanton
14 Walton Heath
15 Wentworth
16 Royal Worlington and Newmarket
17 Royal West Norfolk
18 Woodhall Spa
19 Notts
20 Slaley Hall
21 Woburn
22 Lahinch
23 Killarney
24 Waterville
25 Tralee

Europe

26 Rungsted
27 Falkenstein
28 Frankfurter
29 Schloss Nippenburg
30 Palmerston Golf Resort
31 Golf de Saint-Nom-la-Bretèche
32 Seignosse
33 Barbaroux
34 Royal Mougins
35 Royal Haagsche
36 Royal Belgique
37 Royal Waterloo
38 Crans-sur-Sierre
39 Seefeld Wildmoos
40 Rome
41 Pevero
42 Biella
43 Glyfada
44 La Manga
45 Club de Campo
46 El Prat
47 Quinta do Lago
48 Penha Longa
49 Estoril
50 Penina

North and Central America

51 Bay Hill
52 Sahalee
53 TPC of Scottdale
54 Doral
55 Jupiter Hills
56 Ponte Vedra
57 Sea Island
58 Palmetto Dunes
59 Peachtree
60 Dunes
61 Wild Dunes
62 Country Club of North Carolina
63 Cascades
64 Quaker Ridge
65 Baltimore
66 Westchester
67 Concord
68 Canterbury
69 Scioto
70 NCR
71 Shoal Creek
72 Lakewood
73 Chicago
74 Butler National
75 Sentry World
76 The Honors
77 Hazeltine
78 Interlachen
79 Prairie Dunes
80 Oak Tree
81 Cherry Hills
82 Colonial
83 Castle Pines
84 Pasatiempo
85 Country Club
86 Spyglass Hill
87 Riviera
88 Poppy Hills
89 Edgewood
90 Mauna Kea
91 Princeville
92 Hamilton
93 St George's
94 Vancouver
95 Jasper
96 Vallescondido
97 Port Royal

South America and Caribbean

98 Lucaya
99 Divi Bahamas
100 Carambola
101 Cerromar
102 Tryall
103 Tobago
104 Club Lagos de Caujaral

Africa

105 Emirates
106 Karen
107 Houghton
108 Gary Player

Asia and Australasia

109 Kasugai
110 Nasu International
111 Yomiuri
112 Wack Wack
113 Navatanee
114 Delhi
115 New South Wales
116 Kingston Heath
117 Lake Karrinyup
118 Auckland
119 Christchurch

UK and Eire

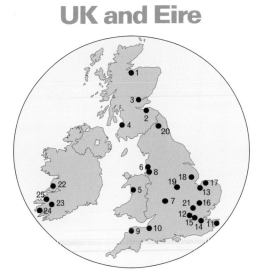

South America and Caribbean

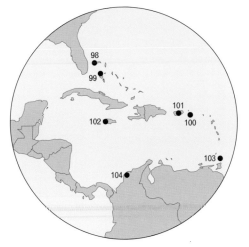

Europe

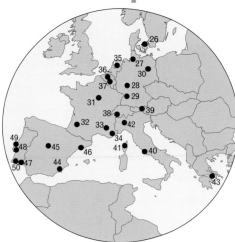

Africa

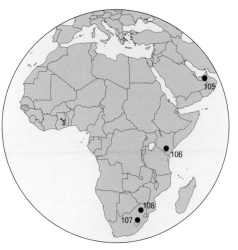

North and Central America

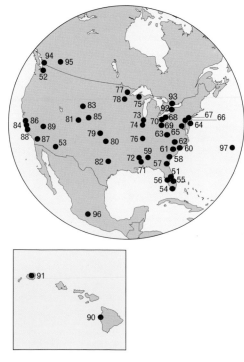

Asia and Australasia

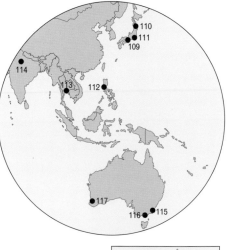

1 Nairn GC, Inverness

The Nairn course was originally laid out on natural linksland by Archie Simpson in 1887 and modified two years later by Old Tom Morris and James Braid. It features large, undulating greens and deep bunkers, with panoramic views across the entrance of the Moray Firth to the mountains of Caithness. The sea plays its own part in the hazards at Nairn, and nowhere more than at the 5th – called Nets after the salmon nets on the shore. The tee shot over the beach needs judgement – and a long carry of 175 to 200 yards – to set up the best line for an exacting second shot to a semi-plateau green that is protected by bunkers to the front and side. The hardest holes are the 12th to the 14th which make an excursion inland onto attractive heathland, and the 15th is deceptively treacherous. In 1899 it became the first Scottish club to make an admission charge for a golf match. A century later it witnessed a memorable home Walker Cup win.

Nairn Card of the course

Hole	Yards	Par			
1	395	4	10	536	5
2	486	5	11	160	3
3	396	4	12	444	4
4	144	3	13	431	4
5	385	4	14	219	3
6	183	3	15	306	4
7	550	5	16	425	4
8	355	4	17	377	4
9	359	4	18	554	5
Out	**3,253**	**36**	**In**	**3,452**	**36**
			Total	**6,705**	**72**

2 Gullane GC, East Lothian

Gullane No 1, the best of this small village's three fine courses, is often claimed to be the equal of nearby Muirfield. Certainly it has the same fine turf and true greens, plus the bonus of breathtaking views over the Firth of Forth to the hills of Fife. The 7th hole starts from the top of Gullane Hill, the course's highest point, and falls to the green 398 yards away. The back nine starts with a series of long, exacting holes. The 10th and 11th are both par-fours of 466 and 471 yards — and they are followed by a very short par-five of 480 yards set at cliff height, which is the lowest point on the course. Golf was played at Gullane from the start of the seventeenth century, and seven holes were laid down by 1844. Forty years later a full eighteen holes were in play, with two courses completed by 1900 and three by 1910

Record: 64, J. B. Carr, Open Qualifying 1959

Gullane No1 Card of the course

Hole	Yards	Par			
1	302	4	10	466	4
2	379	4	11	471	4
3	496	5	12	480	5
4	144	3	13	170	3
5	450	4	14	435	4
6	324	4	15	537	5
7	398	4	16	186	3
8	332	4	17	390	4
9	151	3	18	355	4
Out	**2,976**	**35**	**In**	**3,490**	**36**
			Total	**6,466**	**71**

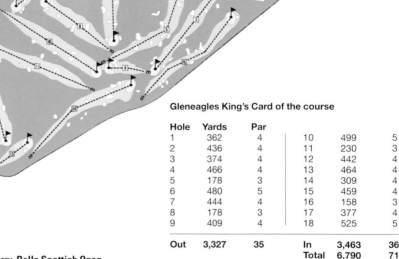

3 The Gleneagles Hotel, Perthshire

Designed by the legendary James Braid and Major C. K. Hutchinson, the King's course is one of four set on a sheltered moorland plateau. It is carved out of superb natural golfing country of rising hills splashed with purple heather and golden gorse, with sculptured bunkers that sparkle against tall stands of dark pine. The firm turf and immaculate greens combine to form a sequence of well-designed, memorable holes. The best is probably the 464-yard 13th, Braid's Brawest, where the fairway rolls narrowly away from the tee like an ocean swell between heather and bracken, demanding a long, straight drive to carry a ridge set with two deep bunkers. The PGA Centenary Course, designed by Jack Nicklaus, hosts the Scottish PGA Championship and is the chosen venue for the 2014 Ryder Cup.

Record: 60, Paul Curry, Bells Scottish Open

Gleneagles King's Card of the course

Hole	Yards	Par			
1	362	4	10	499	5
2	436	4	11	230	3
3	374	4	12	442	4
4	466	4	13	464	4
5	178	3	14	309	4
6	480	5	15	459	4
7	444	4	16	158	3
8	178	3	17	377	4
9	409	4	18	525	5
Out	**3,327**	**35**	**In**	**3,463**	**36**
			Total	**6,790**	**71**

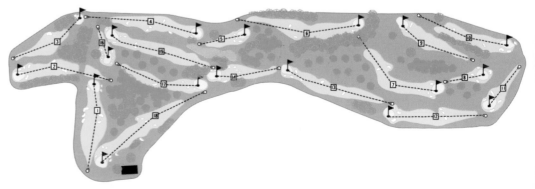

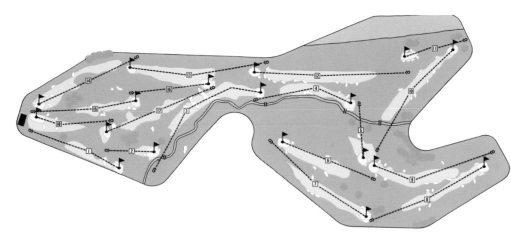

Prestwick Card of the course

Hole	Yards	Par			
1	346	4	10	454	4
2	167	3	11	195	3
3	482	5	12	513	5
4	382	4	13	460	4
5	206	3	14	362	4
6	362	4	15	347	4
7	430	4	16	288	4
8	431	4	17	391	4
9	444	4	18	284	4
Out	**3,250**	**35**	**In**	**3,294**	**36**
			Total	**6,544**	**71**

4 Prestwick GC, Ayrshire

Prestwick Golf Club was host to the first Open championship in 1860 and twenty-three more thereafter, the last in 1925. There is a fascination in tackling these fabled holes, many of them little changed since those early days; the ghosts of Young Tom Morris, Braid, Taylor and Vardon seem to stalk its narrow fairways still. The course lies on typical hard, humpy linksland, with deep bunkers, wild rough, a winding burn and many blind shots over sandhills to the tiny greens. The most famous hole is probably the 482-yard par-five 3rd, the Cardinal. Its main feature is a massive bunker set right on the dog-leg, which has to be carried in the face of a solid revetment of uncompromising railway sleepers.

5 Royal St David's GC, Harlech, Gwynedd

Overlooked by the magnificent Harlech Castle, on reclaimed land of links-like character that is separated from the sea by sandhills, the Royal St David's course is renowned for its beauty and its superb, large greens. The finishing stretch includes two of the finest holes, the 15th and 17th, both of similar length but requiring contrasting strategies. The 15th, with Mount Snowdon in the background, is bunkerless. The fairway is slightly dog-legged right, winds between sandhills and narrows towards a hollow just short of the green; it takes two good shots to get there against the prevailing wind. The 17th, usually downwind, needs extreme accuracy from the tee because of bunkers on the right of the narrow fairway and cross-bunkers that guard the green.

Record: 64, K. Stables, C. Platt

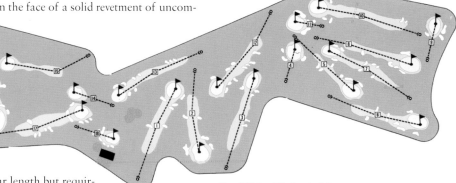

Royal St David's Card of the course

Hole	Yards	Par			
1	443	4	10	453	4
2	376	4	11	153	3
3	468	4	12	436	4
4	188	3	13	450	4
5	378	4	14	222	3
6	403	4	15	432	4
7	494	5	16	354	4
8	517	5	17	428	4
9	175	3	18	201	3
Out	**3,442**	**36**	**In**	**3,129**	**33**
			Total	**6,571**	**69**

6 Southport and Ainsdale GC, Merseyside

Embedded amongst the magnificent sandhills that reach down much of the South Lancashire coast are several courses of championship quality. The Southport and Ainsdale, or S & A links, is one of them. In 1906 there were nine rather undistinguished holes, but sixteen years later, with the help of James Braid, a tournament-class arena was built on a new site. Its challenging and demanding character is most apparent at the 16th, Gumbleys. This is a 510-yard par-five, almost invariably played into the prevailing wind and requiring a tee shot between tight fairway bunkers to avoid the out-of-bounds railway area on the right. The second shot must clear the towering sandhills, or else an enormous, sleeper-faced bunker. In 1933 Great Britain and Ireland won a rare Ryder Cup victory on this course and every time the Open is at Birkdale it is used as a qualifying course.

Record: 62, Chris Moody, 1991

Southport and Ainsdale Card of the course

Hole	Yards	Par
1	200	3
2	520	5
3	418	4
4	316	4
5	447	4
6	386	4
7	480	5
8	157	3
9	482	5
Out	**3,406**	**37**
10	160	3
11	447	4
12	401	4
13	154	3
14	383	4
15	353	4
16	510	5
17	443	4
18	355	4
In	**3,206**	**35**
Total	**6,612**	**72**

7 Little Aston GC, Birmingham

As a true parkland course, set in splendid isolation within a few miles of the centre of Birmingham, Little Aston offers more room for error from the tee than most courses of championship standard. This does not mean it presents a lesser test of golf, for the course demands accuracy of iron play to achieve anything like a good score. The holes were laid out in 1908 by Harry Vardon, who made full use of the excellent subsoil of sand and gravel. Three fine two-shotters, the 6th, 7th and 8th, zig-zag through the course, providing a challenging run to even the most accomplished of golfers. The 362-yard 7th is a classic short par four where both fairway traps and severe bunkering in front of the green must be avoided. The Dunlop Masters was held there five times, with such celebrated winners as Harry Weetman in 1953 and Bernard Hunt in 1963.

Little Aston Card of the course

Hole	Yards	Par	Hole	Yards	Par
1	388	4	10	438	4
2	435	4	11	394	4
3	503	5	12	487	5
4	317	4	13	160	3
5	158	3	14	320	4
6	423	4	15	548	5
7	362	4	16	400	4
8	391	4	17	366	4
9	193	3	18	387	4
Out	**3,170**	**35**	**In**	**3,500**	**37**
			Total	**6,670**	**72**

8 Formby GC, Merseyside

When golf started at Formby in 1884 the membership was limited to twenty-five, who paid one guinea a year for the privilege of playing nine completely natural holes. The site remains basically unchanged apart from the addition of nine more holes, a fine, sandy stretch between railway and sea and it was the sea that forced changes in 1978 to the 8th, 9th and 10th holes. The first hole is typical of the course: the drive is menaced by an out-of-bounds railway on the right and the second shot requires extreme accuracy to find a flat, well-bunkered green. It was here that Sam Snead won his second World Senior title in 1965 by beating Charley Ward at the 37th hole. Formby has three times played host to the Amateur Championship, with Reid Jack and American Bob Dickson taking the honours in 1957 and 1967. In 1984 Jose-Maria Olazabal won a memorable final against Colin Montgomerie.

Record: 68, D. J. Russell

Formby GC Card of the course

Hole	Yards	Par
1	435	4
2	403	4
3	538	5
4	312	4
5	183	3
6	428	4
7	388	4
8	493	5
9	450	4
Out	**3,630**	**37**
10	215	3
11	422	4
12	421	4
13	431	4
14	431	4
15	403	4
16	127	3
17	494	5
18	419	4
In	**3,363**	**35**
Total	**6,993**	**72**

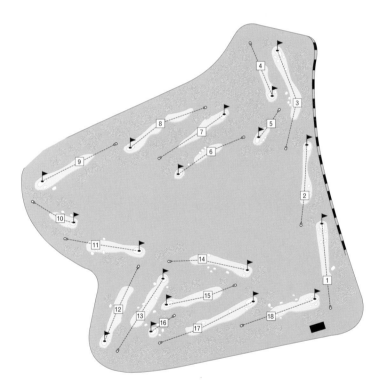

9 Saunton GC, North Devon

As early as 1893 a nine-hole course existed in the fields of Braunton Burrows near Saunton, and in the 1920s it was developed into an 18-hole links by Herbert Fowler. Built amongst the sandhills, scrubland and rushes, the course was closed in 1939; however, with the help of C. K. Cotton it was reopened in 1950 with new 1st, 17th and 18th holes. The start is severe – there is only one par-three in the first twelve holes – but the toughest hole at Saunton is the 16th. This 434-yard par-four requires the drive to carry a high sandhill and draw to the left, following the dog-leg. The long second is hit over a deep bunker into an elevated green wedged between sandhills, which disguise a subtle slope to the right.

Record: 65, M. Treleaven, D. Park, G. Ogilvy

Saunton East Course Card of the course

Hole	Yards	Par
1	478	4
2	476	5
8	402	4
4	441	4
5	122	3
6	370	4
7	428	4
8	380	4
9	392	4
Out	**3,489**	**36**
10	337	4
11	362	4
12	414	4
13	145	3
14	455	4
15	478	5
16	434	4
17	207	3
18	408	4
In	**3,240**	**35**
Total	**6,729**	**71**

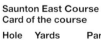

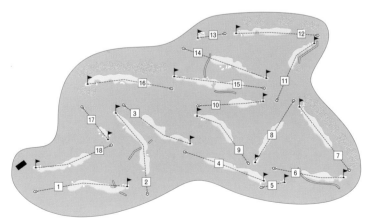

10 Burnham and Berrow GC, Burnham-on-Sea

This is traditional links golf at its best – over and through the massive sandhills which skirt the north Somerset coast, with views of the Bristol Channel and the distant Glamorgan shore. Golf started here in 1891, and significant changes have been made over the intervening years to eliminate many of the blind shots that abounded at the turn of the century. Changes are still being made today. The finishing stretch of four holes is truly exacting with the 15th, a 440-yard par-four, followed by a short par-four, which demands a fine pitch shot when approaching the small raised green. The 200-yard 17th usually needs a wooden club and at the final hole trouble awaits the misplaced drive in the shape of sandy hills; an errant second shot usually finishes in a deep bunker.

Burnham and Berrow Card of the course

Hole	Yards	Par		Hole	Yards	Par
1	380	4		10	375	4
2	421	4		11	438	4
3	376	4		12	401	4
4	511	5		13	530	5
5	158	3		14	192	3
6	434	4		15	440	4
7	450	4		16	344	4
8	494	5		17	200	3
9	170	3		18	445	4
Out	**3,394**	**36**		**In**	**3,365**	**35**
				Total	**6,759**	**71**

11 Royal Cinque Ports GC, Deal

This superb natural links, one of the most challenging courses in Britain, opened in 1895. It has heavily bunkered fairways and well-protected greens. The only major alteration to the original layout occurred in 1938–9, when the direction of the 4th hole was reversed. Minor changes were also made to the 5th, 9th and 14th holes. But the 16th, a 508-yard par-five, is considered to be the best hole. The drive is uphill, requiring a carry of 150 yards to clear strategically placed fairway bunkers. An accurate approach shot must then be struck to pass through a channelled entrance on to the well-elevated green. The course was the setting for two early Open Championships; J. H. Taylor won his fourth Open victory there in 1909 and, in 1920, George Duncan carried off the title by two strokes.

Record: 63, Gordon Manson, 1981

Royal Cinque Ports Card of the course

Hole	Yards	Par		Hole	Yards	Par
1	357	4		10	364	4
2	399	4		11	401	4
3	489	5		12	440	4
4	150	3		13	423	4
5	501	5		14	223	3
6	314	4		15	447	4
7	381	4		16	508	5
8	166	3		17	371	4
9	410	4		18	410	4
Out	**3,167**	**36**		**In**	**3,587**	**36**
				Total	**6,754**	**72**

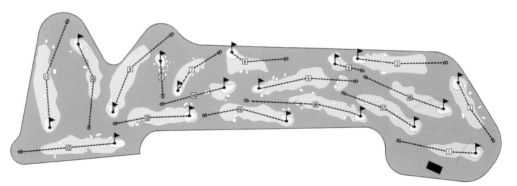

12 Berkshire GC, Ascot

In 1928 Herbert Fowler built thirty-six splendid holes for the Berkshire club, in the heart of rural England. The Red and Blue courses wind over rolling heathland and through quiet woods of pine, silver birch and chestnut. The Red is unusual in that its 18 holes are comprised of six par-fives, six par-fours, and six par-threes; of the short holes, the finest is the 221 yard 16th, where the outstanding plateau green can only be reached and held with a tightly controlled shot to its centre. Equally uncompromising is the 10th, all-or-nothing across a valley. The 8th is the most difficult of the longer holes. The drive must be faced around the pines to leave the way clear for the second over a shallow valley on to the green.

Berkshire Red Course Card of the course

Hole	Yards	Par		Hole	Yards	Par
1	517	5		10	188	3
2	147	3		11	350	4
3	480	5		12	328	4
4	395	4		13	486	5
5	178	3		14	434	4
6	360	4		15	477	5
7	195	3		16	221	3
8	428	4		17	532	5
9	488	5		18	175	3
Out	**3,188**	**36**		**In**	**3,191**	**36**
				Total	**6,379**	**72**

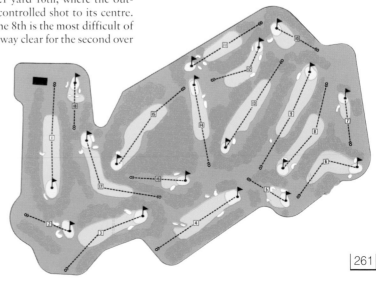

13 Hunstanton GC, Norfolk

This is an excellent example of open seaside golf, especially when played in the brisk winds common to this northern Norfolk coast. The course, laid out over gentle undulating linksland was first played in 1892. Improvements over the next fifty years, mainly under the guidance of James Braid and James Sherlock, brought it up to championship standard. The front nine includes a fine short hole – the 7th – where the ball is driven from a raised tee, 166 yards over a deep hollow to a small, exposed plateau green guarded by an enormous forward bunker. On the back nine, sandhills cradle the fairways and punish any mis-hit stroke. The 13th, a 387-yard par-four, is a testing hole where the dog-leg to the left must be conquered by two long shots – the first from the tee and the second to carry some very rough country to an island target. The 16th needs a dropping shot over a large diagonal sandtrap invitingly positioned just short of the green. On May 31, 1974, and on the following two consecutive days, this hole was aced three times by a Leicestershire player, R. J. Taylor.

Record: 65, Malcolm Gregson, Schweppes PGA championship 1967

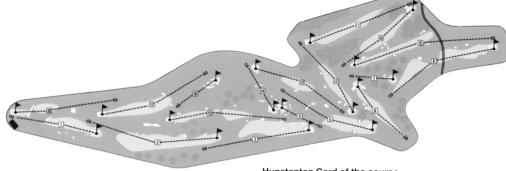

Hunstanton Card of the course

Hole	Yards	Par	Hole	Yards	Par
1	343	4	10	375	4
2	532	5	11	439	4
3	443	4	12	358	4
4	172	3	13	387	4
5	436	4	14	219	3
6	337	4	15	478	5
7	166	3	16	189	3
8	505	5	17	445	4
9	513	5	18	398	4
Out	**3,447**	**37**	**In**	**3,288**	**35**
			Total	**6,735**	**72**

14 Walton Heath GC, Tadworth

The Old Course was designed by Herbert Fowler in 1904, and his additional nine holes were later extended to become the New Course. Both resemble seaside courses in design and quality of turf, even though forty miles from the English Channel. The bunkers are large and deep, while the greens are big and consistent in pace in all weathers. The short and gentle first hole of the Old course belies the trials which follow, and the finish from the 14th is daunting. The 16th, a 510-yard par-five, is critical, needing a long drive down a narrow heather-lined fairway and then a full-blooded shot to a green that is cut into a left-to-right slope, with a large bunker eating into the right-hand edge. It is played as a long par-4 by the professionals. Walton Heath was the venue of the 1981 Ryder Cup when arguably the strongest American side of all time demolished the Europeans. A composite course taken from the Old and New is used for such events.

Walton Heath Old Course Card of the course

Hole	Yards	Par
1	235	3
2	458	4
3	289	4
4	441	4
5	437	4
6	440	4
7	183	3
8	494	5
9	400	4
Out	**3,377**	**35**
10	417	4
11	198	3
12	396	4
13	529	5
14	569	5
15	426	4
16	510	5
17	193	3
18	404	4
In	**3,642**	**37**
Total	**7,019**	**72**

15 Wentworth GC, Virginia Water

Rolling woodland and sandy subsoil create great golf courses and Wentworth, in Surrey's exclusive Virginia Water area, is an outstanding example. Designed by H. S. Colt, the East course, a delightful layout, opened in the early 1920s and was followed soon after by the West, the championship course. Playing the West requires a combination of length and accurate placement of the tee. Twice a year it stages events on the European Tour: in the Spring it is the Volvo PGA Championship; in the Autumn it dons its colours of browns and golds to form a wonderful backdrop to the World Matchplay Championship. The 17th is one of the great bunkerless holes, needing considerable accuracy from the tee.

Wentworth West Course Card of the course

Hole	Yards	Par	Hole	Yards	Par
1	473	5	10	184	3
2	154	3	11	403	4
3	447	4	12	509	5
4	497	5	13	442	4
5	191	3	14	179	3
6	354	4	15	481	4
7	396	4	16	383	4
8	400	4	17	571	5
9	452	4	18	531	5
Out	**3,364**	**36**	**In**	**3,683**	**37**
			Total	**7,047**	**73**

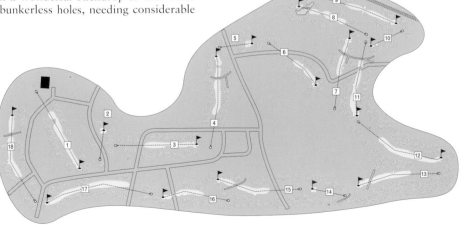

16 Royal Worlington and Newmarket, Suffolk

Acclaimed as the best and most distinguished nine hole course in the country, this inland gem was constructed in 1890 under the guidance of Captain A. M. Ross, a local golfer, on a base of light sandy soil. This has enhanced the quality of the turf and led to true and unusually fast greens. The 5th is a stunning, bunkerless short hole which can be played with anything from a five to a nine iron, and where the overlong shot is punished by the trees behind the green. The 7th is another fine par three, with a classic saucer green leaving only the top of the pin visible from the tee. In 1907 J. F. Ireland achieved the rare double of an ace at both the 5th and the 7th in the same round.

Record: 28, J. A. Floyd, 1949

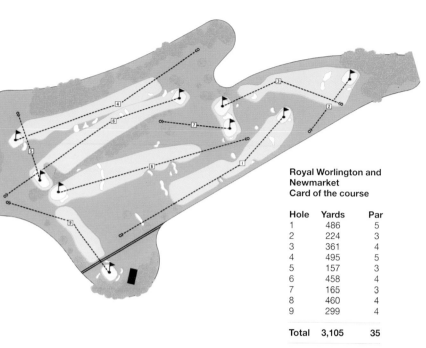

Royal Worlington and Newmarket Card of the course

Hole	Yards	Par
1	486	5
2	224	3
3	361	4
4	495	5
5	157	3
6	458	4
7	165	3
8	460	4
9	299	4
Total	**3,105**	**35**

Royal West Norfolk Card of the course

Hole	Yards	Par			
1	413	4	10	147	3
2	442	4	11	474	5
3	401	4	12	377	4
4	122	3	13	304	4
5	415	4	14	428	4
6	182	3	15	186	3
7	481	5	16	335	4
8	492	5	17	390	4
9	403	4	18	379	4
Out	**3,351**	**36**	**In**	**3,020**	**35**
			Total	**6,371**	**71**

17 Royal West Norfolk GC, Brancaster

The vast, sleeper-faced bunkers, unyielding greens and savage rough at this Brancaster course suggest all the elements of early links golf. A mixture of tidal marsh and undulating sand-dunes threaten the often windswept fairways and form a formidable array of hazards for the erring shot. Horace Hutchinson and Holcombe Ingleby laid down the course in 1891, and despite alterations to their design, by C. K. Hutchinson in 1928, its character remains little changed. The start is from an ancient rambling clubhouse out along the shoreline to its most easterly point, where the turn is taken. The 8th is on islands in the marsh; the harder and straighter the tee shot, the shorter and easier the second will be. At 492 yards, this par-five needs heroism and strength. The 9th is a fine right-hand dog-leg, a 403-yard par-four, again played over the marsh, but this time with the added hazard of a creek short of the green. The back nine is some 331 yards shorter than the outward half, but is generally played into a strong wind, which compensates for the lack of length.

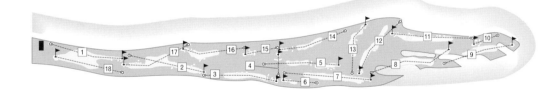

18 Woodhall Spa GC, Lincolnshire

Woodhall Spa is built on sandy soil and abounds in heather, silver birch and pine trees. It features some of the most formidable bunkers in the country, particularly those which guard the three short holes, the 5th, 8th and 12th. Against the wind, the 584-yard 9th is doubly severe, for the fairway is completely cut by a line of bunkers set 340 yards from the tee. Failure to clear this hazard, or playing short and safe, means that it is nearly impossible to reach the closely guarded green in three. Many championships have been held here, including the Brabazon Trophy and the ladies' home internationals, played between the countries of Great Britain and Ireland. The original Harry Vardon layout of 1905 was altered by H. S. Colt in 1912, and completely redesigned in the late 1920s by the owner, Colonel S. V. Hotchkin. It is now the home of the English Golf Union and a second course has been constructed on adjoining land.

Record: 67, G. Wolstenholme

Woodhall Spa Card of the course

Hole	Yards	Par			
1	361	4	10	338	4
2	442	4	11	437	4
3	415	4	12	172	3
4	414	4	13	451	4
5	148	3	14	521	5
6	526	5	15	321	4
7	470	4	16	395	4
8	209	3	17	336	4
9	584	5	18	540	5
Out	**3,569**	**36**	**In**	**3,511**	**36**
			Total	**7,080**	**73**

19 Notts GC, Hollinwell

The spacious and testing Notts course was designed by Willie Park Jr, with the bunkers added by J. H. Taylor. The typical heathland course, opened in 1900, winds among silver birch, oak, gorse and heather. At the difficult 8th, a 408-yard par-four, the drive is crucial, requiring a 200-yard carry across Hollinwell lake and through a funnel of trees. The 228-yard 13th is played from an elevated tee down into a valley to a heavily bunkered green. Notts has hosted many professional and amateur events over the years, including the first and only British staging of the European Mid-Amateur (in 2000), while the English Amateur returns in 2004.

Record: 64, J. Bland

20 De Vere Slaley Hall, Northumberland

Two courses, both over 7,000 yards in length and quite different in character, give Slaley Hall one of the most comprehensive golfing tests in the north of England. The surrounding scenery is uplifting with glorious views over the grouse moors of Northumberland and the rolling hills of Hadrian's Wall country. The Hunting Course is the one used for the Great North Open on the European Tour, played in June when the rhododendrons are a blaze of colour. With many holes plunging through woods, punctuated by lakes, ponds and streams it is no surprise to find it dubbed "The Augusta of the North". Dave Thomas's design uses the natural contours to great effect with a number of charming dog-legs such as the 2nd, 3rd, 8th and 16th. Top marks for beauty and difficulty go to the 9th, a sterling par-4 on which trees, rhododendrons and a stream call for great precision on a steeply rising hole on which power is also a requirement.

Slaley Hall Hunting Course Card of the Course

Hole	Yards	Par		Hole	Yards	Par
1	429	4		10	362	4
2	429	4		11	562	5
3	412	4		12	531	5
4	521	5		13	395	4
5	382	4		14	179	3
6	205	3		15	331	4
7	432	4		16	395	4
8	423	4		17	184	3
9	453	4		18	463	4
Out	**3,686**	**36**		**In**	**3,402**	**36**
				Total	**7,088**	**72**

21 Woburn Golf & Country Club, Milton Keynes

Set in glorious rolling woodland on the edge of the estate of the Dukes of Bedford, Woburn's three courses are among England's most beautiful. The Duke's and Duchess Courses hosted no fewer than 36 professional tournaments or championships between them over 25 years. Now the mantle of European Tour events has been taken on by the new Marquess Course, already hailed as a jewel, and lauded by the professionals as one of the finest courses they play all year. With almost every hole lined by tall trees, inaccurate driving is severely punished, although the hardest hole against par has turned out to be the short 14th, exposed to the wind and with a deceptively tricky green.

Woburn Marquess Course Card of the course

Hole	Yards	Par		Hole	Yards	Par
1	395	4		10	374	4
2	506	5		11	579	5
3	473	4		12	343	4
4	425	4		13	467	4
5	415	4		14	219	3
6	159	3		15	575	5
7	538	5		16	450	4
8	188	3		17	176	3
9	473	4		18	425	4
Out	**3,572**	**36**		**In**	**3,608**	**36**
				Total	**7,180**	**72**

Notts Card of the course

Hole	Yards	Par
1	376	4
2	428	4
3	547	5
4	454	4
5	189	3
6	582	5
7	398	4
8	408	4
9	178	3
Out	**3,560**	**36**
10	364	4
11	360	4
12	433	4
13	228	3
14	403	4
15	439	4
16	353	4
17	501	5
18	457	4
In	**3,538**	**36**
Total	**7,098**	**72**

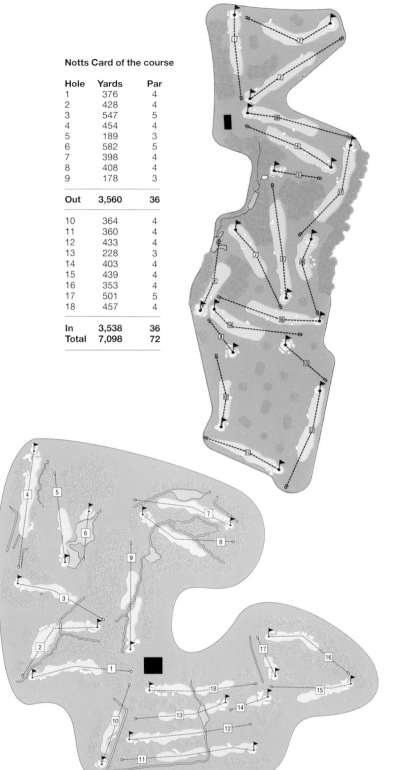

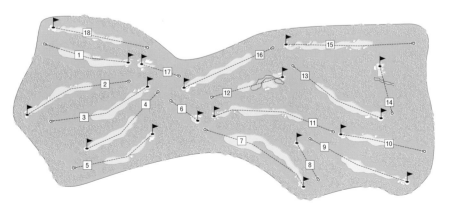

22 Lahinch GC, Country Clare

A barometer with hands hangs in the entrance to Lahinch Golf Club. Across its face is a message which reads "See goats" – for if they are in the lee of the clubhouse foul weather is on the way and barometric pressures are neither here nor there. Laid out in 1893 by Old Tom Morris and remodelled thirty-three years later by Alister Mackenzie, it is characterized by massive sandhills, views of the ocean and the dramatic Cliffs of Moher. Oddly, the most celebrated hole, the 155 yard 6th, The Dell, is probably the worst of a course that is stern yet essentially fair. From the tee the green is totally hidden and a mid-iron shot must be played over a hill. Judge the distance correctly and the ball is on the green in the hollow beyond; short or long and the next shot is from a precipitous bank. Club member John Burke was eight times Irish Amateur champion, an Irish international from 1930 to 1949 and a member of the Walker Cup side in 1932.

Record: 67, Christy O'Connor, Irish Professional Championship 1961

Lahinch Card of the course

Hole	Yards	Par			
1	385	4	10	451	4
2	512	5	11	138	3
3	151	3	12	475	4
4	428	4	13	274	4
5	483	5	14	488	5
6	156	3	15	462	4
7	399	4	16	195	3
8	350	4	17	438	4
9	384	4	18	533	5
Out	**3,248**	**36**	**In**	**3,454**	**36**
			Total	**6,702**	**72**

Killarney Card of the course (Mahony's Point – 'round' holes)

Hole	Yards	Par			
1	373	4	10	376	4
2	442	4	11	466	4
3	472	4	12	235	3
4	154	3	13	476	5
5	490	5	14	376	4
6	394	4	15	293	4
7	185	3	16	501	5
8	582	5	17	408	4
9	324	4	18	196	3
Out	**3,416**	**36**	**In**	**3,327**	**36**
			Total	**6,743**	**72**

Killarney Card of the course (Killeen – 'square' holes)

Hole	Yards	Par			
1	380	4	10	170	3
2	380	4	11	509	5
3	196	3	12	475	4
4	414	4	13	442	4
5	470	4	14	386	4
6	201	3	15	421	4
7	488	5	16	520	5
8	414	4	17	387	4
9	382	4	18	450	4
Out	**3,325**	**35**	**In**	**3,760**	**37**
			Total	**7,085**	**72**

23 Killarney Golf and Fishing Club, County Kerry

Golf is played in few surroundings more romantic than Killarney's lakes and mountains, and it has been played here since 1891 on part of the vast estate of the Earl of Kenmare. In the 1930s Lord Castlerosse, London socialite and heir to the estate, invited Sir Guy Campbell to lay out a new 18-hole course, assisted by his journalist friend Henry Longhurst. That course opened in 1939, but over the next four years Castlerosse altered eight holes and built five new ones, turning a good course into a great one. When the Irish Tourist Board funded an expansion in the late 1960s the original course was divided up between the resulting new courses, Mahony's Point and Killeen, Castlerosse's gems now becoming the 3rd and 13th of Killeen, and 13th of Mahony's Point. Campbell's stunning finishing trio now close Mahony's Point. The Irish Open was held over the Killeen Course in 1991 and 1992, Nick Faldo running away with the former, but having to birdie the 18th in 1992 to force a play off with South African Wayne Westner, Faldo only triumphing on the 4th extra hole. Henry Longhurst summed up Killarney perfectly, "What a lovely place to die!"

Waterville card of the course

Hole	Yards	Par
1	430	4
2	469	4
3	417	4
4	179	3
5	595	5
6	387	4
7	178	3
8	435	4
9	445	4
Out	**3,535**	**35**
10	475	4
11	506	5
12	200	3
13	518	5
14	456	4
15	407	4
16	350	4
17	196	3
18	582	5
In	**3,690**	**37**
Total	**7,225**	**72**

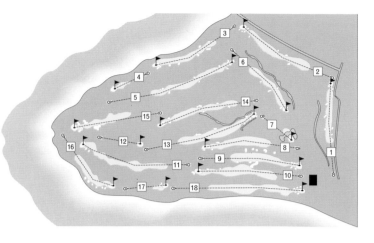

24 Waterville House & Golf Links, County Kerry

Golf had been played at Waterville as long ago as 1889, but when the Irish-born New Yorker, John Mulcahy, came to Waterville in the early 1970s the old links lay fallow. He recognised the potential of the site and enlisted the gentle Irishman Eddie Hackett to help him lay out the course of his dreams. Hackett revamped the original nine holes to form the current front nine, adding a second nine through some of the finest linksland imaginable. With stunning views to sea over Ballinskelligs Bay and inland to the mountains of the Ring of Kerry, Waterville is outstandingly beautiful. It is also a great test of golf, and Els, O'Meara, Stewart, Woods and Duval are among the world stars who have come here to sharpen up their game before the Open Championship. Gary Player described the bunkerless 11th as 'the most beautiful and satisfying par 5 of them all.' Waterville's tour professional of the 70s and 80s, the long-hitting Liam Higgins, once aced the par-4 16th with a prodigious drive straight over the sandhills, necessitating a carry of some 270 yards. This, of course, was in an era before today's more powerful clubs and balls.

25 Tralee Golf Club, Co Kerry

As a golf club, Tralee goes back to 1896, but its present links course dates from 1980, when Arnold Palmer was brought in to lay it out. "I designed the first nine, but surely God designed the back nine," said Palmer. "I have never come across a piece of land so ideally suited for the building of a golf course." The course tumbles over and between mountainous dunes, it hugs the rocky shoreline, and in a wind it is merciless, yet the surrounding mountain and ocean scenery is so magnificent that no golfer, however savagely treated by the course, could bear the slightest malice towards it. Going out, the 2nd and 3rd, along the clifftops, are a slicer's nightmare, and the 7th and 8th punish the hook equally severely. There are several dramatic carries on the back nine, with both par 3s requiring all-or-nothing shots, and an extraordinary catalogue of misfortunes awaiting almost any drive which misses the fairway.

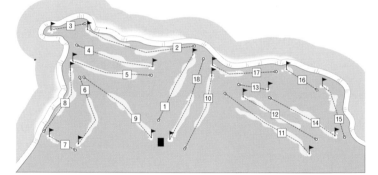

Tralee Card of the Course

Hole	Yards	Par		Hole	Yards	Par
1	402	4		10	427	4
2	594	5		11	570	5
3	194	3		12	444	4
4	425	4		13	158	3
5	428	4		14	400	4
6	416	4		15	303	4
7	154	3		16	196	3
8	382	4		17	351	4
9	493	5		18	462	4
Out	**3,488**	**36**		**In**	**3,311**	**35**
				Total	**6,799**	**71**

26 Rungsted GC, Rungsted Kyst

The scene of many Scandinavian championships, Rungsted is distinguished by the problems of hilly terrain with deep ravines and encroaching beech woods. The magnificent sweep of holes such as the 4th and 5th is uplifting, and the strategic problems of the dogleg 7th, 8th and 9th demand intelligent play. Work is in hand to strengthen the middle part of the back nine, building to a climax at the 17th. The drive here is threatened by out-of-bounds on the left and, as the ball loses height, it clears a belt of sheltering trees and may be caught by the prevailing westerly wind and carried into deep rough or the woods that lie on the right of the narrow fairway. Pinpoint accuracy from the tee is essential for any chance to attack the target with the second shot, which must negotiate trees short of the raised green. Ravines on either side await any ball that is slightly off the target, which is pear-shaped with possibilities for very difficult pin placings. Rungsted was designed by C. K. Mackenzie and opened in 1937. O. Bojensen made slight alterations to the course in 1969.
Record: 69, Olle Dahlgren, Johnnie Walker Cup 1973

Rungsted Card of the course

Hole	Yards	Par
1	435	4
2	379	4
3	174	3
4	453	4
5	387	4
6	181	3
7	406	4
8	389	4
9	373	4
Out	**3,177**	**34**
10	405	4
11	494	5
12	324	4
13	341	4
14	358	4
15	121	3
16	524	5
17	397	4
18	486	5
In	**3,450**	**38**
Total	**6,627**	**72**

27 Falkenstein Course, Hamburger GC

A fine natural course showing obvious signs of the game's Scottish origins, Falkenstein was laid out in 1930 by architects Alison and Morrison, on gently undulating ground with quick draining sandy subsoil which encourages the growth of heather, pines and silver birch. Alterations were made later by Dr Bernard von Limburger. The course features many well contrived dog-leg holes, with the sparing but intelligent use of sandtraps. The massive 2nd, just under 550 yards, swings to the left past a giant bunker and presents the handicap golfer with a difficult third shot to a green that is guarded by sand on both sides. The 17th, another par-five, is eighty yards shorter yet has vast areas of heather in front of the tee and crossing the fairway short of the green. It was at Falkenstein in 1981 that Bernhard Langer became the first home winner of the German Open in the tournament's 77-year history, setting up his victory with a stunning, third round 64, containing eight birdies.

Record: 63, Sam Torrance, 1981

Falkenstein Card of the course

Hole	Yards	Par
1	321	4
2	549	5
3	233	3
4	474	5
5	399	4
6	410	4
7	354	4
8	177	3
9	421	4
Out	**3,338**	**36**
10	171	3
11	438	4
12	400	4
13	363	4
14	348	4
15	155	3
16	329	4
17	478	5
18	366	4
In	**3,048**	**35**
Total	**6,386**	**71**

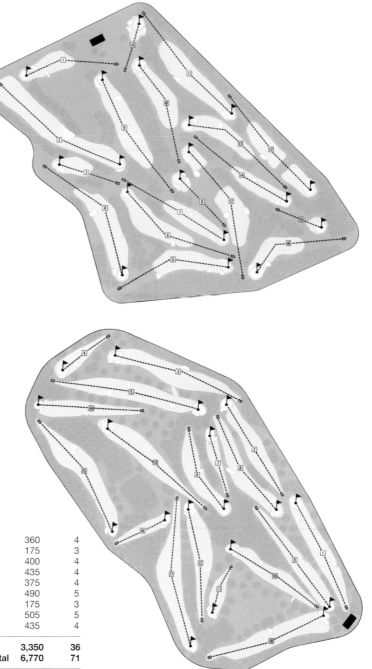

28 Frankfurter GC, Frankfurt

With a total length of just under 6,800 yards, the Frankfurter Golf Club is decidedly short by modern championship standards. The difficulty here is in overcoming the very large greens, which demand second shot accuracy to get near the pin. The course is essentially flat, but the fairways are carved through forest and the problems set by the trees add to the scoring difficulties. The best hole is probably the 7th, a 220-yard par-three that is flanked on the lip of the green by left and right bunkers; it requires a full-blooded tee shot into the heart of the target. Little has been done to the original H. S. Colt and John Morrison layout of 1928, and the course attracts a great international following because it is within easy reach of the city. The German Open has been held here on a number of occasions, including 1938, when Henry Cotton won the second of his hat-trick of victories.

Record: 63, Dale Hayes, German Open 1969

Frankfurter Card of the course

Hole	Yards	Par			
1	415	4	10	360	4
2	425	4	11	175	3
3	465	4	12	400	4
4	170	3	13	435	4
5	555	5	14	375	4
6	335	4	15	490	5
7	220	3	16	175	3
8	410	4	17	505	5
9	425	4	18	435	4
Out	**3,420**	**35**	**In**	**3,350**	**36**
			Total	**6,770**	**71**

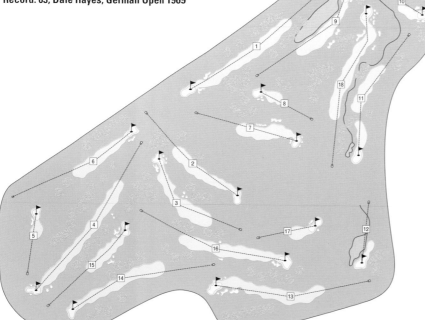

29 Schloss Nippenburg ETC

Schloss Nippenburg is Germany's first stadium golf course and has rightly won the title of PGA European Tour Course. Designed by Bernhard Langer, it was built upon derelict farmland and opened in June 1994. However it is not without its critics. After an amazing day of under-par scores at the 1996 Volvo German Open in which Paul Broadhurst hit a 62, Seve Ballesteros commented: "...it was no challenge".

Record: 62, Paul Broadhurst, German Open 1996

Schloss Nippenburg Card of the course

Hole	Yards	Par			
1	541	5	10	170	3
2	388	4	11	430	4
3	376	4	12	222	3
4	597	5	13	516	5
5	187	3	14	464	4
6	444	4	15	344	4
7	335	4	16	476	4
8	194	3	17	205	3
9	439	4	18	522	5
Out	**3,501**	**36**	**In**	**3,349**	**35**
			Total	**6,850**	**71**

30 Palmerston Golf Resort, Bad Saarow

Nick Faldo's entry into the profession of golf architecture has been no less impressive than his record in the majors. Having cut his teeth in the Far East and at Chart Hills in Kent he was commissioned to put his name to a course laid out on a windswept clearing in what was until recently golf-deprived East Germany. It resembles a lunar landscape, all humps and bumps and pot-bunkers, 130 of them. Quite intentionally it is very different from Arnold Palmer's woodland course at the same hotel complex, while the Silberberg Course is a much gentler affair, less punishing to the beginner. Every Sporting Club activity has a "designer label" – riding, sailing, tennis, even the beauty parlour. Already the Nick Faldo Course is ranked No.1 in Germany and has already hosted the German Open European Tour event. Unusually for a contemporary course, water comes into consideration on only two holes, and there are plenty of shorter par-4s. England's Gary Evans took full advantage of them in the 1999 German Open, setting a course record 62. The top amateur events, the 2000 Eisenhower and Espirito Santo Trophies, were played over the Faldo and Palmer Courses.

Palmerston Golf Resort, Nick Faldo Course.
Card of the course

Hole	Yards	Par
1	548	5
2	414	4
3	186	3
4	379	4
5	212	3
6	533	5
7	441	4
8	383	4
9	449	4
Out	**3,545**	**36**
10	552	5
11	570	5
12	376	4
13	233	3
14	415	4
15	388	4
16	360	4
17	189	3
18	458	4
In	**3,541**	**36**
Total	**7,086**	**72**

31 Golf de Saint-Nom-la-Bretèche, Versailles

In 1959 Fred Hawtree transformed what had been a somewhat run-down, muddy farm into two fine golf courses, undulating agreeably though rather open and featureless at first. As the trees have grown over the intervening years the Red and Blue courses have matured, matching for beauty the cuisine served in the sumptuous clubhouse. For most of the year the golf is social, the province of wealthy Parisians, but once a year a dazzling field of the cream of professional golf assembles for one of the glittering occasions of the European golf calendar, the Trophée Lancôme. The list of winners reads like a Who's Who: Jacklin, Palmer, Miller, Casper, Player, Ballesteros (four times), Trevino, Price, Langer, Olazábal, Montgomerie, O'Meara and so on. A composite course stretching to over 7,000 yards is used for the Lancôme, the front nine mostly drawn from the Blue, the back nine utilising the outward half of the Red, so culminating in a charming, but treacherous, downhill par-3 (Red 9th) guarded by a pond. The professionals play their 14th (Red 5th) as a 467-yard par-4, already a tough dog-leg to an elevated green until five new bunkers added in 1999 further spiced things up.

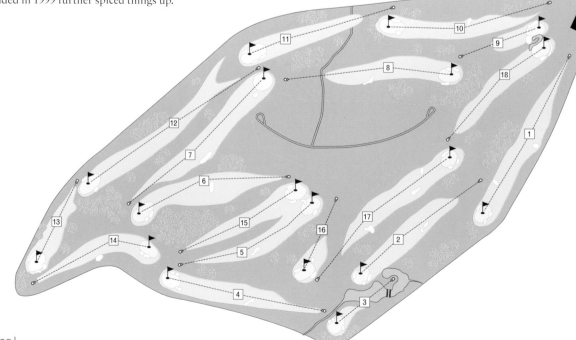

Saint-Nom-la-Bretèche (Red Course)
Card of the course

Hole	Yards	Par
1	365	4
2	394	4
3	179	3
4	394	4
5	476	5
6	437	4
7	504	5
8	420	4
9	205	3
Out	**3,374**	**36**
10	409	4
11	371	4
12	544	5
13	205	3
14	359	4
15	388	4
16	170	3
17	519	5
18	368	4
In	**3,333**	**36**
Total	**6,707**	**72**

32 Hôtel Blue Green, Seignosse

Opening in 1989, Seignosse was immediately voted one of the best tests of golfing technique in France. It is not unduly long, yet Robert Von Hagge's layout, winding through the pine-clad sand-hills of the Basque country, demands considerable accuracy. Von Hagge has supplemented nature with links-like humps and sleepered greens. Here the hills are steep, the ravines natural, and the golf strenuous from the back tees. The view down the 11th is spectacular, the tee 150 feet above the narrow, snaking fairway, trees on either side leaving no margin for error. Target golf is required on three of the short holes and on the approaches to many greens, such as the 17th, raised up alongside a pond.

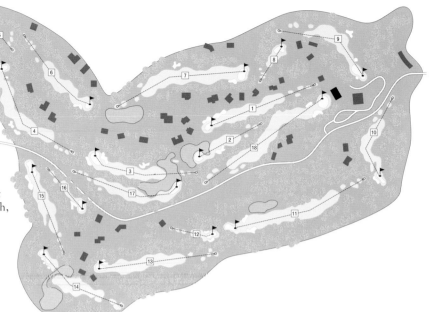

Seignosse Card of the course

Hole	Yards	Par		Hole	Yards	Par
1	447	4		10	344	4
2	326	4		11	578	5
3	401	4		12	128	3
4	486	5		13	461	4
5	144	3		14	359	4
6	387	4		15	350	4
7	542	5		16	202	3
8	133	3		17	399	4
9	398	4		18	614	5
Out	**3,264**	**36**		**In**	**3,435**	**36**
				Total	**6,699**	**72**

33 Barbaroux, Provence

For his third major foray into Europe Pete Dye chose to work at Barbaroux with his son Paul Burke Dye. They contrived to incorporate all their usual trademarks, railway sleepers, bulk-headed lakes, and extraordinarily contoured greens, into a layout which is nevertheless at one with the deep valleys and wooded hillsides of the Massif des Maures which provides a glorious backdrop. Oaks, chestnuts and olives frame many holes, while others cling precariously to the mountainside, giving great variety to the round. Length is rarely at a premium, extreme accuracy being more valuable with so much trouble just off the fairway. The most spectacular section comes on the outward half, the walled green of the par-5 5th set above a hundred-foot drop into a chasm capable of inducing vertigo.

Golf de Barbaroux Card of the course

Hole	Yards	Par		Hole	Yards	Par
1	387	4		10	353	4
2	357	4		11	325	4
3	510	5		12	546	5
4	161	3		13	433	4
5	535	5		14	315	4
6	438	4		15	187	3
7	291	4		16	410	4
8	177	3		17	572	5
9	429	4		18	212	3
Out	**3,285**	**36**		**In**	**3,353**	**36**
				Total	**6,638**	**72**

34 Royal Mougins GC

Robert Von Hagge laid out Royal Mougins in the Vallon de l'Oeuf amongst the olives and pines of the gentle hills of the Côte d'Azur. Lakes, streams and waterfalls contribute to the strategy particularly on the par-5s where the long hitter is dared to accept the challenge of reaching the greens in two shots. Unusually, one of the strongest holes is a par-3, the 2nd, Le Saut de l'Ange, Angel's Dive, which falls almost 100 feet from its elevated tee to a green on the far side of a lake. In the late 1990s the European Tour played a number of Cannes Opens here.

Royal Mougins Golf Club, Cannes Card of the course

Hole	Yards	Par		Hole	Yards	Par
1	347	4		10	137	3
2	200	3		11	421	4
3	524	5		12	326	4
4	501	5		13	432	4
5	212	3		14	388	4
6	391	4		15	579	5
7	369	4		16	419	4
8	196	3		17	139	3
9	424	4		18	563	5
Out	**3,164**	**35**		**In**	**3,404**	**36**
				Total	**6,568**	**71**

35 Royal Haagsche Golf & Country Club, Wassenaar

The Dutch coastline is similar in many places to the best links country of the British Isles, and the Haagsche course is ideally sited for capitalizing on the best features of seaside golf. Designed in 1939 by British architects Colt, Alison and Morrison, it has needed very little change. The 481-yard par-five 6th is the best example of the course's exacting qualities. However, it was here, during the 1972 Dutch Open, that Jack Newton hit a spectacular shot. His massive second rolled across the green and into the cup for a double-eagle.

Record: 64, Peter Oosterhuis, Netherlands Open 1972

Haagsche Card of the course

Hole	Yards	Par		Hole	Yards	Par
1	503	5		10	480	5
2	383	4		11	414	4
3	366	4		12	167	3
4	221	3		13	412	4
5	482	5		14	420	4
6	481	5		15	412	4
7	341	4		16	383	4
8	229	3		17	156	3
9	359	4		18	508	5
Out	**3,365**	**37**		**In**	**3,352**	**36**
				Total	**6,717**	**73**

36 Royal Golf Club de Belgique, Tervuren

With a clubhouse that is a national monument and a course that was built by royal command, the Royal Golf Club de Belgique does justice to its auspicious origins. Tom Simpson laid out the eighteen holes on attractively undulating land belonging to the Donation Royale. The King insisted that all the trees lining the fairways should be specially selected to include many rare species from his own arboretum. After almost a century's growth these magnificent trees make this a course of rare beauty. Over the last ten years many revisions have been made to the course, particularly the bunkering, to bring its challenge into the 21st Century, whilst maintaining the character and shot values of Simpson's masterly course. The conversion of the par-5 15th into a long par-4 has considerably strengthened the finish.

Record: 65, Flory van Donck, Belgian Open 1935

Royal Belgique Card of the course

Hole	Yards	Par		Hole	Yards	Par
1	491	5		10	349	4
2	420	4		11	417	4
3	156	3		12	194	3
4	415	4		13	522	5
5	521	5		14	330	4
6	210	3		15	446	4
7	373	4		16	336	4
8	360	4		17	419	4
9	336	4		18	305	4
Out	**3,282**	**36**		**In**	**3,318**	**36**
				Total	**6,600**	**72**

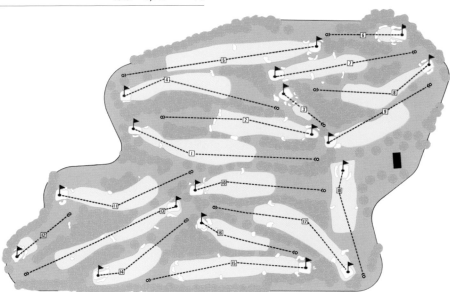

37 Royal Waterloo GC, Ohain

The first of Henry Cotton's three Open Championship victories, in 1934, came when he was the professional at the original Royal Waterloo Golf Club, whose course had been laid out eleven years earlier. In 1960 a new 18 holes were designed by Fred Hawtree on a site at Ohain near Brussels. Hawtree's course has since been supplemented by the addition a further championship course, Le Lion. The first ten holes and the finishing pair run over a wide, undulating plain with a scattering of small trees, but the 11th to the 16th climb and drop through a high beech wood. The dramatic contrast is best seen at the 13th, a 408 yard par-four dog-leg running through a wooded valley – a claustrophobic hole after the open plains. For many years the course record was 67, set by Donald Swaelens, the club's professional until his untimely death while still in his thirties.

Record: 65, Nick Faldo

Royal Waterloo (La Marache) Card of the course

Hole	Yards	Par
1	411	4
2	361	4
3	529	5
4	189	3
5	514	5
6	427	4
7	161	3
8	359	4
9	421	4
Out	**3,372**	**36**
10	392	4
11	418	4
12	193	3
13	408	4
14	392	4
15	157	3
16	476	5
17	527	5
18	486	5
In	**3,449**	**37**
Total	**6,821**	**73**

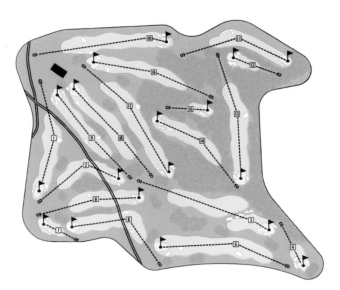

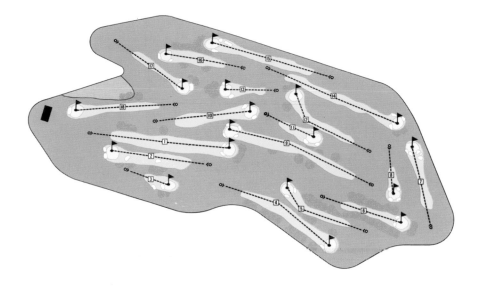

39 Seefeld Wildmoos GC, Tirol

A major ski resort needs steep mountain slopes at high altitude, often densely wooded, with the longest possible snow season. Seefeld not only meets these criteria but also boasts a spectacular golf course. Designed by British architect Donald Harradine and located at 4,300 feet, it is carved out of some of the most fiendish golfing country imaginable. After the early holes over relatively level ground, the course climbs and plunges through forests of pine and birch, presenting some extraordinarily tight holes. Most memorable are the 9th, only 186 yards but a good 200 feet straight down the mountainside; and the 14th, a 656-yard par-five running sharply downhill through the woods and reachable with two accurate long shots. Although under several feet of snow for almost half the year, the playing conditions in summer are excellent, the result of Herculean efforts by the club. Their endeavours have preserved a tight course where the emphasis is on percentage golf, particularly when approaching the elevated greens.

Record: 68 Gerhard König, Seefeld Pro-Am 1975

Seefeld Wildmoos Card of the course

Hole	Yards	Par		Hole	Yards	Par
1	519	5		10	405	4
2	437	4		11	317	4
3	328	4		12	520	5
4	388	4		13	180	3
5	252	3		14	656	5
6	388	4		15	416	4
7	574	5		16	335	4
8	284	4		17	191	3
9	186	3		18	372	4
Out	**3,356**	**36**		**In**	**3,396**	**36**
				Total	**6,752**	**72**

38 Crans-sur-Sierre GC, Valais

Set on a mountain plateau high in the Berner Oberland, Crans-sur-Sierre enjoys the most spectacular scenery of any course on the European Tour. Completely encircled by high, snow-capped peaks and set off against tall stands of dark pines it has always attracted one of the best fields of the year to compete for the European Masters. In the clear mountain air at an altitude of 5,000 feet the ball flies far and scoring has traditionally been low. In 1996 Colin Montgomerie played the 3rd and 4th rounds in a tour record 18 under par on his way to setting a new tournament record low score of 260.

Record: 60, B. Dassu, Swiss Open 1971

Crans-sur-Sierre Card of the course

Hole	Yards	Par		Hole	Yards	Par
1	540	5		10	405	4
2	438	4		11	205	3
3	191	3		12	410	4
4	525	4		13	195	3
5	339	4		14	595	5
6	324	4		15	516	5
7	332	4		16	347	4
8	175	3		17	386	4
9	629	5		18	403	4
Out	**3,493**	**36**		**In**	**3,466**	**36**
				Total	**6,959**	**72**

40 Rome GC, Aquasanta

Golf has been played at Aquasanta, with its reputedly medicinal waters, for more than seventy years. Here the Rome Golf Club, set in low hills and crossed by meandering streams, offers luxuriant golf in historic surroundings, with views of old aqueducts and the legendary Appian Way. The course is short by championship standards but tight enough to be testing. Strategically placed pines and other trees guard the fairways, and the network of streams form a hazard at several holes. The condition of this well-watered course is always superb, as might be expected of such an exclusive club. It is fairly level to play, with particularly featureless and deceptive greens.

Rome Card of the course

Hole	Yards	Par		Hole	Yards	Par
1	334	4		10	470	4
2	137	3		11	129	3
3	350	4		12	439	4
4	387	4		13	379	4
5	211	3		14	359	4
6	378	4		15	365	4
7	544	5		16	350	4
8	394	4		17	417	4
9	427	4		18	400	4
Out	**3,162**	**35**		**In**	**3,308**	**35**
				Total	**6,470**	**70**

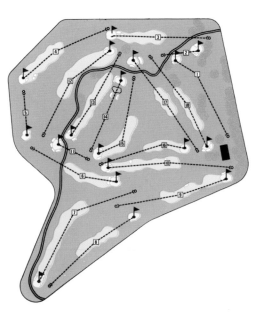

41 Pevero GC, Sardinia

The terrain at Pevero is so imposing and unyielding that it forced the architect, Robert Trent Jones, to follow its contours, developing nature's own golf holes rather than reshaping and building them with machines. The 4th, at 384 yards, starts an exhilarating sequence, plunging into a valley with distant views of Corsica to a green set along one slope. It is followed by a downhill par-three with an enormous rock outcrop guarding the right and a lake to the left. The 6th is a par-four, along, and across a lake, and it is succeeded by a 182-yard short hole back across the lake to a shallow green bunkered front and rear.

Pevero card of the course

Hole	Yards	Par				
1	411	4		10	185	3
2	383	4		11	531	5
3	519	5		12	384	4
4	384	4		13	387	4
5	191	3		14	186	3
6	335	4		15	477	5
7	182	3		16	287	4
8	317	4		17	144	3
9	497	5		18	535	5
Out	**3,219**	**36**		**In**	**2,986**	**36**
				Total	**6,205**	**72**

42 Biella GC, Regione Valcarozza

Dating from 1958, Biella was one of John Morrison's last designs. He had worked closely with Colt on Wentworth. There is an English feel to the course, its fairways laid out through the avenues of birches which give it its familiar name, Le Betulle. Biella has been lengthened over the years to maintain its challenge for the best players, largely retaining Morrison's original shot values. Of the par-fives, the 16th is particularly handsome, driving out of a chute of trees onto an elevated fairway, before plunging downhill past rocks to a well-bunkered green set off in front of a splendid mountain backdrop.

Golf Club Biella, Card of the course

Hole	Yards	Par				
1	401	4		10	201	3
2	179	3		11	466	5
3	400	4		12	377	4
4	359	4		13	344	4
5	193	3		14	386	4
6	373	4		15	340	4
7	476	5		16	522	5
8	368	4		17	172	3
9	474	5		18	466	5
Out	**3,223**	**36**		**In**	**3,274**	**37**
				Total	**6,497**	**73**

43 Glyfada GC, Athens

Set between gently rolling mountain slopes and the sparkling Saronic Gulf, Glyfada is Greece's premier course. The eighteen holes, constructed in 1967, were designed by Donald Harradine, who cleverly lined each hole with umbrella pines to create the chief hazards. Athens airport, a mere 500 yards from the practice tee, is a source of constant noise and can become an almost intolerable distraction. Nevertheless, the course's narrow doglegs, fast greens and pine-dominated rough provide excellent surroundings for Mediterranean-type golf. From the back tees there is enough length to test the best, making the course very tight and favouring players with powerful drives. The toughest hole is the 9th, a 414-yard par-four, gently bending to the left with a deep hollow, often filled with water for tournament play, before the green.

Record: 67, Tony Lema

Glyfada Golf Club, Athens Card of the course

Hole	Yards	Par				
1	397	4		10	494	5
2	350	4		11	399	4
3	509	5		12	203	3
4	394	4		13	395	4
5	163	3		14	458	4
6	440	4		15	492	5
7	559	5		16	142	3
8	179	3		17	361	4
9	414	4		18	419	4
Out	**3,405**	**36**		**In**	**3,363**	**36**
				Total	**6,768**	**72**

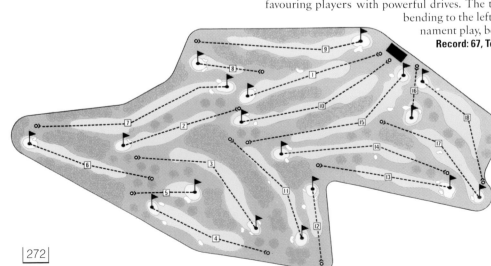

44 Hyatt La Manga, Murcia

Fifty-four holes of golf are amongst the many leisure facilities currently available at La Manga, a 1,400 acre estate close to both the Mar Menor and the Mediterranean. David Thomas's recent West Course is set in the rolling hills overlooking the club and provides a shorter, more undulating foil to the original courses of 1971. The South Course, designed by Robert Dean Putnam, remains the championship layout, long and searching. Palm trees, large bunkers, lakes and barrancas (deep ravines) form the main hazards, though the greens present generously expansive targets and are fairly straightforward. Its high profile was established soon after it opened with a run of five Spanish Opens in succession, Arnold Palmer the winner in 1975. Water threatens on each of the par-3s, and no fewer than seven bunkers now attend the 17th green. The 18th is a great gambler's hole, a par-5 reachable in two shots, with water both sides of the drive and a ravine 80 yards short of the green. But it is not sufficient simply to clear the ravine for there is a huge semi-circular bunker running round the front of the green lying in wait for the shot that nearly makes it but not quite.

La Manga, South Course Card of the course

Hole	Yards	Par	Hole	Yards	Par
1	401	4	10	368	4
2	400	4	11	393	4
3	540	5	12	133	3
4	433	4	13	555	5
5	220	3	14	361	4
6	400	4	15	440	4
7	429	4	16	370	4
8	218	3	17	222	3
9	591	5	18	485	5
Out	**3,632**	**36**	**In**	**3,327**	**36**
			Total	**6,959**	**72**

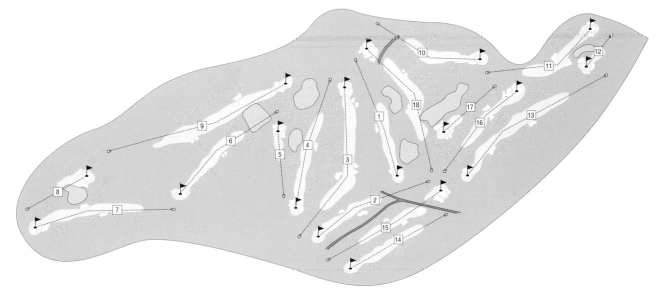

45 Club de Campo, Villa de Madrid

Just a couple of miles north-west of Madrid city centre, on the Carratera de Castilla, is one of Spain's great clubs, offering, amongst many sporting activities, polo, tennis, hockey, swimming and golf at the highest level. It lies just across the valley from Madrid's other famous course, Puerta de Hierro, both frequent hosts to the Spanish Open. Max Faulkner won the first to be held at Club de Campo in 1957, shortly after Javier Arana's new course opened. The 1991 Spanish Open ended in a tie, Argentina's Eduardo Romero needing seven play-off holes to overcome Severiano Ballesteros, but in 1995 Ballesteros triumphed alone, in what may well prove to be his last tour victory. The club operates a notable caddie school, Ryder Cup stars Mañuel Pinero, José-Maria Canizares and Antonio Garrido amongst its distinguished alumni. The opening hole is tough, a long par-4 with an angled fairway running through trees to a well-protected, sloping green. One of the best holes is the 6th, a sharp dog-leg climbing to a two-level, hill-top green, again well bunkered. The climb to the green at the par-5 12th is rewarded with superb views over the city of Madrid.

Club de Campo Villa de Madrid Card of the course

Hole	Yards	Par	Hole	Yards	Par
1	467	4	10	400	4
2	442	4	11	214	3
3	207	3	12	477	5
4	508	5	13	442	4
5	409	4	14	537	5
6	441	4	15	377	4
7	538	5	16	423	4
8	372	4	17	152	3
9	170	3	18	353	4
Out	**3,554**	**36**	**In**	**3,375**	**36**
			Total	**6,929**	**72**

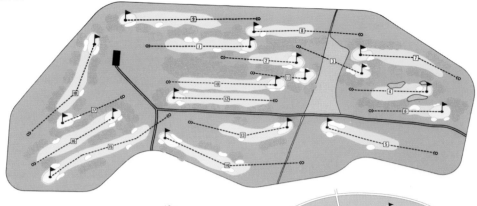

46 Real Club de Golf "El Prat", Barcelona

The late Javier Arana created this quite untypical Spanish course in 1954 on a flat coastal stretch close to Barcelona airport. The emphasis is on strategic positioning from the tee, with subtle moulding around the greens and minimal but significant bunkering. On the sterner second nine the 14th epitomises the whole course, a par-4 needing a long-iron second to a beautifully shaped green.

El Prat Card of the course

Hole	Yards	Par				
1	415	4		10	508	5
2	288	4		11	171	3
3	171	3		12	497	5
4	326	4		13	357	4
5	408	4		14	455	4
6	224	3		15	547	5
7	397	4		16	435	4
8	376	4		17	181	3
9	490	5		18	396	4
Out	**3,095**	**35**		**In**	**3,547**	**37**
				Total	**6,642**	**72**

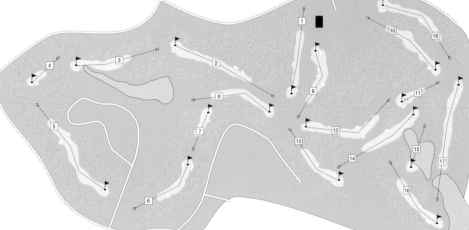

47 Quinta do Lago, Almancil

In the few miles between Albufeira and Faro in the Algarve is an astonishing concentration of highly-rated golf courses, including Pine Cliffs, Vilamoura, Vila Sol, Vale de Lobo, Pinheiros Altos, San Lorenzo and Quinta do Lago. 36 holes of golf wander through a 2,000 acre estate of exclusive housing and leisure facilities, but as part of it lies within the 45,000 acre Ria Formosa Nature Reserve it is still a place of peace and beauty. The initial 27 holes are the only European work of American architect William Mitchell who died shortly after their completion in 1974. Nine further holes were added by Joseph Lee to complete what is now known as the Ria Formosa course. Seven Portuguese Opens were held here, the 1989 event giving Scot Colin Montgomerie his first European tour victory. The 8th on the championship course is a tricky hole with a sloping fairway and the green cut into a steep bank, and the 10th is testing with the approach difficult to judge over a depression. With a bunker and pines in the angle, the dog-leg 18th is a good finisher. But the hole everyone remembers is the 15th with its lake and wooden bridge.

Quinta do Lago Card of the course

Hole	Yards	Par				
1	427	4		10	449	4
2	547	5		11	208	3
3	423	4		12	503	5
4	187	3		13	356	4
5	552	5		14	419	4
6	383	4		15	219	3
7	199	3		16	407	4
8	421	4		17	558	5
9	388	4		18	452	4
Out	**3,527**	**36**		**In**	**3,571**	**36**
				Total	**7,098**	**72**

48 Penha Longa, Sintra

Built in the grounds of a 14th-century Hieronymite monastery by Robert Trent Jones Jnr., Penha Longa journeys out and back through the foothills of the majestic Sintra Mountains. From the championship tees it is a stern challenge, which tested the fields of the Portuguese Opens in 1994 and 1995. Part of the charm is the fact that only the 1st and 18th can be seen from the clubhouse, giving the player an experience of eager anticipation during the round, with the early and late holes running through a valley of pine trees and granite rocks. The remains of an ancient aqueduct and water-tower bordering the fairway on the par-5 6th provide a historical distraction. On the other side of the walls the 7th is a testing par-3 protected by water and sand. The handsome 15th is equally tricky, the start of a tough finish, of which the 16th is probably the hardest hole of all, with a downhill drive to a well-bunkered fairway and long uphill approach shot.

Penha Longa Golf Club Card of the course

Hole	Yards	Par				
1	366	4		10	418	4
2	396	4		11	393	4
3	354	4		12	495	5
4	434	4		13	352	4
5	209	3		14	417	4
6	498	5		15	197	3
7	199	3		16	440	4
8	556	5		17	204	3
9	409	4		18	542	5
Out	**3,421**	**36**		**In**	**3,458**	**36**
				Total	**6,879**	**72**

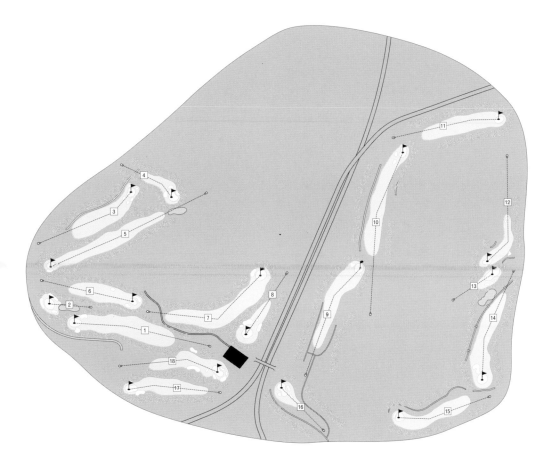

49 Golf do Estoril, Lisbon

Scotsman Mackenzie Ross designed this short but characterful course in 1945 before turning to his masterpiece, the restoration of Turnberry. It is set on high ground behind the fashionable resort. With the advent of Portugal's new breed of championship courses, Estoril is no longer the automatic choice for the Portuguese Open, an event it hosted no fewer than twenty times, with Flory van Donck, Peter Alliss, Ken Bousfield, and Ramon Sota amongst its illustrious winners. Like an English parkland course in feel, its narrow fairways put a premium on accuracy. Extreme length is rarely an advantage, though few will reach the 517-yard 5th in two shots, for it runs steeply uphill. The building of a motorway through the course has necessitated the alteration of several holes and the construction of a lovely new hole, the short 13th. It is entirely in keeping with the strategic nature of the course as a whole, a narrow target through a gap in the trees, the green sloping towards bunkers and water. From here the finish may not be lengthy, but ditches and trees punish the errant.

Record: 61, Robert Lee, Portuguese Open 1987

Estoril Card of the course

Hole	Yards	Par			
1	385	4	10	502	4
2	156	3	11	415	5
3	319	4	12	339	4
4	177	3	13	167	4
5	517	5	14	396	4
6	266	4	15	326	4
7	419	4	16	201	3
8	216	3	17	298	4
9	379	4	18	278	4
Out	**2,834**	**34**	**In**	**2,922**	**35**
			Total	**5,756**	**69**

50 Penina GC, Algarve

The brainchild of Henry Cotton, Penina was opened in 1966, making it the first in an impressive line of Portuguese resort courses. Cotton made the most of a flat, damp ricefield, planting more than 350,000 trees, constructing expansive sandtraps and using the many drainage canals to strategic advantage. His teeing grounds were up to 100 yards long enabling the course to be extended to enormous lengths for tournament play, and the Portuguese Open was held at Penina five times during the 1970s and 80s and it hosted prestigious amateur events such as the 1973 European Amateur Team Championship and 1976 Eisenhower Trophy. In the last few years it has been completely upgraded and refurbished, bringing, in 1998, the return of the Portuguese Open after a twenty year gap, Peter Mitchell the winner by a stroke. Penina is unusual in that four of its five long holes occur on the back nine, the last hole the easiest of them, comfortably eagled by Gary Orr in winning the 2000 Portuguese Open. Water ensures that the most demanding approaches are those to the 2nd and 12th, contributing also to the allure and difficulty of the short 13th and 16th.

Penina Card of the course

Hole	Yards	Par			
1	445	4	10	545	5
2	424	4	11	540	5
3	335	4	12	421	4
4	386	4	13	202	3
5	493	5	14	392	4
6	193	3	15	329	4
7	339	4	16	210	3
8	187	3	17	521	5
9	422	4	18	477	5
Out	**3,224**	**35**	**In**	**3,637**	**38**
			Total	**7,041**	**73**

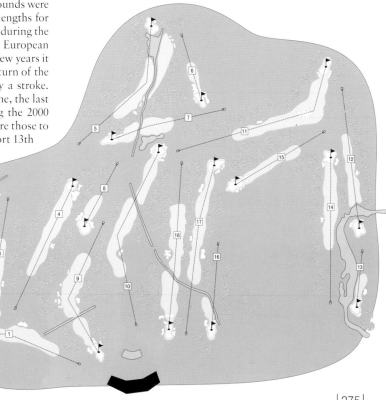

51 Bay Hill Club and Lodge, Orlando, Fla.

The field for the Bay Hill Invitational is always one of the strongest of the year on the PGA Tour. They are attracted by the quality of the course and by the magnetism of Arnold Palmer who has presided over the tournament since it moved here in 1979. Palmer first played the course in an exhibition match in 1965 and was so impressed by the quality of architect Dick Wilson's work that he bought it! Since then he has been steadily improving the design to make it a tougher test, especially in a wind. Dog-legs and water holes invite the player to gamble (very much in the Palmer spirit) and the finish from the 16th is one of the strongest on tour, the 17th being notably unforgiving. Tiger Woods captured the Bay Hill Trophy (a replica Scottish Claymore) three times in a row 2000 to 2002.

Bay Hill Club and Lodge Card of the course

Hole	Yards	Par	Hole	Yards	Par
1	441	4	10	400	4
2	218	3	11	438	4
3	395	4	12	580	5
4	530	5	13	364	4
5	384	4	14	206	3
6	558	5	15	425	4
7	197	3	16	517	5
8	459	4	17	219	3
9	467	4	18	441	4
Out	**3,649**	**36**	**In**	**3,590**	**36**
			Total	**7,239**	**72**

52 Sahalee Country Club, Redmond, Wa.

Sahalee, meaning 'High Heavenly Grounds' in the language of the Chinook, was the name chosen in the 1960s by the founders of a new club near Seattle which they intended to be of national championship standard. They located a tract of beautifully wooded, rolling ground on the Sammamish Plateau, east of Redmond, engaging the Californian architect Ted Robinson as the course designer. They also appointed former PGA champion Paul Runyan as their first professional. Their aspirations were fulfilled when Sahalee was awarded the 1998 US PGA, for which Rees Jones oversaw the redesign of the bunkering and a few key strategic features. The Fijian Vijay Singh at last broke through to win his first Major. Tall trees lining most fairways dictate that the player must be able to shape tee shots both ways, with a fade the ideal drive on the tough 8th, for instance, and a draw needed to open up the 2nd green beyond a pond.

Sahalee Card of the course

Hole	Yards	Par	Hole	Yards	Par
1	406	4	10	401	4
2	507	5	11	546	5
3	415	4	12	458	4
4	386	4	13	176	3
5	195	3	14	374	4
6	480	4	15	417	4
7	421	4	16	377	4
8	444	4	17	215	3
9	213	3	18	475	4
Out	**3,467**	**35**	**In**	**3,439**	**35**
			Total	**6,906**	**70**

53 TPC of Scottsdale, Az.

Tom Weiskopf and Jay Morrish have become experts in the art of designing desert courses. They were commissioned by the City of Scottsdale to create a course which would host the Phoenix Open on the PGA Tour, yet still be playable by the thousands of handicap golfers who visit every year, for this is a public course – one of the best in America. The backdrop of the McDowell Mountains is handsome, but the course itself had to be created out of barren, flat desert. Two large lakes were excavated and thousands of tons of dirt moved to create raised greens and ample spectator mounds. The 11th and 14th are toughest against par, while the approach to the 15th is reminiscent of the approach to Augusta's 13th. Mark Calcavecchia set a new PGA Tour record of 256 when he took the Phoenix Open title for the third time in 2001.

TPC of Scottsdale Stadium Card of the course

Hole	Yards	Par	Hole	Yards	Par
1	410	4	10	404	4
2	416	4	11	469	4
3	554	5	12	195	3
4	150	3	13	576	5
5	453	4	14	444	4
6	389	4	15	501	5
7	215	3	16	162	3
8	470	4	17	332	4
9	415	4	18	438	4
Out	**3,472**	**35**	**In**	**3,520**	**36**
			Total	**6,992**	**71**

Doral Blue course
Card of the course

Hole	Yards	Par
1	529	5
2	376	4
3	409	4
4	236	3
5	394	4
6	442	4
7	428	4
8	528	5
9	169	3
Out	**3,511**	**36**
10	551	5
11	363	4
12	603	5
13	245	3
14	443	4
15	175	3
16	372	4
17	419	4
18	443	4
In	**3,614**	**36**
Total	**7,125**	**72**

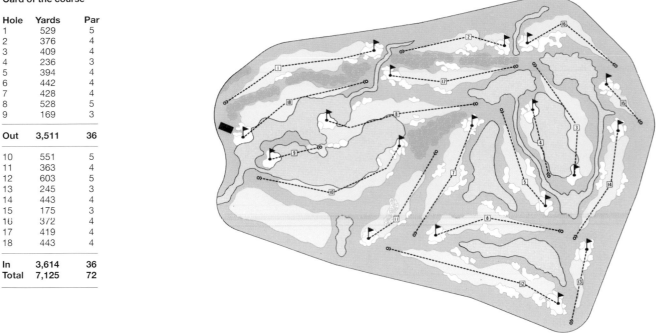

54 Doral CC, Miami, Fla.

Doral is the epitome of Florida resort golf. Ninety per cent of the golfers who play there are winter vacationers, yet none of its six courses is in any way easy, the Blue undeniably being of championship calibre. Nicknamed the "Blue Monster" by professionals, largely because of the remarkable final hole, this Dick Wilson inspired layout also has a stunning 9th. The 443-yard par-four 18th is an absolute dream of design, where water, on the left, has to be carried twice on the run in to a green half encircled by the same lake. In all, Wilson built eight lakes during construction and the holes, interspersed by a few palm trees, were tailored around them. A programme of upgrading over the last few years has seen the bunkering altered significantly to keep it relevant to the modern professional game. The 2002 Genuity Championship saw Ernie Els desperately trying to defend an 8-stroke lead against an attack from a rampant Tiger Woods. Els hung on – just!

Jupiter Hills Card of the course

Hole	Yards	Par			
1	512	5	10	389	4
2	439	4	11	198	3
3	176	3	12	415	4
4	573	5	13	536	5
5	421	4	14	225	3
6	379	4	15	399	4
7	411	4	16	336	4
8	384	4	17	508	5
9	192	3	18	429	4
Out	**3,487**	**36**	**In**	**3,435**	**36**
			Total	**6,922**	**72**

55 Jupiter Hills Club, Tequesta, Fla.

The ultra-exclusive Jupiter Hills Club was a joint financial venture between golf architect George Fazio, comedian Bob Hope and motor industrialist William Ford. It was one of Fazio's favourite courses, to which he frequently returned to make subtle improvements. Jupiter Hills hosted the 1987 US Amateur Championship, with the current PGA Tour player, Billy Mayfair, emerging as the winner. The 11th was one of Fazio's favourite holes, a delightful par-3 with a positively Machiavellian twist to its design. It has six tees and can be played at virtually any length between 198 yards and 120 yards, but it is the different angles of approach that the two tees offer that make the hole. The green is long and narrow and on one line straight away from the tees: on the other it is slightly angled and therefore easier to hit, though protected by water. But the outstanding characteristic of the course is that it is hilly – a full sixty feet from its lowest to its highest point, an unheard of amount of "drop" in the flatness of Florida's "golf coast" stretching from the Palm Beaches to Miami.

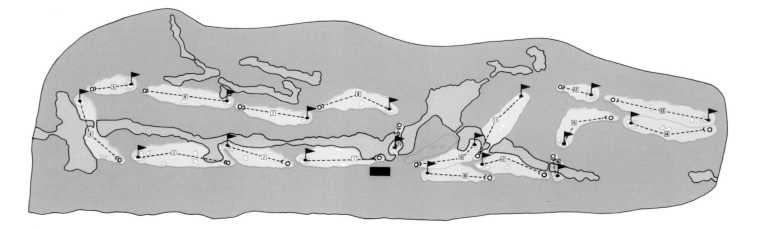

56 Ponte Vedra Inn & Club (Ocean Course), Ponte Vedra Beach, Fla.

Ponte Vedra Inn & Club is on Florida's Atlantic coast between Jacksonville and St. Augustine. Its Ocean Course was designed by the British-born architect Herbert Strong, opened in 1933, and modified by Robert Trent Jones in the late 1940s. Jones made further changes in 1961 and added nine more holes, which in 1977 were joined to nine new holes designed by Joe Lee to create the Lagoon Course. The Ocean Course is a 6,484 yard test of skill featuring large mounds as backdrops for the fresh water lagoons that wind through the course. Water is only the most obvious hazard: fifteen to twenty-foot high mounds break up the otherwise flat Florida landscape and frequently obscure the greens. Ocean breezes can be brisk. The 4th hole, at 427 yards, is a difficult par-four with water on either side of the fairway and in front of the green. The 11th, which tees off over water, is no easier, but perhaps the best known is the infamous "Island Ninth". A deceptively short par-three at 140 yards, it features a green surrounded, except for a narrow walkway, by golf ball (and possibly alligator!) infested water. A short approach area offers a safe landing to those who underclub.

Ponte Vedra Ocean Course Card of the course

Hole	Yards	Par			
1	397	4	10	355	4
2	363	4	11	400	4
3	516	5	12	174	3
4	427	4	13	529	5
5	216	3	14	466	5
6	475	5	15	387	4
7	383	4	16	128	3
8	401	4	17	382	4
9	140	3	18	345	4
Out	**3,318**	**36**	**In**	**3,166**	**36**
			Total	**6,484**	**72**

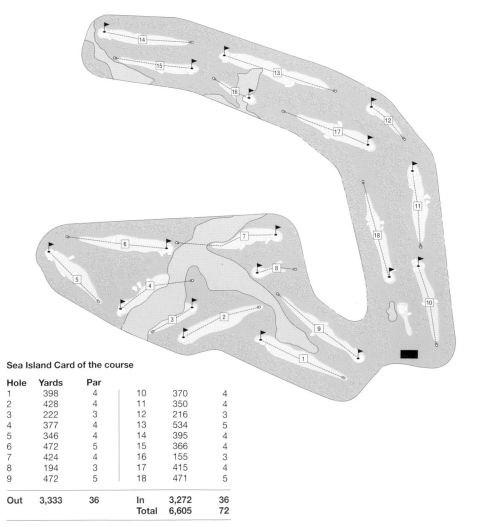

57 Sea Island GC, Sea Is, Ga.

Sea Island's oceanside golf course was laid out in 1927 and 1929 on the Retreat Plantation–an early nineteenth century cotton farm – by the English architects H. S. Colt and Charles Alison. They designed two nine-holers which now form eighteen of the club's thirty-six holes. The Seaside is the front nine and rolls over the broad undulating fairways set amongst the dunes, edged by the ocean and surrounded by waterways and marshland. The Plantation course, which makes up the back nine, scythes through great forests of oak and pine, occasionally touching the marsh and often crossing or playing alongside the lagoons. The greens are well elevated and trapped on all sides. The 7th hole, White Heron, is a real equalizer, as the drive has to carry a broad marsh inlet where a stiff breeze can nudge the ball into the inlet. The alternative is to play to a thin peninsula of fairway, which leaves the second shot blind over two large bunkers with the brackish marsh threatening on the left. Bobby Jones first focused national attention on the club and his record of 67 stood for many years.

Record: 63, Sam Snead, 1958

Sea Island Card of the course

Hole	Yards	Par			
1	398	4	10	370	4
2	428	4	11	350	4
3	222	3	12	216	3
4	377	4	13	534	5
5	346	4	14	395	4
6	472	5	15	366	4
7	424	4	16	155	3
8	194	3	17	415	4
9	472	5	18	471	5
Out	**3,333**	**36**	**In**	**3,272**	**36**
			Total	**6,605**	**72**

58 Palmetto Dunes Resort, Hilton Head, SC

At the George Fazio course at Palmetto Dunes, in the South Carolina golfing Mecca of Hilton Head Island, each fairway runs parallel to another on its right and, with the exception of the 3rd and 16th, there is out of bounds on the left of every hole. A mark of Fazio's work was his extravagant shaping of teeing areas. Not for him the square-cut tees so common in golf. At Palmetto they sweep in elegant curves around lakes, while others are circular and laid one after another like giant stepping stones. At the par three 17th the terraced tees advance down a slope to the lagoon, leaving the rolling green 230 yards away and protected by a large sandtrap. At the 421-yard parfour 9th a massive oak tree blocks any approach to the green from the right side of the fairway, and the short 4th green is split into three distinct levels. Oak, magnolia and palmetto trees, together with the ever-present threat of water, add to the danger and beauty of this most unusual course. Two further courses by Arthur Hills and one by Trent Jones give 72 holes of outstanding golf.

Palmetto Dunes, George Fazio Card of the course

Hole	Yards	Par
1	432	4
2	562	5
3	412	4
4	205	3
5	389	4
6	180	3
7	414	4
8	431	4
9	421	4
Out	**3,446**	**35**
10	513	5
11	354	4
12	387	4
13	386	4
14	185	3
15	445	4
16	425	4
17	230	3
18	462	4
In	**3,427**	**35**
Total	**6,873**	**70**

Record : 66 Buddy Alexander, 1975

59 Peachtree GC, Atlanta, Ga.

To speak of Peachtree in Atlanta is to speak of Bobby Jones, for it was he who was the inspiration behind it. His ideas were followed by architect Robert Trent Jones, and Peachtree has ever since been one of the premier golf clubs of Atlanta and the place that Bobby Jones considered his golfing home in his later years. The course was built during the late 1940s amongst azaleas and dogwood in the typically hilly countryside around Atlanta. Marching up and down these hills in the hot summer months can make it purgatory to play, but the anguish is more than compensated for during the other seasons – particularly the spring. The start is awesome, with an initial 391-yard par-four, with two bunkers set in the dog-leg which force the drive out to the right of the fairway. The 2nd is simple but superb. A 527-yard par-five, it is bunkerless but has a green protected in front by a lake and stream. In 1989 Peachtree played host to a historic Walker Cup - the first victory on American soil by a side representing Great Britain and Ireland.

Peachtree Card of the course

Hole	Yards	Par			
1	391	4	10	516	5
2	527	5	11	224	3
3	409	4	12	440	4
4	166	3	13	421	4
5	529	5	14	180	3
6	216	3	15	452	4
7	434	4	16	532	5
8	369	4	17	446	4
9	392	4	18	401	4
Out	**3,433**	**36**	**In**	**3,612**	**36**
			Total	**7,045**	**72**

Dunes Card of the course

Hole	Yards	Par			
1	425	4	10	380	4
2	425	4	11	430	4
3	435	4	12	245	3
4	505	5	13	590	5
5	205	3	14	450	4
6	435	4	15	535	5
7	400	4	16	365	4
8	525	5	17	185	3
9	200	3	18	430	4
Out	**3,555**	**36**	**In**	**3,610**	**36**
			Total	**7,165**	**72**

60 The Dunes G & BC, Myrtle Beach, SC

Dunes was designed by Robert Trent Jones back in 1947. He built the course on land with a colourful history; it was a deer and turkey hunting ground before becoming an Air Force target range during World War II – somewhat hazardous territory to plough up into a golf course. Jones incorporated in the layout his favourite design features: long tees, well-defined fairway traps to give the player a target off the tee, and huge, elevated, sometimes tiered greens. The 13th, a 575-yard par-five, is the most outstanding hole on the course. It dog-legs so severely around Singleton Lake that the golfer feels he is going back on his tracks. The hole bends a full 110 degrees through the line of play, and to add to the difficulty the approach to the green is between two flanking green sidetraps supported by a single bunker on the far side. To make the green in two is a rare feat. Dunes has hosted six Senior Tour Championships in the 1990s, the 1973 PGA Tour Q-school (won by Ben Crenshaw), and the 1962 US Women's Open in which Murle Lindstrom emerged victorious.

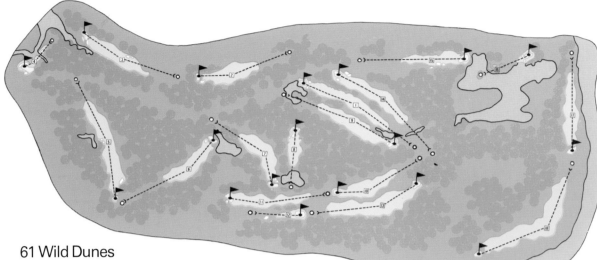

61 Wild Dunes Resort (Links Course), SC

Both the Links and Harbor Courses at Wild Dunes are impressive achievements from designer Tom Fazio on land he described as an "architect's dream". The Links Course, opened in 1980, winds through marsh and sand for most of its 6,772 yards. Most of the elements of the course come into play on the par-three 170-yard 4th hole: marshland at the edge of the tee and along the right side of the fairway; magnolia, oak, palm, and cedar trees in abundance; and a combination grass and sand bunker front and right of the green. The 10th hole begins a series of complete dune holes, which required no major earthwork to create. The 11th, 12th, and 13th also come with ocean views from the tees. The 15th brings back the marshland, which also borders the par-three, 175-yard 16th, where the championship tee is placed on a small peninsula in the salt-water lake. From there it's all carry over water and marshland to the green. The 17th and 18th are true links holes, with wild rolling dunes swept by strong ocean winds.

62 CC of North Carolina, Pinehurst, N.C.

Standing apart and aloof on the Sandhills of Pinehurst, the exclusive private Country Club of North Carolina has two eighteen-hole courses set amidst an expanse of trees and water. The championship course is known as Dogwood, while the Cardinal course, designed in part by Robert Trent Jones, was extended to eighteen holes in 1981. The back nine of the championship layout is strengthened by the abundant water hazards, which affect all but the 10th and 12th. At the 206 yard 16th, the carry is all water to a green guarded to the front and back by enormous sandtraps. For the timid, a piece of fairway on the right offers refuge from the endless water, but taking the safe route may mean dropping a shot. The lake runs alongside the two home holes from the 17th tee and encroaches on to the final fairway before drifting away to leave an unhindered approach to the last green.

63 Cascades GC, Hot Springs, Virginia

One of the world's most elegant and successful golf swings – that of Sam Snead – was created on this demanding course at The Homestead, Virginia. Built in 1923 by William Flynn, it was rated by Snead as the best training course for budding professionals because it demands every shot in the book from an infinite variety of hilly lies. The first twelve holes are very tight, sloping fairways such as the 2nd tricky to hold. It was on these early holes that Bill Campbell built an unassailable lead in the final of the 1980 Senior Amateur Championship. A narrow dog-leg, the 12th is one of the most difficult holes. It was here that Snead began his professional career in 1934 and where, in 1967, French girl Catherine Lacoste became the first non-American, the first amateur and the youngest winner of the US Women's Open.

Wild Dunes Links Card of the course

Hole	Yards	Par
1	501	5
2	370	4
3	420	4
4	170	3
5	505	5
6	421	4
7	359	4
8	203	3
9	451	4
Out	**3,400**	**36**
10	331	4
11	376	4
12	192	3
13	427	4
14	489	5
15	426	4
16	175	3
17	405	4
18	501	5
In	**3,322**	**36**
Total	**6,722**	**72**

CC of North Carolina Card of the course

Hole	Yards	Par
1	425	4
2	421	4
3	160	3
4	382	4
5	513	5
6	441	4
7	450	4
8	221	3
9	578	5
Out	**3,591**	**36**
10	386	4
11	417	4
12	548	5
13	190	3
14	445	4
15	441	4
16	206	3
17	420	4
18	510	5
In	**3,563**	**36**
Total	**7,154**	**72**

Cascades Card of the course

Hole	Yards	Par
1	394	4
2	412	4
3	283	4
4	198	3
5	576	5
6	369	4
7	425	4
8	141	3
9	450	4
Out	**3,248**	**35**
10	375	4
11	191	3
12	476	5
13	438	4
14	408	4
15	222	5
16	525	5
17	491	5
18	192	3
In	**3,318**	**36**
Total	**6,566**	**71**

64 Quaker Ridge GC, Scarsdale, NY

Designed by A. W. Tillinghast in 1916, this exacting course in rolling, heavily wooded country a short distance from New York is relatively unknown compared with its neighbour, Winged Foot. It is said that there are eighteen 'signature holes' at Quaker Ridge, and, certainly, the short holes are ingeniously varied. Driving is tough with a string of difficult par-4s from the 2nd, with the narrow 6th fairway the hardest to hit. It favours a left-to-right player, as does the only real dog-leg on the course, the 7th. The shorter, par-four 11th is distinguished by a stream which crosses in front of the tee, threatens the left side of the fairway and snakes back around the right side of the green. For good measure trees overhang the left side of the putting surface. Quaker Ridge has shunned the limelight of the big tournament circuit, but did play host to the Walker Cup in 1997, with the home side winning handsomely.

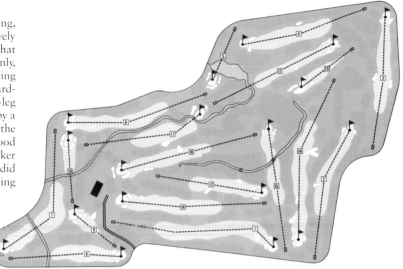

Quaker Ridge Card of the course

Hole	Yards	Par		Hole	Yards	Par
1	527	5		10	201	3
2	425	4		11	387	4
3	441	4		12	437	4
4	430	4		13	234	3
5	185	3		14	545	5
6	446	4		15	394	4
7	431	4		16	427	4
8	359	4		17	362	4
9	164	3		18	440	4
Out	**3,408**	**35**		**In**	**3,427**	**35**
				Total	**6,835**	**70**

65 Baltimore CC, Baltimore, Md.

Five Farms, which was once just the suburban course of the Baltimore Country Club, is now the hub of the club. It sits amid the rolling hills of Maryland's "huntcountry", where horses have always been the major sport but from which golf is fast taking over. Designed by the late, great genius of architecture, A. W. Tillinghast, the course is not overly bunkered and neither is it tremendously long. But those hills present numerous sidehill lies after mis-hit drives and the greens can get fearsomely slick, although remaining awesomely true. Baltimore has hosted a number of major events, including the exciting 1965 Walker Cup in which Britain and Ireland tied the US team, so breaking a string of losses dating back to 1938. In 1988 the Women's Open was held there, and was won by the Swede Liselotte Neumann.

Baltimore Card of the course

Hole	Yards	Par
1	424	4
2	433	4
3	387	4
4	163	3
5	425	4
6	575	5
7	349	4
8	355	4
9	193	3
Out	**3,304**	**35**
10	378	4
11	424	4
12	388	4
13	158	3
14	500	5
15	425	4
16	422	4
17	175	3
18	385	4
In	**3,355**	**35**
Total	**6,659**	**70**

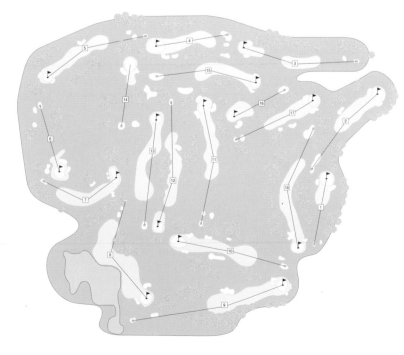

Westchester, CC Card of the course

Hole	Yards	Par
1	190	3
2	384	4
3	408	4
4	419	4
5	565	5
6	133	3
7	326	4
8	464	4
9	505	5
Out	**3,394**	**36**
10	314	4
11	442	4
12	473	4
13	379	4
14	154	3
15	462	4
16	204	3
17	374	4
18	526	5
In	**3,328**	**35**
Total	**6,722**	**71**

66 Westchester CC, New York

Westchester County, a snug New York suburb within easy reach of the bustle of Manhattan, has more than its share of excellent golf courses and in particular Westchester Country Club, together with its near neighbours Quaker Ridge and Winged Foot, comprise a formidable trinity. The venue each year for the Buick Classic on the USPGA tour, the Westchester course is not long at a shade under 6,800 yards, yet the formidable 12th is perennially one of the hardest holes on the tour. Tight fairways and subtly contoured greens are married together to form a classic layout, one that eminently appeals to the game's shotmakers: Vijay Singh and Ernie Els have each won there twice in recent times.

67 Concord GC, Kiamesha Lake, NY

The Concord Hotel and its two eighteen-hole courses are set in the woods of the Catskill Mountains about two hours' drive north of New York City. Before 1964 the resort had an eighteen-hole layout, the International, and a small nine-holer, the Challenger. To these the Texan architect Joe Finger added the Monster. This course is incredibly long, measuring, from the back tee, a standard 7,471 yards – which can be stretched to 7,650 yards in exceptional circumstances. Finger wanted the longer distance to be played only when there was a strong following wind, blowing off the mountains. The course borders on Kiamesha Lake and fine, though not extravagant, use of the water has been made on eight of the holes. The greens are grand, sprawling areas and the bunkering is subtle, in the true Finger style. At the 610-yard par-five 4th, a lateral water hazard runs for 220 yards down the left-hand side, gradually encroaching on to the fairway and making the 4th a hole that even the elite find hard to master.

Concord Monster Course Card of the course

Hole	Yards	Par			
1	555	5	10	416	4
2	458	4	11	198	3
3	467	4	12	529	5
4	610	5	13	392	4
5	224	3	14	177	3
6	380	4	15	481	4
7	231	3	16	572	5
8	443	4	17	420	4
9	442	4	18	476	4
Out	**3,810**	**36**	In	3,661	36
			Total	7,471	72

70 NCR CC, Kettering, Ohio

The NCR Country Club's South Course was one of two courses originally built in 1954 for the employees of the NCR Corporation. This 6,824-yard course, designed by Dick Wilson, has frequently been called a "thinking-man's course" because the premium here is on accuracy. The course winds through heavily wooded areas and rolling terrain and has no water hazards – a lack more than compensated for by the trees, traps, dog-legs and rough. The scenic 10th, a 528-yard par-five, is a dog-leg to a gorgeous green set in the face of a hill, surrounded by six traps. The toughest par three, the 228-yard 15th hole, calls for a demanding tee shot uphill to another heavily trapped green. Gary Player has suggested that golf architects today "could learn a lesson from this course", and Jack Nicklaus, admiring the sloping green of the 13th hole, said "What a job that architect Dick Wilson did!" NCR hosted the 1969 PGA Championship, won by Raymond Floyd, and the 1986 Women's Open, won by Jane Geddes.
Record: 66, Mike Podolski

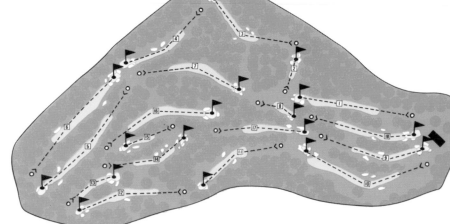

NCR Country Club Card of the course

Hole	Yards	Par			
1	447	4	10	528	5
2	168	3	11	375	4
3	418	4	12	439	4
4	378	4	13	200	3
5	538	5	14	373	4
6	529	5	15	228	3
7	410	4	16	450	4
8	170	3	17	348	4
9	416	4	18	409	4
Out	**3,474**	**36**	In	3,350	35
			Total	6,824	71

Canterbury
Card of the course

Hole	Yards	Par
1	432	4
2	367	4
3	177	3
4	452	4
5	412	4
6	522	5
7	201	3
8	410	4
9	552	5
Out	**3,525**	**36**
10	344	4
11	180	3
12	373	4
13	490	5
14	384	4
15	367	4
16	611	5
17	229	3
18	439	4
In	**3,417**	**36**
Total	**6,942**	**72**

68 Canterbury GC, Cleveland, Ohio

Ten miles from Cleveland, the Canterbury course was designed by English émigré Herbert Strong in 1922 and modified a few years later by the club's professional, Jack Way. It is not excessively long, but the problems caused by the fourteen dog-legs and the wind that blows off Lake Erie produce a course that favours the long hitter. From the 16th, a 611-yard monster, the run-in is very tough and has sealed the fate of many a player. When played into the wind the short, 229-yard 17th can require a wood to reach the raised double-tiered green, flanked by bunkers and guarded by out of bounds on the right. Then comes Canterbury's last and most difficult hole, its fairway uphill for 439 yards and lined with trees, with out of bounds to the right and a viciously trapped green. It is often said that if par is held on these three holes then victory is almost assured. The course has seen two US Opens, in 1940 and 1946, the 1973 USPGA, 1964 and 1979 US Amateur, and 1996 US Senior Open.
Record: 66, Bobby Clampett, 1979

69 Scioto CC, Columbus, Ohio

Scioto is the course where Jack Nicklaus developed from a pudgy junior to a world beater. Designed by Donald Ross in 1916, it carries all the hallmarks of his best works – greens nestling into the terrain, gentle slopes on the approaches, full use of the ground's natural contours and plenty of subtle problems which demand thought rather than power. The 438-yard 2nd is one of the great Ross holes. A stream crosses in front of the tee and runs up the left side of the fairway, which is bordered by trees and out-of-bounds on the right. Bunkers protect the tee shot landing area and the sloping green is guarded at the front. All four par-three holes on this magnificent course offer a stiff challenge. Toughest of all is the 238-yard 14th, a deceptive hole with a long carry over a rolling fairway. Scioto staged the 1926 US Open (won by Bobby Jones), the Ryder Cup matches of 1931 and both the American PGA and Amateur Championships.

Scioto Card of the course

Hole	Yards	Par
1	410	4
2	438	4
3	377	4
4	194	3
5	438	4
6	527	5
7	372	4
8	505	5
9	162	3
Out	**3,423**	**36**
10	424	4
11	365	4
12	545	5
13	435	4
14	238	3
15	408	4
16	425	4
17	209	3
18	445	4
In	**3,494**	**35**
Total	**6,917**	**71**

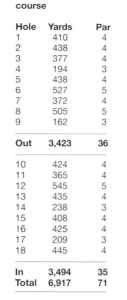

71 Shoal Creek, Birmingham, Ala.

Opened in 1977, Shoal Creek soon hosted two prestigious events: the 1984 PGA Championship and the 1986 US Amateur. Cradled in the lap of Oak and Double Oak Mountains, this sparkling Jack Nicklaus-designed course plays at 7,145 yards without a weak hole. Nicklaus describes the 555 yard 6th as the best par-five he has created. The serpentine Shoal Creek meanders through the fairway and must be negotiated twice before reaching a slender, undulating green. The 428-yard, par-four 9th is a slight dog-leg left, bunkered right at the turn, with water to the right of the fairway and on three sides of the green. The 10th and 11th holes both feature multi-tiered greens and the further windings of Shoal Creek. The 539-yard par-five 17th is called the "Waterfall Hole", for the pond and waterfall that guard the front of the shallow green. To reach it in two requires shots both long and accurate to avoid the large bunker and woodlands on the right of the fairway and a large dogwood tree in the left centre. The green, apparently flat has several subtle breaks in the centre.

Shoal Creek Card of the course

Hole	Yards	Par	Hole	Yards	Par
1	409	4	10	415	4
2	424	4	11	517	5
3	530	5	12	452	4
4	458	4	13	177	3
5	189	3	14	383	4
6	554	5	15	407	4
7	443	4	16	197	3
8	177	3	17	539	5
9	428	4	18	446	4
Out	**3,612**	**36**	**In**	**3,533**	**36**
			Total	**7,145**	**72**

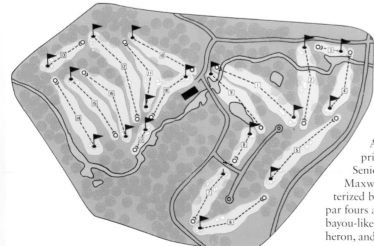

72 Lakewood GC, Point Clear, Ala.

Lakewood Golf Club is located on the eastern shore of Mobile Bay at the 140-year old Grand Hotel, now owned by Marriott. Lakewood offers thirty-six holes of golf, the original eighteen holes designed by Perry Maxwell in 1946; nine holes added by Joe Lee in 1966; and nine more designed by Ron Garl in 1986. They are arranged in the Azalea and Dogwood courses, and the eighteen holes comprising the Dogwood course were the venue for the 1986 USGA Senior Women's Amateur Champion-ship. A combination of the Maxwell and Lee designs, the Dogwood is 6,676 yards. It is characterized by pine trees and moss-draped oaks lining the fairways. The par fours and fives generally dog-leg to some degree and lead through bayou-like vegetation that provides a natural habitat for beaver, duck, heron, and alligator.

Lakewood GC (Dogwood Course) Card of the course

Hole	Yards	Par
1	500	5
2	444	4
3	158	3
4	380	4
5	522	5
6	413	4
7	327	4
8	190	3
9	396	4
Out	**3,330**	**36**
10	388	4
11	430	4
12	530	5
13	236	3
14	438	4
15	406	4
16	436	4
17	145	3
18	337	4
In	**3,346**	**35**
Total	**6,676**	**71**

73 Chicago GC, Wheaton, Ill.

Chicago was one of the five clubs which formed the US Golf Association in 1894 – the same year that the club moved to its present site at Wheaton from Belmont, where it had been inaugurated two years earlier. The guiding light in those times was the famed Charles Blair Macdonald, who constructed the first course before it was completely redesigned and rebuilt during 1921 with the assistance of Seth Raynor. At 413 yards, the 8th is slightly double dog-legged and scarred by eight sandtraps, of which three abut a green that has a gently rolling surface and is set obliquely to the fairway. The club staged many early championships, including the US Open three times and the US Amateur on four occasions.
Record: 66, Bobby Jones, Walker Cup, 1928

Chicago GC Card of the course

Hole	Yards	Par			
1	450	4	10	139	3
2	440	4	11	410	4
3	219	3	12	414	4
4	536	5	13	149	3
5	320	4	14	351	4
6	395	4	15	393	4
7	207	3	16	525	5
8	413	4	17	382	4
9	406	4	18	425	4
Out	3,386	35	In	3,188	35
			Total	6,574	70

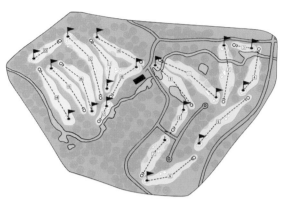

74 Butler National GC, Chicago, Ill.

Located in the Oak Brook suburb of Chicago, Butler National, designed by George Fazio, is a new course which demands patience and precision from the tee. The greens have become renowned for their mysterious undulations, so tricky that they defeat even those most familiar with them. Water has been used imaginatively, coming into play at eleven holes. It creates a potent problem from the back tee at the par-three 5th, where a 240-yard carry is needed to hit a peninsula green which is also backed on the right side by water. At the 435-yard par-four 14th the same body of water has to be crossed twice en route to the green, making it the most challenging hole on the course.

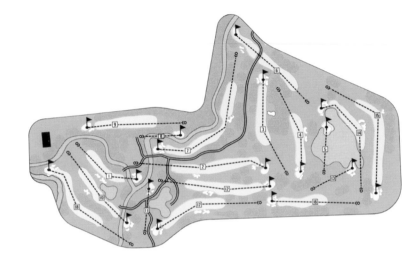

75 Sentry World GC, Stevens Point, Wisc.

Designed by Robert Trent Jones, Jr., Sentry World opened in late summer of 1982. It is a public course owned by Wisconsin's Sentry Insurance. Jones has described the 6,951-yard course as "very possibly my Mona Lisa", and it is easy to see why when surveying the spring-fed lakes and Sentry World's special characteristic, the five acres of flower beds. There are many tests for a golfer's game, with sinister bogs, sand traps (83 in all, including one that measures a full half-acre), hungry lakes and multi-tiered greens. The par-five, 507-yard 5th hole is exciting, as it hooks around an island in one of the lakes to a peninsular green that can be reached by two daring long shots. Another kind of hazard is provided by the gorgeous par-three 16th, the "Flower Hole": 90,000 multi-coloured blooms hem both fairway and green. The flower beds are like water hazards, in that balls that stray into the marigolds and petunias cannot be retrieved.

Butler National Card of the course

Hole	Yards	Par			
1	392	4	10	433	4
2	552	5	11	190	3
3	433	4	12	469	4
4	400	4	13	193	3
5	240	3	14	435	4
6	442	4	15	578	5
7	603	5	16	385	4
8	195	3	17	454	4
9	427	4	18	470	4
Out	3,684	36	In	3,607	35
			Total	7,291	71

Sentry World Golf Course Card of the course

Hole	Yards	Par			
1	387	4	10	392	4
2	416	4	11	545	5
3	405	4	12	223	3
4	187	3	13	395	4
5	507	5	14	523	5
6	409	4	15	457	4
7	202	3	16	173	3
8	368	4	17	412	4
9	502	5	18	448	4
Out	3,383	36	In	3,568	36
			Total	6,951	72

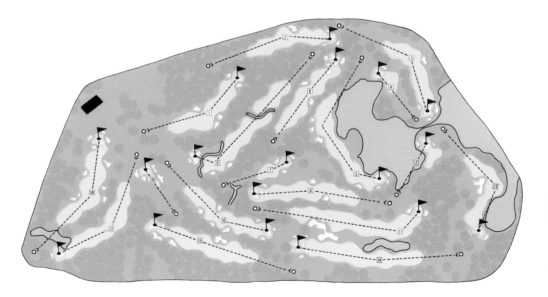

76 The Honors Course, Chattanooga, Tenn.

Architect Pete Dye was given more than 200 acres of East Tennessee countryside to create The Honors Course, allowing him to design a course that reflects his belief that the architect must mould his idea to conform to the land. But Dye is not too much of a purist — The Honors called for the creation of two lakes, one larger than 20 acres in size. At 7,024 yards, the layout offers plenty of privacy among its widely-spaced fairways. Players need to be free of distractions when facing the tricky, par-three 16th, with trees and a deep but subtle grass bunker to the left and one of the lakes to the right. Dye expects "many safe and somewhat timid" shots to find the bunker, facing "an interesting pitch back to the small green, since the lake still stands on the other side, ready for any missed shot." The 18th, a long, 451-yard par-four, is crossed by two ravines en route to the large, severely contoured green surrounded by bunkers. The Honors Course tests every club in the bag and every shot in the repertoire of the seasoned golfer.

The Honors Course Card of the course

Hole	Yards	Par		Hole	Yards	Par
1	401	4		10	435	4
2	520	5		11	562	5
3	195	3		12	355	4
4	433	4		13	394	4
5	459	4		14	156	3
6	546	5		15	443	4
7	437	4		16	208	3
8	206	3		17	494	5
9	369	4		18	451	4
Out	**3,566**	**36**		**In**	**3,498**	**36**
				Total	**7,064**	**72**

77 Hazeltine National GC, Chaska, Minn.

Hazeltine National is an unusual club in that it only has 290 members, with a mission that includes hosting national championships. Its strong commitment to equal access and the promotion of junior golf has been recognised with recent national awards. Founded in the 1960s, its first Major was the 1970 US Open, won decisively by Tony Jacklin. Then came Payne Stewart's popular Open win in 1991. By then Robert Trent Jones's course, built in the 1960s, had been considerably altered, and further changes were made for the 2002 US PGA, substantially lengthening the course. Dangerous, despite its modest length, is the 16th, with a 220-yard carry over water to the fairway, which is itself flanked by water. The approach is then an all-or-nothing shot to a peninsula green. A stroke picked up on the long 15th is readily lost here.

Interlachen Country Club Card of the course

Hole	Yards	Par		Hole	Yards	Par
1	531	5		10	341	4
2	351	4		11	476	5
3	195	3		12	541	5
4	509	5		13	195	3
5	171	3		14	440	4
6	350	4		15	414	4
7	346	4		16	318	4
8	412	4		17	226	3
9	520	5		18	397	4
Out	**3,385**	**37**		**In**	**3,348**	**36**
				Total	**6,733**	**73**

Hazeltine National GC Card of the course

Hole	Yards	Par		Hole	Yards	Par
1	460	4		10	410	4
2	435	4		11	597	5
3	636	5		12	465	4
4	196	3		13	204	3
5	412	4		14	357	4
6	405	4		15	586	5
7	542	5		16	402	4
8	178	3		17	182	3
9	436	4		18	457	4
Out	**3,700**	**36**		**In**	**3,660**	**36**
				Total	**7,360**	**72**

78 Interlachen CC, Edina, Minn.

Interlachen Country Club lies just west of the city of Minneapolis, in the suburb of Edina, and is blessed with an abundance and wide variety of trees. This is hallowed ground, the course having been designed by the legendary Donald Ross (1920) and having served as the site of the 1930 US Open, won by Bobby Jones as the third leg of his "Grand Slam" that year. In 1930, Interlachen's 17th hole was the longest par-three (262 yards) in Open history. The best Jones could do in four rounds was a bogey four (in the entire Open, the 17th gave up but two birdies). During the mid-1980s, Interlachen was restored by Geoffrey Cornish, holding to Ross's original concepts. It is customary to use the words "rolling fairways" to describe almost any golf course, but in the case of Interlachen, they may be taken literally, and no fewer than ten holes have elevated greens. Both factors proved too much for Great Britain and Ireland's Walker Cup team in 1993 – they were demolished 19–5 by the USA.

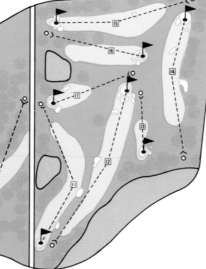

79 Prairie Dunes GC, Hutchinson, Kans.

Prairie Dunes could hardly be farther from the sea, yet the superb course is played across rolling sandhills characteristic of a true Scottish links – an impression heightened by the severe rough, so unusual on American golf courses. Originally a nine-hole course, designed in 1937 by Perry Maxwell, it was extended to 6,339 yards over a period of twenty years by his son, J. Press Maxwell. The 420-yard dog-legged 8th is a classic. Thick rough prevents any thought of a short cut and a long iron second is necessary to reach a well-trapped, two-tier plateau green. The 169-yard 10th – played downwind, with a scrub-covered dune on the left, a cavernous bunker in front, a steep drop to deep rough on the right and more bushes beyond – is a hole Scotland would be proud to own. Perhaps it was because Prairie Dunes reminded them of home that Great Britain and Ireland's Curtis Cup team achieved their historic first victory on American soil by the astonishingly comfortable margin of 13–5 in 1986.

Prairie Dunes Card of the course

Hole	Yards	Par			
1	424	4	10	169	3
2	150	3	11	450	4
3	325	4	12	327	4
4	160	3	13	357	4
5	439	4	14	337	4
6	382	4	15	197	3
7	507	5	16	420	4
8	420	4	17	497	5
9	399	4	18	379	4
Out	**3,206**	**35**	**In**	**3,133**	**35**
			Total	**6,339**	**70**

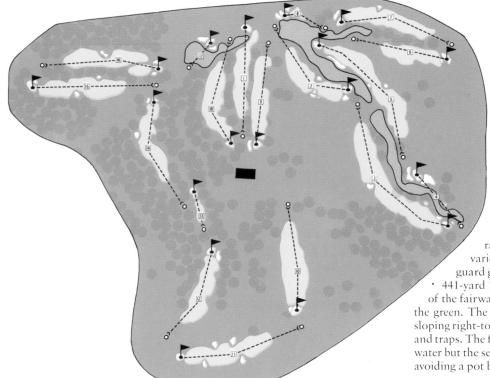

80 Oak Tree GC, Edmond, Okla.

Architect Pete Dye calls his course at Oak Tree "the finest inland golf course I have ever built". Consistently acclaimed as one of America's best and host of the 1988 PGA Championship (won by Jeff Sluman), the Oak Tree course features not only the massive old oaks that give it its name, but also railroad ties, rock walls and bridges that provide a variety of hazards. Large sand traps, strategically placed, guard greens that tend to slope right to left. On the par-four, 441-yard 1st, it's important to keep your drive to the right side of the fairway, away from the trees, for a clear shot over the lake to the green. The par-three 4th features the lake again, as well as the sloping right-to-left green. The back nine has its fair share of bunkers and traps. The finishing hole, a par four, 406-yard effort, tees off over water but the second shot should be played to the center of the green, avoiding a pot bunker to the right.

Oak Tree Card of the course

Hole	Yards	Par			
1	441	4	10	379	4
2	392	4	11	466	4
3	584	5	12	445	4
4	200	3	13	149	3
5	590	5	14	453	4
6	377	4	15	434	4
7	440	4	16	499	5
8	171	3	17	200	3
9	429	4	18	406	4
Out	**3,624**	**36**	**In**	**3,391**	**35**
			Total	**7,015**	**71**

81 Cherry Hills CC, Denver, Colo.

Denver is the "mile-high" city and in its rarefied atmosphere the 7,088 yards of the Cherry Hills course play shorter than they read on the card. Designed by William Flynn in 1922 it was here, thirty-eight years later, that Arnold Palmer won his only US Open. Ben Hogan named the 483-yard 14th one of the most difficult par-fours in America. Its fairway rises from the tee with trees and out of bounds on the right; on the left, thick rough falls away to a creek. The hole then swings sharply to the left, offering a narrow opening to the green set between a deep bunker on the right and the ever-threatening creek which curls round and behind the left edge. The 14th starts a demanding finish which includes a 215-yard par-three to a very small green encircled by sand and trees. Then comes a testing par-four 16th that demands supreme accuracy; an exacting 555-yard par-five to an island green; and finally the 480-yard 18th often described as one of golf's finest last holes.

Record: 63, Doug Wherry

Cherry Hills Card of the course

Hole	Yards	Par			
1	346	4	10	439	4
2	421	4	11	577	5
3	328	4	12	207	3
4	437	4	13	387	4
5	543	5	14	483	4
6	171	3	15	215	3
7	394	4	16	433	4
8	234	3	17	555	5
9	438	4	18	480	4
Out	**3,312**	**35**	**In**	**3,776**	**36**
			Total	**7,088**	**71**

82 Colonial CC, Fort Worth, Tex.

It is often said that Ben Hogan's success was partly due to the fact that, having played his early golf at Colonial, every other course in the world was easy in comparison. Designed in 1935 by John Bredemus and embellished by Perry Maxwell for the 1941 US Open, it is 7,080 yards with a par of 70. Its trees, bunkers and river do not allow an all-out attack from the tee – placement rather than pure length being the key to success at every hole. This puts a premium on long, accurate second shots as at the 5th, a 459-yard par-four dog-leg to the right. A power fade from the tee may find the Trinity River under the trees, a long straight tee shot could overrun the fairway's bend into thick trees on the left. The 5th signals the welcome end of the notorious 'Horrible Horseshoe', the three hardest holes on the course.

Record: 61, Keith Clearwater 1993

Colonial Card of the course

Hole	Yards	Par		Hole	Yards	Par
1	565	5		10	404	4
2	400	4		11	609	5
3	476	4		12	433	4
4	246	3		13	178	3
5	470	4		14	457	4
6	393	4		15	430	4
7	427	4		16	188	3
8	192	3		17	383	4
9	402	4		18	427	4
Out	**3,571**	**35**		**In**	**3,509**	**35**
				Total	**7,080**	**70**

83 Castle Pines GC, Castle Rock, Colo.

Carved by Jack Nicklaus out of a scrub oak and pine forest north of Castle Rock, Colorado (near Denver), Castle Pines' 7,503-yard layout does not seem so long in the thin air of 6,600 feet above sea level. Here the ball carries about 10 per cent farther than normal. Nicklaus disturbed very little of the terrain to create this course, in which fourteen holes are generally wooded, and the remaining four are open links with a Scottish flavour. On twelve of the eighteen holes, no other is visible. The most difficult hole is the 5th, a 477-yard par four that climbs to an elevated green guarded by mounds, five traps, and a collection bunker waiting in the front centre of the green to punish any less than perfect approaches. Castle Pines is the home each year to one of the more unusual tournaments on the PGA Tour – the International – with its modified stableford format. Its roll call of winners includes Greg Norman, Davis Love, Jose-Maria Olazabal, and Phil Mickelson.

Castle Pines GC Card of the course

Hole	Yards	Par		Hole	Yards	Par
1	644	5		10	485	4
2	408	4		11	197	3
3	452	4		12	422	4
4	205	3		13	439	4
5	477	4		14	595	5
6	417	4		15	403	4
7	185	3		16	209	3
8	535	5		17	492	5
9	458	4		18	480	4
Out	**3,781**	**36**		**In**	**3,722**	**36**
				Total	**7,503**	**72**

84 Pasatiempo GC, Santa Cruz, Calif.

Pasatiempo, the brainchild of champion horsewoman and lady golfer Marion Hollins, was designed by Alister MacKenzie and completed in 1929. It is a 6,528-yard course that sprawls over the Santa Cruz hills. The front nine, deceptively simple holes that offer straight fairways flanked by trees and bunkers, don't prepare the golfer for the arroyos and dry stream of the back nine. Barrancas (ravines) dot the fairways and guard the greens. A par-four, 445-yard, dog-legged 10th hole sets the tone for the incoming nine. After a drive that must carry some 170–180 yards over a barranca, the player must use another wood for a downhill shot to a sloping fairway. A huge eucalyptus tree guards the green to the right and many a shot falls onto a bare lie among tree roots, caught by the extending branches. The 17th may offer some respite before the par three, 187-yard closing hole, with towering trees on the right and a deep barranca on the way to a very tricky green.

Pasatiempo Golf Club Card of the course

Hole	Yards	Par
1	497	5
2	438	4
3	218	3
4	394	4
5	197	3
6	518	5
7	345	4
8	178	3
9	491	5
Out	**3,276**	**36**
10	445	4
11	406	4
12	386	4
13	490	5
14	422	4
15	145	3
16	408	4
17	363	4
18	187	3
In	**3,252**	**35**
Total	**6,528**	**71**

85 Country Club of the Rockies, Edwards, Colo.

Situated high in the Rocky Mountains west of Vail, Colorado, the course at the Country Club of the Rockies, designed by Jack Nicklaus, has been acclaimed since its opening in 1985. The 7,000 foot elevation means both that the ball carries farther than normal in the thin mountain air and that the course is playable during the months of April through October only. The rest of the year, herds of deer and elk graze over the site, as they have for centuries. During the warm seasons, the 7,317-yard course boasts a Scottish links style layout with the mounds, characteristic of Nicklaus designs, that define fairways and protect greens. The par-four, 477-yard 12th hole plays downhill off the tee with mounds on either side. The second shot must cross the Eagle River, which comes into play and must be crossed on the 13th, 14th, and 15th holes as well.

Record: 67, Craig Stadler, Jerry Ford Invitational, 1986

Country Club of the Rockies Card of the course

Hole	Yards	Par	Hole	Yards	Par
1	453	4	10	446	4
2	389	4	11	180	3
3	566	5	12	477	4
4	209	3	13	573	5
5	429	4	14	156	3
6	427	4	15	415	4
7	571	5	16	463	4
8	162	3	17	586	5
9	400	4	18	415	4
Out	**3,606**	**36**	**In**	**3,711**	**36**
			Total	**7,317**	**72**

86 Spyglass Hill GC, Pebble Beach, Calif.

Spyglass Hill is possibly the hardest of the courses on the Monterey Peninsula. Statistics recorded over the 1991–93 seasons showed Spyglass to be the toughest course on the PGA Tour, with an average score of 73.957 per round. The 8th and 16th were rated 2nd and 3rd most difficult holes on tour. The infuriating thing is that it is so beautiful. The hilly land tumbles down towards the sea, leaving fairways lined with windswept cypress trees and Californian pines liberally laced with areas of brilliant white sand. The course, designed by Robert Trent Jones and opened in 1966, makes heavy demands on both the mental and physical resources of those who play. On a windy day it can become almost impossible and in fact is rarely played at its full championship length of 6,888 yards. The opening holes are a fearsome introduction to the course's difficulties. The 1st is an enormous 595 yards that needs thunderous stroke play even to approach a par. The course returns inland at the 6th, but trees now compound the problems set by the wind.

Spyglass Hill Card of the course

Hole	Yards	Par
1	595	5
2	349	4
3	152	3
4	370	4
5	209	3
6	416	4
7	529	5
8	399	4
9	431	4
Out	**3,450**	**36**
10	407	4
11	528	5
12	178	3
13	445	4
14	560	5
15	125	3
16	462	4
17	325	4
18	408	4
In	**3,438**	**36**
Total	**6,888**	**72**

87 Riviera CC, Pacific Palisades, Calif.

The golfing domain of show-business stars since its opening in 1927, this great Californian course, designed by George Thomas, plays host almost every year to the Nissan (formerly the LA) Open. It was here that Ben Hogan set his US Open record of 276, which stood for nineteen years, and, in 1950, made his historic comeback to golf after a near-fatal car crash. Massive reconstruction work was undertaken in 1974 to restore the small meandering stream which had become, over fifty years, a 40ft deep ravine; seventeen acres of land were reclaimed and the course was returned to its original glory. The spongy quality of the turf does not allow the ball to roll far and this makes the par fives extremely difficult, particularly the massive, 576-yard 17th. Yet power is not the only requirement, for there are subtle problems set by the winding barranca and the arrangement of bunkers. At the 175-yard 6th, sandtraps proliferate. The first bunker lies in the dead centre of the fairway just short of the target; on the green itself there is a small shallow trap, and at the back a hillside bunker to swallow the over-clubbed stroke.

Riviera Card of the course

Hole	Yards	Par
1	503	5
2	463	4
3	434	4
4	236	3
5	419	4
6	175	3
7	408	4
8	416	4
9	420	4
Out	**3,474**	**35**
10	315	4
11	564	5
12	410	4
13	438	4
14	176	3
15	443	4
16	166	3
17	576	5
18	451	4
In	**3,539**	**36**
Total	**7,013**	**71**

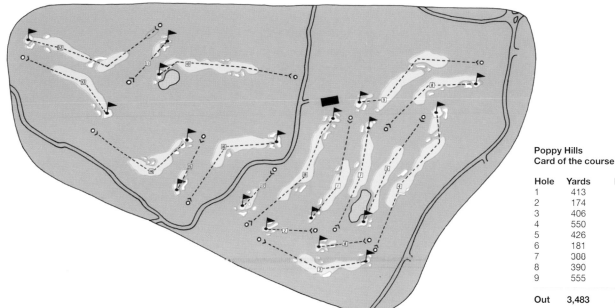

88 Poppy Hills GC, Pebble Beach, Calif.

Located on California's Monterey Peninsula, an area with an abundance of great golf courses, including the famed Spyglass Hill only a mile away, Poppy Hills Golf Course is in the Del Monte Forest. A public course designed by Robert Trent Jones, Jr., Poppy Hills opened in 1986. The course is close to the sea but incorporates water hazards with spare efficiency: the long (426-yard) par-four 5th offers a difficult second shot to the irregularly shaped green guarded by a pond on the right and bunkers to the left. The par five 10th hole, at 511 yards, challenges the best golfer's approach shot as the green is nestled behind water. The back nine has its share of doglegs, including the 90 degree left dog-leg on the 14th hole and a sharp right dog-leg on the 439-yard par-four 16th. Greens are typical of Robert Trent Jones, Jr., designs – large and rolling.

Poppy Hills
Card of the course

Hole	Yards	Par
1	413	4
2	174	3
3	406	4
4	550	5
5	426	4
6	181	3
7	300	4
8	390	4
9	555	5
Out	**3,483**	**36**
10	511	5
11	203	3
12	531	5
13	393	4
14	400	4
15	210	3
16	439	4
17	163	3
18	500	5
In	**3,350**	**36**
Total	**6,833**	**72**

89 Edgewood Tahoe, Stateline, Nev.

This public course, designed by George Fazio, opened for play in 1968. Adjacent to Lake Tahoe and at a breath-shortening elevation of 6,200 feet, the 7,725 yard course is as challenging as it is visually appealing. The 438-yard par four starting hole offers a wide landing area and a large green, but the second, a 493-yard par four, leads to a more severe two-tiered putting green. The toughest hole on the front nine, the 471-yard 9th, requires a long to mid-iron second shot after the dog-leg right to make the par-four. The 11th and 12th holes, par four and three respectively, offer fair chances for birdies, but swirling winds make the 14th a challenge, and the winds combine with trees and water for the spectacular final three holes. Edgewood Tahoe hosted the 1985 US Senior Open, won by Miller Barber.

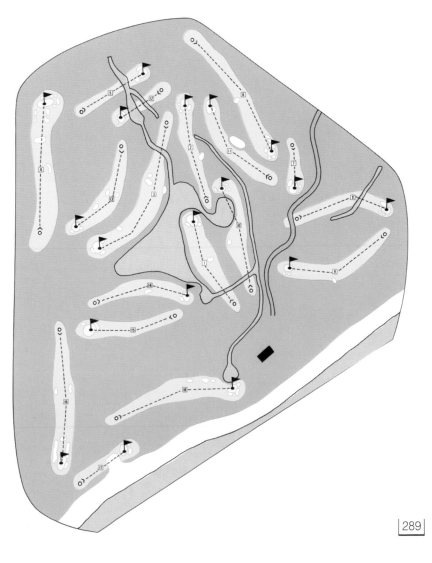

Edgewood Tahoe Card of the course

Hole	Yards	Par		Hole	Yards	Par
1	438	4		10	447	4
2	493	4		11	427	4
3	608	5		12	214	3
4	638	5		13	442	4
5	240	3		14	441	4
6	463	4		15	375	4
7	179	3		16	575	5
8	463	4		17	220	3
9	471	4		18	591	5
Out	**3,993**	**36**		**In**	**3,732**	**36**
				Total	**7,725**	**72**

Mauna Kea
Card of the course

Hole	Yards	Par
1	383	4
2	394	4
3	210	3
4	413	4
5	593	5
6	344	4
7	204	3
8	530	5
9	427	4
Out	**3,498**	**36**
10	554	5
11	247	3
12	387	4
13	409	4
14	413	4
15	201	3
16	422	4
17	555	5
18	428	4
In	**3,616**	**36**
Total	**7,114**	**72**

90 Mauna Kea GC, Hawaii

Robert Trent Jones's incredibly tough masterpiece at Mauna Kea on the Big Island of Hawaii has been refined by his son Robert from a course which only the elite among playing professionals could hope to master. The younger Jones adapted the layout so that it became acceptable for the average player – though even without some of its original savagery it still presents a number of formidable challenges. Carved out of desolate volcanic lava beds beside the ocean and over the foothills of vast mountains, it has developed the lush beauty to be expected on these scenic islands. The 3rd, with its view over the pounding Pacific to a green perched above volcanic rock 210 yards away, is not solved in one shot. The green carries the Trent Jones characteristic of sharp borrows and lightning speed, which rewards only the lightest of touches. But not every hole is as severe.

Record: 64, Terry Dill, 1969

Princeville Ocean Card of the course			Princeville Woods Card of the course			Princeville Lake Card of the course		
Hole	Yards	Par	Hole	Yards	Par	Hole	Yards	Par
1	410	4	1	360	4	1	346	4
2	602	5	2	185	3	2	497	5
3	173	3	3	517	5	3	440	4
4	359	4	4	393	4	4	222	3
5	506	5	5	376	4	5	308	4
6	419	4	6	442	4	6	404	4
7	197	3	7	427	4	7	200	3
8	345	4	8	185	3	8	436	4
9	390	4	9	492	5	9	510	5
Ocean 3,401		**36**	**Woods 3,377**		**36**	**Lake 3,363**		**36**

91 Princeville Makai GC, Hawaii

Built as three separate nines – Ocean, Lake and Woods – on a beautiful tract of land on Kauai, this is undoubtedly one of the most outstanding courses designed by Robert Trent Jones Jnr. Vast tees and large greens allow many combinations, lengths and degrees of difficulty over a layout of rolling fairways, strategic bunkers and generous use of lakes. The championship course is a combination of any two nines, depending on the strength and direction of the 15–20 mph trade winds – the effect of which can be judged from the professionals' choice of clubs at the 173-yard par-three 3rd on the Ocean course. A fourth course, the 18-hole Prince, opened in 1988. Enjoying spectacular vistas, it is 7,309 yards long (the shortest of its four par-fives is 554 yards!).

Hamilton
Card of the course

Hole	Yards	Par
1	425	4
2	457	4
3	401	4
4	543	5
5	321	4
6	216	3
7	394	4
8	195	3
9	423	4
Out	**3,375**	**35**
10	343	4
11	451	4
12	385	4
13	220	3
14	424	4
15	381	4
16	181	3
17	550	5
18	440	4
In	**3,375**	**35**
Total	**6,750**	**70**

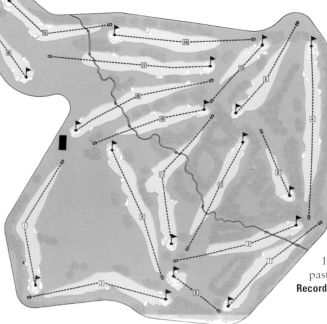

92 Hamilton G & CC, Ancaster, Ont.

Ancaster, as Hamilton is commonly known, epitomizes the country club ambience. The turf is lush and springy, while the heavily wooded surroundings give the property an elegant seclusion. The championship layout takes its front nine from the West course and the remainder from the South. Both were designed as nine-hole courses by H. S. Colt in 1914, and in 1974 an extra nine-holer, the East, was added by Robbie Robinson. From a promontory, the opulent clubhouse overlooks the strong finishing hole, a 440-yard par four where the fairway winds around an S-shaped stream to a saucer-like green. Because of the water, the tee shot is normally played as a lay-up and the approach to the large green calls for a wood or a low iron for even the longest hitter. The Bell Canadian Open returns to Hamilton in 2003. New tees are under construction for this event adding 50 to 100 yards to certain holes, and pushing the total length past 7,000 yards.

Record: 62, Warren Sye, Ontario Amateur Championship 1991

93 St George's GC, Islington, Ont.

St George's is distinguished by its tight fairways and rolling terrain. Situated in downtown Toronto, the course was designed by Stanley Thompson and opened for play in 1928. It was known as the Royal York and associated with the Canadian Pacific Railway until the company relinquished its interest after World War II. Not only the fairways twist and roll – even a putt over a flat surface is a rare treat on the well-trapped greens. At the 14th, a 446-yard par-four, the drive must avoid out of bounds on the left and carry a knoll, leaving a mid-iron second shot down the hill to a green that is banked on the right and trapped on the left. The problems are intensified by a river which runs down the right side of the fairway and crosses just in front of the green. In the 1933 Canadian Open Joe Kirkwood, the eventual winner, was stymied behind a large oak at the 5th. He hit the ball out of the right and produced a total roundhouse hook to land the ball eight feet from the pin, and holed out for a birdie.

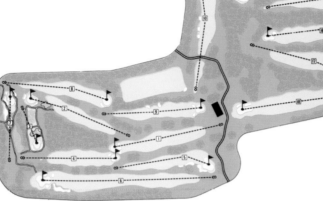

Record: 64, George Knudson, Canadian Open 1968

St George's Card of the course

Hole	Yards	Par			
1	378	4	10	377	4
2	420	4	11	517	5
3	201	3	12	383	4
4	480	5	13	214	3
5	403	4	14	446	4
6	146	3	15	580	5
7	442	4	16	203	3
8	217	3	17	447	4
9	543	5	18	400	4
Out	**3,230**	**35**	**In**	**3,567**	**36**
			Total	**6,797**	**71**

94 Vancouver GC, Coquitlam, BC

Inspired by emigrant Scots, the Vancouver course was laid out in 1910 on a stretch of densely wooded, rolling coastal land. Giant pines and cedars line the narrow fairways, increasing the difficulty of the course and offering compensation for its lack of length. The front nine is considered the easier although the 6th is more than 600 yards and needs a subtle approach shot to an irregularly shaped green, protected by a small pond that lies in front and just off to the left. On the back nine, the 16th – aptly called Graves – is a deceptive par-four of 371 yards. The hole dog-legs sharply left, leaving the green unsighted from the championship tee. The drive must reach the crook of the fairway, where the second shot needs a firm blast with a mid-iron to make the small green, which sulks behind a single bunker and is encircled by trees. Before the urbanization of Vancouver, it took quite a trek through the British Columbian wilds to reach the club, which explains the old segregated dormitory accommodation in the original clubhouse.

Vancouver Card of the course

Hole	Yards	Par			
1	395	4	10	460	4
2	378	4	11	373	4
3	134	3	12	190	3
4	357	4	13	520	5
5	343	4	14	381	4
6	616	5	15	372	4
7	192	3	16	371	4
8	383	4	17	396	4
9	354	4	18	446	4
Out	**3,152**	**35**	**In**	**3,509**	**36**
			Total	**6,661**	**71**

95 Jasper Park Lodge GC, Alberta

It took 50 teams of horses and 200 men to clear the site of huge quantities of timber and rocks to enable Stanley Thompson to create one of the most individual courses of its age; Jasper Park opened to huge acclaim in 1925. Here Thompson indulged his sense of humour, for instance designing the par-3 9th to resemble a woman, and naming it Cleopatra. He formed bunkers into the patterns of the snow formations on the surrounding mountains and created mounds to replicate the skyline, with many holes lined up on the principal peaks. Each short hole has the possibility of a birdie, but a double bogey or worse is likely to follow any misjudgement from the tee. The mountains complicate depth perception on many shots, and Thompson's bunkering is prolific, notably on the par-5s. A beautiful three-hole stretch on a peninsula, jutting out into Lac Beauvert, culminates in a testing pitch over its waters to the 16th green.

Jasper Park Card of the course

Hole	Yards	Par			
1	391	4	10	492	5
2	488	5	11	403	4
3	454	4	12	181	3
4	240	3	13	603	5
5	480	5	14	361	4
6	393	4	15	138	3
7	178	3	16	380	4
8	434	4	17	360	4
9	231	3	18	463	4
Out	**3,289**	**35**	**In**	**3,381**	**36**
			Total	**6,670**	**71**

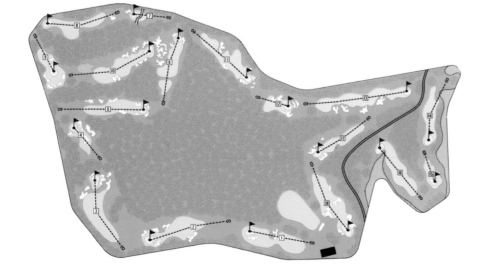

96 Vallescondido GC, Mexico City

Vallescondido is a superior private course designed by Percy Clifford, with a membership that is restricted to 750 members. Situated just outside Mexico City, it sprawls over a beautiful valley; oak trees closely line the fairways and a meandering stream affects play on eight of the holes. The gently undulating ground means that sidehill lies often result from less than accurately positioned shots. This rolling nature of the layout means that good club selection can lead to the gaining of important yardage. On the front nine a small pond comes into play at the 165-yard par three 8th, while on the back nine a solitary lake affects the 10th, a 496-yard par-five, and another small pond enters into the strategy of the short 15th. The 408-yard 4th ends with the green ninety degrees away from the initial line of play; the right of the fairway is flanked by sand and the green is effectively protected in front by a vast sandtrap.

Record: 68, Roberto de Vicenzo, 1975

Vallescondido Card of the course

Hole	Yards	Par			
1	408	4	10	496	5
2	323	4	11	359	4
3	668	5	12	218	3
4	408	4	13	468	4
5	219	3	14	574	5
6	400	4	15	255	3
7	530	5	16	420	4
8	165	3	17	443	4
9	434	4	18	405	4
Out	**3,455**	**36**	**In**	**3,638**	**36**
			Total	**7,093**	**72**

97 Port Royal GC, Southampton

Bermuda has so much golf to offer within its 21 square miles of land that it has been described as virtually one big golf club. Built in 1970, Port Royal was designed by Robert Trent Jones on high ground sweeping down to cliff edges overlooking the Atlantic, presenting a challenge considerably less lethal than many of his other designs. The greens are vast but gently contoured, and the surrounding bunkers do offer some leeway. From a tee on the cliff edge the spectacular short, 176-yard 16th is played across a yawning gap to a promontory which holds nothing more than the green, edged on three sides by sand. The course is over pleasantly undulating land where 200,000 new trees have been planted to blend in with the massive originals which survived the constructions. Three small lakes play their part – before the green at the 1st, on the left of the short 3rd and left again of the driving area at the sweeping dog-leg 17th.

Port Royal Card of the course

Hole	Yards	Par			
1	432	4	10	325	4
2	563	5	11	442	4
3	149	3	12	161	3
4	403	4	13	386	4
5	382	4	14	384	4
6	362	4	15	387	4
7	531	5	16	176	3
8	200	3	17	507	5
9	366	4	18	405	4
Out	**3,388**	**36**	**In**	**3,173**	**35**
			Total	**6,561**	**71**

98 Lucaya G & CC, Freeport

The towns of Lucaya and Freeport are the centres of the gambling enterprises that lure so many people to the Bahamas. However, the Lucaya Golf and Country Club is far from being a gambler's paradise: it is a conservative club with a membership largely composed of American and Canadian businessmen. The course, designed by Dick Wilson and opened in 1964, sits on a natural hilly area overlooking the Bell Channel. One of its most interesting features is the extraordinary natural hazard of white coral rock that lies off the fairway beyond the normal rough. If the ball lands here, finding it is a minor problem compared to the difficulties of playing out. There is only one lake on the course and this runs the final 200 yards down the left-hand side of the 17th to haunt any hook-prone right-hander. Lucaya was the last club which the late, vastly admired American professional Craig Wood represented. It was here that he shot a 66 a matter of days before his sixty-sixth birthday.

Lucaya Card of the course

Hole	Yards	Par
1	373	4
2	170	3
3	540	5
4	431	4
5	383	4
6	389	4
7	210	3
8	489	5
9	429	4
Out	**3,414**	**36**
10	419	4
11	199	3
12	469	5
13	169	3
14	405	4
15	427	4
16	560	5
17	374	4
18	388	4
In	**3,410**	**36**
Total	**6,824**	**72**

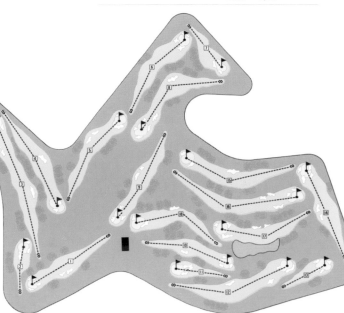

Divi Bahamas
Card of the course

Hole	Yards	Par
1	517	5
2	404	4
3	385	4
4	168	3
5	396	4
6	510	5
7	343	4
8	235	3
9	422	4
Out	**3,380**	**36**
10	530	5
11	118	3
12	413	4
13	407	4
14	386	4
15	165	3
16	528	5
17	354	4
18	426	4
In	**3,327**	**36**
Total	**6,707**	**72**

99 Divi Bahamas Beach Resort and Country Club, Nassau, New Providence

Designed by Joe Lee and completed in 1971, Divi Bahamas is one of the best of the Bahamian courses. Situated on New Providence Island near Nassau, the capital, it has eighteen holes of completely separate and iden- tifiable character, cut through dense tropical jungle. Water comes into play at seven holes and the vast greens are matched by enormous areas of sand, some with trees in the middle, a trademark of Lee's work. He has also resisted the modern temptation to make every par-three a test of power rather than accuracy, and the 118-yard 11th – to an elongated green whose entrance is flanked by bunkers – is a welcome change, if no less demanding. Of the par-fives, the 528 yard 16th is virtually a double dog-leg, first round a lake on the right, then skirting a second stretch of water on the left before pitching to a green that is protected by four bunkers.

Record: 68, Lee Elder, Pro-Am 1973

100 Carambola Beach Resort and Golf Club, St Croix

At St Croix on the Virgin Islands, an American protectorate, Robert Trent Jones has built a course of outstanding beauty and charm. Carambola is on the floor of a valley that is filled with trees, water and ravines, offering an awe-inspiring collection of views. Subtle teeing grounds are the key feature of the design, especially on the four short holes, three of which must be carried from the back tees, although alternative tees reduce the problem for the less accomplished. The first short hole is the 175-yard 5th, where the tees jut farther and farther out into the lake. From the champi- onship teeing ground the shot requires a clear carry over the water, whereas from the ladies' tee the lake runs adjacent to the fairway, threatening any shot that is slightly hooked. The large green is trapped to the rear, penal- izing those who over-club to ensure clearing the lake. Trade winds in the horseshoe-shaped valley both cool the course and add to its problems.

Carambola Card of the course

Hole	Yards	Par		Hole	Yards	Par
1	510	5		10	395	4
2	400	4		11	487	5
3	407	4		12	310	4
4	467	4		13	470	5
5	175	3		14	190	3
6	595	5		15	400	4
7	419	4		16	389	4
8	180	3		17	235	3
9	470	4		18	410	4
Out	**3,623**	**36**		**In**	**3,286**	**36**
				Total	**6,909**	**72**

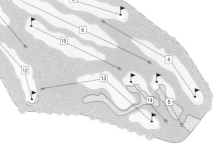

101 Cerromar Beach Hotel GC, Dorado

When Robert Trent Jones was invited to design a North and South course at Cerromar, just a short walk from his famous thirty-six hole complex at Dorado Beach, the challenge to produce equally good-look- ing golf of a totally different style was irresistible. He achieved this by the more discreet use of the abundant water, particularly on the par-three and par-five holes, and by varying the greens from the large, contoured, sparsely bunkered type to the smaller, flatter, sand-surrounded designs. Although the combination of trees and water makes skilful shotmaking essential on many holes, these hazards are pulled back from the line of play at others to offer scenically exciting and less demanding golf. The North course is used for championship play and its outstanding par threes call for the best strokemaking. At the 187-yard 4th the green is particularly narrow, well protected by inviting bunkers and flanked by water on the right. The 11th is played from a raised tee 193 yards away and into the prevailing wind, with a lateral water hazard threat- ening on the left of the green and a large bunker protecting the right side.

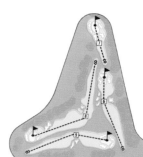

Cerromar Beach
North Course Card of the course

Hole	Yards	Par		Hole	Yards	Par
1	507	5		10	378	4
2	406	4		11	193	3
3	393	4		12	548	5
4	187	3		13	428	4
5	397	4		14	408	4
6	373	4		15	394	4
7	175	3		16	445	4
8	519	5		17	185	3
9	400	4		18	505	5
Out	**3,357**	**36**		**In**	**3,484**	**36**
				Total	**6,841**	**72**

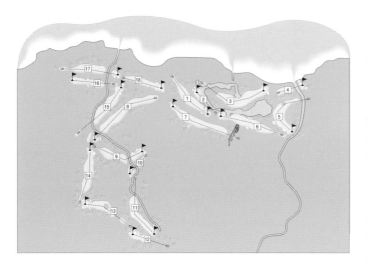

102 Tryall Golf, Tennis and Beach Club, Hanover, Jamaica

Sandy Bay lies on the western tip of Jamaica on near-mountainous land that has superb views over the ocean. Here, in the breach of the trade winds, is the Tryall course, a fine layout that was conceived by Ralph Plummer. It was radically rebuilt to prepare it for the Johnnie Walker World Championship, a big-money end of season tournament which attracted star-studded fields to Jamaica in the early 1990s. The basic character of Plummer's layout has been retained but many of the low-lying holes along the Caribbean shore now feature water hazards. On the higher ground of the back nine there are stunning seaward views, especially on the 12th and 14th, and the breezes bring a refreshing relief from the kitchen-hot valleys. Tryall's newest hole is the 4th, a dangerous short hole with the sea on the left, the Flint River just in front of the green and, almost invariably, a tricky breeze off the sea. The most unusual hole is the 7th, on which the drive from the blue tee is made through the stone arches of an aqueduct. It is a stern uphill par-4. Tougher still from the back plates is the 8th, but visitors play it as a par-5 when it is a more manageable proposition.

Tryall
Card of the course

Hole	Yards	Par
1	373	4
2	193	3
3	521	5
4	175	3
5	367	4
6	519	5
7	434	4
8	482	4
9	404	4
Out	**3,459**	**36**
10	170	3
11	500	5
12	213	3
13	373	4
14	450	4
15	445	4
16	429	4
17	391	4
18	342	4
In	**3,313**	**35**
Total	**6,772**	**71**

103 Tobago GC, Tobago

Commander John D. Harris has a string of designs in more than thirty countries to his credit, and the Tobago course at Mount Irvine Bay is one of his classics. Set in gently rising country along the coast, there are sea views from every hole, fine water features and an abundance of massive palm trees. The sharply dog-legged 472-yard 9th is played from an elevated tee so that those who attempt the shortcut can clearly see the lake, trees and sand which stand in their way. This is a feature of Harris's designs – he believes that every hazard should be visible, acting as lighthouses to guide the player along the correct path. The five par-three holes are particularly challenging; only two are less than 200 yards. The 215-yard 7th is considered the best. The shot is to a long, narrow green with sand on the right and a drop to a lake on the left. The lush tees, fairways and greens, all grassed in tifton, are amply watered by the course's subterranean irrigation network.

Tobago
Card of the course

Hole	Yards	Par
1	464	4
2	540	5
3	170	3
4	360	4
5	405	4
6	535	5
7	215	3
8	335	4
9	472	4
Out	**3,496**	**36**
10	485	5
11	445	4
12	215	3
13	510	5
14	225	3
15	445	4
16	445	5
17	195	3
18	395	4
In	**3,360**	**36**
Total	**6,856**	**72**

104 Lagos de Caujaral GC, Barranquilla

Designer Joe Lee built many problems into this beautiful course; nine holes feature water – several of them threatened on both sides – while three par-fives have double dog-legs, and three other holes have a seventy-five foot drop from tee to fairway. Mercifully, at 6,585 yards, the length is not too demanding. Yet the strong trade winds can make even the most modest par-four a drive and long-iron for the majority of golfers. The view from the elevated 1st tee is of a narrow fairway between dense trees to a well-trapped green – and this is the widest fairway on the course. The double water hazard is first featured at the 370-yard 4th, where the tee shot must carry 200 yards to an island fairway and counteract the prevailing wind pushing the ball towards the water on the right. It is then necessary to cross the water again to reach a green which is also virtually surrounded by two lakes, with bunkers to the left rear and right front.

Lagos de Caujaral Card of the course

Hole	Yards	Par		Hole	Yards	Par
1	490	5		10	430	4
2	410	4		11	210	3
3	375	4		12	520	5
4	370	4		13	360	4
5	140	3		14	155	3
6	555	5		15	360	4
7	370	4		16	335	4
8	175	3		17	430	4
9	395	4		18	505	5
Out	**3,280**	**36**		**In**	**3,305**	**36**
				Total	**6,585**	**72**

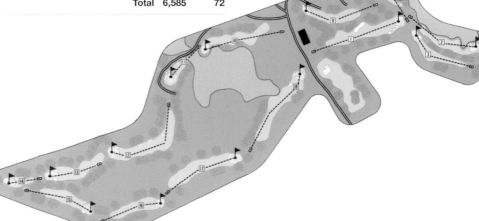

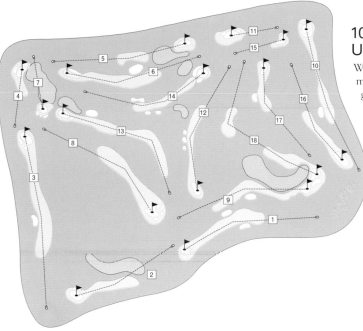

105 Emirates Golf Club, Dubai, United Arab Emirates

With daytime temperatures soaring to 120°F, more than 4 million litres of water must be pumped through 500 sprinkler heads every day simply to keep the grass growing on the Majlis Course. It was a member of Dubai's ruling family, Sheikh Mohammed bin Rashid Al Maktoum, who conceived the idea of building a golf course in such an inhospitable landscape, engaging the American architect Karl Litten for the design work. The Majlis Course opened for play in 1988 and almost every year since then it has hosted the Dubai Desert Classic with Ballesteros, Els, Couples, Montgomery and Olazábal among past winners. The key to success is to stay on the fairways with several lakes and huge expanses of virgin desert awaiting the slightest error. There is now a second course, the Wadi, equally long, and the clubhouse, resembling a group of Bedouin tents, is stunning.

Emirates Golf Club, Majlis Course
Card of the course

Hole	Yards	Par			
1	433	4	10	549	5
2	351	4	11	169	3
3	530	5	12	467	4
4	184	3	13	550	4
5	436	4	14	434	4
6	450	4	15	177	3
7	184	3	16	392	4
8	434	4	17	351	4
9	463	4	18	547	5
Out	**3,465**	**35**	**In**	**3,636**	**37**
			Total	**7,101**	**72**

106 Karen CC, Nairobi

Founded in 1937 in the wooded residential district of Karen, twelve miles south of Nairobi, much of the course was laid out on the former coffee estate of Baroness Karen von Blixen, after whom the district takes its name and where she wrote her classic novel *Out of Africa*. Situated at an altitude of 6,000 feet on rolling terrain, with a backdrop of the Ngong Hills, the course is handsome at all times of the year, with its rich variety of native trees, flowering shrubs, and noisy animal and bird life. An extensive irrigation system and sand-based greens ensure excellent conditions, and with Nairobi's temperate climate they can be enjoyed 365 days a year. At 580 yards, the 2nd is a stern hole, its huge dog-leg demanding drives of great length and perfect positioning. The 14th is a mere 137 yards in length, but its environmentally protected water hazards call for pin-point accuracy.

Karen Card of the course

Hole	Yards	Par
1	350	4
2	580	5
3	538	5
4	387	4
5	186	3
6	475	4
7	166	3
8	384	4
9	443	4
Out	**3,509**	**36**
10	362	4
11	395	4
12	301	4
13	457	4
14	137	3
15	561	5
16	195	3
17	458	4
18	559	5
In	**3,425**	**36**
Total	**6,934**	**72**

107 Houghton GC, Johannesburg

As with so many of the early South African courses, Houghton – first played in 1926 – was designed by the club professional, A. M. Copland. It was built on 155 acres of prime residential land which is now only three miles from Johannesburg City Hall. There are only three par-threes, and in the rarefied atmosphere of the Transvaal highveld (almost 6,000 feet above sea-level) even the mediocre golfer finds himself suddenly two clubs longer. A few par-4s only require a drive and short iron onto the green, but the accuracy of the tee shot is crucial because of the narrow, tree-lined fairways, and well-positioned bunkers guarding the greens. Particularly outstanding holes are the 9th, 13th and 14th, each rewarding only the finest shot-maker. In the 2002 Dunhill Championship, Justin Rose (who, as a teenage amateur, so nearly won the 1998 Open at Royal Birkdale) held off the challenge of US PGA Champion Retief Goosen to record his first European Tour win. Rose stamped his authority with a brilliant 35-yard bunker shot, over a ridge to the 16th green.

Houghton
Card of the course

Hole	Yards	Par
1	369	4
2	417	4
3	604	5
4	438	4
5	529	5
6	190	3
7	421	4
8	155	3
9	476	4
Out	**3,599**	**36**
10	430	4
11	429	4
12	160	3
13	469	4
14	498	4
15	225	3
16	523	5
17	406	4
18	572	5
In	**3,712**	**36**
Total	**7,311**	**72**

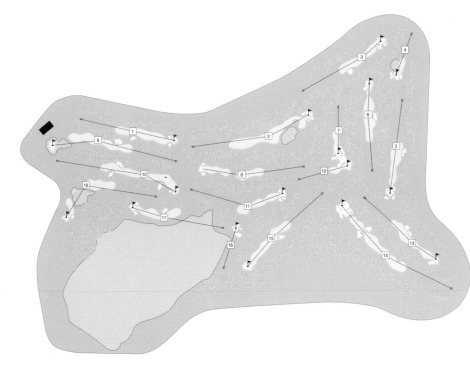

108 Gary Player CC, South Africa

From the pyramid hotel that dominates the skyline to the lush, opulent greens it is plain to see that this course is not just soaked in sun, but it is also drenched in money. The course is famous for the Nedbank Million Dollar Golf Challenge that invites just 12 professionals to what many believe to be an exhibition of mere money-grabbing. Gary Player's course does, however, house some impressive holes. The par-five 545-yard ninth is one of them. The drive must be straight to avoid trees on the left and a bunker on the right. The professional big-hitter could hit the green in two, however, staying on it is a different matter. The hole is a raised island and lies on the upper level of a split-level lake. The lay-up is advisable.

Gary Player Card of the course

Hole	Yards	Par			
1	403	4	10	518	5
2	503	5	11	419	4
3	395	4	12	207	3
4	195	3	13	395	4
5	400	4	14	550	5
6	363	4	15	417	4
7	206	3	16	195	3
8	431	4	17	374	4
9	545	5	18	422	4
Out	**3,441**	**36**	**In**	**3,497**	**36**
			Total	**6,938**	**72**

Kasugai East Card of the course

Hole	Yards	Par
1	415	4
2	395	4
3	498	5
4	179	3
5	416	4
6	460	4
7	182	3
8	511	5
9	407	4
Out	**3,463**	**36**
10	362	4
11	368	4
12	174	3
13	503	5
14	435	4
15	189	3
16	427	4
17	525	5
18	410	4
In	**3,393**	**36**
Total	**6,856**	**72**

109 Kasugai CC, Nagoya

Kasugai's East and West courses were designed by Japan's leading architect Seichi Inoue in the hills to the west of Nagoya. Giant earth-moving machines were used in cutting off the tops of hills and filling the valleys to make the fairways – a common method of construction in Japan. What is left is still undulating and decidedly steep in places, which is much to the Japanese liking. The clubhouse, perched on the highest point, overlooks both layouts, which are well defined by many young conifers and small decorative ponds. These obstacles also serve to provide some challenge. For the 1975 Japan Open, played on the East course, additional fairway sandtraps and temporary trees were arranged to provide extra difficulty. Korai grass is used for the putting surfaces, giving the greens much variation in both texture and colour from season to season. The East course is 6,856 yards of rambling holes over many hills, some of which are quite steep by world championship standards. This provides a problem of distance – an advantage to the long hitters but frustrating for those who have less power.

110 Nasu International CC, Tochigi

Situated on Japan's northernmost island, Nasu International Country Club is distinguished by its year-round, one-green putting system, which is contrary to the usual Japanese practice of providing winter and summer greens. The course has been carved through steep, hilly wood land which eventually makes the 6,825 yards play longer than the card reads, an effect exaggerated by the almost constant cross-winds and numerous sidehill lies. On the 6th and 7th, both par-fours, the drive is blind, the fairways rising to a crest before dipping to well-trapped greens. The long, uphill 13th dog-legs to the right around a bunker strategically placed to catch the sliced or the over-ambitious drive. The lay-up second then has to contend with the severe gusting winds to leave an untroubled short-iron to the target.

Nasu Card of the course

Hole	Yards	Par
1	505	5
2	175	3
3	400	4
4	525	5
5	423	4
6	430	4
7	385	4
8	200	3
9	380	4
Out	**3,423**	**36**
10	490	5
11	360	4
12	200	3
13	500	5
14	412	4
15	460	4
16	410	4
17	150	3
18	420	4
In	**3,402**	**36**
Total	**6,825**	**72**

111 Yomiuri CC, Tokyo

The Yomiuri Country Club, to the west of Tokyo, is part of a huge sporting complex built by the Yomiuri Newspaper Group. The course, which is of the highest class, was designed in 1964 by Seichi Inoue. He used his considerable experience to create holes that are adventurous without being unreasonable, avoiding a drawback that mar many courses in this mountainous country. At 6,962 yards it is well set for distance, particularly in the lushness that follows the mid-year wet season. It has a two-green system which slightly interferes with the greenside trapping, but generally sand areas are punishing and fearsome. There are a number of blind shots from the teeing areas and many shots have to carry deep valleys, which are grassed as rough and where the wind can play strange tricks with the ball. Yomiuri has a high reputation amongst the professionals and top-class amateurs – a sentiment reflected by the decision of the Japan Golf Association to stage the World Cup there in 1966.

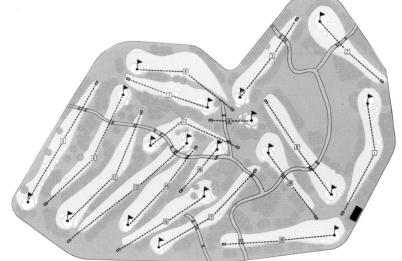

Yomiuri Card of the course

Hole	Yards	Par			
1	396	4	10	425	4
2	180	3	11	507	5
3	403	4	12	432	4
4	508	5	13	450	4
5	384	4	14	364	4
6	541	5	15	194	3
7	389	4	16	410	4
8	197	3	17	510	5
9	448	4	18	224	3
Out	**3,446**	**36**	**In**	**3,516**	**36**
			Total	**6,962**	**72**

112 Wack Wack G & CC, Manila

Wack Wack was founded in 1930 by Bill Shaw, an American whose aim was to build a golf course for all races. The necessary capital was swiftly raised – those who could not pay immediately were allowed to pay by instalments – and Jim Black, an American professional, was hired to lay out the course. The name, Wack Wack, was inspired by the noise made by the many crows that habitually preside over golf here. A second course was added later, but it was over the original East Course that the Philippine Open was played more than 40 times up to 1990, attracting players like the American stars Mangrum, Oliver, Burke, Harrison and Furgol. The Philippine Open returned here in 2001 for its 86th staging. Black's course has been much improved over the years, notably the greens, and the creeks have been dammed to provide a number of serious water carries. The World Cup of Golf was held at Wack Wack in 1977, when Gary Player won the individual title, while the team honours went to Spain, with a youthful Severiano Ballesteros partnering Antonio Garrido.

Wack Wack East Course Card of the course

Hole	Yards	Par
1	421	4
2	384	4
3	357	4
4	354	4
5	585	5
6	429	4
7	343	4
8	168	3
9	428	4
Out	**3,469**	**36**
10	384	4
11	375	4
12	441	4
13	515	5
14	433	4
15	382	4
16	207	3
17	412	4
18	435	4
In	**3,584**	**36**
Total	**7,053**	**72**

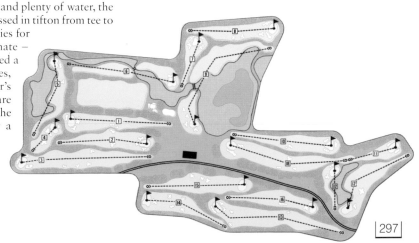

Navatanee Card of the course

Hole	Yards	Par
1	424	4
2	380	4
3	555	5
4	133	3
5	347	4
6	457	4
7	218	3
8	370	4
9	559	5
Out	**3,443**	**36**
10	428	4
11	230	3
12	379	4
13	578	5
14	357	4
15	412	4
16	381	4
17	159	3
18	539	5
In	**3,463**	**36**
Total	**6,906**	**72**

113 Navatanee CC, Bangkok

Navatanee Golf Club possesses by far the best course in Thailand. Designed by Robert Trent Jones for its owner, Sukhum Navapan, this 6,906 yard par-72 layout entertained the 1975 World Cup, from which all players departed with high praise for its championship qualities. The course construction converted a large swamp of rice paddies and wasteland into a vista of green fairways, white sandtraps and plenty of water, the familiar Trent Jones trademark. It is grassed in tifton from tee to cup, providing a lush carpet of superb lies for fairway play and – for such a hot climate – smooth putting surfaces. Jones has placed a variety of teeing grounds for most holes, so adapting the layout to suit every golfer's needs. For tournament play the nines are reversed making for a thrilling finish to the round, with disaster lying in wait for a false step – especially at the 559-yard final hole where a double water carry is particularly fearsome in any kind of wind.

114 Delhi GC, New Delhi

Built on the rubble of the old Mogul metropolis, the Delhi course, set amidst the grandeur of such ancient architectural monuments, has a fascination and beauty all of its own. The fairways of pure couch grass – and the natural jungle rough have a verdant greenness after the monsoon rains which suggests coolness in an otherwise torrid climate. The layout has undergone several changes. At one time it ranged over wider territory, but the club now confines twenty-seven holes within a tight boundary, the main eighteen forming a championship course of high merit. It combines a need for length with a demand for extreme directness. Drives that curl into the wild bush rough are invariably unplayable, so necessitating the almost mandatory employment of an "agi-wallah", who performs the function of a fore-caddie while understudying the more responsible job of caddie. The club is a delightful meeting place for many of Delhi's sporting citizens and diplomats. Davidoff Tour events are frequently played here, with India's Vijay Kumar beating an international field for the 2002 Indian Open.

Delhi GC Card of the course

Hole	Yards	Par
1	530	5
2	420	4
3	390	4
4	450	4
5	413	4
6	188	3
7	540	5
8	412	4
9	175	3
Out	3,518	36
10	416	4
11	455	4
12	160	3
13	375	4
14	512	5
15	373	4
16	393	4
17	153	3
18	530	5
In	3,367	36
Total	6,885	72

115 New South Wales GC, Matraville

Laid out by Alister Mackenzie in 1928, the New South Wales course at Sydney offers magnificent, panoramic views over the Pacific Ocean to the east and Botany Bay to the south; the spot where Captain Cook landed in 1770 is less than a par-four from the clubhouse. The land presents an unrivalled site for a course and the wind, ever-changing in both direction and strength, produces a stern challenge to golfers of all categories. Mackenzie's layout cleverly ensures that the wind must be tackled from every quarter, with the par-3s and par-5s running to all four points of the compass, and the punishing undulations, serious rough and deep bunkers give many a tough shot. The strong par-4s from the 13th to the 16th form a demanding sequence, but pride of place goes to the par-3 6th down on the headland, with an all-or-nothing shot to be played over the water, a distinguished forerunner of Cypress Point's 16th.

New South Wales Card of the course

Hole	Yards	Par
1	321	4
2	201	3
3	416	4
4	428	4
5	512	5
6	194	3
7	411	4
8	552	5
9	372	4
Out	3,407	36
10	394	4
11	163	3
12	527	5
13	410	4
14	353	4
15	407	4
16	441	4
17	167	3
18	548	5
In	3,410	36
Total	6,817	72

Kingston Heath Card of the course

Hole	Yards	Par
1	458	4
2	365	4
3	296	4
4	389	4
5	189	3
6	434	4
7	502	5
8	431	4
9	354	4
Out	3,418	36
10	143	3
11	403	4
12	484	5
13	354	4
14	549	5
15	155	3
16	422	4
17	457	4
18	428	4
In	3,395	36
Total	6,813	72

116 Kingston Heath GC, Melbourne

Like many old clubs, Kingston Heath was born of necessity: an established club was forced off its course on municipal land near Melbourne city edge and so, faced with extinction, its members sought land farther out where the price was right and soil conducive. They chose a site for Kingston Heath on the same sandy tract of land as Royal Melbourne, and the eventual result looks like its half-brother. The design in 1925, was by Sydney professional Dan Souter, but three years later Alister Mackenzie undertook the bunkering. It is now a delightful mixture of flat and rising land, making easy walking and interesting golf. The holes vary in theme and, played for the first time, may even surprise. The fairways, lined by eucalyptus and tea-trees, are almost pure couch grass and lead on to greens that have fine surfaces of seaside bent, browntop and fescue mixed. The three par-threes are classic in conception and offer a fine challenge for perceptive strokemaking. The course is on the regular championship roster and has accommodated the Open three times.

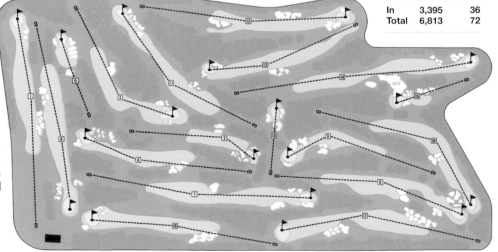

117 Lake Karrinyup CC, Western Australia

As its name suggests, Lake Karrinyup is constructed around a lake set in a natural basin surrounded by sandhills. The lake is the home of many forms of wildlife and from any angle mirrors the beauty of the course. Created by Alex Russell in 1927, it bears a marked similarity to his home course of Royal Melbourne in the arrangement of the generously wide, couch grass fairways, the grand sandtraps and the large, flowing greens. Eucalyptus and many species of native wild flowers flourish in the sandy soil, forming an indigenous and attractive setting for each hole. A wind from the Indian Ocean can affect the scores by adding to the problems already set by the water and the bush. The 8th, a 219-yard par-three, is the only hole that is played directly over the lake and a strong low-iron tee shot is often required when playing into the wind. The course is a popular venue for the Australian Open and amateur championships, Retief Goosen demolishing a high-class field to land the 2002 Johnnie Walker Classic with stunning play.

Lake Karrinyup Card of the course

Hole	Yards	Par
1	298	4
2	470	4
3	542	5
4	427	4
5	178	3
6	446	4
7	603	5
8	219	3
9	372	4
Out	**3,555**	**36**
10	372	4
11	522	5
12	164	3
13	421	4
14	284	4
15	531	5
16	469	4
17	197	3
18	405	4
In	**3,365**	**36**
Total	**6,920**	**72**

118 Auckland GC, Middlemore

Middlemore, as the Auckland Golf Club is known, after the district in which it thrives, has an atmosphere that is both special and unique, even for New Zealand. Its comfortable, colonial-style clubhouse looks out on a parkland setting of exemplary tidiness and tranquillity, the course having been laid out by the professional, E.G. Hood. Tall rows of mature pines define some fairways, while others are wide open to the sky and the wind. For all these parkland qualities, Middlemore also maintains rough, malevolent enough under normal conditions, but allowed to grow in further for major events – Auckland has hosted the New Zealand Open seven times since it moved to this site in 1910, and will do so again in January 2003. The club itself, though, is older, having celebrated its centenary in 1994.

Auckland Card of the course

Hole	Yards	Par
1	362	4
2	381	4
3	404	4
4	510	5
5	404	4
6	407	4
7	198	3
8	401	4
9	592	5
Out	**3,659**	**37**
10	110	3
11	272	4
12	358	4
13	214	3
14	359	4
15	458	4
16	404	4
17	480	5
18	373	4
In	**3,028**	**35**
Total	**6,687**	**72**

119 Christchurch GC, Shirley

Christchurch Golf Club has a golfing tradition stretching back to 1873 when, like many a similar club in distant British colonies, it began on another site, sparked by the enthusiasm of a handful of Scots. It moved to its present home, 5km from the city centre, in 1900. Some years ago several holes were abandoned and three strong new ones added, the 5th, 6th and 7th. The course is essentially flat, but there are sufficient undulations not to be dull, while the trees are a delight to the eye. Frequently during the round the player is uncomfortably aware of the proximity of boundary fences: this is no place for the persistent slicer! The long 4th, for instance, runs perilously close to Horseshoe Lake Road for its entire length before ending at a green with the indignity of out-of-bounds on three sides! From the championship tees Christchurch demands strong nerves and a sure technique.

Christchurch Card of the course

Hole	Yards	Par	Hole	Yards	Par
1	361	4	10	435	4
2	330	4	11	142	3
3	146	3	12	454	4
4	535	5	13	430	4
5	590	5	14	365	4
6	400	4	15	445	4
7	200	3	16	525	5
8	426	4	17	375	4
9	480	4	18	350	4
Out	**3,468**	**36**	**In**	**3,521**	**36**
			Total	**6,989**	**72**

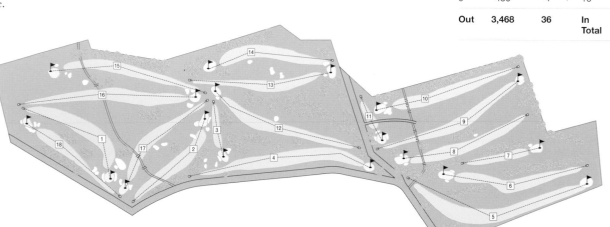

Index

ACKNOWLEDGEMENTS
The publishers would like to thank the following organizations and individuals for their kind permission to reproduce the photographs in this book:

Allsport/Simon Bruty 115
/David Cannon 8-9, 12-13, 24-25, 67, 81, 112-113, 145, 235
/Vandystadt/Christian Petit 99
/Andrew Redington 240-241, 245
St Andrews Links Trust/Massakuni Akiyama 27, 29, 30-31
Banff Springs Golf Course 196
Bridgeman Art Library/National Gallery 87
The Celtic Manor Resort 4-5, 6
Corbis UK Ltd 156, 191 left
/Arthur Jones 47
Peter Dazeley 7 top, 39, 41, 50, 53, 70-71, 85, 123, 230, 233, 247
Falsterbo Golfklubb/Bjorn Hillarp 91

Golf Monthly/Press Association 59
The Golf Picture Library 148 top, 183
/Chris Cole 134
Golf Picture Bank/Nick Walker 75, 158, 190
Hailey Sports Photographic 125, 126 Top, 126 bottom, 254
Halmstad Golklubb Tylosand 93
The Matthew Harris Golf Picture Library 10-11, 19, 20-21, 23, 34, 48, 77, 119, 147, 211, 215
Hulton Archive 26
K Club 83
L. C. Lambrecht 144
Le Golf National 2-3, 96-97
Brian Morgan Golf Photography 14-15 bottom, 118-119, 176, 179, 186, 216, 223, 225, 236, 248-249
Pinehurst Resort & County Club/Henedry 148 bottom
Tony Roberts Photography 226, 239
Sea Pines Company , Inc. 140
/David S. Soliday 14-15 top
Phil Sheldon 1, 7 bottom, 10 left, 13 right, 18-19, 28, 33, 35,

37, 38, 44-45, 46, 57, 65, 70 top, 102, 105, 118, 120, 121, 127, 129, 137, 139, 149 left, 155, 163 top, 162, 163 bottom, 165 bottom, 166, 167 Top, 167 bottom, 170, 171 top, 171 bottom, 181, 186-187, 188, 192-193, 193 right, 195, 205, 219, 221, 228-229, 243
/Karina Hoskyns 101
/Larry Petrillo 152-153, 253
/Jan Traylen 61
Unknown 16-17, 69, 70 bottom left, 116 left, 117, 150
U.S.G.A. 132, 135, 149 right, 151, 152 left, 184, 185, 191 right
Club Zur Vahr 94
Vilamoura 111
Visions in Golf/Mark Newcombe 31, 51, 58, 72, 79, 108, 165 Top, 200, 202-203, 208-209, 213